Theory and Ideology in Indian Sociology

Theory and Ideology in Indian Sociology

Essays in Honour of Professor Yogendra Singh

Edited by
Narendra K. Singhi

RAWAT PUBLICATIONS
Jaipur • New Delhi • Bangalore • Guwahati • Kolkata

ISBN 978-81-7033-304-3

Reprinted, 2018

Published by
Prem Rawat for **Rawat Publications**
Satyam Apts., Sector 3, Jawahar Nagar, Jaipur 302 004 (India)
Phone: 0141 265 1748 / 7006 Fax: 0141 265 1748
E-mail: info@rawatbooks.com
Website: www.rawatbooks.com

New Delhi Office
4858/24, Ansari Road, Daryaganj, New Delhi 110 002
Phone: 011-23263290

Also at *Bangalore, Guwahati* and *Kolkata*

Typeset by Rawat Computers, Jaipur
Printed at Nice Printing Press, New Delhi

Contents

PREFACE

The first volume in honour of Professor Yogendra Singh, edited by Professor K.L. Sharma and entitled as *Social Inequality in India* was released on the occasion of the XXI All India Sociological Conference held at the Centre for the Study of Social Systems, New Delhi, in 1994.

Theory and Ideology in Indian Sociology is the second volume in the series of five volumes planned by me and Professor K.L. Sharma, in honour of Professor Singh, who has been our PhD supervisor.

It is difficult for me to express my intellectual debt to Professor Singh, with whom conversation about any phenomenon gets converted into sociologically meaningful discourse. In his intellectual company, many have learnt different cognitive facets of sociological enterprise. I feel privileged to have had many opportunities to discuss and learn from his erudite exposition. This volume is a symbol of our reverence for Professor Singh, who has influenced many of us, not only as an erudite scholar but also as a person in whom we found profound human qualities.

Professor Singh has done serious and significant work in the area of theory and ideology in Indian sociology. This volume is dedicated to him with profound respect and a sense of deep appreciation for his academic contribution, scholarship and human qualities.

I am grateful to all the contributors for granting permission to include their articles in this volume and for encouraging our efforts. The publishers of the journals and volumes, wherein these articles have appeared are duly being thankfully acknowledged. My sincere thanks are due to Shri Kailash Rawat of Rawat Publications with whom the idea of publishing five volumes as a tribute to Professor Singh got its first initiation. I particularly appreciate the efforts of Shri Pranit Rawat whose commitment to publication augurs well for the house of Rawat Publications.

Narendra K. Singhi

PRINCIPAL WORKS OF PROF. YOGENDRA SINGH

Articles Published in Journals

1958 'Land Reform and Social Tensions in Villages', *Journal of Social Sciences*, Vol. I, No. 2, Institute of Social Sciences, Agra University, Agra.

1959 'Group Status of Factions in Rural Community', *Journal of Social Sciences*, Vol. II, No. 1, Institute of Social Sciences, Agra University, Agra.

1959 'Institutional Factors in Land Reform Policy', paper presented at 42nd Annual Conference of Indian Economic Association and published in Conference Number of the *Journal of Indian Economic Association*.

1960 'Role of Sociology in Planning', paper presented at the Social Planning Seminar, organized by the Institute of Social Sciences, Agra University, Agra, and published in *Journal of Social Sciences Supplement*, Institute of Social Sciences, Agra University, Agra.

1960 'Social Change and Social Problems: A Study of Crime in Six Villages of UP', *Journal of Social Sciences*, Vol. II, No. 2, Institute of Social Sciences, Agra University, Agra.

1960 'Youth Problem and Welfare: A Sociological Approach', *The Economic Weekly*, Vol. XII, No. 45, Bombay.

1960 'Development of Caste Consciousness in Indian Children from 4 to 10' (with S.D. Singh and K. Singh), *Journal of Research (Letters)*, Vol. VIII, Part. 1, Agra University, Agra.

1961 'Changing Caste Stratification and Problem of Integration of Indian Society', *Journal of Social Sciences*, Supplement Volume.

1964 'Cultural Integration and Changing Values', *Sociological Bulletin*, Vol. XIII, No. 2, September 1964.

1965 'Processes and Problems of Social Change in India', *Political Science Review*, Vol. 4, No. 1, Department of Political Science, University of Rajasthan, Jaipur.

1965 'Disciplinary Growth of Sociology and Its Teachings in India', *Sociology in India*, Seminar Volume.

1968 'Caste and Class: Some Aspects of Continuity and Change', *Sociological Bulletin*, Vol. XVII, No. 2.

1968 'Academic Colonialism: Sociological Issues', *Seminar* 112, Delhi.

1970 'Indian Council of Social Science Research: Its Promise and Dilemmas', *Economic and Political Weekly*, Vol. V, No. 16.

1970 'Modernization: Political Aspects', *Seminar*, April 1970.

1970 'For a Sociology of India', *Contributions to Indian Sociology*, No. 4.

1973 'The Role of Social Sciences in India: A Sociology of Knowledge', *Sociological Bulletin*, Vol. 22, No. 1, March 1973.

1975 'Social Contents of Scientific and Technological Revolution', *Philosophy and Social Action*, Inaugural Issue, January 1973.

1979 'Constraints, Contradictions and Inter-disciplinary Orientations: The Indian Context', *International Social Science* Journal, Vol. XXXI, No. 1.

1984 'Relevant Sociology (I): Conceptual Issues', *Relevant Sociology*, Vol. 1, No. 1, April 1984.

1984 'Relevant Sociology (II): Conceptual Issues', *Relevant Sociology*, Vol. 1, No. 2, October 1984.

1986 'Law and Social Change in India: A Sociological Perspective', *Relevant Sociology*, Vol. III, No. 1–2, April-October 1986.

1988 'Quest for Relevance: Teaching and Research on Sociology', *Indian Journal of Social Sciences*, Vol. I, No. 1, January-March 1988.

1988 'Literature and Social Change: A Sociological Perspective', *New Horizon*, ICCR, New Delhi.

Articles Published in Books

'Academic Role Structure and Modernization', published in Satish Saberwal (ed.), *Beyond Village*, Indian Institute of Advanced Studies, Simla.

'Country-Town Nexus: Social Transformation in Contemporary Indian Society' in K.L. Sharma and Dipankar Gupta (ed.), *Country-Town Nexus*, Rawat Publications, Jaipur, 1990.

'Economic Development and the Changing Family System: The Indian Experience', Christian Academy of Social Sciences, Seoul, 1989–90.

'Ideology, Theory and Methods in Indian Sociology' in Stien Rokken (ed.), *Quarter of a Century of Social Sciences*, 1952–77, Paris, 1977.

'Modernization of Higher Education in India', review article in Higher Education in India, A.B. Shah (ed.), *Sociology of Education*, Delhi, 1969.

'Process of Socialization of Education' in I.P. Desai and M.S. Gore (eds.), *Sociology of Education in India*, NCERT, New Delhi.

'Processes of Socialization and Education', paper presented at the Seminar on Sociology of Education, organized jointly by the Tata Institute of Social Sciences, Bombay and the Education Commission, Government of India, Winter 1965.

'Relevance of Max Weber for the Understanding of Indian Reality' in Krishna Bhardwaj and Sudipto Kaviraj (eds.).

'Social Process and Dimensions of Indian Nationalism (I.P. Desai Memorial Lecture)', Surat, Centre for Social Studies, 1988.

'Some Emerging Issues in the Indian Sociology of Social Stratification' in K.L. Sharma (ed.), *Social Stratification in India*, Manohar, Delhi, 1986.

'The Class Structure and Political Processes in Village India', paper presented at the Seminar on Panchyati Raj, organized by the Department of Political Science, University of Rajasthan, Jaipur.

'The Scope and Method of Sociology in India' in T.K.N. Unnithan et. al (eds.), *Sociology for India*, Prentice Hall of India, New Delhi, 1965.

'Traditional Culture Pattern of India and Industrial Change' in A.B. Shah and C.R.M. Rao (eds.), *Tradition and Modernity in India*, P.C. Manaktala and Sons, Pvt. Ltd., Bombay, 1965.

Reports

Jaipur City, A Study of Selected Sociological and Economic Aspects, Vol. I, *Ajmer City* Vol. II, and *Kota City*, Vol III, reports of a survey directed jointly with Prof. T.K.N. Unnithan for Government of Rajasthan.

Modernisation of Syllabi in Sociology and Social Anthropology, report based on core regional workshops organized by the UGC Panel on Sociology and Social Anthropology, UGC, New Delhi, 1977.

Traditional Socio-Cultural Systems and Economic Growth in Developing Countries in Asia and the Pacific Region: The Case of India, prepared for the Asian Development Bank, Manila, Philippines, 1978.

Books

1. *Towards a Sociology of Culture in India* (ed.) with T.K.N. Unnithan et. al., New Delhi: Prentice Hall of India, 1965.
2. *For a Sociology of India* (ed.), with T.K.N. Unnithan et. al., New Delhi: Prentice Hall of India, 1967.
3. *Sociology of Non-violence and Peace* (co-author) with T.K.N. Unnithan, New Delhi: Council for Social Development, 1968.
4. *Tradition of Non-Violence* (co-author) with T.K.N. Unnithan, New Delhi: Heinmann, 1972.
5. *Modernization of Indian Tradition*, New Delhi: Thompson Press, 1973.
6. *Essays on Modernization*, New Delhi: Manohar Publications, 1977.
7. *Social Stratification and Social Change in India*, New Delhi: Manohar Publications, 1978.

8. *Social Aspects of Scientific and Technological Revolution* (co-author) with Ralph Dahrendorf et. al., London: Sage Publications, 1978.
9. *Image of Man: Ideology and Theory in Indian Sociology*, New Delhi: Chanakya Publications, 1984.
10. *Indian Sociology: Social Conditioning and Emerging Concerns*, New Delhi: Vistaar Publications, 1987.
11. *The Sociology of Culture* (co-author) with Boris Erasov, Moscow: Progress Publishers, 1991.
12. *Social Change in India: Crisis and Resilience*, New Delhi: Har Anand Publications, 1993.

INTRODUCTION

NARENDRA K. SINGHI

The Indian sociology, as an emergent distinctive discipline during colonial and post-colonial phase, has been significantly influenced, and patterned on western paradigm. The conceptual usage, articulation and exposition; the theoretical perspective, approach and construction; and the methodological orientation, application and use, became integral part of the academic and professional institutionalization of sociology in India.

Thus, the processes and patterns of emergence and development of sociology in India led to certain cognitive consequences leading to intellectual dissonance, gaps, neglect and misrepresentation of Indian social reality in relation to themes, perspectives, theory, methodology, interpretation and ideology. The historicity of Indian society, as reflected in its cumulative adaptive continuity, can be comprehended in terms of micro-local, macro-regional and meso-national as distinct categories of analysis and local-regional-national in terms of to mutuality of linkages. This would necessitate understanding of classical Sanskritic scriptures, regional-language texts, records, documents and other historical data, and folk, oral and living traditions as formulated in ideal normative construct, empirical pragmatic praxis, belief systems, social institutions and cultural practices. Expanded space and temporal continuity is built through cognitive-psychic acceptance of pluralism, adaptability, assimilation and tolerance. Thus, composite cultural construction of India has been weaved through diversities and openness. It also suggests predominance of culture over polity.

The grand sociological construction of Indian society and culture thus needs to be attempted at different levels: (a) spatial-locale-oriented construction, (b) spatial-macro-societal construction, (c) temporal periodo-processual construction, (d) normative-ideal construction, (e) empirical-operative construction, (f) pluralistic-heterogeneous construction, (g) unified-homogeneous construction, (h) composite-harmonic construction, (i) conflictual-divisive construction, (j) physical-vital construction, (k) transcendental-spiritual construction, (l) continuity-replicational construction, (m) change-transformational construction, (n) evaluative valuational construction, (o) insider-outsider construction, (p) integral-holistic construction, (q) ethno-cognitive construction, (r) universalistic-cognitive construction, and (s) Anekantvad-relativistic construction.

The conceptual dimensions necessitate use of terms as used and discussed in classical texts, folklore and literature, everyday usage of common man, regional words, western concepts and neologisms of Indian social scientists. There is lack of cognitive discourses and debates about the construction and use of concepts which reveal local, regional and trans-regional realities by Indian scholars. The conceptual articulation thus necessitates use of terms, idioms and expressions which reveal the social reality as perceived and experienced – individually and collectively. Although experiences have unique characteristics of being subjective, they become part of collectively sharedness through linguistic symbols. The external experiences are converted into internal meaning giving process through a dialectical relationship of ideals, values, norm, evaluation and judgement. Life experiences are not merely empirical sensory experiences but tend to be placed into more complex meanings with imagined or cogniticized non-cognitive psychic or spiritual revelations. Such dimensions have social meanings as they determine belief systems, ideals, practices and govern the mundane dimensions of individual and collective life. In certain sense, pluralistic meanings determine diversity of social and cultural life in the Indian context.

There is significant and rich tradition of classificatory and typological schema of concepts in classical texts. The intellectual traditions reveal significant and rich contribution in all areas which men have created, experienced and imagined. These areas include specific texts oriented to skills, systems of thought and systems governing human relationships in the realm of polity, economy, culture, society and religion. There are texts which deal with architect, sex life, art of thieving, grammar, theatre and acting, policy, economy, medicine, and all that which man has created, thought of and visualized. There are texts on as diverse themes as omens, wrestling, and birds.

The *Natya Shastra*, *Shanti Parva* of *Mahabharata*, Panini's grammar, *Arthasastra*, *Charak Samhita*, and *Vastu Sastra* illustrate the commonly known literature. However, there are millions of manuscripts, written in *Prakrit*, *Pali* and regional languages, which have not been studied and translated. Obviously, such an intellectual heritage remains unexplored by sociologists and other scholars. Study of such literature can help in the formulation and articulation of appropriate concepts and conceptual schema for social scientists.

Besides the classical texts, the study of regional-local documents, folk literature and grasp of oral and living traditions can help in the analysis of deeper meanings and nuisances of the patterns and processes of everyday life and institutions which led to continuity and change in Indian society.

The conceptical formulation thus has several sources which can be categorized as:

(1) Classical-textual
(2) Regional-semi-textual
(3) Local-folklorist
(4) Integral-universalistic
(5) Composite-national

The use of concepts should be related to the level of reality which is being constructed and communicated. All concepts need not be universalistic. Conceptual categories need to be viewed within the framework of historical relativism and evolutionary universalism. Certain concepts remain inappropriate for understanding the changed reality while others tend to have significance in terms of replication of reality at a particular temporal-spatial contextuality.

Thus, conceptual articulation is a dynamic process and has to keep pace with changes in society and preceding and successive cognitive constructions. There is a great deal of intellectual temptation in stating the same reality in different linguistic/stylistic mode of articulation. Terms are substituted and styles are changed, so that the presentation appears to be original, significant and stimulating. Intellectual fashions are as attractive as fads in attire, they delight but do not lead to original contribution in the realm of knowledge.

At a fundamental level, ideology constitutes the normative principle that enter into the construction of social reality.[1] The normative principles which entered into the construction of classical Indian social reality had generally transcendental reference. The mundane was not seen as the Ultimate nor the Real. The concepts of *dharma, artha, kama, moksha, atman, karma, punrajanma, punya, papa, ashrama*, etc., provided a significant and specific meaning to life and ordering of its goals.

At other level ideology provides a path to be pursued in a particular manner. Ideology is a complex construct of values and meanings, based on theoretical exposition and tend to be oriented towards a schema of praxis. There has been very little effort on the part of sociologists in India to pursue the cognitive task of the analysis of the ideological-theoretical dimensions of intellectual traditions of India.

Almost all sociologists in India have taken up studies on the theoretical paradigm of Durkheim, Weber, Marx, Parsons, or have adopted philosophical theoretical orientation. Culturological orientation, structural theoretic orientation, dialectical historical orientation, and its variations.[2]

Such a sociological orientation within sociology has been explained on the basis of sociology of knowledge. Sociology, as a distinct discipline in India, was introduced during the second decade of this century. Colonialism and its impact on the intellectual and cultural traditions of India provide an important historical backdrop for theoretic ideological and professional growth of sociology. The cognitive and paradigmatic tension of Indian sociology during 1952–77 bear imprints of the socio-historical forces released during the freedom struggle which shaped the responses of Indian intellectuals to the categories and structures of ideas in social sciences and sociology.[3] In the initial years descriptive and evolutionary studies of caste, social customs, folklore, land systems and village community were undertaken. The choice of the theme was determined by the colonial scholars from outside India, for whom the 'typical' and the 'different' looked interesting and worth reporting. The Indian society in this perspective was interpreted by western scholars. Such sociology alienated the scholars who belonged to its own culture.

Scholars like Radhakamal Mukherjee, B.N. Seal and B.N. Sarkar were critical of western cognitive interpretation and found western categories inadequate for interpretation of the Indian reality. However, there was no effort to 'do' sociology in the mould which could provide an alternative model. The academic institutionalization of sociology as a discipline in colleges and universities further strengthened the western impact. The anthropological traditions of British sociologists and historical research methods were over-powered by the positivistic-empirical mode of data collection of the US.

Although Singh has periodicized the process of growth of sociology into four time-spans, i.e., 1952 to 1960, period of adaptive changes; 1960 to 1965, period of significant shifts in theoretic priorities and beginning of some critical tensions in theory; 1965 to 1970, period of marked sociological self-awareness and growth of new directions in theoretical and substantive directions; and finally 1970–77, period of new maturity and new horizons of knowledge, the schema seems to be arbitrary, optimistic and unsubstantiated. It is true that lot of empirical work has been done during past few decades but it would be difficult to suggest that sociology has gained theoretical maturity of its own in India. New areas of research have multiplied but the theoretical rigour and depth of interpretation seem to be lacking. The contribution of earlier generations of sociologists continue to be regarded and recognized as rigorous and significant by serious scholars.[4]

Singh's typology of four major theoretic orientations is significant and logically coherent. The philosophical orientation in Indian sociology is associated with the contributions of Radhakamal Mukherjee, D.P. Mukerji and A.K. Saran. This orientation has not made a significant impact on the theoretical nature of Indian sociology according to Singh.[5] It is interesting to note that despite the profoundness of scholarship of these scholars, the impact is minimal. The impact of western sociology was becoming more and more enveloping and empirical bases of societal understanding looked more simpler than the rigour of philosophy and pain of meaningfully digging the past; that to swim with the current stream was easy sociological course, than the cognitive grasp of complex historical past.

Emergence of sociology as a profession denied and negated the scholastic rigour. Searching sociology in classical texts necessitated more self-discipline, hard work and sharpness of intellect. On the other hand, hardly any attempt was made to examine the contributions of contemporary thinkers like Sri Aurobindo, Ambedkar, Tilak and Gandhi in sociological sense.

Sri Aurobindo's contribution to *Human Cycle, Foundations of Indian Culture* and other writings provides an ideological construct of Indian society with profound erudition. Gandhi's writings provide empathetic understanding of Indian society through a direct, simple, down to earth narratives. Indian sociologists have now tried to make some efforts to give sociological interpretations to their contributions after western scholars started cognitive interpretation of their contributions. In a sense it is yet another example of sociological colonialism and academic imperialism.

There is a great deal of distortion of Indian society and culture by western scholars. These scholars saw the Indian society from their perspective – a perspective which was developed within their social and cultural milieu. The hegemonic tendencies and superiority of power made them look at the dominant Indian institutions as problematic. Some scholars glorified the philosophical-metaphysical dimensions of Indian religion and eulogized certain Sanskritic writings and literature, and also their relevance in applicability. But the pertinent point relates to the politics and ideology of orientalist projects, emphasizing their relations with the colonial expansion. There is a significant relationship between knowledge and power. Orientalism paved the way for political power through a distinct construction of Indian society. There are traps and contradictions in the critique of orientalism of colonialism and orientalism of imperialism. The critique itself uses western academic theory, its terminology, classificatory typology and methodology.[6] Under the garb of positivistic knowledge, there is systematic misconceptions and willful construction of 'the other' via orientalism.

The culturological orientation begins with the work of Srinivas, 'Religion and Society Among the Coorgs of South India', Brahmanization, Sanskritization and westernization were major concepts derived from this study. Sanskritization characterized a change within the framework of Indian tradition.

The term 'secularization' has also been used by Srinivas to denote ideological formulation after independence which was incorporated in the formal-legal-constitutional text. Sanskritization and westernization seem to be only the conceptual contribution made by Indian sociologists. The impact of this concept was found beyond the discipline of sociology as it did appeal to indologists, historians and social anthropologists.[7] The other concepts which have been often used in the context of cultural dimensions of social change are 'Little and Great Traditions'.[8]

The other theoretic orientation has been termed as structural theoretic orientation. The structural studies focus on power structure, social stratification, family structure, demography and similar aspects which reveal patterns, arrangements and repetitiveness. The empirical aspects are converted into abstracted concepts, models and categories. The structural studies have also taken comparative framework.

The dialectical historical orientation is primarily on Marxist approach and method for the analysis of social reality.[9]

The dialectical method has not been termed as Marxist, as adaptations have been made keeping in view the Indian social reality. It is however a less developed branch of Indian sociology. D.P. Mukherji and Ramkrishna Mukherjee emphasized the significance of dialectical model.[10] A.R. Desai had consistently used dialectical-historical approach with ideological fervour and commitment. He has consistently exposed contradictions in policies and programmes of change. The dialectical-historical theoretic orientation grew rapidly in the seventies, when micro-empirical realities were subjected to class observation along with macro-structural social and economic processes in India.[11]

These theoretical-orientations basically have implicit or explicit ideological connotation. The implications can be discerned at the level of *analysis,* which as a critique rejects the way social reality is managed or justifies the formation of social reality as it has come to be, manipulated and constructed. At other level, they imply need for alternatives, modifications and corrections. Knowledge-neutrality is contradicting in terms. Evaluation and analysis of social reality reveals systematic formulation of scattered, diverse and immediate impressions which are mediated through common man's impressionistic perceptions and views. At the third level, dominance of theoretical orientations generated institutionally tends to lead to negation and blinding of our own intellectual traditions.

Apart from the question of theory and ideology, the issue of methodology and ideology assumes significance in the context of Indian sociology.[12] The process of inquiry necessitates a research design which helps in its systematization from initiation to completion. Methodology in natural science is independent of and is not determined by the nature of natural reality. However, the methodology in social sciences necessitates taking into account the nature of social reality inclusive of norms, values, institutions and such cultural and social forces which lead to distinct social formation in a locale. The conceptual categories at certain level necessitate use of indigenous terms which through abstracted format are converted into concepts. The use of western concepts can fix our mind-set to see indigenous-particular nuances in a specific manner. This obviously leads to distortion of reality. Caste and class are abstracted concepts for concrete social realities although both connote social stratification. The former is peculiarly Indian phenomenon. Historical records have great significance for a society which has long and recorded past. Mythology, folklore and oral tradition reveal nature of social reality of pre-literate societies.

The techniques of interview, schedule and questionnaire need to be used with different skill and understanding. Biographies and life histories can help a great deal in qualitative understanding of individual's life experiences and through that construction of social structures and their impact on individuals and vice versa. In a society which gives primacy to collectivity than to self, and in which family, kin, community play important part, group-participatory interviews assume significance. It is necessary to understand the place of privacy, shame, ideals, norms, particularistic values, status, honour, stigma, contextual reality, local dialect, belief systems, customs, gender, caste, and relationships based on age categories as they operate in Indian society at micro and macro levels.

Methodological problems also need to be viewed in terms of ethical questions related to interference in and exploitation of respondents. The methodological contributions made by Indian sociology have been examined at two levels: first with reference to the types of methods and techniques of research that have been used; and secondly, the types of reflections that sociologists have made on their own methodological craft, looking at it from a new context of post-facto objectivity.[13] Observation as a tool of research in social anthropology and survey research design for urban studies or studies of social categories have been common in the sixties. The application of cybernetic model, set theory, and matrix algebra has been rare in Indian sociology. The sophistication of quantitative methods of research in sociology in India is not very common.

The self-reflection by sociologists on their studies reveals subjective and ideological issues which have influenced their writings.[14]

The categories of knowledge, their meaning, content and the methodology of their construction bear the deep imprint of their social and historical forces of the time.[15] In the Indian context, the colonial experience did not lead to any significant cognitive formulation reflecting the need for freedom on the part of sociologists. India had remarkable leaders who were actively involved in the struggle for freedom and had contributed through ideas and ideals, the need for freedom through struggle and mass movement. At the intellectual level, however, the role of sociologists in this arena was marginal. Absence of systematic and critical construction of colonial experience is also quite evident. Intellectually, ideology necessitates fearlessness and ability to take risks. Such fearlessness, sacrifice and moral uprightness came from activists, freedom fighters, national leaders like Gandhi, Nehru, Tilak, Sri Aurobindo, but not from professional sociologists.

Sociologists failed to mirror the social reality, social tensions and social concerns of Indian society. After independence, despite professional and disciplinary expansion, sociologists remained devoid of ideology in the sense of being critique of government, its policies nor provided any alternative for policies and programmes, which could help in providing a direction to Indian society or help in tackling its problematics. The grip of colonial and western sociology has been so profound that for sociologists, the colonial cognitive conditioning in the realm of theory and methodology acutely so socialized the sociologists, that they were almost insensitive to the real concerns of Indian society. No wonder, journalists and non-disciplinary scholars and literatures were able to analyze and focus upon the problematics of Indian society in a deeper and meaningful manner than professional sociologists.

Thus, in the ultimate analysis, the impact of colonial cognitive model and western paradigm was more powerful than the reality of social forces, in the writings of Indian sociologists. The professional work of Indian sociologists is far below the contribution of concerned non-sociologists, such that it is difficult to cite any single work, which could be termed as a classic which has been produced by any Indian sociologist. This is not to undermine their works, but to point out the critical concern and to opt for formulation of alternative sociological paradigm which would provide greater freedom, autonomy and inspiration to see Indian society from a perspective which is free from colonial-western-imperial-cognitive forces. The relationship between knowledge production and cognitive conditioning is different from the relationship of knowledge and social forces. It is, thus, not the social forces which determined knowledge but colonial cognitive forces which created particular mind-set of Indian sociologists.

Such an ideology at best is the ideology of imitation and conformity and at worst that of intellectual slavery. It alienates scholars from their own roots and moorings. It makes them insensitive, kills their ability to be critical and makes them incapable of providing alternatives based on critique of establishment. In this sense, 'ideology' is missing from the writings of Indian sociologists.

This is not to deny the analysis of some social scientists who have revealed sensitive concern for specific dimensions of problematics of Indian social reality. Scholarly traditions in history and in the ethnography of India have provided significant insights into the peasant and tribal movements. Subaltern historiography seeks to restore a balance by highlighting the role of the politics of the people as against elite politics played in Indian history.[16] The contributions made by masses in making society has gone unrecognized and unwritten due to their social placement and ignorance regarding means and mechanisms of seeking recognition.[17] Subaltern historiography treats 'people' (subalternity) as autonomous who are not dependent upon elite. The ideological element in the subaltern domain is not uniform in quality and density and at times sectional and sectorial interests have been pursued. Guha has used ideology in subaltern studies as a schema of interpretation of the past in order to change the present world and that such a change involves a radical transformation of consciousness.[18] Tribal or peasant insurgents have not to be seen as a merely 'objects' of inquiry but makers of their own history.[19] The influence is obviously Marxist. Acceptance of Marxism as an ideology has been much easier for Indian sociologists for several reasons. Marxism provided a profound theoretical as well as ideological framework with its rigorous logical and neat framework for alternative society. It had both cognitive and emotive appeals for concerned intellectuals. The existence of abundant literature in the area helped the critique of western imperialism to find solace and shelter in the paradigm of Marxism.

The subaltern studies have immense possibilities of projecting, constructing and analyzing the people's lives, institutions, problems, movements, values and the processes of their formation, structuration and restructuration at local and regional levels. The meanings thus need not be viewed from Marxist perspective but from Indian historigraphical and culturological perspective. In fact, at theoretical and ideological levels, it can provide the basis for explanation of social existence of Indian people and the way people managed their lives. The Indian culturology can be constructed at ideological, theoretical and empirical levels in terms of continuity and change through analysis of classical texts and folk-rural commonality of existence. The relationship between the two provides significant framework to understand the Indian social, cultural and personality systems, at local micro-level and trans-regional macro-level. It further provides a scheme to relate past with present, empirical with ideological, segmental with pluralism and mundane with transcendental.

The focus on peasants and workers' movements by the subaltern studies reveals only one-dimensionality of cognitive form which could be constructed from sociology of people. Movement is a form of protest and assumes significance in the context of relationship of subordination, exploitation, suppression and organized efforts to protest against such a situation ideologically. However, people's lives are influenced by several ideologies which operate through religion, social institutions, polity and cultural practices.

The role of ideologues in the form of local heroes, community leaders, revered individuals, and aesthetic and literary figures needs to be understood in the context of role of ideology, not in terms of its content and ideas but also in terms of their influence on the lives of people in everyday life, in their existence itself.

Populist discourse refers primarily to 'people' or masses.[20] The significance of ideology needs not be seen merely in terms of dialectical tension between the people and the classes and through it formulation of conflictual situations, but also as a framework for composite, integral world-view and life-ways wherein the self and society; self, society and transcendence; and diversities and conflicts are viewed holistically at a certain level of meaning construction.

Obviously, such a proposition raises several uncomfortable questions for sociology as a discipline at the level of generality of academics, and Indian sociology at the level of history of ideas in a specific society in terms of relationship of ideas and social forces and ideas in terms of their content. Ideas and ideologies are developed by people in society but not necessarily and always as consequence of social existence and social forces. Knowledge is also construction of cognitive consciousness which is creative and delinks itself from socially induced consciousness.

The diversities in knowledge and co-existence of opposite cognitive contentions, both in Indian society and cognitive system, need to be understood sociologically.

Sociology, as an academic discipline, had developed in West and was obviously a result of intellectual response to the existential conditions as they operated there. Such a sociology obviously did not take into account the world-view and life-meanings of people of the non-traditional societies. A discipline has to grow not merely in terms of concepts, theories, researches and teaching but also in terms of its own perspective, definition and coverage. Professionalization of sociology has led to its conditioning in certain ways. Intellectual journeys need freedom, not barriers or closures. Cognitive game has rules but not boundaries. Its terrain is vast and rich. Travelling on the known paths is easier but one reaches the known destinations. Unknown destinations require new searches, new paths and even new vehicles.

Indian sociology needs to enlarge the framework of its inquiry, free itself from such concepts and theoretical approaches of the West which have created trained incapacity to look beyond the given framework. Conformity to western paradigm did provide respectability which goes with westernization of life-style. But it deeply alienated sociologists from understanding and analyzing what society and social life are made of, why they continue and change, and how they continue and change.

Cultural uniqueness and similarities bring in the issue of levels of understanding social reality. Institutions like family and marriage reveal universality, yet these institutions have great deal of variations. Emotions like love and hate are universal, yet their modes of expression and institutionalized forms have variations. Relationships of power and social inequality are also universal but the ways in which they are accepted, rejected or legitimatized reveal cultural and structural variations.

The long historical continuity of Indian society necessitates understanding of cumulative forces which shape, alter and integrate the past with the present.

Thus, sociology in India imitated approaches of colonial masters. Studies of village, tribes, castes, family, and kinship dominated the work of Indian sociologists. Microcosmic empirical investigation led to obsession for fieldwork.[21] Despite the fact that Indian social institutions have had a long evolutionary history, most of the professional sociologists were committed to functionalism. Present became significant for sociological understanding, which was evidence of profound ignorance about the relationship between past and present and the processes which create continuity and change.

The use of history has to be made in relation to the understanding of meanings which historians have missed and which sociologists are capable of. Sociology has focused on the 'contemporary' and has not made systematic and academically institutionalized efforts to understand the past through sociological-historical approach and methodology. The use of classical texts and folk literature, myths and legends and diverse historical records and manuscripts can provide significant information and data in understanding the deeper and apparent meanings related to conformity to certain values and formation of specific institutions in Indian society, as it existed at national, regional and local levels.[22] Singhi has identified certain crucial aspects of studying Indian society, which are as under:

(1) The historicity of Indian society: Socio-historiography.
(2) The nature of Indian social reality: Spatial-temporal coverage.
(3) The relationship of text and context: The dialectics of hermeneutics and empiricism.
(4) The ideal normative and actual-empirical: The dialects of ideology and life reality.

(5) The structural and cultural continuum: The generality and specificities.
(6) The colonial-imperial construction: The orientalistic, subaltern and populistic critique.
(7) Theoretico-methodological appropriateness: The consonance between ontology and epistemology.
(8) The compositiveness of Indian society: The pluralistic ethos.[23]

Apart from pure academic formation, its ideology and its critique, the emergence of large number of action groups which have been trying to educate and mobilize different deprived and marginalized sections, particularly the poor, has been the most important development in India since 1960s.[24] The activist groups have taken up feminist, environmental, health and issues like literacy as their focus of work. There is plethora of micro-level empirical studies related to developmental programmes of government. There has been shift of focus from conventional to the new and emerging areas of change. ICSSR has sponsored and supported researches on poverty, scheduled castes, tribes, women, movements, and similar such areas. Despite large scale funding and adequate facilities, there is accumulation of data but not really any breakthrough in theoretical-methodological dimension or any significant revealing understanding of Indian social reality. There is no new paradigm, no indigenous conceptual formulation nor new paths in sociological journey.

Ideology in Indian sociology needs to be viewed within the proposed paradigm, which is suggestive and open-ended:

(1) Ideology of a society can be abstracted through the processual unfolding of the dominant assumptions which shape, guide and provide basis for its continuity and change.

The ideological bases, assumptions and forms of Indian society need to be constructed by sociologists. Such a construction necessitates study of classical and regional texts, local records, folklore and folk narratives, oral traditions, macro-level empirical generality, micro-level contextual reality, historicity and contemporaneity and their interactional linkages.

Sociology in the context of Indian society should subsume study of culture or culturology. The study of classical ancient languages like Sanskrit, Prakrit, Pali and other regional languages and dialects provides rich basis of such a construction. Incidentally, this is a neglected area of work amongst sociologists. Apart from social dimensions of language and dialect, the symbols, the rituals, the dress, the food habits, and the cultural and structural linkages between environment and community reveal distinctive reality of Indian society.

(2) Indian sociology under the influence of positivism has neglected the normative role of knowledge – sociological knowledge. In Indian society, knowledge in its textual form, through folk wisdom and oral narratives, stories, proverbs, mythology, has played dominant role in the formulation of norms, values, and principles which serve as guiding framework for individual and collective action in diverse areas of life. Traditionally, community, culture and social institutions were instrumentalities through which actions, beliefs and practices were normatively managed. The normative framework gave direction to human actions and activities.

The role of intellectuals, both as a critique of society and as formulators of norms, needs not only to be recognized but realized. Although role of intellectuals as a critique of society has been generally recognized, and strongly expected, Indian intellectuals have not played this role effectively. Knowledge as 'power' necessitates profoundness of articulation, rigour of thinking and relevance to people. The intellectuals have to be free from the lure of recognition by state or have to refrain from mercenary and other considerations which might come as life comforts to them in lieu of, or as bargain for freedom and self-respect. In growing power of market forces, human potentials and creativity tend to be converted into purchasable commodities; hence instead of intellectual risk taking, intellectuals run the risk of selling the soul by accommodating their mental creations to the demands of power.

On the other hand, under the impact of positivism, sociologists have been committed to ethical-neutrality. Academic structure and ethos negate the idea of norm-construction, norm-propagation, formulation of alternative systems and thereby focuses on 'what is', and not what 'ought to be' and how 'ought to be' can be realized.

The implantation of western institutions in the major areas of life organization like administration, judiciary, education, medicine, polity and economy have negated and discarded the traditional ways and means of organizing collective and individual life in Indian society. The colonial bureaucracy, based on Weberian model, was manipulated and oriented towards maintenance of British hegemony on the Indian masses.

After independence, despite the drastic change in goals of the government, the bureaucratic structure remained the same. This led to structural dissonance between the continuity of colonial bureaucracy and new goals. Post-independence era reveals increasing expansion of the space of the state and de-communiticization of the people.

The replacement of traditional panchayats by codified legal system has led to delay in justice, its formal, non-participatory distancing from people, its commercialization and mystification.

The western medicinal system has marginalized indigenous medicinal system. Health and medicine were not seen as business for profiteering in India. The evils of western medicine can be discerned both in terms of its long term impact on the quality of life as well as the commercialization of medical profession and commodification of patients.

The educational institutions have been based on western model. The cognitive contents, theoretical approaches and conceptual categories have been replicated for Indian students. The academic socialization was devoid of understanding of India's intellectual heritage. Higher education was imparted in English for many years and in almost all the universities.

Formal democracy and consumeristic-oriented economy were yet other aspects which were adopted in independent India. Sociologists could have analyzed the relationship and relevance of these institutions within the context of Indian social reality. The purpose of this discussion is not to debunk the western institutions, but to examine the need for their appropriateness for Indian society. The sociologists, therefore, should perform the role of norm-formulation, which is an essential input of ideology.

The ethical-normative formulation does not come from political elites, nor from business, administrative and other elites. The intellectual and non-political leaders-thinkers can play significant role in nomos building processes and instrumentalities. It has been the traditional role of intellectuals in India. Intellectuals have the cognitive ability to comprehend reality, anticipate certain consequences and provide direction and path to pursue. Thus, sociologists should be concerned with formulation of appropriate norms which would provide proper direction for the institutional functioning. In absence of any normative guidance, there is a situation of anomie at the level of society and alienation at the level of individual, which need to be filled up through appropriate normative construction. In the wake of post-colonial situation, as an emergent consequence of independence of the country, significant alterations have taken place. Apart from the law there are no means to regulate, guide and provide direction to the people in the changed milieu.

Sociologists can cognitively construct ideologies from the speeches and writings of thinkers, activists, social and religious reformers which have received only marginal attention from some sociologists in their writings. The ideas of Gandhi, Ambedkar, Sri Aurobindo, Vivekanand, Tilak, and literateurs like Premchand, can be converted into systematic sociological normative formulations.

There are strong normative-ethical and spiritual dimensions in the writings of these scholars. Gandhi had strong emphathic understanding of Indian social reality as it was reflected in the lives of people. His writings and speeches have touched upon almost all aspects of people of India. With central focus on freedom struggle through instrumentalities of non-violence, *satyagraha,* non-cooperation and truth, his discourse provides normative framework for decenteredness of power, non-exploitative economic system, concern for downtrodden, gender equality, religious tolerance and harmony between man and nature.

His charisma was all-pervasive. Gandhi did not make any dichotomy between thought and practice in his everyday life and experimented with ideas and ideals through self-practice.

Sri Aurobindo's construction of India was based on abstracted cognitive formulation. He reinterpreted Indian culture, ideals and ideology through deeper spiritual-metaphysical schema. The range and depth of his scholarship reveals profoundness of intellect. Sri Aurobindo wrote on all major themes which affect human life with a clear vision of the direction the human society should be taking.

While Gandhi had mass appeal, Sri Aurobindo's influence was restricted to educated enlightened individuals, scholars and spiritual seekers. Their ideologies and converge differ – as both sought truth in different ways. Gandhi sought truth in mundane with reference to transcendence while Sri Aurobindo sought truth through transformation linked to transcendence, with reference point being mundane. Thus, India's intellectual traditions and social formation depict profound pluralism. Pluralism, as an ideology, has been the basis for diversities in Indian society in all its manifestations – ideas, practices, belief systems, institutions and values.

The *Anekantvad* of Jain religion focuses on the need for understanding a phenomenon from different perspectives. To understand any phenomenon from any one singularistic perspective is part of imperfection. A phenomenon has innumerable traits. A fruit has a size, colour, smell, touch, characteristic to satiate others, curative traits and so on. It implies relativism in contentions. *Syadvad* explains relativism at theoretical level. When a phenomenon is analyzed, different possibilities can be put forward. Any phenomenon from one aspect is *sat* and from another point of view *asat*; from one perspective it is useful, from other it is not useful. There are seven possibilities in a such a schematic paradigm.

(1) *Syadasti* – Every phenomenon from one of the perspective of its character, space, time and situational contextuality is true – *sat*.
(2) *Synasti* – The same phenomenon from the perspective of other space, different time, space, and context is untrue.
(3) *Syadasti-nasti* – When both the interpretations are kept in sequence, the phenomenon is true and untrue also.
(4) *Syadvaktavya* – When both the expectations are kept simultaneously, then nothing can be said as speaking is sequential. If both the interpretations are put together, then it is *Avakatvya*.
(5) *Syadasti Avakatvya* – A phenomenon is true from one perspective and *Avakatvya* from another.
(6) *Syannasti Avakatvya* – A phenomenon is untrue from one perspective and *Avakatvya* from another.
(7) *Syadasti Nasti Avakatvya* – A phenomenon is true from one perspective, untrue from another perspective and is *Avakatvya* from yet another perspective.

Like true and untrue, there can be similar combinations for perennial and transitory, general and specific, and similar and different.

The *Syadvad* signifies the theoretical dimensions of pluralism of perspective and thus, encompass contradictory propositions as true or false as seen from different angles. For sociologists, *Syadvad* becomes base for the explanation of diversities of approaches, contextuality of truth and cognitive-relatives.

(1) *Spatial-locale Oriented Construction*

The specificities of a particular region in terms of structure and culture reveal the mechanisms of social forces as they operate in an autonomous way. The local deities, customs, rituals, heroes, dialect, ecology, systems of stratification, marriage, family and institutions of governance, conflict management and livelihood, reflect local-regional creativity, adaptation and accommodation. Understanding of such micro-level realities are significant both at their own levels of linkages as well as in relation to wider societal linkages.

(2) *Spatial-macro Societal Construction*

The spatial-macro societal construction takes a broader coverage and goes beyond local-contextual. The great traditions, encompassing the totality of India, illustrate the point.

(3) *Temporal-period Processual Construction*
In such a construction, the processuality of time becomes the focal point for analysis of social reality. The process of time can be viewed at micro-spatial-local level as well as macro-spatial-societal level. The time can be periodized or could be seen non-sequentially to put phenomena in a sequence despite temporal dissociation.

Recurrence and regularity of societal phenomenon can be examined in relation to time interval, frequency and span.

(4) *Normative-ideal Construction*
The human existence necessitates schema and institutionalization of norms which mediate between individual and external objects – physical, social, cultural and transcendental. Values and norms provide the basis for realization of different goals. The ideal normative construction of a society in terms of continuity and change can be attempted through analysis of classical texts, religious scriptures, fables, mythological stories, folklore and ethical-narratives.

The worldview of Indian society is characterized by transcendental references in all mundane spheres. The schema of life has been characterized in terms of *dharma, artha, kama* and *moksha*. The pursuits of material-utilitarian goals, sensory enjoyment, moral obligations and salvation encompass fulfilment of worldly and other-worldly goals within the framework of defined principles.

The ideal-normative construct includes the division of life into four-fold stages called *ashramas*. These are *brahmacharya*, which is stage of learning and celibacy; *grahastha*, stage of familial life; *vanaprastha*, stage of withdrawal from familial ties and altruistic work with deprived and isolated communities; and *sanyasa*, devotion to spiritual values and its propagation amongst non-familiar section of the society. These values and norms were part of ideological-motivational phenomena and did not find their articulation in the institutional-organizational framework of the society. The obligation were relative to space (*desha*), time (*kala*), ability to make *sharma* (effort) and innate *guna*(endowments of the individuals).[25]

The theory of *karma* is another important attribute of Hindu view of life. The assumption is that soul is immortal, and rebirth is a continuous process determined by *karmas*. The salvation is the ultimate destiny of the soul.

(5) *Empirical-operative Construction*
The empirical-operative construction is the reality of society as it discerns, works and takes place in a society. The institutional, structural, processual, group and individual manifestations of such

realities are reflection of the mediation of forces in their generality and contextuality. These realities differ from situation to situation and also reveal a pattern which is in flux.

The empirical reality of Indian society has varied spatially and temporally. The institutional, structural, normative and cultural aspects of Indian society reveal pluralism, differentiation, conflict, co-operation, and all such patterns and processes which individuals and collectivities are capable of.

The existential operative reality as manifested objectively has been determined by social, ecological, valuational and other forces and circumstances necessitating adaptation and adjustment. The dress, food habits, customs, rituals, belief system, patterns of marriage, language and the conduct, morality and behaviour of individuals signify the encompassing possibility of everything.

(6) *Pluralistic-heterogeneous Construction*

The pluralistic-heterogeneous construction focuses on differentiated dimensions of Indian society, both at ideal-normative and actual-empirical levels.

(7) *Unified Homogenous Construction*

The unified-homogeneous construction provides a framework for integration of similar structural and cultural traits of Indian society. It focuses on identical items and ignores diversities.

(8) *Composite-harmonic Construction*

The diversity in Indian society reveals the essential unity and harmony which reflects its fundamental ethos.

(9) *Conflictual-divisive Construction*

The diversities of Indian society have been constructed and converted into divisiveness, both at abstracted-cognitive level and operative-empirical level.

(10) *Physical-vital Construction*

The physical-vital construction focuses on external observable dimensions of reality through empiricism.

(11) *Transcendental-spiritual Construction*

Transcendental-spiritual construction gives ontological priority to the primordial, other-worldly, ultimate and all mundane existence is explained with reference to the trans-mundane.

(12) *Continuity-replicational Construction*

Such a construction reveals the dimensions of continuity and similarities of different dimensions of Indian social reality.

(13) *Change-transformational Construction*
This construction highlights the processes, patterns and factors of societal changes which have been both endogenous as well as exogenous.

(14) *Evaluative-valuational Construction*
This approach focuses on the ethical and moral evaluation of Indian society.

(15) *Insider-outsider Construction*
The way in which Indians have constructed their own reality and the way on which outsiders have constructed the Indian reality, differ due to variations in perception, point of view and location in a particular society.

(16) *Integral-holistic Construction*
This construction takes into account all dimensions of societal reality and establishes linkages between local and universal, mundane and transcendental, individual and collectivity, process and pattern, harmony and conflict, subjective and objective, and scientific and humanistic.

(17) *Ethno-cognitive Construction*
The ethno-cognitive construction focuses on contextual, local-regional, specific and people's perception and understanding of existentially experienced and acted upon reality.

(18) *Universalistic-cognitive Construction*
The universalistic-cognitive construction deals with essential-universalistic dimensions which are not found by temporal and spatial constraints. They are true for all societies, all people and all times.

(19) *Anekantvad-relativistic Construction*
Anekant implies multiplicity of perspectives for understanding the reality. Every perspective is partial, hence incomplete. Each phenomenon has unlimited traits. For example, a fruit has form, smell, structure, taste, effect on body, etc. *Aekantvad* implies use of 'only' while *Anekantvad* connotes 'also'.

There is always relativism in statements, formulations and interpretations. A person says, 'I am small; smaller than whom?'

From the viewpoint of relativism, an object is both big and small. Relativism also implies permanency of essence. Gold can be converted into a ring, a bangle or a chain and despite change in form and size, the gold remains gold.

All religions are true, despite variations in forms and objective expressions on the basis of relativism. *Syadvad* is the linguistic discourse of *Anekantvad*'s perspective. The former has linguistic orientation while the later is oriented towards ideas. Till a perspective dwells in the realm of ideas, it is a *Anekantvad*, and when it is couched in language it is *Syadvad*.

Saptabhangi is the mode of expression of *Syadvad*. There are seven modes of expression of *Syadvad*:

(1) *Syadasti*: A phenomenon is true in accordance with its own time, feeling, locale and personality.
(2) *Syanasti*: But the some phenomenon is 'not true' from the standpoint of other locale, other feeling, other time, etc.
(3) *Syadasti-Nasti*: If both the assumptions are placed sequentially, it is *sat* as well as *asat*.
(4) *Syad-Avaktvya*: If both the assumptions are placed simultaneously, then it is undescribable. Since all speaking is sequential, two contradictory assumptions cannot be conveyed simultaneously.
(5) *Syadasti-Avaktvya*: A phenomenon is true from one perspective and undescribable from other perspective.
(6) *Syanasti-Avakatvya*: A phenomenon is not true from one perspective and undescribable from other.
(7) *Syadasti-Nasti Avakatvya*: A phenomenon is true from one perspective, and not true from other perspective, but cannot be described so simultaneously.

As there are seven possible combinations on the bases of true-untrue, similar combinations are possible on the basis of (a) permanent-transitory, (b) uniformity-differentiation and (c) general-special.

II

In this section, various articles of the volume are being summarized. Arguments and themes in many articles reveal similarity as well as dissimilarities. Variant perspectives and schema of classification have been outlined taking each article independently for epitomization.

Jaganath Pathy's article on 'In Pursuit of Indigenization: Trends and Issues in Building Sociology for India' emphasizes the need for demystification of the western mainstream sociology along with critical evaluation of the so-called indigenous paradigms. The mainstream sociology has performed the ideological functions of the ruling capitalist class, dominated by the world capitalism and embroiled in the vicissitudes of politics of the establishment. This has resulted into mystification of social consciousness and blunted critical impulse. The concealment of unpalatable truths of domination is constantly obfuscated through repetition of platitudes and disguised propaganda. The ideological commitment to scienticism, objectivity and ethical neutrality have led to alienation of sociologists from their surroundings. It has led to status-quoism. Quantification focuses on appearances and external form and thus neglects the inner-structural relationships between objects, the consciousness and struggles of the subjects. It is the dialectics between inductive and deductive processes that unfold the laws of existence and change, and bring unity between history and structure, quality and quantity, and universal and particular.

The mainstream sociology in India is wedded to objectivity and neutrality. Institution of academic sociology in the positivistic mould has led to culture of silence, paradigm of conformity and intellectual slavery. This has led to status-quoism brought through western sociology and its theoretical approaches. The author opines that if sociology has to be relevant both in terms of conceptual articulation at theoretical level and policy formulation at pragmatic level, it must free itself from the suffocative 'global' sociology and unshackle the paradigm imposed by imperialism which distorts the understanding of the Indian reality and obstructs the praxis-oriented activities of liberation, justice and humanism.

The distinctiveness of India society, in terms of its historicity, diversity, pluralism, catholicity and assimilation capacity, led to the debate on Indian sociology, ethno-sociology and indigenization. India has unique cognitive and cultural traditions. Both indological determinism and crash empiricism could not deal with internal dynamics of structural and cultural transformation.

The author examines the contention of Dumont, Meillassoux, and Hawthorn in relation to the above assumption. Indian culture contains both the dominant Brahmanic traditions and the counter-traditions of peasants, tribes and other ethnic groups. There was autonomy of each tradition and unity in pluralistic modes of life. Indian tradition was neither static nor frozen, it was continuously embedded with counter-cultures. There are several versions of each epic. Hinduism itself is too fragmented in terms of social structure, value system and ideology. There has always been inter-tradition interactions. There is need for critical evaluation of indigenization. The overwhelming majority of the Indian subalterns need to be given its due place.

The author decries the tendency for sectarian glorification and romanticization of the traditional institutions, associated with Hinduism. At a time when there is unprecedented threat to the diversity, the effort at indigenization in terms of Brahmanical order amounts to playing in the hands of chauvinism and fascism.

Developing conceptual schema and theoretical formulations in accordance with historical and cultural specificities of India is yet another dimension of indigenization. This is not to reject the western models and paradigms, but to use them appropriately and selectively, along with internal innovative cognitive categories which fits into the social reality of India. However, not much has emerged in this intellectual realm, despite its ideological acceptance. Indigenization has faltered because it failed to emphasize social justice and economic concerns, although these issues have existed in the tradition.

The emancipation of inarticulate people needs to be emphasized. The author is critical of intellectual dependence of sociology in India. Orthodox academic magnets may not relish revision of their pet views, blatant propaganda, ideological coyness and methodological ascerticism. There is a need to be critical of international capitalism and control of state apparatus. There is a scope for a praxis-oriented sociology through the process of conscientization. Western sociology's false notion of internationalism should be demystified and debunked. The aim is not to completely discard the western paradigm – both the wholesale adoption and wholesale rejection is detrimental to sociological liberation. Comparative perspective and critical evaluation, with concern for both universal and contextual, are important aspects of the new approach. Concepts and theories are bound by time and space. Distortion of culture for domination which perpetuates unequal exchanges is done through intellectual mode of interpretation. Sociology should offer social criticism. The endogenous knowledge has its own structural causality and rationality.

People's knowledge should be understood, organized, preserved and used. After all, it is the people who are subjects of their own transformation and authors of their own history.

The tragedy for sociology in India, both neo-colonial and indigenous varieties, is its alienation from the people, the motive forces of history. A decolonized sociology and indigenous research demand collective reflection and action.

Thus, sociology for India should strive to demystify both the alien and the indigenous dominant ideologies in terms of commitment to the liberation of oppressed and provide praxiological thrust into their sociological activities. There is need for free and frequent interaction between disciplines, commitment to history, and use of a comparative paradigm. People's fight for liberation should decide research issues and that would produce a relevant sociology; and also contribute to alternative humane social order.

The second article by **Suresh Chandra Shukla** deals with 'Pluralism and Education in India: Problems and Possibilities'. The author has raised the question: 'What is India?' The notion of India as a geographical, political and cultural entity has been debated by different cognitive streams of constructing India. The question of pluralism assumes significance at various levels of its expression. The author raises the issue of secularism in the context of educational institutions run by religious organizations. The ideological orientations of parties in power in different states have influenced the changes in curricula, grants-in-aid and nominations in boards of education. The rewriting of history has not been merely influenced by political ideology of certain parties but has also been motivated by orientalist critique of colonial cognitive paradigm of the construction of Indian society.

The contributions of people in different walks of life necessitated a nationalistic-civilization approach, rather than regional-civilizational. The National Council of Educational Research and Training (NCERT) involved scholars in writing the comprehensive history for school students. Such attempts have their critics too. Updating of history came under attack as it was felt that the 'pseudo-secularists' are seeking to glorify the post-independence leadership of the largely secular Congress party which has been running the country almost on its own.

Religious denominations, particularly among Muslims, and later Sikhs, have also promoted fully religious associations, totally unaided by the state. The schools of Christian minority have tended to be elite because they were the first English-language schools. The 'secular' provisions of the Constitution have tended to be interpreted in favour of both elitism and parochialism. There is little religious or formally sanctioned segregation. However, gender segregation is permissible wherever desired. The formal structure of education offers very little scope for particularistic tendencies or even much pluralism. They provide uniformity which leads to homogenization. The parochial institutions receive grants-in-aid from the state. It is the contention of author that with the rise of BJP as party in power in certain states, the picture of education could change.

The largest scope for the propagation of particularistic tendencies of a different religious and cultural complexion lies in traditional family and religious institutions, the political system and the emerging mass media.

The RSS, the Tablighi movement and the Jamaati-Islami movement perform educational functions according to their beliefs, which counter the spirit of national and cultural integration. The face-to-face and person-to-person organizational links which these communities are developing exercise a supra-educational influence in a separatist and non-liberal direction, which it would seem naive to categorize as pluralist. Separate schools would serve to strengthen these tendencies and minimize the possibilities of understanding which is the basis of real pluralism.

Hindi has been a unifying and integrating force through films, but television has taken more communal character according to the author. The assertive homogeneity and recalling ancient past through TV in response to wider socio-political tendencies have communal implications. The *Ramayana* has glorified Hindu identity. Only half of the 11 year-olds receive schooling. Polity and socio-cultural systems are less affected by the educational system. The pressures of divisiveness have been created by converting differentiation into divides. There is centralized network in educational system, through prescribed syllabi and examinations, which has ensured broad uniformity. The state agency finances education but it consists of professionals and academics of all denominations and persuasions.

The third article by **Dipankar Gupta** is entitled 'Sociologism, Marxism and the Anthropological Imagination'. The author is skeptical about the universal opinion that anthropology is the study of primitive societies while sociology is the study of modern ones. There is pure sociology and pure anthropology despite overlapping concerns. How and why the lack of anthropological imagination inhibits the development of sociology and anthropology as truly humanistic discipline is the major thrust of the article.

Marxism has been credited with upholding the anthropological imagination and for the transition from blind humanism to enlightened humanism. The early anthropologists such as Tylor, Boas, down to Malinowski, were interested in the study of Man – the Universal Man. Their concern was to show the commonality of mental apparatus of 'primitive' with 'civilized' man. Analysis of social structure assumed secondary importance. Sociology, on the other hand, is concerned with the study of social structure. Since man is not its primary concern, it could be termed as 'anti-humanist' or 'ahumanist' discipline.

The essence of man can be demonstrated through anthropological imagination, which demonstrates the unity of man and views, customs and traditions as contextual in terms of time, space and intervening circumstances. These customs and traditions get modified, altered, bypassed, subverted and resisted. Anthropological imagination believes in essential unity and similarity of the human mind.

The author, through anthropological imagination, brings out a strong critique of Durkheimian sociology. This specific sociology has been termed sociology due to its dominant influence in the mainstream sociology.

Discussing Marx and Althusser, the author states that by denying man a legitimate role, Althusser takes away from Marxism the vitality of praxis. The anthropological imagination is an essential element of Marxism. From any point in the social formation, man is both dependent and independent. A pure man is not only conceptually a sociological absurdity but empirical impossibility. There is nothing like complete freedom in society – it is because choices are limited and man has to be the universal man of the anthropological imagination.

The ideological elements and ideological systems are outgrowth of the material world. It is only in the structuration that ideological elements get a semantic content and meaning. Anthropological imagination can go a long way towards showing up the doctrinaire and undialectical nature of certain formulations by few Marxist scholars. Once it is acknowledged that neither structure nor superstructure can determine causality in society, we are close to an appreciation of the various ways by which man manipulate his social environment to his advantage. Man manipulate the ideological heritage in consonance with his 'lived in' relation in the world. In Marx, there is detailed treatment of the unconscious structure and also the notion of men making their history unconsciously.

The author states, through examples of Dumont and Godelier, that once the anthropological imagination is given up and along with it the anthropological man, despite diversities of theoretical and methodological preferences, conclusions would be the same.

Sociological imagination demands a conjecture between historical and biographical investigation, whereby one is able to understand the social and historical processes that separate individuals and alienate them from one another.

Social forces must work through man, hence anthropological imagination encompasses sociological imagination. 'At the root of man is man himself' – it is the 'reflexive cogito', which mediates through social forces. The sociological imagination tells us of the deep structure that binds men together only to differentiate them, while through anthropological imagination mankind can again be united. Sociology can become a true humanistic discipline through anthropology.

The fourth article entitled 'Reciprocity in Social Science: Gender Issues' by **Patricia Uberoi** deals with construction of social science knowledge about women's lives in India and China. The basic questions raised in this context relate to the way in which narratives of past and present have been constructed, social science knowledge created, and empirical data collected, regarding changes in the status of women.

Access to knowledge is akin to access to property, where intellectual products become 'capital', to which certain groups and individuals have better access than others. This leads to 'power' to exercise control over others.

The problem of non-reciprocity in the production and authorization of social knowledge has assumed significance. Women studies have been inspired by feminist theory, and is the outcome of the western feminist movement of the 1960s and the 1970s. Women are supposed to have better insight into other women's lives. Men are excluded from feminist forums.

The 'homogenization' of women, as an analytical category, has come under scrutiny of late. Black women are constructing their own understanding of the feminine condition. They see themselves as being exploited by both white men and white women, undercutting gender solidarity. The white women, along with white men, have been beneficiary of the system of racial inequality. Similar affinity can be seen in the caste system. Lower caste women are exploited by higher caste men, who are careful to monitor the sexuality of their own women. The system rested on the notion of purity-purity of higher caste women. The various social measures taken during the colonial period really helped the higher caste women, such as abolition of *sati*, widow remarriage, raising the age of marriage, etc.

The bulk of the literature on women in India presents a homogenized account of the Indian women – upper caste, bourgeois and Hindu. Despite parasitic dependence of academic agenda of women's studies on the First World, the Third World women have been challenging the preoccupations of the First World women, as irrelevant to their own needs. The author, quoting Ashis Nandy, states that women's liberation movement on the lines of that in the West, is irrelevant in India, as Indian women need to seek liberation from their sons. It is the mother-son bond which is of crucial significance, unlike the conjugal bond of the West. Indian feminists have found the question of sexuality disquieting.

The Indian feminists have ambivalent attitude towards the state. The burden of population control falls on women. The modern state is duplicitous on gender issues, giving lip-service to the cause of women, while actually acting in the interests of men. Progressive legislation remains on the 'statue book'.

The inappropriateness of feminism in the Indian context reveals the misplaced emphasis on issues which are not of real concern in India and neglects those that are. Indian women scholars have not made any contribution on theoretical and methodological aspects of women's movement. Work is available on theoretical positions generated elsewhere, but not endogenously.

The space for self-expression for Indian women has come through religion, specially through *bhakti*. The other issue relates to the colonial construct of Indian women as victims of inhuman practices. The author believes that this line of reasoning has come closer to even romanticizing the several ignoble customs.

The deconstruction of the colonial discourse on women has certain hazards. A text is termed as based on colonial perspective, hence colonial knowledge. But does it invalidate the message of the text? The other problem relates to using critique of colonialism as a mechanism to avoid self-blame which has been used as a means of transference. There is dearth of discourse on position of women in princely states which were not directly ruled by British.

There is a need to debate several issues. In what sense the Indian feminism is parasitic on western paradigm? Can we understand the position of Indian women, unmediated by factors of caste, class, community and culture region? Sudhir Kakkar's and Ashish Nandy's writings lead to unacceptable homogenizing and unauthenticated commonality. How do we study Indian woman in her own terms, in her own language, on her own ground and through her own categories of understanding.

Discussing eco-feminism, the author states that Indian scholars have made significant contribution in this area, both at the theory and social action levels. The second area of indigenous conceptualization relates to female power (*shakti*), associated with Mother Goddess. The third area relates to the principle of *Ardhanarishwar* (the deity as half-male and half-female). Gandhi saw his strategy of non-violence as linked to the cultivation of the 'feminine within' is no longer seen as eccentricity. Conversely, contemporary militant discourse related to women in Punjab focuses on the masculinist reaffirmation of aggression, and the repudiation of the feminine within.

The plurality of the definitions of femininity is yet another area necessitating discourse. Associating religion with femininity raises several significant issues. To conclude, the author points out that the original question remains. There are structural asymmetries in the present-day world order and given this situation how do we achieve complementarity, or reciprocity in the construction of social science knowledge in the context of indigenous experience.

The fifth article by **I.P. Desai** is entitled as 'Craft of Sociology in India: An Autobiographical Perspective'. This essay is both historical and autobiographical. It is divided into five parts: part one deals with academic socialization of a second generation student of sociology; part two describes the author's trainings in the tradition of the founders and the beginning of his career; part three deals with author's first research; part four deals with new trends in British and American sociology; and part five makes some general and specific observations having a bearing on the past as well as the future of sociological research in India.

Desai was educated at Bombay University. G.S. Ghurye and N.A. Thoothi were his teachers. Post-graduate degree was given by research as well as papers. It was possible to take four papers of sociology and four in economics which Desai opted for. Research methodology was not taught as a separate course at Bombay. Sociology was not understood as a science as it is understood today and it was supposed to have a bearing on practical life and was future-oriented.

The second generation sociologists were trained differently but were teaching sociology of a new kind. Theory was taught as it prevailed in Britain and now as it is in the US political independence has not made any difference to academic colonialism. If one were to remember any method it was comparative method. The emphasis was on impartial and adequate observation, logical reasoning based on evidence and cultivation of scientific attitude.

Desai got his PhD in 1942 on the thesis entitled 'Social Bases of Crime'. All books related to the theme were procured. As research assistant of Ghurye, he did fieldwork wherein there were no samples, no schedule and the interviews were unstructured.

Desai was appointed as a teacher in 1945 in Samaldas College at Bhavnagar. In 1951, he joined Deccan Post Graduate College and Research Institute at Poona.

His research procedure and methods on his first work were determined by sociological reasoning and sound commonsense, devoid of technical format, in which Desai had no training. He was against fetishism of methodology. This study never saw the light of the day but Desai gained a lot about the processual dimensions of research.

The next study by Desai was on high school students of Poona. He was now better in sampling and tabulation. Desai learnt things through doing those – hard but direct learning of permanent value. His experience of handling data single-handedly helped him later, guiding and supervising research work.

While at Baroda, Desai was exposed to Parsons and Merton. There he did his project on Mahuva, which was published as 'Some Aspects of Family in Mahuva'. These studies made Desai aware about conceptualization and categorization in research studies. Deadlines of projects lead to rushing and certain pressures. But setting time limit is part of managing research, otherwise it can never be completed.

The section on 'Retrospective and Perspective' does not represent the profession but is evaluation of his own work. There were new trends of visits abroad and foreigners coming to India. This priestly category has been so termed by Desai in a functional sense and not in a derogatory sense. What they said was accepted without debates.

The establishment of Indian Sociological Society was an indication of professionalization of sociology as an academic discipline.

The theories of independent origin and of culture contact influenced the studies of society and culture. However there was hardly any criticism of 'old' and 'new' thought. D.P. Mukherjee, A.R. Wadia, D.N. Majumdar, G.S. Ghurye and Radhakamal Mukherjee boldly expressed their views. The founders were diagnostic. The substantive areas of their study included tribes, castes, family, marriage education, *taluka* surveys and surveys of women clerks, farmers, untouchables, religious communities, etc. These works were based on fieldwork and written records – historical and contemporary, statistical and non-statistical. These were largely descriptive studies. The concepts used were normative and not analytical. This went on till 1950.

Srinivas brought some critical changes in the trend of sociology. He was not for social philosophy nor social work. He talked of severance of sociology from evolutionary theories. His focus was on synchronic studies and change and the field of studies from tribal to peasant societies. Srinivas was against questionnaire and statistical tests.

There was hardly any serious critique of American paradigms. Sociology and anthropology were not seen as different disciplines in those days in India. Methodology is not an exclusive prerogative of sociologists. It is common to all social sciences.

The emphasis on policy research and social change was the result of social forces and their demands. The new technology by itself has no meaning in research. Training in craftsmanship is necessary. Technology of methodology helps but it should not be made fetish. It should he made serviceable to the researchers.

The sixth article by **S.C. Dube** deals with 'Indian Sociology at the Turning Point'. The author raises several relevant issues related to the state of dissatisfaction within Indian sociology. He terms questioning of prevalent paradigms and theoretical approaches as healthy self-awareness and professional desire to redefine its goals. Obviously, such a situation is a turning point in Indian sociology.

The author makes a case for critical awareness of Indian sociological tradition, identification of weakness, assessment of reasons for absence of response of sociology to freedom struggle, and training of independence so that it could become more sensitive to changing needs.

Dube explodes several myths and taken for granted meanings of India's intellectual heritage. *Shastras* and *Smritis* were not merely metaphysical. They were also concerned with existential reality of the time. *Dharma* was related to *kala* (time), *desa* (place), and *patra* (persons, social category). The knowledge base was wide and comprehensive. It did not confine itself to *dharma*, but also *arthashastra* and *kamashastra*. The knowledge provided an integral view of life, encompassing mundane and transcendental. Empirical traditions were part of knowing society. In *Arthashastra* (324–296 B.C.), the king was advised to ensure collection of data about society to ensure proper policy formulations. *Charak*'s masterpiece on art of and science of healing, dates back to eight century B.C. and takes into account social, cultural and ecological bases of medicine. This work is based on carefully collected empirical data.

The question of ultimate reality was seen both within this world and also through transcendence. The materialistic approach did exist, so also skepticism. Social philosophy and social reality were linked together. Travellers and chronicles also gave account of India based on observation. This reflected shift from philosophy to narratives.

The Asiatic Society of Bengal was founded in 1784 which regarded history, science and art as the trinity of human knowledge. Ram Mohan Roy was a great social thinker and reformer. Dutta,

Vidyasagar and Mitra were constructing social reality of their time. Several other organizations were established for understanding and analysis of social reality which had practical and scientific concerns. There was western influence and also that of indigenous intellectual traditions.

The civil servants during colonial rule collected massive data about India. The officials wrote on history, anthropology, sociology, linguistics, and archaeology. The census operation also collected significant data. In 1857, the first three universities were established. The Bombay University established Department of Sociology and Civics in 1920. Within the university system and outside, the social sciences gained respectability and independence.

Post-independence sociology in India bears the impress of three major styles: (a) Traditions of empirical research as they developed in the West. Conceptual rigour and methodological rigour were introduced in the discipline. (b) Concern for indigenous formulations – conceptual and theoretical – to grasp the specificities of Indian society. (c) Radical criticism of the structure of society, partly through Marxism.

The author feels that even after three decades of independence, both teaching and research in sociology continue to be cast in the colonial mould. We have had 'captive mind'; ours was sociology of borrowed concepts and methods. Western paradigms were uncritically accepted. It stunted the growth of sociology.

There is great deal of mismeaning of tribe, caste, *varna, jati, gotra, dharma, vikas, kutumba, parampara, devta, devi,* etc. Besides the priorities of research were not in consonance with reality. Disciplinary boundaries got hardened and battles were passionately fought about autonomous domain of sovereign disciplines.

Dube rejects the deliberate severance of sociology and social anthropology and history and ideology. The depth of knowledge is achieved through a more wider perspective where artificial boundaries become irrelevant. The distinction between pure and applied research is also unnecessary. The mask of 'profound' scholarship often hides puerile and vicarious ideas. Sociology in India has to be autonomous and not dependent as a satellite system.

Sociology has to clean itself from colonial virus, focus on major social concerns, ensure disciplinary growth, encourage interdisciplinary dialogue, and develop strategies for the effective utilization of sociological research. The message is clear – stop chasing the mirage of high prestige models and avoid the quick sands of pseudo-intellection. Both uncritical acceptance of western sociology is bad as uncritical rejection. We ought to resolve our own problems through creative response from within. Research cannot be done without reflection. Dube suggests areas related to development, quality of life, interface between freedom, equality and social justice, as relevant themes for research.

To conclude, the author states that Indian sociology has yet to establish its credibility with the people and policy-makers. The need for problem-solving capabilities should be strengthened. The role of intellectuals has been undermined due to emphasis on immediacy and action. The need is to play a pivotal role in national reconstruction. Posterity will judge us by the degree to which we respond creatively to the challenges of contemporary social reality.

The seventh article by **P.C. Joshi** is entitled as 'Reflections on Social Science Research in India'. The main aim of this paper, according to the author, is to highlight the gaps and deficiencies of social science research in India rather than to assess and identify its achievements. The author has started with the discussion on context for social science in India. The development of social science in India has been viewed as the response to challenges confronting Indian society since independence. The thrust for social transformation and planned national development provided a new context for social science in India after independence. The Indian national leadership provided a broad framework based on democracy, social equality and mass welfare. Nehru realized that transformation of human society necessitated commitment to scientific approach. The context of India reveals influences of contradictory nature; on the one hand, breakdown of the colonial systems and emergence of national political force necessitated continuation of anti-colonial and anti-feudal revolution at the intellectual and cultural frame, and on the other, the exposure of the national intelligentia to international influences after independence was essentially based on western academics. The western dominance was also reflected in the political and economic institutions which were largely replication of western model without any appropriate changes necessitated by the specificity of historical, social and cultural forces. There has been a tendency for mechanical imitation rather than bold attempt at innovations of new approaches, concepts, theories and research methodologies. The social scientists in India are also gripping with problems which are considered important in the western world and not with issues which are relevant and are agitating the people in the country. This lack of sensitivity and inadequate response to the needs, problems and aspirations of the people of the country led to the alienation of intellectuals from the masses and their real issues. With few exceptions, most of the sociological studies continue to project India as a land, dominated by religion, joint family, caste and the village community. These institutions and issues related to them have not been treated from a dynamic perspective, but largely in a static setting. The caste and religion have been often stated as the ideological systems without reference to the impact of economic, political and technological forces. There is a separation of micro studies from the macro studies. There is absence of any theoretical approach to link the micro with the macro and interplay of forces between them. Thus, nationalism, peasant movement, intelligentia, the middle class, rural-urban interaction, the emergence of new activized conscience, the process of economic globalization and economic liberalization and similar other issues have not been dealt with adequately by the social scientists of India. The process of emergence of new India through social conflicts and movements through the release of creative energies of the Indian people after independence have not yet found an adequate reflection in the work of sociologists. Neither the sociologist nor the sociology played any significant role in the creation of new worldview or conscience.

Some feel that the very scope of social science research and the course of his development has been influenced directly or indirectly by the class society. The absence of literacy and education amongst have-nots in the past had thwarted the development of critical intelligentia from amongst the have-nots. The use of English language and insufficient development of regional languages as medium of teaching and research have favoured the select elite class in Indian society who essentially were alienated from the masses.

India does not lack the intellectual and cultural traditions but it did lack, according to the author, the scientific tradition amongst the intellectuals. The traditional social structure did not encourage dissent and the intellectual tradition was largely metaphysical, idealistic and materialistic. It was more speculative rather than empirical.

The independence movement for the first time created new awareness and raised several new questions and began organized protest movement. Several intellectuals with strong sense of commitment and the profound sense of sensitivity got involved into the agitation in independence, which was lost in building scientific scholarship during the freedom movement. D.P. Mukerji often drew attention to the contrary tendencies of our national movement – its emancipating as well as constraining effect on the social science. His favourite remark was, 'The intellectual problems of the national movement were taken care by Gandhi's own voice, and those of the left movement by the party line.' In certain sense politics was not adequately intellectualized although it was idealized. The mindlessness of the politics was to have lasting impact on the policy formulation of the country in times to come. After independence, the mindlessness of the politics has become far more acute.

The author has raised question of involvement or neutrality in the pursuance of knowledge by the social scientists. Social concerns help creativity if they lead to the choice of meaningful problems. The academic freedom without social concern has produced technocrats and/or light-weights, rather than genuine social scientists. Contemporary India is full of challenging problems waiting to be tackled by social scientists, yet they have failed even to perceive them in a proper perspective, let alone tackle them largely because of lack of sympathy and interaction with the indigenous people. Indian sociologists need self-examination and soul-searching, and should seek answer as to why the problems of social inequality, mass poverty, national development and cultural renewal have not received either adequate attention or profound treatment. The independence of social science can be maintained through commitment, devotion and integrity – both at the level of personality and at the level of ideas. It is significant to note that there has been erosion of values and formation of academic cliques for mutual admiration or mutual denigration. Early social scientists have done much serious and important work despite few higher positions available in the universities and much less funds to pursue researches. It is a quality of mind which ultimately creates knowledge and not mediocrity and manageriality. It is also significant to note that there has to be conscious effort for the promotion of social scientists from the lower class and lower castes and from the rural areas, so that their perception, experience and worldview can be made visible through articulation and writings. It is easy to promote political agitators and activists from the lower sections of the society than to provide them encouragement and transforming them into intellectuals.

The author raises the question of scientific ethos, which is different from the scientific methods. Scientific culture includes cultivation of values, attitudes, norms and methods appropriate to the growth of social sciences and also to the fulfilment of its humanistic objects. There is a need for special emphasis on the development of scientific culture due to the threat of scientific values from commercialization and bureaucratization which are impinging upon all spheres of life. The new types of research structure is emerging where grants, sponsorship and recruitment of large number of people in a project determine the status of intellectual, rather than his contribution in the field of knowledge. The fieldwork is done by hired people and reports are written by people other than the author. Under such circumstances, no work of distinction and originality is likely to emerge. Sponsored research, quite often, is a research not in the service of truth, but is a research for people in power. Under these circumstances, the scientific community has to create, observe and enforce the rules for the scientific game played in the arena of knowledge. Ideological fanaticism also poses serious obstacle to the growth of social science. The fanaticism is not merely confined to the 'traditionals' but also the 'modernists'. The fanaticism of the modernist is much more dangerous and difficult to detect as it works in a subtle manner and tends to be maneuvered systematically.

The author discusses the relationship between politics and social science. He believes that there is no aspect free from the influence of politics in the contemporary world. The influence operates both in subtle and negative ways. It has both beneficial and adverse effects on the growth of social science. The politics of knowledge can convert battles of interests into battles of ideas. The interaction of politicians and social scientists could either lead to their cross-fertilization or cross-sterilization. The interaction of politics in social science is one of the most challenging areas of research in developing countries.

Institution-building for social science research has created new instrumentality to promote and encourage research. Institution-building has to be taken as a creative challenge in the Indian context. The scientific and democratic traditions, with freedom and fearlessness to pursue knowledge, are necessary prerequisites of research institutions. One does not have to create institutions which could lead to generating Hindu '*Maths*'. It is important to recommend that 'fruit bearing research' and 'light bearing research', policy-oriented research and fundamental research, short-term research and long-term research ought to be seen with different perspective of knowledge rather than in the light of extra academic benefits. Quite often, this dichotomy is irrelevant. All knowledge properly, systematically and scientifically pursued are relevant by any standard of game of the knowledge. It is necessary that developing countries like India which is entering in the industrial age in the latter part of the twentieth century perhaps need the revolution in human science much more than the developed countries. There is a need for reconstruction of a new world-view. What is important is to understand the need for interdependence between the socio-economic reconstruction and cultural restructuration.

The eighth article by **T.K. Oommen** is entitled as 'Sociology in India: A Plea for Contexualization'. The author, while distinguishing meanings between sociology *in* India, sociology *of* India and sociology *for* India, raises certain relevant questions in the above context: Which central concern has dominated Indian sociology: order or change? Is directionality of change important for Indian sociologists? What are the appropriate units for analysis? What are the preferred techniques of investigation? To what extent Indian sociologists have succeeded in developing conceptual categories and theoretical formulations for studying Indian society? Have Indian sociologists given adequate attention to the specificity of Indian social reality? What is the nature and impact of academic colonialism? Have Indian sociologists played second fiddle to the establishment? Why some substantive themes have not been analyzed? Why there is predominance of studies in certain areas?

There are broadly five streams of thought in this context:

(1) Those who focus on specificity of Indian society historically: The Traditionists.
(2) Those who do not consider Indian society unique but do recognize its specificity. They believe in emancipation from influence of outsiders: The Nationalists.
(3) Those who argue for native concepts and categories to reconstruct social reality as people perceive it: The Nativists.
(4) Those who see Indian society essentially same as elsewhere, hence universalistic paradigm for study: The Cosmopolitans.
(5) Those who believe in the transformation of society through intervention: The Radicals.

There is not only multiplicity of perspectives but also a real identity crisis of the discipline. The problematic involved in contextualization of sociology in India may be viewed as a series of tensions.

The attempt to reduce Indian values to those contained in Hindu texts is untenable. It is largely Brahmanical in nature and fervour. A substantial population of India like *adivasis, dalits,* and even peasantry have oral history. Historical records and narrations have ignored the commonality of common man. Study of past helps the present but study of present equally helps the future. In this sense, present sociology becomes history for future.

The academic colonialism and international reference model of Indian sociologists deny them their autonomy. It happens because there are willing buyers. Rejection of international model leads to academic 'nationalism' and academic 'communalism'. The question, however remains: Whose international model?

Study of one's category provides depth but also inbuilt biases. Studies by others are equally important. The idea is not to promote and produce one's own sociology! Balance of studies by insiders and outsiders can help in building cognitive dialectics. The author is critical of academic feudalism and scholastic parochialism that reign the Indian sociology. Patronage and network linkages are detrimental and lead to internal academic parochialism.

The author raises the issue of motivation for entry into the profession which are (a) instrumental, (b) professional, and (c) existential. Expansion in teaching sociology helped students of sociology to get jobs. So also recruitment in jobs by the state. The professionals are careerists who seek prestige and power not through academics alone but means other than academics. They neglect concern for our immediate environment in the broader perspective of humanism. One's existential conditions and life experiences lead him/her to take up sociology as a mission. The author feels that sociologists in India are without a goal and this is the reason for their failure to meaningful response to the critical human issues of their times and milieu. There is no serious study of partition and its consequences. There is no sociography of untouchability in various regions in India. Poverty has been largely seen as political and economic problem rather than sociological. The issue of nationality is paramount, yet there is no comprehensive study about it.

The issue of unit of analysis assumes significance in the context of India's multiplicity of regional societies and non-regional cultural pluralism. There is need to establish linkages between village, region and nation. This raises the question of appropriateness of techniques.

The need is to use appropriate technique and not be wedded to techniquism or methodologism. The context of study should determine the use of concepts – universal or indigenous. The western epistemological dualism does not fit Indian social reality.

There are reasons for lack of innovations. There are contradictions in societal values and constitutional-legal norms. There cannot be sudden displacement but appropriate adaptations. It has to be recognized that tradition contains both assets and liabilities. We should accept appropriate values and institutions from other societies and culture. This should be done keeping in view the central tendency of a reconciliation and adaptation. Transformation may be slow but it shall be enduring. Mobilization and styles of protest ought to be specifically Indian. It should be based on appropriateness of retention, borrowing and judicious mutation.

The ninth article by **Nirmal Singh** is on 'Ramkrishna Mukherjee's Sociology: A Sociological View'. The author first delineates common characteristics of social sciences and modes of pursuing knowledge within the framework of certain rules. These are: (a) collection of relevant and reliable facts, (b) formulation of propositions, (c) eliminate contradictory statements which cannot be true simultaneously, and (d) share rules of logic.

The role of sociology is not to predict and control social situations. It has to be tolerant, pluralist and liberative and against control of others' lives. It is the centrality of question which sociologists ask which distinguishes the discipline from other social sciences. The principles of interpretation are also different. It studies human action – past, present, material, cultural, own society, other societies, different groups, hopes, fears, motivations and aspirations.

In contrast to pre-independence period, development of sociology in India in the fifties and sixties has been characterized by greater academic status, theoretical orientations, specialization, American influence and responsive to the needs of development. Srinivas, Desai and Ramkrishna Mukherjee who started sociology on the eve of independence did not represent commonality of perspectives or concerns. Desai was an activist, addressed himself to the question of social background of Indian National Movement. His sociology was troublesome to establishment, imperialism and capitalist development.

Mukherjee started his academic career with investigating famine of 1943, effect of destitution and food crisis. His later studies include *The Rise and Fall of East India Company, The Problem of Uganda: A Study in Acculturation*, and *The Dynamics of Rural Society*. The focus was on to make viable the invisible social forces and taking a diagnostic view of change. Such a sociology could not work as handmaid of power-wielders.

He shifted his interest in the direction of methodology. He does not clarify issues when he pleads for 'disparity' and 'conflict' instead of mere 'inequality', 'deprivation' and 'exploitation' instead of just 'poverty', and 'class contradiction' against weaker sections. Scientists should not only reveal the social reality but also change it according to their value judgement. Mukherjee started with many categories and operations shown from Marxist tradition in his early studies, but later advocated 'inductive inferential' method, which is equally relevant to Marxist and non-Marxist analysis in sociology.

The main contribution of Ramkrishna Mukherjee to the development of sociology in India lays in his early work, both for substantive conclusions and for methodological perspective. Mukherjee's interest in mathematical-statistical procedures was as old as the humanist emancipatory appeal of Marxism.

The tenth article by **R.S. Shrivastava** deals with 'Justice Model and Social Conflicts in Contemporary India'. The author opines that even after more than four decades of independence, Indian society is confronted with concept, content, and direction of economic, social and political transformation. Terminological equipments like 'breakdown of modernization', 'contradiction of development', 'discontinuities', and 'national disintegration' have been used for the characterization of the existential social reality of Indian society. There have been several protest movements, communal and caste riots, emergence of terrorism, loss of credibility, perpetuation of inequities, shrinking of educational and economic opportunities, corruption, and criminalization of polity and economy.

Analysis of group conflicts in India necessitates understanding of historico-social conditions in their cumulative-continuity character. The developmental model of any other country shall be inadequate for Indian society. The major difference between the 'western' and Indian situation is that in West, economic growth preceded the emergence of values of social justice, welfare ideology while in the case of India, justice model preceded economic growth. In fact, the slogan has been economic growth with social justice. However, this could not be transformed into practice.

There has been intensification and overt expression of conflicts amongst collectivities based on primordial loyalties such as caste, religion and language. Besides these, conflicts in politics, universities, and labour management are also self-evident. Group conflicts are the result of clash of interests.

The justice model as depicted by the author focuses on providing equal life chances to every member of society. It underlines distribution of power and influence in rational manner. There are three principal models which have discussed this issue. First, the 'ruling class' conception which believes that power lies with those who rule. They suppress the 'masses' for their hegemony. The second model is 'pluralistic model' which asserts that multiplicity of groups or 'pressure groups' compete with each other for power and privilege. No particular group holds the key to all decisions and influences. They often come in conflict for opposing interests. The third model is the 'elite conception' of social power, which suggests that power is unequally distributed amongst different elites. None of these models can explain the complex Indian situation. It is useful to accept selectively and appropriately underlying assumptions of each of these models for analyzing the Indian society. The concept of justice is linked with that of equality and at certain point both could come in conflict.

The author says that sometimes certain fundamental values of a society may not be consistent with each other. This is the case with India where the concepts of justice and equality lead to divisiveness and conflicts in a society. Both these values have been enshrined in the Constitution but their feasibility has not been explored. The traditional structure lacked egalitarian values. The earlier principle of hierarchy and modern exposition of equality have led to group conflicts. The principle of holism is seen as in contradiction to the institution of democracy and citizenship. The justice principle enjoins reservation or preferential treatment to historically and structurally deprived categories of people, while the principle of equality raises certain pertinent questions about it. The defense of reservation is being conceptualized as 'compensatory justice' granting special privileges and opportunities on the basis of collectivity and not individual situation, is also questioned. There have been anti-reservation agitations. The present-day generation of youth questions punishment to them for wrongs perpetuated by earlier generation. Besides collectivism which is inherent in social justice it is against the canons of procedural justice. Further benefits are cornered by the select few who are privileged, amongst the underprivileged collectivity.

These privileged amongst the underprivileged act as middle man between the state and their group and serve their interests. Such privileges lead to a sense of inferiority, entails loss of dignity and self-respect and may be efficiency. The processes of 'expansionism' and 'exclusiveness' on the part of cultural mainstream, coupled with primordial collectivism in instrumental terms, give rise to peculiar nature and types of social tensions and protests.

In the eleventh article by **Sheo Kumar Lal** on 'Time and Value', the author discusses Hegel and Marx in relation to fact and reality. Contradiction became the hypothesis of philosophical inquiry of Marx. The equation of fact and value is possible for the essential connection in history. Marx had strong ethical concerns along with action. Belief in the nobility of ethical ideals constitutes the theory of praxis of Marx. The human needs have normative character. Ethics is not intuition but ideal – it is an agency of struggle. The ideas of ethics are rooted in history, in time. And what is rooted in time is also limited by it. Every age has its own standards of judgement and evaluation. What happens in history is necessary and in a way good. *What is, was to be and ought to be*. This is historical inevitability.

The criticism to this idea is that survival alone cannot constitute the standard of right. Historical relativism suggests that history is the ultimate criterion of right and wrong. In this way, 'right' is determined by history not morality. It should be noted that history in the hands of Marx has been reduced to science. Science deals with the process of causation and discovers laws which govern the process.

Marx was a social scientist of history, of class struggles, of moral ideas. Science is incomplete without praxis and it does not merely interpret but also evaluates. The author divides Marx's system of ideas into (a) activist-analytical and interpretive type, and (b) revolutionary and activist type. Marx forged a union of historicism, sociologism and activism.

Morals of a time reflect the economic stage which society has reached at that point. There is nothing like eternal moral laws, yet there has to be moral standard to serve as an ultimate criterion of morality. To Marx and Engles, a society free from all exploitation and contradiction will provide highest morality. Thus, in the course of history, morals and values have been shown to depend upon economic or technological progress of society. It is humanitarianism which has lent colour and vitality to Marxist thought.

The twelfth article by **S.L. Sharma** is entitled as 'Ethnic Challenge to Indian Identity: Rethinking Culture-Polity Interface'. The author raises the issue of nature of Indian identity in the context of ethnicity. Is it cultural or political? Is it composite or unitary? What are the sources of ethnic dynamics, is yet another question which has been raised. Is it a consequence of the culture of modern rationalism? Is it a result of the distortions of development? About its implications the author asks: Does it represent a challenge to national unity? At the practical level, one may ask: Can the ethnic issue be resolved amicably? If yes, how? At a theoretical level, the posers are: Is there a relationship of equivalence or polyvalence between culture and polity? Does the culture of modern nationalism suit multi-ethnic societies?

There are two identities in India – cultural and political – according to the author. The essence of India's cultural identity lies in its plural character and of political identity in its federal format. Both these identities have come under severe strain of secessionist-ethnic movements. The solution lies in giving primacy to culture over polity and pluralism over unitarianism. The article is divided into five parts. The first part deals with the concept of ethnicity. In the generic sense, ethnicity refers to an identity construct based on a set of objective cultural markers – common ancestry, religion, language and territory. There is consciousness of cultural differentiation. When this consciousness of cultural differentiation turns into political differentiation, it represents the emergent conception of ethnicity. The former implies 'ethnicity-in-itself', the latter signifies the idea of 'ethnicity-for-itself'. In its dormant form, ethnicity provides cultural identity. While in its salient form, ethnicity implies urge for political power. The author further discusses allied concepts of nation and state. Nation has been used both as a cultural entity as well as political entity. State has no cultural reference. It is a political instrument having space, sovereignty and legal and administrative apparatus. The second part deals with ethnic dynamics of India. Both ethnicity and nationalism came to India as colonial constructs. Preparation of ethnography of India and census data helped colonial power to divide people. There have been several conflicts on ethnic basis in post-independence India. Ethno-linguistic upheavals, tribal eruptions, nativistic movement in Assam, ethno-regional movements for separate statehood such as Bodoland, Gorkhaland, Jharkhand, Vidarbha, etc., illustrate the variety of strifes and grouping. Most of these movements are for greater autonomy than secession. Religio-communal movements have asked for separate statehood. The author believes that emergence of such tendencies is due to contradictions within our polity. The Indian State has been able to achieve neither the cultural rights of different people nor creating a civil society. According to the author, centralization, politicization and development orientation of Indian polity has led to ethnic resurgence.

The third part deals with the nature of Indian identity. The author feels that since our sense of nationalism is only skin deep, there is danger to territorial integrity. On the other hand, the model of modern nation-state in India is a threat to our national heritage of ethnic diversity. It has stimulated ethnic reactivity. Ethnic bellicosity is a function of state repression. Ethnic pride is not a threat to national integrity, but modern nation state is.

The fourth part deals with reflections on culture-polity linkage. There are three models of culture-polity interface: uni-ethnic, uniformitarian, and pluralist. In uni-ethnic model, there is one-to-one correspondence between ethnicity and polity. Uniformitarian model characterizes multi-ethnic countries. This model stresses on the supremacy of civic culture which renders cultural diversities insignificant. Pluralist model postulates a framework of flexible and responsive polity which can hold diverse ethnic groups under one polity.

Ethnic identities should be recognized and respected. India has resolved the issues related to linguistic identity effectively. The question of regional identity needs to be tackled more effectively. Communal identity needs still greater care in handling as politicization of religion is a dangerous trend. Each identity should be tackled differently through institutional instrumentalities. There are two kinds of identity in India – cultural and political. The former is rooted in its fathomless past while the latter is of recent origin. One type of cultural identity is organic, based on transcendence, other-worldliness and spirituality. Other Indian cultural identity is composite, adaptive tolerant and accommodative. The political identities are also of two types. India was never a nation; instead there were several kingdoms. The other view was that India was always a nation. However, there is primacy of cultural identity. India has political identity as one of the biggest democracies in the world, but it is struggling to evolve a viable national identity.

The fifth part deals with the implications of this for India's integrity. Ethnicism seems to represent a threat to India's integrity and identity. Ethnic invigoration poses no challenge to India's spiritual cultural identity. *Hindutva* represents a serious threat to composite socio-cultural identity of India. It is the majority ethnicism which seems to be of greater danger to the heritage of ethnic mix. The recent demolition of Babri Masjid is a grim reminder of the potential of majority ethnicism to tear apart India's composite socio-cultural identity.

The thirteenth article by **Ramkrishna Mukherjee** is entitled as 'Study of Social Change and Social Development in the Developing Societies'. The author first discusses the conceptual dimensions of the terms. Understanding of social change is usually based on the following premises. An 'alteration' observed in economic, technological, demographic, political, psychological aspects of the societal arrangement alteration in a social arrangement modify behaviour pattern of the people, in the form of emergence, revision or disappearance. The altered behaviour pattern will have repercussions on other behaviour pattern. The emergence of new social groups will replace previously existing groupings. The author discusses the fallacies inherent in the above formulation. He illustrates the fallacy as it operates in the concept of developing and developed nations.

The indicators of social change need to be formulated with specific reference to place, time and the object of change.

The opinion, attitude, idea and the belief of the people are in a state of flux and causality in social change work in several ways. People learn in one way at home, another way at school, realities may compel them to think in the third way when they grow up, and act in the fourth way. The industrial and rural development, urbanization and spread of education have influenced the behaviour pattern but the chain does not follow expected, logical or imitative course. The above forces have not destroyed the joint family and the caste system. Changes are taking place in Indian society but they do not necessarily destroy the existing social systems. New forms of joint family and new *jatis* have emerged in the wake of forces of change.

The author suggests that it is necessary to distinguish between studies of social change from the historical or the contemporary perspective, and as an explanatory or a diagnostic proposition. According to the author, a deductive approach to the social change for developing societies is inadequate, consequently inadequacy of all such theories which emerge out of it. A-contextual and imitative application of a theory cannot be universal. Current theories of social change need to be examined empirically.

In order to draw objective and unambiguous generalizations from such an approach, it is necessary to have a commonly agreed frame of reference which locates a set of hierarchically structured units of observation, analysis and inference. Social action is the smallest unit of observation. Proceeding on this basis, we may consider a set of mutually distinct but analogous behaviour patterns to denote specific social relationships. Following therefrom, a set of mutually distinct but analogous social relationships will denote an institution. Particular characteristics of a set of mutually distinct but analogous institutions will refer to a specific social group. The tiers of social action, behaviour patterns, social relationships, institutions, and social groups express the mechanisms of any society.

The field may comprise one or more than one society, provided they are identified in terms of their place, time and object dimensions. The course of research will necessitate infinite but innumerable varieties of social action, null hypothesis, alternative hypotheses and a priori knowledge of the society under reference. The test of hypotheses will require a research design, based on the concept of statistical probability.

The author then discusses the concept of social development. Social change was a value loaded concept, according to the author, because it also implicitly meant social development. But development is also value-charged concept. Attempts have been made by economists and statisticians to enumerate the content of social development under subject categories as nutrition, health, shelter, education, and security. However, this would not eliminate values. The values are imposed by social philosophies of development. Welfare society, or from tradition to modernity concepts also are not value-free.

To conclude, the author states that appraisal of any course of social development will primarily require answering certain questions, a few of which are as under: (a) What is the goal of social development and why that goal has been chosen? (b) What is the immediate target of social development and the successive targets and how are they sequentially related? (c) What are the necessary social actions, behaviour patterns, social relationships, institutions and social groups for the realization of the successive targets?

The development of sociology in each society will have a specificity of its own. It will require an intrinsic knowledge of each society with reference to what it was, what it is and what it should be.

The fourteenth article by **A.M. Shah** deals with 'History and Sociology'. The author states that the core of the disciplines of sociology and anthropology consists of the analysis of contemporary behaviour of groups, through interview, survey, census and observation. The synchronic analysis of society is usually guided by the idea of structure, which entails the notion of continuity. Structuralists often deny the value of history in understanding society and culture. Students of social change accept the value of history in studying social change. However, often scholars borrow from text-book history and construct historical myths.

Social sciences in India should be rooted in history, for it has a continuous historical past. Moreover, every society has a historical consciousness. In India, articulators of historical past dates back to Vedic times. The *Rgvedic* society had two major articulators – the Brahman and the bard. The latter transmitted genealogies and myths – both oral and written. The same institutions have survived with different names in different parts of India.

While a great deal has been written about the Brahman's role, there is little analysis of the role of the non-Brahman legitimizers of status like the bard who have operated through a basically historical medium and idiom. The modern secular history has created yet another historical consciousness of the people of India. There is far more historical consciousness amongst common people in India then what most people realize. How then sociologists can miss it or neglect it!

The author moves on to identify what historians have missed. They have missed the sensitivity to Indian ethnography. Historical sources are silent about certain sections of the people. In the recent years, Indian historians have rightly moved from unique events such as wars and elites, like kings, queens and generals to the ordinary people.

If we miss the type of history we want, the solution is not to reject the history but to enter into dialogue with historians. Sociologists should make use of unused records for writing social history, if need be, sociologically.

The fifteenth article by **Narendra K. Singhi** is titled as 'Gandhian Social Thought in Relation to Non-Violence and Social Change'. The author first discusses the concept of social change and ideology. He further explains the factors of social change. The ideology contains both cognitive and emotive traits and is oriented towards efforts for ushering societal change for transformation. Gandhi's ideology is based on non-violence. It is the instrumentality to bring societal changes.

Gandhi's concept of non-violence has been analyzed in the following terms: (a) interpretation of Gandhian non-violence at conceptual theoretical level; (b) delineation of major areas wherein Gandhian instrumentality of non-violence was to be operationalized; (c) Gandhi's strategy of social change with its instruments of overt action; (d) Gandhi's charismatic impact and operative failure of ideology; (e) explanation for the operative failure of ideology; and (f) the relation of structural changes to the psychic-spiritual development of man.

The concept of non-violence has been analyzed in its various dimensions: (a) the mystical-theological level, (b) the philosophical level, (c) the ethical level, and (d) the sociological and psychological level. The analysis in the paper is confined to the sociological dimensions of the concept. Certain level of non-violence is a functional prerequisite for the maintenance of social order. However, no society has completely eliminated non-violence. The positive tradition of non-violence is activistic. It inculcates value of kindness, love, and brotherhood for the regulation of human relationships. Non-violence in its passive form refers to non-killing at physical level and refraining from hurting others, through speech and action at social level and not to entertain non-violent thoughts at psychological level.

Non-violence for Gandhi was an instrumentality of action, a supreme human value, the psychic force and has a transcendental reference. It has been equated with truth and God by him. Gandhi preached and practised non-violence in political field, social field and economic field.

Gandhi's ideology is not a conscious intellectual systematization of theoretical ideas by him, but a construct by scholars and followers. Gandhi's personality formation was based on a continuous search for truth through experimentations in real life.

He was involved in mass movement wherein people of all types were involved. *Satyagraha* was his instrumentality of action against aggression, injustice and violence. It was moral equivalent of war. Fasting was the most potent armory of *satyagraha*.

Gandhi had a charismatic influence and could mobilize all sections of society, in one way or the other, for the independence and social transformation. After independence Gandhi's ideas did not find proper place in the constitutional, legal and administrative framework of polity and policy.

The author explains the reasons for the operative failure of ideologies. Quoting Sri Aurobindo, the author suggests that the social transformation necessitates transformation of consciousness without negation of matter. Collective possession and individual freedom to pursue action and work which could maximize one's creative potential, ought to be the existential basis for social formations. In such a scheme, transcendence and mundane are merged, so also communism and individual freedom.

The sixteenth article by **J.S. Gandhi** is entitled as 'Professions and their Co-optation in State and Polity: The Case of Legal Profession' The author brings out the increasing extension of state domain in civil and social life of people.

The central thesis of the article relates to co-optation of professionals in the Indian polity, particularly lawyers. The case of Indian lawyers reveals that such a phenomenon exists due to 'individual-personal' interest and not capitalistic interest in the Marxian sense nor professional interests in the functional sense.

The author supports his thesis through empirical evidence by quoting figures of professionals (lawyers, teachers, medicos, engineers) in eight Lok Sabhas. Thereafter, he gives data of selected state legislatures in support of his thesis.

The role of lawyers in pre-independence and immediately after independence has been highlighted. Lawyers have played an important role in the freedom movement of India. Their role in constitution-making was significant and important. The author provides evidence from Nepal also. There have been lately some confrontationists' posture on the part of legal profession. The activists orientation of judges and many liberal-minded lawyers has led to protest against state on issues of *dalits* and oppressed. The principle of *locus standi* was waived by the judges in the case of public interest litigation.

Simple post-cards sent by mail were treated by judges as 'petitions' and given priority listing. However, there were no enduring norms created out of such prayers. Such reactions are individual or sectarian and do not represent the dominant ethos of the contemporary legal profession.

The seventeenth article by **T.N. Madan** is entitled as 'Dialectic of Tradition and Modernity in the Sociology of D.P. Mukerji'. The article deals with some central ideas in the works of the late Prof. Dhurajati Prasad Mukerji. DP was one of the founding fathers of sociology in India, an effective teacher and an original thinker.

The author has examined the relationship of tradition and modernity in DP's thought. DP's two books, *Personality and the Social Sciences* (1942) and *Basic Concepts in Sociology* (1932) were considered by him as 'personal documents'. For DP', knowledge and knower ought to be seen together. Knowledge has to be philosophic, albeit based on empirical data. It transcendents disciplinary boundaries. The Indian intellectuals had borrowed worldview, based on western liberal outlook. The element of 'purpose' has been stressed as 'progress' is not a stage in automatic self-generating evolution. Progress is a movement of freedom. For DP', progress involves balancing of values and he draws from religious scriptures to identify the hierarchy of values.

Emphasis in his works has changed through passage of time. DP was very sensitive and was influenced by the environment around him. He drew from traditional culture as well as modern. *Modern Indian Culture: A Sociological Study* was first published in 1942 and its revised edition in 1947 – the year of partitioned-independence. Synthesis has been the dominant organizing principle of Indian culture. British rule provided a real turning point to Indian society. The middle class helped in the consolidation of British rule in India, but later challenged it successfully. DP's vision of India was a peaceful, progressive India born out of 'union' of diverse elements, of distinctive regional cultures. Reorientation to tradition was an essential condition of moving forward. DP denied that he was Marxist, he claimed to be only a 'Marxologist'.

The national movement was anti-intellectual, although it generated idealism and moral fervour. He concluded, 'Politics has ruined our culture.' DP believed that no genuine modernization is possible through imitation. He feared cultural imperialism. Modernization is a process of expansion, elevation, revitalization of traditional values and cultural patterns. Tradition is a principle of continuity. It gives us freedom to choose from different alternatives. Modernity should be defined in relation to, and not in denial of, tradition.

DP's arguments have been criticized. Saran has pointed out that DP does not subject the socialist order itself to analysis and takes its benign character on trust. He fails to realize that a technology-oriented society can not easily be non-exploitative and not anti-man; that the traditional and the modern worldviews are rooted in different conceptions of time.

DP's concern is seen by author as that of westernized Hindu intellectual. There is need to read DP, reprint his works and examine his ideas, concludes the author.

The eighteenth article by **C.N. Venugopal** is entitled as 'G.S. Ghurye on Culture and Nation-building'. The author discusses Ghurye's perspective on nation-building. Ghurye averred that culture and polity could not be separated.

Ghurye's approach has been described as an exercise in the sociology of knowledge. In general, sociology of knowledge is the critique of positivistic epistemology. Human life, in contrast to nature, is infinitely variable. It is characterized by reflexivity, contingency and collective subjectivist perception, leading to relativism, rather than absolute certification of knowledge. India's intellectual traditions reflect theoretical-speculative knowledge. There were variations in approaches related to validity of knowledge. *Vedanta* and *Mahayana* Buddhism followed an idealistic epistemology, with distrust of empirical knowledge. *Lokayata, Sanakhya, Vaiseseka* and *Mimamsa* followed an empirical epistemology in varying degrees. The *Jainas* followed a relativistic epistemology which led to the doctrine of multiplicity and partiality of truth.

Ghurye wrote a number of essays on the sociology of knowledge. His works on caste, ethnicity, religion and culture can be placed within the sociology of knowledge. He viewed the growth of knowledge in India in relation to contingent (historical and cultural) factors and used plural sources of knowledge. His collection of essays reveals his nationalistic sentiments.

Ghurye was interested in the description of caste in its various aspects – the processes of fission and fusion included. He was upset over the proliferation of caste-sponsored associations. The inter-caste rivalries and the rise of numerous caste blocks were undermining the national unity. Ghurye's ethnography of caste included both detailed and specific works. He advocated a policy of assimilation of tribes into the mainstream, not merely in economic terms but also in moral and cultural terms. He, however, omitted to mention the role of Christian missions in the ethical reform of tribals. For the tribes of north-east, Ghurye, proposed a programme for their political assimilation. He did not adequately appreciate the contribution of Buddhism and Jainism to cultural nationalism in India and also did not document the contribution of Muslims and Christians to India's nation-building. Ghurye collected vast data on social tensions in free India. He resorted to a reductive approach in his assessment of communal tensions.

Ghurye showed his deep concern for the unity of India. *Brahmi* script and Sanskrit language unified India. *Asvemedha* sacrifice provided ritualistic unity to the monarchic power. Such instances, symbols and practices led to cultural nationalism. The unity of India stemmed from the acculturative processes. Despite this, Ghurye's thinking was slanted in favour of Hinduism. There was a sort of cognitive dissociation with non-Hindu cultural motifs.

In his treatment of values, Ghurye mainly relied on the Hindu tradition. He noted two interludes in the evolution of Indian values – the *Upanishadic* quest for inner perfection and the Ashokan policy of compassion and goodwill towards all sentient beings. The continuous interaction between folk and elite groups in India gave rise to a syncretic culture. Ghurye concludes his discussion of Indian values by referring to *jatras*, gambling and drinking which were popular amongst both folk and elite.

The Indian system of knowledge called *vidyas* was designed to cater to the elite groups – most of whom belonged to the three upper *varnas*. The learning was based on *guru-shishya* relationship. It was imparted in hermitages in austere surroundings. In a heterogeneous society like India, there are different dominant groups and multiple hierarchies. The Indian, *vidyas* have arisen from pluralistic sources: economic, religious and literary.

Self-criticism was inherent in the intellectual paradigm of traditional India. *Vidyas* were revised six times. There were thirty-two *vidyas*, containing compendium of different topics such as marital and practical sciences, speculative and ritualistic knowledge. They were thus responsive to the changing needs. The fact that the Indian nation has survived numerous economic and political crises, has shown that the composite culture of India has a great tenacity.

Cultural revitalization and political will, both are the needs for India's strength.

The nineteenth article on 'Toward Reconstructing National Traditions in Sociology' by **Dan A. Chekki** emphasizes that sociology can only be relevant if its theory and methodology is appropriate to a socio-cultural milieu of a nation. The article examines the endogenous and exogenous forces that have influenced the development of sociology in India. The identifiable Indian sociology movement is the result of emergence of nationalization issue within the discipline.

Based on the framework of ab-intra intrinsic and ab-extra extrinsic bases of knowledge, the paper examines the relationship of thought and society, and thought as an emergent property from thought. The process of institutionalization of sociology and socialization of sociologists in India has been examined in the above perspective. Sociology in India has developed not only as a response to its milieu but also by western sociology. The trend towards universalization is in effect Americanization of sociology everywhere. American sociology is also culture-bound and ethnocentric. Is this sociology relevant to the cultural milieu of India?

There are different models to view the growth of sociology. The institutional model considers sociology within the context of educational institutions – university structure. The ideological congruence model demonstrates the influence of native societal values and ideologies in the conception and development of sociology. The depending model has emerged on the basis of the imitation of the main centres of sociological dominance, power and prestige. The hegemony of the external disciplinary community leads to dependency. Academic colonialism and academic imperialism are some of its prominent versions. In the context of world system theory, American sociology forms the core, whereas sociology in India and Canada tends to be *peripheral*.

The renaissance, revolution and independence in India consist of the names of Sri Aurobindo Ghosh, B.K. Sarkar, Tilak, Gokhale, Ranade, and Gandhi, who linked sociology to transcendence and religion. The formal disciplinary growth of sociology in India was marked by the western influence.

After independence, sociology developed as a profession. The discipline was taught in many universities and colleges and research grants were made available through UGC and ICSSR. The influence of American sociology can be discerned in data collection and identification of priorities in research, as viewed and defined by outsiders.

The development of Indian sociology has been classified into time sequence of 1920–40 and the 1950s, 1960s and 1970s with the 'pioneers', 'modernizers', 'insiders', and 'pace-makers' versus non-conformists playing distinctive roles in their respective periods.

There has been unprecedented growth of sociology in India in the post-independence era. The need for modernization of syllabi with Indian contents has been accepted by all. It is also felt that at higher level, there is a need for greater diversification with emphasis on regional, national and international comparative approaches. Indian sociologists have also recognized that standardized uniform syllabi for all regions of the country is not desirable, although a basic minimum is necessary. There is a dearth of appropriate teaching material. The regional language teaching has started, but there is paucity of standard textbooks in these languages.

On the other hand, post-1950 period has witnessed greater Americanization of sociology. However, during the 1970s, the influence has been selective and adaptive. Indian sociology has been growing as a mixture of various endogenous and exogenous intellectual traditions. Indian sociology is more tolerant. Its contribution to world sociology is yet to be forcefully recognized. There have been series of studies on deprived categories since 1970s. The decline of American scholars after 1970s is the consequence of CIA-funded researches.

The weaknesses of Indian sociology have been ably brought out by sociologists. Need for academic decolonization, effort to nationalize our problems and focus on problematics of India, as perceived from below, have been emphasized by many scholars.

The debate about sociology 'in', 'for', 'of' India has led to different advocacies. There are three different cognitive advocacies: (a) advocacy of distinctive conceptual-theoretical paradigm which would be appropriate and relevant in understanding Indian reality; (b) advocacy of universality of sociology; and (c) advocacy of adaptation and integration.

It is reasonable to argue that whereas nationalism in science is unscholarly, the comprehension of national societies is not. There is a need to 'do' Indian sociology rather than continue to debate the issue. The author opines that Indian sociology should be historically informed, theoretically sophisticated, and comparatively oriented.

The twentieth article by **Y.B. Damle** is entitled as 'Dialectics Between Theory and Social Reality'. Sociology has to deal with both logical and non-logical actions of man. Action has to be viewed within the framework of system.

Theory is a set of logically interrelated concepts and propositions about social reality. It provides a comprehensive description of existing social reality in its complexities and interrelatedness. It has to be exploratory and inductive.

The basic premises on which theory is based has been questioned by several thinkers. Personal reality should be taken into account, rather than social reality, in the construction of social theory. Having examined the theoretical issues, the author discusses the Indian social reality. He describes the development of sociology in India. G.S. Ghurye, Radhakamal Mukherjee and D.P. Mukerji have been mentioned in this context.

The author states that Indian society cannot be understood except in terms of sub-structures and the various levels at which it operates. There are varieties of social mechanisms which regulate social institutions and multiple styles of life. Indian society must be seen in terms of space and time. The author thinks that division of labour based on caste was anomic in its character and did not provide support to the composite culture of India. The career of a ruler or that of a cultivator was open to everyone.

The process of development in India has not been coherent and congruent. In India, there is state intervention rather than welfare state. The common civil code has not been accepted, keeping in mind its impact on voting pattern. Social structure has to be treated as a point of departure rather than as an existing and acceptable reality.

The twenty-first article by **H.C. Srivastava** is entitled as 'Indian Social Reality: For Paradigm-Bridging'. The author begins by raising the question: Is 'tradition' fix the logical universal of Indian sociology. Several questions emanate from this paper. What is the character of knowledge in Indian sociology? Is there any reigning-paradigm or multiple-paradigm scheme? What is the presupposition of sociology in India? What are the epistemological categories frequently employed in explanation? In Indian sociology, what is tradition – great-little, ritual-secular, east-west, specific-universal?

Tradition remains the core context of Indian sociology. Other things are externalities. The search for 'Indian' has been sloganized. Residual category of transcendental is the basic format of Indian society and culture. The author states that sociology needs not commit suicide in search for the ultimate symbol. For them Indianness is bliss. The author has no quarrel with them, but he says, sociology is wrong place for them.

Modernization of Indian Tradition is the first and the last work in social historicism. Social thought is not identical with 'culture' or 'society'. The art of sociology in India confused the image of value as image of 'fact'. Colonial history has no relevance to many sociologists. Many rural studies were devoid of human actors – the peasants. The early Marxist trend was brushed aside. For Indian sociology, India-in-history does not exist, only history of ideas exists as *India*.

'Convergence' and 'influence' on sociology are the terms used to denote what has been consistently done in other social science disciplines. The debate on the dominant mode of production in Indian agriculture, differentiation of peasantry, ancient and medieval social history and subaltern studies in social movement could be cited as illustrations. The author states that there is neither 'convergence' nor 'influence' but a lag to be bridged. The viable propositions could be paradigm-bridging or integrated insights from different paradigms.

There are several areas of study of sociological relevance which have not been taken up. The role of state in recombination of Indian society remains a neglected field in Indian sociology. Caste remains the 'pope theory' of Indian sociology. Sociology in India has to give adequate analytical significance to the 'response' of the nation-state and to the world system factors and theory.

A 'paradigmatic break' is not to suggest a new paradigm. Sociology cannot start a-new. Paradigm-bridging is an attempt to resolve the anomalies, gaps, lags and inadequacies which the earlier paradigms failed to do and an effort to integrate the possibles.

The last article by late **Surendra Sharma** is entitled as 'Sociology in India: A Sociology of Knowledge Perspective'. The emphasis of the debate is: Whether sociology in India should concern itself with the study of values or it should study relations? The corollary of this question is: Whether the approach would be indological or comparative? D.P. Mukerji had used 'positive-cum-subjective' approach by combining the view from within (study of tradition) and the view from without (Marxology). This point is related to the nature of Indian sociology in regard to its universal versus specific nature. What is the nature of sociology in India? There are, several answers to it. Has it been Hindu sociology or Indian sociology? Is it culturological or universal? Does it has the hangover of British colonialism and the academic hegemony of the West, or is it nationalistic?

Unity of ideas and values reflects Indian society. Unity in relationships is reflected through caste system. Dumont and Pocock's thesis assumes: (a) India is one, (b) Indology is representative of people's behaviour, (c) unity in ideas and values is *social* in nature, and (d) people's mode of thinking and not their modes of actual relations should be taken as data. Bailey considers this perspective as narrow.

Dumont and Pocock do not make distinction between cultural and social facts. Bailey states that there can be no 'Indian' sociology except in a vague geographical sense, any more than there are distinctive Indian principles in chemistry or biology. The author summarizes the debate by responses of Dumont and Pocock and comments of Saran and Madan. There cannot be more than one sociology according to Dumont.

According to Yogendra Singh, the tensions in Indian sociology are between (a) the 'general theory' and 'conceptual schemes', (b) 'universalism' of concepts and propositions and their contextuality, and (c) role of ideology in theory construction. Singh has periodized the theoretical developments in Indian sociology into: (i) philosophical, (ii) culturological, (iii) structural, (iv) dialectical, and (v) historical. However, the author says that periodization does not synchronize with the dominance of any of these approaches. Singh's skill for categorization overpowers his care for factual data.

There have been two co-existent traditions in Indian sociology: (a) the colonialists, and (b) the imperialists. The nationalist tradition has not emerged from a challenge to one or the other or both. Singh emphasizes greater use of history and cautions against the international or western social science 'reference model'.

The author discusses in details the Marxist and non-Marxist dispositions in Indian sociology. He discusses Ramkrishna Mukherjee, P.C. Joshi, A.R. Desai, K.P. Gupta, D.A. Chekki, and R.S. Khare amongst others. Most of the discussions of these writers have been enumerated in this volume. The author has summarized the major contentions of these thinkers within the framework of sociology of knowledge perspective.

The summarization of the above articles has been intended to highlight relevant issues and major contentions, basically in authors own cognitive thought and linguistic mould. There has been conscious effort for self-control and therefore even when the ideas of authors were making stimulating series of impacts, refrain was difficult but desirable act on my part for this edited volume.

The refrain to react has been diverted by making certain formulations in the first section and certain risky observations in the third section, so that the issue of theory and ideology in Indian sociology is further articulated – both through doing sociology and reflecting over it. The debate should go on and discourses should continue between scholars.

III

It is a difficult cognitive enterprise to debate upon theory and ideology in Indian sociology. But it is an intellectual risk, worth taking, as it might sensitize and stimulate younger scholars to raise questions; enter into meaningful discourse in this area; identify gaps in knowledge in Indian sociology; encounter history, philosophy, metaphysics; motivate them to read classical texts not only written in Sanskrit, but also in *Pali, Prakrit* and regional languages; help them in analyzing local-regional social realities and establishing linkages between past and present at micro and macro levels; and encourage them in making choices for transformation of Indian society through understanding or activism.

Doing sociology through teaching, research and reflection makes me feel that its perspective is all-encompassing, as any phenomenon – natural or human – can be sociologically analyzed, if it is viewed within its framework or is seen as socially meaningful and relevant. All phenomena get social meaning and have impact on individuals, groups, collectivities and society – from water to plants, from transcendence to mundane, from body to thoughts, from past to present to future, from values to objects, and from feelings to rationality.

Sociology consists of facts and their interpretations, concepts and their articulation, theories and their interpretations, approaches and their usages, data and mode of their collection, themes and their understanding, problems and their resolution, and can be accordingly categorized, classified, debated and debunked. Cognitive pluralism is the strength of the discipline.

The sociology-paradigm reveals description, construction and interpretation of reality in terms of world-system theory linking centre and periphery. It stresses a holistic, systemic approach. One cannot speak of India in isolation from the world economy as a whole. The 'subaltern studies' provide counter view to the 'official' or 'elitist' history of India, to see the concrete and particular historical struggles of the 'subaltern' masses in India. It focuses on microscopic and local or regional issues. The modernization-secularization theorizing consists of the tradition of modern, liberal social scientific work. The orientalist theorizing pertains to non-western traditions, including philology, archaeology, language, literature, and history of religion. It focuses on the classical and essentialist formulations coming from the past of the world's great non-western civilizations and religions as they are set forth primarily in textual, art historical and archaeological sources. Religionization theorizing focuses on the high salience of religious experience, not merely in terms of its manifestations in historical, social, economic and political contexts, but also in terms of its substantive content, that is, its basic intellectual and spiritual claims.[26] All these theories provide a distinctive perspective, world-view, an approach to understand and analyze India.

In terms of further divisions of coverage, approach and meta-theory, the sociology-paradigm could emphasize commonality and specificity; micro and macro; textual and contextual; continuity and change; processes and patterns; historical and contemporary; mundane and transcendental; subjectivity and objectivity; structural and ethnomethodological; positivistic, idealistic and realistic world-views, activism and passivism; autonomy and constraint; universal and indigenous; holistic and sectorial; subaltern and supertern; values and facts; insider and outsider; ethical-neutrality and normativeness. The list can be expanded and various permutations and combinations can be built.

Methodologically, social meanings can be derived through observation, interviewing, sensing, perceiving, and reflecting not only human actions but the meanings which people give to physical objects, cultural objects, social objects and transcendental objects. Social meanings can be constructed through body-gestures, dress, architect, dwelling area, art, craft, as also through social practices, social institutions and location of power.

Meanings need not be definitive, fixed, uniform and one-dimensional. One's own social location, self as constructed through social forces, group interests, interest of self, academic training and socialization influence the meaning giving processes – consciously, subconsciously and unconsciously. Social reality is made, modified and reconstructed. So also the streams of knowledge.

To me, sociology, philosophy, including philosophy of science, and history, including history of ideas are essential for creation of knowledge for every academic discipline. The formal disciplinary boundaries beyond a point are barriers to the intellectual growth. Boundary maintenance is part of politics of knowledge and not academics of knowledge. Sociology brings interdisciplinarity by its perspective and methodology.

It is also necessary to emphasize here that the classificatory scheme of knowledge has been changing. Sociology, as a distinct discipline within the knowledge system, did not exist in the schema of traditional knowledge system in India. This does not imply that study of society, construction of social reality and concern for social transformation were not intellectually dealt with and debated. Nor does it mean that sociology and other academic disciplines are final schema of categorization in the cognitive meta-theory. Sociology by the present nomenclature may wither away and substituted by some other nomenclature, model, paradigm, theory, methodology and perspective.

Acceptance of finality in the realm of knowledge is its death or its ultimate realization. Ultimate knowledge is the stage of *nirvana* and tends to be beyond mind. Knowledge is always a mental construct and not realization of the Ultimate Truth. Seeking is mental but arrival is supramental. Curiosity, quest, concern and commitment are means and motivations for seeking answers to questions.

Sociology in India needs to be examined in terms of its normative role. In the West, norms and values have legal-formal sanction and have become part of civil society. In India, the pluralistic mode of styles of life, values, norms and institutions had autonomy through caste, community, polity and religion which performed the tasks of norm-formulation and norm-internalization. With the acceptance of western institutions based on universalistic principles amidst contextual particularism of Indian society, the formulation of norms became a very delicate issue. Sociologists ought to take up the task of formulation of appropriate norms, which would be in consonance with changed circumstances, marked by contradictory forces. Sociology should function as nomos building instrumentality and thus provide direction to individuals and institutions in realm which fall outside the right of control of the state. This would also make the path and course of development facile and firm.

The institutional and organizational dimensions of teaching and research of sociology in India are yet other aspects which ought to be discussed seriously. Career in sociology is alright but not careerism. Absence of ideology, imitation of western sociology, lack of rigour in indigenous conceptualization, and incapacity for theoretical break-through ultimately reflect our inappropriate knowledge systems. Sociology can be, and has been, done by the so-called non-sociologists. Restructuring of course contents, training in rigorous fieldwork, commitment to ethics of profession, studies in neglected areas of inquiry, innovation in methodology, and search for meanings in plethora of symbols can vitalize the mediocrity of sociology in India. Creativity necessitates dissatisfaction. Dissatisfaction assumes sensitive mind. Sensitive mind assumes critical self-consciousness. The academic milieu of sociology should help in promoting the above values and traits.

There are levels of societal existence, hence levels of social reality. The perspective of people from below and that of people from above need to be carefully understood. Power should not determine the dominant view. The dominant reality is the reality of people and not the elite. The subaltern studies, *dalit* literature, the common man's conversation, the ordinary man's biography, the experience of everyday life, and the studies of women, children, and people of deprivation help in understanding how power operates in the creation of inequality, oppression and exploitation. The invisible but real structures need to be unearthed along with demystification.

The impact of colonialism, imperialism, partition, independence, terrorism, constitution, development and similar themes need to be sociologically analyzed. The sociological analysis of the ancient thought and that of the ideas of Gandhi, Sri Aurobindo, Tilak, Ambedkar, Phule, Vivekanand, Nehru and other visionaries are relevant areas of study for sociologists. National, regional and local cultural, structural and ideational realities should be examined in terms of their linkages as well as in terms of their autonomous existence.

The Indian mind and Indian psyche are the products of its society. The Indians are culturally different. India as a country has variant ecological setting. The historical continuity of Indian society is unique experience in civilization. The course of history has witnessed light and darkness but never an eclipse. Society is built on what has existed in past, what present is and what is being done for future. Both in terms of time and space, India presents vast canvas of issues and themes. It needs sociological signatures.

Notes

1. Yogendra Singh, *Image of Man*, Chanakya Publications, Delhi, p. 6.
2. Ibid., pp. 81–101.
3. Ibid., pp. 77–78.
4. Ibid., p. 80.
5. Ibid., p. 81.
6. A. Breekenridge and Peter van der Veer, *Orientalism and the Postcolonial Predicament*, Oxford University Press, Delhi, 1994, pp. 9–17.
7. Singh, op. cit., p. 92.

8. Ibid., p. 92.
9. Ibid., p. 98.
10. Ibid., p. 99.
11. Ibid., p. 101.
12. Ibid., pp. 104–05.
13. Ibid., p. 105.
14. Andre Beteille and T.N. Madan, *Encounter and Experience: The Personal Dimension of Social Anthropological Field Work*, Vikas, Delhi, 1975.
15. Yogendra Singh, *Indian Sociology*, Vistaar, New Delhi, 1986, p. 1.
16. D.N. Dhanagare, *Themes and Perspectives in Indian Sociology*, Rawat Publications, Jaipur, 1993, p. 133.
17. Ibid.
18. Ibid., p. 132.
19. Ranajit Guha, *Elementary Aspects of Peasant Insurgency in Colonial India*, Oxford University Press, Delhi, 1983.
20. Ernesto Laclau, *Politics and Ideology in Marxist Theory*, Verso Publications, London, 1979.
21. Dhanagare, op. cit., pp. 21–26.
22. N.K. Singhi, Bahi-Paddhati: A Middle Range Methodology, in *Folk, Faith and Feudalism* by N.K. Singhi and Rajendra Joshi (eds.), Rawat Publications, Jaipur, 1995, p. 349.
23. Ibid., p. 350.
24. Dhanagare, op. cit., p. 154.
25. Yogendra Singh, *Modernization of Indian Tradition*, Thompson, New Delhi, 1973, pp. 33–35.
26. Gerold James Larson, *India's Agony over Religion*, State University of New York Press, Albany, 1995, pp. 38–42.

1

In Pursuit of Indigenization
Trends and Issues on Building Sociology for India

Jaganath Pathy

For the last three decades and more, there has been an ongoing quest for indigenization of sociology. The respective presidents of the Indian Sociological Society have almost invariably exhorted the urgency for indigenization of sociological concepts, theories and methods to synchronize with the historical specificity of Indian social structure and cultural tradition. The interminable debate whether 'sociology *for* India' is a more appropriate formulation than either 'sociology *in* India' or 'sociology *of* India' has generated a profusion of literature. But alas, in spite of such a prolonged professional concern, one is sure to be lost looking for any genuine articulation of sociology for India. The domination of the so-called global sociology persists overwhelmingly and constitutes the incontrovertible in the profession. Ironically, the cognitive impetus for the very debate toward indigenization of sociology has remained closely attuned to the developments in and contributions of western sociology. This paper attempts to indicate that while it is essential to demystify the western mainstream sociology, no less crucial is the need to critically evaluate and expose the so-called indigenous paradigms, if at all, we wish to alter the character of sociology.

The mainstream sociology being born as a response to challenges posed by the growth of industrial capitalism in the West and the associated violence and estrangement, from all traditional conditions of coexistence, has energetically performed the ideological functions of the ruling capitalist class, dominated by the world capitalism. It has remained embroiled in the vicissitudes of politics of the establishment. Through a set of intensively cultivated myths like instrumental neutrality, capitalist rationality and universal applicability, it has earnestly endeavoured to bring the broadest sections of the people of the world into capitalist spheres of influence. Such an overt or covert indulgement in the persistent process of reification has contributed to the mystification of social consciousness and blunted critical impulse. To conceal the unpalatable truths of domination, subjugation and mutilation of people and culture, the reality is constantly obfuscated through exultant technicalities, repetition of platitudes and disguised propaganda, mostly emanating from the sociological Mecca – the United States.

The basic tenet, through which the western sociology has made itself acceptable to the world of the deprived, is the mask of value neutrality and wig of objectivity. Sociological need for objectivity has somehow mixed up with the notion of academic neutrality. The doctrine of ethical neutrality inhibited critical stance and reflexive loyalty, and reproduced the fertile conditions for alienation of sociologists from the surrounding context. The notion of detached observers is of course naive. There is no neutral data, no neutral observer. In the final analysis, sociological exercises seem as marshalling data for partisan ends. The problem of objectivity therefore can be overcome to some extent by confronting, and not by denying the values and value judgements. The ultra-positivist sociology from the time of Comte onward, with abstruse and arcane findings, has been the traditional mode of ideological legitimation of the status-quo. Empiricist theory of knowledge and the bogey of quantification deliberately ignore that the observable facts cannot be independent by themselves but are only logically connected constituents of an entirely invisible reality. The dogma that only those which can be counted worth investigation is a superstition and falsehood. Obsession for precision and exactitude refuses consideration of crucial issues on the ground that the relevant factors cannot be measured. In any case, the starting point of quantification being appearance, it cannot discover innerstructural relationships between objects, the consciousness and struggles of the subjects. Positivism deliberately or otherwise strives to divert the attention from the fundamental contradictions and problems in the system, and seeks to bring order to a turbulent situation. It is the dialectics between the inductive and deductive processes that unfolds the laws of existence and change, and brings unity between history and structure, quality and quantity, and universal and particular. The question thus is not a total nihilistic dismissal of all positivistic – empirical sociology but of placing it in the appropriate realm.

Despite Indian universities have had departments of sociology for seven decades and there are nineteenth century precursors too

(Mukherjee, 1977), the mainstream Indian sociology follows the dictates of the nineteenth century positivism and believes in objective and value-neutral sociology. Sociology is not only a foreign implant but also nurtured in somewhat feigned way. The alienating character of sociology in India is manifest in the fact that it is used most often as an instrument of domination and tyranny rather than as a pursuit for liberation. The sociological teaching contributes to the perpetuation of a culture of silence and internalization of domination, where the dignity of men and women is lost in conformity and inaction. After four decades of national independence, western conservative models, methods, values and prejudices continue to be unblushingly imitated without any critical scrutiny (Pathy, 1982: 39–48). A whole generation of 'captive minds' have contributed to the reproduction of neo-colonial domination. The satellite character of sociology can hardly make itself productive or relevant, small wonder, judged from the point of conceptual creativity, theoretical advancement, methodological refinements, and more particularly analytical handling of the gut issues of the contemporary Indian social reality. Sociology in India reveals a grotesque existence. The same false assertions of neutrality and obscurantistic social practices dominate the profession. In the process of domesticating and emulating alien products of high prestige centres of learning in the West with adulation, the dominant neo-colonial sociology has actively denigrated indigenous popular culture, knowledge, institutions and traditions accumulated over centuries of observation, practice and reflection. Needless to reiterate that in order to participate and convert the sociological profession into a relevant sociology for India, we must demystify theoretical generalizations, conceptual categories and research methods of the suffocative 'global' sociology and unshackle the paradigm imposed by imperialism which distorts the understanding of the Indian reality and obstructs the praxis-oriented project of liberation and construction of a just society and human order.

As a response to the neo-colonial sociological hegemonism, indianization has been promoted by a variety of mechanisms. The major stream of the debate on sociology for India stresses the distinctiveness of Indian sociology due to unique cognitive and cultural tradition of India, based on the principle of hierarchy and holism as against the western principle of equality and individualism. Indians being conditioned in the ideology of caste system have allegedly a peculiar mystic predilection for thinking and constructing rigid hierarchical structures. Hence, sociology for India should essentially be a sociology of values, the values of Hinduism or more appropriately Brahmanism. Curiously, these Eurocentric reductionist and cultural relativist notions, consigning Indian society forever to the limits of timelessness and stagnation was the starting point for the genesis of sociology for India.

At the risk of repeating the well known, notorious debate between Dumont-Pocock, and Bailey is worth recalling (Dumont-Pocock, 1957: 1–25; Bailey, 1959: 88–101). The former overemphasized indological texts such as the epics while the later reflected continuing academic neo-colonialism. It was primarily an ideological discourse between idealistic and western anti-Marxist positions, shared by a whole generation of Indian sociologists, both ending up pretty much the same way. The former rooted in indological determinism while the later in imported crash empiricism, and neither paradigms could pay attention to the internal potentialities of structural transformation. Though Bailey challenged the obsession with caste, kinship and religion, and the equating of indologically constructed Hinduism with the unity of India as well as overstressing the uniqueness of Indian society, his seminal study on Orissa remains essentially a study of the process of Sanskritization, appearing as mechanism to restore the traditional caste equilibrium (Curie, 1986: 1–20). In his *Caste and the Economic Frontier*, the uniqueness of caste continues its attraction, and though he deals with the changing patterns of land control in the studied village (Bailey, 1957), class does not figure even once in the index of the book. The position he adopts is essentially ambivalent and contentious.

Be that alone, Indianization of sociology happens to be more influenced by Dumont than anyone else. Pleading for forging meaningful links between indology and sociology, Dumont examines Indian society in terms of an abstract formalized structure of values of Hinduism or Brahmanism. This is ideational and reductionist. By focusing only on abstract formal hierarchy, he fails to grasp the underlying material structural relationships, which constitute the essence of social reality (Meillassoux, 1973: 89–111). Not only that he denies to consider the structures of economic and political power but also his thesis is allegedly based on distortion of facts and misuse of evidence (Hawthorn, 1982: 206). His attempt to establish the uniqueness of the Indian ethos in terms of 'individual-out-of-this world' as against the Christian notion of 'individual-in-the-world' (Dumont, 1960: 21–45) constitutes a dehumanized mystification of the reality. Castes are simply treated as cultural entities and defined as closed status groups, and considered more important than production relations. Implicit are the assumptions of inherent rationality of the economic system, and that the individual has little autonomy of his own, except as a member of an ascriptive group. After all we are also told that caste system is less exploitative than the democratic society. Caste and class coexist, and at the level of ideological legitimation caste can and has reinforced relations of domination and subordination. Any sane person cannot escape noticing the exploitative dimensions and inhumanity of the caste system. Obviously, this perspective of indigenization is a defender of social conservation, and seeks to bring order to an already crisis-ridden, turbulent context by diverting attention from the fundamental contradictions and problems in the Indian society. In short, this exclusive concern with the supposedly pristine Brahmanic Hindu civilization is disastrous for building a responsive sociology for India.

The tragedy of this perspective is its failure to take account of the country's socio-cultural diversity and multiple centres of culture. Indian culture contains both the dominant Brahmanic tradition and the counter-traditions of peasants, oppressed castes, tribes and other religions minorities. These counter-cultures are not simply localized as 'little traditions' or 'foreign traditions' rather they have had an all-India spread. Thus, it does violence to reality and is invidious to treat the culture of the twice-born Hindus of the Indo-Gangetic plain as representing the cultural mainstream. Brahmanical legitimation for subjugating and exploiting the lower castes and minorities cannot be called the structure of the indigenous. This approach apparently suits the post-colonial Indian leadership in its insatiable urge to increasing centralization of power, bureaucracy, education, communication, etc., by eroding in bit by bit the cultural and political autonomy of federal units. A retreat from diversity would eventually undermine the Indian unity and its democratic polity. Where then this sort of sociology for India is leading us?

Rootness to the Indian tradition and history is crucial for the survival of Indian sociology with creative dignity. The history, however, should not be viewed as a frozen reality of the dominants but as an integral part of the process of unfolding the contemporary reality and the desirable future. Unfortunately, Indianization and Sanskritization have often been treated as of the same genre. Such identities are questionable, to say the least. Sanskritization is though a specifically Indian historical process, this is only one among several historical processes of Indian tradition, even when claimed as the dominant component in the historical landscape. Indian tradition is thus problematic. It was never frozen and continuously embedded with counter-cultures. A wide variety of literary texts and inscriptions have effectively shown that Brahmanical ideology did not remain static and indeed as early as the fourth century A.D., the traditional Brahmanical order was weakened by social crisis (Jha, 1987). There are many versions of epics representing counter-cultures. For instance, *Ramayan* of Valmiki, of Tulsi, the Tamil version, and Michael Madhusudan Dutt's Bengali epic *Meghanad Badh Kavya*, are all distinct. In fact, Hinduism itself is too fragmented in terms of social structure, value, system, and ideology to provide a single encompassing model (Gangadharan, 1970). Besides the non-Sanskritic forces of the tribals, *dalits*, Dravidians, Muslims, Christians, Buddhists, Sikhs etc., with their regional and all-Indian configurations, Indian history and contemporary context does amply demonstrate both the de-Sanskritization process and continued inter-tradition interactions. Witness the large number of anti-Brahman movements in the West and the South India. The obsessive concern with the mainstream has led to the conspicuous neglect of the dialectic of cultural development of the people. Kosambi (1975) rightly observed: 'The entire course of Indian history shows tribal elements being fused into a general society'. And there were historical rises and falls in various constellations of knowledge and factors articulated according to the social classes competing for power (Kuhn, 1973: 23). Pointing out the limitations of the Brahmanic perspective and emphasis, does not follow that sociology for India should be the sociology of Hindus, Muslims, Christians, tribals, *dalits* etc., for that would surely demolish the very root of Indian sociology (Ahmad, 1972: 172–78). Instead, it is crucial to comprehend the dynamics of inter-cultural interactions, especially in their co-operative, competitive and hostile aspects. Such an exercise necessarily demands analysis of the power structures of the ethnic communities and in the Indian society as a whole. This neither amounts to promoting the all pervasive evolutionary perspective of castes becoming classes nor a crude economic determinism denying the relevance of ideological structures in legitimating and moulding material relationship. Those who relate *varna* to the so-called Asiatic mode of production and *jati* to the feudal mode of production (Gupta, 1980) beg both methodological and substantive questions. It is important to analyze degrees of domination and subordination of ethnic groups, castes, genders and classes, and the complex interrelationship between these four categories. The scope of this paper, however, prohibits us to deal on this important issue.

Be that alone, critical evaluation of such a perspective of indigenization is highly relevant at the moment when the cultural and social diversity which had been the basis of Indian unity and integrity has been threatened by the rise of Hindi revivalism. Recent political developments in India indicate a systematic suppression of linguistic and religious minorities, tribals, *dalits* and other subjugated groups, who constitute the overwhelming majority of the Indian subalterns. There is thus a precipitous fall in the level of mutual tolerance and understanding between the groups, living together for centuries. Ignoring the unity in the multilayered process of autonomy with disjunctions and conjunctions in the various identities and traditions, Hinduism has been increasingly equated to Indian nationalism, and an aggressive assimilation policy is pursued. Pity is an increasing number of intellectuals in the name of countering the baneful influences of neo-colonial academic hegemony are involving in sectarian glorification and romanticization of the traditional institutions associated with Hinduism.

It is true that such resurrection of the past, sanctified by the claims of truth and salvation in the sacred texts, appeared quite often in the Indian history, especially during the late nineteenth and early decades of this century. The ideal of resuscitation of a Hindu *rashtravad* (the Ram Raj) was directed more against the Muslim colonizers than the British colonizers. Bankim Chandra's *Anandamath* allowed Hindus to learn from the British but prohibited adoption of any element from the Muslim tradition. Balganagadhar Tilak extolled the greatness and strength of India in Vedic times and urged to consolidate all sects into a mighty Hindu nation. His invention of Shivaji and Ganapati festivals in the late nineteenth century was directed at building a controlled Hindu communal front. Obviously, the nationalist leader opposed anything that violated the caste system, like inter-caste marriage. Max Mueller provided the credence for the Brahmanical supremacy through the theory of Aryan racial origin, and therefore, received applause from Tilak, Vivekanand, Dayanand Saraswati, Aurobindo Ghosh, Bankim Chandra, B.C. Pal, Justice Ranade and a host of other nationalist intellectuals of the time. This theory buttressed their social supremacy over the low caste Sudras and elated the Indian reactionary elite. The revivalism was an integral ideological component of the early nationalist attitudes in India. Subsequent modification notwithstanding, the very ideal of the national unity could not escape from being presented in the form of communal identity.

The contemporary scenario is however much more grave. Though communal riots and ruthless suppression of *dalits* and tribals have been an ongoing feature of the Indian society; in the last five years or so, these have become widespread and recurrent. The attack on Sikhs in late 1984, the anti-Muslim riots after Babri Masjid court decision, the RSS threat to converted tribals *ad infinitum* reflect a perilous central trend of the Indian reality. The Hindu fanatics and organizations like the RSS, Shiv Shakti Dal, Viswa Hindu Parishad, Shiv Sena, etc., have been aggressively campaigning for equating the Hindu chauvinistic ideology with Indian nationalism. Accordingly, the non-Hindus are often branded as aliens, the enemies of the country. Actually religious fundamentalism has also been increasingly evident among the minorities but basically as a defensive order. The two thus cannot be equated without a risk of not distinguishing between assault and defence, cause and effect. Preservation of minority identity is a fundamental human rights question. To treat it as false consciousness typically amounts to supporting the dominant community. In short, what is argued here is that at a time when there is an unprecedented threat to the diversity, the effort at indigenization in terms of Brahmanical order amounts to playing in the hands of the forces of chauvinism and fascism.

In addition to this predominant trend, some scholars have noted the positive aspects of indigenization, namely, the importance of developing paradigms with special regard to the historical and cultural specificities of India, better use of native categories of thought, and moreover establishment of distinct intellectual identity. They contend that any serious effort at indigenization should be viewed as a necessary for deparochialization of western sociology and striving to build genuine internationalization (Atal, 1981: 189–97; Dube, 1980). This approach does not reject models and methods simply because they emanated from the West but urges to establish appropriate and meaningful interaction between national social traditions and international trends by building self-reliance in theory (Uberoi, 1974: 135–51), among other dimensions. But all their attempts have not yet resulted in any interesting body of knowledge. There is a seemingly unbridgeable gap between rhetoric and reality. The pace of internal reform has been far too slow and has fallen victim to either repressive organs within and outside or outright apathy and unconcern. Indigenization has faltered because it failed to emphasize democratic rights, and the concerned have apparently lost faith in the power of social justice and fundamental economic reforms.

The need is not only to counter the weight of the ideas of imperial and obscurantist forces masquerading as objective sociological knowledge but also to act to insurrect the sociology in order to make it relevant to the emancipation of the oppressed nations and peoples of the world. The crisis in society has activised some to demystify the credentials of their prized 'value-free' discipline with unprecedented openness. The disastrous impact of the world capitalism on sociological teaching and research is being unraveled and an increasing number of committed students of science of society are striving to demonstrate that academic sociology in some sense has been a conspiracy of the imperial powers, exploiting classes, castes, races and gender. There is something polemical, but nonetheless essential to demystify the mainstream theoretical generalizations, conceptual categories and research methods. The mainstream can no more treat this trend as an outmoded shibboleth. Perhaps, there rests the seeds of the 'New'.

This approach is distinct in the sense that it neither accepts nor rejects the global or indigenous versions outrightly but critically endeavours to formulate a sociology concerned with the emancipation of the inarticulate peoples. The insurrection sociology plunges into the burning issues of the time, in the service of the present and future. This may be accused of being partisan by the orthodox academic magnets who can hardly relish revision of their pet views, blatant propaganda, ideological coyness and methodological ascerticism. The following deals briefly on this trend.

The intellectual dependence ought to be analyzed within the global framework of international capitalist relations. The major domestic contradictions cannot be grasped in isolation from the major world contradictions. Fundamental issues like peace and survival rights are truly international and cannot be understood in an isolated manner. The social basis of indoctrination and reproduction of 'captive mind' in sociology has survived due to the present international and national political economy. Hence, without unleashing a comprehensive and systematic struggle against the international capitalism and control of the state apparatus, radical changes in the sociological profession is difficult to conceive of. At the risk of digression, it may be recalled that under the influence of the national movement, some of the first generation sociologists of India responded skeptically to the Eurocentric ideological formulations of Indian reality by the western scholars. Similarly, the rising social movements in the early 1970s, both within and abroad, generated a new awareness in history and social criticism in sociological paradigms. In other words, struggles of the people often produce a few critical scholars in the profession. There is, however, scope for a praxis-oriented sociology stimulating just struggles of the exploited through the process of conscientization, provided of course a decisive attempt is made to break the self-imposed barrier of the mandarins and address to a wider audience in comprehensible terms.

Western sociology's false notion of internationalism should be demystified and debunked. The problem with indigenization is that it readily becomes a self-conscious attempt at shaking of all 'western ideas'. And this is equally detrimental to the advancement and liberation of the sociology as colonial wholesale adoption of the same. The task however is to discard many and restructure several of the western theoretical categories and conceptual structures in the light of the evidence and critical evaluation of classical traditions, history and contemporary context in a comparative perspective. Such a theoretical innovativeness of delinking from ideologically dominating theoretical universe must root in the current crisis and popular movements, and strive to be applicable to any people's tradition and time. This does, of course, entail a rejection of a complacent ahistorical, mechanistically empiricist structural-functionalism so dominant in the mainstream sociology in India.

True, concepts and theories being bound by time and space cannot be adequate reflection of the essence and process of phenomena in all social spaces and times. And hence uncritical application of alien concepts and theories under the guise of the falsehoods of universality and neutrality need to be challenged. But, at the same time, it must be acknowledged that neither there is a single conceptual structure in the West nor even in the Indian sub-continent. Instead, there are inter-regional and intra-regional diversities associated with diverse historical conditions and ideological preferences. In other words, it is not simply due to different historical and cultural roots but also of sponsoring and emphasizing of a specific conceptual apparatus, paradigms and analytical tools that put severe limits on the validity of the western originated concepts and theories in the Indian context; and are eventually used to dominate, depoliticize and deculturalize the peoples and societies. Similarly, the local ways of conceptualizing objects and categories in their existence and dynamics are not necessarily comprehensive or superior, precisely because of different sets of conceptualization and knowledge among the dominants and the deprived on the one hand and the archaic dehumanizing values of the traditionally dominant sections on the other. Indeed, there is also an increasing articulation of the world capitalism into the internal ruling classes. The resolution of the problem then rests not in replacing one by the other, but in evaluating all categories and structures in terms of a set of explicit value premises in conformity with the time, trend and their relevance, necessity and comprehensiveness to cognize the context and achieve the desired social objectives. In the process the endogenous categories will of course have more relevance but so also those concepts and theories outside the western mainstream. However, it does not belittle the significance of the urgency of demystifying those exogenous concepts, theories, cognitive structures and methods that distort cultures for domination and perpetuate unequal exchanges between the western mainstream sociology and Indian social thought. After all, one of the most important and desirable functions of sociology is to offer social criticism aimed at demystifying the ruling class ideology (Bottomore, 1974: 90–94).

Needless to stress that the concepts and cognitive structures are not necessarily the property of intellectual elite; rather much more widespread among the subalterns who cannot but have those in order to comprehend the objects around them. Though not codified in the accepted manner of the profession, the endogenous knowledge has its own structural causality and rationality (Fals-Borda, 1982: 25–40), and that has allowed them to survive, interpret, produce and reproduce over the centuries. Effort should be made to critically recover and systematically reconstruct the diverse, and at times contradictory, indigenous knowledge stored by people and promote the growth of endogenous creativity of masses. After all, it is the people who are subjects of their own transformation and authors of their own history. In sum, it is not the dichotomy between emic and etic, or endogenous and exogenous, rather a need for dialectically unifying those with reference to an explicit value system. It is quite relevant to attempt to change a situation in which truth is made to appear as the monopoly of a particular nation, culture or minority. Decolonization implies not only defeat of hegemonic ideologies of dominant classes, communities and nations but also intellectual self-emancipation.

The tragedy for sociology in India, both neo-colonial and indigenous varieties, is its alienation from the people, the motive forces of history. The mandarins of sociology deliberately opt a cloistered existence within their charmed circle and least bother the wider audience. The continued chasm between intellectuals and history making subjects, the asymmetrical relationship between the two, prohibit self-reflection of the masses and consequently obstruct genuine production of knowledge. If social research has to become a tool in the transformation of society, it cannot be just an academic exercise monopolized by the academics (Stavenhagen, 1971). A decolonized sociology and indigenous research demand collective reflection and action. There should be thus greater interaction between theory and social practices; for no theory, howsoever sophisticated may be, can enjoy any significance and relevance, without the intervention of the active people. As Marx put it: 'It is not enough that thought should seek to realize itself, reality must strive towards thought. It is only when consciousness stands in relation to reality can theory and practice be united. For this to happen emergence of consciousness must become the decisive step. The historical function of theory is to make this step a practical possibility' (Marx, 1970; Lukacs, 1971).

In short, in order to be meaningful, sociologists concerned with sociology for India should strive to demystify both the alien and the indigenous dominant ideologies in terms of an open commitment to the liberation of the oppressed people and nations, and extend a praxiological thrust into their sociological activities. It is also equally important to critically recover the popular knowledge, and document case studies of democratic, progressive, relevant and unambiguous concepts and cognitive structures of the common people. This, of course, requires a free interaction between disciplines, across the disciplinary frontiers, and a commitment to history and to a comparative approach in which issues and processes are systematically compared with other oppressed nations and peoples. Such a liberation of sociology is not possible merely through indigenization, in which even the Ford Foundation is involved, but by breaking the continuing asymmetrical relationship between the sociologists and the toiling peoples, the unorganized labourers, castes, tribes, women, minorities, and all disadvantaged. People's struggles for peace, survival rights and against domination and coercion shall decide issues of research and that would produce not only a different sociological knowledge but can contribute to the eventual establishment of a humane order for all. The point is not to reinterpret or redirect domination in sociology but to strive to end it. And the task is formidable.

References

Ahmad, Imtiaz, 1972, 'For a Sociology of India', *Contributions to Indian Sociology*, No. VI.

Atal, Yogesh, 1981, 'The Call for Indigenization', *International Social Science Journal*, Vol. 33.

Bailey, F.G., 1957, *Caste and the Economic Frontier*, Manchester, The University Press.

—, 1959, 'For a Sociology of India', *Contributions to Indian Sociology*, No. III, July.

Bottomore, T., 1974, *Sociology as Social Criticism*, New York, Pantheon Books.

Curie, Catherine, 1986, 'Caste and Class in India: Revolution or Stagnation in Anthropology', *Journal of the Institute of Asian Studies*, Vol. IV, No. 1.

Dube, S.C., 1980, 'Indigenization of the Social Sciences', in J.J. Loubser (ed.), *The Indigenization of the Social Sciences in Asia*, IFFSO, Occasional Paper No. 1.

Dumont, Louis, 1960, 'World Renunciation in Indian Religious', *Contributions to Indian Sociology* (Old Series), No. IV; and 1970, *Homo Hierarchicus: The Caste System and Its Implications*, London, Weidenfeld and Nicolson.

Dumont, Louis and D. Pocock, 1957, 'For a Sociology of India', *Contributions to Indian Sociology* (Old Series), No. 1.

Fals-Borda, Orlando, 1982, 'Participatory Research and Rural Social Change', *Journal of Rural Co-operation*, Vol. X, No. 1.

Gangadharan, K.K., 1970, *Sociology of Revivalism*, New Delhi, Kalamkar Prakashan.

Gupta, Dipankar, 1980, 'From Varna to Jati: The Indian Caste System from the Asiatic to Feudal Mode of Production', *Journal of Contemporary Asia*, Vol. X, No. 3.

Hawthorn, G., 1982, 'Caste and Politics in India Since 1947', in D. McGilvray (ed.), *Caste, Ideology and Interaction*, Cambridge, The University Press.

Jha, D.N. (ed.), 1987, *Feudal Formations in Early India*, Delhi, Chanakya Publications.

Kosambi, D.D., 1975, *An Introduction to the Study of Indian History*, Bombay, Popular Prakashan.

Kuhn, T.H., 1973, *The Structure of Scientific Revolutions*, Chicago, Macmillan.

Lukacs, George, 1971, *History and Class Consciousness*, London, Merlin Press.

Marx, Karl, 1970, *The Origin of Hegel's Philosophy of Right*, Cambridge, The University Press.

Meillassoux, C., 1973, 'Are There Castes in India?', *Economy and Society*, Vol. II, No. 1.

Mukherjee, Ramkrishna, 1977, 'Trends in Indian Sociology', *Current Sociology*, Vol. 25, No. 3.

Pathy, Jaganath, 1982, 'Social Anthropology in India', *Association of Third World Anthropologists Research Bulletin*, Vol. III, No. 1–2.

Stavenhagen, Rudolfo, 1971, 'Decolonializing Applied Social Sciences', *Human Organization*, Vol. 30, No. 4.

Uberoi, J.S., 1974, 'For a Sociology of India: New Outlines of Structural Sociology, 1945–1970', *Contributions to Indian Sociology*, No. 8.

2

PLURALISM AND EDUCATION IN INDIA

Problems and Possibilities

SURESH CHANDRA SHUKLA

It is a difficult time to write about pluralism and related matters, when the perspective today is so fast-changing and it is unclear where both the issue itself and the way it is likely to be viewed by the many parties involved will stand even five years from now. And, indeed, there are also important cross-cultural and cross-national differences of historical experience which affect the very presentation of the matter in different societies.

Pluralism is for the most part a liberal response – although, of course, not the only liberal response – to a condition of immigrants coming from poorer countries and former colonies or lesser developed minority groups living in a country with a reasonably developed economy and/or a confident forward-looking elite. Pluralism sometimes also emerges from a history of the need for a determined united struggle against colonial domination. Sometimes, however, this could also give rise to an imperative of uniformity or homogeneity, viewing expressions of distinctness or distinctive characteristics of minority groups as separatism, parochialism or, in current Indian terminology, communalism or linguism, which are inimical to the common enterprise of national independence, cultural identity and even development. The liberal prescription, then, is unity-in-diversity opposed by extremists at either end and favouring uniformity (and assimilation) or parochialism respectively.

India has been battling with dilemmas of this kind for at least a century, and may well be poised today for a decisive and qualitative redefinition of these questions along more than one dimension: religious, linguistic or, more broadly, cultural. Education, clearly, is involved as both cause and effect. The problems in this domain are both general and specific to India's own cultural and historical circumstances.

The question of education as a factor for change, as opposed to its tendency to perpetuate the status quo, has long been discussed in various ways by social scientists and others. It is also important to note here the tendency of education itself to remain basically unaltered in its essential structure and content (Shukla, 1968; 1992), a quality which has important bearings on its capacity to promote either pluralism or cohesion. This static, constant quality of education may be stronger in countries and cultures with a long history of domination (under colonialism, for example) and conflict.

This has obvious implications for our discussion, as education would tend to reinforce and even perpetuate existing distinctions, even though it has some tendency to the contrary, and even as economic modernization of recent times, political developments (in particular, democracy) and recent advances in communications, albeit with some limitations, push in the direction of homogenization or integration.

INDIA

The question 'What is India?' has been raised repeatedly and from many perspectives over the years. Some British rulers called it a mere geographical expression. Indian nationalists have contradicted this position for over a century in many ways.

The present Indian state, with its present geographical boundaries, was formed in 1947. The larger British Indian empire which preceded it included today's Myanmar, Pakistan and Bangladesh as well, but at the same time allowed the existence of 562 states with varying degrees of suzerainty to paramount authority. There had not been such an extensive unified authority or domain before. On the other hand, Greater India, extending from Cambodia to Kabul and of basically Hindu and Buddhist cultural influence, could be traced back to over a millennium earlier and consisted of many sovereign states with changing boundaries. The arrival of the Christian and Zoroastrian faiths in the early period made a much smaller difference to India than the later arrival of Islam – and its monarchs, who built new dynasties and brought the Persian and Arabic languages, with their wealth of culture and learning as well as new ways of family and economic life. The existence over a long period of these influences, however, has not prevented the more extreme proponents of unity and integration, even uniformity, to proclaim today a pan-Indian identity, citing Hindu places of pilgrimage in the extreme north, south, east and west of the sub-continent and use of Sanskrit by the Brahmin upper caste and the literati in general. The *Vedas* have occasionally been cited as the sole source of Indian civilization (Jain, 1991) and the carrying over of such Hindu characteristics as caste and social stratification among the convert-followers of Islam and Christianity is seen by many as justification for an essentially Hindu hegemonic character of India. On the other hand, the assertion of Islam as a basis for nationhood, which led to the formation of Pakistan – itself somewhat ambivalent about this, as exemplified by founder- President Jinnah's inaugural address to the Constituent Assembly, by an early official publication, *5000 Years of Pakistan* (Wheeler, 1949) and by the later, language-based split by the originally secular nationalism of Bangladesh – continues to present the Indian identity with its most serious problem.

The formation of the present Indian state came about at the conclusion of a long struggle against British rule, through a movement which was at once political and cultural. It contended with an effort – which was bitter and keenly contested – to identify religion as the basis of nationality. Even as the state of Pakistan, with its Muslim majority, was carved out in the wake of communal riots and the cross-border migrations of millions of people in both directions, with over a million people killed, the strong Hindu hegemonistic impulse in India, which still had over 50 million Muslims (there are now 100 million), was overcome by the stronger of the two trends – that is, secular or multicultural motives as opposed to Hindu hegemonic forces – in the movement for independence. India thus framed a constitution (in 1950) which essentially separated the state and religion (including the barring of religious instruction in state-sponsored or financed institutions) and which constitutionally entrenched the right of minorities – religious or linguistic – to organize with public support educational institutions of their choice on a par with all others. Concessions to majority Hindu beliefs, for example the protection of cows and better management of cattle, or even such modern secular proposals as a uniform civil code for marriage, were only designated as directive principles of state policy. Thus, the basis for religious and linguistic pluralism in education was laid and persists today. It was strengthened through later amendments to the constitution in which secularism, socialism and scientific spirit (the former two defined in India's own peculiar manner) were prescribed as fundamental duties of a citizen, with ample reference to the ideals of the national struggle, 'common brotherhood transcending religious, linguistic, regional or sectional diversities' and the value of 'the rich heritage of our composite culture' (Constitution of India, Part IVA).

India's diversity of language is evident from the list of fifteen languages in part VIII of the schedule of the constitution, which describes the languages of the major regions as follows: English, the language of the elite all over the country; Sanskrit, rather like Latin in Europe, the classical language of the ancient period spoken by no one in everyday life but used in institutions of classical learning and the source of a great number of words and literary riches in most other Indian languages; Urdu, spoken (like Hindi), the language of almost 40 per cent of the people of northern India, but also of many Muslims elsewhere, with a vocabulary relying heavily on Persian and Arabic and using their script, and possessing an extremely rich literature; and Sindhi, a later addition, whose region of origin is now in Pakistan but which is used by Hindu Sindhi immigrants to India. In fact, this list in the constitution understates the case, for there are many other languages, such as Maithili in Bihar, Konkani in Goa and Nepali in north-eastern India, pushing their claims to inclusion in the part VIII schedule, and dialects such as Bhojpuri, Avadhi and Brij – to give examples only from the Hindi region – which are widely spoken and have literature in the common Hindi script. The Central Institute of Indian Languages lists almost 200 languages, an obvious overstatement by academic practitioners of the science of linguistics for any practical purposes, since twenty-two of those spoken by over 1.5 million people in fact cover 548 million people, or 93 per cent of the population (Vanaik, 1990). It nevertheless serves to highlight the reality of linguistic diversity.

It is to be expected that ethnic diversity, in a country of over 850 million people, will be great. But what is important for our present purposes is not so much the distinction between the Dravidian south and the rest of the country (although in other circumstances it could be so) but the persistence of tribalism, particularly in the north-east where other national frontiers – with China, Myanmar and Bangladesh – exist on every side. These people had not only experienced little participation in any organized central national state but were under the sovereignty of the British government of India and were also the object of organized Christian missionary work. This marked them out from the rest of the country, not only by loose administrative association but also by religion and ethnicity. Educational problems arising from these have, however, been more or less successfully negotiated through restraint in the spread of Hindi, a greater use of English and, in some cases, the private management of education.

Some questions related to pluralism or multiculturalism or any other variant of the basic notion of accepting diversity as important to harmonious living together are, on the other hand, rather more intractable. These relate mostly to religion and religion-based cultural-political matters in which language is also involved, particularly in northern India. Here, Urdu is associated with Muslims – although not in fact correctly – and Punjabi is equally inaccurately associated with Sikhs; these have become bones of contention with conservative sections of Hindu opinion. It is through elucidation of this (Hindu) syndrome that one can best clarify the question of pluralism.

HISTORY: THE HINDUS AND OTHERS

Many overlapping strands, which do not completely coincide, contribute towards the now strident assertion of a national unity with a specifically Hindu complexion.

The identification of India – particularly its nationalism or national identity – with Hindus and Hinduism (a term which many consider a misnomer as there is no single text which all Hindus accept as the source of their beliefs or practices) has a somewhat complicated history. In opposing imperial rule, many, although not all, nationalists who were born as Hindus used Hindu tradition and sometimes even Hindu religious symbolism, even though not all of them were either very religious or 'communal' (just as many Indian Muslims used the idea of *dar-ul harb*, anti-Islamic state, as a basis for rebelling against British rule in their capacity as true Muslims). In seeking to contest notions of inferiority vis-à-vis the colonizing power, a long past was evoked. Also, many tribal and originally non-Hindu groups were incorporated in Hindu society, along with their Gods and Goddesses, as one more caste. This was facilitated by the caste structure of Hindu society in which hundreds of castes coexisted and were grouped in a loose hierarchy of four *varnas*. Some recent conceptual advances in the recording of India's history have also tended to offer bases for questioning the Indian state as a secular national identity and provided room for support to the Hindu state. Thus, notions of India as a civilizational state (Kumar, 1991) would supersede the nation from above, as it were, and that of community as more fundamental than nation (Freitag, 1990), undermining it from below, are capable of use by proponents of India as basically a Hindu nation. The most militant and assertive proponents of a Hindu India have only recently begun to publicly exhort pride in being Hindu but they have long raised the slogan: 'Hindi-Hindu-Hindustan'.

Contemporary reaction against positivism and scientific rationalism in the social sciences, not without its own justification and rationale in a basic theoretical sense, has been invoked by many Indians to question secularism itself (Joshi, 1991; Verma, 1991).

We should also note the contribution to this question made by Islam, followed by a minority of Indians, many of whom also retained memories of periods of Muslim rulers in many parts of India – including the crucial northern capital of Delhi – and of Muslim ascendance in society and culture. A history of proselytization within the country, the maintenance of separate systems of learning and instruction in Arabic *madrasas*, Persian and mosque schools and a religious faith governing social and personal life to varying degrees, alongside a Muslim aristocracy or other higher social strata, had accompanied centuries of Muslim rule. There were also religious and educational links with other Islamic countries. This history had brought with it a legacy of a shared culture and life, a common struggle against the British and a similar history of competition, strife and separateness.

All this has obvious implications for what history will be taught and what kind of civil society (in which the young are expected to live the rest of their lives) is visualized. Thus, among the Hindu majority, in a development process covering many decades, the educational organization of the Hindu ideological volunteer organization, Rashtriya Swayamsevak Sangh (RSS), or Vidya Bharati, at a recent conference set up a committee to draft a syllabus depicting the Muslim rulers in Indian history in an uncomplimentary light, in fact the opposite of the hitherto accepted view of them as notable contributors to the culture, economy and general life of the country. This history would trace India's unity to the *Vedas* as the only source of Indian civilization and contest the hitherto dominant view that the Aryans migrated from the north a few thousand years ago, giving India as their original home. This and similar notions, to use the description of an eminent (non-Hindu, non-Hindi-speaking) sociologist, are expected to promote the concept of a national 'mainstream' which is 'twice-born, i.e., upper-caste Hindi-speaking Hindu' (Oommen, 1986). As is to be expected, there is considerable ambiguity and casuistry alongside much aggressive expression on these questions. One way of identifying non-Hindu minorities acceptable to many strident Hindu 'nationalists' is to refer to all Indians as 'Hindu-and-Muslims' or 'Muhammadi Hindus' – since Hindu was the term used by Muslims as well as by the British when they first came to India, for all who lived in Hindustan (India). That this use of the term 'Hindu' is not a pluralist or liberal one is evident from the fact that those who use it have also been responsible for a call for 'Indianization' or even 'Hinduization' of Muslims, Christians, etc., and for insisting on Ram – the Hindu God – as a common object of veneration, citing the example of Indonesia – a Muslim country – where the *Ramayana* – the epic story of Hindus, has been incorporated into national tradition and most names still bear Sanskrit origins.

To return to the more Hindu version of Indian history for school curricula, it is important to note that the Vidya Bharati and its associate organization Saraswati Shishu Mandir run almost 10,000 schools at various levels from kindergarten to senior secondary, among social groups varying from tribal, rural and poor to high fee-paying city dwellers. In view of the external examination-dominated character of the Indian school system, such efforts could so far only have had a partial effect through co-curricular activities, supplementary reading, etc. However, the 1991 elections have put in governments in four northern Hindi states, under the Bharatiya Janata Party (BJP) that is committed to this programme. Liberal grants-in-aid to voluntary organizations running schools, combined with their influence on state boards of secondary education which set curricula and conduct examinations, could also promote these ideas to a very substantial degree.

As a Marxist commentator has noted: 'The progressive legitimization of Hindu cultural nationalism can only make the minorities insecure and promote among them a sense of being culturally inferior ... the birth of a self-conscious Hindu identity marks the beginning of a Hindu community-in-the-making' (Vanaik, 1990: 149–51). The reference here is to the fact that there is no codified Hindu faith but a myriad of sectors, all of whom share the common social stratification of caste, or *varna*. Further, he adds: 'In the West religious sects have finally learnt to live and let live... . This is obviously not the case in India' (Vanaik, 1990).

Such a situation had been foreseen by forward-looking, secular and liberal leaders of Indian opinion and policy. The teaching of history had been reformed for other reasons as well, namely, to erase the traces of domination and inferiority vis-à-vis the former western rulers, to bring into relief the ideas of Indian enlightenment and independence in the nineteenth and twentieth centuries and to familiarize the young with the advances of all mankind in scientific and social domains. But a prime objective was what in Indian parlance is called national integration and 'secularism'. The country discovered that, as school children, people in many parts of India had not even learnt the main contours of the history of their country, but only those of their own regions, leading to a narrowness of outlook and prejudice against other regions or communities or the followers of other religions. Such people would tend to develop a false sense of superiority and be unable to appreciate the contributions of people from different regions and communities to contemporary Indian life and culture or the similarity of the many faiths and their intermingling and mutual influence at many levels. To remedy this, a more scientific and comprehensive history syllabus using the skills of contemporary scholarship was worked out in the 1970s by the National Council of Educational Research and Training (NCERT). This was recommended to the states and enforced in the small proportion of (elite) schools affiliated with, first, the Central Board of Secondary Education, then the countrywide State Boards of Secondary Education. This raised the level of instruction but also attracted considerable comment, to the effect that the state was intervening in what, according to traditional liberal tenets, did not concern it (Rudolph and Rudolph, 1983; Shukla, 1991). In the wake of the attempted Hinduization of Indian history by Vidya Bharati and the four BJP-ruled states noted earlier, India's Union Education (now called Human Resource Development) Ministry sought again, late in 1991, the assistance of recognized historians to write a syllabus which would also bring history up to date, well into the post-independence period. This has come under similar attack, with the added point that 'pseudo-secularists' are seeking to glorify the post-independence leadership of the largely secular Congress party which had been running the country almost on its own.

EDUCATIONAL ADMINISTRATION AND POLITICS

India's national movement had, notwithstanding notable Muslim and Parsi contributions, understandably started with a majority Hindu leadership, but held a broadly pluralist position on the shape of free India's polity even as, as noted earlier, many strands in it would glorify India's (Hindu) past and show that much Hindu philosophy and thought was equal to any in the West. By the time of independence, there was considerable agreement on a policy of 'live let live' between people of various denominations and faiths; indeed, the most vocal elements, led by Nehru, expected science and industrialization to dissolve differences and lead to a 'modern rational' outlook that would push religion into the background if not make it disappear altogether. However, as the leadership had been vehemently opposed to the partition of the country along ostensibly religious lines, it took great care to ensure that minority groups were able to preserve their faith and way of life. Hence, not only was the state to be secular, not connected institutionally to any religion, but a concept of specifically Indian origin – 'secularism' – has tended to emerge. This has been variously understood to mean the acceptance of long-term separateness and the distinct modes of life of different communities, or the acceptance and even promotion of such distinctions with the expectation that industrialization, democracy, science, etc., would help minimize and even eradicate them (Shukla, 1974). A third, very small minority opinion promoted a totally non-religious or anti-religious view of life. In this context, some minority educational institutions have received state recognition and financial support on equal terms, on condition that no religious instruction is provided during official school hours (with the exception of institutions like Aligarh Muslim and Benares Hindu Universities, whose pre-constitution legislation permitted or even enjoined religious education). Specifically indigenous educational institutions of Sanskrit, Arabic and Persian have also been supported. These cannot but have strong religious associations. Religious denominations, particularly among Muslims, and later Sikhs, have also promoted fully religious schools, totally unaided by the state. The schools of the Christian minority (including Anglo-Indians) have tended to be elite because they were the first English-language schools. Some of them were connected with internationally established groups such as the Jesuits. Their right to establish and maintain institutions of their choice, if they so desired, has been interpreted by the judiciary to include enrolling even a majority of those belonging to other denominations, thus preserving the all-elite character of English-medium schooling, and to admit up to 50 per cent children from their own denomination so as to maintain exclusiveness. Thus, the 'secular' provisions of the constitution have tended to be interpreted in favour of both elitism and parochialism. There are, however, large numbers of other denominational institutions of Muslims, Sikhs, etc., which command neither state political authority nor elite monopoly. Large numbers of these conform to the broad official educational system, but there has also been much growth in mosque-based or other traditional institutions.

National integration has been an important concern, particularly since the disturbances, which began in the 1960s, along linguistic or communal lines. This concern is the natural successor to the concern for national unity during the struggle for independence. But, as noted earlier, there is considerable divergence on the interpretation of integration. Pluralist integration corresponding to either interpretation of secularism noted above would allow for considerable variety in languages of instruction – a matter particularly relevant to northern India, where urdu and Punjabi coexist with Hindi as the commonly used language. To the extent that this involves the segregation of children from different religious denominations into separate schools or classes, this encourages particularistic tendencies. This has been most vociferously opposed by those proponents of integration who are inclined to produce a somewhat forced uniformity, which would lead in fact to the alienation of minority groups through neglect of their language and culture. This happened to Urdu in many northern states following independence. Later, however, renewed emphasis – through watchdog functions performed by the Commissioner for Linguistic Minorities or exhortation of the union government and National Integration Council – has tended to ensure that any group of ten pupils using one language were provided with schooling in that language. There have, indeed, still been problems with the registration of such languages or the non-availability of proper teachers or textbooks in them. Most schools using Indian languages tend to develop a particularistic school culture, more in keeping with the broader social norms of the groups involved. On the other hand, in the elite sections of the school system, a more modern westernized climate prevails and children from all communities participate in it.

PAROCHIAL AND LIBERAL TRENDS

It has to be remembered, of course, that this differentiation takes place within the framework of a common syllabus prescribed by state education departments and evaluated through a uniform written examination. This explains the vehemence of the debate over the syllabus in, for example, history. There are, however, more pervasive problems, arising from the fact that courses in language and literature also draw upon the same culture and history. To the extent that these rely on the writing from sources located in the hitherto established social groups, e.g. upper castes, particularly Brahmins, for the ancient period – and ignore lower groups and castes, school curricula could alienate pupils from social groups and classes just entering the educational system. This has been the view of many *dalit* (ex-untouchable castes) spokesmen. It is difficult, however, to imagine either the possibility of adequately changing syllabi in this direction or the desirability of establishing caste schools. We may note here that, as a measure of tribal welfare, separate residential *ashram* schools have been established as a matter of policy to enable tribal children to acquire education in a homogeneous atmosphere. This does not involve, however, the imposition of an educational apartheid which prevents them from entering common schools. Indeed, they follow the common syllabus and prepare for entry to common higher education.

Little religious or formally sanctioned segregation is observable. However, segregation of the sexes is permissible wherever desired. This is fairly common, especially among Muslims. There is also some tendency in all communities to lower the requirements in mathematics and emphasize domestic science for women. This is also perhaps more prevalent among Muslims.

Thus, we see that the formal structure of education as such offers relatively little scope for any great particularistic tendencies or even much pluralism. However, the wide scope for private initiative in establishing and managing educational institutions has offered the possibility (widely utilized by denominational and caste groups) of creating resources, buildings, employment opportunities, organizational infrastructure and a school culture and climate that can be used in the service of such goals. This effort has been eligible for considerable state financial support as grants-in-aid for education. What has developed is thus not exactly pluralism in education but the use of education for social pluralism or, if circumstances so dictate, divisions within the society. For the last forty or so years, the professedly 'secular' leadership of the governments has led to an educational structure that formally lays great emphasis on national integration of a tolerant – even pluralist – nature, as permitted and even financially assisted by the government grants-in-aid generally available to parochial institutions. With the rise of the BJP as a significant political party, controlling as it does many state governments and in a position to influence national policy-making, combined with the decline of the traditional ruling Congress party (or, in some states, left-wing parties), this picture could change, and a more Hindu national integration, more assimilationist in character, could emerge. Whether it would permit minority groups to have their own more distinct systems, supported by state funds, appears problematic. This is still in the realm of speculation, as the long tradition of the national movement and the existence of a very large modern intelligentsia could in the prevailing politically democratic context offer strong resistance to such an educational prescription, even though the competitive politics of democracy could increasingly accentuate these divisions.

It is useful to note at this stage that as long as the national government retains a broadly secular character, even a particularistic state government educational policy can be checked. For while all education, with the exception of co-ordination and determination of standards of higher education and research, is within the purview of states, in 1976 the constitution was amended to bring it within the concurrent jurisdiction of both state and central governments. Although this provision has not been used since its incorporation in 1976, a parliamentary decree – with, of course, its political costs in party terms, as well as in terms of encroaching on state autonomy – can enforce any educational measure nationwide.

It is this kind of authority, which the constitution initially afforded to the union government in respect of determination and co-ordination of standards of higher education and research, not to mention the substantial finances it commands and passes on to states for educational schemes, that has enabled it to enforce more or less effectively broad uniformity at the school level. While individual universities incorporated by national or state legislation possess autonomy and can set their own syllabi, these are subject to union level co-ordination effected through a statutory autonomous University Grants Commission (UGC), which works through both consultative expert committees and financial assistance set up by union legislation. As these institutions are all based on public legislation they cannot be denominational in character. Some leeway does exist, however, since UGC also has authority to recommend the Government of India to consider certain institutions as universities. Recently, some such recognition has gone to foundations which are quasi-religious, even though they offer only secular courses.

OTHER EDUCATIONAL INFLUENCES

The largest scope for the propagation of particularistic tendencies of a different religious and cultural complexion thus lies in traditional family and religious institutions, the political system or the newly emerging mass media. We must note here the emergence not only of the Hindu BJP but also a variety of political parties of Muslim and Sikh denominations – although they do not necessarily claim the allegiance of all or even a majority of the adherents of their respective faiths. The RSS of the Hindus, the *tablighi* movement and the Jamaati-i-Islami movement perform educational functions according to their beliefs, which counter the spirit of national and cultural integration.

The point to note particularly about RSS and the Jamaat is their quasi-military character and their effort to homogenize and unify the community, cutting across some traditional divisions, e.g., the RSS effort to erase caste and even language distinctions dividing Hindus, in order to produce a contemporary political-cultural entity legitimizing all its ideas in the name of the reinstatement of the basic message of the hallowed traditions. This runs counter to the development of a modern nation in which individuals and communities of minority groups can participate as cultural and political equals. It also tends, in practice, and more often than not in theory as well, to buttress and strengthen some old inequalities, e.g., of women or lower castes, in the name of cultural identity and solidarity. Thus, as a concession to the pluralist proclivity for recognizing and legitimizing cultural identities, these movements could, in the name of the rights of communities to assert and develop their identity, end up by negating the individual human rights both of women as equals in work and politics and of the lower orders and rival communities or individuals. Freedom of conscience, including the acceptance of other beliefs and overt disavowal of faith, and individual freedoms – whether relatively trivial or minor ones such as particular hairstyles, forms of dress, greetings, etc., or major ones such as marriage outside the religious community – are similarly questioned. The face-to-face and person-to-person organizational links which these communities are developing exercise a supra-educational influence in a separatist and illiberal direction, which it would seem naive or deceptive to categorize as pluralist, a term we began by defining as essentially liberal and permissive. Separate schools would serve to strengthen these tendencies and minimize the possibilities of understanding – the basis of real pluralism.

This struggle between liberal and illiberal influences, effective as it is at individual and organizational levels, is also visible now at a mass level in the mass media, which are no minor influence. Newspapers (55 million copies published daily), even in a less than half-literate society like India, are read by hundreds of millions of people (Government of India, 1990). The growth of television extends now to over 30 million sets (29.2 million in 1990, expected to rise to 45 million in 1992) (*Manorama Yearbook*, 1990), while the much older radio network is much more extensive but perhaps, today, less influential. Nationwide broadcasts of *Ramayana* created a more clearly articulated Hindu consciousness in a year and a half than had ever been the case before – images transcend the language barrier – and the current weekly programme *Chanakya*, glorifying the leadership of that ancient Indian Machiavellian figure with his saffron robes (associated with Hindu priests and aspirations) and repeated hostile references to the invading forces of Alexander, contributes to the creation of a largely aggressive or oppressive Hindu identity for India.

It might be convenient, at this point, to examine the differential place of English, Hindi and the other Indian languages in the context of pluralism, and the more widely prevalent Indian concepts of secularism and communalism. The visual media influence users of English and those of Indian languages other than Hindi as much as those who use Hindi alone. Hindi has been a unifying and integrating influence through films for over a quarter of a century. But television has tended to concentrate messages a great deal and, presumably in response to wider socio-political tendencies, has taken on a more pronounced communal character, relying in part on the currently felt need to recall an ancient past or, worse, reinforce assertive homogeneity.

This is a very recent phenomenon, for even popular TV serials had, until *Ramayana*, stuck to secular and even liberal integrationist themes. The important point is that now the English-speaking intelligentsia has also been very substantially influenced by the serials glorifying a Hindu identity. This is in contrast to the former situation in which only a small minority (about 5–10% of schools used English as a teaching medium) risked being exposed to more modern and fewer religious messages of their own faith, the religious message in Christian schools understandably being ineffective or uninfluential.

The language question is also related to pluralism and communalism as well as modernity in another manner. The movement to use Indian languages in education and other business of everyday life was essentially one of democratic and popular inspiration which also corresponded to the urge to discover and develop the identity of a people. However, through the circumstance of dependency under British rule, administration, business, science and technology were increasingly monopolized by the English language and an all-Indian English-using elite emerged. For reasons of convenience, and also because of the inability of groups of the different linguistic origins within this elite to agree on one common Indian language, the pre-independence stress on Hindi, the language of over 40 per cent of Indians, and on other Indian languages has progressively decreased.

Although formally pronounced as the main official language of the union, with English as associate official language (a position which prevails even today, with only the political assurance that English will continue to be used by the union government as long as any state so desires), any move to promote the use of Hindi (or other

Indian languages) in administration or business science or technology comes up against understandable opposition, in addition to the expected technical problems it encounters. Thus, the small English-using population has access to a great deal more new knowledge and modern thought. Through professional association it forms almost the only cohesive all-India intelligentsia, leaving those who do not use English relatively less informed and modern and more isolated from other language groups. The conundrum of all-India elite integration versus popular linguistic separateness is also reflected in terms of more traditional and perhaps therefore somewhat more parochial divisive culture and socialization offered by language education and a more western-oriented one for education through English. Those in the latter category occupy elite managerial and technical positions in society, even if democratic politics does produce some non-English-using leaders. This brings about a situation of quasi-colonial domination in the spheres of culture and even of political economy.

CONCLUSION

The implications for pluralism in both its liberal and conservative interpretations are somewhat mixed. With a substantial proportion of the population living below the poverty line and the economy still affected only in some parts by the market, only about half the 11-year-olds have received schooling. Thus, the polity and the prevailing socio-cultural system are less affected by the educational system, which enrols over 150 million young people. In a late developing society with unequal relationships with the developed world, and with a labour surplus economy with more than 20 million high-school graduates looking for jobs, the urge for upward social mobility is pressing. Competition is severe – there is the pull of the West as well as of West Asia – and the pull of culture and language is thus strong. In this country of so many religions and languages, therefore, the pressures for divisiveness are very much in evidence, even though unification of the national labour market, a participatory democratic political system and nationwide public communication and educational systems are basically centripetal and integrating. The structure of the educational system, operating in conjunction with social and political processes, tends to produce a broad unifying tendency, allows for differences and encourages interaction, tolerance, and the coexistence of distinct ethnic and religious identities, and still provides for interaction. Regional-linguistic as well as religious-cultural distinctions are provided for through some differentiation of curricula and the possibility of instruction at the highest levels in the major Indian languages, while the pre-eminent position of English yields a somewhat western-oriented, quite unified all-India elite. But this could by now be subject to strains based on religious identity. This could be related partly to a sharpening of contradictions and conflict in situations of scarcity and competition, and partly to the tendency of some Hindu ideologies to define Indian nationality and integration in terms of their own symbolism and idiom. They justify this by pointing to the scores of nation-states that are doing the same thing in the name of other faiths, either explicitly or under the guise of a cultural situation of modernity, rationality or even atheism, with symbols and structures of thought related to faith and ethnicity evident just under the surface. There is a serious dispute going on at present between the proponents of rationality, universalism or liberal pluralism as the basic content and orientation of education and those of the opposite tendency, that is, divisive pluralism, segregation and particularism or even majoritarian integration alongside its minority counterpart, that is, separatism and parochialism.

We have not noticed the political and international situation or factors influencing the question in any great measure, particularly as regards the rise of ethnicity over the last decade or two and the decline, successively, of the more earthly ideologies of national liberation, development or equality (we include socialism here) before it. Education may have contributed to all these in the past, but certainly today it is feeling the impact of the latest phenomenon – the ethnic component. India is no exception to this trend.

Similarly, it was tempting, and potentially extremely stimulating, to explore whether India has had its own variant of such phenomena of world outlook and identity as to distinguish it from the modern West and examine its implications for the plurality that constitutes this nation. The notion of negritude in Africa, the view that colonial scholarship has invented the Orient so as to be able to dominate it or, for that matter, the subject of Indian historical scholarship pioneered by the Subaltern School (Guha, 1982) could perhaps have been explored in the context of pluralism in Indian education. We have, however, had to keep our discussion close to the ground in the existing educational situation. Here we do not notice any major reflections of such concepts. Perhaps because of a 200–year-long imperial domination, in which a numerous and sophisticated intelligentsia has cast itself in the mould of western education – the more so because education was linked to the hierarchies and rewards (and demands) of the new system of power and occupation that emerged under British rule – we only have relatively minor distinctions and segregations within the context of a unified structure. Totally isolated systems which do not take cognizance of each other at all do not exist. The closest one comes to such a situation is the recent *dalit* literature of ex-untouchable intellectuals, mainly in Maharashtra. But their implications for education are not apparent. We also have in existence the continuing promotion of indigenous learning and instruction in Sanskrit and Arabic Islamic institutions which retain little contact with the main organized formal educational system. Apart from these minor exceptions, the situation is one of a large, somewhat centralized network which, through centrally prescribed syllabi and examinations, ensures broad uniformity and allows much cultural specificity in institutions recognized, and even financially assisted and inspected, by the state agency, which is itself very largely composed of professionals and academics of all denominations and persuasions.

References

Ahmed, R., 1981, *The Bengal Muslims, Eighteen Seventy-One to Nineteen Six: A Quest for Identity*, New Delhi, Oxford University Press.

Bhattacharya, N.K., 1988, 'Tribal Identity', *Economic and Political Weekly* (Bombay), No. XXIII, pp. 19–23.

Carre, A.G., 1987, *Islam and the State in the World Today*, Delhi, Manohar Publications.

Chalam, K.S., 1988, *Education and Weaker Sections*, New Delhi, Inter-India Publications.

Chatterjee, P., 1986, *Nationalist Thought and the Colonial World: A Derivative Discourse*, New Delhi, Oxford University Press.

Engineer, A.A., 1980, *The Islamic State*, New Delhi, Vikas Publishers.

Frankel, F. and Rao, M.S.A. (eds.), 1989, *Dominance and State Power in India*, New Delhi, Oxford University Press.

Freitag, S., 1990, *Collective Action and Community*, New Delhi, Oxford University Press.

Government of India, 1971, *Census of India*.

—, 1983, *Report of the Committee on Value-oriented Education*.

—, 1990, *India 1990: A Reference Annual*.

—, 1991, *Constitution of India 1950* (as amended up to 1991).

Guha, R. (ed.), 1982, *Subaltern Studies*, New Delhi, Oxford University Press.

Gupta, D., 1991, 'Communalism and Fundamentalism – Some Notes on the Nature of Ethnic Politics in India', *EPW*, Annual Number XXVI, pp. 11–12.

Hashmi, M.A.A., 1989, *Muslim Response to Western Education*, New Delhi, Commonwealth Publishers.

Hussain, S.S., 1978, *The National Culture of India*, New Delhi, National Book Trust.

Jain, G., 1991, 'Culture and Civilization', *Times of India* (Delhi), 17 December.

Jha, A., 1968, *Modernization and the Hindu Socio-culture*, New Delhi, B.R. Publishing.

Joshi, S., 1991, 'Some Theoretical Problems: Religion and Marxism', *EPW*, Vol. XXVI, No. 45.

Kaur, K., 1990, *Madrasa Education in India*, Chandigarh, Centre for Research in Rural and Industrial Development.

Kumar, K., 1991, *Political Agenda of Education: A Study of Colonialism and Nationalist Ideas*, New Delhi, Sage Publications.

Kumar, R., 1991, 'India's Political Identity', *Times of India*, 26 August.

Manorama Yearbook, 1990, Trivandrum, Malayalam Manorama Publication.

Oommen, T.K., 1986, 'Insiders and Outsiders in India: Primordial Collectivity and Cultural Pluralism in Nation-building', *International Sociology* (Cardiff), Vol. I, No. 1.

Patil, S., 1981, *Dasa Shudra Slavery*, Bombay, Allied Publications.

Roy, A.K., 1983, *The Islamic Syncretic Tradition in Bengal*, Princeton, N.J., Princeton University Press.

Roy, S., 1979, *Freedom Movement and Indian Muslims*, New Delhi, Peoples Publishing House.

Rudolph, L.I. and Rudolph, S.H., 1983, 'Rethinking Secularism: Genesis and Implications of the Textbook Controversy: 1977–79', *Pacific Affairs*, Vol. 56, No. 1.

Sarkar, T., 1991, 'The Woman as Communal Subject – *Rashtrasevika Samiti and the Ram Janm Bhoomi* Movement', *EPW*, Vol. XXVI, No. 35.

Satyamurthy, T.V., 1983, *Nationalism in the Contemporary World*, London, Frances Pinter.

Sharma, K.D., 1978, *The Education of a National Minority*, New Delhi, Kalamkar Prakashan.

Shibutani, K. and Kian, M.K., 1965, *Ethnic Stratification: A Comparative Approach*, New York, Macmillan.

Shukla, S., 1968, 'Educational Techniques and Educational Planning', *Educational Sciences*, Vol. II, No. 1., London, Pergamon.

—, 1974, 'Secular and Non-Secular Elements in Indian Education', *Teacher Today*, April-June (paper prepared for Indian Institute of Advanced Studies).

—, 1975, 'Indian Muslims and Education', in I. Zafar (ed.), *Muslims in India*, New Delhi.

—, 1991, 'Education and Ethnocentrism: Asian Perspective', *Bildung und Erziehung*, No. XVIV (proceedings of the International Conference in the Unity of Sciences, Los Angeles, 1988) (in German).

—, 1992, 'Reconsidering Education', *Seminar* (Delhi), No. 337.

Shukla, S. and Kumar, K. (eds.), 1985, *Sociological Perspectives in Education: A Reader*, New Delhi, Chanakya Publications.

Singh, K.S. 1990, *Ethnicity, Identity and Development*, New Delhi, Manohar Publications.

Taneja, N., 1991, 'India: More Than a Civilization', *Times of India*, 12 September.

Thapar, R., 1969, *Past and Prejudice*, New Delhi, Indian Council of Cultural Relations.

Vanaik, A., 1990, *The Painful Transition*, London, Verso.

Verma, N., 1991, 'The India of My Dreams', *Times of India*, 29 December.

Wheeler, A.M., 1949, *5000 Years of Pakistan*, Karachi, Government of Pakistan.

3

Sociologism, Marxism and the Anthropological Imagination

Dipankar Gupta

I have some difficulty in accepting the universal opinion that anthropology is the study of primitive societies while sociology is the study of modern ones. If this is all there is to the distinction between the two disciplines then it does not seem worthwhile carrying on with either of them. I believe, however, that there is a yet more fundamental difference between anthropology and sociology. This difference though it does not preclude either discipline from having overlapping concerns does demarcate the objectives of sociology from those of anthropology in their pure form. It is important to separate pure anthropology from pure sociology, if only as an abstraction, if the interaction between the two is to be purposive and imaginative. The term 'social anthropology' has in many senses been rather unfortunate. It has etiolated the fundamental concerns of anthropology under what appeared to be a compromise formula while involvement with primarily sociologistic concerns has allowed the anthropological imagination to atrophy. This, I contend, is evidenced in studies of the caste system over the past several decades, notwithstanding the two recent and apparently novel thrusts of Louis Dumont (1972) and Maurice Godelier (1972; 1977), whose theoretical perspectives have gained great prestige of late amongst students of the caste system. How and why the lack of *anthropological imagination* inhibits the development of sociology and anthropology as truly humanist discipline will be discussed in the following pages.

As it is *de rigueur* in academic work to warn the reader of what to expect in the pages that follow, a hint of things to come can probably begin with a quick introduction of the term 'anthropological imagination'. This term was chosen not so much to add to the silo of neologisms, as to grasp at once the nimbus of anthropology, immanent as it were in its etymology and to denote its neglect under the tyranny of sociologism which apotheosizes the standardized social fact. That lodestar of the anthropological imagination is the concept of the universal Man who with his essences intact constantly reflects and performs an action upon his social environment. In this process he strives to maximize to his advantage the limited options available to him as a member of the society, and thereby provides a social identity to what are commonly perceived as immobile social facts. But it is only by sheer imagination that a scientist can first transcend the contrary populist tendencies that separate and divide mankind, and it is also by imagination *alone* that he can accept the essence of man as a fundamental principle even without a single social fact *openly* canvassing in its favour. But the imagination gets recognition and maintains itself not by courtesy of opaque social phenomena which so obsequiously fawn on populist notions, but by recognizing in turn the *essence*, or the infrastructure, of a social formation. The acceptance of the imagination is first an act of faith, an assertion of blind humanism, which after careering through a variety of symbolic universes and theoretical schema finally finds fulfilment in Marxism, and in the Marxian insistence on separating appearance from essence. It is not as if this paper, or the anthropological imagination, seeks to uphold Marxism, but it is Marxism that upholds the anthropological imagination and makes possible the transition from blind humanism to enlightened humanism. The essence of man is retained and enriched through this mediation and is severed from all notions of the transcendental individual thus making it possible for one to reach out towards a true humanist social science.

Some cautionary remarks need also to be appended to this preface. By Man (with a capital 'M') I do not mean the individual. This is a central distinction. Second, sociologism, and the sociolatory that it propagates, is not the same as sociology, but refers on the other hand only to a specific tradition in sociology. Finally, this paper is not a reworked charter of the Frankfurt School (or the critical theorists), with which our position bears only a superficial resemblance. It is true that the essence of man as has been accepted here was also accepted by that school. But, as I hope to show later, our differences are substantial not least of all because for the Frankfurt School, more specifically for Horkheimer, Marcuse and Adorno, the essence of man was a utopian vision that was only realizable in a more rational order of the future, and therefore, served only as a spectral antipode that threatened the present and thus facilitated a critique of the current 'irrational' social order. The position that has been taken here quite unambiguously rejects this postulation in the belief that the stuff of *praxis* and the understanding of the present cannot be premised on a threat. We shall have occasion to develop this theme later on. But the bulk of this paper is devoted to the development of the anthropological imagination and to those who constantly threaten it or deny the validity of the imagination in sociology and anthropology.

THE ANTHROPOLOGICAL IMAGINATION AND HUMANISM

> ... The organization of mind is practically identical among all races of man; that mental activity follows the same laws everywhere but that its manifestations depend upon the character of individual experience that is subjected to the action of these laws. (Boas, 1911: 99)

> ... it is really the same mental attitude which makes us value our heirlooms, and makes the natives in New Guinea value their *yaygu'a*. (Malinowski, 1922: 90–91)

The early anthropologists such as Tylor, Boas down to Malinowski, in an almost uninterrupted tradition, were interested primarily in the study of Man – the universal Man. Their primary concern was to demonstrate that 'primitive' man shared with so-called 'civilized' man a common mental apparatus. They then analyzed, through diverse theoretical perspectives, how in spite of this fundamental unity, societies were so diverse. An analysis of the social structure was thus secondary to their concern. And if any analysis was undertaken at this level, as by Malinowski (1922), it was to debunk the search for exotic items while stressing the need to understand such exotica in terms of the total system of relationships existing in that society. Only then Malinowski believed could what appeared strange, unfamiliar and exotic be viewed as akin to some of the institutions and customs that the so-called civilized also cherish. He went on to say:

> To pause for a moment before a quaint and singular fact; to be amused by it, and see its outward strangeness; to look at it as a curio and collect it into the museum of one's memory or into one's store of ancedotes – this attitude of mind has always been foreign and repugnant to me. Some people are unable to grasp the inner

> meaning and psychological reality of all that is outwardly strange, at first sight incomprehensible, in a different culture. These people are not born to be ethnologists. It is in the love of the final synthesis... that lies the test of the real worker in the true science of Man. (ibid.: 517)

Strong words, and yet how soon after Malinowski, anthropology was to be defined, not as the study of Man, but as the study of primitive societies. The outcome of this post-Malinowskian understanding of anthropology was to study societies rather than Man, while unfamiliar practices and customs were soon legitimized as valid exotic objects rendered fixed and immobile by the close intermeshing of social structures. This was a result of the influence of sociology *sans* sociological imagination.

In contrast to anthropology, sociology is primarily devoted to the study of social structures. The concern with man is not uppermost and it can therefore perhaps be called an anti-humanist (perhaps 'ahumanist' is a better word) discipline. The basis for such a conception was best put forward by Durkheim who rejected the notion that the 'entire succession of men, through the whole course of ages must be regarded as one man, always living and incessantly learning' (see Rex, 1961: 8; Durkheim, 1966: 77–78). Durkheim, therefore, concluded that one cannot study humanity but only societies (ibid.). It was Durkheim's approach coupled with his versatile scholarship on primitive and modern societies now undertaken for the first time on a grand scale that obfuscated the distinction between sociology and anthropology. After Durkheim, barring the Malinowskian interregnum of the 1920s and early 1930s, Radcliffe Brown became the most systematic proponent of Durkheimian thinking in British anthropology and it was through him that the dominant anthropological trend in India, and indeed the world over, received legitimacy and succour.

Now, the approach towards primitive societies became excessively formal. Every ceremonial custom was seen as formally fulfilling some essential functional imperative of the social structure. Durkheim's (1966: 3) rigid insistence that social facts are external to individuals. While it did provide a secure emplacement from which the sociologist could combat idealism, methodological individualism and unexamined prejudices, nevertheless also reduced man to the status of an unreflexive subject of the social structure (Durkheim, 1966: Lvi). 'It would thus appear' as Yogendra Singh (n.d.: 16) writes, 'that functional sociology both in its systematic postulates such as those of Parsons and Merton or in its micro-systematic form as in Homans has rendered man a peripheral concept. Man is treated not in the fullness of his existential being, but as an abstraction or as a process.' Each cultural institution, rite, custom and belief was deemed to exist in its pure form and was seen to exercise a pristine influence on the actions of man. There is not in Durkheim either, what Adam Kuper (1973: 59) correctly pointed out in the case of Radcliffe Brown, that 'whiff of reality' that is to be found in Malinowski's minor masterpiece *Balona* or in his magnum opus *Argonauts of the Western Pacific*. The logical order of symbolic representations were considered to be 'so rigid, the power of constraint of these categories on the mind ... so strong' (Durkheim and Mauss, 1970: 16) that 'the individual ... at every moment of time conforms to it. These ways of thinking and acting exist in their own right. The individual finds them completely formed and he cannot evade or change them' (Durkheim, 1966: LVI). The anthropological imagination thus fell into desuetude. Mankind became differentiated on a cultural determinant, and the search for exotic items got a fresh lease of life.

The anthropological imagination which begins with the fundamental concern of demonstrating the unity of Man is forever perceptive in noting how customs and traditions do not exercise a permanent and undiluted influence over men. It examines, on the other hand, how these customs are modified, altered, bypassed, subverted and resisted when men find it in their interest to do so. It brings in, in other words, the essential man. As Marret said: 'The immobility of custom, I believe, is largely the effect of distance. Look more closely and you will see perpetual modification in process' (quoted in Kuper, 1973: 31). This could stand, as Kuper said, as the 'motto to any of Malinowski's Trobriand monographs' (ibid.). In fact, Malinowski himself wrote that 'the description in familiar terms of exotic customs' is the task of anthropologists, and only then will come the recognition that what may seem 'strange at first sight are essentially cognate to very universal and fundamentally cultural items' (Malinowski, 1944: 41). Elsewhere he said that 'whenever the native can evade his obligations without loss of prestige, or without the prospective loss of gain he does so exactly as a civilized business man would' (Malinowski, 1926: 30). Where Radcliffe Brown would have stressed the unquestioning attitude of the 'primitives' towards their customs and rules, Malinowski detailed how it was typical that 'a rule very stringently formulated by all informants when you ask about it, yet in reality often observed with laxity' (Malinowski, 1922: 155). For Malinowski then 'man was down to earth, reasonable, rather unimaginative, perhaps, but able to discern his long term interests' (Kuper, 1973: 40). To appreciate this and to utilize it requires, I believe, an essential quality of mind which is crucial to anthropology, and which I call the *anthropological imagination*. It is this anthropological imagination which marked the works of Boas, Tylor and Frazer, and united them with Malinowski in one tradition for they all believed with him 'in the essential similarity of the human mind' (Malinowski, 1944: 212).

THE ANTHROPOLOGICAL IMAGINATION AND SOCIAL STRUCTURE

Looking back from the short distance we have traversed I can foresee some of the immediate objections they may arise in the minds of the readers to some of my bold statements regarding the fundamental difference between sociology and anthropology, or even more to my suggestion that sociology has dimmed if not desiccated the anthropological imagination.

The only admission I am prepared to make now regarding the first objection is that the distinction between anthropology and sociology, as I have formulated it, is abstract, and that it is highly likely, and even favourable, that a sociologist may also possess the anthropological imagination. There can and should be overlapping concerns between anthropology and sociology, but it is essential at the same time to reiterate and keep active and fundamental concern of anthropology via anthropological imagination.

The second objection and the set of reservations that this alone might spawn, deserve a more lengthy elaboration. How exactly has sociology set the clock back on the progress made by Malinowskian anthropology? Has sociology nothing to offer?

I should perhaps make clear that by sociology and the sociological tradition which militates against the anthropological concern, I am referring to sociology of a specific type – Durkheimian sociology. The reason why I used the blanket term sociology in the first place was because Durkheimian sociology, with several refinements, has provided an aureole to the dominant trend in the teaching of sociology and in sociological research over the last several decades. An entirely new generation of sociologists has been brought up with an unquestioning faith in the Durkheimian method. And with time the carapace has hardened to automatically deflect any suggestion of reviving with profit Boas or even Malinowski.

The fundamental quest of the Durkheimian sociological approach, which has been adopted by anthropologists, is the study of social structures. And how is this to be undertaken? Here again, the Durkheimian influence is predominant. The two important steps that need to be taken so as to understand social structure according to Durkheim are: (i) description of the *normal type* after a study of many cases; and (ii) classification into species, genera, etc. (Durkheim, 1966: 78ff.; Durkheim and Mauss, 1970: 20). How is the normal type to be arrived at? The answer lies in discovering the average of each of the main features of the observed specimens and in constructing a type which possesses all these average features (Rex, 1961: 9). On the basis of this then proceed to differentiate and classify societies.

The understanding of society thus emerged would be on the basis of observed regularities. No one observation in all its contours would be presented, nor would the many divergences from the norm be documented. Hence, the question of a theoretical accounting of deviations from the norm would not arise as a valid problem. If all the deviations are of a normal type, then they would not be considered as deviations at all. They would be deemed as part of normal behaviour. If the deviations are varied, then they would not be presented at all, as in this case the normal type cannot be arrived at. So the understanding of the social structure is primarily dependent upon a statistical average of observations which is then mapped out in a manner not unlike a histogram, with each block representing institutions. These institutions are then presented as the fundamental blocks of society. All this is pure Durkheimian sociology. After this point there might be disagreements between those whom I would still call for the purpose of this paper, Durkheimians, as to how these institutions are related to one another: organically, mechanically or mysteriously. Therein lies their inner debate (see Stark, 1962). But by this time, for the anthropologist following such a route, the damage has already been done.[1]

There is yet another understanding of structure in sociology. The structure in this case is not a statistical norm of observed human behaviour which then, at the hands of social anthropologists, turns on its masters and shackles them. Structure in this case is not the visible structure, but the deeper reality, the essential logic of a social formation. The structure is also objective, outside human consciousness as such, and works behind the minds of men. Such an understanding of structure finds its full and systematic elaboration in Marxism, and is the leitmotif of the Marxian insistence to separate appearance from essence. But this understanding of structure does not negate man as the 'reflexive cogito'. The unconscious structure defines the logic and the limits of a system, of which men are not directly aware, and therefore does not limit human responses in a fixed and determined manner. The structure here sets the limits and determines the potentialities of human action, but does not manifest them directly. An understanding then of structure and process in Marxian terms must be mediated by the constant interaction of varying interests of different segments of society. This exertion of the human element on the logic of the structure is the distinctive character of Marxism.

Sartre (1976: 36) once said: 'If we do not wish the dialectic to become a divine law again, a metaphysical fate, it must proceed *from individuals* and not from some kind of supra-individual ensemble.' This statement might easily arouse fears of a voluntaristic, privatized, solipsistic and a purely ethical intercalation of the individual into the objective science of Marxism. But Sartre puts his finger quite accurately on the failure of many Marxists who view social processes as a concatenation of necessary events, almost as if they were ectoplasmic emanations of the logic of the structure itself. Conscious intervention by man is viewed then simply as 'chance' or accident, and as occurrences outside the scientific dialectical tempo of Marxism. The emphasis on *matter* to the exclusion of everything else, and the consequent slogan – 'the insurmountable character of historical laws' – is foreign to Marxism, and thoroughly negates the very essence of Marxian *praxis* which captures the dialectical moment. As Marx (1969: 14) said: 'The materialist doctrine that men are the product of circumstances and education, that changed men are therefore products of other circumstances and of a different education, forgets that circumstances are in fact changed by men and that the educator must himself be educated.' Or to take a more direct commitment from Marx himself on the anthropological imagination we find him saying in *Critique of Hegel's Philosophy of Right*: 'To be radical is to go to the root of the matter. For man, however, the root is man himself.'

To take away this element of anthropology from Marx, and or to deny the 'universal essence of man', as Althusser does, leaves historical materialism without its prime integrator – social praxis. As Thompson (1978: 201) points out in his lengthy critique of Althusser: 'What Althusser overlooks is the dialogue between social being and social consciousness.' Althusser replaces this dialogue with his notion of 'hierarchy of structures' and thus takes us back effectively to the Plekhanovian views of Marxism, where each level develops automatically with a logic that is extrinsic to the logic of the infrastructure. It is for this reason that Althusser like Plekhanov is 'incapable of seeing the moment of *conscious* intervention or action except as a factor in a mathematical sum or more precisely, insofar as it represents a truly individual phenomenon, in terms of mere *accident* revealed at the point of necessary processes' (see Colletti, 1978: 31), such as in Russia in 1917, China in 1949 and Cuba in 1958 (Althusser, 1969: 207). Therefore, Althusser's mode of cleansing and purifying Marxism by blanching it of its humanist dimensions, actually succeeds in denying man his role as a conscious agent, and man's faculties the capacity for reflexive cogitation. It debases him finally to the position of a mere support or bearer (Trager) of structures (Althusser, 1970: 252; see also Veltmeyer, 1974–75: 396–97).

By denying Man a legitimate role Althusser takes away from Marxism the vitality of *praxis* and of practical sensuous activity. This denial prevents Althusser from making a contribution to the study of the interaction between structure and superstructure and in making an unequivocal breakthrough in his stated objective of combating reductionism. For if there is no anthropology in Marxism, and if men are only the bearer of structures, then the different levels of social reality, the different moments of social existence, viz., ideological, economic, scientific, etc., can never be mediated. The 'historically specific conjuncture' becomes a historically specific conjuncture, because Althusser says so. And this is in fact not very far from what Althusser does say when he studies the 'conjuncture' in Russia in 1917 (with 1905 seen only as a dress rehearsal), China in 1949 or Cuba in 1958 (Althusser, 1969: 207). The revolutions took place on these occasions because they were the necessary denouement of an objective 'fusion' because of the given conditions, i.e., they were the outcome of a mechanistic and obstinate assertion of materiality, *sans praxis* or practical sensuous activity. The result is then a *post festum* assertion of pure causality. Mechanical, yes; perhaps Hegelian too. Did not Hegel say, 'What is actual is necessary in itself' (see Lukacs, 1971: 16). As Lukacs pointed out, Marx criticized Hegel because for the latter, 'knowledge is no more than knowledge about an essentially alien material. It was not the case that this material, human society, came to know itself… . The philosopher's role in history is thus limited to this subsequent consciousness, for the real movement is executed unconsciously by the absolute spirit. Thus, the philosopher arrived *post festum*' (ibid.). We thus see, that movements away from Marx's insistence on Man, result except for a slight twist here and a statement of faith there in conclusions identical with positivism at one extreme, and idealism at the other.

It is not as if by bringing back the anthropological man we are forgetting the epochal constraints of society. Or that we are going back again to methodological individualism and forcefully conjuring up a relation between it and Marxism. Or even that we are denying that the individual in Marxism is really the historically conditioned individual.

All these objections are false though the concern with epochal constraints and with the historically conditioned individual, is valid. (We must be by this time quite tuned to accept paradoxes). The legitimacy of this concern however as expressed in its current form is only a partial, though undoubtedly an important aspect of Marxism. It is true that what separates Marxism from idealism and positivism, and what prevents it from ahistoric reifications, is Marx's insistence on epochal constraints and on historical materialism. But in stressing these aspects alone without integrating them with the dialectic we are still left with a superficial understanding of Marxism, which by the logic of its own incompleteness slides back into the more complete methodological systems of the positivists and the idealists. Whereas it is true that Marxism talks of the historical individual, this individual is not denied his practical and sensuous dimensions. The individual interrogates his own social existence, reflects on its and maximizes his options. It is incorrect then merely to uphold the historically determined individual and then to predetermine his existence as a subject of transcendental material forces (a paradox again). The historically determined individuals, or classes, are concepts which underline the *finality* of social existence, but never presuppose the *causality* of social moments.

We come back to Sartre again. Not the Sartre of *Being and Nothingness* but to the author of *The Critique of Dialectical Reason*. Marxists, when they have taken Man into account have sometimes, as we said earlier, either reduced him to an accident or to an objective interpolation necessitated by the *dictat* of structures. 'Sartre's argument is that no collectivity of individuals can possibly grasp its surrounding material field as a whole, perform an action on it, alter it and so meet human needs – unless *each* individual can do it' (Aronson, 1978: 220). But is Sartre reducing our Man to an individual, forgetting, as Aronson points out that praxis is always social praxis (ibid.: 223)? If placed in its proper context, one notes that Sartre's individual is already integrated into the dialectic (Sartre, 1976: 80–81). His individual is not an isolate, but an anthropological practical sensuous man, whose activities are preordained by the dialectic. He has also internalized the total, with its interstices, and constantly reflects and acts upon the given (not the 'ever pre-given' of Althusser), in order to transcend it and transform it. The transcendence and transformation of the given is not necessarily envisaged in a totalizing manner but from the vantage point at which individuals find themselves. And 'in the course of this transformation', as Lukacs points out, '"pure" economics are naturally transcended though this does not mean we must appeal to transcendental forces' (Lukacs, 1971: 15). But Sartre is not fully able to overcome the lingering remains of solipsism even in *The Critique of Dialectical Reason*. This is probably because he defines praxis as serialized individual *praxis*, and thus opens himself to criticisms, such as that of Aronson's. When Sartre set out to reconquer Man within Marxism, he would have been less equivocal and solipsistic had he begun with the unconscious infrastructure and its dialectic with the anthropological man, instead of advancing via the existentialist schemata, which even in its altered form, considers *praxis* as a plural inflexion of individual *praxis*. By underplaying the role of the infrastructure which unites heterogeneous elements in its field of force, Sartre, who has come a long way since his postulation that 'hell is other people', now apparently believes that *structure is other people*. The dialectic, undoubtedly, is there in Sartre. But the dialectic is now between individual *praxis* and serialized *praxis*, which without the unconscious infrastructural logic of Marxism, still leans towards solipsism and leaves his goal of reconquering man within Marxism unfinished. But Sartre certainly succeeds in bringing about the reappearance of man, and therefore the anthropological imagination should give him his due.

STRUCTURE, TYPIFICATION AND ANTHROPOLOGICAL IMAGINATION

The anthropological imagination is to my mind an essential element of Marxism whether or not Marxists are studying pre-capitalist or capitalist societies. In pre-capitalist societies, or in societies undergoing transition, the urgency is perhaps greater in view of the careless manner in which the members of these societies are generally characterized by scholars, both Marxists and otherwise. It is the anthropological imagination alone which helps one capture the essence of dialectics. The imagination underpins and informs (or should in any case), the friction between necessity and freedom and between structure and Man. The fact that men believe they are free, and yet behind their backs the structure bends to assert a finality to their actions is the *true* dialectic of Marxism.

In the Durkheimian understanding of structure, observed behaviour is standardized to become the objective determinant of human behaviour. Here we have a pure case of positivistic determinism or causality. Even Malinowski in his later period, when he was unexpectedly appreciative of Durkheim, complained against his 'sociological one sidedness ...' (Malinowski, 1944: 24). This sociological one sidedness of Durkheim leads to an understanding of social structure which, to steal a phrase from Simmel, is actually 'the lowest common denominator of individuals'. But whereas Simmel scorned society, Durkheim upheld it as pre-eminent reality. And in consonance with his sociologism, the lowest common denominator was not only given the lofty designation, social structure, but was also in the same swift motion empowered to issue a comprehensive protocol for human behaviour. So, along with societies, individuals also receive their appropriate classificatory labels. A similar fate awaits man in the idealist tradition, pre-Hegelian and Hegelian, which has influenced much of sociology from Montesquieu downwards. After all Hegel himself in the *Philosophy of Right* constantly praised Montesquieu. In the idealist tradition subjective attitudes harden to form objective institutions, and it is on the basis of subjective attitudes, say, for instance, the attitude towards freedom, that mankind can be bracketed. The Germans, Hegel (1944: 347) found, cherished independence and freedom, and that was therefore their determining trait. And not unlike Tacitus before him, Hegel believed that it was this characteristic that distinguished German society from other societies and the German period from the Oriental, Greek and Roman periods of History (ibid.). Montesquieu too subscribed to such a view though Hegel was to develop it more fully. Like his predecessor Count Henri de Boulanvilliers, Montesquieu believed that all notions of political freedom come from the 'Germanic strain'. In fact, he went so far as to state that the 'beautiful system' of freedom embodied in the English parliament had been actually 'invented in the forests of Germany' (Barzun, 1965: 19). It is necessary to know this aspect of Montesquieu for all too often Montesquieu is understood as the precursor of positivist sociology. This should also indicate why idealist notions can easily be incorporated into positivistic sociology without an alarm being sounded for theoretical caution.

The sociologism of Durkheim (or positivism), and idealism in spite of their diverse origins converge insofar as they seek to typify man and society. In Durkheim we proceed from typifying society to typifying social beings, while in idealism we begin by typifying the attitudes of men and then move on to the typification of society.[2] In both cases the margin that distinguishes one from the other is very thin and can be frequently combined with profit as was done by Talcott Parsons. But does Marxism also succeed in typifying man? Is sociology no matter of what genre fundamentally against the anthropological imagination?

The mode of production in Marxism is known to encapsulate the unconscious structure we alluded to earlier. But the mode of production of any historical period can be compared to the social structure of Durkheim, as can the open ended paradigm of Kuhn to the fixed grammatical structure (Kuhn, 1970: 23). The mode of production is like an open ended paradigm for it does not enable one to project what would be the concrete character of the whole social formation. The paradigm, or the mode of production provides the underlying logic of the system, in abstraction it is made to stand apart, but in reality it forms the limits consequent upon the determinate relations men enter into in producing and reproducing their material life. This logic loops the multitude of social actions with centripetal and conservative pressure, but it has also constantly to shift its position and enlarge its options in order not to destroy itself. Social action is therefore always burdened with this logic, but never fully determined. From any point in the social formation man is both dependent and independent, but his energies are more frequently concerned with the area of independence that the logic grants him – the 'give' so to say of the logic itself. The anthropological man, in Marxism, epitomizes the attribute to freedom, of decision and of choice, which becomes relevant and assumes importance because the logic of the system curtails sizeable chunks of it. A pure free man is not only conceptually a sociological absurdity, but is also empirically a mentally certifiable case. It is because there is no complete freedom in society, it is because choices are limited and options mostly closed that man as Man must exercise his faculties and be one with the universal man of the anthropological imagination.

But this has not always been considered by Marxists in their understanding of the mode of production, or of structure. An outcome, as we have tried to show earlier, of denying *praxis* its rightful position at the core of the Marxian dialectic. When this happens, men become only standard bearers of structure, changes occur because of pure objective forces (the 'current situation' of Althusser), and what is more the superstructure, which Althusser variantly assigns a dependent and independent role, becomes in the 'current situation', a slithery lubricant, objectively determined by the objective forces of the current situation. Apart from the paradoxes this gives rise to, it also gives credibility to certain arguments which go along the following lines: if there be a given superstructure, then that superstructure, as it is an objective condition, part of the 'current situation', etc., must also be borne in its entirety by men. Men therefore are bearers of both structure and superstructure and perform only as pre-coded automatons. They are capable of neither reflection nor contemplation. After this is done, it matters little whether the superstructure has its own 'time scale and mode of evolution' as per Godelier (1972: 92), nor whether the structure is an 'absent presence' in the superstructure, for on all occasions men can be called up to fulfil their mute roles. Thus, we see that instead of moving away from reductionism, Althusser's Marxism is doubly inflicted with reductionism, or as Thompson (1978: 290) put it, it is a system of closure. Instead of combating idealist and positivist assaults on man, Althusser's Marxism helps in typing man by the standard whose 'bearer' he is deemed to be. This variant of Marxism, after having demolished the reflexive cogito, can now pronounce with equal facility that the logic of the 'current situation' is in the infrastructure or superstructure. This is precisely what Godelier does leaning on Althusser. If men are mute bearers of structures (plural), the distinction between infrastructure and superstructure loses its significance. And as is often the case infrastructure can also be superstructure and vice versa (Godelier, 1978). Beginning by granting superstructural moments their own levels and autonomy, we end up by positing the two as interchangeable. In between, as we have not managed to locate the subject of the various structures we have also moved towards ideationalism, and structural functionalism (Thompson, 1978: 237, 253, 268 and *passim*), and also if Glucksmann is to be believed, sound like Spinoza for a while (Glucksmann, 1974: 101–02). The structure is the 'insurmountable given', and can only destroy (overcome) itself by its own agency, about which we are told nothing but that we should in all likelihood know about *post festum*, i.e., after the 'historically specific conjuncture'.

The point in being unseemly about all this is that anthropology cannot be fractured from Marxism without Marxism becoming both all and nothing. But the problem does not end with a simple and extraneous avowal of anthropology by Marxists without fully integrating into Marxism the reflexive cogito, and without fully recognizing it as a vital constituent of *praxis*. This has indeed been the case with Horkheimer, Adorno and Marcuse, who recognized the essence of Man but only as suppressed potentiality to be revealed in the promised order of the future. The Frankfurt School had consistently maintained that the faculty of reason with which Man had been gifted could not realize itself in an irrational social order. By implication this meant that if society was irrational so was man, which gave credence to the 'copy theory' of perception which the Frankfurt School had all along opposed (Jay, 1976: 75, 89).

But simultaneously it must also be admitted that the recognition of the essence of man as a utopian proposition was also reflected in some of Marx's own works, such as the *Economic and Philosophical Manuscripts*, and related closely to the concept of alienation as first propounded by him. If one is to rely solely on his early texts then alienation refers only to the inability of man to hunt, fish or write poetry any time he pleases. The essence of man is therefore realized only in the indulgence of these rather effete pleasures. But in the later, specifically in *Capital*, the concept of alienation is derived from the transformation in capitalist societies of concrete labour into abstract labour. The concept of alienation is thus sublated of all its Hegelian connotations and is predicated now on labour, concrete labour, and not on an idealist postulation. In the earlier rendition of alienation, as Althusser repeatedly points out, Marx had not been able to extricate himself from the thralldom of the Hegelian system and the essence of man was lodged only in the lofty idealist realm. But this does not provide justification enough, as it does for Althusser, to dismiss humanism entirely from the kernel of Marxism. If one were to take a lesson from Althusser and go on to the later Marx, it becomes quite clear that it is in the abstraction of concrete labour that the product of labour faces man as an alien object, as a commodity, from which his individual imprint has been wiped clean. Therefore, alienation in Marxism does not simply mean that in an irrational social order the essence of man is not realized, but that in an irrational order the essence of man is *not recognized*. That this recognition is not possible either socially or individually does not however mean that man is not actually performing concrete labour. Or, to carry the argument further, the irrationality of society only curtails the number and choice of avenues through which man can realize himself, but, by the same token, it is this irrationality that makes it incumbent upon man to exercise his faculties all the more, to realize his essences fully in order to overcome the handicaps that the social order imposes on him. It is by paying attention to the depth and vitality of these experiences that one finds that manifestations of the essence of man cannot be limited only to some epicurean expressions of man's faculties. True, the quality of life differs vastly from society to society and from section to section within that society, but that is a totally different matter.

STRUCTURE, SUPERSTRUCTURE AND THE ANTHROPOLOGICAL IMAGINATION

It is from material foundations, Marx said, that specific ideas, beliefs, values, etc., emerge. The superstructure does not have an independent existence, but grows out of the material relations men enter into in concrete historical situations. This *methodological* starting point towards an epistemological theory should not however be construed to mean that at any given point in a concrete social formation, every superstructural element has a one to one origin in the basis. To stress an obvious Marxian platitude, elements in the superstructure are not outgrowths of the pure mind, but of the mind contemplating and ratiocinating on and within given social conditions. As Althusser (1969: 232) said: 'Human societies secrete ideology as the very element and atmosphere indispensable to their historical respiration and life'. But the Althusserian system soon asserts that ideologies 'are usually images and occasionally concepts, but it is above all as structures that they impose on the vast majority of men …' (ibid.: 233; emphasis given). So the ideological structure in Althusser receives a coherence, permanence and logic much like the economic structure as it does not impose itself on men 'via their consciousness' (ibid.). Once again men are mere supports.

If for structures and superstructures man is only a support, then we can again type him off in a manner not unlike the positivists and Hegelians. For here again these structures are insurmountable and impervious to the human agency and man must therefore constantly submit to them. This would be the outcome if one were to construct an Althusserian system based on Althusser's contributions. But Althusser's work also provides other theoretical leads. His side glances on the question of 'survivals' (ibid.: 118–19) are pregnant with suggestions that take us away from the simplistic basis – superstructure dialectic and also from the Althusserian system. The Althusserian system, as a coherent system, talks of structural causality only. Though his attack on Hegelian Marxist notions of 'supercession' (ibid.: 197–99), and his insistence that 'categories can no longer have a role and meaning fixed once and for all' (ibid.: 209), cannot be integrated into his system, and sound jarring to one undertaking a 'symptomatic reading' of Althusser, they are nevertheless capable of rendering a service that his system fails to do, i.e., in combating reductionism. It is this other aspect of Althusser that I should like to acknowledge in much of what appears in the following pages.

The ideological elements and ideological systems, needless to say, are outgrowths of the material world. But at no one point can the ideological world attain a structure of its own which can either be as enduring as the logic of a mode of production, or entirely composed of elements that are emanations of the given structure. The past and present in the superstructural elements should be seen rather as 'now past' 'now present', as these elements live beyond the conditions that give them birth (another Marxian platitude). But these elements live on and are structured and restructured, built and shattered, to express and articulate the lived in conditions of men in society, of men placed differently in the constant dynamic of society. As Boas said: '... mythological worlds have been built up, only to be shattered again, and that new worlds were built from the fragments' (quoted in Levi Strauss, 1966: 21). This is why as Althusser (1969: 209) says these elements are not univocal. But this is also why superstructures contrary to what Althusser adumbrates and Godelier develops, do not have their autonomous mode of evolution or time scale. It is because the human mind cannot fully grasp its surroundings, that it treasures the ideological elements of the past, hordes them as one would ancient heirlooms not knowing when, nor for what reason, their value would appreciate. Althusser (ibid.: 116) mentions 'the reactivation of older elements', but only in passing. Also more significantly he does not mention their restructuration, nor also that a particular form of structuration is not lived out in that form during an entire epoch. These 'silences' of Althusser become eloquent when one recalls the resonance of his system, in particular its fundamental principle, that the lonely hour of the last instance, i.e., the economy, never comes (ibid.: 113). If the emissions and the effects of structures are primarily cathodic in quality, emanating upon and lighting up a zone that is a vacuous monad of structure bearers, then the incidence of refraction and mediation of the effects of structures cannot find a symptomatic elaboration within the system.

It is to get away from this form of determinism that the Althusserian system promotes that the recognition of the anthropological imagination is absolutely essential. Not only does man try to maximize his options, straining against the logic of the unconscious economic structure, he also reviews and revises his strategy towards this end continuously. In this process new alliances are created, new obstacles are detected and within the range of novelty that the logic allows, newer ideological structurations emerge which explain to him his life, his purpose, his conditions, and his past and future from the ever shifting standpoint of the present. From here, I think, we can take the plunge towards an affirmation of orthodox Marxism. Not only are elements of the superstructure outgrowths of the basis, but a particular ideological structuration or expression is the result of the manner in which man reviews and plans his programme during a determinable moment in social history.[3] And therefore this expression is not determined by the 'economy in the last instance' (ibid.: 113, 213), but is determined at the start, by the modalities of optimizing one's situation vis-à-vis others within a definite socio-economic formation. The articulation and acclaim of the ideological structure rests primarily on its ability to aspire towards a worldview and to project, by condensation, experimental reflexes learnt from the lived in world as knowledge. But as the lived in world also changes in small microscopic doses, so do experiences. The ideological structure is then a protean phenomenon and therefore it cannot be said that a class has a fixed ideological structure composed to a fixed number of elements. It is only in the structuration that ideological or superstructural elements get a semantic content and meaning. This structuration makes sense because of the selective manner in which certain elements are given salience to provide a charter for class action. At another point different aspects of these non-univocal elements can be activated, or wholly new elements may be brought it. To give an example, sometimes 'casteism' expresses itself in the form of a war between the upper castes and some (not all) members of the untouchable castes, whereas the logic of pure casteism should not have distinguished between different sections among the untouchables. At other times 'casteism' finds expression in a situation of hostility between Hindus and Buddhists, while at other times untouchables and Hindus bury their differences and have a face off with the Muslims. Yet again, two dominant castes are antagonistically ranged against each other with the lower and middle castes either left out of the picture or drawn in at different points; and so it goes on … . This holds true for nativism, chauvinism, regionalism, racism, etc. Also from casteism, the same protagonists, may move over to some other idiom to express their mutual hostility. In this process they may draw in other allies or drop their previous ones. The models change, the elements undergo transformation, depending entirely on the manner in which people in society give meaning to them, in order to maximize their conditioned options.

This understanding should hopefully take us away from two types of gross errors. The error of the first type occurs when Marxists talking of 'survivals' believe that these elements of the past have only a short period of survival ahead of them as the conditions that gave them birth have disappeared. In India, for instance, we are often told that communalism and casteism are pre-capitalist and feudal, and if only the Indian economy had been a fully developed capitalist one they would have withered away. This is a form of evolutionism which has nothing to do with Marxism, and which was long ago effectively debunked by Malinowski. Criticizing Goldenweiser, Malinowski (1994: 29) said: 'There is no doubt that the survival endures because it has acquired a new meaning, a new function... Antiquated types of automobiles are never used simply because they have survived, but because people cannot afford to buy a newer model. The function is economic.' The same is expressed elsewhere when he said: 'Much has been said and written about survival. Yet the survival character of an act is expressed in nothing so well as in the concomitant behaviour in the way in which it is carried out ... (O)bserve and fix the data of their behaviour, and at once the degree of vitality of the act will become clear' (Malinowski, 1922: 30). It is not my intention to slight Marxists by quoting Malinowski, but it is rather to demonstrate that the anthropological imagination can go a long way towards showing up the doctrinaire and undialectical nature of some formulations made by some Marxists. To return to our problem. Elements of the superstructure do not just wither away. They are part of the historic memory of man to be used and revitalized just when they are about to be thought of as defunct, so as to position man and to define his situation vis-à-vis other men in society.

The error of the second type occurs when it is believed that an ideological structure has a clear run, propelled either by its own mode or by the logic of the mode of production. But if man is constantly straining against the overarching logic of the infrastructure, he is at the same time relatively free to apply and reapply ideological elements to express himself via his faculties. Just as the logic of the infrastructure curtails his freedom, the finite elements of the superstructure again relate him, even in the world of ideas, to other men. And as the elements of the superstructure are finite, they cannot be univocal (which does not make them equivocal, as Althusser (1969: 200), rightly said, nor can they be unstructured, for they are called upon to serve a variety of situation. These situations are situations of the lived in world and are therefore denoted in the *first instance* by the 'economic'.

It is true that Althusser admits that elements of the superstructure cannot be reduced directly, i.e., in an etiological sense, to the reigning mode of production. He also says: 'The meaning of this whole, of a particular ideology... depends not on its relations to a *truth* other than itself but on its relation to the existing *ideological field* and on the *social problems and social structure* which sustain the ideology ...' (Althusser, 1969: 62; emphasis given). But his system, as it was shown earlier, goes on to assert the autonomy of the different levels of society, and the superstructure is one of them. He begins by giving this level relative autonomy, but ends up in granting it absolute autonomy. Recall, for instance, Althusser's assertion: 'From the first moment to the last, the lonely hour of the "last instance" (the economic – D.G.) never comes ...' (ibid.: 113). While it is agreed that ideological elements may not find their origin in the existing base, the disagreement with Althusser is on the autonomy he grants the ideological structure. It is because he grants ideology 'more than relative autonomy' (Glucksmann, 1974: 107), that Godelier building up on Althusser, and without destroying his system, is able to say that each level or structure, in particular, the superstructure has 'its own mode and time scale of evolution' (Godelier, 1972: 92). But outside the Althusserian system, Althusser (1969: 63) says: '(T)he developmental motor principle of a particular ideology cannot be found within ideology itself but outside it ...'. This is why the emphasis on Althusser's equivocation, and on the two Althusser's. One of the Althusserian system, which Godelier has appropriated, and one outside it, which has been positively acknowledged here.

Let us return now to our anthropological imagination. Once it is acknowledged that neither structure nor superstructure can determine causality in society we are close to an appreciation of the various ways by which man manipulates his social environment to his advantage. We then also hesitate to designate a prefixed set of behaviour patterns for those belonging to different societies with differing social structures. Nor can we say that the ideological level exists in any one form, but that man manipulates his ideological heritage in consonance with his 'lived in' relation in the world, and from this friction emerges a particular ideological structuration. If one grants the ideological level autonomy we take away the autonomy of man. For how else can ideology express itself but through men? If we believe on the other hand that the social structure is close ended, men are again bearers of a pre-ordained 'transcendental dialectic'. To move imaginatively therefore, in Marxism, and in sociology, the assertion of the anthropological man becomes ineluctable.

THE INFRASTRUCTURE AND ITS METHODOLOGICAL RELEVANCE

In an earlier section it was noted that in mainline sociology of the Durkheimian variety the emphasis is on social structure. This social structure should not be confused with Marx's or Levi Strauss' understanding of infrastructure. For the Durkheimians, structure is the norm of observed behaviour, rules, regulations, beliefs, etc. This is akin to Radcliffe Brown's use of the term 'structural form'. The structure here is not an unconscious structure, but quite plainly a conscious structure (see Godelier, 1972: XVIII).

In Marx, on the other hand, we have a detailed treatment of the unconscious structure. In Marx again, we have the notion of men making their history unconsciously. This is in keeping with his methodological starting point which seeks to separate appearance from essence. As Godelier (1972: 81) rightly says: 'Marx ... brings out the existence of *aspects of reality that do not relate to any consciousness and are not explicable by consciousness*' (emphasis given). For Marx, as for Levi Strauss, to continue with Godelier, 'a structure is not a reality that is *directly* visible, and so directly observable, but *a level of reality* that exists beyond the visible relations between men, and the functioning of which constitutes the underlying logic of the system, the subjacent order by which the apparent order is to be explained' (Godelier, 1972: XIX; emphasis given).

Levi Strauss used the deep structure of the mind which functions on the principle of binary oppositions to understand 'how the human spirit works' (Glucksmann, 1974: 87), notwithstanding the social diversity of human existence. His studies focused especially on the superstructure, i.e., on myths, totemism, 'savage' thought, etc. He said: 'Without questioning the undoubted primacy of infrastructures, I believe that there is always a mediator between *praxis* and practices, namely, the conceptual schema... . It is to this theory of superstructures, scarcely touched upon by Marx, that I hope to make a contribution' (Levi Strauss, 1966: 130). But this superstructure is not a defined and conscious structure. Levi Strauss (ibid.) criticized Balzac who wrote that '(i)deas form a complete system within us, comparable to one of the natural kingdoms', by commenting that, 'more madness than genius would be required for such an enterprise. If, as I have said, the conceptual scheme governs and defines practices, it is because these, which the ethnologist studies as discrete realities placed in time and space and distinctive in their particular modes of life and forms of civilization, are not to be confused with praxis which – and here at least I agree with Sartre – constitutes the fundamental totality for the science of man' (ibid.).

Though it is sometimes construed that for Levi Strauss the social structure is derived from the structure of the mind (Glucksmann, 1974: 72), I think this arises out of an insufficient attention paid to the methodological principles of the Levi Straussian method. Glucksmann cites Levi Strauss' studies on kinship to make this point (ibid.). But if one looks a little closely at Levi Strauss' study on kinship it will be noticed that what Levi Strauss is actually doing is using linguistic theory, and the theoretical insights of linguistic theory – the distinction, for instance, between *language* and *parole* – to bear upon the ordering of relationships of authority and joking relationships in kinship relations, in order to undermine the counter emphasis on conscious interventions in the detailing of kinship relations (Levi Strauss, 1968: Chapter I). Our earlier quotation from Levi Strauss also makes clear that he has no intention of trifling with the economic infrastructure of Marx. His search is for the common properties of the mind. To quote him again: 'If as we believe to be the case, the unconscious activity of the mind consists in imposing form upon content, and these forms are fundamentally the *same for all minds* – it is necessary and sufficient to grasp the unconscious structure underlying each institution and each custom, in order to obtain a principle of interpretation valid for other institutions and customs' (ibid.: 21). It would appear then that Levi Strauss' object of analysis is to study the universality of the human mind via a variety of customs, institutions and practices, and not to emphasize or demonstrate either that the structure of the human mind determines man's concrete socio-economic environs, or that myths, customs, etc., constitute the social infrastructure. His search is for the deep structure behind the superstructure, which would explain the universal attributes of the mind, and also the principle that keeps ordering and reordering the superstructure. All this is important if one is to understand the methodological foundations and aims of structuralism, and distinguish structuralism from the pseudo-structuralism of say, Dumont. As we shall see later, Dumont's structuralism takes on precisely those tasks that Levi Strauss consciously kept out of his purview for he considered them to belong to the genre of 'mad enterprises'.

To write on Marx's understanding of the infrastructure would appear as if we were trying to rediscover the wheel. But given the various interpretations of Marxism it is important to enter into this endeavour. The infrastructure, for Marx, very simply put, is the logic of a given mode of production. This logic can be understood primarily in terms of the relations of production, and it is therefore the relations of exploitation that give us the underlying principle of a particular social formation and set up the final limits for human action. It is because a mode of production does not start off a causal series, that each society, depending on its initial contingent conditions, its peculiar place in ecology and history, manifests a unique social formation. It is this mode of production that serves as the integrator for the heterogeneous elements in a social formation, and brings about a complex unity of its various levels. Poised here, in the deep structure of society, Marxists are able to bring out the friction between the pure logic of the infrastructure and the empirical encumbrances through which the structure must work and which it must finally subjugate. It is against the logic of this structure that, as it was mentioned earlier, the anthropological man strains, stretching it to its utmost, before succumbing to it. And in the process succeeds in altering, even if it be in microscopic details, his concrete social formation.

If this logic is the infrastructure of Marxism, and if this logic exercises a finalist constraint, then it is obvious that it must be able to recharge itself at every point of its social duration. It must in other words reproduce itself. In order to do so it must summon the various levels of society and conscript them for this purpose. Institutions in society are all charged with this responsibility, though their duties are not identical, as they vary with the nature of the expertise of each institution. The contrary trends and tendencies within each institution must also be recognized, but it is in their final contribution vis-à-vis the deep structure that their contribution towards the reproduction of the structure can be understood. It is important, logically, at least, to separate the infrastructure from the other 'levels'. The infrastructure as infrastructure presents a coherent logic. That this logic must also have a reproductive capacity is an axiomatic, or even better, an apodictic truth. But as men in society do not work with a steadfast gaze on this logic, and as they also consider themselves to be free to make certain choices, their subjugation to the logic is never fully external either, i.e., through sheer physical force. There must be a social atmosphere in which this logic must breathe. It takes in some noxious fumes, of course, but on the whole gets enough of the life giving stuff which enabled it to come into existence in the first place. Both the oxygen and the pollutants are supplied by the social formation. Religion for instance emits both what is necessary for the reproduction of the infrastructure and also what undermines it (Gramsci, 1971: 420).[4] So also for family ties and kinship and indeed for every social institution. But logic qua logic, must reproduce itself directly. This occurs only in abstraction. As the logic works itself in society it must work through every level to reproduce itself and also to establish its suzerainty. The distinction then between infrastructure and superstructure is not between two levels of empirical reality, for one most obviously is not visible as an empirical reality. The distinction is analytical, for the purpose of grasping empirical reality (another Marxian homily) and its dynamic. The infrastructure helps one understand visible structure. Then it is an intellectual choice as to what one's universe of study will be: hot societies or cold societies; the structure of myths, beliefs, etc., or concrete social processes. This would then determine the analytical choice as to whether the infrastructure should be located in the mind, in the economy, or in the structure of distribution.

The distinction between infrastructure and superstructure can also not be premised on different functions, as Godelier argues. According to Godelier (1978: 85), the function of the infrastructure is to 'produce and reproduce material means of their (members of society – D.G.) existence'. The disagreement here is that the logic of the infrastructure itself compels all institutions in society with this reproductive function. If Godelier's understanding of infrastructure is to be accepted, then everything is infrastructure. This is precisely why he can maintain that politics, religion, etc., act as both infrastructure and superstructure (ibid.: 88).

This form of reasoning on the distinction, if any, between infrastructure and superstructure gives rise to the notion that all that is not relevant for social reproduction, which in turn means, all that is not relevant for the survival of the logic, is superstructure. This obfuscates the fact that the logic of the infrastructure is an 'absent presence' in Althusser's term, and that a delineation of structures in terms of whether or not they help to reproduce material reality would be too inclusive to be meaningful. If it is concrete reality one is attempting to understand then the economy holds the logic in a near pure form, because that is the foundation of material life. Marx's reasons for positing the logic in economic relations is too well known to suffer repetition. The economic process, the growth of certain economic institutions and practices, price movements, etc., should not be understood as the infrastructure. They can be explained by the infrastructural logic, but as such are the outcome of live social reality, of concrete historical conditions, constrained by the logic of the infrastructure, i.e., by the determinate relations of production. The superstructural levels are those which bridge over the breaks and contradictions of the infrastructure, in the minds of men, so that the contradictions in the economy, i.e., 'pure' class contradictions, are never apparent or existent in their pure form. This, in the final analysis, facilities material reality, in concrete terms, to reproduce itself, a facility that the logic had only in abstraction provided for itself.

It might be possible to misunderstand what we have just said to mean that all that is observable is superstructure and all that is unobservable is infrastructure. Certainly not. What is also observable are manifestations of the logic of the infrastructure: giant conglomerates, technical development, the increasing importance of fixed capital, observable human behaviour and relationships of a wide variety. What we should like to denote as superstructure are precisely those elements that help in masking and concealing the true nature of the contradictions in the basis, so that a comprehension of the 'sensible world in sensible terms' (Levi Strauss, 1966: 16) is arrived at by the members of the society. This is akin to Levi Strauss' understanding of myths where 'the myth as a whole is less a representation of society than a contemplation of the unsatisfactory compromises on which it rests' (Glucksmann, 1974: 80). In class societies with class contradictions, it is in the superstructure that a compromise is attempted in sensible terms to make possible concrete material reproduction. This is precisely why Marxists consider certain 'levels' such as beliefs, values, religion, etc., to belong to the superstructure, and this is also why these levels are not considered unimportant either by Marxists, giving a lie to the common assumption that the superstructure in Marxism is all that is secondary or irrelevant. This would perhaps be the outcome of a strict Godelierian understanding of superstructure – a fate layered with irony in view of Godelier's project to combat reductionism.

The superstructure is a vast store house. There are far too many elements in it to make possible an inventory of the worst sort. But only certain elements of the superstructure are more directly related to the basis or to the infrastructure than others. These more directly relevant ones are those which best hide the basic contradictions in the infrastructure and therefore recur constantly in that epoch. But it is not enough to stop here in one's examination of the superstructure for this would truncate its vast epistemological sweep. Certain elements, it is true, occur again and again in an epoch. But in any of their specific articulations (and they are capable of several, as it was maintained earlier) they must combine with other elements borne more directly out of mundane experiences. These experiences in turn have the menemotechnic effect of revitalizing certain other items from the collective memory, which also go into the combination to form an ideological structuration. The critical assembly that is thus arrived at in the minds of men appears either chaotic or autonomous if superstructural elements are not seen as functioning to conceal infrastructural contradictions, and if the catalyst for the rejuvenation of slices of one's ideological heritage is not located in mundane lived in experiences.

The process of ratiocination of the lived in world, changes the world itself, albeit gently, gently. To add to this the several fractures that exist in the superstructure makes this level extremely dynamic and fluid as man is constantly straining to optimize and maximize his opportunities, and is thus constantly changing and readjusting his ground plan and the symbolic universe on which it rests. Nevertheless the fact that the unconscious structure, or the contradictions of the infrastructure, is invisible and hidden, compels man to comprehend only the sensible world in sensible terms, which assures the continuation of the infrastructural logic, for its deep secret is well hidden and never fully grasped in the minds of men. This objectively sets the final limits of the potentialities of the superstructure, and thus only in this objective sense can certain ideas in the superstructure be considered as ruling class ideas. These ideas are not the preserve, nor always a willful creation of the ruling class.[5] These ideas are such that though they may on occasion jar the logic of the infrastructure, destabilize it and embarrass it, they never threaten to extirpate it.

The superstructure does not have a uniform elaboration of its structure such that it could determine the priorities of all men for all times in an epoch. It also functions to reproduce the material means of society, but does so indirectly by its silences on the contradictions of the infrastructure, and by trying to bridge the contradictions of the known in knowable terms. Man can contemplate upon only objective manifestations of the logic and upon objective and 'dominant contradictions' which allow a multiplicity of explanatory themes depending on the multiplicity of experiences arising out of differential locations at which men are placed in the socio-economic formation.

But the superstructures of each epoch have a definite quality about them, with enough diacritical marks to distinguish them from the superstructures of other epochs. It is by the elaboration of these diacritical notations that we are able to talk of the existence of such superstructural themes as the belief in the caste system, in democracy, in paternalism, etc. The governing elements of each such superstructural theme are intimately related to the basic contradictions of the infrastructure, in the sense that they most effectively conceal these contradictions. But as these elements are finite and not equivocal, it is only within certain limits that they can be used.[6] But as long as they are in existence they do strive to perpetuate the internal logic of the system, and hence material reproduction, though never in a uniform or clearly knowable way. For the anthropological man is ubiquitous and perpetually in his element, reinterpreting elements of any structuration to his own advantage, bringing in different elements, and altering the assembly in such a manner that he can explain the present as well as find hope and a *raison d'etre* for his future existence in society.

The superstructure, if the analysis thus far is accepted, does not have its own autonomous level. It enjoys a relative autonomy of course, but this relative autonomy does not have abundant ideological, free space to indulge in anything more than a privatized carousel on its own steam. The reason why earlier elaborations of this theme sounded so implausible was because the logic of the economy was supposed to govern to the last detail every element of the superstructure and even its structuration, *ab initio*. This not only obfuscated a close study of the peculiarities of the material basis and its prior history, but also standardized the superstructure on a dogmatic principle leaving little for the anthropological man to design and fashion. At the other extreme we have the Althusserian inspiration, where apart from moments of conjuncture when the economy 'selects' from the autonomously elaborated superstructure, the latter like the former has its own tempo and its own autonomy. But what Althusser forgets is that the moments of conjuncture that he finds in recent history were actually 'selected' by the philosopher himself. For the anthropological man, however, the moments of conjuncture are not only 1919, 1949 or 1958,[7] but every moment is a moment of conjuncture as it alters the world ceaselessly in microscopic details.

DUMONT AND GODELIER: TWO RECENT REVERSALS IN THE ANTHROPOLOGICAL IMAGINATION

In making examples of Dumont or Godelier the intention is primarily to demonstrate that once the anthropological imagination is given up and along with it the anthropological man, no matter how diverse one's theoretical origin and one's stated methodological preferences, the conclusions are going to be dreadfully similar. Dumont in his *Homo Hierarchicus* (1972) tries to demonstrate how inadequate Marxism is for the study of Indian reality. And yet Godelier from a clearly stated Marxist position finds it possible to appreciatively quote Dumont, and also to utilize Dumont's formulations as theoretical illustrations. This unity between Dumont and Godelier which might otherwise seem baffling can however be understood by the commonality of their respective orientations towards the understanding of man. For both men are determined by structures. For Dumont the 'conscious model' is the most important level of reality determining in detail how men are to act in a variety of situations. For Godelier the conscious structure is infrastructure in pre-capitalist societies, and hence the most important level of reality in these societies. The second area of agreement between Dumont and Godelier is that neither considers the anthropological man to be capable of functioning as a reflexive cogito, as he is totally determined by the most important level of reality in society. Why do the Indian tribes in the Inca state formation hand over part of their surplus to the Gods? Because, according to Godelier (1977: 35), their religion commands them to do so. It is the religious idea that 'causes thing to happen' (Godelier, 1978: 90). Therefore, politico-religious ideas constitute the infrastructure in the Inca empire. Let us move on to Dumont. Why do Hindus still remain backward in spite of the great strides taken by industrialization elsewhere in the world? Because Dumont avers, the caste system determines just how much to give in to industrialization without endangering its hierarchical principle. The Hindus are allowed to avail of the benefits of industrialization only in areas which the caste system considers unimportant (Dumont, 1970: 228). Godelier then moves swiftly and claims caste as infrastructure (Godelier, 1978: 89; 1972: ix).

It cannot be denied that beliefs play a role in influencing human behaviour. This is a truism that needs not be stated. But what is being disputed here is that these beliefs in the hands of sociologists and anthropologists become absolute determinants of human behaviour and prescribe a set rule of action. Thus, in spite of Dumont's and Godelier's rather novel methods, structuralism and Marxism respectively, they quite unambiguously resurrect Durkheimian sociologism which was debated and contested in the earlier section of this paper. We shall not go into this again, other than to remind the reader why Dumont and Godelier have been chosen as recent instances of the reversal of the anthropological imagination. Perhaps we should also mention again that it is not necessary to go to Marx to be aware of this. He, of course, provides a full theoretical integration of the anthropological man in the study of society. But even Malinowski (1926), with his faltering apparatus was able to see that beliefs, however marginal, must contain a utilitarian core. And as utility is measured and perceived differently by members belonging to different sections of society, one should at least consider the possibility of multiple interpretations of, spontaneous accretions to, and even the rejection of, a particular system of beliefs.

Though Malinowski's work was constantly devalued by later anthropologists who only saw him as a crude functionalist with somewhat naive predilections towards an analysis of social phenomena in terms of psychology and human needs, Malinowski continued to provide massive doses of inspiration to all those who were interested in the study of conflict and tension in social formations. Max Gluckman and Edmund Leach were the foremost in this regard. But because of the complexity of their material, and of their arguments, most anthropologists preferred to take up the simpler, almost rule of thumb and populist approach of Radcliffe Brown instead. This precluded a full elaboration of Malinowski which would have thrown up some of his theoretical weaknesses more fully without losing out on his core concern and without abjuring what I have called the anthropological imagination. Malinowski, Leach and Gluckman are still referred to in essential readings, quoted in passing, but otherwise told to stand in the corner and speak only when spoken to.

It was with Levi Strauss that the anthropological imagination, which was made friable by Malinowski's theoretical weakness, was reassembled again. The impact was devastating. Here was a man able to move freely between Marx, Jakobson, de Saussere, and the anthropological masters. Not many perhaps understood what was happening, a state of incomprehension that at times Levi Strauss seemed deliberately to inspire by his equivocation on some vital issues and also by the subtle dislocations effected by the translation of his works. Also, and most importantly, he chose for himself the study of 'cold societies' and of their myths, beliefs, to arrive at the structure of the superstructures of these societies. All this demanded a great deal of mental ability, as such 'cold societies' are no longer in existence, but are part of our anthropological pre-literate past. But, I think Levi Strauss also implies, that this past can only be forgotten if we are determined to misunderstand ourselves in the present.

Though structuralism gained in stature in anthropology almost wholly due to the unstoppable advance of Levi Strauss' reputation, very many structuralist studies proceeded without the least acknowledgement Levi Strauss had made to the primacy of Marx's infrastructure, and with an audacity and pretentiousness that Levi

Strauss quite specifically resisted. Dumont and Godelier began structuralist studies with several others, and conducted them in a manner that would have been anathema to Levi Strauss. The most egregious departure of such structuralists from the Levi Straussian method, it that for the latter the deep structure, or the infrastructure, was never consciously known. Even Godelier, as it was pointed out earlier, contravened this in claiming conscious cultural beliefs and values to be at the level of the infrastructure 'causing' certain things to happen. Dumont (1972: 76) also believed that the consciously elaborated caste system is a state of mind which is the primary level of Indian social reality.

As was mentioned earlier (recall Levi Strauss' comment on Balzac), Levi Strauss had no intention of suggesting that conscious models determine actual social relations. Also Levi Strauss was actually searching for invariant principles behind all conscious models and nothing more. Two simple quotes from Levi Strauss and Dumont should make clear their vast theoretical differences. To quote Levi Strauss (1966: 117) first:

> 'I do not, at all, mean to suggest that ideological transformations give rise to social ones. *Only the reverse is in fact true*. Men's conception of the relations between nature and culture is a function of modification of their own social relations. But since my aim here is to outline a theory of superstructures, reasons of method require that they should be singled out for attention and that major phenomena which have no place in this programme should seem to be left in brackets or given second place. We are however merely studying the shadows on the wall of the cave forgetting that it is only the attention we give them lends them a semblance of reality'. (emphasis added)

In direct contrast to this Dumont (1972: 71) writes that the 'caste system is a state of mind, a state of mind which is expressed by the emergence, in various situations, of groups of various orders generally called "castes".' The state of mind therefore expresses itself, and is thus instrumental in giving rise to concrete social formations, which is exactly the kind of thing Levi Strauss not only opposed but also considered futile and 'mad'. For Levi Strauss 'the relation between the "representation" of the object to the real non-conceptual object is always transcendental, but not centred in consciousness. The relation between the categories of thought with the elements of reality is transcendental precisely because... it is not an empirical relation of thought to its object – nor can experience ever provide its status as a conceptual object' (D'Amico, 1973: 89). This summing up by D'Amico most accurately represents Levi Strauss' methodological position regarding the relationship between the categories of the mind and empirical reality which again demonstrates the distance between him and Dumont.

Finally, when Levi Strauss employs a binary model for grasping the hidden structure behind the superstructures, he is not talking, in the words of Gehlke of the 'content of mind' but of the 'capacity of mind' (Needham, 1970: xxcv). Nor does he posit that the elements which express these oppositions have an innate quality as such which attaches them to either pole of the opposition. The oppositions only make sense in a system of internal homology and transformations. The semantic content of the superstructure is related to empirical reality only in so much as it permits man to overcome the very unsatisfactory contradictions on which his society rests. For Dumont, on the other hand, the opposition between the pure and impure, by virtue of being an empirical opposition cannot bear a transcendental relation between categories of thought and empirical reality. There is no system of internal homology or transformations in Dumont. It is the opposition alone which is on its beat, searching the society, differentiating it, imprinting it, and constantly adding, over the years, to its combined stockpile of things pure and impure. This method, if anything, bears a strong affinity to the Hegelian system of reasoning and not to Levi Strauss or to structuralism. In this method, loaded semantic categories operate which then raise tricky analytical problems. From one point of view the opposite of pure, is, *not pure*. Anything that is not pure need not be impure, and so on.[8] Moreover, whether or not a certain object should be designated as pure and another as impure, cannot, in the Levi Straussian sense, be understood simply in terms of their *innate properties*, but only in a system of internal homology, which would then allow structural transformations, which would in turn bring in the anthropological child as the father of the man.

CONCLUSION: THE SOCIOLOGICAL AND ANTHROPOLOGICAL IMAGINATION

The sociological imagination primarily demands a conjuncture between historical and biographical investigation whereby one is able to understand the social and historical processes that separate individuals and alienate them from one another. This at least is the way I read C. Wright Mills' *The Sociological Imagination*. An imaginative analysis of this sort, Mills believed, would cross illuminate the method and logic of seemingly timeless, faceless, inert social institutions which conceal the relations that bind man, sectorized and atomized as they are at different, often remote points on the scatter diagram of society.

The sociological imagination brings one to an understanding of our common fate, to multiple social forces in history which shape institutions and classes and separate them from our common consciousness. The anthropological imagination works in a complementary mode, and indeed encompasses all of the insights of the sociological imagination. It starts, however, from the realization that 'at the root of man is man himself'. Social forces must work through man. But because, in the anthropological imagination, man is essentially a 'reflexive cogito', who contemplates and thinks, rationalizes and maximizes, no social force is left entirely in pristine form once it has undergone mediation by men. But to realize itself fully the anthropological imagination must rely on the sociological imagination. The sociological imagination tells us of the deep structure that binds men together only to differentiate them, while the anthropological imagination affords a perspective through which the constant dynamic of society can be grasped and mankind can again be united. This dynamic is propelled in fact by the rational energies of man, by the 'essence'[9] of man, contending with the circumscribing logic of the infrastructure to realize himself. The anthropological imagination that proclaims at the start that '(t)he organization of mind is practically identical among all races of man' (Boas, 1911: 99), and which focuses on the universality of man, makes it possible for the sociological imagination to bring out in richer details the structures that separate and differentiate mankind. It is only via this complementary modality that anthropology can make sociology a true *humanist* science.

Notes

1. Neither does Durkheim's concept of *homo duplex* help to moderate his basic sociologism. This concept tells us that man is made up of two elements. The first is his sociologically conditioned being, and the second is his free floating intellect which toils on pure reason. Mannheim's 'free floating intellectual' striving for the unity of unities, coldly oblivious to history, is akin to this second element. Durkheim's *homo duplex* has often been hailed by later scholars as a precursor to humanist sociology. But a little closer scrutiny will reveal that the *duplex*

actually houses two discrete entities which live amicably for they live by observing avoidance. One entity is governed by positivistic sociologism and the other by intellectual idealism. There is no essential tension between them for they are unrelated to each other as only absolute opposites can. The practical sensuous man never visits this *duplex*, and one is, therefore, left with the option of either developing lasting solidarity with sociologism (as Durkheim did) or with idealism. Durkheim himself seemed to be unaware of this problem and his able exegetist Tiryakian (1962: 47) actually commends this 'double centre of gravity'.

2. Hegel when forced to take cognizance of the relationships that exist between men found it to be no more than '"arbitrary chaos" and its laws... to be "similar to those of the planetary system"' (Lukacs, 1971: 26).
3. By social history I mean the ground between structure and conjuncture. The inspiration is derived from F. Braudel, but as it is not a 'symptomatic' borrowing it should be understood only in the sense that it has been used here.
4. The reader is referred to Gramsci's treatment of 'corporate ideology' and 'trade unionist ideology' which in the purely short run can have a destabilizing effect on society (Gramsci, 1971).
5. Here at least I agree with Godelier when he says that ruling ideas are not only adhered to by the ruling class and that there is a wider consensus on them (Godelier, 1978: 91). But he does not mention that the consensus arises and continues to exist precisely because of the 'silences' in the superstructure regarding the basic contradictions in the infrastructure. This is what separates us theoretically on a wide range of issues.
6. In spite of the fact that there are certain areas of agreement between Laclau (1977) and myself, I would nevertheless differ from his understanding of ideology and popular interpolations on at least two points. Though I believe with him that ideological elements receive their semantic content in their articulation, I very specifically maintain that these elements are not equivocal, and not multifunctional. It is only within certain limits and towards certain ends that they can be effectively used. In Laclau, the emphasis on the other hand is on the equivocal (he calls it neutral) character of ideological elements amenable to all kinds of structurations and class articulations (ibid.: 147).

   The second disagreement is that I believe that the elements in the ideological storehouse that are brought out at a specific point depend entirely on actual class and or situational experiences. In Laclau, elements of popular interpellations have a universal appeal within a given period of time for all members of society no matter where they are situated. It is only the articulation that matters. In my opinion, it is the concrete experiences of men in diverse situations that make certain elements more appealing then others.

7. Althusser (1970: 102) says that a historical fact is 'a fact which causes a mutation in the existing structural relations'.
8. See in this connection Das and Uberoi (1971: 36). They write: 'The whole matrix, sacred and non-sacred, consists of a network of relational oppositions, out of which no one binary opposition can be selected for over emphasis without putting the entire investigation in peril'. Khare (1978: 273) also quite clearly says in his opposition to Dumont's method that purity and impurity are not static values. He goes on to say: 'As linguistic theories demonstrate, contexts are conceived by conjunctions... of relations; and category opposition... is one such conjunction'. But none of these authors bring out sufficiently the fact that the categories in opposition in Levi Strauss and in structuralism are not empirical or conscious categories that they are for Louis Dumont. This major difference cannot be slurred over, and it is this that really puts Dumont's structuralism in peril.
9. This essence of man is not in any way synonymous with the concept of 'human nature' which the sociological imagination specifically denounces (Mills, 1970: 182). The concept of human nature is not the same as the essence of man. Human nature is generally an idealization of a certain norm of observed behaviour wrapped in specific motivations relevant only for a given historical period, which is then extended for all of mankind in a totally ahistoric fashion. Polanyi's (1944: 44) condemnation of the economic man whose only driving force is to truck, barter and sell, is too well known to be repeated here. Malinowski (1922: 60) too demonstrates that the Trobriander 'works promoted by motives of a highly complex, social and traditional nature, and towards aims which are certainly not directed towards the satisfaction of present wants, or to the direct achievement of utilitarian forces purpose'. The anthropological imagination forces us to understand the context within which men act, rather than to judge men by an empirical mode with which one may be more familiar.

References

Althusser, Louis, 1969, *For Marx*, Harmondsworth, Penguin Books.

Althusser, Louis and Etienne Balibar, 1970, *Reading Capital*, London, New Left Books.

Aronson, Ronald, 1978, 'The Individualist Theory of Jean Paul Sartre', in *Western Marxism: A Critical Reader*, London, New Left Books, Verso Edition.

Barzun, Jacques, 1965, *Race: A Study in Superstitution*, New York, The Macmillan, Harper and Row.

Boas, Franz, 1911, *The Mind of Primitive Man*, New York, Macmillan Company.

Colletti, Lucio, 1978, *From Rousseau to Lenin: Studies in Ideology and Society*, Delhi, Oxford University Press.

D'Amico, Robert, 1973, 'The Contours and Coupures of Structuralist Theory', *Telos* No. 17, pp. 70–79.

Das, Veena and J.P.S. Uberoi, 1971, 'The Elementary Structures of Caste', in *Contributions to Indian Sociology* (N.S.), Delhi, No. 5, pp. 33–43.

Dumont, Louis, 1972, *Homo Hierarchicus*, London: Paladin/1970 Edn. Delhi, Vikas.

Durkheim, Emile, 1966, *Rules of Sociological Method*, New York, Free Press.

Durkheim, Emile and Marcel Mauss, 1970, *Primitive Classification*, London, Cohen and West.

Glucksmann, Miriam, 1974, *Structuralist Analysis in Contemporary Social Thought: A Comparison of the Theories of Claude Levi Strauss and Louis Althusser*, London and Boston, Routledge and Kegan Paul.

Godelier, Maurice, 1972, *Rationality and Irrationality in Economics*, New York, Monthly Review Press.

Godelier, Maurice, 1977, *Perspectives in Marxist Anthropology*, Cambridge, Cambridge University Press.

Godelier, Maurice, 1978, 'Infrastructures, Society and History', in *New Left Review* (London), No. 112, pp. 84–96.

Gramsci, Antonio, 1971, *Selections from the Prison Notebooks*, Ed. and Trans. by Quintin Hoare and Geoffrey Nowell Smith, New York, International Publications.

Hegel, G.W.F., 1944, *Philosophy of History*, Trans. by J. Sibreo, New York: Wiley Book Co. Jay, Martin, 1976: *The Dialectical Imagination*, London, Heinemann.

Khare, R.S., 1978, 'Structuralism in India: Some Issues and Observations', in *Contributions to Indian Sociology* (N.S.), Delhi, 12, pp. 253–78.

Kuhn, T.S., 1970, *The Structure of Scientific Revolutions*, Chicago, University of Chicago Press.

Kuper, Adam, 1973, *Anthropologists and Anthropology: The British School 1922–72*,. London, Penguin Books.

Laclau, Ernesto, 1977, *Politics and Ideology in Marxist Theory*, London, New Left Books.

Levi-Strauss, Claude, 1966, *The Savage Mind*, London and Chicago, University of Chicago Press and Weidenfold and Nicholson.

—, 1968, *Structural Anthropology*, Trans. C. Jakobson and B.G. Schoepf, London, Allen Lane, The Penguin Press.

Lukacs, Georg, 1971, *History and Class Consciousness*, Trans. by Rodney Livingstone, London, Merlin Press.

Malinowski, Bronislaw, 1922, *Argonauts of the Western Pacific: An Account of Native Enterprises and Adventure in the Archipelagoes of Melanesian New Guinea*, London, Routledge and Kegan Paul.

—, 1926, *Crime and Custom in Savage Society*, London, Routledge and Kegan Paul.

—, 1944, *A Scientific Theory of Culture and other Essays*, University of North Carolina Press.

—, 1948, *Magic Science and Religion and Other Essays*, Glencoe, Illinois, Free Press.

Marx, Karl, 1969, 'Theses on Feuerbach' in Karl Marx and Fredrick Engels, *Selected Works*, Vol. I, Moscow, Progress Publishers.

Mills, C. Wright, 1970, *The Sociological Imagination*, Harmondsworth, Penguin Books.

Needham, Rodney, 1970, 'Introduction', in Emile Durkheim and Marcel Mauss, *Primitive Classification*, London, Cohen and West.

Polanyi, Karl, 1944, *The Great Transformation*, New York, Rinehart.

Rex, John, 1961, *Key Problems of Sociological Theory* (mimeo), Centre for the Study of Social Systems, Jawaharlal Nehru University, New Delhi.

Sartre, Jean Paul, 1976, *Critique of Dialectical Reason*, London, New Left Books, Trans. by Allan Sheridan-Smith.

Stark, Werner, 1962, *The Fundamental Forms of Social Thought*, London, Routledge and Kegan Paul.

Thompson, E.P., 1978, *The Poverty of Theory and Other Essays*, London, Merlin Press.

Tiryakian, Edward A., 1962, *Sociologism and Existentialism*, New Jersey, Prentice-Hall Inc.

Veltmeyer, Henry, 1974–75, 'Towards an Assessment of the Structuralist Interpretation of Marx: Claude Levi Strauss and Louis Althusser', in *Science and Society* (New York), Vol. 38, pp. 385–421.

4

Reciprocity in Social Science
Gender Issues

Patricia Uberoi

This paper examines some problems and issues in the construction of social scientific knowledge about women's lives in India and China. It seeks to focus on the manner in which the narrative of past and present changes in the position of women in society has been constructed, social scientific knowledge on the theme produced, and empirical data generated. By the same token, it does not seek to review that data in and of itself. Though the primary reference here is to sociological writings on women in India, the material is presented in such a way as to invite a comparison between Indian and China, two major world civilizations whose recent experience has been rather different in terms of the relationship between the state and civil society, but which now face the challenges and dilemmas of liberalization and integration into a world economic system and a restructured multipolar political order.

With these processes under way, presumably irreversibly, we urgently need to assess their costs and benefits from a *gender sensitive* perspective, for there is considerable evidence that their outcomes are not always gender neutral (see, e.g., Smith et al., 1984; Mies et al., 1988; Agarwal, 1988; Desai and Krishnaraj, 1987: Ch. 2), but may involve, for instance, significant readjustments in the domestic, national and international sexual division of labour, enhanced state control over women's productivity and reproductivity, and exacerbated distributive inequalities affecting in particular women and their female children (Sen, 1990; Sen and Sen Gupta, 1983: 855–64; Das Gupta, 1987: 77–100).

Along with a continued monitoring of the development process, a critique that began with the stimulating work of Boserup in the early 1970s (Boserup, 1970; for an update, see Tinker, 1990), we also need to reflect on the modes of apprehension of sociological 'facts', again from an explicitly gender sensitive perspective. For it is widely acknowledged that 'knowledge' is a form of 'capital' to which some individuals and groups have better access than others (Bourdieu and Passeron, 1977); and, moreover, that it is a source of power through which control over others is exercised. As a result, social structure inequalities (as of race, nation, caste, class or gender) correlate with asymmetries in the production, reproduction and deployment of social scientific knowledge. Even cultural and regional *differences* in apperception tend to become hierarchized and translated into asymmetries, with particular modes of understanding coming to dominate over others and lay claim to universal validity (Uberoi, 1984; Merchant, 1980; Shiva, 1988).

The past two decades have witnessed a growing critique of the politics and ethics of the production of knowledge in the human and social sciences, particularly in the context of the relations of ex-colonial powers and erstwhile colonies, or of developed nations and developing societies (see Barnes, 1977; Uberoi, 1968: 119–23). The critique has come partly from scholars in the Third World, and partly from within the First World academies where representatives of the Third World diaspora have conspicuously joined in the symphony of breast-beating and self-reproach.

The discipline of anthropology has led the way in introspection, for its traditional definition as the study of 'other cultures' and 'other peoples' was premised on the objectification of these others for purposes of scientific investigation, and in fact historically assisted their control even as, in many cases, it bore witness to their dying moments (Levi-Strauss, 1966: 124–27). An important trend in contemporary anthropology, following from the critique of the discipline's classical discursive tropes, is the exploration of new modes of 'writing cultures' (Clifford and Marcus, 1986) that would be participatory and dialogic rather than invasive and appropriative.

This is no doubt a worthy aim, but exactly how such a reciprocity of perspective is to be operationalized, and what shape or form it will take, still remain unclear. In fact, a close look at attempts to 'indigenize' the production of social scientific knowledge of Third World societies such as India (as a recent example, see Marriott, 1990) shows the project to be a problematic, even a flawed one, in several respects – conceptual, methodological, practical and, perhaps also, *political*. Nonetheless, the problem of non-reciprocity in the production and authorization of social science knowledge is a real one, for the social and human sciences as a whole, and within them for the newly developed cross-disciplinary area of 'women's studies'.

FEMINISM AND SOCIAL SCIENCE

Academic women's studies was inspired by feminist theory, and is an institutional outcome of the western feminist movement of the 1960s and the 1970s. It assumes gender as a primary contradiction by virtue of the universality of women's oppression or 'secondary status' in all, or almost all, known societies. Women are thereby constituted as a quasi-'class' *in*, and increasingly *for*, themselves, regardless of differences of race, nation, caste, class, culture or region. Assuming the universality and transitivity of women's experience of self and the world, women are automatically assumed to have better insight into other women's lives – again, irrespective of factors of race, nation, caste or class. That is why it often seems self-evident that women should write books about other women, and that academic women's studies should be taught, and offered, mostly by women. In fact, men are sometimes explicitly excluded from feminist forums, and in extreme cases the excursion may apply even to (heterosexual) women who continue to collaborate actively with men in their personal lives and political practice!

The homogenization of 'women' as an analytical category has come under scrutiny of late, not only from self-proclaimed misogynists ever ready to diminish feminism, but also from within the women's movement itself. For instance, in North America, women of colour have increasingly sought to construct their own understanding of the feminine condition. Assuming 'race' as the initial and primary factor in creating their self-identity, they see themselves as historically exploited both by white men *and* by white women, undercutting gender solidarity, as well as by black men with whom, on the other hand, they share the experience of race. And they no longer seek, or want, their white 'sisters' to speak *for* them, to decide on priorities, or to define normalcy and pathology. They claim, and surely quite rightly, that their experience of 'patriarchy' has been mediated in important ways by their location in the racial system of stratification. Historically, the problem for them has been the use and abuse of their sexuality by white (as well as black) men, reinforcing the asymmetry of the sexes, whereas for white women in the same society it was rather the containment and repression of sexuality in the interests of the preservation of the system of racial hierarchy (Beteille, 1990: 489–504). In their protests against male domination, therefore, white and black women do not necessarily share the same concerns and priorities, all the more so because white women as much as their menfolk have been beneficiaries of the system of racial inequality.

As sociologists have often pointed out, caste has affinities with race as a principle of social stratification (Beteille, 1990) and similarly cross-cuts gender solidarity. In the traditional Indian caste system, lower caste women were often, and still are, sexually exploited by men of higher castes, who at the same time vigilantly monitor the sexuality of their own women (Yalman, 1963: 25–58). After all, the preservation of the entire social system rested on assuring the 'purity' of women, or, one might affirm again, the purity of women of *higher* status groups. (The informal sexual availability of women of low status did not threaten the system, and might even have aided its preservation in the same way that prostitution is said to have assisted the perpetuation of Victorian monogamy).

It is important to note that the various social measures that were enacted during the colonial period for the 'uplift' of Indian women were largely directed towards removing the disabilities that constrained the lives of *upper caste* (Hindu) women (the abolition of *sati*, widow remarriage, raising the age of consent, etc., see Chaudhuri, 1993), for *sati* and ascetic widowhood were practised largely by higher status and upwardly mobile groups. In many castes, and in some culture regions, widow remarriage was an accepted social practice (Kolenda, 1983: 172–220; O'Hanlon, 1991: 62–108; Chowdhry, 1989; 1990: 259–74). Similarly, encouragement of female education is viewed as a measure that has brought women out of seclusion and ultimately into the workforce, but in truth small segments of the female population (courtesans and *devadasis*, for instance) were traditionally educated to become independent professionals (Srinivasan, 1988; Oldenburg, 1991: 23–61). A large proportion of the female population traditionally worked for wages outside the home, and paradoxically this proportion has been declining, not increasing, since the turn of the century and the social and economic changes consequent on colonial rule (Government of India, 1974: Ch. V).

The question of class formation and of the relations of caste and class is of some theoretical interest in the sociological literature on social stratification in India (Beteille, 1965; Gupta, 1991: Sections III and IV). It is a matter of practical interest, too, in the light of post-independence policies of affirmative action on behalf of formerly disprivileged groups. In many cases, upwardly mobile groups have attempted to legitimate their claim to higher status by adopting Brahmanical customs. This process, which the well-known sociologist M.N. Srinivas (1989) has termed 'sanskritization', characteristically involved a ban on widow remarriage, giving dowry in place of bride wealth, and a prohibition on exchange marriage, all features which had important implications for women's lives (Srinivas, 1977: 221–38; 1984). In other cases, perhaps in those areas where caste and class status had coincided to a large extent, movements by lower class groups involved the explicit and hostile rejection of Brahmanical customs (though that does not necessarily imply that they were less coercive in respect of women). Other studies have suggested that the process of class formation, linked to the monetization of the economy and the consolidation of a capitalist system, has had several deleterious, disempowering effects on women's lives (Sharma, 1980; 1986; Mies et al., 1988; Shiva, 1988).

Though caste and class based differences in Indian women's experiences are increasingly conceded (World Bank, 1991) and sometimes movingly documented (Gulati, 1982; Karlekar, 1982), the bulk of the literature still presents a relatively homogenized account of *the* Indian woman, upper caste, bourgeois and presumed Hindu, located in a unilinear history of decline from her exalted status in the Vedic period to a position of miserable subjection (Chakravarti, 1989) at the moment when the social reform movements began to 'tropize' the Indian woman as both the symbol of national degeneration and the hope for national regeneration (Uberoi, 1990: 41–48). And where differentiation is allowed to cross-cut sexual hierarchy, it is significantly often along communal lines – Hindu, Muslim, Sikh, Christian, tribal – rather than in terms of caste or class.

Though the majority of accounts of lower caste or lower class Indian women are mediated by upper caste/class or foreing interpreters – and one has no wish to diminish the efforts of such interpreters, without whom these voices might have been lost to memory – *dalit* women are increasingly aspiring to speak for themselves. There is still much to be done in investigating the roles of women in caste based social reform movements – the anti-Brahman and non-Brahman 'self-respect' movements in Tamil Nadu, Kerala and Maharashtra, for instance. Not all of them ran parallel to or fed into the nationalist movement, which has been the dominant interest so far; and not all of them were sanskritizing in their programmes.

As we have already noted, the academic agenda of women's studies in India is parasitic on developments in the First World. Increasingly, however, the Third World women have been challenging the preoccupations of the First World feminism as irrelevant to their own needs and priorities. A special cause of contention is the preoccupation of western feminists with questions of sexual choice and sexual separatism. While critiquing 'patriarchy' as an 'institution', Indian feminists and activists, especially of the Left, have been relatively gentle with men, and personally and politically welcomed their collaboration over women's issues. One is reminded here that, some years ago, psychologist Ashis Nandy had insisted that there could be no scope in India for a women's liberation movement on the lines of that in the West, since it was the mother-son bond, not the conjugal one, which was salient in India. It made precious little sense, Nandy argued, for Indian women to seek liberation from their sons (Nandy, 1980: 32–46). Nandy has a point, for a dispassionate reading of biographical and autobiographical accounts of Indian women's lives over the last century and a half reveals the passion with which they were attempting to establish the legitimacy and primacy of the conjugal bond, over and against the line of patriarchal authority (Karlekar, 1991; see also Das, 1976: 1–30). But it is precisely the conjugal bond, even heterosexuality (Rich, 1980: 631–60), that has been questioned by western feminism in theory and practice. Indian feminists have found its emphasis disquieting and embarrassing, and hesitate to explicitly address themselves to questions of sexuality.

Not so long ago, the failure of Indian feminists to question the conjugal bond and 'compulsory heterosexuality' was made to seem like a defect, which was understandable, if not excusable, in the light of the distinctive history of the Indian women's movement and its special dependent relationship with the nationalist movement (Chitnis, 1988: 81–95; Liddle and Joshi, 1986). The historical argument was similarly used to explain another paradox in the discourse of the contemporary Indian women's movement, namely, a conspicuously ambivalent attitude to the state. On the one hand, the state is constantly petitioned to act on behalf of women – to enact legislation for their protection, to ensure the actuation of measures already on the statue books, to guarantee the gender neutrality of the police and judiciary, etc. 'The government should do such-and-such' is an insistent refrain.

On the other hand, an influential body of writing, particularly from the Left, takes the view that no good can be expected from the state. State formation, it is argued, goes along with the generation of surplus and class formation, and is intimately linked to the institutionalization of male control over women through the immediate agency of the family. Moreover, the modern state is seen to be especially 'patriarchal' to the extent that it now has at its disposal unprecedented resources for the surveillance of populations and intervention in people's lives. Thus, for instance, the burden of population control – whether pronatalist or antinatalist – falls inequitably on women and, in an international context, on women of the Third World. The modern state is essentially duplicitous on gender issues, giving lip-service to the cause of women while actually acting in the interests of men, and this is the reason why even manifestly 'progressive' legislation, often enacted as a result of prolonged struggle by women's groups, remains as the saying goes 'on the statute book', never being seriously enforced (Sarkar, 1984: 3–7).

Reluctance to confront questions of sexuality and ambivalence regarding the role of the state on gender issues, with currently fashionable radical feminist categories overlaid on the earlier rhetoric of the Indian women's movement, are issues which have made it difficult for researchers on the Indian women's movement to classify their subjects according to received categories such as 'radical feminist', 'socialist feminist', 'liberal feminist', and 'Marxist feminist'. They find very few candidates to be placed unequivocally into the 'radical' box, and in many cases a rather disconcerting divorce between theory (stated ideological positions) and practice (the actual programmes of individuals and organizations). To their dismay they note that most activists have only a very shallow acquaintance with the theoretical 'issues at stake' to quote the title of a recent book on the Indian women's movement (see Shah and Gandhi, 1991), and that the best that can be said in their defence is that they are 'inconsistent' rather than plain muddled! Oddly, it does not seem to have occurred to these researchers that the classificatory categories themselves may not be adequate, and that their lack of fit to the Indian context might be not so much a reflection on the authenticity of the women's movement in India as an indication that the categories themselves had better be rethought in relation to the western women's movement as much as in relation to the Indian women's movement.

The inappropriateness of feminism in the Indian context was the theme of a recent and much publicized (not to say, notorious) essay by Madhu Kishwar, founder-editor of India's leading journal about women and society, namely, *Manushi*. In this leading article, brutally entitled 'Why I Do Not Call Myself A Feminist' (1990: 2–8), she argued that feminist theory highlights issues which are not actually of real concern in India, and neglects – or misidentifies – those that are. To this she added a practical consideration, namely, that to assume the label 'feminist' was definitely a tactical mistake for the

Indian women's movement at the present moment. It would give the wrong signals, conjuring up images of militant bra-burning western feminists, and would alienate potential political support.

In a superficial reading, Kishwar's argument pertains mainly to political practice, to the tactics and strategies necessary to sustain a women's movement in India and other countries of the Third World when it is common knowledge that the women's movement in the West in now fragmented, and reeling under the effects of a conservative backlash. But questions of the international politics of knowledge are also implicated and it is this problem that is discussed further in this paper.

I was first made acutely self-conscious of the divorce between metropolitan theory and indigenously generated data a few years ago, when I set out to design a post-graduate course on 'women and society in India'. As conventional with many courses, for reasons long since buried in institutional history, the course was divided into two sections, an introductory section on theory and method, and a substantive section reviewing empirical literature on women in India. It was discouraging, if not a surprise, to find that the theory section contained no readings at all by Indian authors, though the substantive section was relatively even handed (see Uberoi, 1989–90: 279–89). It was as though, in the academy as in the agenda of action for the women's movement, Indian scholars could at best provide illustrations for the women's movement, Indian scholars could at best provide illustrations for theoretical positions generated elsewhere, but not themselves contribute reciprocally to the production, and now regeneration, of feminist theory.

It is in this context that this paper seeks to review some specific moves to 'indigenize' feminist theory in the Indian context – moves which to some extent run parallel to similar trends in Indian social anthropology (Uberoi, 1992). It then proceeds to consider some of the themes in writings on Indian women which may contribute dialogically to the remaking of feminist theory. It must be clarified in advance, however, that there is no assumption that any of these trends are unproblematic, as the subsequent discussion will bear out. In fact, there are some disquieting implications to the themes that are suggested as complementary, even remedial, in the context of contemporary feminist theory. Most importantly, this may be a 'no-win' situation, for the very act of incorporation into contemporary feminist theory is likely to transmute into co-optation, given the centre-periphery asymmetries in the production of social scientific knowledge which constitutes our problem in the first place.

INDIGENIZING FEMINIST THEORY

It is, of course, one of the projects of women's studies to amplify and privilege the hitherto muted voices of women in the historical record and literary canon. In India, the last few years have seen a growing number of researches based on oral history – for instance, the recorded memories of women activists in the Telengana movement (Stree Shakti Sanghatana, 1986) – and the collection, translation and publication of vernacular texts authored by women. A monument to this project is Tharu and Lalita's edited volume of translations of women's writings (1991), the first huge volume, incredibly covering the period 600 BC to AD 1947. No doubt, the women's voices that are thereby heard are mediated by the editors' politics, even by their sense of decency, but the volume at least makes available (to the *English-speaking* audience) a wealth of records of women's lives, thoughts and feelings through history. It makes interesting reading.

It is clear from this volume – and this is an issue that is now explicitly being raised – that Indian women have often found space for self-expression, and experienced a measure of emancipation from normal social constraints, through religion – especially through *bhakti*, with its potential for a personalized, unmediated relationship with the godhead. A number of recent writings have explored the *bhakti* tradition from a gender sensitive perspective* have sought insights into the lives of women saints and contemporary women religious leaders (e.g., Ojha, 1990), and have focused on the gender implications of new religious orders like the Brahma Kumaris (Babb, 1984: 399–416). But the issue of religion is obviously a problematic one in the eyes of many Indian feminists, suspicious of its constraining power, and alive to the ongoing communalization of Indian society (see Sarkar, 1991).

A second issue of contemporary debate – or perhaps one should rather say, disquiet – is the proposition that the portrayal of Indian women as victims of inhumane practices – tropizing the Indian woman as a symbol of a degenerate race and society – is a colonial construct whose latent function was, in the past, to justify the imperial mission, and in the present to endorse the leading role of western feminism in scripting the agenda of the Third World women's movement. (The custom of foot-binding in China played a similar role in 'constructing' the Chinese woman for a prurient

---

* See *Manushi*, Nos. 50–52, 1989 (special issue on Women Bhakta Poets).

western audience, see Uberoi, 1991: 387–405). Rereadings of the literature of the social reform movements of the nineteenth and early twentieth centuries, and of more recent debates as well, have shown that not only *sati* (the obvious case), but also female infanticide, infant marriage, polygamy, *purdah*, temple dedication, ascetic widowhood – even polyandry and matriliny – were read as signifiers of a backward and inhumane society, and thereby justifications of the white man's burden and of state interventions.

While this line of reasoning has produced some important and powerful work, the argument also comes dangerously close to endorsing, even romanticizing, these very customs. It is possible to argue, and a recent paper had done just that, that *sati* is indigenously conceived as a noble form of spiritual exercise (Sharma et al., 1988), and that its interpretation as an inhumane practice is an exogenous and almost deliberate misreading. It may not seem easy to legitimate female infanticide – though some recent pragmatic arguments on behalf of sex selective amniocentesis seem quite close to that (Kumar, 1983: 61–74) but glamorization of the life and art of a courtesan or temple dancer is another matter (see Rao, 1990: 31–39; Oldenburg, 1991: 23–61; Srinivasan, 1988; Petievich, 1990: 25–31). She *lends* herself to sentimentalization, and the popular media routinely do just that. Ambivalence, prurience, and sometimes indignant prudishness are frequent responses to these writings in public presentations, for their implied endorsement of autonomous female sexuality contradicts the received image of the Indian woman: Sita, the chaste wife.

The deconstruction of the colonial discourse on women has other hazards, too. It is easy enough to point out the rhetorical devices that frame and legitimate a text as an artefact of colonial knowledge, but does that necessarily invalidate the message of the text? The reference is to an exercise done some time ago in analyzing the 'Introduction' that frames and authorizes Pandita Ramabai's famous essay, 'The High Caste Hindu Woman' (Sarasvati, 1988), and gives to it the seal of colonial approval as the authentic account of the Other's Other. As a literary exercise, informed also by the 'new ethnology', that analysis seems sound but such a stand would put one in alignment with those who decried and hounded Ramabai after she converted to Christianity, accusing her of presenting a motivatedly hostile interpretation of the Hindu religion and of its treatment of women. That the text continues to resonate today, more than a century on, is evidence, surely, of its containing more than a grain of truth, at least as far as the experience of women of the higher castes goes.

There is another ethical/political problem with the current enthusiasm to deconstruct colonial discourse that should at least be mentioned here, if not developed. In a way, concentrating all fire on colonial discourse is recognizable as the old strategy of passing the blame. It is the common currency of much contemporary analysis of communalism, for instance, blame 'colonialism', and forget to ask, 45 years after independence, why in that case communal riots *still* occur!

Compared to the burgeoning literature on the colonial period's construction of women, there has been very little work on the pre-British state in relation to women, nor for that matter on the experience of princely India. (One has almost forgotten, now, how much of the map of India was not shaded in the pink tones of the British empire). In addition one might hazard the opinion that the discourse of the contemporary Indian state has probably not yet been analyzed with the same rigour that has been applied to colonial discourse, though that is increasingly being attempted.

Finally, one must confront the accusation that contemporary Indian feminism, parasitic on its foreign models, discounts or ignores indigenous understandings of femininity. The problem is, what are (or were) these? Male constructions of femininity, or women's own consciousness, as presented, for instance, in the Tharu and Lalita volume (1991)? Or is the woman's voice, as Veena Das (1989) has recently argued, independent of biological sex, a truth-telling voice that speaks out in moments of 'loss' and 'mourning'? More importantly, adverting to the points made earlier, can there be – should there in fact be – an understanding of Indian femininity unmediated by factors of caste, class, community and culture region? Efforts to arrive at a commonality, as in the writings of psychologists Sudhir Kakar (1978) and Ashis Nandy (1980: 32–46) are fraught with difficulties: the former authorizing his position by appeal to a pot pourri of folk idioms, eclectically selected for apt illustration; the latter tending to generalize from the *bhadralok* (or *bhadramahila*) to 'India'. Such constructions tend to be unacceptably homogenizing and normative.

These are all areas of vigorous debate between activists of the women's movement, and researchers and teachers in the academy. In many ways they evoke the arguments of women of colour within and against the dominant positions of the western feminist movement. They share the common concern that exogenous models may have distorted an understanding of Indian womanhood, which should properly be understood in her own terms, in her own language, on her own ground and through her own categories of understanding.

TOWARDS RECIPROCITY

Writing recently an account of the history of kinship studies in India, I had initially followed the usual strategy of outlining the theoretical moves and controversies in metropolitan anthropology, and then looking for their reflection in studies of family, kinship and marriage in India. I then decided to turn the question around, and try to reflect, dialectically or dialogically, on the history of India in kinship studies. One may be reminded here of Lewis Henry Morgan, whose attention to the similarities of structure of the Dravidian and North American kinship terminologies created kinship studies as a scientific enterprise at the heart of professional anthropology; of Sir Henry Maine, who discovered in the Indian joint family the distinctive features of unilineal descent groups as 'corporations'; or of W.H.R. Rivers, whose work among the Todas of South India demonstrated the functional interrelations of social institutions and the potentiality of the 'genealogical method' of inquiry; or more recently of Claude Levi-Strauss, in whose challenging new theory of kinship the Indian evidence was a crucial input; or of Louis Dumont, whose attempt to articulate the unity of India as a culture area brought important modifications into the alliance theory of kinship (Uberoi, in press).

This is not the place to undertake a critique of the present state of womens' studies, or to discover the reasons for the widespread feeling that the feminist enterprise has become stale and routinized and has lost momentum. Nonetheless, I would like to suggest here that the field of Indian women's studies at present offers some interesting insights towards the remaking of feminist theory. Before I enumerate them, I should reiterate that these areas are not altogether unproblematic, as I shall indicate in the comments that follow.

Eco-feminism

The contemporary development of a sub-study of eco-feminism within the feminist theory was not pioneered in reference to India, nor by Indian scholars. However, India has contributed significantly to its growth (Shiva, 1988; Agarwal, 1986), at the levels of theory and of social action such as the Chipko movement. The crisis of subsistence, especially problems of access to fuel and water, are problems that directly affect the lives and work of women and children, even more than their menfolk, who might well have access to the new cash incomes that state promoted development activities generate.

Conceptually speaking, however, eco-feminism often tends to a sentimentalized essentialism: as mothers, women are deemed closer to nature and therefore, the argument goes, must instinctively seek to protect nature (Shiva, 1988; Merchant, 1980). In this sentimentalization of women's nature, the political economy of subsistence production is soon forgotten (Agarwal, 1992: 119–58); so too is the fact that in many cases these movements are not only a *gender* issue, but also, often primarily, a *class* issue. In fact, identifying the issue as a gender issue may deflect attention from the larger conflict of interests underlying alternative development strategies.

A Concept of Female Power

A second area of interest is the indigenous conceptualization of female power (*shakti*) associated with the so-called Mother Goddess. This points to an important asymmetry in sex role stereotypes between western and Indian societies (see Das and Ghadially, 1988; Rao and Rao, 1988). Psychologists locate this imagery in the experience of Indian childhood – specifically in the mother-son bond, where it borders, in their descriptions, on the pathological (Kakar, 1978; Nandy, 1980: 32–46). But feminists in India and abroad have grasped eagerly at this straw, if not as a mimetic reflection of the reality of women's lives, then at least as a symbolic role model for future empowerment. Here again, there is a danger of romanticization, for what after all, as Americans like to say, is the 'cash value' of this symbolic acknowledgement of female power.

Androgyny

Psychologist C.J. Jung had turned to Oriental societies – not only India, but also China – to explain and illustrate the notion of androgyny, which he believed intrinsic to the human psyche. Against the bitter polarization of the sexes, which the mainstream of western feminism invoked, there opened up a new possibility, an invitation to retrace the historical process of sexual polarization back through the colonial period (Nandy, 1983), and to recapture an almost forgotten possibility. That Gandhi saw his strategy of non-violence as linked to the cultivation of the feminine within is no longer certified as eccentricity (or perversion), but as a psychic gesture evoking the religious principle of Ardhanareshwar (the deity as half male-half female). Conversely, as sociologist Veena Das has recently pointed out, contemporary militant discourse in this region (Punjab, to be precise) focuses on the masculinist reaffirmation of aggression, and the repudiation of the feminine within (Das, 1992: 245–59). This example provides food for reflection.

Pluralism

Finally, one might note the recognition in this region of a plurality of definitions of femininity, taking inspiration from the multiple role models of the Hindu pantheon. It might be recalled that in her provocative book, *The Creation of Patriarchy*, Gerda Lerner (1986) had located the advent of patriarchy in the domain of religion, in a double transition from polytheism to monotheism, and from female Goddesses to an authoritarian male godhead. Unfortunately, there is much that is problematic and speculative in attempts to link the worship of the Mother Goddess in ancient times – whether in China or Mesopotamia or India – with the institution of matriarchy, or even with a high 'status' for women in society, but this should not disqualify *all* reflection on the symbolic meaning and function of the Hindu pantheon. Though it resists a superficial reading, this is an area of genuine theoretical challenge, all the more so because the religions of this region are being continuously rescripted in relation to each other, and increasingly internally homogenized.

In pointing out these four areas, one may be treading on dangerous ground, for in one way or another, more or less explicitly, they all authorize religion as a point of reference for making of the feminist theory. Moreover, they identify the indigenous potentialities of this region with a single religious tradition, namely, Hinduism, which, when posited as the true Indian tradition, has demonstrated often enough in recent times its unattractive face. There is no defence except to plead that we should sometimes try to think, and then to think through, the unthinkable.

But even if one accepts these suggestions (and there has already been some *de facto* acceptance of them), this enterprise involves another danger, namely, of serving in new bottles that old stale wine of 'Eastern Spiritualism *versus* Western Materialism', as the East is once again co-opted to the remaking of western thought.

'Orientalism', in the special meaning that Edward Said (1978) had given it, implies knowledge of the Other to reaffirm the difference, and ultimately the superiority of the Self. But there have been moments in the recent history of European thought when the Other, be (s)he the primitive or the Oriental, has become the inspiration for remaking and rethinking aspects of European culture. One such moment, admittedly a rather minor one, occurred when China of the 1970s was seen to suggest the complete remedy for the pathology of the relations of the sexes in contemporary western society (Kristeva, 1986; Uberoi, 1991: 387–405). There will surely be many more.

But the original question ultimately remains. Given the structural asymmetries of our present world order, can there ever be complementarity, or better still exchange and reciprocity, in the construction of social scientific knowledge, or is co-optation and appropriation inevitable if indigenous experience is to be certified as true knowledge, and not merely surrender to the heat and dust and confusion that is India!

References

Agarwal, Bina, 1986, *Cold Hearths and Barren Slopes: The Woodfuel Crisis in the Third World*, London, Zed Books.

—, 1988, *Structures of Patriarchy: State, Community and Household in Modernizing Asia*, New Delhi, Kali for Women.

—, 1992, 'The Gender and Environment Debate: Lessons from India' *Feminist Studies*, Vol. 18, No. 1.

Babb, L.A., 1984, 'Indigenous Feminism in a Modern Hindu Sect', *Signs*, No. 9.

Barnes, J.A., 1977, *The Ethics of Inquiry in the Social Sciences*, Delhi, Oxford University Press.

Beteille, Andre, 1965, *Caste, Class and Power: Changing Patterns of Stratification in a Tanjore Village*, Berkeley, University of California Press.

—, 1990, 'Race, Caste and Gender', *Man* (N.S.), Vol. 25.

Boserup, E., 1970, *Women's Role in Economic Development*, London, Allen and Unwin.

Bourdieu, Pierre and Passeron, J.C., 1977, *Reproduction in Education, Society and Culture*, Beverly Hills, Sage.

Chakravarti, Uma, 1989, 'Whatever Happened to the Vedic *Dasi*'? Orientalism, Nationalism, and a Script for the Past' in Kumkum Sangari and Sudesh Vaid (eds.), *Recasting Women: Essays in Colonial History*, New Delhi, Kali for Women.

Chaudhuri, Maitrayee, 1993, *Indian Women's Movements: Reform and Revival*, New Delhi, Radiant.

Chitnis, Suma, 1988, 'Feminism: Indian Ethos and Indian Convictions' in Rehana Ghadially (ed.), *Women in Indian Society*, New Delhi, Sage.

Chowdhry, Prem, 1989, 'Customs in a Peasant Economy: Women in Colonial Haryana's in Kumkum Sangari and Sudesh Vaid (eds.), *Recasting Women: Essays in Colonial History*, New Delhi, Kali for Women.

—, 1990, 'An Alternative to the *Sati* Model: Perceptions of a Social Realty in Folklore', *Asian Folklore Studies*, Vol. XLIX, No. 2.

Clifford, James and Marcus, George K., 1986, *Writing Culture: The Poetics and Politics of Ethnography*, Berkeley, University of California Press.

Das, Sukanya and Ghadially, Rehana, 1988, 'Parental Sex Role Orientation and Sex Stereotypes of Children' in R. Ghadially (ed.), *Women in Indian Society: A Reader*, New Delhi, Sage.

Das, Veena, 1976, 'Masks and Faces: An Essay on Punjabi Kinship', *Contributions to Indian Sociology* (N.S.), Vol. 10, No. 1.

—, 1989, 'Narrativising the Male and the Female in Tulasidas' *Ramayana*', paper presented at the Workshop on the Female Body and Gender Identity, Centre for the Study of Social Systems, JNU, 18–19 January.

—, 1992, 'Time, Self and Community: Features of the Sikh Militant Discourse', *Contributions to Indian Sociology* (N.S.), Vol. 26, No. 2.

Das Gupta, Monica, 1987, 'Selective Discrimination against Female Children in Rural Punjab, India', *Population and Development Review*, Vol. 13, No. 1.

Desai, Neera and Krishnaraj Mathreyl, 1987, *Women and Society in India*, Delhi, Ajanta.

Government of India, 1974, *Towards Equality: Report of the Committee on the Status of Women*, New Delhi, Ministry of Education and Social Welfare.

Gulati, Leela, 1982, *Profiles in Female Poverty*, New Delhi, Hindustan.

Gupta, Dipankar (ed.), 1991, *Social Stratification*, Delhi, Oxford University Press.

Kakar, Sudhir, 1978, *The Inner World*, Delhi, Oxford University Press.

Karlekar, Malavika, 1982, *Poverty and Women's Work*, New Delhi, Vikas.

—, 1991, *Voices from Within: Personal Narratives of Women in Early Nineteenth Century Bengal*. Delhi, Oxford University Press.

Kishwar, Madhu, 1990, 'Why I do not Call Myself a Feminist', *Manushi*, No. 6.

Kolenda, Pauline, 1983, 'Widowhood among the "Untouchable" Chuhras' in Akos Ostor, Lina Fruzzetti and Steve Barnett (eds.), *Concepts of Persons: Kinship, Caste and Marriage in India*, Delhi, Oxford University Press.

Kristeva, Julia, 1986, *About Chinese Women*, New York, Marion Boyars.

Kumar, Dharma, 1983, 'Male Utopias or Nightmares?', *Economic and Political Weekly*, Vol. XVIII, No. 3.

Lerner, Gerda, 1986, *The Creation of Patriarchy*, New York, Oxford University Press.

Levi-Strauss, Claude, 1966, 'Anthropology: Its Achievements and Future', *Current Anthropology*, Vol. 7, No. 2.

Liddle, J. and Joshi, Rama, 1986, *Daughters of Independence: Gender, Caste and Class in India*, New Delhi, Kali for Women.

Marriott, McKim (ed.), 1990, *Indian through Hindu Categories*, New Delhi, Sage.

Merchant, Carolyn, 1980, *The Death of Nature: Women, Ecology and the Scientific Revolution*, San Fancisco, Harper and Row.

Mies, Maria, Bennholdt-Thomsen, Veronika and Von Werlhof, Claudia, 1988, *Women: The Last Colony*, London, Zed Books.

Nandy, Ashis, 1980, 'Woman *versus* Womanliness in India: An Essay in Cultural and Political Psychology' in Ashis Nandy, *At the Edge of Psychology*, Delhi, Oxford University Press.

—, 1983, *The Intimate Enemy: Loss and Recovery of Self under Colonialism*, Delhi, Oxford University Press.

O'Hanlon, Rosalind, 1991, 'Issues of Widowhood: Gender and Resistance in Colonial Western India' in Douglas Haynes and Gyan Prakash (eds.), *Contesting Power: Resistance and Everyday Social Relations in South Asia*, Delhi, Oxford University Press.

Ojha, Catherine Clementin, 1990, *La divinite conquise: Carriere d'une sainte*, Nanterre, Societie d'Ethnologie.

Oldenburg, Veena Talwar, 1991, 'Lifestyle as Resistance: The Case of the Courtesans of Lucknow' in Douglas Haynes and Gyan Prakash (eds.), *Contesting Power: Resistance and Everyday Social Relations in South Asia*, Delhi, Oxford University Press.

Petievich, Carla, 1990, 'The Feminine Voice in the Urdu Ghazal', *Indian Horizons*, Vol. 39, Nos. 1–2.

Rao, Prakasa and Rao, V. Nandini, 1988, 'Sex Role Attitudes of College Students in India' in Rehana Ghadially (ed.), *Women in Indian Society*, New Delhi, Sage.

Rao Vidya, 1990, '*Thumri* as Feminine Voice', *Economic and Political Weekly*, Vol. XXV, No. 17.

Rich, Adrienne, 1980, 'Compulsory Heterosexuality and Lesbian Experience', *Signs*, Vol. 5.

Said, Edward, 1978, *Orientalism*, London, Routledge and Kegan Paul.

Sarasvati, Pundita Ramabai, 1888, *The High Caste Hindu Woman*, Philadelphia (reprint, New Delhi, Inter-India).

Sarkar, Lotika, 1984, 'Women's Rights', *Religion and Society*, Vol. 31, No. 1.

Sarkar, Tanika, 1991, 'The Woman as Communal Subject: Rashtra Sevika Samiti and Ram Janmabhoomi Movement', *Economic and Political Weekly*, Vol. 26, No. 35.

Sen, Amrtya, 1990, 'Gender and Co-operative Conflicts' in Irene Tinker (ed.), *Persistent Inequalities*, New York, Oxford University Press.

Sen, Amartya and Sen Gupta, S. 1983, 'Malnutrition of Rural Children and the Sex Bias', *Economic and Political Weekly*, Vol. 18 (Annual Number).

Shah, Nandita and Gandhi, Nandita, 1991, *The Issues at State: Theory and Practice in the Contemporary Women's Movement in India*, New Delhi, Kali for Women.

Sharma, Arvind et al., 1988, *Sati: Historical and Phenomenological Essays*, Delhi, Motilal Banarsidass.

Sharma, Ursula, 1980, *Women, Work and Property in Northwest India*, London, Tavistock.

—, 1986, *Women's Work, Class and the Urban Household: A Study of Shimla, North India*, London, Tavistock.

Shiva, Vandana, 1988, *Staying Alive: Women, Ecology and Survival*, London, Zed Books.

Smith, Joan, Wallerstein, Immanuel and Hans-Dieter, Evers (eds.), 1984, *Households and the World Economy*, Beverly Hills, Sage.

Srinivas, M.N., 1977, 'The Changing Position of Indian Women', *Man* (N.S.), Vol. 12, No. 2.

—, 1984, *Some Reflections on Dowry*, Delhi, Oxford University Press.

—, 1989, *The Cohesive Role of Sanskritization and Other Essays*, Delhi, Oxford University Press.

Srinivasan, Amrit, 1988, 'Reform or Conformity: Temple Prostitution and the Community in the Madras Presidency' in Bina Agarwal (ed.), *Structures of Patriarchy*, New Delhi, Kali for Women.

Stree Shakti Sanghatana, 1986, *We Were Making History... Life History of Women in the Telengana People's Struggle*, New Delhi, Kali for Women.

Tharu, Suzie, and Lalita, K. (eds.), 1991, *Women Writing in India*, Delhi, Oxford University Press.

Tinker, Irene (ed.), 1990, *Persistent Inequalities: Women and World Development*, New York, Oxford University Press.

Uberoi, J.P.S., 1968, 'Science and Swaraj', *Contributions to Indian Sociology* (N.S.), Vol. 2.

—, 1984, *The Other Mind of Europe: Goethe as a Scientist*, Delhi, Oxford University Press.

Uberoi, Patricia, 1989–90, 'Some Reflections on Teaching the Sociology of Gender', *Samya Shakti*, Vols. 4 and 5.

—, 1990, 'Feminine Identity and National Ethos in Indian Calendar Art', *Economic and Political Weekly*, Vol. XXV, No. 17.

—, 1991, '[The] Chinese Woman in the Construction of Western Feminism', *Alternatives*, No. 16.

—, 1992, 'Indigenizing Feminist Theory in Indian Anthropology', paper presented at the XIX Annual Conference of the Canadian Anthropological Society, Montreal, 9–12 May.

—, In Press, 'Introduction' in Patricia Uberoi (ed.), *Family, Kinship and Marriage in India*, Delhi, Oxford University Press.

World Bank, 1991, *Gender and Poverty in India*, Washington D.C.: World Bank.

Yalman, Nur, 1963, 'On the Purity and Sexuality of Women in the Castes of Ceylon and Malabar', *Journal of the Royal Anthropological Institute*, Vol. 93, No. 1.

5

Craft of Sociology in India

An Autobiographical Perspective

I.P. Desai

The present state of sociological research in India cannot be understood without inquiring into its historical background. This is equally true of the work of an individual which too has to be viewed in the context of the development of the discipline and the involvement of the individual researcher in that development.

This essay, which is both historical and autobiographical, attempts, by considering the author's own education, training and research as a 'case study', to present a retrospective and perspective of sociological research in India. It is in five parts. Part I describes the sociological equipment which a student of the second generation of Indian sociology, like the author, acquired. Part II delineates the author's training in the tradition of the founders and the beginnings of his professional career. Part III describes his first efforts in independent research. Part IV deals with the new trends in British and American sociology which influenced the author between 1952 and 1956. Part V makes some general and specific observations having a bearing on the past as well as the future of sociological research in India.

I
THE FOUNDERS: ORIENTATION AND EQUIPMENT

The Bombay University where I studied in the mid-1930s was then the only university in India which provided for a Master's degree in sociology entirely by research. Alternatively, a student could offer four papers in sociology along with four papers in some other subjects such as economics and political science. In 1934, when I joined the post-graduate programme, I offered four papers in sociology and four in economics. Three of the four sociology papers dealt with (1) Principles of

Sociology, (2) Caste Rank, Marriage and Family, and (3) Pre-History, Indian Ethnology and Archaeology. In addition, there was a fourth paper – Essay – which was not specifically taught.

There were two teachers in sociology – G.S. Ghurye and N.A. Thoothi. The former was trained at Cambridge and the latter at Oxford. Those who had registered for MA degree by research were more influenced by the outlook and approaches of these teachers. Thoothi was strongly influenced by Patrick Geddes, R.R. Merret, J.L. Myres, J. Arthur Thomson, Peake and Fleure. His general approach is partly indicated by the series which be edited and titled as 'Regional and Sociological Studies (mainly Indian)'. His outlook and approach were also reflected in his lectures on 'Principles of Sociology'.[1] Ghurye lectured on 'Caste-rank and Marriage', 'Indian Ethnology' and 'Archaeology and World Pre-History'. He also gave a few introductory lectures on sociology. On sociological thought the book suggested was 'Development of Social Theory' (1923) by Lichtenberger. On marriage we were recommended 'History of Human Marriage' (1891) by Westermarck. Some of the books mentioned during the course of lectures were R. Briffaults's 'The Mothers' (1927), V.F. Calverton's 'Bankruptcy of Marriage' (1927), Hobhouse's 'Morals in Evolution' (1906), Russell's 'Marriage and Morals' (1929) and C.C. North's 'Social Differentiation' (1926). The students interested in these books would read them, the rest could rely on Ghurye's lectures for examination. My opinion is that the students in general in those days were as much degree and examination oriented as they are today.

Ghurye's view was that all that sociology could do was to create an enlightened public opinion. It was not that only sociologists marshalled evidence for different views; but he did have a view of his own to bring about the desired change in society. This can be seen from his writings. Thoothi (1935) was more explicit on this issue. In the general introduction to the series he was editing he wrote: 'The studies bear upon problems of human life in its various aspects – regional, economic, institutional, cultural and philosophical – with a view to advance constructive suggestions concerning the complicated problems that confront us at the present day. Such an understanding necessitates the treatment of facts and ideas in a scientific manner and spirit. Only patient investigation can yield results that prove valuable for the guidance of life. Every problem has its practical bearings. Hence, to understand a problem we must study it with reference to its past as well as its present in order that we may be enabled to estimate its future. Vague and unscientific endeavour are worse than useless for they not merely vitiate human effort but frustrate purpose and aspirations, and paralyze our hope to shape the future.'

The points that emerge from the foregoing are that (1) methodology as a separate course was not learnt by any one of the sociologists of the second generation from Bombay University and it would not be incorrect to say that such was the case for sociologists from other universities in India as well; (2) sociology was not understood as a science as it is understood today; and (3) sociology was supposed to have a bearing on practical life and was future-oriented, that is, change-oriented.

All the sociologists of second generation who were trained in the tradition of the founders, and all those trained under the second generation of sociologists carry the imprint of their tradition and outlook. It is necessary to recognize this fact. The new post-war sociology was being grafted during the last twenty years on this climate of thought and on that tradition of knowledge and training with which the sociologists of second generation were imbued. Their sociological outlook and training was of a specific kind. But they were required to teach and practise sociology of a new kind. The present generation of sociologists and the sociological research is the result of the interaction between these two traditions. We shall see later how the new trends appeared. Here it may suffice to say that, as in the past, the new trends have the same two sources – Britain and the United States.

Sociology in the United States in the pre-World War II period could be described as 'all branches and no trunk', and the sociologist could be described as 'a person who knows less and less of more and more and ends up with knowing nothing of everything'. The sociology that we are aiming at is a specialism and the sociologist a specialist. I was and still am at a loss to answer the question: 'What have you specialized in?' or 'what is your department specializing in?'

To return to the point was it then that sociologists of the second generation were not trained to be scientific or methodological? I shall try to answer the question by narrating what actually happened at Bombay when I was a student.

What is called the methodology course today was not taught either at MA or as pre-PhD training. As for sociological theory, it was taught as it prevailed in Britain and the United States. Our model then was Britain as now it is the United States. Political independence has not made much difference in our colonial status in this regard. The research problem was suggested by the teachers. For quite sometime the teacher and the student remained vague and uncertain. In our terminology we distinguished between library studies and field studies. The student would read and meet the teacher and discuss. They would then arrive at a problem and the student would begin the work on his dissertation. Sometimes they did not arrive at a problem and the student left.

It is interesting to note here that even today, after 'modernizing' our under-graduate and post-graduate courses, introducing tutorials, seminars and many such innovations, many teachers complain that they do not get students who are aware of the problems they want to research in for PhD work.

It was not uncommon that a student would keep in this view some work or dissertation previously done for his guidance, particularly in the case of the field work studies.[2] There were no books on theory and methodology as we understand them today. The library studies were mostly historical. There were interpretations or judgments according to the 'theory' or 'views' that one held. That is how a student doing library thesis understood his task and that was also expected of him. The teacher's role was to see that sufficient and relevant evidence was collected. He would see that the evidence in the contrary was not suppressed or ignored. He would examine the logic of interpretation and would also counter the views of the student, if necessary.

In the field studies the prevailing categorizations and classifications were used both for non-quantitative and quantitative studies. Here also the teacher watched whether the observations were precise and sufficient in number. Largely, the interpretations were based on percentage differences, even in the case of bivariate tables. It was not that the teachers did not know mean variations, standard deviations and chi square. But the students rarely learnt them or used them.

If one were to name the method that was used, it was the method of comparison. The emphasis was on impartial and adequate observations, on logical reasoning based on evidence and cultivation of scientific attitude. All this was imbibed through the talks with the teachers and from the practice of others who had done similar work. It was more a disciplining of the mind than training into a craft.

In general, a student was offered an opportunity to develop a world-view and scientific outlook according to his ability and interest. He was being prepared to become a 'generalist' rather than a 'specialist'. That is how the second generation of sociologists trained at Bombay might be characterized. In my opinion that was also true of the students coming out of Lucknow and other universities who became the teachers of the next generation.

I was awarded the PhD degree in 1942 for a thesis entitled 'Social Bases of Crime'. It was a 'table thesis', based largely on the material from the 'primitive' tribes. I must have gone through monographs on about 200 tribes from different parts of the world and selected nearly a hundred tribes for inclusion in my work. The selection was not by a random sample. It depends on whether there was adequate information about certain crimes among these tribes. I would read a monograph and if I came across a reference to another book, all that I had to do was to suggest it to Ghurye and he would recommend the book to the librarian for purchasing it. This is what every student could do. I would also get references from *Man* and from *Journal of Royal Anthropological Institute*. It was through these two journals and through *Nature* that I came across references to the monographs written by Malinowski's students and others. I do not remember whether I read American journals or not. But I had recommended all the monographs on American tribes to be procured by the library. The publications of Smithsonian Institute and of Peabody Museum were also acquired. So far as building up the library was concerned the teachers had no prejudices. The simple rule that was followed but never enunciated was that the university library must have anything that was published. I believe that Bombay University library must be having one of the richest collections of literature on tribes in the country.

Additionally, books on criminology and penology, criminal law, civil law, jurisprudence and sociology of law, etc., were also purchased. Some were read and some were just browsed through. The idea was that the student must have at least a nodding acquaintance with the relevant literature of the subject he was working on. Similarly, other students working on other subjects would replenish the library through the same process.

The literature on the tribes was mostly ethnographic. Some was ethnological. New trends had begun to appear with Malinowski and his students. But we were not able to appreciate the significance of these trends then.

The model that I had adopted for my study was from the 'Material Culture and Social Institutions of Peoples: An Essay in Correlation' by Hobbouse, Wheeler and Ginsberg (1915) and 'Sexual Regulation and Cultural Behaviour' by J.D. Unwin (1935). Unwin had not done field work but used the field work data of others. Unwin's book left an indelible impression on me. Hobhouse was Martin White

Professor of Sociology at London. But within ten years of my 'parading' as a sociologist he was being dubbed as unscientific and wrong.

I did not conduct any field work for my PhD degree but I got the opportunity to do it when I was appointed as a research assistant to Ghurye. He had a project for collecting data regarding the fast, feasts and festivals of Hindus all over India. M.N. Srinivas was the first to do such work in South India for Ghurye. When Srinivas left for Oxford I replaced him. I had to go to Bihar and Orissa for that work. The data were to be taken castewise. There was no sampling of castes or of individuals, any one who knew the customs and would be responsive could be the respondent. There was no schedule – open-ended or closed. The interview was unstructured. The respondent would talk and I would ask probing questions for additional information or clarification. I took down notes on the spot and wrote them out later. That method of collecting information is still my favourite, though of course, with necessary modification.

With this kind of personal research experience I joined Samaldas College at Bhavanagar, then a princely state, as a teacher in November 1945. Sociology was not a subject at under-graduate level in Bombay University to which this college was affiliated then. The course, however, was on the anvil and one of Ghurye's students who was in a senior position in the state's administration was eager to introduce it in that college. It was expected that the course would come through within a year or two and I was appointed in the economics department in anticipation. When sociology was introduced two years later it was called 'Social Institutions' and the back prescribed was Hobhouse's *Morals in Evolution* (1906). Keller's *Societal Evolution* (1915), *Society* (1950) by MacIver and Page, and Daryll Forde's *Habitat, Economy and Society* (1934) were introduced later.

Though I had to teach 13 to 14 hours a week there was enough leisure. I had to read up for the lectures for the first one or two years and communicate this to about 150 students in the class. In the evenings I played cricket, hockey and tennis according to seasons. Most students came from rural areas and were very thrilled by the descriptions of the tribes, their customs and activities. They were constantly suggesting that there was a tribe called Padhars in that region and that we should visit them.

We went there, stayed for less than a week and took notes and photographs. But everything was unplanned and *ad hoc* for the simple reason that I did not know what I was about. So it was more a pleasure trip than a study trip. But I took another blind step and applied to Bombay University for a research grant for the study of Padhars, entirely in a spirit of adventure. The grant was sanctioned, but by then I had shifted to Poona and so I could not accept it.

This episode, though seemingly insignificant, made me realize that a PhD degree or teaching in the classroom did not prepare a person for doing research on his own. The episode also made me realize how difficult the task of the research supervisors must be.

II
FIRST INDEPENDENT RESEARCH

In 1951 I joined Deccan Post-Graduate College and Research Institute at Poona, where one had to justify one's existence primarily by research. I had to teach only two hours a week, to a small class of twenty MA students. What could I do the rest of the time? The only thing that I knew about research was that I had to do it. Every five years a committee came to observe the work of the institute and of individual researchers. I knew of a case in which a man did absolutely nothing and had to leave. In the institute itself there were prominent persons in their own fields: linguistics, archaeology, history, sanskrit and sociology. Outside the institute there were equally eminent persons in other fields. To be anywhere near them was itself a difficult challenge. There was also some difficulty in my securing recognition as a post-graduate teacher. D.R. Gadgil who was an active member of the board of management of the institute sent me a message that I need not bother about teaching at the university and that I could carry on research.

My reading of the monographs on tribes and knowledge of studies of urban areas such as 'Middle Town' by Lynd and Lynd (1929), 'Poona: A Socio-Economic Survey' by Gadgil and Sovani (1952) and 'A Survey of Social Structure of England and Wales' by Carr-Saunders and Caradog (1927) were of no avail even for deciding the area of my research, let alone the problem. The interest in sociological theories as they are understood now did not exist in India then. If I read them or about them in foreign journals and books, they went over my head.

Any thing that informed me about social change interested me. Social reform and political movements were the focus of my attention then. Writings, lectures and gossip connected with them were the concern of that generation.

In those days Poona University which was hardly five years old had started a new experiment in the organization of under-graduate teaching. It was called centralized teaching. All students, whatever colleges they belonged to, had to go to the teachers who were considered proficient in their subjects, irrespective of the college affiliation. The lectures were held at one place at the concerned college. There was a controversy whether that type of organization was good and whether it should be continued. Teachers, students and the public were involved in that controversy. I smelt some meat there. Some students and teachers promised help if I carried out an inquiry concerning students. That decided the problem of my research.

But with that decision my responsibilities and difficulties as a research worker increased. There were two initial problems: what to ask, and whom to ask. These were the problems of questionnaire making and sampling.

The question regarding sampling was tied with the problem whether the students would respond or not. Ultimately, the procedure of broadcast distribution was decided upon. Teachers would distribute the questionnaires in their classes and the students would put them after completing, into locked boxes with slits, kept in the colleges. The technical questions, such as the adequacy or representativeness of the sample, its stratification, randomness and systematization, never occurred either to the group or to me. The whole attitude was to face the problems as and when they cropped up.

When I began going through the completed questionnaires, the issue did arise: How far the opinions or conditions of the students as reflected in the questionnaires were representative in the sense that they reflected the conditions of the student community as a whole? When the percentages were clearly in favour of one or the other view, there was not much difficulty. But when the difference was not glaring what would one do? I told the students and teachers that in such cases we might simply report that 'this is the situation'. Stating the facts with 'accuracy' and 'confidence' is better than puerile hypothesis testing. I believe that even for descriptive purpose a good sampling design is the *sine qua non*.

The next task was construction of questionnaire. There were two problems: what we should ask, and how we should ask. The tendency in regard to the first was to be all inclusive. The question of inclusiveness could be answered in terms of relevance to the problem at hand. But we had no well-defined problem. Our apprehension was that the students might not respond at all or not respond carefully if too many questions were asked. But the difficulty continued even when we agreed on what was worth asking. This came to include questions on students' social conditions and their opinions, not only on organization of university teaching but also on considerations in the choice of marriage partner, etc. Ultimately, the questions were decided in a purely *ad hoc* manner.

The next problem was how to ask the questions. Here, a very healthy common sense objection was raised to particular questions. Will they not understand the questions in the sense different from ours? Will they have accurate information on the point? Attempt was made to make the questionnaire more accurate. Despite this care I would not be able to say how well our questionnaire would stand the present tests of a good questionnaire.

It may be relevant here to mention that I had not read anything on methodology. The only book I knew was one by Stuart Rice (1931). Then, there were not so many books on methodology as there are today. Even after I was convinced of the need and usefulness of certain techniques, I have not studied a book on methodology like other books. For the last few years I am controlling my irrational prejudice against what is called methodology. But I must also say that it is a reaction against the fetishism of method and fussiness and or of superiority evidenced on this account in some social scientists.

I began to experience the real difficulties due to my ignorance of techniques regarding sampling, questionnaire making, tabulation and calculation, as I began to process my data. There were about 600 questionnaires. What does one do with all that data of good, bad and indifferent quality? I was thinking hard about how to bring order out of this jungle of data. Organizing the data is a problem in research and I also now realize that the problem has to be thought of before you launch your field work.

Before I could organize my data some persons involved in the university controversy began to ask for information on the matters of their specific interest. I became cautious. I consulted the director of the institute who advised me not to give information to individuals and also to go slow about the tabulation. That suited me. I did not tabulate the data in Poona and I brought them with me to Baroda with the hope to work on them some day. But that day never came. That was the end of that adventure.

But I learnt several lessons out of this experience. First, I was convinced that the respondents do not always lie. Secondly, I realized that questionnaire making was not so easy and was not a matter of just asking questions. In addition to these lessons I gained some confidence for doing research in spite of the failure; I also struck upon a field for research – the problems of students.

III
STUDY OF HIGH SCHOOL STUDENTS IN POONA

The next victims of my research were the high school students in Poona. For finance I approached the director of the institute, S.M. Katre and he at once agreed. He asked me to submit a budget without which it will be difficult to find money. He was right both administratively and academically. A budget means thinking of some research problem first and then estimating the expenses. That was precisely the difficulty with me. However, this problem was solved. Katre not only gave me money but also went with me personally to introduce me to the principals of many schools.

The questionnaire was prepared in English. Though I could speak and read Marathi satisfactorily, I had to take the help of others for translating the questionnaire into Marathi. It was a self-administered questionnaire. In about 20 schools, out of 25 covered by the inquiry, I personally administered the questionnaire. The questionnaire was indeed and improvement on the previous one and has been printed in the monograph, 'High School Students in Poona' (1953).

I was better this time in regard to sampling and tabulation. I took a systematic random sample of 20 per cent. The total number of respondents came to 849 students (boys and girls) distributed over 25 schools. I now think that 10 per cent sample would have been enough. The idea then was that larger the number more 'representative' it is. I still have that notion. I still believe that a sufficiently large number of respondents randomly selected covers most of the varieties in the population. I did not know 'stratification' as a sampling device then. Having known about it now my understanding of sampling is modified. But even today I understand stratified sampling as a technique which takes us nearer to reality by covering large number of significant variations. I must say that though sampling is the technique borrowed from statistics it is the most useful and fruitful part of modern research technology which has come to stay with us for good and to our benefit. Even those who believe in nine months intensive field work staying in a village might find it useful.

I got the questionnaire filled in alright. The next problem was: What am I going to do with the information? How was I going to bring order into the information?

I had gone through each and every questionnaire carefully. While going through them I was visualizing some broad classifications and the relations between two classes of facts from the figures. Also, questions concerning the difference between a teacher's opinion of the student and the student's opinion of himself occurred to me. The distribution of schools was very instructive from the beginning. Most of them came from areas inhabited by advanced castes, and most of them were also managed by the associations of such castes. Other questions also arose: How many of the Brahmin boys were 'good students'? Were the students of different qualities distributed over different occupational groups? So in addition to simple frequency, some data had to be organized on the lines of cross tables. At that time, I knew the expression 'variable', but not its precise meaning.

An economist friend in Bombay suggested that the work could be better done on machine. He would put me in touch with the person who would do it. That person fortunately turned out to be interested in his work and he had respect for academic pursuits and persons. He came down to Poona from Bombay, stayed with me for two days and we arrived at the scheme for transferring the data on what we now call 'code sheets'.[3] The most part of the data from 849 questionnaires were transferred by me single-handed. That did take time. Objectively, that experience was very useful in supervising and guiding others afterwards.

After the data were transferred to the sheets they were sent for punching and sorting. The results were brought to me in much shorter time than I took in transforming the data. I again decoded the sheets and made nearly seventy tables. Most of them were simple frequency tables and I prepared them myself.

The monograph was distinctly divided into two parts. What I wrote followed from the description of Poona High School students. Only some aspects of the students were selected for comments. The grounds on which selections were made gave the relevance to the monograph. I had not thought of them before I began the research. As I have already said my interest in students as the field of research was influenced by the environment in Poona of that time. There were no theoretical assumptions behind the study because I had no theory. If there was anything in the sense of abstract generalization, it was by way of my world-view and outlook. Despite this, in the conclusion, I noted that the students' acceptance of family regulation was a 'striking feature of our results'. Why? Why do I relate them to caste and village community? Why do I say that 'apparent status distinctions find their *explanation* in the political and economic history of the castes in Poona which is in turn based upon the traditional caste hierarchy of India'?

The answer may lie in the environment and climate prevailing among the professional sociologist in those days and in the manner in which questions of 'relevance' and 'theory' were understood then, to arrive at a theory and not to articulate it. Today, they are articulated.

In the first section of the monograph entitled 'About This Inquiry', a different type of relevance may be seen. It begins: 'The educational system of a society is part of the whole social system. Being a part of the whole, it is interrelated with other parts of the society.' Then follows a quotation from an address by A.J. Allaway 'Social and Educational Change Since 1900' from *The Sociological Review* (1951). Then, there is a paragraph illustrating the relationship between the educational system as a part of the social system in India by which I stand even today.

But the important question is: What is the relation between the 'relevance' as formulated in the introduction and the 'relevance' as discussed in the conclusion of the monograph? I may confess that there is no relationship. Though I stand by the contents of what I have said in the introduction and in the conclusion, they are decorative pieces introduced after the questionnaire was framed and after 'the data were analyzed', if one may say so. But I must also say that those pieces remained with me in the kitbag of my thinking. One may start without being very clear about relevance. One might or might not see it even at the end of one's research. That was the situation then.

Now about the 'quality'. I followed certain general principles of science: You should be sure that you observe what you want to observe and observe it correctly and precisely. You should not argue beyond the limits of your facts. Your conclusions should follow from your facts. While arguing you must see that you do not allow your irrelevant unconscious biases in your interpretation and that your interpretations reflect only such 'biases' of which you are conscious. In short, it may be said that one must strictly follow the general rules of reasoning. It is a mental discipline which might be called scientific attitude. My opinion now is that modern technology of research combined with this attitude would give better results.

To return to the specific issue of methodology the conclusion says: 'We reject the extravagant claims for the questionnaire method as the chief method of sociological research. We believe that questionnaire should be used in close collaboration with field work, each in turn suggesting questions which the other may satisfactorily answer and this particularly in the complexity of urban studies... . From all these examples it will be seen that at no time the distinction between methods is absolute.'

I stand by the last sentence quoted above even today. The other things might need modifications and qualifications.

The whole monograph was written while I was in Baroda where I moved in August 1952. By that time methodology perhaps was advancing in India and Baroda was an important centre propelling that movement. M.N. Srinivas was holding seminars and putting the students to do field work and was also writing in newspapers and journals about sociology and field work and also against questionnaire method. But for this new development in sociology I might not have written on 'methodology' in the conclusion of the monograph.

IV
NEW EXPERIENCES

While at Baroda I did not come in personal contact with American sociology and its field work orientation. But through books and journals I was becoming more and more aware of the way in which sociology was developing in the United States. I do not exactly remember how I came to know about 'Towards a General Theory of Action', edited by Parsons and others (1962) and 'Social Theory and Social Structure' (1948) by Merton. These were my first acquaintance with new developments in American sociology. I do not remember whether they were part of the MA course; but I made the MA students read and discuss them with me. We did not have more than two or three students in the MA class, if we had five students, we thought the class was big. That there was M.N. Srinivas, a social anthropologist, as the head of the department did not come in my way of buying American books for library and teaching them. The MA student was conversant with both American sociology and British sociology or social anthropology. I found it very fruitful to have another teacher with different sociological outlook in the department.[4]

Teaching in Poona could not be called a load; but in Baroda it was heavy not merely in terms of hours but in terms of variety also. The department was teaching sociology in the faculties of Home Science and Social Work apart from the two years BA and MA sociology course. Srinivas and I were the only two teachers. This continued up to 1955–56. During this period, Srinivas went to Britain for a year as Simon Fraser fellow. He was away again for some time. Very little time and inclination was left for my personal empirical research, though I found time for cricket and tennis.

After I left Poona, I spent one or two vacations in Poona at Deccan College. There I met D.P. Pandit who had been my colleague at Bhavnagar. She told me that the President of Mahuva Municipality was interested in economic research of Mahuva and that she was thinking about it. After the discussions with her we agreed to expand it and also make it sociological. I made a trip to Mahuva at my own expense and met the president who was a leader in that area. It turned out that the municipality was not in a position to spend more than two or three thousand rupees for the research. So, for a while nothing concrete happened.

Around this time a high official in the Rockefeller Foundation had a meeting with Srinivas at Ahmedabad. On his return, Srinivas said that the Rockefeller Foundation would finance research which had a bearing on practical affairs. He asked if I would do something regarding Mahuva. Both as a departmental head and as a friend he encouraged me to prepare a proposal. I did that and the grant came.

This time it was different from the earlier adventures. There were expectations from the sponsors and we have some vague ideas. The only specific thing was the place – Mahuva; and frankly it was a hotch-potch proposal meant to be acceptable to the sponsors. I do not have a copy of that proposal, though I had preserved it.[5]

I had some vague ideas about what we wanted to do. Initially, D.P. Pandit and S.N. Ranade, then in the faculty of social work at Baroda, were participating in thinking. But both of them went out of India just when the work began. I do not remember to have discussed with anyone whether the report would be one book or more than one. But after the data were collected I found myself overwhelmed by them and for quite sometime, I was at a loss to decide how to accommodate the data in one volume. The organization of data was thought about after the data were collected, and that created the problem.

Ultimately I decided to write separate books on different aspects or problems. In addition to my book on family, D.P. Pandit published 'Earning One's Livelihood in Mahuva' (1965). A third book was planned on 'The Settlement Pattern of the Town, House Patterns and Allied Problems'. It was nearly completed. But now there are only a few line blocks prepared by the press. The rest of it along with schedules and notes were washed away in the Surat floods of 1968.

The choice of writing on family was not accidental. It was a continuation of my interest. I had published a paper entitled 'Joint Family in India: An Analysis' (1956). My emphasis was on jointness which is very much alive in spite of separate households and division of property and, I would like to add, in spite of inter-caste, inter-state and even inter-religious marriages. It may be that the co-ordinates are different but the qualitative change is not much.

Like the 'High School Students in Poona', 'Some Aspects of Family in Mahuva' is also an exploratory work. But there is a marked difference both in regard to quality and relevance. Before I deal with them I should like to point out a serious omission. Nowhere in the book is a mention of how the sample was selected. I cannot explain how I missed it. There is a story behind sampling which needs to be told, because our record keeping even today is as indifferent as it was in 1956.

The 1951 census had prepared a 'national register'. It contained information about each household and about each member in the household. The registers were kept with the Taluka Mamlatdar (Tehsildar). When we first visited Mahuva we saw the registers for two wards and were told that the registers for the remaining two wards were also there. But these registers were not traceable. That created the problem for sampling. We had to lake a census and prepare the list of all members. From that list we selected the household of every 56th member. That delayed our work and increased the cost. We had to prepare new forms and take the help of the students from the town for taking the census.

We used both the scheduled and the open-ended interviews for getting the information. We got good information by our informal and casual talks with the respondents and other people. Though, in the beginning, there was some suspicion that investigators were from income tax department, very soon it evaporated and on informal occasions, the members of the team were not considered outsiders.

In the beginning someone also spread the runner that we were recruiting agents for the army. On one occasion, T.N. Sheth was saved from being beaten up by the timely arrival of a local teacher.

Four out of the five investigators were my students and, except one, all of them were from my BA class. Among the men T.N. Sheth, D.L. Sheth and Edwin Masihi were with me from the time the schedules and talking point were being prepared. All three of them have kept up their academic attitudes. The two women investigators – Pratibha Pandya and Hansa Bhatt – are married and are 'keeping home'.

Most of the investigators had not passed their BA examination when I employed them. We were working during the vacation only. The university registrar's office did not like them receiving Rs. 250 per month. But the then Vice Chancellor, Hansa Mehta, just did not listen to them and gave all freedom to me regarding the choice of the investigators, their pay and my expenses. I recommended the names without advertisement and the university approved them. Srinivas played his role in instilling that attitude in her. We also proved equal to the trust that she placed in us. However, the university bureaucracy had the upper hand after Hansa Mehta's term came to an end.

The processing and transferring of the data from the schedules to the code-sheets was done by the investigators. The expressions, coding and code-sheets were then in vogue but had not become the part of my vocabulary, and I did not know what a code-book was. However, since three of the investigators had to do the work of transferring the data, it had to be seen that every one of them understood every item of the answer in the code-book the same way. The answers had to be standardized. So the code-book was prepared without giving it such a name. I saw a code-book for the first time with M.S. Gore when he was in Delhi. I did not ask him anything about it but I took it with me to Baroda.

Surprisingly, there is a scale of jointness in my book under the title 'degree of jointness'. Not only was the index of the jointness made without knowing what it was but I also related it to other 'variables'. Now I find that the other variables are also similarly arranged in descending or ascending order. I have argued about the relationship between the two on percentage figures. I know by then from my talks with a statistician that there were techniques to measure the relationships between variables and their degrees for which one did not require the knowledge of mathematics.

Procedurally, I became more precise now than when I conducted the survey on the high school students in Poona. I became aware that the terms and categories that I use must be properly defined.

So far as the relevance is concerned I think the monograph touches on many such points. It deals with the phenomenon of 'jointness' in family or household. Jointness can exist irrespective of the type of household. A joint household can be a joint family but a joint family does not necessarily mean a joint household. Jointness can exist between the members of nuclear or elementary families. Similarly, joint property does indicate jointness but jointness does not necessarily mean joint property. Jointness is a sentiment that exists between the relatives. The relationship between the members of the families of two business partners cannot be called the joint family relationship. The circles of relatives and the areas of the relationships may change from time to time. But the joint family sentiment may persist. When we talk of the break up of joint family we miss these points.

Once we understand jointness as a system of rights and obligations and observe the behaviour or interactions of the members of a household or a circle of the relatives, the terms of our analysis and interpretation also need to be appropriate to that observation. In this regard, the influence of developments in American sociology is obvious in the monograph. The orientation of actions, the norms governing the actions and the mutual role expectations are used for distinguishing jointness from nuclearity.

During vacations I used to go to my village and each time I observed the differences compared to the village of my youth. The most striking thing was the number of closed houses and presence of tenants in some houses. The houses closed were those of the highest caste in the village – Anavil Brahmins referred to as Desais in popular parlance.

During my student days, the village was very lively, particularly the Desai locality, which I primarily identified as my 'village'. We always went to the village as soon as the school or the college was closed. Those working in Bombay would manage to get leave during the college vacations. We, about twenty youngmen, used to gather from the morning under the banyan tree. As the time passed, this scene disappeared although the number of graduates, matriculates and the high school and college students was much larger now than before. How did it happen? It was not difficult to mark out and select from observation the differentiating factors. These factors could be marked out from my knowledge of the village and the knowledge of the similar phenomenon elsewhere gathered from books and talks.

With this background I undertook the study which led to the publication of 'The Patterns of Migration and Occupation in a South Gujarat Village' (1964). The method of collecting data was the same as the field worker uses. It was talking to the people and to the persons selected as informants. But there was no regular schedule. The points of information were very very limited and all the information collected was kept in the form of notes about each family. Now I think that the schedule and code-book would have been more economical both in terms of time and the handling of the data while writing. But, even today, my mind is not disciplined that way. Tradition dies hard.

If I had written the monograph some time later, it would have been different. But I do not also rule out the other possibility that I would not have written it at all. In fact, in all the cases of published and unpublished reports, I have worked under pressure of finishing them in time. My experience of myself and of others is that if we do not set a time limit beforehand, sometimes the report might never be submitted. I must say that our sponsoring agencies have been very liberal on this point. Under the circumstances in which we work – the organization of research in our universities, lack of financial support to purely research institutions or indiscriminate support to them, and 'the reference models' for the social sciences as discussed by Yogendra Singh (1973) – I also think that it is a reasonable attitude.

V
RETROSPECTIVE AND PERSPECTIVE

This is an attempt by one particular researcher to reflect upon his work and evaluate it. It does not represent the profession. In fact, I doubt if any single researcher would be representative of the state of sociological researches in our country.

The significance of the present case is that it is of a member of the second generation of sociologists, a generation which has held important positions in most universities in our country. The sociology as it was taught to them and learnt by them therefore is both quantitatively and qualitatively an important tributary stream to the mainstream of sociological thinking and research in India.

Moreover, the break with tradition also comes from among the members of this generation. From among the members of the second generation and of the third generation some went to the United States and some to Britain after independence. Of those who went to foreign universities, some were uprooted from their Indian experience of sociology and were transformed; some were neither uprooted nor transformed but were half-baked. Some others came back as they went. But all these persons formed a category and did influence sociological tradition in India, by introducing the new trends. For academic position, a foreign degree, or even a stay abroad without any degree, was considered more acceptable by the universities and they filled up many positions in the university departments.

The new trend was reinforced by the visit of the foreigners to India, again a very large number from the United States and a smaller number from Britain.

This category can be called a 'priestly' category, not in a derogatory sense but in a functional sense. Feeble voices from the generation of the founders were raised at this development. But on the whole, there was no academic controversy and what those in the influential category said and did was largely accepted without debate.

One indication of sociology attaining the professional level was the establishment of the Indian Sociological Society, followed by a number of organizations at national and local levels. The growth of profession in terms of mere numbers also creates the possibility of varieties in thinking and outlook. These signs are visible among the members of the third generation of sociologists. In fact, such differences began in the second generation itself. I have already described in Section I what an MA or PhD degree-holder was equipped with by way of 'theory' and 'methodology'. Both theory and methodology in those days were not understood as they are today. Studies of single societies or parts of them as advocated by the social anthropologists were also not in vogue in those days.

The single societies were studied as the part of the whole humanity *via* the concepts of culture and civilization. Ethnology, archaeology, linguistics and such other disciplines contributed to the identification of each society as a whole in terms of its culture and civilization and helped place it on a scale of development. But that involved comparison; and the question of explaining the similarities and differences was inherent in such comparison. Leaving aside other explanations in terms of race or geography, two theories were in vogue: the theory of independent development of each society and the theory of culture or civilization having originated in one centre and spreading to other societies through contact. They are known as theories of independent origin and of culture contact.

One of the important items of comparison was custom. Malinowski's contribution lay in his exploding the belief in what he called the understanding of primitive society as a cake of custom. He demonstrated that each custom had a function in maintaining a particular part and through it the whole society. Leaving aside his contribution to the techniques of field study, his views gave importance to the study of single societies or parts of them with a new orientation. Radcliffe-Brown propagated what he called 'structure-function' studies leading to the emphasis on social structure. Evans Pritchard and others developed different line of studies. For anyone who was acquainted with the writing of Herbert Spencer the terms structure and function were not new. What was new was 'social' acquired from Durkheim.

We of the second generation, though aware of Durkheim as a name, knew nothing about his theoretical work. But for those acquainted with Hobhouse's article on sociology in the 'Encyclopedia of Religion and Ethics', or with his 'Social Development' and with Ginsberg's writings, the concept of society as a 'network' of parts was not so new. A critical study of the inherited thought and the new thought was necessary. But no one in India had done that. The scholarship of the 'founders' was of one type and the scholarship of the innovators was limited to the new monographs on tribes.

Consequently, there was no critical examination of the old and new thought. Intellectually and psychologically, some of us of the second generation were hesitant to accept the new. The propagators of the new were more polemical than scholarly; they simply dismissed the tradition of the 'founders'.

If we understand the theory and practice of sociology as was prevalent in Britain then we shall appreciate better the courses of study and the work of the 'founders'.

Ghurye went to Sindh and Saurashtra and himself did the digging to find the spread of Buddhistic and Mohen-Jo-Daro culture not because he was not a sociologist, but because he was a sociologist as understood in those days. It is also not surprising that Aiyappan became the curator of Madras Museum. D.N. Majumdar's interest in Himalayan expeditions and anthropometry were not career-oriented, but was consistent with the theory and practice of his discipline of the time. Similarly, Radhakamal Mukherjee, D.P. Mukherjee and A.R. Wadia were not doing irrelevant or speculative studies. They too had their value premises and boldly expressed their views.

The founders of sociology in India were neither unsociological nor unscientific; they were also not specifically patriotic if they related their work to policy or practical problems. While dealing with practical problems they were not merely concerned with social reforms but also with the change in the type of society. These were their concerns precisely because they were sociologists. We are free to disown them. But we should also be prepared and willing to be disowned as sociologists and scientists by a generation after us. Ramkrishna Mukherjee (1972) argues that now our researchers need to be more diagnostic. I agree. But I do not agree with his reasons. He believes that we have passed the descriptive and analytical stages in our researches and must now enter the diagnostic stage. That is not true.

The 'founders' were nothing if not diagnostic. The substantive areas of their study were tribes, castes, family, marriage, education, taluka surveys and surveys of women clerks, farmers, untouchable workers, religious communities, etc. These studies were based on both field work and written records, historical and contemporary, statistical and non-statistical. They were largely descriptive or narrative studies. They were classificatory. The concepts used were normative and not analytical and it was a customary practice that there were prescriptions at the end of the study. It was not difficult to find out the value biases. That was the state of sociological research roughly up to 1950. The change came during and after the 1950s.

I first became aware of the change through M.N. Srinivas. What I am writing about the new trend is therefore based on my understanding of Srinivas' position.[6]

There were two aspects to his view of the tasks that he undertook: negative and positive. It is necessary to destroy the old or at least parts of it if you want to construct something new. His first point in this regard was that what was going on as sociology in the country was not sociology. It was at one end social philosophy and at the other end social work. Therefore, it had to be made a science. If you want to make it a science it followed that it must break with all value-connection or what was considered as a desirable future state. He did not believe in the possibility of prediction. It further follows from that position that you must break with the considerations of change and practical problems. Even when Srinivas participated in the discussion regarding policy or practice oriented researches his emphasis was always on fundamental theoretical knowledge. He believed that the rest would follow.

The second point in the negative aspect of his tasks was that he advocated the severance of sociology from evolutionary theories. That was consistent with his position against the study of change.

His positive stand was that we should take up synchronic studies and not diachronic studies, at least for some time. Synchronic studies meant unfolding the relationships between parts or between different systems of a society. The issue is: if one is studying kinship systems, political systems, religious systems, knowledge systems, etc., does one stop at exposing their interrelationships or does he go beyond and try to make general statements regarding the given society as a whole? For a given society the interrelationships could be understood through the concept of social structure. To me the term social structure never meant more than a label useful for the study of Indian society whether by Indians or foreign scholars.

The reason, as I understand, is that sociologists favouring synchronic studies were not sure or clear about the type of generalization that such studies would throw up. In fact, Srinivas did not bother much about this question. He thought it was a speculative question and it did not matter much if we did not take decision on it or even did not discuss it. He gave us to read in manuscript from Radcliffe-Brown's 'Methods in Social Anthropology' (edited by Srinivas, 1958) and Evans Pritchards' 'Social Anthropology' (1956). The two did not share the same views. If we go by the former we go to universalistic types of generalizations on the lines of natural science. The latter questions the possibility of such generalizations, though generalizations of limited nature could be possible.

Srinivas did not, however, bother much about such questions, which according to him, were long-term problems. His immediate concept and mission was to start the tradition of synchronic studies and change the field of study of social anthropology from tribal to peasant societies. A number of American and British scholars came to India and did such studies. A sample of such studies is 'India's Villages' edited by Srinivas (1955).

The new field work studies were meant to test a hypothesis and were not just descriptive. The new field work tradition did not mean only staying for a long time in a village and observing the details of life; it also meant a selective and more purposive observation. Another advantage of this long stay was that one could observe many things besides the specific area of observation and that gave the opportunity of opening up new or further points and areas of study. In addition, the investigator actually experienced the system in its day-to-day functioning and understood it better.

Side by side with this positive and constructive thought and activity, Srinivas was attacking the techniques of questionnaire, statistics and other 'methods' with the vigour of a missionary.

What Srinivas was doing or preaching was against everything that I was doing and thinking and all that I had learnt and taught. It was under this situation that I was to write the conclusion of the monograph 'High School Students in Poona' (1953) which was based on questionnaire. I was not unnerved. But I was set to thinking. D.F. Pocock was doing similar field work in Gujarat at that time. I had long discussions with him and the concluding remarks regarding method in my monograph were the result of that discussion.

The debunking of all my academic views began from 1950 when Srinivas joined Baroda. He published his views in a national newspaper which evoked several letters to the editor. Srinivas himself wrote to me when I was in Poona that he had also received many personal letters. Though the campaign had started from 1950, I did not grasp its meaning or its significance until I joined Baroda University.

Between 1950 and 1955 when I began to think seriously about Mahuva project, my beliefs regarding sociology and sociological theories were to receive another shock from another direction. This time it was from American development.

Y.B. Damle and I had written an article for the volume presented to Ghurye, and Damle suggested that we might give it to M.S. Gore for reading. I did not know Gore though I had heard about him from the teachers in the Bombay University's department of sociology. He had returned from the United States.

During the meeting with Gore, which was my first meeting with him, he mentioned the paper on change that he had written. That interested me and I asked him if he would give me that for reading. He agreed and sent it to me from Delhi.

I had thought that it might be on the lines that I had read and that I would quickly dispose of it. But when I read it, I found it difficult. Gore had applied Merton's analysis about which I knew nothing. I had to read Merton's book first and then understand Gore's application of his theory to Indian situation.

Reading Merton's book 'Social Theory and Social Structure' (1948) and Gore's paper were exercises in tight-rope walking. So I wrote to Gore that I would take sometime and that if I agreed with him I would have to blaspheme myself. Gore wrote to me that my reactions were quite interesting and that I could take my own time. He also wrote to me to refer to Parsons and Shils' 'Towards a General Theory of Action' (1962). But by that time I had already started looking into the books by Merton and Parsons. My interest in them and other American sociologists increased.

In my opinion, the spread of American sociology in India took place not by the influence of a single American book or author. Unlike the British influence there was not one single person writing or speaking on behalf of it. It spread largely through the persons who went to the United States and returned to occupy positions in the Indian universities. Also, a number of Americans came to India and many of them held positions in the government as well as in the foundations. They offered opportunities for employment and funds for research. The demand for persons trained to handle practical problems on a larger scale than the anthropologists were trained to handle increased. Anthropologists in India were not trained to work in a team and the problems posed by the government and the foundations required working in a team and in larger areas than a tribe, or a village or a single city. The new tasks required training in the measurement of the phenomenon and the cognate techniques of research. That is how the new developments in American sociology came to spread in India.

The old guards were in position when these developments were taking place. But no critical appraisal of the American development or its spread in India came from any one of them. A feeble voice was raised by D.P. Mukherji. Srinivas publicly expressed his fear of losing the academic freedom and relegating fundamental knowledge and theory to the background through the overemphasis on applied research sponsored by some public agencies. So far as I was concerned I did not develop uncritical opposition or acceptance of the new pincer movement of which one arm was social anthropology (both British and American) and the other had new developments in American sociology.

Before I deal with these developments, however, I must make it clear that anthropologists and sociologists were never understood as two 'castes' as they are understood today. The simple distinction that was made between anthropology and sociology was that the former was the study of primitive tribes and the latter was the study of the civilized societies of the past and the present. The sociologist and the anthropologist could study either of the areas. Sociology and anthropology in these days had a common theoretical outlook, namely, evolutionism. The primitive societies were taken as the early forms of human society. So in terms of theory there was nothing to distinguish between anthropology and sociology. In fact, sociology was something amorphous at least as it was practised then in India and probably elsewhere too. There were no books on sociological theory as such. The books available to us were the books on the history of 'theories'. The two books which I read were Lowie's *History of Ethnological Theories* (1937) and Haddon's *History of Anthropology* (1949).

Until 1950 there were no distinctions between anthropology and sociology in India. K.P. Chattopadhyaya came to be treated as an anthropologist because he was appointed in the department of anthropology. He would have become a sociologist if he was appointed in department of sociology. Similarly, Iravati Karve, a practicing anthropologist, was in the department of sociology and M.N. Srinivas had throughout held chairs in the department of sociology.

Further, there was no intellectual or academic ground for the separation of anthropology and sociology. The number of universities and the number of departments of anthropology or sociology could be counted on fingertips. Though there could be competition between anthropologists and sociologists, conflict between the two would benefit neither. There was tolerance of each other if not co-operation between the two. It is significant as Ghurye mentions that though the department of anthropology was developing under K.P. Chattopadhyaya and that of sociology under his guidance, both of them were the branches of the same trunk – W.H.R. Rivers.

It was under this intellectual climate inherited by me that Srinivas confronted me with social anthropology. Neither Srinivas not I made much of the difference between the terminology though Srinivas held that social anthropology was the true or real sociology. He went beyond the understanding that anthropology was merely concerned with the primitive societies by encouraging the study of villages and peasant societies. His position even then was that it could also study more complex societies. For instance, he often mentioned the book by Fustel de Coulange on 'Ancient City' (1864). He was thus introducing what he called 'history' into the studies in social anthropology. His student A.M. Shah had started working with this frame of reference. But my understanding of history was different from his understanding. I had inherited the study of history from the evolutionists or of developmentalists and it was also influenced by Marxist writers, though not exclusively by Marx. It interrelated the past, present and future and was something nearer to what is now called 'continuity and change'. Srinivas' main target of attack was all such understanding that smacked of evolutionary change and Marxism. He and the American and British scholars who came to India in the 1950s accused Marxists as being dogmatic. Indeed, they were no less dogmatic in their anti-Marxism. This attitude of theirs did not enhance my respect for them.

Srinivas treated the societies or civilizations of the past and the contemporary complex urban societies as laboratories to verify some of the findings from the studies of the tribal or peasant societies. These findings were worth testing according to him on two counts: (1) their contribution to the theory of society or to the demolition of existing theory; and (2) their validity or soundness.

On neither of these counts I differed from Srinivas. However, his understanding of 'theory' was not the one which I had inherited. Theory always implies to me some wider application to human society and to show how society changes from one stage to another. Srinivas viewed such understanding with suspicion. It was natural, therefore, that the findings of the social anthropologists would not look impressive to me. Nevertheless, they had an attraction for me for their 'destructive' role of questioning the speculative generalizations. In their role of constructing a theory, however, as I understood it, they were inadequate.

Srinivas' strong point was his emphasis on field work method. I too had recognized its usefulness in the conclusion of my study of 'High School Students in Poona' (1953). Srinivas, however, held, at least at that time, that intensive field work was the sole method of getting reliable knowledge of society or social phenomenon.[7] I was neither convinced of this position then, nor I am now. I used the underlying principles of this method in my own way in my study of Mahuva and subsequent work.

In these studies, the data were collected according to a somewhat modified method of social anthropology. The analysis of data, however, went beyond this framework and used a method which I would attribute to social sciences. I do not call it sociological method because psychologists, political scientists and even some social anthropologists can and do make use of this method. My position then was and still is that what data you want and what you do with them depends on the questions that you ask about what you are studying.

We might say that how one collects data and what one does with them depends on the problem that one formulates or one's substantive interest. Interest might vary from the description or knowing 'what the thing is' to arriving at some propositions of generalized nature. I was concerned in my Mahuva study with knowing the prevalence of family jointness, of how it was changing and, if it was changing, in what direction. The scheme of classification of families had the usefulness for knowing the direction of change. At one time I thought that these forms might have some order. But now I do not think so, and for studying the direction of change I would not use them. This kind of understanding of the problem had its roots in my academic heritage. But, in the book, there is clear influence of the new developments in American sociology. Yet, it would be incorrect to say that I belong to this or that school of thought.

Two influences were working on my 'heritage'. One was of a social anthropology as it was developing in Britain about which I learnt from Srinivas and Pocock. Pocock's understanding was different from that of Srinivas and also his influence on me. The other influence was that of the developments in American sociology during the 1950s and subsequent years up to 1966.

None of these influences swept me off my feet, though they did unsettle me intellectually. I think this has happened to most of us of the second and also of the third generation of sociologists. Most of us of the second generation are out of university positions. The members of the third generation are practically in charge of training the future sociologists. What now matters most, therefore, is their intellectual heritage and position.

The question is what role can 'methodology' play in resettling us, the Indian sociologists or social scientists, to our tasks. Before answering the question, it is necessary to note the changes in the substantive areas of research which also help us in resettling. The current emphasis is on the problems of change and the problems of social policy or applied problems. For me this is a heartening situation. In terms of the direction of studies, what else were the founders or the first generation sociologists doing? One is welcome to say that they had no concepts, and their theories are outmoded. But we cannot deny the general direction of their work.

While we may say that they worked on inadequate data, or that the data they collected were not precise, or that their techniques of data collection left much to be desired, it would be incorrect to say that they were not empirical unless we assume that empirical means only observations by oneself.

While criticizing our predecessors we threw away the baby with the bath water. Instead of building upon what they did we started anew. But what was the new based on?

The question can be answered better by inquiring into the sources of the recent formulation of the 'new' or the problems of change. Has it arisen out of the inadequacies of the theories and concepts which we subscribed to and propagated during the last 25 years? Was it the result of our intellectual quest? My submission is that our emphasis on change and policy research has two sources. One is the expectation of the government and the public to help them in their efforts towards reconstruction of society. This social pressure has been one reason for the change in the orientation of our studies. Secondly, the problems of change began to be emphasized as a result of similar developments in America and Britain.

Here, we must also observe the difference in the situation of our predecessors and that of ours today. They were living in the period of political nationalism when political independence has been achieved. 'Indian' in the colonial political sense is probably no longer relevant for us except as an empirical reality. Today, the question of the type of future society we want to build is more difficult to formulate than it was for our predecessors. The 'western', in the sense of foreign, and 'Indian' can no longer be taken as given. The nineteenth century or early twentieth century picture of western society is no longer relevant. We cannot emulate that society today, though our international context today is more effective. But our cognition of that context is changing. The substantive tasks of choosing the theories and concepts have to be based on this reality. If our substantive researches look trivial, irrelevant and fruitless it is because we are ignoring this new context. The new situation demands change in our concerns and outlook.

We may now return to the question of methodology as a new concern and its role in helping to change our orientations. What goes on under the title of methodology in India as evident from the syllabi of different university departments and from what is done in the methodology courses organized by the ICSSR is the technology of research or training in craftsmanship.

There is dissatisfaction about this development. Some do not like it because it is American; others do not like it because they do not like a particular technologist, and still others grumble against the cliquishness of a few such technologists. Leaving aside such grumblings, the question of the spread of technology needs to be discussed on its own merits.

Before I deal with the issue, I may touch upon the subject of measurement. If one considers measurement as an essential attribute, or even an attribute for estimating the course of future events, the case of the modern technology of research follows from it. But if one understands science as a method of looking at the world as distinguished from the methods or theory, metaphysics and aesthetics, the case for technology of research can still follow from it but it will not be of the same nature as in the first case.

In the first case, the tendency will be to omit anything that is not amenable to measurement and therefore to the particular technology of research. Only those concepts and propositions will be considered real and valid which are amenable to this sort of treatment. Ultimately and in the long run that might lead to equations, formulae and models as in economics. No one should be sorry if that happens in future and in the long run. But along with it goes the attitude that anyone who is not using that technology and the view of science underlying it is not scientific and is not a sociologist. This I do not agree with. In a country where science is still in the process of development, it would be harmful to entertain the belief that the ultimate nature of sociology as science will be realized by only one particular view of science.

In the context of our needs in this country, will the new technology and the narrow attitude entertained by some users of that technology help us in deciding the concerns of our sociological research? The answer is clearly in the negative. Is the new technology in itself and by itself capable of giving us a model of that new society? The answer is no. Much less do the practitioners of new technology of research have to offer by way of building up such a model of society. This is so, even if we grant the precision their technology offers for describing Indian reality.

While rejecting the possibility of a precise model of the future society – mathematical or non-mathematical – do we reject the new technology also? No. It has its uses if we can make it serviceable to the formulation of the problem at hand, and not in the choice of the problem itself; also if we believe that the training in the craftsmanship also disciplines the mind. This latter aspect of the new technology of research has either not been realized by its proponents and propagators or is not sufficiently emphasized. If this aspect of the training in new technology is accepted and practised, we shall be gaining in the training of mind which our predecessors tried in their person-to-person style of training. If the proponents and the practitioners of the new technology fail to do that, they will have accepted the view that they are training craftsmen or technicians and not scientists.

The new technology of research has come to stay in sociology in India not because of its upholders but in spite of them. Sociologists who were most unwilling to accept the new technology were those who preferred to call themselves and were also known to others as social anthropologists. The leading lights among them have come to recognize the need and usefulness of the new technology now. This is a welcome development for which the credit goes to the social anthropologists. They have not accepted it through lectures on methodology. They have accepted it because of the problems that they faced in their work. For them it has an instrumental value and not an end value. If they use new technology rationally, they are likely to contribute much more than what they have already done.

This new development can be turned to the maximum advantage of sociology by a two-way traffic. The new technologists should understand the problems that the sociologists of all varieties are handling, their immediate and minimum needs for new technology and help them in handling the problems in their own way. They need not make a fetish of their technology. They should see how much of their technology others can take at any particular moment. The researcher too should first formulate the problems in his own way and then look for new technology or go to the technologist for consultation.

The point that I am making is that co-operation and collaboration in work will give us the maximum benefit in addition to training courses. At the moment, the need seems to be to make the technology serviceable to the researchers. The temptation to emphasize the complex and most recent developments and their abracadabra might have to be curbed.

Notes

1. In order to appreciate Thoothi one should study his book 'The Vaishnavas of Gujarat' (1935) and also consult the MA and PhD dissertations done under his supervision.

2. From 1930 to 1932, I was an active political worker. I moved about in the villages of the present Surat and Valsad districts and that 'field work' experience was enhanced afterwards by my field trips to Bihar and Orissa. This experience in addition to my village upbringing has helped me as a sociologist more than the books by the pundits.
3. I do not remember what sort of 'code-book' was prepared, but I do remember that I did not know that there could be a code-book.
4. The personal element in this relationship must be mentioned. Srinivas and I have been together from 1937 as students in Bombay. The friendship grew at Baroda and continues. Whatever intellectual differences we had were cooled by cracking jokes on our orientational preferences.
5. My books, papers and other belongings were washed away in a flood in 1968 at Surat.
6. Srinivas is not responsible for my understanding of his position. I am not referring to other reactions to his position from sociologists from other parts of the country because I am not well acquainted with the development in Lucknow and Calcutta. Mysore had ceased to be effective by 1950.
7. He relented from that position subsequently.

References

Allaway, A.J., 1951, 'Social and Educational Change Since 1900', *The Sociological Review*, Volume XLIII, Number 8.

Briffault, R., 1927, *The Mothers*, Allen and Unwin, London.

Calverton, V.F., 1927, *Bankruptcy of Marriage*, Modern Library, New York.

Carr-Saunders, A.M. and Jones, D. Caradog, 1927, *A Survey of the Social Structure of England and Wales*, Oxford University Press, London.

De Coulanges, Fustel, 1864, *Ancient City*, Gordon Press, New York.

Desai, I.P., 1953, *High School Students in Poona*, Deccan College Post Graduate and Research Institute, Poona.

—, 1956, 'Joint Family in India: An Analysis', *Sociological Bulletin*, Volume V, Number 2.

—, 1964, *Some Aspects of Family in Mahuva*, Asia Publishing House, Bombay.

—, 1964, *The Pattern of Migration and Occupation in a South Gujarat Village*, Deccan College Post Graduate and Research Institute, Poona.

Durant, Will, 1953, *The Story of Civilisation*, Simon and Schuster, New York.

Forde Daryll, C., 1934, *Habitat, Economy and Society*, Methuen, London.

Gadgil, D.R. and Sovani, N.V., 1952, *Poona: A Socio-Economic Survey*, Gokhale Institute of Politics and Economics, Poona.

Giddings, F.H., 1896, *Principles of Sociology*, MacMillan, New York.

Ginsberg, M., 1932, *Studies in Sociology*, Mercury, London.

—, 1934, *Sociology*, Oxford University Press, London.

Haddon, Alfred C., 1949, *History of Anthropology*, Watts, London.

Hobhouse, L.T., 1906, *Morals in Evolution: A Study in Comparative Ethics*, Champman and Hall, London.

—, 1924, *Social Development*, George Allen and Unwin, London.

Hobhouse, L.T., Wheeler G.C. and Ginsberg, M., 1915, *The Material Culture and Social Institution of the Simpler Peoples*, Routledge and Kegan Paul, London.

Keller, A.G., 1915, *Societal Evolution*, Yale University Press, New Haven.

Lichtenberger, James P., 1923, *Development of Social Theory*, Century, New York.

Lowie, Robert H., 1937, *The History of Ethnological Theory*, Halt, Rinehart and Winston, New York.

Lynd, Robert and Lynd H., 1929, *Middletown*, Harcourt and Brace, New York.

MacIver, R.M., and Page, C.H., 1950, *Society*, MacMillan, London.

Merton, Robert K., 1948, *Social Theory and Social Structure*, The Free Press, Glencoe.

Mukherjee, Ramkrishna, 1972, 'On the Mode of Social Research', *The Indian Journal of Sociology*, Volume III, Numbers 1 and 2.

North, C.C., 1926, *Social Differentiation*, Oxford University Press, London.

Pandit, D.P., 1965, *Earnings One's Livelihood in Mahuva*, Asia, Bombay.

Parsons, Talcott, 1947, *The Structure of Social Action, The Free Press*, Glencoe.

Parsons, Talcott and Shils, Edward A., 1962, *Towards a General Theory of Action*, Harper, New York.

Prichard, Evans, 1956, *Social Anthropology*, Cohen and West, London.

Rice, Stuart, 1931, *Methods in Social Research*, University of Chicago Press, Chicago.

Russell, Bertrand, 1929, *Marriage and Morals*, George Allen and Unwin, London.

Singh, Yogendra, 1973, 'The Role of Social Sciences in India', *Sociological Bulletin*, Volume 22, Number 1.

Srinivas, M.N., 1955, *India's Villages*, Asia, Bombay.

— (Ed.) 1958, *Methods in Social Anthropology: Selected Essays by Radcliffe-Brown*, The University of Chicago Press, Chicago.

Summer, W.G. and Keller, A.G., 1927, 'Folkways and Mores', *Science of Society*, Volume 1.

Thoothi, M.A., 1935, *Vaishnavas of Gujarat*, (Regional and Sociological Studies), Longman Green, London.

Unwin, J.D., 1935, *Sexual Regulations and Cultural Behaviour*.

Westermarch, Edward, 1891, *The History of Human Marriage*, London.

6

INDIAN SOCIOLOGY AT THE TURNING POINT

S.C. DUBE

During the last decade, there has been a visible unease within Indian sociology about its direction and purpose. Many of the cherished assumptions that informed and inspired the discipline now leave us cold and unconvinced, some of the coveted theoretical models and conceptual frames of reference have been the subject of doubt and debate, and the appropriateness of several of the extant methods of research, to comprehend the social reality of India and to unravel its complexity, is open to question. This represents the prevailing mood; it is not the cry only of the malcontent. The trend reflects neither morbid introspection nor pathological self-pity; it is a manifestation, in the main, of a healthy self-awareness and of the profession's desire and capacity to redefine its goals and set its course straight. Having reached the moment of truth, as it were, Indian sociology today is at a turning point; it is all set to break loose from the colonial bonds that set limits to its range, constricted its vision, and blunted its purpose.

This, I think, is an occasion for the celebration of awareness. It would be self-defeating to let it turn into an orgy of iconoclastic vandalism: denial of the academic heritage, denigration of intellectual progenitors, and showering of invectives at peers and contemporaries would only worsen the confusion. This is no time also for sulking over social events overtaking the social sciences, for shedding tears over an 'ungrateful' new generation dissenting from, doubting, and even denying the assumptions and formulations of its predecessors, or for burying ostrich-like our heads in the shimmering sands of scholarly creations refusing to accept that anything has

Presidential address delivered at the Indian Sociological Conference, Chandigarh on 26th December, 1976.

changed. A critical awareness of the Indian sociological tradition is essential for an appreciation of its growth points and also for the identification of weaknesses that have led to a blurring of objectives and misdirection of endeavour. In retrospect, we also have to examine why the response of Indian sociology to the travail and trauma of independence was so feeble and why its efforts to deal with the ferment and convulsions characterizing the post-independence decade were so half-hearted. To restore purpose to our scholarly activity and to make Indian sociology more sensitive and responsive to changing social needs, such an exercise in the form of a wide-ranging debate is necessary.

India has an old and established tradition of reflection and writing on man and society. Some of the ancient Indian classics represent high intellectual achievement in the realms of social philosophy and normative social thought. Some stereotypes have persisted about Indian contributions of this period. First, it is believed that this thought was deeply rooted in metaphysics and ethics, and was far removed from social reality. Secondly, there is an implicit assumption that the ethos of the age allowed little or no scope for development of an empirical tradition in respect of knowledge relating to man and society. Thirdly, the ascription of inviolabe sanctity to the ancient texts, it is assumed, inhibited the growth of independent thought in later periods. These stereotypes, at best, represent only partial truth; they do emphasize certain central tendencies but underplay other currents which were by no means feeble and inconsequential.

Though the ancient texts – the *shastras* and the *smritis* – stand out for their philosophic content and metaphysical heights, it would be incorrect to assert that they concerned themselves exclusively with eternal verities and neglected the existential reality of the time. Even Manu's *Dharmashastra* was no a utopia – an outline of an idealized normative order rooted in a system of philosophy and having no organic links with the institutions and norms of society. This work abstracted and schematized from a wide range of elements in the prevailing social system. The assumptions and principles underlying even the concept of *dharma* related to *kala* (time), *desa* (place/country), and *patra* (person/social category). Several dimensions of the social reality, thus, were central even to the understanding and explication of *dharma*. To comprehend *dharma* it was not enough only to know its philosophy; its empirical referents were also crucial for its true understanding. It is often forgotten that the pattern of ancient social thought was wide; besides *dharmashastras*, it also produced *arthashastras* and *kamashastras*. These works undeniably had metaphysical and ethical undertones, but at the same time they had an integral vision of life which did not discount social reality.

Nor is it wholly true that the empirical tradition was absent or discouraged. In Kautilaya's *Arthashastra* (324–296 B.C.), the king was strongly advised to ensure collection of all possible information, about different parts of the country and different segments of its population, in the interest of efficient administration and successful implementation of state policies. Charak's masterpiece on the art and science of healing, dating back to the eighth century B.C., takes account of the social and cultural foundations of the practice of medicine. This work is based on carefully and painstakingly gathered empirical data. He advised other healers not to lose sight of the values, norms, and customs of the people to whom they sought to offer relief.

Although the concern for understanding the Ultimate Reality was dominant and other-worldliness characterized a great deal of early Indian social thought, contrary views were also articulated. The Lokayat philosophers were frankly skeptical about the established (and prevailing) modes of thought and the wisdom they contained. They questioned the understanding of the Ultimate Reality and the goals of life derived from it. They were unmistakably materialistic in their approach. Traces of such skepticism are noticeable in Upanishadic literature of the sixth century B.C., although the earliest propagators of materialistic philosophy and skepticism first openly voiced their opinions in the seventh and eighth centuries B.C. Ajit Kesamkambalan, a contemporary of Buddha, is credited with being the first among the philosophers to preach complete materialism. Elements of materialism persisted in Indian thought and anti-religious philosophical texts continued to be produced.

All this, of course, was not sociology as we understand the discipline today, but it did represent the emergence of an intellectual tradition in which social philosophy was linked with social reality, the need for understanding cultural norms and social institutions was emphasized, and freedom of enquiry was vigorously asserted at least by a minority.

More solid empirical foundations for an understanding of Indian society were provided by a number of travellers and chroniclers who observed Indian life closely and wrote about it at fair length. Their records cannot be dismissed as travellers' tales; they examine the institutional framework of society and portray the manners and customs of the time. The ambassador of a Greek king, Megasthenes, who spent many years at the court of Chandragupta Maurya (324–300 B.C.) and wrote about Indian society was in a sense a precursor of the empirical traditional which was to gain strength later. He described the seven classes in which Indian society was divided and made many interesting comments on Indian beliefs and practices. Three Chinese travellers – Fa-hsien (A.D. 400–11), Yuan Chwang (A.D. 629–44), and I-Tsing (A.D. 671–95) – have described the conditions of life in meticulous detail. Examined in chronological order, their works present some valuable perspectives on change in Indian society. A number of Arab scholars also visited India and have left behind records based on acute observation. Al-Biruni, a gifted scholar with many talents, wrote knowledgeably about Indian social and cultural life. His work on India, completed around A.D. 1030, shows his close familiarity with Indian systems of thought as well as with the religion, sciences, and customs and manners of the Hindus. His comments on the ethnocentric predicament of the Hindus are perceptive. There is little doubt that his approach was sociological. Ibn Batuta, an Arab traveller from Morocco, came to India in A.D. 1333 and lived here until 1347. The narrative left by him contains valuable information on the geography of the land, on social and cultural conditions, and on the daily life of the people. For South India we get useful information in the chronicles of Marco Polo who visited this part of the country around A.D. 1293 and in Farishtah who completed his work in A.D. 1609. The narratives of these travellers are classified today as history, but when they were written they merited being rated as sociography. These chroniclers were not writing about the past, nor were they using documents and records as sources. They were observing life and recording what they saw and heard. Bernier, a French traveller, has left a vivid and minute description of the customs, manners, and cultural and social life in the country during the reign of Shahjahan and Aurangzeb. He even addressed himself to the important sociological question pertaining to the causes of the retardation of Indian society. He was anxious to find out why it had failed to keep pace with the West. Several natives of India, either by birth or by adoption, also had a close look at the society in their time and recorded their observations. The most outstanding among them was Abul Fazl who wrote about Akbar and his times and provided substantial factual information about society in Akbar's empire. He was an empiricist par excellence and covered the widest spectrum of society, not excluding even the remote Ahoms and the inaccessible Gonds. The writers of this genre were not sociologists and social anthropologists in the modern sense, nonetheless their work marks a shift from social philosophy to detailed observation of social life. They were keen observers of the social scene, often also perceptive social analysts. In a rudimentary form they produced the stuff out of which sociology and social anthropology are made.

The impact of the West created a ferment and Indian intellectuals reacted to it in several diverse ways. A happy consequence of it was the growth of social science activity in the sub-continent. The Asiatic Society of Bengal was founded in 1784. Sir William Jones, the moving spirit behind this society, regarded history, science, and art as the trinity of human knowledge. The society held weekly meetings at which original papers were presented and discussed. Men of learning contributed papers for publication in the *Asiatick Miscellany* which was brought out once a year. The society encouraged work in the fields of history and anthropology and its activities generally covered a wide range of social institutions and problems. In 1828, the Academic Association was started in Calcutta under the inspiration of Henry Derozio. Among its members were a number of distinguished Indians of the time. Notable among them were Pyari Chand Mitra, Dakshina Ranjan Mukherjee, and Rev. K.M. Banerjee. Although it was a debating club, besides discussing literary and philosophical questions it also took up social problems for study and discussion. The active but short-lived Society for the Acquisition of General Knowledge, which came into existence in 1838, deserves note. Besides literature and philosophy its activities covered history, geography, language, and social conditions also. Its transactions included themes like prostitution, the Hindu widow, and female education. Unfortunately, it ceased to exist in 1843. Another important society of the time, also in Calcutta, was the Tattwa Bodhini Sabha. Established in 1839, it discussed social conditions and problems and questioned some of the established customs and institutions. Rammohan Roy (1777–1833) was a great social thinker and reformer. His writings had considerable sociological content. His views on religion, caste, position of women, and rural society anticipated some of the major concerns that were to characterize Indian sociology later. Other notable social thinkers and reformers of the time were Akshay Kumar Dutta (1820–86), Ishwar Chandra Vidyasagar (1820–41), and Pyari Chand Mitra (1840–83). They were all contemplating the social reality of their time and their writings were informed by intimate knowledge of the prevailing conditions. Such activities were not confined to Bengal alone. There were active associations in Bombay, Madras, and other cities also. As early as 1820 a comprehensive empirical survey of a small town – Lon – was presented before the Literary Society of Bombay. It was published in the *Transactions of the Literary Society of Bombay* (1823) and presented information on demographic structure, institutions, hereditary castes, cultivators, food, religion, and other aspects of the life of the town. A comparable statistical survey of the 'Pergunnah of Jumboosur' was also published in the same volume. The *Madras Journal of Literature and Science*, which appeared in 1935, published historical and ethnographic studies and also surveys of cities and villages. The Bethune Society, established in 1851, contributed significantly to social science studies. Its activities covered general education, literature and philosophy, science and art, medical and sanitary improvement, sociology, and female education. It may be noted that a section on sociology was formed in the society in 1859, in recognition of the subject's elevation to the rank of a 'science' and of the fact that it was 'replete with practical benefits to man'. It was in this society that in 1861 Rev. James Long presented his paper comprising '500 questions on the subjects requiring investigation in the social condition of the natives'. A wide variety of papers on different aspects of the social situation were presented and discussed at the meeting of this society. There is evidence of comparable associations functioning elsewhere also. The Benares Institute, founded in 1861 and reorganized in 1864, was popular and active. Its section on 'social progress' attracted important papers on ethnography and social problems. The Oudh Scientific Society of Lucknow was also concerned with social problems. In 1867, a paper on 'Sociology for India' was presented before it by Syed Shurrafoodin. A Society for Sociological Studies was established in Jaipur in 1869. The most notable among the institutions concerned with the social sciences was the Bengal Social Science Association (1867–78). The objective of the association was 'to collect, arrange and classify series of facts bearing upon the social, moral and intellectual conditions of the people of Bengal and by such means to assist in the promotion of measures for the good of the country'. Its programmes were to be practical and scientific and it was to dedicate itself to the promotion of the development of social science in the presidency of Bengal. The principal departments of the association were jurisprudence and law, education, public health, and economy and trade. Indians formed an important part of the members of the association's council. Through questionnaires it collected a great deal of empirical data. The papers presented at its meetings also represented an effort to systematize and analyze facts about Bengal and India.

A close scrutiny of the sociological papers and documents prepared during this period and presented to voluntary associations dedicated to the cultivation of the social sciences reveals many interesting trends. A small section of those involved in this activity were completely overwhelmed by the West; a few, on the contrary, were drawn to the traditional heritage. But nearly all recognized the necessity and desirability of understanding the social situation. The question with many was neither of uncritical acceptance nor of blind rejection of attributes and elements of the West, it was one of comprehending the social situation prior to doing something about it. Systematically gathered facts were considered to be of paramount importance and at the heart of this research activity was a deep social concern. The society had to be reformed and energized.

For purposes of administration also a great deal of information on the social and cultural conditions was needed. Much of this was collected by civil servants. The data gathered by semi-literate lower level officials could not have been very accurate, but this was considered adequate. The pace of administration being slow, some of the higher civil servants found themselves with ample leisure to indulge in scholarship as a hobby. Their chosen fields were anthropology, sociology, linguistics, and archaeology. With official support some interested civil servants assembled the monumental tribes and castes volumes for different provinces of India. It goes to their credit that a number of them produced outstanding monographs on individual tribes and castes. In addition, there were two official organizations for collecting social science data, the more important of which was the Census of India. Although the census operations were of an *ad hoc* nature and their technical quality was much less sophisticated than it is now, they set a tradition for collection of useful social data. The other organization was the Ethnographic Survey of India which came into being in 1901. Its activities lacked a focus; nor were its methods of investigation above reproach. But it did nevertheless assemble a mass of crude data. Official sociology and social anthropology of the early period left its impress on the development of these subjects as academic disciplines. In fact, even to this day they have not been able to shake off this legacy totally.

In 1857, the first three universities were set up in the presidency capitals. The first department of anthropology was established in 1920 in Calcutta University. With a grant from the Government of India, the Bombay University started some courses in sociology and social sciences in 1914; a department of sociology and civics was established in 1919. In 1924, Bombay initiated a full master's level course in sociology. A doctoral programme was started in 1936 and the first PhD degree in sociology was awarded in 1938. Despite the early start in two leading university centres, the acceptance of sociology and social anthropology in the academic system of India was slow. In most other centres they were first linked to economics, philosophy, history, or political science and had to strive hard to attain for themselves an independent and autonomous status. The courses drew heavily from the British system. Though in a limited measure, they provided also for teaching of Indian social thought. Few universities had adequate funds for research, but operating even on shoe-string budgets some of them produced work of impressive quality. The scholarship of this period is not characterized by an excessive concern either for theory or for method. It had a rich data base and presented some significant analyses.

Within the university system and outside, the social sciences gained respectability after independence. There were sizeable additions to the workforce of sociologists and social anthropologists. Funds for research were made available on an unprecedented scale. Trained manpower in sociology and social anthropology grew in size and the volume of publications in these fields increased enormously. This was a welcome development but it was not without its problems. A critical look at this activity is needed to assess its direction, purpose, and utility.

Post-independence sociology in India bears the impress of three major styles. The strongest of these approximates closely to the traditions of empirical research as they developed in the West and were currently being practised there. The American and the British models made a powerful impact and sociology as well as socio-cultural anthropology endeavoured to adopt their conceptual frameworks and modes of enquiry. Objectivity and value neutrality were emphasized. From wider social concerns the focus of the disciplines was narrowed to specific but limited questions of theory and method. Scienticism prevailed as the dominant mode for sometime. In the process, conceptual precision and methodological rigour were introduced into the disciplines. In the best of Indian work, developments parallel to those of the better works in the United Kingdom and the United States were in evidence. This trend, however, had some negative and non-functional aspects, to which we shall turn in a moment.

The second trend, represented by a small group, shows keen awareness of the Indianness of the situation – a fact which apparently calls for skills and insights not available in existing sociology. This group felt that the ethos and special cultural contexts of India necessitated a conceptual and methodological apparatus different from the one which was accepted as international. Regrettably those belonging to this group never articulated themselves with much clarity and precision; while they expressed with some vigour the need of a different approach to the understanding of Indian society, they never proceeded to demonstrate convincingly what the approach might be and how it could be applied in actual practice. Thus, all we have from them is a series of personal statements regarding the inadequacy of western paradigms and of the need for an alternative approach. No solid work is available to test the strength of the alternative model. The late D.P. Mukherjee's sane ideas regarding the study of tradition were not pursued with resolve and dedication. Time and again it was reiterated by some of the exponents of this school that the concepts of *dharma, karma, moksha*, and rebirth make a difference to Indian society, but how these doctrines alter the operation of the institutions and processes of society was never convincingly demonstrated in a major work. Alongside, by gimmicks of logic, efforts were made to prove the impossibility of sociology. Many of these arguments have been repeated for over two decades in seminars and conferences, but they have made little impact on the discipline as a whole. It is indeed curious that the larger works of representatives of this school conform to the western empirical tradition and do not reflect the position taken up by them in their theoretical argument regarding the nature of Indian society and an alternative approach to it. The deficiencies of this approach notwithstanding, it should be credited with the limited achievement of having focused attention on some of the limitations of empiricism and of bringing home to Indian sociology the importance of native categories of thought that get distorted in the efforts to fit them into an accepted international framework. This school also suggested rethinking the relationship of sociology with indology and history.

The third style is reflected in radical criticism of the structure of society as well as of the approaches to studying and analyzing it. This was inspired partly by the rediscovery of Marxism in western sociology and partly by the disaffection of the younger intellectuals with the over-scientific and consequently dehumanized tone of much of contemporary sociology. Criticism from this point of view has generated some serious rethinking. Relationships of production and the class bases of social relations are being recognized as legitimate fields of enquiry, and in consequence the importance of ritual considerations and caste is being underplayed. But even this approach has not registered a major thrust. A doctrinaire and somewhat scriptural acceptance of Marxism has limited its power to penetrate and probe into the inner workings of society. Beyond creating a critical awareness, this style of sociology has as yet not much to show for itself. Its dynamic potential remains to be realized.

The expression of dissatisfaction about the content and direction of sociology in India is timely and understandable. It augurs well for the future of the discipline. It has brought us to the turning point leading to a more relevant and meaningful sociology – a science imbued with social concerns, a discipline with a human meaning and purpose.

Even after three decades of independence, both teaching and research in sociology continue to be cast in the colonial mould. It is incredible but true that the sociologists in India did not react to the advent of freedom in any significant manner. In fact, they began imitating the western pattern under the guise of cultivating 'international science' without any sense of guilt or even qualms of conscience. In this they showed unmistakable symptoms of what S.H. Alatas, the distinguished Malaysian sociologist, calls the 'captive mind'. Ours was (and to an extent continues to be) largely a sociology of borrowed concepts and methods. High prestige centres of learning in the affluent West, especially in the United Kingdom and the United States, determined the kind of sociology that should be taught and the type of problems that should be researched. Foreign models and techniques were accepted uncritically without assessing their relevance or suitability to Indian conditions. This led to distortions in the perspectives of Indian sociology and also to its stunted growth.

The implantation on Indian data of categories of analysis successfully employed elsewhere has led to some avoidable confusion. The notion of 'tribe' in India, detached from the larger civilizational context, has acquired a meaning that is not warranted by the social reality. There is a great deal of uncertainty about different categories and types of domestic groups. Caste and sub-caste do not necessarily subsume *varna* and *jati*. *Gotra* is often erroneously used in reference to the Hindu social system; it is not clan. In fact, the model of the Indian social system as visualized by western observers is in some ways also a distortion of the reality. It is not as uniform and immobile as it had been made out. Caste, for example, is not a fixed and permanent category. Ritual criteria significantly enter into determination of rank and status, but at the same time economic and political determinants cannot be discounted. It would be naive in the extreme to assume that affluence and poverty make no difference to the social position of a caste. Because of the oppressive influence of foreign models native categories of thought have had to undergo transfers of meaning and in the process they now represent something which is far removed from their original intent.

Imitation has had some other injurious side-effects also. Priorities of research have often been determined in reference to the kind of work that enjoys popularity and prestige elsewhere rather than in terms of what the country needs. Indeed a significant part of our work was addressed not to the people or even professional colleagues in India but to peers and mentors abroad. Most of this work was done in a foreign language with which a bare two per cent of our population had any familiarity. The audience for work of the so-called international standard was confined to a few hundred academics in less than half a dozen English-speaking countries. Some other habits of mind were also uncritically picked up. Disciplinary boundaries were hardened and battles were passionately fought about autonomous domains of sovereign disciplines. Consider the meaningless quarrel over the respective spheres and importance of sociology and social anthropology in India. Consider also the deliberate severance of connection between sociology and social anthropology on the one hand and history and indology on the other. How much more meaningful the notions of sanskritization and dominant caste would have been, had they had historical specificity and depth? Consider also the artificial distinction made between 'pure' and 'applied' research, the former enjoying unquestionable superiority. Through a series of logical acrobatics, tortuous statistical procedures, and mystifying model building we appear to arrive at convoluted generalizations that often turn out to be statements of the obvious, their pseudo-profound terminology notwithstanding. What are left unattended are problems whose solution can be helped measurably by meaningful sociological inputs. The mask of 'profound' scholarship often hides puerile and vacuous ideas, it only offers terminological satisfaction with no operational guidelines.

The discipline finds itself in this tragic situation because it has opted to function within a framework of dependency, as a satellite system rather than an autonomous one. Happily this phase is passing. A new awareness is restoring purpose to sociology.

To realize its potential and make a genuine contribution to the solution of pressing national problems, Indian sociology will have to contemplate a series of imaginative steps – cleansing of thought-ways and work-ways of the colonial virus, bringing back the focus on major social concerns, ensuring disciplinary growth, encouraging interdisciplinary dialogue and collaboration, increasing the credibility of the discipline, and developing strategies for the effective utilization of sociological research.

The colonial virus, although it generated some false euphoria, has greatly debilitated Indian sociology by sapping its creativity. It is time we stop chasing the mirage of high prestige models and avoid the quicksands of pseudo-intellection. It is evident that we have consciously cultivated only a few styles of sociology and invested far too much effort in the pursuit of the trite and the trivial. In planning instructional programmes and in determining priorities of research it is essential that we hear our own voice and be guided by our national needs. Of course, it is *not* being suggested that we close ourselves to powerful currents of thought emanating from outside for that would be a fatal error. If uncritical acceptance of western sociology was wrong, its uncritical rejection would be equally wrong. But such exposure should not be weighted in favour of only a few approaches; we should draw from the widest spectrum of experience and thought. There is a great deal in the experience of the socialist countries and the Third World that has meaning and significance for us: this experience needs to be analyzed and evaluated. In doing so we have to bear in mind that recipes for contemporary Indian problems do not exist anywhere else, they must be derived from our own creative response.

Our sociology will have to address itself to the living concerns of today and tomorrow. For this we shall have to identify critical problems, pose the right questions, and devise appropriate procedures of investigation in respect of them. Research and reflection will have to go together. Unless this is done we shall not be able to contribute meaningfully towards resolving the many dilemmas of development. Let us invest more research effort and thought into such areas as indicators of social development, content of quality of life, problems and processes of the toughening of a 'soft state', and the interface between freedom, equality, and social justice. In respect of the future a return to the tradition of normative thinking and a new approach to social philosophy is indicated.

To be able to carry out a mission of this magnitude, the disciplinary growth of Indian sociology will have to be ensured, both in respect of theory and method. Simultaneously, interdisciplinary dialogue and collaboration will have to be encouraged. One cannot legislate for such developments; they require building up opinion, selective support, a reward system for innovation, and understanding and tolerance for failures.

Indian sociology has yet to establish its credibility with the people and the policy makers. To this end it should work towards enlarging the consciousness of the people at large and also towards sharpening the problem-solving capability of the policy makers with sociological insights. An adequate strategy for the effective utilization of sociological inputs remains to be devised. These problems require cool and collected thinking.

India is passing through a difficult phase. Appeals of populism and calls to action often discount the role of the academic and the intellectual. But this precisely is the time when he is needed most. Action without reflection can lead the country into a blind alley. This is one danger which must be avoided at all costs. To intervene meaningfully in this baffling situation the sociologist will have to shed his narcissism and misdirected quests. He will have to relate himself directly to the people and their problems. Intellectual elitism in the situation is bound to be counter-productive; permanent dissent and constant anger will lead us nowhere. Without discarding the function of the critic of social trends and policies, we shall have to assume a more direct role in the challenging task of national reconstruction. Our best contribution evidently can only be our analytic insights. Towards this end we shall have to activate the entire profession. If we let events overtake us there is a danger of our being left behind. But if the present ferment within the profession is a true indication of our mood, we are poised for a change in the right direction. We have the manpower and the resources, and now we are also gathering the will to take up the task with seriousness and commitment. Posterity will judge us by the degree to which we respond creatively to the challenges of contemporary social reality.

7

REFLECTIONS ON SOCIAL SCIENCE RESEARCH IN INDIA

P.C. JOSHI

This paper presents reflections on certain issues pertaining to social science research in India with illustrations mainly from sociology. Thoughts expressed in this paper should be treated as strictly tentative and exploratory in character since the purpose of the paper is to provoke further thinking and discussion on issues raised here. For this purpose the author has drawn upon his own experiences ranging over a period of about twenty-five years in four eminent centres of social science research in India. It should also be stated that the main aim of this paper is to highlight the gaps and deficiencies of social science research in India rather than its achievements. A certain one-sidedness which may be found in this paper is, therefore, deliberate. The author feels that gaps and deficiencies can be overcome only when they are brought to light in a sharp way. And Indian social science is entering a phase of maturity when it can overcome them.

CONTEXT FOR SOCIAL SCIENCE IN INDIA

The development of social sciences in India has to be viewed and appraised as a response (or lack of response) to challenges confronting Indian society since independence. The challenge of planned national development and social transformation provided a new context for social science after India's independence. The Indian

Thanks are due to many scholars with whom I have discussed issues raised in this paper in the course of informal Discussions, specially to Prof. Andre Beteille and Prof. C.H. Hanumantha Rao. Repeated references to D.P. Mukerji have been made in this paper because he is one of the very few who made a heroic struggle to evolve an *Indian* perspective in social science.

national leadership put forward before the Indian people the perspective of development and transformation within a democratic framework and with maximum regard for social equality and mass welfare. Few would disagree that this was an ambitious perspective without precedent in world history. In the conception of leaders like Jawaharlal Nehru, the realization of such a perspective was not possible without total commitment to the scientific approach. With his unerring sense of history Nehru understood the process of change in India after independence in terms of the Great Transition from a traditional to the modern age. In the West this historic transition was associated with the break from traditionalism (Durkheim, 1960) and, consequently, with the emergence of the scientific spirit. In countries suffering from arrested development, this transition calls for a far greater utilization of the revolutionary potential of science including social science. *This is because development in the case of the latecomers is a process of conscious planning rather than of unconscious adaptation to elemental forces released in the course of a break-up of the old order and the emergence of a new order.* The institutionalization of scientific activity has assumed a new significance and received a tremendous impetus in this background.

It should be noted that this social context of underdeveloped countries like India exercises a contradictory influence on the growth of social science. On the one hand, the breakdown of the colonial system and the emergence of national-revolutionary political forces require the continuation of an anti-colonial and anti-feudal revolution to the intellectual and cultural plane. On the other hand, the exposure of the national intelligentsia of the underdeveloped countries like India to international influences after independence has meant exposure essentially to western influences. Indeed, internationalization of social science and its professionalization is still based primarily on western dominance (Pieris, 1969: 433–45). To challenge western cultural and intellectual dominance is, therefore, far more difficult and exacting than it was to challenge western dominance on the political plane.

What appears as intellectual dominance of western world from one point of view should also be seen as lack of adequate intellectual independence among the social scientists of the underdeveloped world. Certain adverse consequences of this lack of intellectual independence in the field of social science research are specially noteworthy. Firstly, a distinction is not always drawn between the scientific method on the one hand and the western conceptual and theoretical structures on the other. Questioning of these inherited structures on the basis of the scientific method and in the light of the conditions and requirements of the underdeveloped countries is still not very common in India. This has often resulted in tendencies of mechanical imitation than in bold attempts at innovations of new approaches, concepts, theories and research methodologies. Secondly, social scientists are often grappling with such problems as are considered important in the western world and not with issues agitating one's own national community. This inadequate responsiveness to the challenges of one's own society is at the root of insufficient release of the creative spirit among the social scientists in India. The identification with these challenges would have facilitated independent growth of social sciences as it did to some extent during the period of the nationalist struggle for independence.

The consequences of these tendencies of imitation rather than independence, alienation from rather than identification with social challenges, have been quite pronounced. In many parts of the underdeveloped world like Latin America of Africa, sociology and social anthropology have been a vehicle of national resurgence and social awakening. In contrast, Indian sociologists and social anthropologists have, with few exceptions, not yet made a decisive break from colonial and semi-feudal perspectives. These obscurantist and backward-looking perspectives have resulted in the general neglect of dynamic processes at the macro-level and the preoccupation with micro-situations within a framework of statics. As a result the forward movement and dynamism of Indian society or the conflict between the old and the new society after colonial rule have been underplayed and certain retrogressive tendencies (e.g., casteism and sanskritization) have emerged as the main tendencies of Indian society. With few exceptions, most sociological and social anthropological studies continue to project India as a land dominated by religion, joint family, caste and the village. Even these problem areas are treated not from a dynamic perspective but in a static setting. For instance, religion is studied without reference to the growing differentiation within religion between the religion of the priesthood and the religion of the reformer. The distinction between the religion of the upper castes and that of the peasant castes has also been seldom explored in depth. Caste is studied without reference to the contradictory tendencies within the caste system as represented by the forward-looking casteism of the low castes and the backward-looking casteism of the upper castes. Further, caste and religion are often studied as ideological systems without reference to the impact of economic, political and technological forces. Thus, even when the regional variations of caste system are conceded, the concept of variation does not become meaningful without reference to the variations in its techno-economic or political basis.

The gravest weakness of sociological and social anthropological approach to the study of social institutions is that it detaches the enquiry into *specific* features of the institutions of a particular country from an enquiry into the *general* processes of social change common to many countries. Thus, the emphasis on the specificity of caste can lead to recognizing caste as a variant of social inequality and subject to inequality reducing influences of modern forces like education, industrialization, secularization, etc. It can also lead to overplaying the uniqueness of caste, its immunity from the equality-promoting impact of modern forces and, therefore, from the general processes of modernization. The separation of the study of social institutions from an enquiry into their techno-economic bases facilities the commitment to a perspective of *exceptionalism*. The lack of development of economic anthropology and the separation of anthropology from history have contributed to the conservative and anti-developmental tendencies which have become characteristic of the mainstream of Indian sociology and social anthropology.

The above tendencies have also become strengthened because of a separation of the micro-studies from the macro-perspective. Certain major forces influencing the dynamics of Indian society at the macro-level have not yet received adequate attention from sociologists and social anthropologists. Thus, nationalism, peasant movements and revolts, the emergence of new forces like the working class, the intelligentsia, the middle classes and the *bourgeoisie*, the disintegration of the classes based on pre-capitalist modes of exploitation, the changing character and role of the towns and of rural-urban interaction since independence, the emergence of regional social patterns within the national framework, the breakdown of fatalism and the emergence of a new activist consciousness and of new ideologies, the emergence of a new nation-state with new sanctions and instruments of authority, the impact on India of the world socialist system and of a resilient Third World – in brief, *the processes of the emergence of a new India through social conflicts, and movements and through the release of creative energies of the Indian people after independence – have not yet found an adequate reflection in the work of sociologists*. Nor has sociology played any significant role in the creation of a new worldview or consciousness as outstanding sociologists like Comte, Marx, Weber, Durkheim, etc., did in the nineteenth century or as Luckacs, Sorokin, Wright Mills, Myrdal, Ossowski, etc., have done in the twentieth century. Or as Radhakamal Mukherjee, D.P. Mukerji, N.K. Bose, etc., did in India itself in the pre-independence period. Sociologists have not played a positive role of this type in India because they have not attempted a sharp questioning of colonialist and conservative assumptions about Indian society and its evolution and they have not identified themselves adequately with the new currents of India's resurgence after the end of foreign rule. They have not so far even evolved a language of the discipline which is their own.

Having taken note of the constraints on scientific development arising out of the uncritical acceptance of western approaches and out of lack of deep roots in the national social milieu, one should also take cognizance of the constraints for social science arising in recent years out of the division of one's own society into the haves and the have-nots. Questions were most often raised in social science from the standpoint of the haves rather than from that of the have-nots. The *critical* potentialities of social science have been undermined by the existence of class divisions and by the alienation of social scientists from the have-nots. Thus, the very scope of social science research and the course of its development have often been influenced in direct and indirect ways by a class society. The absence of literacy, education and enlightenment among the have-nots in the past had thwarted the development of a critical intelligentsia from among the have-nots. Further, the continuing use of English for scientific investigations and insufficient development of regional languages as medium of teaching and research continued to favour the growth of an intelligentsia alienated from the people. Owing to these factors, even the new intellectual elements emerging from amongst low castes have been rapidly absorbed into the old type of intellectual elite. These factors have decisively influenced the direction and scope of social science research in favour of the haves. Moreover, the have-nots in India may be illiterate but they have their own cultural traditions, though these are mostly unwritten and oral. A systematic exploration of these oral traditions has not formed an important part of the research programmes of most Indian universities and other academic centres.

It should be obvious from the above that the utilization of the potentialities of the social sciences for national development and social transformation cannot be a spontaneous or an autonomous process. It has to be a conscious process requiring social stimulus from outside social science, that is from the forces of national development and social transformation in the underdeveloped world.

Promoting social science research is therefore desirable and necessary if policies and programmes for it are formulated and implemented in response to the needs of social transformation and national development and if they are based on the initiative, support and sanction specially of the enlightened, critical and responsible sections of the scientific community itself.

There are formidable social structural and cultural barriers to the growth of social science in countries like India. There are, for instance, historical constraints, the most important being the weakness if not the absence of a tradition of scientific enquiry in India. India did not lack an intellectual or a cultural tradition. In fact, a highly sophisticated intelligentsia or *literati* existed and functioned in different phases of Indian history. But an *intellectual* tradition was one thing and a *scientific* tradition was quite another. A social environment affirming a critical and questioning attitude of mind is one of the essential requirements of scientific progress. In western countries the break-up of the medieval social order and the intellectual demands of industrialization created a favourable context for progress of natural and social sciences.

In India, the traditional social structure and culture did provide for development of thought and, also to some extent, for tolerance of dissent. But Indian thought perhaps was more metaphysical and idealistic than materialistic. It was more speculative than empirical. It did not raise searching questions leading to enquiry into regularities underlying the physical world and the social reality in such a pronounced way as to provide an autonomous basis for development of the sciences. Further, while the Indian elite was almost entirely divorced from the production system, the productive classes of artisans and peasants were divorced from culture and, therefore, incapable of throwing up an intelligentsia of their own. In other words, in India, neither the demands of a dynamic economy nor those of protest against the old order ever assumed such sweep and momentum as to serve as a stimulus for a scientific breakthrough. The anti-imperialist movement for the first time created such a stimulus. But the over-riding demands of the nationalist struggle diverted the scientific talent into the sphere of agitation for independence. This explains Bernal's famous statement that India's best scientific talent is to be found in the ranks of agitators for India's freedom. Further, nationalism also promoted contradictory tendencies of intellectual stimulation as well as anti-intellectualism. These reflected the existence within the national movement of an intelligentsia as well as of an illiterate peasantry. The latter are the strongholds of superstition and of fear of enlightenment. They provide an environment unfavourable to doubt and questioning so necessary for scientific advance.

D.P. Mukerji often drew attention to the contradictory tendencies of our national movement – its emancipating as well as constraining effect on social science. His favourite remark was that 'the intellectual problems of the national movement were taken care of by Gandhi's inner voice and those of the Left movement by the party line!'* He believed that such anti-intellectualism was bound to result in great harm and aberrations. One had to pay the price for ignoring the demands of reason. Considering the growth of mindlessness as a rising menace in the Indian context, D.P. Mukerji's observations appear to have a prophetic quality.

The existence of an illiterate and unenlightened peasantry continues to act as a brake on scientific advance. This is specially so when political forces of a reactionary nature are always trying to exploit their cultural backwardness and to resist any movement against it. To a large extent the excessive preoccupation with politics in India reflected an escape from the hard challenges of a cultural and intellectual renewal. Again, as D.P. Mukerji (1958: 190) put it, 'our politics has ruined our culture'. The danger of mindlessness of politics has become far greater after independence than before. In fact, the political elite of the post-independence period has yet to acquire deep cultural and intellectual moorings. It has, therefore, often tended to function more as a *mindless* than as a *thinking* elite. In this background growth of social science depends as much on development of scientific skills as on dissemination of respect for thought, for a scientific outlook and for a *questioning* attitude among the widest sections of the Indian society. The absence of an organized church in India does not mean that obstacles to the growth of a scientific attitude are non-existent. The strength of the forces of intellectual inertia, if not total mindlessness, in Indian society rules out the prospect of a spontaneous development of social science. Institutions and organizations have therefore to play an important role in promoting scientific growth and development. There is need in this background for a national policy for social science promotion in the country.

---

* D.P. Mukerji made this observation time and again in the course of his class lectures to us during 1947–49.

SOCIAL SCIENTIST: INVOLVED OR DETACHED

On the question of social policy for growth of science, one must take note of the view expressed by many that a social scientist should be socially detached rather than socially involved. Fundamentally speaking, there is no conflict between responsibility of social scientists to their society and their responsibility to social science itself. In fact, no genuine social science can emerge (or has ever emerged) if the social scientists are not responsive to the problems thrown up by their *own* society and *their* times. Those who believe that the rootedness of a social scientist in his country has no contribution to make to his quality as a social scientist are taking a very superficial view of what contributes to the making of good scientists. Social sympathies and concerns help scientific advance by leading social scientists towards enquiry into unexplored and neglected, meaningful and relevant, problem areas. No doubt, there is also the danger of social sympathy generating bias or partisanship. But not to have social sympathies has also its dangers. It may lead to the preoccupation with technical virtuosity at the expense of challenging social questions. Economics in India provides the best illustration both of sterility resulting from the pursuit of value-free economic science and of a spurt of creativity resulting from concern with problems of Indian economic development or eradication of poverty.

Social concerns help creativity if they lead to the choice of meaningful problems. They hinder creativity if they influence the enquiry or analysis of the problem in a pre-determined direction. In this background, it is much better, therefore, to be aware of the social forces which shape the development of science rather than be blindly influenced or overpowered by them. Social influence can be controlled not by remaining ignorant of social forces but by developing an awareness of these forces. Further, social science research would suffer only if social scientists of one type of ideological or value orientation are given stimulus or encouragement. If research from diverse ideological standpoints is encouraged and stimulated, the inadequacy and partiality of one standpoint would be corrected by confrontation with other standpoints.

There has not been enough study of the question of how social concerns of social scientists have influenced the development of social sciences in India since independence. To what extent this influence has been beneficial to the development of social science sand to what extent it has distorted its development? And how far academic freedom without social concerns has produced mainly technocrats or careerists or lightweights rather then genuine social scientists? These are relevant questions which need to be squarely asked and debated.

Contemporary India is full of challenging problems waiting to be tackled by social scientists. And yet they have failed even to perceive them, let alone tackle them, largely because of a lack of sympathy and interaction with the indigenous environment. They are prone to tackle problems which are raised by western, especially American and British, social scientists. They are indifferent to problems which are genuinely agitating their own national community. Myrdal made an immortal contribution to social science by writing a classic on the Negro problem called *The American Dilemma*. The problem of untouchability has yet to find a Myrdal who could undertake a study of this problem on the scale of Myrdal's classic.

Indian sociologists need to engage in some self-examination as to why their scientific attention has not been drawn to such crying problems of their society as the problems of national development, cultural renewal, social inequality and mass poverty. In the recent period, so many studies of caste have appeared but they do not add up to an insight into the inegalitarian social order comparable to Myrdal's *The American Dilemma* or *Asian Drama*. The themes of anti-colonial and anti-feudal revolutions in the Third World also do not figure prominently among subjects studied by social scientists in India. Those taking up these themes are often dubbed as propagandists and not recognized as scholars. Thus, A.R. Desai, one of the few Indians who took up the study of Indian nationalism, has been a target for unfair criticism by an outstanding French sociologist, it seems, for combining social analysis with a critical standpoint (Dumout, 1964).

In the above background if social forces and agencies impinge on professional social science and bring it closer to the study of burning social questions, they play a positive role in the development of social science.

It may be asked whether social involvement may not threaten the very independence of the social scientists. A deeper examination would show that the only guarantee of the independence of social science is the integrity, hard work and dedication of social scientists to science. What respect is accorded by society to science would depend on whether there are scholars who have devoted or have the ambition of devoting a lifetime of hard work to the study of meaningful problems. It should be the task of a vigilant community of social scientists to distinguish between the scholar and the *dilettante*.

It should not be overlooked that after independence there has been a tremendous expansion of academic opportunities in India. While earlier so few professorship, readerships and lecturerships were available, now the number of these posts has increased phenomenally without a corresponding increase in the number of qualified and competent persons. As a result, one of the basic maladies today is that many a *dilettante* passes for a scholar and many a dabbler passes for a professional. It is only by combining appreciation of merit with continuous criticism of deficiencies that one can contribute towards social science development. Centres of research in India, however, tend to oscillate between forming 'mutual admiration societies' and 'mutual denigration societies'. This does not permit either the healthy growth of institutions or individuals.

The question of quality assumes a lot of significance in this background. At the same time one must not allow an 'elitist' approach to the question of quality. There can be no going back to the good old days when the scientific community was a very restricted and closed group. The question of quality has to be resolved without restricting access from lower classes to the scientific community and without resisting innovation in methodology and approaches in response to the needs of the Indian situation. In the coming years conscious effort should be made to promote social scientists from the lower classes specially from the lower castes in the rural areas. It should at the same time be fully appreciated that promoting the growth of a class of intellectuals from the lower classes is not the same thing as promoting a class of political agitators and activists from them. The former is thousand times more difficult and also therefore more rewarding even for the realization of the fundamental social aims of political movement itself.

THE QUESTION OF SCIENTIFIC ETHOS

The concern for quality of social science is vitally linked to the development of what may be *called the development of scientific culture or ethos as distinguished from the development of scientific skills, even though the two are not unrelated*. Scientific culture should include the cultivation of values, attitudes, norms and methods appropriate to the growth of social science and also to the fulfilment of its humanist objectives.

Special emphasis on the development of a scientific culture is required today because of the threat to scientific values from commercialization and bureaucratization which are encroaching upon all spheres of life. In the pre-independence period, the temptations and allurements of a non-academic type did not exist on a large scale for academicians. It should be asked how far the pursuit of wealth or power is compatible with the demands of a life genuinely devoted to scientific pursuits. There exist today vast opportunities in the government sector or the private sector or in international agencies offering both money and influence and also creating the illusion of a scientific career. Experts thus are needed now on a vast scale in the service of political, administrative and business establishments. And a massive drain of talent from academic to non-academic fields is a serious problem confronting scientific institutions. Within the academic fields also the *lone scholar* today belongs to a vanishing tribe. What are taking his place are academic establishments. In fact, the old type of social scientist now constitutes a tribe which is fast being over-shadowed by a new tribe. The latter comprises smart and slick academic bosses and brokers of scientific research, controlling enormous funds and heading vast establishments of academic business. In their style of life and intellectual disposition they now approximate much less to the unworldly and absent-minded professor of olden times. They are now cast in the same mould as the wordly-wise, self-advertising and efficient bureaucrats or business executives occupied with disbursing money and patronage and throwing their weight about. Now academic values are fast getting eroded by bureaucratic and commercial values.

A serious discussion on this entire field of scientific values and institutionalization of research is, therefore, necessary. Some of the grave dangers emanating from the emergence of research empires are specially noteworthy. Pointed attention to these has been drawn by Stanislav Andreski in this recent book *Social Sciences as Sorcery* (1972). The most important tendencies associated with bureaucratic organization of research are growth of orthodoxy and conformism on the one hand and what Andreski characterizes as the 'law of lighter weights rising to the top' on the other. Andreski (1972: 190) remarks that concentration of control over research not only imposes orthodoxy but 'also alters the mechanisms of selection for positions of influence. This is because power and big money attract a special kind of man, seldom distinguished by a passion for the pursuit of truth. Even in physics and mathematics, where the threshold of acceptability demands real knowledge and intelligence, the increase in the scale of research has given prominence to the operator at the expense of the thinker'. Andreski further explains why the inferior rather than the superior minds tend to rise to the top under organized research. To quote: 'In the subjects concerned with human behaviour, where well-founded standards of excellence hardly exist, nothing debars selections for positions of power without the slightest regard for intellectual quality. Where the prizes are appetizing but the rules of the games are so vague that honest play can hardly be distinguished from cheating, it is not very likely that the idealists and the impractical seekers after truth will get to the top; and the larger the sums which come into question, the more ruthless is the scramble and the greater the chances that anti-intellectual manipulators will win it' (ibid.: 192). Andreski argues further that the availability of vast funds for social science research is not always a boon but often a liability. 'In physics or technology there are urgent problems which cannot be tackled without a vast outlay on expensive machinery, but there are no such thresholds in the social sciences, apart from the collection of demographic and economic statistics which requires a large organization. In other branches of the study of man in society we not only have the law of diminishing returns, but even a law of negative returns, whereby a large expenditure may produce less knowledge than a smaller one' (ibid.: 196).

Andreski's observations are borne out in ample measure by Indian experience in recent years. The availability of vast funds for social science research in India has not been an unmixed blessing. With research becoming a lucrative business patronized by non-academic agencies, a new category of managers of research has been multiplying faster than that of genuine research workers. When research was not a paying proposition, only those having a genuine interest in research were attracted towards it. Now the less genuine have tended to overwhelm the more genuine elements by sheer numbers. Further, when vast amounts of money were not available, a researcher had to be his own field workers and investigators. Today hired hands are engaged for field work resulting in sharp decline in the quality of field work and, therefore, of quality of research work. Srinivas (1962: 146–47) has drawn attention to the threat to social science posed by this 'new type of research structure'. He has even warned that '*under these conditions no work of distinction and originality is likely to emerge in the near future in social anthropology or in any other social science*' (ibid.).

Last but not the least, the intrusion of political and money power in the sphere of social science research results in proliferation of all kinds of research establishments not always for genuine fact-finding but often for lending support to vested interests within the private sector or the governmental structure. Sponsored research is thus very often research not in the service of truth but research open to extra-scientific pressures. They only guarantee against such vulgarization of scientific research and its adaptation to extra-scientific ends is the existence of a scientific community strictly observing and enforcing the rules of the scientific game.

Apart from commercialism and bureaucratization, ideological fanaticism is another factor which constitutes a serious obstacle to the growth of social science. Existing both in open and disguised forms, it is an evil legacy from cold war days. A phenomenon akin to fanaticism is also that of 'partisanship' which also became most pronounced during the cold war and as part of Stalinism in the communist movement. Fanaticism is not entirely alien to India's cultural tradition itself. As a mental aberration, it is thus characteristic not only of radical ideologies but also of conservative and traditionalist ideologies. In fact, the fanaticism of the traditionalists and the conservatives is perhaps more pervasive in India than the fanaticism of the progressives and the modernists.

Both types of fanaticism constitute a serious danger to growth of scientific culture and of social science in India. There is, however, an important difference in the two forms of fanaticism. The fanaticism of the traditionalists is easier to detect than the fanaticism of the modernists, since the irrationalism of the former assumes more naked forms. The latter are formally committed to a rationalist outlook but depart from it in various ways which are often subtle and cannot be easily identified as forms of irrationalism.

A distinction should, however, be drawn between having social and political ideas and convictions and being a fanatic and a partisan in regard to one's own ideas. A fanatic and partisan is not willing to submit his ideas and convictions to examination by others. Further, in the case of the fanatic and the partisan, the conclusions of the study are pre-determined, they do not emerge from the process of scientific investigation. Fanaticism and partisanship therefore negate the very spirit and vitiate the very style of scientific enquiry. They promote a theological rather than a critical approach to problems. Scientific debate in this way degenerates into a dialogue between the judge and the accused, between the priests and sinners.

The fanatics and the partisans are hostile to the battle of ideas and opinions without which there can be no progress of science. They substitute abuse in place of argument, assertion in place of investigation and rigidity in place of receptivity to new developments in reality. In the name of opposing departure from basic truths, fanaticism and partisanship in effect idealize intellectual inertia and conformism. They are satisfied with yesterday's answers to today's and tomorrow's problems. Wherever these tendencies are strong, the inevitable consequence has been stagnation of social science research. Tendencies of conformism have, therefore, been condemned in the strongest terms by creative thinkers all over the world. 'Doubt everything', was the basic maxim of Karl Marx who showed how to pursue revolutionary causes without sacrificing scientific objectivity. For Marx he alone deserved to be called an intellectual who had a 'free and fearless mind'. Mao once gave the slogan 'without investigation, no right to speak' as a corrective to the malady of dogmatism in Chinese intellectual circles. Gramsci (1971: 343) in a classic passage quoted below suggests that to engage in a scientific discussion means to give due weight to counterviews and even to incorporate the insights of one's adversary into ones own analytical structure:

> 'In the formulation of historico-critical problems it is wrong to conceive of scientific discussion as a process at law in which there is an accused and a public prosecutor whose professional duty is to demonstrate that the accused is guilty and has to be put out of circulation. In scientific discussion, since it is assumed that the purpose of discussion is the pursuit of truth and the progress of science, the person who shows himself most "advanced" is the one who takes up the point of view that his adversary may well be expressing a need which should be incorporated, if only as a subordinate aspect in his own construction. To understand and to evaluate realistically one's adversary's position and his reasons (and sometimes one's "adversary" is the whole of past thought) means precisely to be liberated from the prison of ideologies in the bad sense of the word – that of blind ideological fanaticism. It means taking up a point of view that is "critical", which for the purpose of scientific research is the only fertile one.'

What must be emphasized once again is that an atmosphere in which questioning of established ideas and opinions is discouraged or suppressed is not favourable to scientific discussion and to growth of social science. The tyranny of outmoded ideas is the worst tyranny and it becomes still worse if re-enforced by extra-scientific authority wielded by vested interests in the governmental or in party agencies or by the academic priesthood. Further, the very fear of being ridiculed or censured for departing from accepted truths or for committing mistakes often prevents many from vigorously pursuing their scientific enquiry to its logical conclusion. As Raymond Aron (1968: 88) has very aptly remarked: '...minds capable of facing the disapproval of their peers whether conservative or revolutionary are few in any society'. One must, therefore, recognize the importance of promoting a social climate favourable to the clash and contest of opinions and to the tolerance of dissent. It is also necessary to appreciate that the right to err is fundamental to scientific enquiry (Lange, 1970: 435) and that it may be 'necessary' to commit ten errors in order to arrive at one correct point.

POLITICS AND SOCIAL SCIENCE

The interaction of politics and social science also deserves special mention on account of its far-reaching implications for development of social science. It should be noted that there is no escape from the influence of politics on social science in the contemporary world. This influence operates both in subtle and naked ways. It has both beneficial and adverse effects on the growth of social science in the same country in different periods. One can refer to the countries of the socialist world including the Soviet Union and the East European countries. In these countries politics stimulated social science research in the earlier phase. But it led to the virtual stagnation and sterility of social science under the influence of Stalinism in the subsequent period (Lange, 1970). Even de-Stalinization has not entirely succeeded in neutralizing the disastrous impact of Stalinism on social science. In many countries of the Third World also the influence of politics on social science has been detrimental to the growth of social science. Even Marxism which was a product of the Enlightenment and introduced the scientific approach to the study of social phenomena has been denuded of its scientific potential in many countries (Joshi, 1974). How to maximize the beneficial and minimize the adverse effects of the politics on social science has in this background emerged as an important problem especially in many underdeveloped countries.

It can be suggested that politics has a stimulating effect on social science if it seeks a knowledge of the hidden aspects of the social system, that is, if it makes demands on social science in terms of the critique of the social system. Politics has a retarding effect on social science when it seeks mere rationalization of the existing social system. When that happens the influence of politics on social science is positively harmful to the growth of social science. Social science can be rescued from such a state of stagnation resulting from its identification with apologetics only by a massive shock which can be administered by critical social forces and socio-political processes. It can be said that the conditions favourable to revolt against Stalinism on the intellectual plane were created by new socio-political processes. The Twentieth Congress of the Communist Party of Soviet Union which initiated the revolt against Stalinism had a liberating impact on social science. Even though it did not go far enough in the direction of removing the constraints created by Stalinism, it set new forces in motion favourable to social science research. The growth of social science is thus linked up with the conflicts and tensions of socio-political transformation itself.

There is another kind of dampening effect on social science resulting not so much from the domination of politics by vested interests but from the very *style of politics*. There are two alternative ways of conducting a political battle which is essentially a battle of interests. In the first case those engaged in the battle of interests from both sides try to raise it from a merely polemical and journalistic to a theoretical and philosophical plane. The battle of interests is thereby transformed into a battle of ideas. In the second case, the participants in the battle are not able to raise it to a higher plane; the battle in this case is fought out only on a lower or non-theoretical plane. While in the first case politics draws upon social science to the fullest extent and raises the quality of political discussion to a scientific level, in the second case the reverse happens. The quality of scientific discussion is brought down to the level of ordinary political discussion. In the first case social science gains from interaction with politics; in the second case it is the loser from such an interaction. The distinction between science and non-science is eliminated.

Gramsci (1971: 432–33) has shown a brilliant insight into the consequences following the importation of the methods of political and military warfare into the scientific arena. Gramsci observes how the rules of the game which lead to victory in the political and military spheres do not ensure success when followed in the scientific sphere. In political and military affairs success is ensured by striking the enemy *at its weakest point*. In contrast success in the scientific sphere is ensured only when the 'enemy' is confronted *at its strongest point*. Thus, in the scientific sphere, one must take cudgels with the strongest and the best exponents of the 'enemy' point of view. In other words, the 'enemy' in scientific matters is not a person but a system of thought or ideas. Moreover, to confront the 'enemy' on the scientific plane is not merely to engage in the *negative* task of demolishing the intellectual edifice created by one's intellectual rival. Much more essential, though difficult, is the *positive* task of creating an alternative thought system and an alternative methodology which is superior to that contributed by one's 'enemy'. To quote Gramsci: '*A new science proves its efficiency and vitality when it demonstrates that it is capable of confronting the great champions of the tendencies opposed to it and when it either resolves by its own means the vital questions which they have posed or demonstrates, in peremptory fashion, that these questions are false problems'* (1971: 432–33; emphasis added).

Gramsci's formulation of rules of the game for scientific activity assumes great significance in so far as it comes not from an arm-chair academician hostile to politics but from an active political being who was conscious of the political significance of scientific activity.

In a nutshell, the interaction of politics and social science can either lead to their cross-fertilization or cross-sterilization. The significance of what happens in the sphere of politics to the sphere of social science is thus very great in many underdeveloped countries. This is because politics attracts some of the best minds who were (and are) capable of making an outstanding contribution to social science. They can however make this contribution only if conscious effort is made to invest politics with an intellectual content and significance. If this conscious attempt to *intellectualize* politics is not made, anti-intellectualism makes subtle inroads into the sphere of social science itself. Far from imparting a critical and intellectual tone to politics, social science itself becomes a force for rationalization of dominant trends in politics. What is worse, instead of providing illumination on urgent problems facing underdeveloped countries, social scientists themselves get fragmented into partisans and rationalizers of this or that political group, or of this or that political personality.

The interaction of politics and social science is one of the most challenging areas of research in underdeveloped countries.

INSTITUTION-BUILDING FOR SOCIAL SCIENCE RESEARCH

With the institutionalization of social science research and the emergence of centres of organized research, the question of institution-building has assumed great importance. It must be realized that the growth of knowledge is a cumulative and collective process; that peaks of individual excellence can seldom emerge without a tradition of scientific culture and of a viable institutional framework. The individual 'genius' in this sense is a collective product rather than entirely an accident. The 'genius' is like a flower or a fruit which grows in a healthy tree. It should be noted that in a dynamic and growing institution even third-raters can grow into second-raters and second-raters may succeed in becoming first-raters. If the institutional life declines, even first-raters deteriorate into second-raters and second-raters into third-raters. Institution-building, therefore, has to be taken as a creative challenge in the Indian context.

India's problems are in basic respects different from the problems of western societies. It would be futile, therefore, to try reproducing Cambridge, Oxford, London School of Economics, Harvard or MIT in the Indian environment. Whenever such attempt was made, one sometimes reproduced grotesque caricatures of these western institutional forms.

In the absence of scientific and democratic traditions, many academic institutions in India have either taken the shape of classical Hindu *mathas* or of *zamindaris*. These institutions resemble the former in their remoteness from the living problems of society, they also resemble the latter in so far as they represent private empires emerging not from academic impulses but from acquisitive and power drives. Moreover, the inner life of these institutions is often vitiated by an unacademic and unproductive ethos.

The social science scene has also some bright spots. India has been very fortunate in having produced a few outstanding institution-builders in the field of social science who have put the country on the social science map of the world. The history of these few social science research centres provides rich lessons in institution-building which need to be explored and grasped.

The very strength and weakness of institution-building in the past has been that each of these social science research centres has revolved round one individual of outstanding ability who has been its founder. This prominence of a single individual grew sometimes into 'a cult of personality'. This was bound to create problems for a research centre once the individual was no more there at the helm of affairs. This is not a criticism of the outstanding individuals who built these research centres. It is more a recognition of the complex problems of building academic institutions in a country having a colonial past and a strong semi-feudal social background.

The institution-builders themselves had a contradictory personality. On the one hand they emerged as highly creative individuals responsive to the dynamic urges of the national movement and the progressive urges of a new society. Promoting social science research for them was not a mere academic task. It was conceived as part and parcel of the national endeavour to make a decisive break from the colonial and feudal past. On the other hand, the institution-builders were also the products of a colonial tradition and a semi-feudal social structure. They were themselves conditioned by its negative pressures and influences. It may be noted that the very process of institution-building in its formative phase required a cohesive system of values and a ready-made mould of academic organization. In a traditionalist social milieu social science institutes and departments reproduced at their best the main features of the Hindu joint family with the builder assuming the role of the *karta*. At their worst they reproduced the structure of a feudal estate. Whatever usefulness these patterns may have had in the earlier period, their harmful influences on academic life should also be recorded. These patterns were not favourable to the formation of a positive intellectual personality or a self-reliant community of research workers. They produced tendencies of servility and timidity in some and of rebelliousness in some others. Experience has confirmed that only that institutional pattern helps social science growth on a long-term basis as is based on freedom of dissent, on strict observance of academic criteria in recruitment and in the distribution of honours and awards and finally on willingness of persons in higher positions to be intellectually challenged and superseded by promising elements in lower positions. Just as in a joint family some members of the family enjoy privileges not by doing honest and meritorious work but by exploiting the *karta*, so in academic centres based on the joint family pattern lightweights sometimes rose and prospered on the same principle. Further, elements of a courtier mentality characteristic of a feudal estate rather than an academic dignity characteristic of a centre of learning intruded into some research institutions. Some back, A.K. Saran (1962: 167–69) wrote with deep anguish about the corruption of intellectual life and the absence of 'a truly academic life' in Indian universities. What he says about universities is true in various degrees of research institutions also.

The erstwhile colonial background of the country also left its impress on institution-building in the past. This impress was mainly reflected in unconscious leaning towards hierarchical and bureaucratized organization of research and in insufficient assertion of autonomy in relation to intellectual centres in the developed world. The great importance given to foreign degrees and to experience of work in foreign countries in recruitment policy was, in some though not in all cases, an intrusion of the colonial past into the present.

Any objective assessment of the contribution of institution-builders, however, must give the positive elements of their legacy far greater weightage than the negative elements. The imagination, organizational drive and dedication to social science as revealed in the work of these builders will always be gratefully remembered by the succeeding generations who profited, and continue to profit, from this work. Moreover, the institutions founded by them have enough resilience to overcome the negative elements and to ensure a new flowering of social science research.

NEW PERSPECTIVES OF SOCIAL SCIENCE RESEARCH

Among the intricate problems left by the formative stage of institution-building for social sciences, an important question is that of the nature of financing of research institutions and its influence on the organization of research. In the formative stage the builders of research organization approached specific ministries of the government with proposals for forming social science research centres with the assurance that research work done by these centres would also be useful for policy-making purposes. Since each ministry of the government has to justify the expenditure on research in terms of its direct utility to the government, the research centres were eager to give priority to 'quick-maturing' rather than 'long-gestation' research work. They were also eager to give precedence to such types of research programmes as were 'fruit-bearing' and not just 'light-bearing'. A constraint favouring relatively short-term rather than relatively long-term and favouring 'policy-oriented' rather than 'fundamental' studies was thus inherent in the research programmes of these research centres. This constraint was also inherent in research programmes which were supported financially by international agencies. If this constraint did not always work against basic studies and if these centres also produced some important studies on the structure and processes of Indian economy and society, it is due to the intellectual stature of the founders of these centres who could get away with these deviations from the norm. Moreover, the credit also goes to the academic commitments of administrators looking after organization of research from the government side and of the research workers who were recruited by the builders of these institutions.

A stage has come, however, when this whole question of ensuring a balance between basic and applied, fruit-bearing and light-bearing studies in social sciences needs to be thoroughly appraised. It needs to be appreciated that the enthusiasm for research having immediate utility has had not very desirable consequences in the field of social science. This enthusiasm has resulted in giving a technocratic orientation to economics and transformed it from a study of *man* which it originally was into study of *things*. One is reminded of D.P. Mukerji's famous warning against this trend in his *Lament for Economics* written during his last days (1959: 1541–42).

One reason why the attempt to make social science research directly utilitarian has not produced desirable consequences is that a clear dividing line does not exist in social science between the 'fruit-bearing' research on the one hand and the 'light-bearing' research on the other. A clear criterion does not exist also for drawing a line between 'policy-oriented' and the 'fundamental' research. Decisions regarding allocation of funds or personnel to this rather than that problem area therefore reflect a personal preference or subjective judgement or even plain ignorance of those taking these decisions rather than the use of objective yardsticks. At best a preference for problem areas regarded as having some usefulness for economic planning and development can be said to be the only objective yardstick used consciously or unconsciously by the decision-makers in recent years.

Not much thought has been given by social scientists to the influence of these habits of mind reflected in decision-making on the development of social science research in the country. Certain tentative thoughts are being expressed here for stimulating discussion on this very vital subject. Our main proposition is that this insistence on choice of problems that are immediately relevant to development has been carried too far so that the scope of development studies has been very much narrowed down resulting in their divorce from the study of man in the broadest sense of the term. It should be noted that in the world as a whole the twentieth century has been marked by remarkable advances in *science and technology* on the one hand and a retarded growth of the *human sciences* on the other. As a result of this lag in the development of the human sciences, the conscious adjustment of man to the challenges of a second industrial and technological revolution of the twentieth century has also been seriously hampered.

Developing countries like India entering the industrial age in the latter part of the twentieth century perhaps need a revolution in human sciences much more than the developed countries of the world. In the absence of a breakthrough in human sciences these countries are trying to grapple with problems of today and tomorrow with the intellectual tools as it were of yesterday and day-before-yesterday. It is in this background that this direct or indirect insistence on choice of problems having immediate utility for development does not allow social scientists to view the problems of development from a broader perspective of the reconstruction of a new society. This very insistence in the background of excessive specialization is social science has not allowed man to be put in the centre of the stage as the *subject* rather than the *object* of history. It would be unrealistic for social scientists to expect the leadership for a creative re-definition of the role of social science to come from outside. But the imaginative elements among social scientists would have to cultivate an awareness of the new urges stirring the Indian people and of the vision of a new Indian as articulated by its leaders. They would also have to respond to India's new challenges at the *intellectual* level by providing *intellectual* substance to them. This can only be done by the reconstruction of a new worldview suited to the new period.

Linking human sciences with the broader task of creation of a new worldview has assumed urgency in the context of objective process operating within and outside the country. It should be noted that in countries like India the old order is disintegrating at a pace much faster than the emergence of a new order. This has resulted not only in a deep economic crisis but also in the loss of a unifying traditional worldview for the vast masses of society. Moreover, the deep crisis of liberal ideology and the tensions within Marxist thought as prevalent during the twentieth century have left the thinking sections of society also without a worldview – without even viable categories of thought and analysis. Such an intellectual crisis both at the level of the elite and the masses has all the ominous potential of landing the country into a sway of mindlessness which is at the root of all forms of political and social obscurantism.

Here is then a new role for human sciences as creators of a new framework of thought assisting the conscious transition of the latecomers into the modern age. Such a framework has to be created by utilizing all the vital intellectual achievements of other countries and by assimilating the enduring elements from the past tradition of one's own country. The coming years are sure to reveal more and more the interdependence between *socio-economic reconstruction* on the one hand and *cultural reconstruction* on the other. This task of cultural reconstruction cannot be undertaken without putting an end to the state of excessive compartmentalization within social sciences themselves. We conclude this paper therefore with D.P. Mukerji's call to his social science colleagues in his last days: *'To recollect the umpteen human or social disciplines into a human science is a worthy human effort'* (1959: 1542; emphasis added).

References

Andreski, Stanislav, 1972, *Social Sciences as Sorcery*, New York, St. Martins Press.

Aron, Raymond, 1968, *Progress and Disillusion*, London, Pall Mall Press.

Bernal, J.D., 1939, *The Social Function of Science*, London, George Routledge and Sons Ltd.

Dumont, Louis, 1964, 'Nationalism and Communalism', in L. Dumont and D.F. Pocock (eds.), *Contributions to Indian Sociology*, VIII, Paris, Mouton and Co.

Durkheim, Emile, 1960, 'Sociology' (translated by J.D. Folkman) in K. Wolf (ed.), *Emile Durkheim, 1858–1917*, Columbia, Ohio State University Press.

Gramsci, Antonio, 1971, *Selections from the Prison Notebooks*, New York, International Publishers.

Joshi, P.C., 1974, 'Indian Marxism: Towards a Renewal', *Seminar*, No. 178.

Kothari, Rajni, 1970, *Politics in India*, New Delhi, Orient Longman.

Lange, Oscar, 1970, *Papers in Economics and Sociology*, 1930–60, Warszawa Pergamon Press.

Lazarsfeld, Paul F. and Barnard Berlson, 1955, *The People's Choices*, New York, Columbia University Press.

Leighton, Alexander, 1945, *The Governing of Men*, Princeton University Press.

Little, Kenneth, 1965, *West African Urbanization: A Study of Voluntary Association in Social Change*, Cambridge University Press.

Mayo, Elton, 1949, *Social Problems of an Industrial Civilization*, London, Routledge and Kegan Paul.

Mukerji, D.P., 1958, *Diversities*, Delhi, Peoples Publishing House.

—, 1959, 'Lament for Economics: Old and New', *The Economic Weekly*, XI (46).

Myrdal, Gunnar, 1944, *The American Dilemma*, New York, Harper and Row.

—, 1971, *Asian Drama: An Enquiry into the Poverty of Nations*, London, Allen Lane Penguin Press.

Oommen, T.K., 1969(a), 'Mahila Mandals in Rural Delhi', *Social Welfare*, 16 August.

—, 1969(b), 'Youth Clubs in Rural Delhi', *Kurukshetra*, 17 September.

Palisi, Bartolomeo J., 1968, 'A Critical Analysis of the Voluntary Association Concept', *Sociology and Social Research*, 52 July.

Pieris, Ralph, 1969, 'The Implantation of Sociology in Asia', *International Social Science Journal*, XXI(3).

Presthues, Robert, 1964, *Men at the Top*, New York, Oxford University Press.

Richardson, F.L.W., 1945, 'First Principles of Rural Rehabilitation', *Applied Anthropology*, 4 October.

Rose, Arnold M., 1954, *Theory and Method in the Social Sciences*, Minneapolis, The University of Minnesota Press.

Rudolph, L. and Susanne Rudolph, 1967, *The Modernity of Indian Tradition*, Bombay, Orient Longmans.

Saran, A.K., 1962, 'D.P. Mukerji', *The Eastern Anthropologist*, XV(2).

Scott, John C. (Jr.), 1957, 'Membership and Participation in Voluntary Association', *American Sociological Review*, 22 June.

Sillis, David L., 1957, *The Volunteers*, Illinois, The Free Press.

Singh, Yogendra, 1973, *Modernization of Indian Tradition*, Jaipur, Rawat Publications.

Srinivas, M.N., 1962, 'The Study of Rural and Urban Society', *Caste in Indian and other Essays*, Delhi, Asia Publishing House.

—, 1972, *Social Change in Modern India*, New Delhi, Orient Longman.

Streeton, Paul, 1974, 'Social Science Research on Development: Some Problems in the Use and Transfer of an Intellectual Technology', *The Journal of Economic Literature*, XII(4).

Stouffer, Samuel et al., 1949, *The American Soldier: Combat and its Aftermath*, II, Princeton University Press.

Thrasher, Fiederick, 1963, *The Gang: A Study of 1313 Gangs in Chicago*, Chicago University Press.

Tocqueville, Alexis de, 1899, *Democracy in America*, New York, Colonial Press.

Tocqueville, Alexis de, 1964, *Democracy in America*, II, Bombay, Popular Prakashan.

Warner, Lloyd W. and J.O. Low, 1947, *The Social System of the Modern Factory*, New Haven, Yale University Press.

Warner, Lloyd W. and Paul S. Lunt, 1950, *The Social Life of a Modern Community*, New Haven, Yale University Press.

Whitehead, T.N., 1938, *The Industrial Worker*, Harvard, Harvard University Press.

8

SOCIOLOGY IN INDIA
A Plea for Contextualization

T.K. OOMMEN

Academic sociology[1] has been in existence in India only for six decades, although sociological thinking and empirical research did exist in India since the nineteenth century (see, Dutta Gupta, 1972). And since the 1950s discussions on sociology *in*, *of* and *for* India have been taking place.[2] While sociology *in* India deals with the professional activities of sociologists, the state of the art in the country, discussion on sociology *of* India concerns itself with approaches to the study of Indian society, as a space-time chunk. In the case of sociology *for* India, the effort seems to be one of postulating a set of concepts and theories suitable to study Indian social reality. A perusal of the writings on Indian sociology in all these contexts would unfold that the leading questions posed have been the following:

1. The central concerns of sociology being with order and change, which of these have had predominance in Indian sociology and why?
2. Is the concern for change, as and when it surfaced, buttressed with a preference for the directionality of change?
3. What are the appropriate units of analysis for sociological investigations in India?
4. What are the techniques of data collection preferred and employed?
5. How far did Indian sociologists succeed in developing a conceptual baggage and a set of theoretical propositions which are relevant for India?
6. Did Indian sociology give adequate attention to the specificity (historicity) of Indian social reality?
7. How far Indian sociologists are victims of academic colonialism?
8. Is it that Indian sociologists invariably accepted state patronage and played second fiddle to the establishment?

9. Why is it that sociologists in India failed to investigate some of the substantive themes?
10. How can we explain the predominance of studies in certain substantive areas?

The above questions, and perhaps many more of them have been 'answered' several rounds over by several sociologists and I have no intention to attempt answers to these questions. However, as a starting point, it is necessary to note *how* are these questions answered?

Broadly speaking, one or more of these questions have been answered by sociologists in terms of their understanding of sociology in India as a nation-specific or transnational enterprise. Presently, let us recognize the broad strands of thinking involved:

1. Those who look at India as a unique society, culture or civilization, thereby emphasizing the need to focus on the specificity of Indian society. Pursuantly, they advocate the need to study Indian society as a whole and this entails delving deep into India's hoary past through indology and ancient history: The Traditionists.
2. Those who do not consider Indian society as unique but recognize that as in other cases it has a specificity of its own and argue that this specificity can be understood only through an analysis of Indian history and tradition. This orientation calls for the need to emancipate ourselves from the constricting influence of outsiders (academic colonialism is the current catch-phrase) and to reject the international reference model to render ourselves nationally relevant: The Nationalists.
3. Those who argue for the use of native concepts and categories so as to reconstruct social reality as people perceive it. This perspective implies that there are as many versions of social reality as there are socio-cultural variations and hence what is emphasized is local history and tradition: The Nativists.
4. Those who consider Indian society essentially as the same anywhere else and hence believe that concepts, theories, techniques and methods are universally applicable in spite of the variations in the contexts of their origin. Emphasizing the need to focus on the general and the present, they tend to be ahistorical: The Cosmopolitans.
5. Those who attest the position that transformation of societies everywhere falls into a grand evolutionary schema to be accelerated through conscious human intervention. The advocacy of intervention inevitably calls for an understanding of the past

experiences and the need to take clear value position, a prerequisite to pursue desired goals. Those who pursue this strand of thinking also call for a selective rejection of the outside influences, those of the capitalist First World: The Radicals.

The ongoing debate in Indian sociology discerned both in terms of the questions posed and perspectives postulated points not simply to the multiplicity of orientations of its practitioners but a real identity crisis of the discipline. The fact that Indian sociologists have been discussing the problems that beset the discipline for the past three decades is a healthy sign. To recall the pertinent words of the review committee of Indian Council of Social Science Research: 'Much of the current research effort has *no relevance* to contemporary social and national problems.... It is not yet emancipated to develop research tools, designs and models of its own *appropriate to the Indian situation'* (ICSSR, 1973: 9; emphasis added). I submit that in order to get out of this impasse we need to *contextualize* sociology in India.

I

The problematic involved in contextualization of sociology in India may be viewed as a series of tensions. The first of these is articulated through the differential emphasis accorded to the study of past and present, indology and sociology, tradition and change. Notwithstanding D.P. Mukerji's (1958: 228–41) emphasis on the seminal importance of tradition in the study of Indian society, it is the provocative statement made by Dumont (1957: 7) that '...a sociology of India lies at the point of confluence of sociology and indology', which triggered off the hitherto unsettled controversy in this context. Those who emphasize the study of indology suggest that this is the surest way to apprehend the Indian social reality as a whole. But to the extent the texts which are actually studied or recommended to be studied are invariably Hindu texts what we get at, even if the argument is conceded, is in effect Hindu sociology.[3] I am not suggesting that this is not a worthwhile exercise but only pointing to the implications involved.

Those who invoke Hindu religious texts to understand the values of Indian society, if not the facts, assume that Hinduism is the most ancient religion of India, an assumption not entirely uncontested. It is necessary to refer here to the religions in India in terms of their *sources of presence*. They may be categorized as follows:[4]

1. The primal vision of indigenous social categories such as the *adivasis* and *dalits*.[5]

2. The earliest migrant religion which got 'nativised' and emerged as the dominant religion: Hinduism.[6]
3. The religions which emerged as the resultant of protest against Hinduism: Jainism, Buddhism, Sikhism.
4. The religions which are perceived to be the products of conquest or colonization: Islam and Christianity.[7]
5. The religious groups which came as migrants: Jews, Zorastrians and followers of Baha'i Faith.

The first three categories of religions are usually reckoned as Indian religions not only in popular perception but also in terms of constitutional provisions: Hindu Code Bill and the application of personal laws. On the other hand, notwithstanding the fact that Christianity came to India in the first century A.D. and Islam is in India for thirteen centuries, they are taken to be alien religions. Similarly, while 80 per cent of world's Zorastrians live in India and Buddhism is practically an expatriate religion from India, the former is perceived as an alien and the latter as an Indian religion. I submit that this is sociologically untenable for a variety of reasons but let me mention just two of them. First, when we refer to India as a geographical-political entity today the reference is to an entity scarcely thirty-five years old. Secondly, it is sociologically untenable to view millions of people who have been inhabiting the very same geographical area for centuries as 'aliens' for the simple reason that they profess religious faiths which originated elsewhere.

It is against this background the implications of the attempt to reduce Indian values to those contained in Hindu texts will have to be seen. Therefore, the contention that the '...the very existence, and influence, of the traditional higher, Sanskritic, civilization demonstrates without question the unity of India... it does not only demonstrate, but actually constitutes it' (Dumont, 1957: 10) is undoubtedly unacceptable not only to Muslims, Christians, Zorastrians, etc., but also to the Dravidians,[8] *adivasis* and *dalits*, who did not share this 'higher' Sanskritic civilization. Even the Buddhists and Sikhs, I am afraid, are not likely to be persuaded to accept the proposition in so far as Pali and Gurumukhi texts are ignored. In the final analysis invoking the route of Hindu texts to arrive at Indian social reality would only give us an understanding of the values of the 'mainstream' people of present-day India: the twice-born Hindus inhabiting Indo-Gangetic plain.

However, is important to note that we can speak of Hindu sociology in another sense, that is, in the sense in which we refer to Hindu Law. But Hindu Law is clearly distinct from say, Muslim Law,

Christian Law, etc. And, in India, the modern state legal system co-exists with varieties of religious/folk legal systems, applicable to and actually applied in the case of different groups. Similarly, in medicine, we have the western allopathic system co-existing with ayurvedic (predominantly Hindu), unani (mainly Muslim) and folk systems of medicine. In the case of academic professions we do not have live competing systems of knowledge such as Hindu economics, sociology, politics, etc., although we can speak of Hindu economic, social and political thought. This situation of knowledge vacuum has inevitably led to the domination by western theory and methodology in social sciences once they were implanted in India. But even in those areas where competing indigenous professions (e.g., medicine and law) did exist, the western brands of it came to dominate over them gradually. I will revert to this point later.

There is yet another reason why sociology in India (for that matter anywhere) could not develop mainly based on analyses of texts – ancient or contemporary. Those who argue for the tapping of Sanskritic sources anchor their argument on the richness and variety of thought contained in Hindu texts. There are others who suggest that precisely because of this, one cannot easily endorse one or another normative pattern or value system as representing the Indian collective conscience. Although, this argument can be countered by suggesting that plurality of thought is the very essence of the Hindu collective conscience (see, Chandra, 1977) the more serious objection that the texts are normative and prescriptive and they do not reflect the behavioural realities cannot be easily met. In fact, excessive dependence on the Book is a characteristic feature of those branches of knowledge, such as theology and law, which attempt norm-setting and value-giving. Therefore, those who are concerned with behaviour tend to argue that the book-view does not reflect reality, and for that, one should resort to the field, to get at 'facts'. Then, the tension between those who focus on the Text and the Field is anchored on their differential emphasis on the ideal and the actual. Viewed thus, the controversy appears to be not only sterile but purile, because one cannot understand the actual without reference to the ideal. Levy (1966: 26) aptly remarks:

> The distinction between ideal and actual structure is one of the most vital and useful tools of analysis of any society, any time, anywhere. In one form or another men have been aware of it since time began for them. It is, however, so obvious and such a humble distinction that many social scientists either neglect it or overlook its importance.

The only sane solution, it seems to me, is to follow the dictum: Render unto the Text that which is the Text's and Render unto the Field that which is the Field's. The constructed estrangement between the Text and the Field, value and fact, does not exist; it is largely an artefact of scholastic craftiness, a manifestation of intellectual trade unionism.

To focus on the Text necessarily entails a focus on the past and to concentrate on the Field willy-nilly implies that the major chunk of attention will have to be on the present. But how much back into the past we should travel in order to illumine our understanding of the present?[9] To the extent the sociologists' concern to understand the past is tempered by his interest to comprehend the present, there is a critical slice in history in which he ought to be interested, not more and not less. Admittedly, this critical slice of relevant history would vary depending upon the problem under investigation, as for example, the study of communalism in India on the one hand or Hindu kinship on the other. That is, the options here are not between indology or sociology and history or sociology, as is usually made out to be, but *how much* indology or history, as the case may be, given the prime concern of the sociologist, namely, understanding and explaining the present.

Having noted earlier that to invoke the study of Sanskritic texts as the route to understand Indian society in effect boils down to confining our attention to the value-systems of twice-born Hindus, I should add here that such an enterprise is beset with another danger: (although it does not follow logically) the tendency to ignore oral traditions.[10] And a substantial proportion of Indian population such as the *adivasis*, *dalits* and even peasantry have had only oral traditions. To the extent their oral traditions are ignored, we cannot speak of an authentic history of the people of India. Even if sincere efforts are made to reconstruct their past through oral history or 'texts', the time chunk that we can 'capture' through this would be rather limited. Here we confront a very basic problem about the very nature of history as a discipline. History that is available to us, in the final analysis, is recorded history. But the actual history is the totality of human activities and events and recorded history forms only an insignificant part of this total range of human events. To complicate matters, what is recorded is often the activities of those who occupied exalted positions – political, economic, socio-cultural – in varieties of situations; recorded history is the history from above. While this is valuable in itself, this history is only part-history and hence this gives only a distorted picture of the past. What we need and what is so miserably missing is the history from below, the history of the oppressed, the wretched of the earth. The new-found enthusiasm to study people's struggles, popular movements, revolutions, etc., while partly correct this distortion, this has not been entirely successful in filling our abysmal ignorance in this regard. Even here the focus of attention and analysis has been invariably on those who led the struggles: the movement elite. It is here that the sociologist with his capital concern for the present is at a tremendous advantage. He can observe and record the present-day events as they happen with the focus on the people; the sociologist should view the *present as history*. But regrettably, even this is not done. If we miss the opportunity *now* the future generations will continue to experience all the disadvantages that we are experiencing presently to understand our past in an authentic manner. That is, the sociologist should not only be concerned with the past to understand the present, but he should be involved in the study of the present precisely to aid the future generations to understand their past.

II

The domination of western knowledge system over the indigenous knowledge system is usually explained in terms of the western colonial intervention. Apparently, this explanation is appealing, nationalistic, even patriotic, but actually it does not measure up to rational considerations or logical arguments. Conquest and colonialism were not unknown in India. The Muslim intrusion in India is twelve centuries old and yet the Muslim thought and knowledge did not pose any significant challenge to the Hindu systems of thought and knowledge; no displacement of the latter occurred. In fact, the interaction between Hindu and Muslim systems of thought gave rise to new and creative synthesis. The fact that the Muslims were not 'imperialists' as they settled down and made India their 'home' should hardly be any solace to those who argue that Sanskritic civilization provided the basic grid to 'Indian' society. And, even the mutations which grew out of the combined Hindu-Muslim thought systems could not successfully resist the intellectual conquest of India by the West.

Western colonialism in India is scarcely two centuries old and yet its impact is staggering. Then, notwithstanding the uniqueness of Hindu and Muslim systems of thought and knowledge and their creative combinations, there is something compelling in the western system of knowledge and its application. Its acceptance seems to be necessary for our very survival in the modern world. It is this, rather than colonialism as such which explains the persistence of western knowledge and professions in India. Secondly, if that which was initially imposed was not basically acceptable and useful and viewed as a yoke and a burden, when the colonial master withdrew, the imposed elements would have been rejected. There is no evidence even after forty-five years of political independence that this is beginning to happen. To argue that it is impossible to emancipate ourselves from the cultural clap-trap of colonialism is to accept that men are mere receivers and creatures of history. But this is only a half-truth; men are as much creators of history. Thirdly, it would be helpful to undertake a mental experiment in this context. If we did not have had the western colonial intervention, could it be that our knowledge systems would have remained essentially indigenous uncontaminated by alien influence? The answer to this question would be in the affirmative if only we visualize insulated social systems. But contemporary societies as they are with frayed edges, loose textures and thin boundaries constantly exposed to alien influences are bound to acculturate and assimilate the values and institutions irrespective of the spatial locus of their origin. Of course, there is a qualitative difference between such voluntary adaptation and the coercive imposition that colonialism implies. Be that as it may, we cannot wish away the facts of history and all that we can do is to reject the undesirable and assimilate the desirable elements from among those which were initially imposed on us. This is more a question of our national and rational potentials and not so much of colonialism.

Instead of perceiving the problem thus the effort often is to 'protect' Indian sociology from external intrusions. This concern is often expressed through the phrase: academic colonialism.[11] The argument that Indian sociologists (as indeed other academics) are mere captives of an international reference model accords monopoly to the knowledge industry located in the West. However, it can be argued with equal force that the knowledge industry operates in a free-market situation. The academic entrepreneur of the West, as his counterpart in industry, would want to sell his products wherever he can. But the transaction can take place only if there are willing buyers. Therefore, the argument that Indian sociologists are mere captives of an international reference model totally denies them of their autonomy. And, the implied assumption that humans are mere victims of their circumstances is only partially correct; they are as much designers of their situations. The point is: academic colonialism is possible not simply because there exists enterprising knowledge producers and hidden persuaders in the West but also because there are willing buyers in the East. At any rate, the answer to this is neither a total rejection of the western knowledge without knowing what it is, nor putting restrictions on the knowledge flow but in developing a critical capacity to discern what is good and relevant for us.

I must make it clear here that the rejection of an international model in the case of knowledge implies academic 'nationalism' and even academic 'communalism', both of which are not without their share of dangers. Academic nationalism, that is, viewing all issues exclusively from the perspective of the interests of a nation-state is not likely to be in the long-term interests of man and society, for several reasons. First, formation and dissolution of nation-states do take place within a short span of history and these are not always likely to be in the best interests of the humans involved in the process. In the last forty-five years, we have witnessed this in ample measure in the Indian sub-continent itself. Secondly, to be 'nationalistic' invariably means supporting the state and the government, that is, the party in power. This, under the conditions prevailing in many nation-states, would mean supporting the structures which perpetuate structural and physical violence. Thirdly, given the near absence of support from voluntary organizations for research in many nation-states the states have near monopoly in defining priorities of research which are ultimately geared to tension-management mechanism, to perpetuate the party in power. Admittedly, only the officially preferred brand of social research would get encouragement and recognition usually, which is detrimental to 'creativity'. Fourthly, as social science research has ideological underpinnings unless diverse orientations are encouraged to creatively confront one another, the distortions and ambiguities created by the state-sponsored perspective cannot be corrected. Finally, to investigate and analyze sociological issues to suit national needs is both a challenge and a danger. It constitutes a danger to the scientific enterprise in that one can easily get into 'patriotic' slants pandering to popular emotions.[12]

It has been frequently pointed out that the handful of sociologists who practised the craft during the colonial period were nationalistic and that they focused on Indian problems (see, Mukherjee, 1979; Joshi, 1975: 139–62). But it is often forgotten that after independence the national goals got diffused as there has been a sea-change in the *historicity of context*. The sociologist, as everybody else, during the colonial regime was a subject and there existed a commonly perceived enemy, namely, imperialism, both of which together invested tremendous legitimacy to a conjoint concern, namely, political freedom. But once political freedom arrived not only that the national goal changed to nation-building, but genuine differences of opinion came to be crystallized as to the *paths* to be pursued to achieve the goal and also in regard to the perception regarding the obstacles to nation-building. Secondly, what has been hitherto perceived as national interests took different manifestations in the forms of 'communal', regional, class or linguistic interests. These differing conceptions and consequent conceptualizations of national interests are reflected in the pursuit of sociology. Therefore, what is reflected in sociology in independence India is not an erosion of national concern but a reconceptualization of national interests; a redefinition of sociologist's constituency. This may not be always clearly articulated but it is easily evident to the discerning eye.

The change in the constituency of sociologist is a welcome one to the extent he/she enthusiastically highlights the issues of the collectivities to which he/she belongs, but it also contains a danger, that of academic communalism, to which I have referred to earlier. Academic communalism implies that sociologists select their specific constituencies based on primordial identities and they tend to study only these and emerge as the spokesmen of their constituencies. Thus, the tendency today is that the women are studied by women, the *dalits* by *dalits*, the Muslims by Muslims, the Punjabis by Punjabis, etc.[13] Indeed, the advantages of building instantaneous rapport and empathy with the people among whom one works is an argument in favour of such a trend. But the advantages of studying social segments to which one does not belong is equally clear and important. First, if the advantages of studying 'other cultures' are well recognized and established, the advantages of investigating the social categories to which one does not belong are self-evident. Second, the pay-offs that a researcher accrues from his being a 'stranger' to one's research constituency cannot be altogether denied (see, Simmel, 1950).[14]

Apart from these advantages there are other reasons why one should not confine attention to one's own social categories because there will be segments of population which cannot throw up their own sociologists – the insane, the deviant, etc. Further, this would mean that the study of marginalized categories – *dalits, adivasis*, unemployed, minorities, the poor, etc. – will get neglected. To a certain extent this has already happened in Indian sociology and academic communalism is often a response to this neglect. On the other hand, the personal background of a sociologist may often be a liability to study certain categories or issues. For instance, the possibility of a sociologist of Brahmin background undertaking a study of *dalits* through participant observation, or a Hindu sociologist investigating the issues of communalism amidst Muslims or vice versa, a male sociologist understanding the 'problems' of women etc., is limited. That is to say, we face a genuine dilemma here: the acute fractionation and extreme segmental indularity of Indian society renders the entry of sociologists into several areas of enquiry extremely difficult. On the other hand, if each social category 'produces' its own sociologists it will lead to academic communalism which is likely to reinforce the prevalent primordial collectivism. Clearly, we need to strike a balance by encouraging studies of social categories both by 'insiders' and 'outsiders'.

This brings me to the last point that I would like to make in this context, namely, academic feudalism and scholastic parochialism that reign in Indian sociology (as indeed in the 'republic' of the Indian Academy). It is not so much the professional hierarchy or gradations which debilitates the profession but the patron-client and network ties. This is evident in the recruitment of academic personnel, distribution of 'rewards', be it membership in committees, conferring of honours, or even referring to the works of fellow sociologists. Let me illustrate with reference to the last of these, which is perhaps the least visible and most intractable. If one were to look at the footnotes and references by Indian sociologists what I am trying to convey will be clear. Depending upon one's positioning in the profession one refers to the works of (and this is invariably reckoned as one's obligation to, reward for, defence to, expression of friendship with, rather than the relevance of) (a) one's patrons/bosses etc., (b) one's clients/students etc., and (c) those who are involved in one's own network: 'ethnic', national and international. This creates a situation of internal academic colonialism, which, to my mind, is much more detrimental than the international academic colonialism. And, paradoxically enough those who beat their breasts about academic colonialism are the easiest prey to this internal colonialism.

While one can be indifferent to or even reject the international reference model, one cannot do so in regard to the internal, that is, the national reference model. Because what sustains one professionally is the recognition one gets from fellow professionals from the same country. It seems to me that it is the frustration generated by the behaviour of professional peers that often drives out at least some of the capable ones to seek asylum either in the international network or in cognate disciplines. What is denied at 'home' is sought after elsewhere.

The argument I put forward is that, academic nationalism is not the answer to academic colonialism and the former contains within it seeds of academic communalism and academic feudalism. The way-out is to develop an authentic concern for man and society, a concern informed of humanism and not simply a concern for fellow-nationals, co-religionists or those who belong to one's speech-community, professional network, etc.

III

While considering the issue of commitment to broad human concerns the problem of motivation for entry into the profession becomes important. We may think of at least three broad types of motivations in this context: (a) instrumental, (b) professional, and (c) existential.

To the vast majority of sociologists entry into the profession is a matter of bread and butter; it is a career and not a calling. (This is not something to be deprecated or denigrated; in all probability they may develop an appropriate orientation through occupational socialization). Two sources have suddenly enlarged the career opportunities of Indian sociologists: (a) introduction of sociology as an undergraduate teaching subject; and (b) recruitment by the state, as collection and analysis of data for policy formulation by the planner and administrator became a prerequisite in the 'socialist'/ 'welfare' state. In the case of most college teachers they look upon themselves mainly as communicators of available knowledge to the students and not as producers of knowledge.

Those who work with the government are expected to collect and analyze data through quick surveys as is evident in the numerous studies of community development, panchayati raj, land reforms, urban problems, studies on scheduled castes and tribes, etc. These sociologists are not involved in, perhaps not even expected to, formulating concepts or build theories and there is no point in decrying their work as is done by some (see, for example, Srinivas and Panini, 1973: 198–99). It is not even correct to characterize them as power-hungry sociologists in search of lucrative positions in the establishment as Dhanagare (1980: 24) does. If a sociologist can be and should be a social critic he can also be involved in social policy formulation and planned development; sociology can be and should be social criticism and a policy science at once. All what one can insist is that the sociologist should consciously choose his role and what role he chooses at a given point in time depends on his evaluation of the 'establishment'.

Even most of those who project themselves as sociologists dedicated to the cause of developing the discipline of sociology – the teachers and researchers of university departments and research institutes – look upon their profession as a platform to demonstrate their intellectual ability to fellow sociologists within India and perhaps more importantly to those abroad, an international community of scholars from whom they search professional recognition, rather than creatively attending to the problems of their immediate environment. To secure the eagerly sought after recognition from this international community, they have to demonstrate their ability in terms of what is valued by that community, which alone can bring in pay-offs; fellowships, visiting assignments, invitation to seminars and conferences, etc. Understandably, we have our share of Weberians, Marxists, Parsonians, ethno-methodologists, etc., involved in the international professional network. (But alas! we do not have, say, Gandhians and if anybody dares to do sociology with reference to Gandhi, he is treated with contempt). In this process we got alienated from the issues and problems which confront us here and now. It is my contention that our concern with issues of our immediate environment in the broader perspective of humanism will render us relevant not only nationally but globally.

Perhaps what I have in mind can be illustrated by referring to the works of Latin American social scientists. The notions of centre and periphery, metropolitan and satellite countries, pedagogy of the oppressed, conscientization, de-schooling, etc. – the 'radical' ideas eagerly devoured in the contemporary West and metropolitan centres of the East – have been developed through an in-depth examination and critical understanding of the Latin American empirical situation and yet they seem to be relevant far beyond the boundaries of Latin America. It is not my intention to suggest that these notions and conceptualizations are necessarily fool-proof; but I do want to affirm that these conceptualizations illustrate the potentiality of theory-building even as one concentrates on one's own specific empirical situation.

The third possible motivation, I have listed, for pursuing sociology as a profession is rooted in one's biography; one's existential conditions and life experiences. While I do not have any data to support this argument, it is my suspicion that most sociologists in India do not enter the profession to fulfil a 'mission' – to bring about social transformation, to revive the past glory of India or to perpetuate the present system. This is perhaps because most of them are middle class climbers whose sense of success and achievements is rooted in upward mobility in material terms. If the recruitment base were predominantly upper class for whom one's profession is not the route to achieve material success, or of lower class/caste origin which prompts one to identify with the miseries of one's fellow-men, or persecuted/marginalized minorities, perhaps the experiential base would have provided a compelling mission to fulfil. (Perhaps, it is not a mere accident that the Jews, the perennial minority of the world have produced many outstanding intellectuals, including of course sociologists). It seems to me that the sociologists in India are without a goal which transcends the immediate mundane needs and aspirations; they are steeped in professional pragmatism. And this, I submit, at least partially explains why the sociologist of independent India does not respond to the critical human issues of his time and environment.

IV

Having suggested that the Indian sociologist is impervious to the critical issues of his time and social milieu it is necessary to pursue the argument so as to demonstrate its validity. This is perhaps best done by citing a few examples. Let me begin with the issues thrown up by the very birth of India as a nation-state: the partition of India and the 'refugee' problem. Between 1946–51, nearly 9 million Hindus and Sikhs came to India from the present territory of Pakistan and 6 million Muslims left India. By any account the holocaust was one of the biggest human uprooting in history. And yet hardly any serious sociological study was attempted on a scale and nature warranted by the event.[15] And the reverberations of partition are still with us: Hindu-Muslim conflicts, Akali and Assamese mobilizations, etc., none of which also is being studied adequately by Indian sociologists. Second, the practice of untouchability has been decried almost universally; social reformers fought against the practice, social legislations are passed to ban it. And yet, the practice continues. In spite of this we do not have even a reliable and accurate sociography of untouchability of the various regions in India.[16] That more than 50 per cent of India's population is below the poverty line is well-known. Typically, and certainly most fallaciously, the problem of poverty is assumed to be an economic and at best a political (in that the poor are also voiceless) one and rarely a sociological issue. Consequently, Indian sociologists hardly paid any attention to the study of poverty. The issue of nationalities in India is admittedly crucial in the ongoing process of nation-building. Notwithstanding the expression of occasional anxiety regarding 'national integration' by both politicians and social scientists, we do not have a single comprehensive study on this problem by a sociologist of Indian origin.

I can go on adding to the above list but that will only increase its bulk. But I do hope the message is communicated. And, what is more: Indian sociologists seem to define the boundary of their substantive concerns rather rigidly and they tend to maintain the same very zealously. If anybody takes the risk of crossing the boundary what awaits him are ridicule and indifference.[17] This attitude of professional peers and elders is highly debilitating for ordinary mortals and new entrants and consequently for the profession, as it is constituted mainly by them.

V

A recurring theme of debate in Indian sociology has been the unit of analysis. This is postulated in terms of micro versus macro studies, a misconstrued juxtaposition (see, Oommen, 1972(b): 62–67). True, India is a nation-state, or if you prefer, a civilization. But it is not one society or culture; we have a multiplicity of cultures and societies co-existing under one political arrangement. Therefore, investigations of 'regional' variations, that is, variations based on culture-zones, are crucial in Indian social enquiry. It should be made clear that what I have in mind is not only states (administrative units) such as Himachal Pradesh, Bihar, etc., but also folk-regions such as Bhojpur, Chattisgarh, Mithila, etc.

What we have in India as of now is either studies of institutions as they operate at the local levels (as if they are not linked with a wider universe) or studies which deal with the nation-state as a whole. While there is no denying the fact that there is a set of all-India structures (e.g., upper echelon of bureaucracy, a few political parties, professions, etc.) two points are to be noted. First, the processes involved in the functioning of these all-India structures may vary from region to region. Second, there are institutions which vary both in terms of structures and processes in different regions: family, caste, agrarian system, etc. The specificities of these institutions can be understood only through studies specifically designed for the purpose. Therefore, we should not juxtapose micro-studies with macro-studies; the postulated polarity between them does not exist. It seems to me that we need to concentrate our attention at three levels, simultaneously. First, studies of villages as they operate at the grass root level but trying to understand their linkages with the wider universe. Second, studies of 'regions' which are more or less culturally homogeneous or politically bounded. Third, studies which consider the country as a whole as the unit of analysis. What is important to be kept in mind is that it is the nature of the enquiry and the substantive theme which would determine the unit of study.

The unit of analysis along with the substantive concerns of a study determine the appropriateness of techniques of data collection to be employed. The inadequate appreciation of this consideration results in arguments for or against a particular technique of data collection. As I have dealt with this issue elsewhere (see, Oommen, 1969: 809–15) I do not intend to elaborate on it here. But I do want to affirm that no technique of data collection is eternally valid or appropriate and, therefore, there is no point in making a fetish of one or another technique. The question is not one of accepting or rejecting the western empirical methods in sociological analysis of India but choosing the appropriate ones, amending the existing ones or innovating, devising new ones depending upon the purpose of study and nature of the theme.

A serious objection that is advanced in this context is that some of the techniques, such as survey research, assume the autonomy of individuals and the Indian individual does not have any autonomy in decision-making. Once again, this is only a half-truth and we get at this conclusion precisely because we assume that the traditional values are completely accepted and internalized even today. It could be argued on the other hand that democratic values are increasingly being accepted and internalized in India, which in turn means that the Indian individual is assuming autonomy in varying degrees in different contexts. But both these remain largely plausible hypotheses as of now in the absence of relevant studies.

The debate on units of analysis entails another issue, the kind of concepts to be employed. Generally speaking, those who undertake micro-studies tend to argue for native concepts and categories. On the other hand, those who grapple with macro-analyses prefer concepts which are abstract in nature, usually concepts originally developed based on western empirical experience. Once again, I submit that it is the context of study which determines the suitability of 'native' or 'western' concepts. Thus, if one is studying a culturally homogeneous unit native concepts can be profitably employed. But if the study envelops a variety of culturally heterogeneous units, the use of native categories is likely to be more confusing than enlightening. The way-out seems to be distinguishing between the form and substance of concepts. While the specific terms used by the people of one cultural region may vary from that of another region, with some specificity of connotations, these terms may share more or less the same meaning across the regions. Admittedly, one can think of a set of abstract concepts which are applicable to a variety of cultural regions although these may not be used by the people as such. Therefore, the advocacy of native concepts is logically linked with the study of culturally homogeneous units and that of abstract concepts go with the analysis of culturally heterogeneous situation.

I must enter a caveat here. Even as we employ concepts of western origin (which I do not think can or need be altogether avoided but need to be redefined to suit our purpose) we must guard ourselves from a possible danger, the tendency to postulate conceptual dichotomies or oppositions, such as caste versus class, joint family versus nuclear family, rural versus urban, tradition versus modern, etc., which persist in sociological writings on India. This assumes a *displacement syndrome* fixated on the western epistemological dualism which does not fit our situation. This has been one of the greatest liabilities in our understanding the nature of social change in India.

VI

To conclude, let me reflect on the reasons for lack of innovativeness and the consequent crisis of relevance in Indian sociology. It has been suggested that social science developments in the west occurred in response to the transformative challenges in western society (Yogendra Singh, 1973: 14–28). Responding to religious thought western secular thought effectively challenged religious values and institutions. this is evident in the emergence of Darwinism, Marxism, positivism, etc. Similar secular trends originated in ancient India, as illustrated by *Lokayats* and *Caravaks* which denied the existence of soul or the *Samkhya* school of thought which was initially atheistic. But these strands of thinking remained intellectual museum pieces and scarcely became powerful ideologies or social forces.

It is useful here to look at the evolution of Indian consciousness in the recent past. By the latter part of the nineteenth and early twentieth centuries the anti-imperialist movement gained strength. And during this period we have *demonized* not only the colonial politico-economic dominance but also the institutions and values of the domestic society of the colonizer; we have indulged in an indictment of western civilization. As a corollary to this, it was necessary to *sacralize* indigenous values and institutions as is evident from Gandhi's *Hind Swaraj,*[18] Bankim Chandra's *Anand Math,*[19] Maithili Saran Gupta's *Bharat Bharati,*[20] etc. Given the fact that the British rule was preceded by several centuries of rule by Muslims, who were also perceived as aliens, it was necessary to invoke the glory of the hoary past of Hinduism. The simultaneous demonization of the western and sacralization of the 'indigenous' values and institutions was only partially functional in that the sources of sacralization were Hindu texts which did not appeal with equal force to the *adivasis, dalits*, etc., not to speak of Dravidians, Muslims, Christians and Sikhs. This tendency had its predictable consequences in the alienation of these collectivities and the one with sufficient political clout managed to get a separate nation-state for itself.

The arrival of freedom heralded our rejection of western political dominance but at the same time we accepted western political institutions, economic values and social goals. Our constitution endorsed these values and institutions – socialism, secularism and democracy. The compelling need of independent India was to repeat the exercise we undertook during the colonial rule, but in the reverse order: Selective *de-sacralization* of ancient Hindu institutions and values as well as *re-sacralization* of the constitutional values so as to bring about a judicious and creative reconciliation between the two. And there is no denying the fact that we have utterly failed in doing this and the crisis that we face in India today is the resultant of this failure. Admittedly, the confusion pervades the whole of Indian society and sociology in India cannot be an exception to this. It is my constention that the failure of sociology in independent India is its inadequate anchorage in a set of authentic values.

Today, we have, in India, two sets of competing value-packages: societal values – hierarchy, holism, pluralism etc., and constitutional values – socialism, secularism and democracy. There is no clear evidence that one set of these values is replacing the other, often one comes across reconciliation in some contexts but contradictions in regard to others. We cannot simply dismiss the frictions thrown up by the confrontations of these value-packages in contemporary Indian society as a mere transitional aberration which will disappear in course of time (see, Oommen, 1983). This is because the displacement syndrome cannot operate effectively in the Indian context. We did not have had in Indian thought the opposition and dualism between subject and object, matter and spirit, state and church, emperor and Pope, etc. Understandably, the process of change comes gradually through adaptation and accretion of structures and values and not through sudden displacement. It is of vital importance that we recognize the pluralist paradigm in Indian thought and the reconciliatory ethos in Indian praxis.

In conclusion, if sociology is to be relevant for India as a discipline it should endorse and its practitioners should internalize the value-package contained in the Indian Constitution, the differing interpretations of these values notwithstanding. Although these values have not originated in India and we have borrowed them from the West, undoubtedly they are basic human values. But our societal ethos does not permit of total displacement of the old and institutionalization of the new, at any rate all on a sudden. Admittedly, the route to and style of implantation of these values will have to be our own. It is here that Indian sociology can and should play a critical role in the process of national reconstruction as a part of its commitment to broader human concerns. It is my submission that it is possible for sociology to play this role though a process of contextualization.

The process of contextualization of sociology in India involves the following dimensions. First, recognition of the fact that tradition/past contains both assets and liabilities viewed in terms of the present needs and aspirations. The ingenuity of a people lies in rejecting the liabilities without apology and accepting the assets unequivocally. Secondly, we should not be shy of adopting appropriate values and institutions from other societies and cultures and should judiciously graft them on to our own society. Thirdly, in doing this, we should take into account the central tendency in our society, which seems to be one of gradual adaptation and reconciliation. At the same time, we should recognize that such a societal ethos is capable of bringing about social transformation only at a slow pace. Therefore, it is necessary to mobilize people to protest against exploitation, injustice and oppression. But the strategy of mobilization and the style of protest will have to be specifically Indian. Fourthly, the social engineering involved here – the selective retention of our tradition, informed borrowing from other cultures and the judicious mutation of the two – will have to be a process peculiar to India. The primary task of Indian sociologists today is to understand, analyze and facilitate this process.

Notes

1. For the present purpose I am not making any distinction between sociology and social anthropology.
2. The earliest of these was Mukherjee and Majumdar (1952: 1135–48). In 1957, Dumont and Pocock started *Contributions to Indian Sociology*. This

was followed by a large number of publications, notably, Saran (1958: 122–35, 1962: 53–58); Saksena; (ed.) (1961, 1965); Bottomore (1962: 98–106); Clinard and Elder (1965: 581–87); Unnithan et al. (1967). By the 1970's we come across almost an uninterrupted discussion on the Sociology of Indian Sociology. The most comprehensive of these to date is Mukherjee (1979).

3. This is recognized latterly. See, for instance, Saberwal (1981: 144–56). But even here the lacuna is seen mainly in terms of the neglect of Muslim texts. One wonders why, Jain, Buddhist, Sikh, Zorastrian or Christian texts are not relevant.
4. This categorization draws from but modifies the one made by Schermerhorn (1978) in regard to 'ethnic' collectivities in India.
5. *Adivasis*, literally means the earliest inhabitants. They have been referred to as 'Girijans' (inhabitants of hilly tracts and mountains) in popular writings and as Scheduled Tribes in the official parlance. However, they prefer to be designated as *adivasis* and hence they are referred to be so here. There are about 400 different groups of *adivasis* in India and according to the 1971 Census of India there are 38 million of them constituting 7 per cent of the total population. *Dalits*, literally means the oppressed, a term preferred by them, although Gandhi called them 'Harijans', the children of God. In the official parlance they are designated as Scheduled Castes and there are about one thousand different castes of this category together numbering 80 million according to the 1971 Census of India constituting 14 per cent of the total population. Today, most of the *adivasis* and the *dalits* are reckoned as belonging to one of the 'world' religions: Hinduism, Buddhism, Sikhism, Christianity or Islam. However, from 1871 to 1931 we come across a religious category designated as 'primitive' or 'tribal' in Indian Census data. But some sociologists, notably Ghurye (1943) consider that *adivasis* are but Hindus, indeed a sociologically untenable proposition. As for *dalits*, notwithstanding the current tendency to include them under the fold of Hinduism, the Purusha Sukta in the Rig Veda which refers to the Hindu theory of origin of man only mentions the Brahmin, the Kshatriya, the Vaishya and the Shudra. The *dalits* reckoned as 'untouchables' traditionally were not accounted in the Chatur Varna Scheme of Hinduism. In all probability they were the indigenous people who resisted the invading Aryans, the latter day Hindus.
6. According to some historians Hinduism it the religion of Aryan migrants, howsoever ancient might be their arrival in India.
7. Christianity came to India in the first century A.D. and Arab migration to the Malabar coast started from the seventh century A.D. onwards. That is pre-colonial Christianity and pre-conquest Islam existed in India and yet in popular perception these religions are products of conquest and colonization. But as W.I. Thomas wrote: 'If men define situations as real, they are real in their consequences', and this is sociologically significant.

8. Dravidians are those whose mother tongue belong to the Dravidian family of languages. There are three main branches of Dravidian languages distributed into four main languages and several dialects, together constituting about 25 per cent of the total Indian population. The Dravidian language came into India centuries before the Indo-Aryan languages, the latter consisting of leading languages such as Hindi, Punjabi, Gujarati, Marathi, Assamese, Bengali, Orriya, Sanskrit, etc. The most numerous and developed Dravidian languages are: Telugu (with 45 million), Tamil (with 38 million), Malayalam and Kannada (with 22 million) each speakers as per the 1971 Census of India.
9. It is conjunctured that *homo sapiens* emerged some three million years ago. It is neither possible nor relevant to pitch our attention at history so far back and hence the need to identify the time-chunk appropriate for attention.
10. Admittedly, I am using the term 'text' in its usual limited sense of written text. While it may be legitimately argued that one can speak of Oral Texts, the difference between the two is clear.
11. This has been articulated in a major way for the first time through a pubic debate (see *Seminar* 112, 1968).
12. This is already evident in many contexts. For example, almost all social researchers in India attest the proposition that Hindu-Muslim conflict in India is the handiwork of the British. If an Indian were to argue that there is a basic cleavage between Hindu and Islamic societies and that the intrigues of colonial policy could not have created it as Dumont (1964: 30–70) did he would be accused of creating obstacles or 'national integration'. Or if one were to argue that the multiplicity of 'nationalities' within the Indian nation-state would call for a highly decentralized political system, it is likely to be viewed as creating obstacles in the nation-building process and is likely to be dubbed as a regional or linguistic chauvinist.
13. There is enormous scope for misinterpreting my position in this context. I am not suggesting for a moment that sociologists should not pursue the studies of the social categories to which they belong but am only indicating that such studies need to be supplemented by studies undertaken by 'outsider' to get at a rounded picture as it were. At the same time, aroused political consciousness of the hitherto marginalized collectives render studies by 'outsiders' increasingly difficult, if not impossible.
14. Simmel writes: '...he (stranger) often receives the most surprising openness – confidences which have the character sometimes of a confessional and which would be carefully withdrawn from a more closely related person' (1950: 404).
15. I could locate only two books by Indian social scientists apart from a few government reports. For details, see Oommen 1982: 41–64.
16. An exception being Desai (1976) who gives a graphic account in regard to Gujarat.

17. Let me illustrate the consequences of deviating from 'mainstream' research by drawing from my own occupational biography. In 1962, I started studying the Bhoodan-Gramdan movement, which was widely acclaimed as a unique and novel method to tackle the agrarian problem, an approach hitherto unknown in history. And in 1963, an eminent Indian sociologist asked me: 'Is it a subject for sociological research?', obviously with ample sarcasm. Of course, those were the days one studied religion, caste, village, family or kinship. Any body who attempted to cross this sacred boundary was a but of ridicule. But even by the 1970's the situation does not seem to have changed much. Thus, another eminent sociologist who undertook an extensive survey of sociology in India in the mid-seventies did not even mention the study although it was published by then (see Oommen, 1972a) and his bibliography had over 700 items! If the references cited in the survey were selected on the basis of their 'quality' perhaps my study would not have qualified for inclusion. But the survey did deal with the emerging trends in Indian sociology including the new areas of investigation. And, my book happens to be the first monograph on a social movement in India by an Indian 'sociologist'?
18. *Hind Swaraj* was first published in 1938 and it was not only an analysis of why the British enslaved India but was an indictment of western civilization and a plea for restructuring Indian society based on its ancient wisdom as contained in Hindu texts.
19. *Ananda Math* was first published in 1882 in Bengali. Several of its Hindi translations appeared subsequently. The first English translation appeared in 1904. The central characters in the novel are Hindus who constitute into bandit gangs and plunder for altruistic purposes, the national cause. It was essentially an invocation to the Hindu psyche to restore the ancient glory of India which was essentially Hindu in character.
20. *Bharat Bharati* published in 1912 was instrumental for the mobilization of peasantry against the British. While the 'national' sentiment invoked by it appealed to all sections of the peasantry in parts of North India, the book was essentially couched in imageries and idioms glorifying the Hindu past.

References

Bottomore, T.B., 1962, 'Sociology in India', *British Journal of Sociology*, Vol. 13(2), 98–106.

Chandra, Pratap, 1977, *The Hindu Mind*, Simla, Indian Institute of Advanced Study.

Chatterjee, Bankim Chandra, 1882, *Anand Math* (in Bengali), Calcutta, Bangadarshan.

Clinard, M.B. and J.W. Elder, 1965, 'Sociology in India: A Study in the Sociology of Knowledge', *American Journal of Sociology,* Vol. 30 (4), 581–87.

Desai, I.P., 1976, *Untouchability in Rural Gujarat*, Bombay, Popular Prakashan.

Dhanagare, D.N., 1980, 'Search for Identity', Symposium on Studying our Society, *Seminar*, 254, 23–26.

Dumont, L., 1957, 'For a Sociology of India', in Dumont, L. and D. Pocock (eds.), *Contributions to Indian Sociology*, 1:7–22.

—, 1964, 'Nationalism and Communalism', *Contributions to Indian Sociology*, 7–30–70.

Duttagupta, B., 1972, *Sociology in India: An Enquiry into Sociological Thinking and Empirical Social Research in the 19th Century with Special Reference to Bengal*, Calcutta, Centre for Sociological Research.

Gandhi, M.K., 1938, *Hind Swaraj*, Ahmedabad, Navajivan Publishing House.

Ghurye, G.S., 1943, *The Aborigines – To Called – and Their Future*, Poona, Gokhale Institute of Politics and Economics.

Gupta, Maithili Saran, 1912, *Bharat Bharati* (in Hindi), Jhansi, Sahitya Sadan.

Indian Council of Social Sciences Research, 1973, *Report* of the ICSSR Committee, New Delhi.

Joshi, P.C., 1975, 'Reflections on Social Science Research in India', *Sociological Bulletin*, Vol. 24 (2), 139–62.

Levy, Marion J., 1966, *Modernization and the Structure of Societies*, Vol. I, Princeton, Princeton University Press.

Mukherji, D.P., 1958, 'Indian Tradition and Social Change', in D.P. Mukherjee, *Diversities*, New Delhi, People's Publishing House, 228–41.

Mukherjee, R., 1979, *Sociology of Indian Sociology*, New Delhi, Allied Publishers Private Limited.

Mukherjee, R.K. and Haridas Majumdar, 1952, 'Sociology in India', in Becker, H. and H.E. Barnes (eds.), *Social Thought from Lore to Science*, Vol. II, Washington, Haven Press, 1135–48.

Oommen, T.K., 1969, 'Data Collection Telephones: The Case of Sociology and Social Anthropology', *Economic and Political* Weekly, Vol. IV (19), 809–15.

Oommen, T.K., 1972(a), *Charisma, Stability and Change: An Analysis of Bhoodan-Gramdan Movement in India,* New Delhi, Thompson Press.

—, 1972(b), 'On the Distinction between Micro and Macro Studies', in Satish Saberwal (ed). *Beyond the Village*, Simla, Indian Institute of Advanced Study, 62–67.

—, 1982 'Foreigners, Refugees and Outsiders in the Indian Context', *Sociological Bulletin*, Vol. 31 (1), 41–64.

—, 1983, 'Towards Reconciling Traditional and Modern Values: The Indian Experiment', in Deppert, Joachim (ed.), *Indian and the West*, New Delhi, Manohar Publication, 253–63.

Saberwal, Satish, 1981, 'The Sociological Attitude', *Madras Development Seminar Series*, Vol. XI (12), 143–56.

Saran, A.K., 1958, 'India' in J.S. Rouek, (ed.), *Contemporary Sociology*, New York, Philosophical Library 122–35.

—, 1962, 'For a Sociology of India', *Eastern Anthropologist* 15 (1), 53–68.

Saksena, R.N. (ed.), 1961, *Sociology, Social Research and Social Problem in India*, Bombay, Asia Publishing House.

—, 1965, *Sociology in India*, Agra, Institute for Social Sciences.

Schermerhorn, R.A., 1978, *Ethnic Plurality in India*, Tuscon, University of Arizona Press.

Seminar, 1968, *Academic Colonialism*, 112.

Simmel, Georg, 1950, 'The Strangers' in K.H. Wolf (ed.), *The Sociology of Georg Simmel*, Illinois, The Free Press of Glencoe, 403–8.

Singh, Yogendra, 1973, 'The Role of Social Sciences in India: A Sociology of Knowledge', *Sociological Bulletin*, Vol. 22 (1), 14–28.

Srinivas, M.N. and M.N. Panini, 1973, 'The Development of Sociology and Social Anthropology in India', *Sociological Bulletin*, Vol. 22 (2), 179–215.

Unnithan, T.K.N., et.al., 1967, *Sociology for India*, New Delhi, Prentice Hall.

9

RAMKRISHNA MUKHERJEE'S SOCIOLOGY
A Sociological View

NIRMAL SINGH

I

Sociology, as a specialized branch of knowledge about society (part of human-made world), has a number of characteristics in common with all other sciences in general and social sciences in particular. At the same time, it also is marked by some distinctive features that make it stand apart as a specialized branch of knowledge, with its own internal divisions according to methodological perspectives and chosen aspects of social phenomenon, as objects of interest for study.

When dealing with their respective objectives of study all sciences claim obedience to the same rules of conduct; (a) to collect relevant facts, information checked and rechecked for reliability; (b) represent them in propositions through clear and unambiguous terms so that they become testable by evidence, they claim to cover or derive from; (c) to avoid or eliminate statements that cannot be true at the same time; the way that leads to the truth and be prepared for public scrutiny and criticism; and (d) to share the general rules of logic to draw and validate (or invalidate) conclusions from the amassed verified facts and draw inferences about unknown facts. These are very broad areas of commonality with a large measure of differences of nuances and interpretations (Bauman, 1990: 1–19).

The bases of dissimilarity with natural sciences springs from the fact that for social sciences studying human produced reality epistemologically on separation of the knower and the object of study is possible. This puts the social sciences simultaneously in a privileged and a precarious position (Andreski, 1974: 25). Shutz has put the position succinctly. Whereas natural science involves having concepts about things, social science involves having concepts about things which have concepts (quoted in Rex, 1973). Society, of which social scientists are a constituent part, is to be understood as an ongoing dialectics of the three moments of externalization, objectivation and internalization (Berger and Luckmann, 1967: 149). To be in society is to participate in its dialectics. This involves simultaneously sensing feeling and activist intervention or one following the other in all possible permutations. Attempts at any clear role separation between observer, analyst and activist, beyond a convenient division of labour, lead to false starts. The basic procedures for ordinary actors' knowledge of society and professional social scientists' knowledge of society as a form of common sense, are the same, and common sense and social science feed each other knowledge or quackery as the case may be (Maurice Roche, 1973: 311).

This intermeshing of common sense and social sciences (sociology in particular) has been rightly underlined by Zygmunt Bauman (1990: 1–9): 'To live in the company of other people, we need a lot of knowledge, and common sense is the name of that knowledge.' Raw material for sociological findings is the ordinary people's everyday life experience and in principle, though not always in practice, this experience can be had by everybody. The experience that social scientists study has already been lived by some one else – a person not trained in social science language and methodology. Sociology finds its relationship with rich disorganized, non-systematic and often inarticulate and ineffable knowledge, called common sense, probably more than other social science, fraught with problems decisive for its standing and practice. As Bauman has stated, the sovereignty of sociology over social knowledge, its right to make authoritative pronouncements on the subject, may always be contested. The experience that it deals with is always the experience of some common actor, the language and concepts representing then is in the main common with everyday language already in use and many competing generalizations are already afloat. So sociology has to establish its authority and authenticity by being marked by a distinct refinement over common sense. Some of these could be enumerated as:

(1) Sociology subordinates itself to the *rigorous rules of responsible speech*, an attribute of all science, distinguishing between provisional untested guesses, ideas ground in mere beliefs and statements corroborated by available experience open to public scrutiny both for evidence and procedures of arriving at them and relationship with other findings.

(2) Sociology *broadens the horizon of experience*, drawn from multitude of life-worlds, complex network of dependencies and interconnection. Its material for drawing final conclusions goes beyond the singular biographies.

(3) It *demonstrates that the common metaphor of a motivated individual as the key to the understanding* of the human world – including our own thoroughly personal and private thoughts and deeds – *is inappropriate*. Both our motives and the effects of their motivations are explained by making sense of the human conditions through analyzing the manifold webs of interdependencies.

(4) Sociology *questions the familiar taken for granted truths*. Things and people may not be truly as they are accepted to be. The daily way of life and the routine acceptances are brought under scrutiny. Thus, sociology acts as a meddlesome and often irritating stranger.

Thus, sociology, basing itself upon common sense, tries to overcome its limitations. 'Sociology is a refinement on that knowledge, we possess and employ in our daily life – in as much as it brings into open some further distinctions and some not immediately evident connections which an unaided eye would fail to locate. Sociology charts more details on our world map; it also extends the map beyond the horizon of our own daily experience, so that we can also see how the territories, we inhabit, fit into the world, we have had no chance to explore ourselves. The difference between what we know without sociology and what we known after we have heard its comments, is not the difference between error and truth... it is rather than difference between believing that what we experience can be described and explained in one way and in one way only, and knowing that the possible – and plausible – interpretations are plentiful.... It has been said that the best service sociology may offer is to "prod sluggish imagination" – by showing apparently familiar things from unexpected angles and thus undermining all routine and self-confidence' (Bauman, 1990: 214–15).

We have developed erroneous ideas about sociology's role as a social science. Its capacity to predict and control our social situation to our purpose has been, unreasonably, overestimated and to control other people's behaviour has earned it the protest of the powerless as being the instrument of perpetuating existing inequalities. Sociology's unseverable umblical cord with everyday knowledge and language makes sociology inexorably open and plural in its social function. It undermines the trust in the exclusivity and completeness of any integration, including 'authoritative' postures from within.

The plurality of human experiences and diversity of forms of life and common sense rooted in them, makes claims in sociology's behalf to be a science of societal management untenable. Sociology cannot but be pluralist, tolerant and liberative against abortive attempts to build knowledge for control of others lives.

As one branch of knowledge, sociology could have only a broad commonality with natural science in terms of evidence-based propositions, openness to correction and negation by public scrutiny, avoidance of contradictory propositions and interplay of experience and logic for justification. With other social sciences, like history, economics, political science, psychology, anthropology, law, etc., its relationship is of having a common object of study – society as a human product. The boundaries cannot be too rigidly drawn. Sociology does not have any subject matter distinct from other social sciences but its mark of distinction is the centrality of the questions that it asks, of the same human action, and its principles of interpretation of the very same social reality. It tries to figure out human action – past or present, material or cultural resources and goods, our own society or distant societies, influencing or coercing differentially different groups of people or individuals, means of control or consensus, hopes and fears or motivations and aspirations – as elements of wider figurations, 'of a non-random assembly of actors locked together in a web of mutual dependency.' Sociology looks for and unravels these configurations, webs of mutual dependence, reciprocal conditioning of action and expansion or confinement of actors' freedom. To bring out the social in the individual, the general in the particular, individual biographies intertwined with history, ideas and values situated in interrelated human groupings cementing or undermining these structures, relatedness of continuities and change connections between personal troubles, and public issues are but aspects of sociological imagination of situating every social phenomenon at the trisection of biography history/and social structure (Wright-Mills, 1959). Sociology is inconceivable without a continuous cross-breeding from other social sciences. As a narrowly conceived exclusive specialization it is a non-starter. D.P. Mukherji underlined this interdependence when he wrote: 'Sociology has a floor and ceiling, like any other science, but its speciality consists in its floor being the ground floor of all types of social disciplines, and its ceiling remaining open to the sky… . But a stage comes when exclusiveness ceases to pay for the living' (Oommen and Mukherji, 1986: 1–15).

This may be a coherent picture when we scan the development of sociology in the rest of the world, specially since the mid-sixties, but what is the picture that emerges in India?

II

It is commonly acknowledged that the development of sociology and social anthropology in India could not be seen as development of two separate disciplines, in spite of their distinct origins and methodological thrust. To start with Srinivas and Panani wrote that the two disciplines passing through two earlier phases 1773–1900 and 1901–1950 in the post-independence phase, have become indistinct and so also Saberwal lumps them together (Oommen and Mukherji, 1986: 16–55 and 214–32). The motivation for early studies was that 'the administrative needs of the British rulers led them to collect information about the economic, social and religious life of people' and 'it provided the stimulus for not only social anthropology and sociology but Indology'. Studies by Orientalists and Christian missionaries were not exactly motivated by the same motives but they objectively dovetailed the colonial design. This led to a nationalist response and the past and contemporary social reality was attempted to be reconstructed to lend support to the movement to instill self-confidence among the colonized people. It has also been observed that 'the discovery of India's past, and the antiquity, richness and versatility of its heritage, gave self-confidence to the elite and the material necessary for national myth-making'. The same information was also used for achieving mobility by many groups among Indians (Srinivas and Panini, 1973; Singh, 1986; Mukherjee, 1977).

The point being noted is that development of sociology and social anthropology in India could not be discussed separately. From the very beginning these cognitive efforts were closely related with the needs felt by different groups of people involved for their practical life purposes and the generated knowledge, including images were put to diverse or even opposing purposes.

The early institutionalization of sociological and anthropological studies in the universities of Calcutta, Bombay, Mysore and Lucknow starting with 1914 also indicated that persons with diverse training in philosophy, sanskrit, economics pioneered the development, moving quite freely between their parent interest, sociology and anthropology. So also the governmental support, general diversification of modern education transplanted from Europe and nationalist urge for seeking support in viable traditions had all given fillip to the development.

The development of anthropology from Calcutta was greatly helped by the contributions of K.P. Chattopadhyaya and N.K. Bose who along with their academic interests kept a life-long activist stance in social transformation. An interesting case is of Varrier Elvin, who came as a Christian missionary but settled down as an Indian producing valuable monographs on various tribes of Madhya Pradesh and Orissa and propounded a philosophy for NEFA and worked with the Government of India for tribal welfare.

By the time India became free in 1947, sociology and social anthropology had become established as university departments in half a dozen universities with a dozen teaching posts in these disciplines. The Anthropological Survey of India, a governmental outfit, was the most important research organization for anthropology. A number of journals were also established but these disciplines did not have the academic prestige of economics or even political science. This was partly due to direct contribution that economics and political science made to the nationalist cause and partly because sociology was not recognized in UK and anthropology was suspect as a colonial instrument to divide Indian people and keep the tribes away from nationalist stream. Yet it was noted that it would not be an exaggeration to say that though in the pre-independence period sociologists and anthropologists were few in number, they did make their presence felt as teachers, researchers and critics. This they did when, their disciplines were without prestige, when funds for research were conspicuous by their absence… . Research was indeed an extra activity (Srinivas and Panini, 1973).

III

In contrast to pre-independence period, development of sociology in India in the fifties and sixties has been seen as marked by (a) achievement of greater academic status and an identity of its own, (b) being focused in theoretical orientation and diversified in its specializations, (c) it was related to the growing needs of development in independent India, colonial economy perceived to have become a thing of the past and democracy having been ushered at all levels, and (d) American sociological traditions had become a major intellectual influence, replacing current theoretical concerns in UK, with French, German and Marxian influences *also* having an impact (UGC Panel, 1980). The changed national and international socio-political context has been noted with differential emphasis by various commentators on the development of sociology in India (Oommen and Mukherji, 1986; Singh, 1986; Mukherjee, 1977).

Oommen pointed out that the context had got completely altered. 'Once political freedom arrived not only that the nation's goal changed to nation-building, but genuine differences of opinion came to be crystallized as to the *paths*... and also in regard to the perception regarding the obstacle to nation-building.' Probably the perception that the sociologists who practised the craft during the colonial period were nationalistic and they shared the perception of imperialism as the common enemy and legitimacy of political freedom concern, did not quite reflect the factual position. Similarly, divergent positions on paths of development seem to be a projection of seventies and eighties situation on to the first two decades of independence. But, certainly, the changed context after independence made certain closures and other openings, within the officially projected ideology and programmes for development of sociology, more profitable. The perspectives and concerns inherited from pre-independence were not quite homogeneously constructed and those that flourished afterward too did not go unchallenged and internal logic of the discipline did not decide the outcome.

M.N. Srinivas, A.R. Desai and Ramkrishna Mukherjee had all started their sociological interests and concerns on the eve of independence and did not represent commonality of perspective or concern to start with and pursued divergent paths in their sociological careers. Srinivas launched his sociology on a single village study through participant observation to unravel caste mobility in culturological terms, completely innocent of inequalities of economic class and power structure even at the village level, leave apart the concepts, and reality represented by 'feudalism', 'capitalism' or 'imperialism'. As Saberwal has noted the rigours of field work involved had no affinity with those connected with British anthropologists studying distant 'other' cultures in Africa, Asia and elsewhere. The sociology was no trouble either to the village power holders or to the imperialist rulers or to the government of independent India that followed. When the switchover to American social science from British anthropology as models took place after independence, the soft methodology was quite malleable. The data gathered and reported under the functionalist frame could easily adjust itself to the instrumental junior role, in Government of India's modernist planning and relatively senior role given to economists. All these favourable factors, to a great extent, explain the flourishing of Srinivas sociology in fifties and sixties till modernization itself stood deadlocked and American supremacy got into trouble in late sixties.

A.R. Desai, an activist from the peasant movement, addressed himself to the question of social background of Indian National Movement. The scope and the sense of history that it demanded, needed a different confluence of philosophy, source material sensitivity and engagement. His sociology was troublesome, not only to the colonial rulers, establishment disciplines in the universities in India, and western academic models but also to the aspirants to power in independent India. When India became independent Desai type of sociology could not be adjusted easily to the demands of modernization pursued by the new rulers. For this sociology to get wider audience, the modernization process itself had to be played out. So this sociology in its development started and stayed with radical opposition to imperialism and flawed capitalist development.

Ramakrishna Mukherjee started his academic career with interest in investigating famine of 1943, effect of destitution and food crisis and disintegration of education in mid-forties. He also dealt with concentration of agriculture income in Bengal and surveyed six villages (now in Bangladesh) for unravelling economic structure in rural Bengal. He was not organically linked with any activism but collaboration with senior anthropologist K.P. Chattopadhyay and sympathies with Gandhian N.K. Bose, along with the choice of topics and field for research and a broad Marxist frame for analysis indicated the influence of left radical social milieu of Calcutta. His early training in and use of sophisticated mathematical statistical tools of analysis informed his sociology from the very beginning. Such a sociology could not be neutral towards foreign rulers or rural usurping castes and classes, nor could it be practised by soft scholars who were weary of all conceptual and theoretical issues of global societal transformation. His later studies of sociological appraisal of *The Rise and Fall of East India Company*, *The Problem of Uganda: A Study in Acculturation*, and *The Dynamics of Rural Society* conducted in the fifties, clearly brought out his awareness of emancipatory direction of global history revealed through specificities of *sthan-kal-patra* (place-time-people), the historic task of sociology to make visible the invisible social forces (specially class interests and formations in Marxist sense) behind images, evaluations and ideologies (including social scientists conclusions) and taking a diagnostic view making probabilistic and contingent predictions about future developments and suggestive course of actions for human groups to move in the direction of all-round emancipation. Such a sociology could not work as handmaid of power-wielders on the world scale and the national level either. The publication of these books from Berlin rather than

UK or USA also contributed to their being passed over in silence. Mukherjee's not being the head of an important university department with institutional control of men and resources, must have also contributed to the relative neglect of his work. As we have already noted he kept a sustained interest in mathematical statistical modelling and as tools of analysis. The sudden increase in demand for sociologists, as data-gatherers for planners, foreign academics or as management tools in the first decades of India's independence, did not attract the best scientific minds to sociology and for gifted young persons, economics, exact sciences, technology and professional courses were more lucrative and academically satisfying. So Mukherjee had little readership among this generation of sociologists. No wonder that Srinivas survey of 1973 of development of sociology in India has only one mention of Mukherjee and that is the exceptional case with P.N. Rastogi of having used advanced statistical techniques.

Mukherjee, unlike Desai, has not stayed with the type of sociology, he started with in pre-independence days and flourished into in fifties. He gradually but surely shifted his interest in the direction of methodology, conceived more as a technology of validating or invalidating competing hypotheses than broader issues within methodology of domain assumptions, choice of problematics, concepts and theories, standards of evaluation and norms of evaluation of evidence, rules of logic and role or limits of knowledge etc. Superficial recognition comes easy as it costs next to nothing to other sociologists to say that he is our best methodologists but there are no followers. He must have been rubbed in the wrong by 'super-radicals' for him to write. 'I have been labelled a "bourgeois-Marxist" or a "Marxist-bourgeois", or merely a dilettante or purist, for I harp on the necessity to "clean" our ideology and equip ourselves with a rigorous education to unfold the social reality.' In seventies he propounded: 'In any case, it (research and quest for knowledge) will not promote an emotional upsurge or help to devise catchy political slogans either for the establishment or for the opposition. But science is not the handmaiden of politics, or of any power-sacred or secular – other than of knowledge itself. No doubt, to speak of the role of science in this manner has almost become a cliche, but the cliche has a topical relevance today.' He wanted the sociologists to discard 'popular' labels of 'universal' appeal like 'poverty', 'weaker sections' and 'inequality' or 'futurology' for these being value-loaded, ill-defined and mere symptoms and deal with issues which involve such concepts and definitions as are tangible, observable, measurable, deducible and inferential on a strictly objective and probability basis. He does not clarify issues when he pleads for disparity and conflict instead of mere 'inequality', deprivation and expropriation instead of just 'poverty', class collaboration and contradiction against vague 'weaker sections', unequal exchange and alienation instead of 'national integration' etc. Do his preferred terms help in exposing the disease behind the symptoms or do they answer to the demand of being 'tangible, observable, measurable, deducible and inferential' as he wanted? An affirmative answer is not very obvious. His advice or attempted practice, to move from 'deductive-positive' methodology to 'inductive-inferential' approach, wherein any hypothesis drawn from Marx or Weber on value-free plane or a value-loaded manner will cumulatively lead to a symptotic approach of social science knowledge to truth, is nothing but a recession to Popperian neopositivism and he resents the label. He concludes by quoting in the same breath from Mao and *Kenopanishad* to the effect that 'relations of production, theory and the superstructure in turn manifest themselves in the principal and decisive role, to reject even development and I do not think I know very well nor that I do not know'. This was his way of disarming 'highest form' of materialists and idealists both who desire to change society and controvert quest for knowledge by saying that the scientist should not only reveal the social reality but also change it according to their value judgement (Mukherjee, 1974).

Mukherjee's *Social Indicators* (1975a) is a response to an ICSSR request to prepare a full-scale report on the concept, method and programme for the study of social indicators in India. He himself says that its scope is not restricted to India or any one particular society. This programmatic report stops short of construction of social indicators, testing their validity etc., as that would, according to Mukherjee, open up a different area of discussion and at the current state of our knowledge in the social sciences the attempt may only generate futile polemics. He thought that the discussion on the concept, method and programme taken up in this book may pave the way for construction of the indicators and their validation. The hope of the author has not been fulfilled, though more than fifteen years have elapsed since the book's publication in 1975. Chapter 4 is an attempt to illustrate the programmatic effort to study programme and/or policy documents from five political parties of India for goal, strategy and priorities for development as envisaged by these five parties. The hope was that by taking into account all the value-loads, it could be examined over time whether the Indian society or its specific segments are moving towards one of the extreme right or left or fluctuating around the central tendency. We could also record the change in the alignment of the political parties. Except for the author himself, no other social scientist seems to follow the lead. There was very little substantive information obtained through the effort, that was not otherwise available to social science, even when we take into account *The Quality of Life* (1989: Ch. 2) where the author has pursued with the technique to discuss elite perspective: what do people need. The inductive approach towards systematization of value-load of concepts like 'development' seems to be based on the assumption that social indicators can be objectively built across different approaches to discover points of concentration or scatter on a continuum. The universalizing role of 'scientific methodology' accepted by Mukherjee is obvious. But when it is recognized that the development attributes and indicators must be *culture-specific* both in intra-society and inter-society contexts, unsurmountable difficulties arise about the objective and cross-cultural indicators, when it is known that multi-cultural character of Indian society has many dimensional bases in religious, linguistic, regional, caste and class stratification etc., apart from political-ideological divides. Part explanation of the low acceptability of proposed methodological advance is that it tries to serve irreconcilable conflicting power interests by 'scientific' reconcilement.

Yogendra Singh (1986: 21) is justified in writing that Mukherjee started with many categories and operation drawn from Marxist tradition in his early studies, but later advocated what he called an 'inductive inferential' method which was equally relevant to Marxist or non-Marxist analysis in sociology. The view of society in mid-forties and fifties and seen from Midnapur, Noakhali and Muslim dominated North Bengal villages and from Uganda (Africa) does not correspond the viewpoint from Paris and New York in late eighties, even if earlier views are not completely obliterated. The position of *Quality of Life* almost absolutizes the *inductive-inferential* sociology to *sciencing society*. Different social theories advancing distinct explanations of place-time-people bound configurations of society, stem from one or another form of translating the cardinal values into ordinal value structures. These theories are not disparate, although mutually distinct, complementarily or contradictorily, because of their common origin from the cardinal values." He traces the role of global reality relevant to world capitalism, its role in Asia and Africa in eighteenth and nineteenth centuries as a necessary condition to humanity in the twentieth century and the emergence of socialist world apart from the capitalist after World War I, and the three worlds after World War II. The increasing economic and political global transactions and remarkable accumulation of information on respective configurations of world society have broken disciplinary barriers but multiple theories and practices emerged. Consensus vs. conflict, nation-states vs. sub-national entities perspective, development theories vs. world-system theorists, have resulted in some attempts to conjugate different appraisals by interfacing them, but the dominate note continued to evaluation of world society in different and sometimes antagonistic ways. He writes: 'However, the world range of variability in translating the cardinal values into ordinal valuations points to various ways of exploring the value space on social reality in the context of a better future for humankind. Social science has attained the stage at which the data space for social research is more and more revealed as representing the primary space of selecting items from the information space and the secondary value space for differently evaluating the items of information. Therefore, contemporary social research will be productive if the social theories presenting allied or opposed value structures are interrelated in a systematic manner in place of generating futile or less rewarding polemics by considering them disparately' (1989: 224–28). Thus, *sciencing society* comes within the purview of the quality of life research, as the relative relevance of theories will be indicated by their efficiency in realizing the cardinal values, which is independent of their relative elite-mass relevance.

Mukherjee traces in all sciences including physics, biology etc., and through selective quotes from path-finders in social science like Marx and Weber, Bertrand Russel and Karl Popper the movement from value-neutrality to value-acceptance to value-adjustment and that is the prospect of inductive, inferential and value-accommodation approach and orientation to social research. Gone is the approach when destitution and famine conditions in rural Bengal could be exposed as denial of (quality of) life by usurping feudal classes and upper castes and imperialist ruling classes or when the miseries of the Black Ugandans were depicted as a historical product of British colonials who maintained the historically outplayed social and political forces from among African society and proposed up Indian middle class estranged from Africans and yet denied any real share in power. The shift in Mukherjee's sociological discourse is partly attributable to his accepting the dominant international social science community through UN agencies and upper echelon of International Sociological Association as his addresses abandoning Indian 'poor', 'weaker sections' and other labouring masses and upper class university educated, classes having been monopolized by 'modernizers' and 'pacesetters' as he called the dominant sociologists of India of 'fifties and sixties' (1977).

The above discussion does not do justice to *The Quality of Life* study as such. The study has tried to overcome the one-sidedness of earlier studies which relied entirely on experts assessment of needs or masses questioned for their wants and also the ticklish question of objective and subjective aspects of *Quality of Life*, taking quantitative or qualitative aspects. It recognized 'the joint performance of the wills of the elite as change promoters and of the masses as change recipients and actors cannot but induce and infuse change in the social processes and yield a better quality of life' (1989: 46). The will of the majority of the masses coinciding with the will of a formidable section of the elite is attempted by ascertaining what people need from elite perspective and what people want from mass perspective and juxtaposing them in the last chapter on 'Elite-Mass Perspective' synchronizing the value-loads in the two separate perspectives. The question whether 'the spectrum of valuations of a better quality of life cannot be formidably antagonistic in respect of elites and the masses in one configuration of world society, because the configuration would then burst as under' as asserted by Mukherjee remains wide open. The empirical results of synchronization to a small family of 3–4 children is interesting but the discussion in the mass remains a pleading for a methodological switch by drawing supportive evidence from readings rather than the data collected for the book.

It remains to be said that the main contribution of Ramkrishna Mukherjee to the development of sociology in India lays in his early work both for substantive conclusions and for methodological perspective.

In *The Rise and Fall of the East India Company*, he defined the task of sociology to 'give an interpretation of the facts collected by historians and other social scientists in order to explain the social *forces behind* the rise and fall of the East India Company and the effects they produced in India'. He discusses the early rise of the mercantile bourgeoisie in the womb of the English feudal society, the conflicts and contradictions in different sections of the same class and with other classes. Similar developments were taking place on other European societies, giving rise to national rivalries often leading to wars and adjustments between different European powers, when each tried to secure monopoly to buy cheap in and sell dear to India and other would be colonies. The external trade monopoly and state support were the common traits of the consolidated mercantile bourgeoisie in all countries. Similar emergence of new forces had taken place in India also. Indian rulers and traders too needed trade partners but at terms beneficial to themselves. The change of the Company from peaceful traders to usurpers of state power, war or compromise, deceit or 'friendly' adjustment was not an accident, nor newly developed psychological traits but calculated instruments of advancing class interests. Who won in the conflict was also determined by balance of material power and appropriate tactics to attain the goals. As the Company became the ruler using their own material and armed strength and fostering disruption in the tottering Indian society and state under the impact of newer social classes, artisans traders and industry was successively destroyed to convert India into 'Agriculture Farm of England'. The economic drain from India and loot from agricultural produce not only ruined the Indian people but the primary accumulation in England converted the mercantile bourgeoisie into industrial bourgeoisie. So the very success led to the fall of the Company and the Crown took over the Indian government. The whole long story gives a great sociological understanding of social transformation in India unravelling the intermeshing of politics, economics, culture, traditional and new forces, indigenous and exogenous forces, correcting many fallacious views based on the surface facts neglecting underlying *social forces*. Use of Marx's writings and concepts like feudalism and capitalism was not a mechanical transplant. Indian feudalism not being a manorial one but military and fiscal and historically resting on self-sufficient village community, hereditary elementary division of labour in the form of caste system and sustained on the caste ideology of *jati-dharma*, is one example of concepts arising from specificity of society. Similarly, discarding four-fold *varna* classification in favour of three-fold *usurping*, *producing* and *serving* castes was an attempt to adapt caste to class analysis and vice versa.

The Problem of Uganda benefiting from the experience and analysis of British colonialism in India combined anthropological field experience with extensive reading of secondary sources. Mukherjee wrote that sympathetic understanding opened the gate to the mind of the African people and then came out in flood torrent the pathos of their present life, their aspirations for a future of prosperity and progress, to live in his own country as his own master. He unmasked the mirage of civilizing mission of the British colonialists and their social science objective accomplices including Lucy Mair and Malinowski. The different ethnic entities living in the Protectorate called Uganda were in the process of coming out of tribal state.

The entry of the White intruders only tried to prop up and perpetuate retrogressive native institutions and checked their natural evolution out of tribalism chiefs were removed or imposed with only one view that is to strengthen the British control. The economy was led into a blind alley by demanding agriculture produce as cheap raw material for British industries and later extraction of mineral wealth. Transportation and communication were developed to facilitate this exist of wealth. The class structure of Uganda was analyzed as Whites with total control of real power and economic resources living on African wealth and labour and the Black Africans deprived of political power and control of their own resources, then there were the Indians managing small trade allied to the British but not sharing any real power. Mukherjee also discussed the developmental of struggle for independence. About Indians he advised that they ally with Africans in their independence struggle otherwise when the colonizers are expelled they too would have to leave. Unlike South Africa, India continued to side in Uganda with the British and Mukherjee's prediction later came true (Oommen and Mukherji, 1986: 87–88). The British rulers tried to divert peoples anger in Uganda from their direction towards foreign intermediaries, i.e., Indians and so also the ethnic tensions between different peoples in Uganda in 1955 was shown by the author both as a natural evolution of identities and also the accentuations by the British. He discussed all important communities separately and also the tensions between the communities, giving a lie to the accusation that culture and community were the exclusive domains of scientists innocent of Marx.

The Dynamics of a Rural Society (1957) was another land-mark, whose reading could still trail further research in rural India, taking up where it left. It has tried to show that dynamics of a society could not be revealed without an analysis of its economic structure, even in all case of 'primitive' and peasant societies. First, the economic sphere is taken to show that true nature of the economy is not known without an analysis of economic structure and then it is shown that social organization of socio-ideological aspect is significantly affected by the economic structure. He adopts a novel methodological device by first building nine-fold classification of rural occupations irrespective of religious application and then reduces them to three analytically meaningful classes. Class I is composed of the occupational groups of landholders and supervising farmers. Class II mainly comprised the self-sufficient peasant cultivators but artisans and traders are also included as they mostly maintained self-sufficient existence partly based on land. Class III was made of sharecroppers, agricultural labourers, service-holders and others, i.e., depending on working for others. Thus, statistical categories were converted into meaningful economic hierarchy. Then he is able to show that British rule had resulted in differentiating class II into I and III, with a great majority being forced into the third category through land being made into a commodity, landlordism and disintegration of village community system (1958a). Then how and why of the emergence of this differentiation is discussed in detail to show the new relationship between propertied and propertyless classes at the expense of self-cultivating group. He brings in the concept of semi-feudalism to indicate share-cropping, primitive means of production but wage labour emerging, combined with indebtedness and usury capital keeping the economy down. Then, caste system is discussed with historical development and finally three groups of castes representing more or less the economic structure. Thus, the dynamics of caste systems among Hindus as well as other religious groups and accompanied ideological stance and social organization is explained with the help of three-class structure. This puts lots of facts discovered by other caste-oriented sociologists in a new light.

We have not discussed a number of other works by Mukherjee, by and large they spring from these positions of early works in ingenious Marxist mould or and mature 'science society' mould. His interest in mathematical statistical procedures was as old as the humanist emancipatory appeal of Marxist approach. The break down of modernization and attendant-ideology informing social scientists in India and crises in western sociology in late sixties created interest in works like early Mukherjee but by then he had already moved on to 'sciencing society'.

References

Andreshi, Starislave, 1974, *Social Science as Soveresey*, London, Penguin.

Bauman, Zygmunt, 1990, *Thinking Sociology* Oxford, Basil Blackwell.

Berger, Peter L. and Luckmann, Thomas, 1967, *The Social Construction of Reality*, London, Allen Lane Penguin.

Mukherjee, Ramkrishna, 1944 (a), 'Effects of the Food Crises of 1943 on the Rural Population of Noakhali, Bengal', *Science and Culture*, Calcutta.

—, 1944 (b), 'Destitution at Contai Thana, Midnapur', *Modern Review*, Calcutta.

—, 1945, with K.P. Chattopadhyay, 'Famine and Disintegration of Education in Rural Bengal' *Science and Culture*, Calcutta.

—, 1946 (a), with M.M. Mukherjee, 'A Note on the Concentration of Agricultural Income in Bengal', *Sankhya*, 7 (4), Calcutta.

—, 1946 (b), with P.C. Mahalonibis and Ambi Ghosh, 'A Sample Survey of the After Effects of the Bengal Famine of 1943', *Sankhya*, 7 (4), Calcutta.

—, 1946 (c), with K.P. Chattopadhyay, *A Plan for Rehabilitation of Bengal*, Statistical Publication Society, Calcutta.

—, 1948, 'Economic Structure in Rural Bengal: A Survey of Six Villages', *American Sociological Review*, December 1948.

—, 1949 (a), 'The Economic Structure and Social Life in Six Villages of Bengal', *American Sociological Review*, June 1949.

—, 1949 (b), with F.K. Girling 'Social Survey of Two Breton Villages, *Rural Sociology*, USA, 14 (4).

—, 1950, with F.K. Girling, 'Breton Family and Economic Structure', *Rural Sociology*, USA, 15 (1).

—, 1954, 'Analysis of Data on Social Mobility', in D.V. Glass, *Social Mobility in Britain*, London, Routledge and Kegan Paul.

—, 1956, *The Problem of Uganda: A Study in Acculturation*, Berlin, Akademie-Verlag.

—, 1957, *The Dynamics of Rural Society*, Berlin, Akademie-Verlag.

—, 1958 (a), *The Rise and Fall of the East India Company: A Sociological Appraisal*, Berlin, Verlag Der Wissenchaften.

—, 1958 (b), 'Six Villages of Bengal: A Socio-economic Survey', *Journal of Asian Society of Bengal*, XXIV (1) and (2), Calcutta.

—, 1960, 'Some Consideration, on Social Research', *Eastern Anthropologist*, XIII (3), Lucknow.

—, 1961 (a), 'A Note on Village as Unit or Variable for Studies of Rural Society', *Eastern Anthropologist*, XVI (1), Lucknow.

—, 1961 (b), with Suraj Bandyopadhyay, K. Chattopadhyay and Narain Singh, 'Motivation and Communication Aspects of Family Planning in West Bengal and Bihar', *Social Research Unit of I.S.I.*, Calcutta.

—, 1961 (c), 'Caste and Economic Structure in West Bengal in Present Times' in R.N. Saxena (ed.), *Sociology, Social Research and Social Problems in India*, Bombay, Asia.

—, 1962, 'On Classification of Family Structures Dimensions – Kinship Composition in T.N. Madan and Gopala Sarana (eds.), *Indian Anthropologist*, Bombay, Asia.

—, 1963, 'A Note on Measurement of Kinship Distance', *Indian Journal of Social Research*, IV (1), Meerut.

—, 'A Minority/Marginal group in Calcutta', *Transactions of the Fifth World Congress of Sociology* (Eds and Publishers), International Sociological Association, Lou vain Belgium, Vol. III.

—, 1965, *The Sociologist and Social Change in India Today*, New Delhi, Prentice-Hall.

—, 1971, *Six Villages of Bengal*, Bombay, Popular Prakashan.

—, 1972, 'Nation-building and State Formation in Bangladesh' in S.P. Verma and Iqbal Narain (eds.), *Pakistan Political System in Crisis*, Jaipur, Rajasthan University.

—, 1973, 'Indian Sociology: Historical Development and Present Problems', *Sociological Bulletin*, 22 (1).

—, 1974, 'The Sociologist and the Social Reality', *Sociological Bulletin*, 23 (2).

—, 1975 (a), *Social Indicators*, New Delhi, Orient Longman.

—, 1975 (b), *Family and Planning in India*, New Delhi, Macmillan.

—, 1977, 'Trends in Indian Sociology', *Current Sociology* 25 (3).

—, 1979, *What Will It Be? Explanations in Inductive Sociology* New Delhi, Allied.

—, 1981, 'Realities of Agrarian Relation in India', *Economic and Political Weekly*, 16 (4).

—, 1985, *Uganda: An Historical Accident? Class, Nation, State Formation*, Trenton, African World Press.

—, 1989, *The Quality of Life: Valuation in Social Research*, New Delhi, Sage.

Oommen, T.K. and Mukherji, Partha (eds.), 1986, *Indian Sociology: Reflection and Introspections*, Bombay, Popular Prakashan.

Rex, John, 1973, *Discovering Sociology, Studies in Sociological Theory and Method*, London, Routledge and Kegan Paul.

Roche, Maurice, 1973, *Phenomenology, Language, and the Social Sciences*, London, Routledge and Kegan Paul.

Saberwal, Satish, 1982, 'Uncertain Transplants: Anthropology and Sociology in India' in Oommen and Mukherji, 1986, pp. 214–32.

Singh, Yogendra, 1986, 'Indian Sociology', *Current Sociology*, 34 (2), pp. 1–150.

Srinivas, M.N. and Panini, M.N., 1973, The Development of Sociology in India' in Oommen and Mukherji, 1986, pp. 16–55.

UGC Panel 1980, *Report on the Status of Teaching of Sociology and Social Anthropology*, New Delhi, University Grants Commission.

Wright-Mills, C., 1959, *The Sociological Imagination*, New York, Oxford University Press.

10

Justice Model and Social Conflicts in Contemporary India

R.S. Shrivastava

Four decades after gaining freedom Indian society is confronted with some serious issues regarding the whole concept, content, and direction of economic, social, and political transformation. Whether we may describe it as 'breakdown of modernization', 'contradictions of development', 'discontinuities' or simply as 'national disintegration and disorganization', the fact is that it is not a symptom of any coming crisis; the crisis has already overtaken us. A cool and critical reflection over current Indian scene would make it amply clear that the process of transformation has lacked seriousness of purpose, clarity of goals, and certainty of direction. The contradictions of development are symbolized by various protests, conflicts, and violence at several levels and in different sectors of society. There are growing conflicts across several collectivities, spurt of communal and caste-related violence, revival of violent agitations, emergence of terrorism, loss of credibility and even legitimacy of legal and political institutions, perpetuation of traditional inequities, shrinking of educational and economic opportunities for a large section of population, and growing discontent, corruption, and criminalization of polity and economy. To understand the nature and emergence of group conflicts in India it is necessary to keep in mind the peculiar historico-social conditions prevailing here. The development model of any other society will be inadequate to the Indian reality. The major difference between the Indian and the 'western' situation has been that whereas in western societies modern economic growth preceded the emergence of the values of social justice, welfare ideology and justice model became deeply-ingrained in the Indian ethos much before the processes of economic modernization could be set in motion. It is not insignificant to note in this context that 'economic growth with social justice' became the leading symbol of the desired social and economic transformation of the social order in India. That this was little transformed into practice remains the crucial issue.

FRAMEWORK

Increase in situations of intergroup and interclass conflicts is concomitant with the transformation of a segmented society with inter-structural autonomy into a more participative, encompassing, and interdependent system. Indian society has traditionally been plural, with various groups and communities enjoying relative structural autonomy and independence from other sub-systems, and possessing their own specific plural traditions. As a result of cultural and structural changes in the wake of modernization the traditional groups and collectivities are brought together into the central spheres of political and social activities (Eisenstadt, 1969: 21). A traditional society, with latent structural tensions, but in-built mechanisms to contain their conflictual and violent expression, is transformed into a plural society with multiplicity of groups based on sectional and opposing interests, competing with each other for economic, social, and political resources, power, and privileges. As Eisenstadt notes, the conflicts become more centralized, uniting potentially opposing groups, acquiring encompassing character, symbolizing not only social and political identification in new dispensations, but also demonstrating group power, and making demands on the political system (1969: 22). There is not only an intensification and overt expression of conflict among collectivities based on primordial loyalties such as caste, religion, and language, but also a proliferation of conflict situations in many other spheres like politics, labour management, university campuses, regional collectivities, etc. The cultural and structural changes attendant on the processes of modernization tend to replace the existing well-defined interpersonal and intergroup relationships with conflicting and uncertain norms governing the same. As different groups are involved in changing situations, the established normative patterns are no longer applicable. Each group is called upon, in varying degrees, to readjust itself – its values, norms, ideologies, aspirations, and habit patterns – to the demands of new, emerging cultural values and structural patterns. The readjustment involves considerable stresses and strains in interpersonal and intergroup relationships and transformation of felt community needs. Conflict situations arise mainly as a result of resistance on the part of groups well entrenched in positions of power and privilege to efforts for betterment made by other groups traditionally deprived, but which are now drawn into the central spheres of social system as a result of certain cultural changes in the realm of values. The contradictions between the 'logic of values' and the 'logic of facts' inevitably force the groups into situations in which conflict and unpredictability characterize their relationships with each other. The fight is obviously between those who have every stake in existing arrangements and those who have 'nothing to lose'.

THE JUSTICE MODEL

In a highly stratified society in which certain individuals and groups occupy positions of power and privilege, while others are distanced from such positions and are consigned to structured deprivations, the concept of a just society is either unattractive to the privileged, or acquires a weird meaning. The justice model visualizes affording equal life chances (with certain qualifications) to every member of society for his well-being – socially, economically, and politically. In order, however, for justice model not to hang in air, as it were, it is necessary to relate it to the issue of the distribution and exercise of power and influence in society. Though the issue is not settled in sociology and leads to endless controversies, for the purpose of the present discussion it may be pointed out that the various dialogues can be subsumed under three principal models: first, there is the 'ruling class' conception claiming that the ruling class (whatever may be its composition) exercises power and influence to suppress and control the 'masses', and is guided solely by its class interest; second, there is also what may be called the pluralistic model (Dahl, 1961). It is asserted that in a society there is a multiplicity of groups, interest groups or 'pressure groups' that compete with each other for power and privilege. No particular group holds the key to all decisions and influence and they often come into conflict for opposing interests; and third, the 'elitist' conception of social power and influence advanced by Mills. Mills (1956: 30) argued that power is unequally distributed in society, with select persons and groups, the 'power elite', exercising real power in society. They monopolize the use of power and 'possess more than do others of whatever there is locally to possess'. This select elite group generally consists of corporate, business, government, and military leaders. In so far as the Indian situation is concerned it is difficult to visualize how any one of these models, in its purest form, could be applicable, assertions of their respective advocated notwithstanding. Given the very complex, peculiar, and shifting dynamics of Indian society and its historicity, it seems doubtful if any one of these would be wholly adequate to explain all cases. It may be more profitable to utilize some of the varied assumptions of each to analyze the Indian situation and to find empirical support for them. It is not the intention in this paper to examine the relative merits of these models but only to underline the importance of studying Indian society, particularly its social conflict, by borrowing from, and modifying certain assumptions of each of these models. We are, in this discussion, sympathetic to each of these models and shall relate them to the Indian case as and where applicable. The point is only that the dynamics of group conflicts in Indian case can be understood with reference to the justice model and its actualization vis-à-vis the distribution and exercise of power in society. It is from this viewpoint that these models may be relevant and helpful in this discussion. While talking about the justice model, a related question of its relation to equality principle also crops up. Though the principles of justice and of equality inevitably turn upon each other, the two may often prove to be incompatible with each other, both at conceptual and at empirical levels (Barry, 1981: 115–16). Proponents of social justice may also have to justify some forms of inequalities in some cases. Further problems are encountered when we consider the entire family of the concept of justice – procedural, distributive, social – and try to relate them to the concepts of equality, need, desert, etc.

THE INDIAN CASE

The purpose of the above brief description of the problems inherent in conceptualizing the justice model is to show that sometimes some fundamental values accepted by a society may not be consistent with each other. This is precisely the case in India at present where there not only occurs a conflict between the values of justice and of equality, but these principles also lead to divisiveness and conflicts in society, given the specific conditions of social existence. While both justice and equality have been enshrined in the Indian Constitution as fundamental values, the question of their mutual compatibility, even feasibility, has not been fully explored. Traditional Indian society has been characterized, among others, by principles of hierarchy and holism (Singh, 1973). Despite occasional emphasis on equality in historical tradition (such as Bhakti movement) the hierarchical principle has dominated the entire Hindu tradition, now coming into conflict with the professed principle of equality as a result of certain cultural and social changes. By and large, the traditional cultural structure lacked egalitarian values. The paradox existing between the traditional principle of social hierarchy and modern commitment to egalitarianism has important implications for contemporary social conflicts in India. Besides, it may also be pointed out that another principle of holism, which accorded primacy to group over individual, leads to another modern paradox of contradicting the principles of democracy and citizenship. Juxtaposed with the principles of equality and justice (social justice) it resulted in preferential treatment to certain categories or 'classes of citizens', traditionally regarded as economically, socially, or educationally backward or deprived. While the principle of equality implies that every citizen should be treated equally without regard to his caste, sex, religion, etc. The principles of social justice imply preferential and special treatment to certain 'category' of citizens on the basis of its 'collective' backwardness or deprivation (Kuppuswamy, 1975: 394). Social justice requires that a whole group or community be evaluated for justice or injustice. While (individual) citizenship and equality give primacy to transactions between individuals, concept of social justice involves collective dimensions in any assessment of general rules of fair-play and justice. Given the collectivistic dimension, various constitutional and social policy measures have been initiated to afford protection to, and uplift of, the 'weaker sections' of society. These provisions of social justice obviously come into conflict with traditional values and lead to divisiveness and conflict among groups. These provisions, intended to secure social justice, are perceived by other groups and communities as 'protective' or 'reverse discrimination' and violative of the basic principles of equality and citizenship. There are arguments and counter-arguments on both sides (Barry, 1981: 155–56). The policies of reverse discrimination are defended as being no more than 'compensatory justice', that is, compensating for the various injustice and deprivations inflicted on certain groups in the past; to enable them to secure adequate representations in various jobs and occupations; and to secure the end-state equality for them. The critics of the policy of protective discrimination agree that the egalitarianism inherent in such measures is unexceptionable, and also that some account must be taken of the injustices of the past. But they argue that granting of special privileges and opportunities on the basis of collectivity membership is as unjust and discriminatory as denying such privileges and opportunities on same grounds.

In India, the policy of granting special protection and privileges to certain classes is not new. It goes back to the British period. In the post-independence phase they have been further widened and strengthened, giving rise to endemic and ever increasing demands for new rights and privileges. Also, more and more communities and groups have been clamouring for 'backward status'. With inevitable politicization they have also resulted in what are known as 'anti-reservation' agitations in several parts of the country in recent years. All these agitations and conflicts have been prompted by arguments marshalled by critics of 'reserve discrimination' and impinge on the above mentioned controversy between the principles of social justice and those of individual citizenship and equality. It is argued that in any dispensation in which privileges are granted on the basis of collectivity membership, injustice is inevitable, so far as the individual citizenship is concerned. It is also said that the present-day youth belonging to the so-called privileged castes and communities are being unjustifiably punished or deprived for whatever 'wrongs' were perpetuated by their earlier generation. The argument is also that the collectivism inherent in social justice is against the canons of procedural justice. If confers on some, and denies to others, privileges and opportunities irrespective of individual's own (or his family's) economic or educational conditions and needs. Moreover, proceeds the argument, the special privileges and benefits granted by the state on group basis are, more often than not, cornered by a few more articulate and influential individuals while the community or group for whose uplift they were meant, remains deprived. The benefits do not reach the needy ones, and the weakest among them, thereby defeating the very ends of social justice. On the other hand, the 'privileged' beneficiaries of the underprivileged communities develop a vested interest in retaining the deprived or backward status for their group. These articulate members also serve as the 'middlemen' between the state and their group and try to manipulate the benefits, largely to their own advantage in economic, social, and political terms. Keeping these leaders in good humour then remains the sole function of the welfare state. This state of affairs has another implication also. In a democratic society in which certain constitutional and legal rights have been guaranteed to each citizen as 'citizen', the state should be compelled to put them into practice in case of each citizen by a sustained movement. But when each group cares for itself alone, and there is competition to grab the benefits on the basis of group affiliation, the possibility of launching such movement for citizenship rights becomes remote. In any case the clamour for privileges easily makes each group the target of hostility and conflict by others. Preferential treatment for certain groups also fosters feelings of inferiority, entails loss of dignity and self-respect, and possibly also of efficiency, further goes the familiar argument. In response, the 'collectivists' argue that there have been such deep-seated traditional systematic and structure patterns of deprivation which can only be remedied by giving protective privileges at collective (group) level. A strong case is also made for collectivist orientation by arguing that the various primordial collectivities are deprived not only in economic and political terms but also in terms of cultural identity (Oommen, 1986: 55). The processes of 'expansionism' and 'exclusivism' on the part of the cultural mainstream, coupled with 'the expression of primordial collectivism in instrumental terms' give rise to the peculiar nature and types of social tensions, protests, and conflicts in India. Obviously, any concept of nation, or nation-building process cannot exclude or consign a collectivity to any deprived or inferior position.

GROUND REALITIES

The problems of multiple social conflicts in India emerge not only from the rather conceptual confusion of the demands of social justice (at collective level) and the demands of individualized justice and right to equal freedom and opportunities as citizen. The social conflicts crop up at yet another plane. It is the issue of economic growth, particularly uneven economic growth. Indian case presents some hard, and disturbing realities. Economic growth and building-up of a viable economic infrastructure are considered to be great social equalizers. Whether or not this is true may be debatable, but the experiences of several countries of Africa, Asia, and Latin America point out to the fact that 'economic growth has barely touched the surface of traditional forms of social inequality' (Beteille, 1969: 355). Despite this fact, leaders of the Third World pinned their hopes on economic growth to bring about social equality and ensure social justice. In India, as already mentioned, concepts of justice and equality had become deeply ingrained even as part of movement for national independence, and much before a modern economic infrastructure could be evolved. What is generally known as the Gandhi-Nehru vision (despite several inconsistencies and contradictions between them) had been committed to the reduction of social inequalities and injustices in Indian society. However, the gap between profession and practice in this respect has been a perennial source of irritation and discontent at various levels. As the state became the main agency of desired change, and as planned economic development became accepted as a process to bring about balanced development, various groups and regions became restive about sharing the limited resources and 'fruits' of development. In this respect the case of India or for that matter, of any other developing country is different from the developed countries. Where conditions of plenty abound, tension is likely to be less, despite the existence of few pockets of disparity, as the necessary inputs and resources are available to reduce them. The conditions of scarcity, however, make the issues of social and economic justice the real bone of contention among competing groups, especially when people have well-developed ideas about them. On the other hand, the processes of economic growth lead to the propelling of aspirations at still higher levels, without commensurate availability of developmental inputs and resources to satisfy them. This situation of rising aspirations and scarce resources contributes to rising frustrations and offers great scope for tension and conflicts among competing groups, and tend to alienate them from each other (Weiner, 1962). If the political and the bureaucratic infrastructure fails to develop a proper culture of bargaining, and modes of accommodation among various groups, tension and conflicts are intensified as a result of emerging structural inconsistencies. Moreover, economic growth may also lead to new disparities, or deepen existing ones. As Singh (1969: 267–68) observes: 'What gives special significance to the problem of economic disparities in present-day India is that, while these bear a strong heritage from the past, increasingly economic development and consequences flowing from it have become the main casual factor underlying the new disparities'. Referring to the emergence of a sub-national movement of far-reaching consequences due to this factor, Oommen (1977: 18–19) has noted: '...as the benefits of development are to be shared by a population characterized by considerable disparity, understandable anxiety arose as to the basis of distributing the extremely limited developmental inputs... regional disparities and the fear of exploitation by other linguistic groups gave birth to the emergence of a series of sub-national movements within independent India, leading to the reorganization of the Indian states based on language in 1956'. As a corollary to this, several kinds of agitations and movements took place in different parts of the country, including the DMK movement, the Akali movement, the Naga movement, the Mizo movement and the more recent Gorkhaland agitation. Mention may also be made of the several variants of the 'sons of the soil' agitations as a by-product of the same trend. What adds to the complexity of the problem is that, given the deeply-ingrained traditional values and modes of thought which pervade even the bureaucracy and administration which are supposed to implement some of the 'radical' policies, 'planned economic growth has not made as deep an impact towards liberalizing the structural bottlenecks for modernization as should have been expected' (Singh, 1973: 211). It may also be relevant to note here that the compulsions of political democracy and electoral politics often implied the need to satisfy various interest groups, which also, to some extent, vitiated the process of rational economic planning (Aiyar, 1966).

CONCLUSIONS

We have attempted to look at the various kinds of social conflicts in contemporary India within the framework of the justice model. It has been argued that many social conflicts emerged as a result of deep-seated ideas of justice in Indian consciousness and their relatively poor actualization. The problems arise at two levels: first, there remains the unresolved issue of reconciling the contradiction between various concepts comprising the family of justice, as well as various kinds of justice; and secondly, at some points, both at the level of value and at the level of fact, the twin concepts of justice (particularly social justice) and equality and citizenship may stand in opposition to each other. Compounding the problem at the level of operationalization are the factors of uneven economic growth and an anxious scramble for securing the limited resources on the basis of group affiliations. Though the economic and technical progress achieved since independence is considerable, there has not been an equally satisfactory progress in the spheres of justice and equality. New pockets of prosperity and new kinds of disparities have emerged both in rural and urban areas, not only making the task of cultural and structural reconciliation more difficult, but also giving rise to a new 'style of life' and values revolving around opportunism. Corruption, and precedence to illegitimate means over ends. A few issues arise out of this rather depressing scenario: first, given the existing incompatibility between the logic of values and the logic of facts, a search for more effective ways of making actual structures and processes more consistent with desired and desirable values and ideals, or alternatively, to develop the necessary economic infrastructure and 'postpone' the values for the time being; second, getting out of the trap of what Myrdal called the 'combination of radicalism in principle and conservatism in practice', or Moore (1966: 352) referred as 'equalitarian tinge that comes out more strongly in speeches than in results'; third, building up of a new society based on the historicity of social structure and values, rather than on any 'given' route of westernization; fourth, ensuring that the considerable extension of state activity (as a welfare state) does not make the state institutions a means of suppression and coercion but fulfils the purposes for which they are designed; fifth, building up the nation-state keeping in view the cultural pluralism of Indian society and bringing the several collectivities from periphery to the common mainstream. The fate of the Indian polity hangs on the successful resolution of these issues. Some of the conditions of successful resolution are: the need to demolish the traditional feudal base on which the modern democratic-egalitarian edifice has been sought to be erected or superimposed; the need to evolve a strategy of accelerated and persistent change in the social order; the need to ensure continued flexibility of structures and institutions; the need to reinforce the factor of tolerance in social transactions; the need to make state and its institutions accountable and responsive to the people; the need to avoid 'categorical' thinking by eliminating the feelings of marginalization and alienation among groups; and, finally, to recognize the 'religiosity' of the Indian masses and the role religion plays in their life and belief-systems. The attempts to substitute religious 'superstitions' by another set of scientific and technological 'superstitions' will involve great social costs. Any vision of development has to take into account these issues and conditions to avoid the tragedies of social change encountered in the West.

References

Aiyar, S.P., 1966, *Perspectives on the Welfare State*, Bombay, Manaktalas.

Barry, Norman, 1981, *An Introduction to Modern Political Theory*, London, MacMillan Press.

Beteille, A., 1969, 'The Decline of Social Inequality', in his (ed.), *Social Inequality*, Harmondsworth, Penguin Books.

Dahl, R., 1961, *Who Governs? Democracy and Power in an American City*, New Haven, Yale University Press.

Eisenstadt, S.N., 1969, *Modernization: Protest and Change*, New Delhi, Prentice-Hall of India.

Kuppuswamy, B., 1975, *Social Change in India*, Delhi, Vikas Publishing House.

Mills, C. Wright, 1956, *The Power Elite*, New York, Oxford University Press.

Moore, Barrington, 1966, *Social Origins of Dictatorship and Democracy*, Harmondsworth, Penguin Books.

Oommen, T.K., 1977, 'Sociological Issues in The Analysis of Social Movements in Independent India', *Sociological Bulletin*, Vol. 26, March.

—, 1986, 'Insiders and Outsiders in India: Primordial Collectivism and Cultural Pluralism in Nation-Building', *International Sociology*, Vol. 1, No. 1.

Singh, T., 1969, *Towards an Integrated Society*, New Delhi, Orient Longmans.

Singh, Y., 1973, *Modernization of Indian Tradition*, Jaipur, Rawat Publications.

Weiner, M., 1962, *The Politics of Scarcity*, Chicago, University of Chicago Press.

11

Time and Value

Sheo Kumar Lal

Aldous Huxley, in his novel *The Genius and the Goddess,* writes that a fact is a fact is fact. This is perhaps the best definition of fact in that it neither acquaints you with more than you know already about it nor does it substract anything from it. It is an explanation offered in its own terms, a definition expressed in its crudest tautology. Yet it reveals the essential nature of fact. It is a summing up of 'is', of that which is quite independent of us and belongs to the order of nature. By itself it is a mere existence in a chaotic world of events. It has neither connections nor history. It is because it is. At best it is a point of perception through it alone does it enter into a world of connections. Only then it acquires the status of an individual. Through acquisition it attains the status of reality. It was this mysterious character of fact which led Hegel in the *Phenomenology of Mind* to conceive of the whole world as reasonable and constituted of rationality. To Marx, however, it was the former and not the latter which appeared true. Like Hegel he proceeded to explore the necessary connection of facts. But unlike him he posited fact not only as a subject of investigation but also as the ground of critical hypothesis. He did not rest content with the explanation that facts cannot be arranged in a chain of causation. For all practical purposes, Marx believed that the line of reasoning which Hume followed in his tirade against *Formal Logic and Natural Law* came to a stop ever since Kant took up the challenge to refute Hume. It was not that Marx regarded that Kant had offered a satisfactory explanation of the matter. But with Kant began that tradition of the critique which finally overpowered in the writings of Hegel, the infirmities of the Formal Logic and the hesitant sceptical tone of Hume. Hegel's mighty achievement, Marx testifies, lay in the fact that he reduced the whole territory of facts to rational scrutiny.

He believes that it was Hegel, and partly, to some extent, Kant who grasped significant character of the objective world. Once it was shown by Hume that there was absolutely no reason to deduce one order of fact from another, there was no left except to assert that the essential character of objective world was that one set of facts were contained in another. Contradiction became, therefore, the hypothesis of philosophical enquiry. The supreme task of philosophy was then to develop a science of contradiction and demonstrate through that agency their deducible character. At the hands of Hegel, the law of causation forced its entry once more into the realm of speculation; but this was a causation which lifted the essential out of time and reduced time into a mere shadow of that which is timeless. The order of facts, Hegel demonstrated, was the expression of the idea having no habitat in time and space. And his dialectical causality made a bold attempt to demonstrate the movement of the timeless in temporal sequence. Time was for Hegel the autobiography of God. As such, time exemplified not only that which is rationally valuable. The marriage of fact and value was first effected by Hegel in *Modern Philosophy* and his *Lectures on the Philosophy of History* performed the necessary rituals of that marriage. 'That the history of the world', Hegel says while concluding his lectures on the philosophy of history, 'with all the changing scenes which its annals present, is this process of development and the realization of spirit – this is the true Theodicia, the justification of God in history. Only this insight can reconcile spirit with the history of the world, viz., that what has happened, and is happening every day, is not "without God" but essentially His work'.[1] It cannot be denied that Marx was influenced by these views. Yet he did not accept the order of priority which Hegel gave to the concrete Universal or the Timeless. Though Marx disagreed with Hegel, nevertheless, he believed that Hegel was right in demonstrating the essential connection in history which rendered the equation of fact and value possible. Just as the application of dialectical materialism to history is historical materialism, the application of the latter to questions of morals and ethics is moral historicism. Marx was primarily interested in building up a science of society. This was a marked feature of the nineteenth century attempt to explain human community. Ever since Hegel developed the monistic conception of history it became a fashion to reduce all nature and all history to a set of laws. And with what confidence and complacency these thinkers of the nineteenth century predicted the future of man! They surveyed the whole expanse of the universe, their pen wrote down the career of cosmos. Marx just happens to fall in line with these array of thinkers. But Marx was a materialist. Obviously, his attempt to reduce society to science must be after the fashion of naturalistic sciences in the nineteenth century. Acton has suggested that 'for Marx to say that judgements of fact and value are necessarily mixed up with one another would be for him to say that no science of society is possible. Indeed, it would involve him in a scepticism about the truth of natural science too, which, as I judge, he would have found most shocking'.[2] Acton's contention is that a science of society established in the manner of the natural sciences does not merely state that facts are invested with value but that value is reducible to fact. In appears that Acton was trying to draw a fine distinction between the statement that fact has a moral assessment and, therefore, facts are more than mere facts and the statement that value is reducible to fact and, therefore, facts have a generative power of values. He has referred to Hegel's philosophy of Right and to one of its central arguments to enable us to feel the contrast between the two statements. The problem is not whether or not value is reducible to fact but if at all, how exactly can facts lead to the construction of value system. Though not disagreeing with Acton we can presently dismiss the fine distinction which Acton seems to put forth in his Illusion of the Epoch.[3] We, therefore, take it for granted that in Marx's theory of history, fact and value are rolled into one and in all such critical examinations which involve Marxian theory or morality, we shall, however, imply as Marx himself did that values are projection of facts. This dependence on fact is based on this conviction that history presents in its succession a progressive and evolutionary order of institutions, forms of economic production, systems of government and state and different kinds of moral codes and different principles of conduct in different times. Historically speaking, Mary realized, no moral code has ever persisted through history. He opines that it was not possible for human thought to grasp or the erernal. The tirade which Marx began against philosophy is also directed against the barrenness of abstract thinking.

It has often been pointed out that Marx was an inconoclast in ethical matters as he was in philosophy and therefore, soon after his death a legend became current that Marxian thought concedes no place to ethics. The reason why this was associated with Marx was in fact that people attributed to Marx a narrowly mechanical theory of social causation. This is obviously error of judgement. Of all persons, Marx could not have believed in that. Nobody would fail to miss that ethical appeal which characterizes everything that Marx ever wrote. His writings are vibrant with a call to action and his own life was a story of dedication. Moreover, his dream is grounded in the fact that in the distant future man is surely going to be human and acquire complete freedom. That a belief in the nobility of his ethical ideals constitute the core of his theory of praxis is evident from the fact that he described the communist society of his dreams as a society of perfectly liberated individuals. For Marx, it is impossible to conceive of social life without some kind of ethical ideals. What he actually does is to enquire into the roots of these ideals to determine their *locus standi* in their social milieu. He believes that though those ethical ideals are grounded in human need – the middle term between nature and history – they have a normative character. Where he differs from all whom he criticizes as utopian his essential outlook is naturalistic. And he also breaks off with traditional naturalistic ethics in that he consider 'conscious revolutionary practical activity' to be the essential core of ethics. He bids farewell to the Categorical Imperatives of Kant and the Saintly Sermon of the Mount. He never considered that ethics was a species of geometrical demonstration or brand of intuitive flash. It were demands and not demonstrations, ideals and not intuitions which ethics represents. Marxian ethics is a principle of movement and through the uplands of history ethics has forged the weapons of battling armies. It is the ethical summary of the economics of its time and since all through history economics has been fostered with internal class divisions, ethics has been an agency of struggle. It was Marx's conviction that if we rip upon the exterior of all ethical systems the crude material interest of some class shall be revealed. It is, therefore, of its essence that it cannot postulate a neutral position. What a simple logic Marx advances for that. Since men have never been neutral all through history, how is it possible that their ethics shall remain neutral? Partisan ethics is all that men can have, or better still, man wants to have. This characteristic position raises an inevitable question, what then constitutes the criterion of ethical righteousness for Karl Marx. Surely, it is impossible to arrive at a criterion which may keep itself neutral and above the level of social politics. To Marx, this is a futile question. Though much we try, we can never succeed in getting at one such. Nothing can be lifted out of history whether it is men, institutions, ideas, ethical principles, etc., and, therefore, standards of ethical right are necessarily rooted in time. And what is rooted in time also limited by it. Every age has got its own standards and it joins issue with its corresponding classes. In social history, therefore, the search for the absolutely and eternally ethical is also a mechanism of perpetuating the interest of its class. That is how we can interpret ethical changes in history.[4]

Those who believe in some kind of philosophy of history ultimately accept history as the greatest limitation on their thought. Marx was no exception to it. Like Hegel, he believed that history is a record of progress and all that happens in history is necessary, rational and ethical. Human beings are the ultimate vehicle to realize the logic of history. Social stages are progressive steps in that directions and that which cannot maintain itself becomes from all points of view anachronistic and unethical. Curiously, though the only criterion that history can offer for the determination of ethical righteousness is the test of survival. Here, Marx has introduced into social history what Darwin has done in biology. Like Darwin, Marx too believed that what survives was destined to survive and ought to survive. Thus, what happens in history is necessary and in a way good. What is, was to be and ought to be. This equation of 'is, must and ought' introduces some kind of rigourism in Marxian ethics. It is the doctrine of necessity of what Isaiah Berlin describes historical inevitability. Exactly it is this aspect in Marxian theory of ethics which opens it to critical attack for it has been pointed out time and again ever since Marx that survival alone cannot constitute the standard of right. Marx was obviously Darwinian in his account of ethics in relation to social history. In essence, it may also be stated that Marx was heading towards a theory of historical relativism. It is because categories of morals and ethics are supposed to spring from the matrix of contemporary history. As a logical conclusion it is not feasible within the framework of this theory, as Popper suggests, to put the question: 'Is it right to act in such a way?'[5] It would be much better and truer to put the question: 'Is it right, in the sense of fifteenth century feudal morality, to act in such a way?' Or perhaps: 'Is it right, in the sense of nineteenth century proletarian morality, to act in such a way?' Historical relativism, therefore, proceeds from the hypothesis that history is the ultimate criterion of right and wrong. One may alter the phraseology and put forth that what succeeds in history is right. In appearance the theory shifts the responsibility of judging right and wrong from the moralist to history. And once history is accepted as a guide, it is not very difficult to decide in what direction our duties lie. Obviously, one who assists the development of progressive forces of history is on the side of right because right is always on the side which is about to conquer. Future conquest, therefore, guides our action in the present. In a peculiar sense, morals and ethics are supposed to be on the winning side. It is in this sense that facts speak for values. Realm of value is made co-extensive with the realm of victors in history. Deeply rooted in this conviction is the theory that which cannot help in history its own existence does not deserve to be called good. That which has lost is vitality and strength has failed, therefore, to keep pace with history. Since every age produces its own systems of morals and codes of conduct that conform to it they become obsolete when the respective age passes away. Ultimately, one comes to conclude as Dante did in *De monarchia*, 'what is conquered in duel in conquered by right.'

This close identification of value and fact is once again made possible because history at the hands of Marx has been reduced to science. Science deals with the process of causation and discovers laws which govern the process. Marx often described himself a social scientist. He was a social scientist of history, of class struggles, of moral ideas that are weapons in the raging controversy of the classes. It was as through Marx had before him the whole horoscope of man. And dialectics was the cryptic language in which he wrote all human history. He could, therefore, fairly assert why things follow one another in quick succession and since they must follow the old must constantly yield place to the new. It was this deterministic logic which ultimately proved that moral codes and ethical principles were temporary phases in the history of man. The new was bound to assert, the old was bound to crumble into pieces, and the social scientist must take cognizance of the change in process. But he is not there merely to interpret. His is the pious task of transformation. He is a man of science and science is an activity both of recognition and cognition. Science is incomplete without praxis and therefore science does not merely interpret, it also evaluates. It is exactly at this point that Marx sets the valuational seal of history. Every change in history, therefore, becomes change for the better. This purely physical process of flux is depicted to be invested with processive changes in value. We are at a loss to know how exactly a change in process indicates superior value simply because it is happening a little later. Mere succession in time cannot represent a succession in the upgrading of values. This is the central problem which the union of fact and value raises. But those who have some philosophy of history come to accept history as the greatest limitation on their thought do not raise the question as to why purely historical changes determine moral attitudes. Their whole argument is based on empiricism or say, on historical empiricism. Marx was concerned with the sociological origin of moral ideas and concepts, and the application of dialectics to history revealed to him that ethical principles have an unavoidable connection with the respective social system in which they were created. They are integral to the coherence of the age to which they belong. They are basically economic necessities of that period in question. This attitude may fairly be called as Popper suggests 'sociologism'. In accordance with this theory the state of society and history imposes its own judgements and moral standards. Since, so far, there has always been a prevalent system of morality conforming to the interest of the ruling class. The mode of production to Marx determines the relation of man with each other. Surely, Marx would not have believed in the theory in its extreme form. He was also an activist with his eyes on the future. It was impossible for him to be satisfied with a purely historical and sociological explanation of value. Since they lean towards conservation and a blind defence of status quo, Marx would have found them uncomfortable in his system. In this regard as in many others, Marx's system can be divided in two parts: first its activist analytical and interpretative side, and second, its revolutionary and activist side. Marx has forged a union of historicism and sociologism on the one hand and activism on the other. His theory of value, therefore, is not only an account of how values originated but also how they can be shaped consciously by human beings. Thus, Marx represents the dynamics of value operating in a process of dialectical interaction. Dialectics operates not as a lever of mechanical causation but as interpenetrative mechanism. Experience reveals to Marx that this is the only law which organizes the multitudinous facts of history. That is why it is able to explain how moral codes come into being at the crest of revolution and how slowly but regularly they pass into a state of anachronism. Revolution ripens into stabilization, stabilization passes into stagnation; and stagnation dwindles into decomposition and decomposition is finally succeeded by a new revolution. That is the triadic path both of history and morals. And that means, as Engels pointed out: 'That in this process there has on the whole been progress in morality, as in all other branches of human knowledge.'[6] That, for Marx, is the meaning of history.

But has history any meaning? This is a question which value fact identification raises. To postulate that history has got some meaning is to state by implication that history moves in accordance with certain rigid and fixed patterns. It may be contended that there is some kind of formal cause say, the principle of freedom, the liberation of man from bondage or some such other thing – presiding over human history. For no one can fairly assess the superiority of end over fact and regard facts as progressive realization of that end unless one introduces some kind of first principle or theoretical standard for evaluating it. It may be pointed out in passing that like Hegel, Marx did believe that history is a gradual realization of freedom. And if once it is admitted, it becomes the duty of the philosopher of history to weave facts into definite pattern. To what extent it is arbitrary can fairly be found out by picking up at random some isolated facts from history. This procedure of examination finally proves that anybody can impose any kind of meaning on history. On this score, it is as good to assert that human history is a story of man's decline from a blissful state of natural innocence to the organized treachery of civilization as it is to postulate as Spengler did that the history of man resolves itself into the cycle of national cultures. One may almost select any kind of meaning and finally impose it on order of events. What is required in this philosophical act is a tremendous power of generalization. Different philosophies of history since Augustine testify to the fact that history has always been a very unfaithful mistress. It tricked Bodin and Montesquieu into believing that legal relations are of the essence of history. It deceived Spencer in so far as he took history to be a story of man's attempt for survival and increasing inviduation. Perhaps the philosopher of history is bound from the very start to look at the whole thing from the wrong end of the telescope. This is not to deny that the world of history consists of a confused mass of events and accidents. The point we wish to drive home is, however, this: from the nature of events and facts we cannot derive the goals and purposes which man seeks and also we cannot compel facts and events to suit our philosophical conveniences. Indeed, it is thoroughly impossible to get at any meaning in history without introducing some kind of *a priori* element into it. As far as Marx is concerned the *a priori* and the abstraction in him centres round his concept of man. Ultimately, the whole thing boils down to this: we alone can determine our ends and work it out in the process of history. Then alone history can have some meaning for us. How beautifully Popper puts the whole thing: 'This dualism of facts and decisions is, I believe, fundamental. Facts as such have no meaning; they can gain it only through our decisions'. Historicism is only one of many attempts to get over this dualism; it is born of fear, for it shrinks from realizing that we bear the ultimate responsibility even for the standards we choose. But such an attempt seems to me to represent precisely what is usually described as superstition. For it assumes that we can reap where we have not sown; it tries to persuade us that if we merely fall into step with history everything will and must go right, and that no fundamental decision on our part is required; it tries to shift our responsibility on to history, and thereby on to the play of demoniac powers beyond ourselves; it tries to base our actions upon the hidden intentions of these powers, which can be revealed to us only in mystical inspirations and intuitions; and thus puts our actions and ourselves on the moral level of a man who, inspired by horoscopes and dreams, chooses his lucky number in a lottery. Like gambling, historicism is born of our despair in the rationality and responsibility of our actions. It is a debased hope and a debased faith, an attempt to replace the hope and the faith that springs from our moral enthusiasm and the contempt for success by a certainty that springs from a pseudo-science; a pseudo-science of the starts, or of 'human nature, or of historical destiny'.[7] Proper advises that what mankind needs is 'hope: to act to live',[8] and it needs no more than that and he goes to the length of pointing out that it need 'not be given more'.[9] The substance of his argument is somewhat like this: we are human beings and in virtue of this status our ends are to be born out of us. Whatever it may be, whether freedom or progress, we have to act consciously not with this conviction that the forces of history will necessarily act in alliance with us. What is rationally untenable is this belief in objective necessity and what is morally indefensible is the conviction that we should play the role of a prophet and start from the hypothesis that whatever ends or purposes we have conceived, the laws of history will ultimately demonstrate. 'Instead of posing as prophets we must become the makers of our fate.'[10] We can at this stage of our argument very well expect a Marxist to parry back and say, 'you have not given Marx his due for does he not recognize the tremendous importance of conscious human activity in shaping historical destiny. Well, of course, if you believe, he had not a feeling that human activities are all the time shaped by circumstances, so much the worse for you.' He may proceed to cite the famous 'Third Thesis of Marx on Feuerbach' by way of illustration: 'The materialist doctrine concerning the changing of circumstances and upbringing forgets that circumstances are changed by men that it is essential to educate the educator himself. This doctrine must, therefore, divide society into two parts, one of which is superior to society.'

'The coincidence of the changing of circumstances and of human activity or self-changing can be conceived and rationally understood only as revolutionary practice.'[11] There is some element of truth in this rejoinder. For, as it has been pointed out earlier that Marx's theory of history and morals does contain an activist element and though he relies on inexorable laws of history, working perhaps with as mechanical precision as the laws of the natural science, to unfold the future, he, nevertheless, strongly believes that human action added to the laws of dialectics will realize the purpose of history. Marx must have meant also that no amount of human effort can work its way through against the dialectical necessity of history. But, at the same time, he had the conviction also that dialectical necessity will not operate of itself and it requires human agency to assist it with conscious collective action. The objection to Marx's thought on this point is not that he minimizes the role of collective action in history but that he believes fundamentally that history moves in accordance with definite laws. Neither history has got any law nor can these laws determine the ends and purposes of man. In either case, Marx's theory of history appears just as one brand of doctrinaire system which it was the misfortune of the nineteenth century to witness. Just in order to secure to the proletariat better life and richer standards of living, just because Marx was moved by the sincerest passion and the noblest ideal to abolish the ghastly cruelties and the basic immoralities of the capitalist system to which the proletariat of his day was held down. Marx strove to show that the proletariat 'shall inherit the earth'. He was, therefore, obliged to write human history, in terms of his passions. He created an abstraction almost comparable in range to the logic of Hegel, just to fuse, as Sidney Hook remarks, 'the logic of history with poetry of passion'. He stamped on the whole range of history the categories of nineteenth century speculation.

Marxian theory of morals is rooted in the conviction that morals evolve as history changes. This kind of statement implies some such standard in accordance with which a fairly good assessment of history should be made. If morals evolve and that the morals of the present age are superior to that of the preceding one, there must be some fixed standard for collective evaluation of these moralities and if that standard were to be applied to all history then there must be some standard fixed and rigid to make a fairly good assessment of morals and ethical manners in all ages. That standard, therefore, in virtue of its fixity will assume the character of an eternal ethical standard. But Marx and Engles flatly denied that there could be any such. Engles writes: 'If, then, we have not made much progress with truth and error, we can make even less with good and bad. This antithesis belongs exclusively to the domain of morals, that is, a domain drawn from the history of mankind, and it is precisely in this field that final and ultimate truths are most sparsely sown. The conceptions of good and bad have varied so much from nation to nation and from age to age that they have often been in direct contradiction to each other.'[12] Or further, 'we therefore reject every attempt to impose on us any moral dogma whatsoever as an eternal, ultimate and forever immutable moral law on the pretext that the moral world too has its permanent principles which transcend history and the differences between nations. We maintain on the contrary that all former moral theories are the product, in the last analysis, of the economic stage which society had reached at that particular epoch.'[13] These extracts demonstrate that it was quite foreign to the thought or Marx that there should be a series of some eternal and immutable moral laws. If there were no eternal moral standard, it was all the more difficult to work out a comparative assessment of morals and ethical values. In the absence of a standard, it is difficult to determine whether or not there has been a progress in morals. Perhaps Marx and Engles were aware of the importance of a standard to determine progress in morality. That is why while they rejected eternal and immutable moral principles on the one hand, they had to admit of a moral standard to serve as an ultimate criterion of morality. To them a society free from all exploitation and class contradiction will provide the individuals with highest morality. Engels himself testifies to it. 'A really human morality which transcends class antagonisms and their legacies in thought becomes possible only at a stage of society which has not only overcome class contradictions but has even forgotten them in practical life.'[14] This, then, seems to be the standard to judge whether or not a morality has been progressive. It all depends on the capacity of social system to organize itself on a just economic basis. What it implies is the non-moral standard in accordance with which things would be categorized as moral and immoral and good and bad. On this score it may be pointed out that to predicate morality with some such thing which is strictly non-moral in character is to commit what Moore calls 'naturalistic fallacy'.[15] Surely categories of good and bad can never be predicated reasonably with the non-ethical. It seems that Marx and Engles have reduced the conception of morality to the same status to which Spencer and other social Darwinists have reduced morals. If for Marx, morality consisted in the functioning of a classes society and freedom from exploitation, for Spencer it consisted in the pursuance of that which is conducive to the preservation of life. Or to the utilitarians except Henry Sidgwick, it consists in the non-intuitive character of pleasure. In all these cases, morality is equated with 'something' and it is impossible to show reasonably why it should be so. Why after all that something and not other thing be regarded as a standard of morality. Moore's *Principia Ethica* is an attempt to demonstrate that all such theories of good and he has included amongst them even the idealist theory of morals propounded by Kant, Hegel, Green and Bosanquet – which determine and define good in terms of and in relation to some other thing are basically fallacious and this fallacy he chooses to call, 'naturalistic fallacy'. For instance, he writes: 'If I am asked, "What is good?" my answer is that good is good, and that is the end of the matter. Or if I am asked, "How is good to be defined?", my answer is that it cannot be defined, and that is all I have to say about it. But disappointing as these answers may appear, they are of the very last importance.'[16] We, however, do not want to digress on this point as it will lead us into the complex web of philosophical discussions. We only state that firstly, Marx and Engles reject all absolute ethical standards for determination of moral truth; secondly, the question of value for them is bound up with sociology of knowledge and just as eternal truths are not possible in other branches of human knowledge they are also not possible here; thirdly, economics of an age is the only criterion to determine the norm or the values of that age; and fourthly, that this account of morality is presumably based on a structural-functional approach and therefore they fall short of establishing a correct theory of morals.

We have yet not exhausted the confusions involved in Marx's theory of morals. Indeed, there appears to be so much muddle headed thinking on this score. For instance, on the same page where Engels rejects eternal, ultimate and forever immutable moral law, he writes in the preceding paragraphs: 'But nevertheless there is much that is common to the three moral theories mentioned above – is this not at least a portion of a morality which is eternally fixed?'[17] It seems that Marx even though he rejected eternal laws held fast to strict moral decency as a matter of revolutionary necessity.

In course of history, morals and values have been shown to depend upon economic or technological progress of society. This is rather the central point in Marxist theory. The point, however, is how can industrial progress be a constituent, even in the least degree, of moral progress? Technology at best is man's attempt to conquer the forces of nature. And this mastery does not in any way provide man with moral equipment. If morality were to depend on such things and on such things alone then the most powerful man would be the most moral. Does this not mean that morality is identical with might? But why Marx only? Does not Mill write very emphatically: 'Wherever there is an ascendant class, a large portion of the morality of the country emanates from its class interests and its feelings of class superiority.'[18] We admit that Mill's idea of class was different from that of Marx's and that though both recognized class element in morals. Marx went a step ahead of Mill and asserted that since the dominant class governs technology, technical progress is identical with moral progress.

From the rough outline of the Marxist theory of value described here, it appears that Marx was trying to discover some kind of connection between different ages in history and morals. He was seeking that connection in the prevalent economics of the age. In that conviction he was aided by his observations of the contemporary society. Indeed, there was so much hypocrisy and moral degradation in his time and yet how shamelessly the 'high priests of order' proclaimed the principles of eternal justice, or liberty and equality. All through his life Marx has waged a relentless struggle against these forces of hypocrisy and moral deceit. Most of his views on morality were, therefore, bound to be influenced by the moral experience of his age. That is why, it has been rightly pointed out that Marxist thought is from the first to the last a note of moral protest. It is borne out of anguish and a desire to seek the mainstay of unjust and human life. It is this humanitarianism which has lent colour and vitality to Marxist thought even though it bristles with serious logical confusions. The main target of Marxist attack was capitalism with all its brutal inequalities and inhuman conditions of life. Analysis of capitalism and its morals, therefore, form a significant part of Marxist thought. There is an element of fury and bitter moral indignation when Marx describes that capitalism has forced countless millions to live a wretched existence with emaciated looks and with no gleam of future in their eyes.

Notes

1. Hegel, G.W.F., *Lectures on the Philosophy of History*, p. 457.
2. Acton, H.B., *The Illusion of the Epoch*, London, Cochin West Ltd., 1955, p. 191.
3. Ibid., p. 192.
4. Popper, K.R., *The Open Society and its Enemies*, Princeton, Princeton University Press, 1950, p. 388.
5. Ibid.
6. Engels, F., *Anti-Dihring*, Moscow, Foreign Languages Publishing House, 1947, p. 141.
7. Popper, K.R., op. cit., p. 462.
8. Ibid.
9. Ibid.
10. Ibid., p. 463.
11. Marx, K., 'Theses on Fauerbach', in Marx, K. and Engels, F., *The German Ideology*, Moscow, Progress Publishers, 1968, p. 660.

12. Engels, F., op. cit., p. 139.
13. Ibid., pp. 140–41.
14. Ibid., p. 141.
15. Moore, S.E., *Principle Ethics*, Cambridge, The Unit Press, 1971, p. 10.
16. Ibid., p.6.
17. Engels, F., op. cit., p. 140.
18. Mills, J.S., *On Liberty*, London, Watts and Co., 1948, p. 7.

References

Acton, H.B., 1955, *The Illusion of the Epoch*, London, Cohen and West Ltd.

Berlin, S.L., 1962, *Karl Marx*, Home University Library.

Engels, F., 1947, *Anti-Diihring*, Moscow, Foreign Languages Publishing House.

Hegel, G.W.F., 1955, *The Phenomenology of Mind*, London, George Allen and Unwin Ltd.

Huxley, A., 1955, *The Genius And the Goddess*, London, Chatto and Windus.

Marx, K. and Engels, F., 1968, *The German Ideology*, Moscow, Progress Publishers.

Mill, J.S., 1948, *On Liberty*, London, Watts and Co.

Moore, G.E., 1971, *Principia Ethica*, Cambridge, The University Press.

Popper, K.R., 1950, *The Open Society and Its Enemies*, Princeton, Princeton University Press.

12

ETHNIC CHALLENGE TO INDIAN IDENTITY

Rethinking Culture-Polity Interface

S.L. SHARMA

India is confronted today with the challenge of political and cultural fragmentation in a manner as never before. One source of this challenge is the ethnic ferment which has acquired menacing proportions. As such, it raises some very important questions about the nature of Indian identity, sources of ethnic turmoil and its implications for India's integrity. About the nature of Indian identity, the pertinent questions are: Is it cultural or political? Is it composite or unitary? About the sources of ethnic dynamics, it may be asked: Is it a consequence of the culture of modern nationalism? Is it a result of the distortions of development? About its implications, the issues are: Does it signify a threat to India's cultural identity, particularly to its composite identity? Does it represent a challenge to national unity? At a practical level, one may ask: Can the ethnic issues be resolved amicably? If yes, how? At a theoretical level, the posers are: Is there a relationship of equivalence or polyvalence between culture and polity? Does the culture of modern nationalism suit multi-ethnic societies?

As important as these questions are, these have to be confronted in a forthright manner in order to understand the current state of socio-political dynamics in India. This essay makes a modest attempt to grapple with some of these issues. The main argument of the essay is that there are two facets of India's identity – cultural and political. The essence of India's cultural identity lies in its pluralist character and of political identity in its federal compass. Both these identities have come under severe strain of secessionist ethnic movements, majority ethnicism and, above all, unitarian state nationalism. The hope of salvation lies in correcting this distortion in the relationship of culture and polity by according primacy to culture over polity and pluralism over unitarianism. In order to advance this argument, the essay is structured in five parts. Part I explicates the concepts of ethnicity, nation and state. Part II analyzes pattern and causes of ethnic dynamics in post-independent India. Part III examines the nature and sources of Indian identity. Part IV appraises the implications of ethnic upsurge for India's identity and integrity. Part V deals with the theoretic issues pertaining to the relationship between culture and polity in the light of the analysis of ethnic stir in India.

I
CONCEPTUAL FRAME

First about the concept of ethnicity. There are two notable conceptions of it which for purposes of analytical articulation may be called generic and emergent. In its generic sense, ethnicity refers to an identity construct based on a set of objective cultural markers in terms of which the members of a collectivity differentiate themselves from others and are similarly differentiated by others. This set of objective markers includes such attributes as common ancestry or history, religion, language and territory. Thus, an ethnic group is a 'bounded cultural group' marked by a constellation of distinctive features of its own. The accent of the generic conception of ethnicity is on the consciousness of cultural differentiation. When this consciousness of cultural differentiation turns into a consciousness of political differentiation it represents the emergent conception of ethnicity. The accent of the emergent conception of ethnicity is on the transformation of cultural capital into political capital. Phadnis (1989) puts it succinctly when she views ethnicity as 'a summation of impulses and motivations for power and recognition of a group' based upon its sense of cultural distinction. In much the same way, Bentley (1983: 1–6) interprets ethnicity as an emergent process of power struggle.

The differences between these two conceptions of ethnicity are too telling to be ignored. If the generic conception views it as a structurally given entity, the emergent conception projects it as a situational reality. While the former conceptualizes it as merely a cultural construct, the latter defines it as a culturally-based political construct. If the former implies an idea of ethnicity-in-itself, the latter signifies the idea of ethnicity-for-itself to use the well-known Marxian phraseology pertaining to the concept of class.

As a matter of fact, the two conceptions of ethnicity imply a differentiation between two forms of ethnicity, namely, dormant and salient. In its dormant form, ethnicity represents an innocent mode of identification based on certain relatively distinct cultural attributes.

In its salient form, ethnicity signifies an urge for political power based on a sense of cultural distinction, or better still, politically activated cultural consciousness. It is the salient form of ethnicity with which this paper is concerned. Accordingly, it favours emergent conception of ethnicity for purposes of present analysis.

Like ethnicity, the term 'nation' also carries diverse interpretations; two of which are relevant here: nation as a cultural entity and nation as a political entity. A classic example of the cultural conception of nation is the following definition of nation: '...a people, a folk held together by some or all of such more or less immutable characteristics as common descent, territory, history, language, religion, way of life or other attributes that members of a group have from birth onwards' (Peterson, 1975: 181). Notably, this definition of nation is clearly coterminous with the generic conception of ethnicity. In modern times, the term 'nation' has acquired a political connotation, following its link up with state during renaissance in Western Europe, resulting in the concept of nation-state. Thus, as a political entity, nation connotes a political community, involving one or more cultural groups, a political community enjoying a right to self-determination.

Unlike ethnicity and nation, the term 'state' carries no cultural reference. It refers to a political instrument which covers a wide variety of political structures ranging from kingdoms to multi-national states. It is distinguished by three elements: space, sovereignty and legal and administrative apparatus.

There is a conceptual relationship among ethnicity, nation and state which is revealing to note at this point. Ethnicity connotes a distinctive cultural identity which may or may not have turned into an urge for political autonomy. When an ethnic collectivity acquires the right to political self-determination, it turns into a nation. Once a nation demarcates its boundaries, acquires sovereignty over its territory and people and devises a political and administrative arrangement of its own, it becomes a state. In short, what distinguishes nation from ethnicity is the right to political self-determination and what distinguishes state from nation is the element of territorial sovereignty and complete legal and administrative autonomy.

II
ETHNIC DYNAMICS IN INDIA

The beginnings of the contemporary ethnic dynamics in India can be traced to colonial period. Without meaning to blame the colonial rule for the ethnic strife in post-independence era, it remains to be noted that both ethnicity and nationalism came to India as colonial constructs. No doubt, we have had umpteen ethnic groups and communities in pre-colonial times, but they worked mainly as cultural entities. In a bid to consolidate their rule, the colonial administrators got prepared detailed ethnography of India which they used as an instrument for creating ethnic divisions. This helped them to pursue their policy of divide and rule by setting ethnic groups one against the other. As a result, it led to the crystallization of ethnic identities and distinctions.

Having emerged in the colonial period, the trend of ethnic mobilization has picked up momentum in the post-independence era. Ironically, the event of independence itself was marred by ethnic spurt, resulting in partition, leaving deep communal scars on the psyche of the people. In the early phase of independence, India witnessed a wave of ethno-linguistic upheavals in the name of Dravidian movement, raising the demand for linguistic reorganization of the states. This was followed by a round of tribal eruptions in the north-east, notably the Naga and Mizo insurgencies, resulting in the emergence of seven sisters. Then came the nativistic movement in Assam signifying assertion of Assamese identity against the threat of its absorption by the outsiders. Lately, there have appeared several ethno-regional movements for separate statehood within Indian Union such as Bodoland, Gorkhaland, Jharkhand, Uttarakhand, Vidarbha and Saurashtra. In addition, India is also presently facing with at least three secessionist movements, namely, Khalistan, Kashmir and Assam.

An analytical appraisal of the course of ethnic dynamics in India reveals some notable features. Firstly, most of the ethnic movements have appeared here for greater autonomy rather than secession, the number of secessionist movements having been restricted to three. Secondly, by and large, one kind of ethnic identity has prevailed at one point of time, consigning others to background. The various kinds of ethnic identities seem to have taken their turns in a certain order, starting with religious and followed by linguistic, tribal regional and communal. Thirdly, where different kinds of ethnic identities coincide in a movement, such a movement appears to be a stronger candidate for statehood/nationhood. Take, for example, Jharkhand movement for statehood and Assam movement for nationhood. Fourthly, of the various kinds of ethnic identities, the religio-communal appears to be the strongest candidate for independent nationhood. The examples are Khalistan and Kashmir. Finally, secessionist ethnic movements have appeared in border states only. This applies commonly to all the three secessionist movements: Assam, Khalistan and Kashmir.

It is pertinent here to look into the causes of ethnic activism in post-independent India. The primary cause of it is located in an internal contradiction within our polity. On the one hand, our constitution enjoins upon the Indian State to preserve ethnic diversities, a laudable goal indeed, as it is in consonance with our traditional ethos as well as the commitment of the leaders of freedom struggle. On the other hand, we have adopted the western model of modern nation-state which implies creation of a civil society in which the civic culture of modern nationalism will prevail over ethnic diversities. Gellner (1983: 55), the high priest of the culture of modern nationalism, contends: 'Genuine cultural pluralism ceases to be viable under current conditions'. It is this contradiction between the constitutional obligation of the state to grant cultural rights to the people and its intrinsic obligation to build a civil society by dissolving ethnic cultural diversities that lies at the root of the present ethnic unrest.

In actual practice, the Indian State has been able to achieve neither of the two. It has succeeded neither in defending cultural rights of the people nor in creating a civil society. Hindu Code Bill is one example of it, Shahbano case another, raid on Golden Temple a third and demolition of Babri Masjid a fourth. Many more such examples can be advanced to prove this point. Partisan politics seems to have outsmarted the Indian Union if the latter itself is to be spared of the accusation of being a party to the ethnic turbulence.

There are three other features of Indian polity which are of direct relevance for explaining the phenomenon of ethnic resurgence. These are: politicization, centralization and development orientation. It is common knowledge that the process of politicization has gained in spread and strength in post-independence period, thanks to introduction of electoral politics here. For the present purposes, politicization refers to a process which imparts a sense of political significance to a social unit, be it an individual or a group; or to a social object, be it language or religion or region. Motivated by a desire to make quick political fortunes, political parties as well politicians have spared no efforts to politicize ethno-linguistic, regional and communal identities. This has lent to ethnic groups a new awareness of their political significance. Having become aware of their political potential, several ethnic groups have acquired political aspirations for cultural self-determination, if not the craving for liberation. Politicization has thus stimulated ethnic impulse.

Tendency of centralization is another remarkable feature of Indian polity which has a lot to do with ethnic insurgency. Its trappings of a federal system apart, the fact remains that Indian Union is a highly centralized structure. This is evident from the inclusion of a large number of subjects in the union list or in the concurrent list together with the powers given to centre to appoint governors and impose president's rule as and when it deems appropriate. It is evident even more from the manner in which the centre has used its powers to appoint governors and dismiss democratically elected state governments on frivolous grounds. In its anxiety to maintain national unity the centre is always prone to accord primacy to unity over diversity. For the same reason, any evidence of ethnic urge for even a limited measure of autonomy is viewed with misgivings of disunity by the centre. To be sure, autonomy does not necessarily imply disunity but it does in the reckoning of Indian Union. In most of the cases, Indian Union has not taken kindly to demands for greater autonomy by any state or for a right to even cultural self-determination by an ethnic collectivity. This has only served to enhance ethnic tension as well as strain centre-state relations.

The development orientation of the Indian State, nay its capitalist orientation, is another important source of ethnic discontent. Its socialist rhetoric notwithstanding, the Indian State has by and large followed the capitalist path of development. This has generated inter-ethnic disparities in development. While some ethnic groups have grabbed the benefits of development others have remained deprived. A few of those who have acquired prosperity as a result of development have developed political aspirations for autonomy. The deprived ones, particularly those with a sense of perceived discrimination, have resorted to ethnic militancy. In essence, developmental distortions constitute a major stimulant for ethnic assertiveness.

Whatever the causes of ethnic upsurge, it has profound implications for Indian identity and integrity. In order to appraise these implications, it is first necessary to make sense of Indian identity.

III
NATURE OF INDIAN IDENTITY

India has two kinds of identity – cultural and political. The former rooted in its hoary and misty past while the latter is of relatively recent origin. There are two images of cultural identity again which for analytical purposes may be called organic and composite. In terms of its organic cultural identity India is known for its unique tradition of other-worldliness, transcendence and spirituality. It has an internal integrity and organic unity of its own. It is believed to be absolute, immanent and impenetrable. That is why it has been able to survive the onslaught of alien cultures and retain its distinctive identity. Contending that Indian tradition is altogether absolutist, Saran (1969, 1971), for example, maintains that it is not amenable to alien influences. Similarly, Gupta (1974) avers that no alien culture has ever been able to make a dent into the central core of Indian culture. For all practical purposes, the thrust of organic cultural identity is on spiritually unified personality of India.

Unlike this, many other scholars and civic leaders look upon Indian cultural identity as essentially composite. Arguing that Indian tradition has always been synthetic and adaptive, they underline the importance of tolerance, accommodation and co-existence as remarkable features of Indian culture. Singer (1966), for example, maintains that Indian society has been adapting itself to new forces and circumstances throughout ages. Similarly, Srinivas (1968), Mandelbaum (1970) and Singh (1973, 1986) have also highlighted the adaptive and assimilative character of Indian tradition. More recently, Narayanan (1991) has rightly shown the salience of 'tolerance and respect for others views and feelings' as 'the hallmark of Indians over the centuries'. In essence, this conception signifies the pluralist character of Indian cultural identity.

As about cultural identity, so about political identity: there are two viewpoints – India as a nation of recent origin born out of administrative unity imposed on it by British rule; and India as a nation as envisaged by its seers and visionaries throughout centuries. Those who hold the former view maintain that there is no nation in India and that there never was any. Instead, there were hundreds of kingdoms and as many regional ethnic collectivities, each one a nation unto itself. Stretchy, for example, said hundred years ago almost in a prophetic manner: 'There is not and never was an India, no Indian nation, no people of India, of which we hear so much.' As if this was not enough, he added: '...that men of Punjab, Bengal, the North-West Provinces and Madras should ever feel that they belong to one great Indian nation, is impossible.' Similarly, Chaudhari (1990) contends that India was never a nation until the advent of British rule here and that whatever semblance of nationhood one finds is a consequence of administrative and institutional unity fostered and nurtured by British rule. India's unity, according to him, is like 'a case of western icing on the cake' which can easily be taken off. It is a unity pushed down from the top, a unity that cannot be sustained without force. Some others similarly argue that an Indian takes on Indian identity only in an alien setting, while in India one is either a Bengali, a Bihari, a Marwari, a Sikh, a Muslim, a Brahmin, or a Jat, never an Indian. This is indicative of how the identity of India as a nation remains yet to emerge.

As against this, many believe that the vision of India as a nation is ages old. The geo-political unity of India with Himalayas on the one end and seas on the other visualized by many seers and sages. Such a vision of India is not new, it is found in Rig Veda, in Sanskrit literature in the edicts of Asoka, in Buddhist monuments and in myriad other sources. The concepts of *Bharatvarsha* (indigenous name for India), *Ekchhatra Rajya* (under one rule) and *Ekchakradhipatya* (under one command) are proof enough of it. Chalapathi Rau (1992: 7) puts it so eloquently when he says: 'India was there for centuries before anyone gave her a name, as a concept, as a civilization, as a legend which lived in the visions of her sages, and on which the constellations shed their light, a dream of splendour which beckoned the wandering conqueror'. Taking this point to its logical end he adds: 'The achievement of freedom by India is the transformation of a civilization into a nationality and the fulfillment of nationality through the establishment of national sovereignty' (ibid.).

A few analytical remarks will be in order here. First, India's identity is primarily cultural rather than political. In fact, India has been able to retain a strong cultural identity because its 'cultural integrity has never been tied to any particular political framework' (Eisenstadt, 1973: 667). Like the 'relative independence of cultural traditions from the political centre' India's social organization, including its units like castes, villages and communities have always been 'autonomous and self-regulating in terms of their own social and cultural identity' (ibid.: 668). Secondly, it is important to distinguish between spiritual cultural identity and socio-cultural identity. The spiritual-cultural identity is relevant for distinguishing it from the culture of the West. But when it is misapplied to define India's socio-cultural identity in terms of the ideology of *Hindutva*, it represents a distortion. The fact remains that India's socio-cultural identity is not single-stranded, as the ideology of *Hindutva* seeks to project it; it is essentially composite because in the making of it 'many strands of races, languages, cultures and religious communities have mingled to render it the hallmark of an authentic and classic plural society' (Khan, 1992: 6). Thirdly, the question of political identity of India as a nation is too important to be brushed aside. That India has already acquired a sort of political identity as one of the largest democracies of the world cannot be denied. However, it is still struggling to evolve a viable national identity. In fact, the question of national identity in India is caught up at present in the cultural dialectic of unitarianism and pluralism or majority ethnicism and ethnic federalism. Needless to add that it suits India's heritage and ethos to keep up its federal identity.

IV
IMPLICATIONS FOR INDIA'S INTEGRITY

On the face of it, ethnic irredentism seems to represent a threat to India's identity and integrity. This is understandable particularly in view of the emergence of certain secessionist ethnic movements which by all means represent centrifugal forces. A clear scrutiny, however, reveals a different picture. First of all, it is to be noted that ethnic invigoration poses no challenge to India's spiritual-cultural identity, if only because the latter is far too salient to be offset by the rise of any other ethnic identity. Given its pre-eminence all over the world, it can easily make light of any ethnic challenge. It, therefore, faces no danger of minority ethnicism. If anything, its current political reincarnation in terms of *Hindutva* holds out a formidable threat to ethnic minorities in India.

What is more, the current belligerent of *Hindutva* represents a serious threat also to the composite socio-cultural identity of India. By all accounts it appears that it is not the ethnic secessionist movements, let alone those seeking greater autonomy in terms of provincial status, which endanger pluralist cultural identity of India. Instead, it is the trend of majority ethnicism which seems to pose a greater danger to the heritage of ethnic mix. The recent demolition of Babri Masjid is a grim reminder of the potential of majority ethnicism to tear apart India's composite socio-cultural identity.

Coming to the question of national integrity, ethnic discord certainly poses a threat to geo-political unity of India, unless centre mends its repressive ways. The perception of the threat of dismemberment has gained credibility in view of the recent break-up of the Soviet Union. Without entering into the question of implications of the disintegration of the Soviet Union for national integrity of India, it is essential to point out that ethnic danger to territorial integrity of India no longer seems beyond the realm of the possible. This is all the more so because our sense of nationalism is only skin deep, our ethnic and sectarian loyalties carry far greater emotive appeal than our national identity.

While the ethnic threat to territorial integrity of India is widely acknowledged, what is not generally known is the measure of threat that the model of modern nation-state in India holds to our national heritage of ethnic diversity. In its drive to promote culture of modern nationalism along with its postulate of de-ethnicization, the Indian State through its centralized administration has by all means sought to suppress, if not displace, ethnic identities. This has only served to generate a sense of ethnic insecurity which in turn has stimulated ethnic reactivity. Viewed in this way, ethnic stir is only a manifestation of an instinct of ethnic self-preservation against the onslaught of modern nation-state. For the same reasons ethnic bellicosity is a function of state repression, among other things. That apart, the fact remains that it is not ethnic pride that represents a threat to national integrity; on the contrary, it is the modern nation-state that constitutes a threat to ethnic diversity.

The gist of it all is that the ethnic factor in one form or another does pose a challenge to India's identity and integrity. While the fanaticism of some of the ethnic minorities constitutes a formidable challenge to national identity of India, particularly to its territorial integrity, majority ethnicism holds a threat to India's composite socio-cultural identity. But, above all, it is the Indian nation-state which poses the most serious challenge to the pluralist identity of India.

V
REFLECTIONS ON CULTURE-POLITY LINKAGE

Central to the problem of ethnic unrest is the question of relationship between culture and polity. It is possible to think of three models of culture-polity interface: uni-ethnic, uniformitarian, and pluralist. In uni-ethnic polity, there is one-to-one correspondence between ethnicity and polity, i.e., one-ethnic community one-polity. This is what Herder, a German philosopher, considers ideal. But ideals are ideals, usually distant from the real and for the same reason hard to realize.

Moreover, ethnic reality has become so incredibility complex today that it is difficult to speak of ethnic unity or for that matter of a fixed ethnic identity. By analogy, ethnicity can be compared with an onion comprising complex layers of identities including religious, linguistic, regional, caste and sectarian. Each one of these singly or jointly, can serve as a basis of ethnic identity, depending upon the situation. These bases may coincide in some cases and vary in others. As such the same ethnicity may invoke its partial identity sometimes in terms of religion, sometimes in terms of language, and sometimes in terms of region, guided by the consideration of its interests or, more realistically, the interests of its elites. This variability of its identity renders ethnicity as an unstable basis of nationhood. Little wonder that 90 per cent of the nations today are multi-ethnic rather than uni-ethnic. Thus, ethnic unity is an enviable basis of nation-building.

Uniformitarian model, technically known as modern nation-state, is the one that characterizes many multi-ethnic countries today. Implying that state requires a cultural basis for its legitimation, this model lays stress on the supremacy of civic culture which will render ethnic cultural diversities insignificant. The stress in this model is on the unitarian culture of modern nationalism, a culture in which individuals will outgrow their narrow ethnic loyalties and individuate into citizens. But this model draws a flak in actual practice in most parts of the world as neither modernism nor nationalism has succeeded as a solvent of ethnic identities. This is evident from two sets of studies: one focused on the impact of modernism and the other on that of nationalism. A number of studies from various parts of the world, including those of Birks and Sinclair of Arabian Gulf States (1978), Tambiah's of Srilanka (1986), Mombeshara's of Zimbabve (1990) and Sharma's of India (1990) have shown how modernization has failed to decimate ethnicity; on the contrary, it has led to crystallization of ethnic identities. Similarly, several studies including those of Phadnis (1989), Sheth (1989) and Brass (1991) have revealed how the culture of nationalism has failed to produce a civil society in which ethnic factor is believed to take a back seat. These studies have also shown how the majority ethnicity seeks to capture and control the reins of power and manages to dominate the so-called high culture of nationalism. This also is the upshot of the present essay, as it shows how nationalism has prompted a frantic search for narrow ethnic identities. In view of India's experience, Srinivas (1992) strikes a realistic note: 'Those who deplore various forms of sub-nationalism such as ethnicity, communalism, linguistic consciousness and regionalism are unaware that they are all part of the package of nationalism itself when it hits a developing country and the danger that sub-nationalism may overwhelm nationalism is an ever present one'. From all accounts, then, it is clear that uniformitarian model is unsuitable for multi-ethnic societies like India.

That being the case, pluralist model alone seems to hold promise for multi-ethnic countries. Several modalities of it have been worked out by scholars like Smith (1969). But these have little relevance for

Indian situation as they are born of Caribbean experience. Without getting bogged down into them, it will suffice to note that pluralist model postulates a framework of flexible and responsive polity such that it can hold together diverse ethnic and cultural groups. This is possible only under a political structure which envisages a policy of equilateral relationship with all ethnic groups. Such a polity implies provision of three things: cultural rights, decentralized democracy, and egalitarian development with respect to ethnic communities. The provision of cultural rights signifies an approach of ethnic cultural equality on the part of the state. It means that the state shall not discriminate between majority and minority ethnic communities nor between unequal ethnic minorities in respect of maintenance of their cultural identities. Instead, it shall respect cultural sensibilities of all ethnic groups in an even manner and preserve ethnic cultural diversities. The provision of decentralized democracy implies a system of equal accessibility to power structure. Its importance cannot be over-emphasized for a pluralist polity, as this is the only mechanism through which diverse ethnic groups may voice their grievances as well as realize their aspirations. An undemocratic polity cannot hold ethnic fabric for too long. The recent break-up of the Soviet Union is instructive enough of the failure of centralized polity to contain ethnic eruption. Even in India much of the ethnic discontent could be traced to the failure of the polity to provide for ethnic urge for power and autonomy. This shows that mere democracy will not do, more important is decentralization of power structure which can provide a measure of political autonomy within a larger federal framework to the various ethnic groups. In fact, there is a relationship of complementarity between decentralized democracy and ethnic diversity. It is only through a decentralized democratic process that the ethnic demands for political autonomy can be best met. Similarly, a multi-ethnic setting is the best bet for democracy because uni-ethnic countries tend to gravitate towards authoritarian polity. No less important is the provision of egalitarian development, a process of material advancement which ensures equitable distribution of development benefits. Ethnic disparity in development is as important a source of ethnic disharmony as is uneven ethnic accessibility to power structure. In many cases ethnic urge for power is a consequence of ethnic urge for development. Hence, the significance of the provision of egalitarian ethnic development in a pluralist polity. Overall, it shows that what matters for a pluralist polity is not just the preservation of ethnic cultural differences but the larger system of political and economic arrangement into which such differences are fitted.

From the above it is clear that we cannot wish away ethnic identities, they have to be recognized and respected. The important question is what kind of and how much of autonomy can be provided to them. Two forms of autonomy are pertinent in respect of ethnic identities – cultural and political. Cultural autonomy stands for ethnic right to cultural self-determination while political refers to political self-determination. Few will dispute the right of an ethnic entity to cultural self-determination. May be that some aspects of the culture of an ethnic group appear irrational to others, but if the ethnic group values them the state should not interfere with them. Let the realization of their irrationality grow from within the community through the spread of education and other forces of modernization for which the state may provide. But no legal intervention by the state in ethnic cultural matters unless they come into direct conflict with the laws of the land pertaining to maintenance of order. The right to political self-determination raises the question of the extent of autonomy, i.e., autonomy as a separate unit within the union or autonomy as a sovereign country. It is both rational and prudent to grant a measure of separatist political autonomy within a federal framework to such ethnic identities as may manage it. However, the same cannot be said for secessionist autonomy unless there are absolutely valid reasons for it such as blatant denial of religious freedom cultural identity, democratic process and development opportunities to an ethnic community by the state.

In examining the question of autonomy it is further important to distinguish three major kinds of ethnic identities: linguistic, regional, and religious or communal. Not all of them are equally intractable nor are they amenable to be tackled by a common strategy. Each one of them requires a different kind of handling. India has succeeded, for example, in resolving the question of linguistic identities, partly by evolving a three language formula and partly by effecting linguistic reorganization of states. India has also been able to manage somewhat, though not fully nor satisfactorily, the problem of regional identities. India's handling of regional ethnic movements leaves much to be desired. The sooner it contains its posture of centralized authority which has much too frequently resulted in the denial of democratic process to regional identities, the better. This is as much applicable to the question of centre-state relations as to the question of ethnic-regional movements. There is a need to rework constitutional and institutional arrangements for sharing of power and resources between the centre and the states. Similarly, it should be possible to accommodate the political aspirations of ethno-regional identities by conceding the logic of smaller states. Compared to the other ethnic identities, the religious or communal is the more intractable to be managed. This so because it is difficult to work out any institutional arrangement for sharing of power and resources among religious or communal identities. The only constitutional provision that we have is that of secularism which itself has run into deep crisis particularly in the wake of Ayodhya tragedy. What is needed is to contain the dangerous trend of politicization of religion as well as other social categories, if India's pluralist identity is to be preserved. This can be best done by differentiating the various dimensions of ethnic identity, i.e., linguistic, regional and communal and by treating each one of them separately.

References

Bentley, G. Carter, 1983, 'Theoretical Perspectives on Ethnicity and Nationality', *Sage Race Relations Abstracts*, 8 (2).

Berks, J.S. and C.A. Sinclair, 1978, 'Nature and Process of Labour Importing; The Arabian Gulf States of Kuwait, Bahrain, Qatar and the United Arab Emirates', *ILO Working Paper*, Geneva.

Brass, Paul R., 1991, *Ethnicity and Nationalism: Theory and Comparison*, New Delhi, Sage.

Chaudhari, Nirad C., 1990, 'Thy Land Great Anarch', interviewed by L.K. Sharma, *The Sunday Times of India*, December 30, p. 13.

Eisenstadt, S.N., 1973, *Tradition, Change and Modernity*, New York, John Wiley and Sons.

Gellner, Ernest, 1983, *Nations and Nationalism*, Ithaca and London, Cornell University Press.

Gupta, K.P., 1974, 'Sociology of Indian Tradition and Tradition of Indian Sociology', *Sociological Bulletin*, 23 (1).

Khan, Rasheeduddin, 1992, 'Political Integration in Federal India', *The Times of India*, November 19, p. 6.

Mandelbaum, David G., 1970, *Society in India: Change and Continuity*, Bombay, Popular Prakashan.

Mombeshora, Solomon, 1990, 'The Salience of Ethnicity in Political Development: The Case of Zimbabwe', *International Sociology*, 5 (4).

Narayanan, V.N., 1991, 'When Other Isms Fail Try Pluralism', *The Tribune*, December 8, p. 6.

Peterson, W., 1975, 'On the Subnations of Western Europe' in Glazer, N. and Moynihan, D.P. (eds.), *Ethnicity: Theory and Experience*, Cambridge Mass, Harvard University Press.

Phadnis, Urmila, 1989, *Ethnicity and Nation-Building in South Asia*, New Delhi, Sage Publications.

Rau, Chalapathi M., 1992, *Indian Drama: Traditional Societies in Transition*, New Delhi, Allied Publishers.

Saran, A.K., 1969, 'Religion and Society: The Hindu View', *International Yearbook for the Sociology of Religion*.

—, 1969, 'Hinduism in Contemporary India', *Convergence*,Vol. 3.

—, 1971, 'Secular-Sacred Confrontation: A Historical Analysis', *Religion and Society*, Vol. 8.

Sharma, S.L., 1990, 'The Salience of Ethnicity in Modernization: Evidence From India', *Sociological Bulletin*, 39 (1–2).

Sheth, D.L., 1989, 'State, nation and Ethnicity: Experience of Third World Countries', *Economic and Political Weekly*, XXIV (12).

Singer, Milton, 1956, 'Cultural Values in India's Economic Development', *Annals of the American Anthropologist*, Vol. 63.

—, 1966, 'The Modernization of Religious Beliefs' in Myron Weiner (ed.), *Modernization: The Dynamics of Growth*, New York, Basic Books, Inc.

Singh, Yogendra, 1973, *Modernization of Indian Tradition: A Systematic Study of Social Change*, Jaipur, Rawat Publications.

—, 1986, *Indian Sociology: Social Conditioning and Emerging Concerns*, New Delhi, Vistaar Publications.

Smith, M.G., 1969, 'Institutional and Political Conditions of Pluralism' in L. Kuper and M.G. Smith (eds.), *Pluralism in Africa*, Berkeley, University of California Press.

—, 1969, 'Some Developments in Analytic Framework of Pluralism', op. cit.

Srinivas, M.N., 1968, *Social Change in Modern India*, Berkeley and Los Angeles, University of California Press.

—, 1992, *On Living in a Revolution and Other Essays*, London, Oxford University Press.

Tambiah, Stanley J., 1986, *Sri Lanka: Ethnic Fratricide and the Dismantling of Democracy*, Chicago, The University of Chicago Press.

13

STUDY OF SOCIAL CHANGE AND SOCIAL DEVELOPMENT IN THE DEVELOPING SOCIETIES

RAMKRISHNA MUKHERJEE

Social change and social development, which were of prime concern to the pioneers of sociology in India, have re-emerged as key concepts in the usefulness of the discipline in contemporary India. Their relevance to the study of all 'developing societies' has also been stressed in recent times.

Usually, however, the two concepts are not evaluated critically before their application to these societies. In India, this has resulted more in confusing the situation than in clarifying it; similar possibilities have occasionally been pointed out for other 'developing societies'.

In this situation, evaluation of either of the two concepts is required on its content and the manner of its application. Specified in this manner, the two concepts will maintain their universal validity while being useful particularistically: a position which their imitative and a-contextual application to different societies may fail to attain.

The objective of this paper is to initiate discussions on these points.

I

Our understanding of social change is usually based on the following premises:

(1) An 'alteration' observed in a society refers to a societal arrangement which may be economic, technological, demographic, political, cultural, psychological, and so on in character.

(2) An alteration in a societal arrangement will alter a corresponding behaviour pattern of the people, and this will take the form of

emergence, revision, or disappearance of the social category identified in the given context.

(3) The altered behaviour pattern will have repercussions on other behaviour patterns and will ultimately lead to the emergence of those social groups which would represent symbiotically the altered economic, ideological, political, cultural, and other patterns.

(4) The emergence of social groups, representing the new and altered behaviour patterns, will replace the previously existing groupings and, thus, social transformation will take place.

As I have discussed elsewhere (Mukherjee, 1968: 31–55), these premises are relevant to the evaluation of social change but they are not precise enough to permit us to appreciate the phenomenon unequivocally and comprehensively. Fallacies occur with reference to each of these premises. With reference to premise, (a) fallacies are seen to occur in two ways mainly: (i) the imputation of any alteration from the given fact may be wrong, and (ii) the observed alteration may not refer to the societal arrangement it is imputed to refer to. The first is concerned with social research *per se*, viz., to evolve appropriate techniques and methods to study any societal phenomenon.[1] This sort of fallacy, therefore, we need not discuss in exclusive reference to the 'developing societies'. The second kind of fallacy, however, has a distinct relevance to our discussion.

For example, the number of radios per 1,000 population in a nation-state has been used as one of the 'political and social indicators' in an authoritative publication (Russet et al., 1964: 120–25). The obvious assumption is that an increase in the number of radio listeners in a society indicates an alteration in its 'value arrangement' relating to the social, political, and economic orientation of the people. It is known, on the one hand, that an alteration has taken place in the number of radio listeners and on the other, that the transmitting authorities have the communication of a particular set of values as one of their major objectives, and that for this purpose they transmit (in between the music and drama programmes) various kinds of 'talks' and other special programmes designed for factory workers, peasants, students, women, etc. The validity of this assumption, however, is seriously questioned for the 'developing societies' since the listeners in many of these nation-states usually avoid the special radio programmes, as it has been found for India (Mukherjee, 1965: 44–45).

In a 'developed' society, on the other hand, the above assumption may be valid, as in the USA (NORC, 1948: 123–24). For the members of a 'developed' society may make use of their radio-sets more frequently for newscast or special programmes than for the regular music and drama sessions, since they have access to more effective aids for the latter ones (e.g., TV, tape-recorder, etc.) and a large number of them can also afford to visit movies, theatres, concerts, etc., regularly (see, for example, NORC, 1948: 126; BBC, 1959: 6ff; NHK, 1969: 10–14).

The example suggests that the indicators of social change, formulated in one particular social context, cannot automatically attain a universal validity: a point which has also been illustrated by Alatas (1969) from instances in the life and living in southern Asia. Obviously, the indicators will have to be formulated with specific reference to the place, the time, and the object of change: the three dimensions of variation which must be taken into account to appreciate a phenomenon, as expressed in Indian logic under the phrase *sthana-kala-patra*. Afterwards, the indicators obtained from various nation-states may be systematized in a global perspective, which cannot be equated before hand to the situation in one or a few 'developed' nation-states.

Later, we shall have the occasion to discuss further the pernicious effect of the willful or unconscious *imposition* of any meaning to social change and development in the 'developing societies'. To continue presently with the aforesaid four premises of social change, the following major fallacy is associated with premise. (b) The observed alteration may have a bearing upon a societal arrangement but it does not necessarily alter the corresponding behaviour pattern of people, and this for one of two reasons: (i) the alteration observed is casual or transitory, and (ii) although the alteration in the given societal arrangement is lasting, it either does not alter people's behaviour pattern or the results are inconsequential.

The relevance of this fallacy is now fairly obvious with reference to changes in the material culture of a people. Changes to this effect, therefore, are not generally assumed to indicate social change *per se* (as distinct from societal change of any kind), but as having a contingent role to play in the process. The point has to be discussed, however, with regard to the emergence of 'value differentials' in the society, which are often considered to reflect alterations in the value system of a people as they are registered in the structure, function, and process of the people's behaviour patterns. The assumption is fallacious; also to consider 'value differentials' to represent the incubative phase in the course of social change is conjectural.

Obviously, there are four possibilities in reference to (a) the emergence of 'value differentials' in a society, and (b) the corresponding change in the behaviour pattern of the people. These are: (i) the score on both counts is negative; (ii) the score on (a) is positive but on (b) negative; (iii) the score on (a) is negative but on (b) positive; and (iv) the score on both counts is positive.[2] The first possibility is irrelevant to the present discussion. The fourth possibility assigns an explanatory, and not a diagnostic, role to the emergence of 'value differentials' in a society vis-à-vis changes in the behaviour patterns, since the changes are no longer anticipated but have already taken place. As we shall discuss later, this possibility, therefore, is relevant to a historically accomplished phenomenon; viz., when a course of social change, as laid down by the four premises stated at the beginning of this discussion, has taken place. In terms of an ongoing process of social change, on the other hand, only the second and the third possibility are relevant, but they denote an indeterminate situation. India abounds in examples to substantiate this point and draw the following conclusions (Mukherjee, 1968: 34–36, 46):

(1) The inference regarding the emergence of 'value differentials' in the society may be valid, but the alterations are of only casual relevance to changes in the corresponding behaviour patterns of the people. For example, although the informants may state a preference for an alteration at one moment (e.g., to break caste taboos), the stated preference is no longer indicated at the time for the translation of the 'value arrangement' into practice (see, in reference to the caste taboo on commensality, Karve and Ranadive, 1965: 224–25, 228–29, 278–79).

(2) 'Value differentials' may be durably established in regard to some aspects of the society, but they may not alter the corresponding behaviour patterns of the people. For example, the emergence of certain 'value differentials' is seen to have led to the legal sanctioning of a behaviour which was previously prohibited (such as, the passing of the Widow Remarriage Act of 1856), but even a century later this lasting alteration in the societal arrangement did not lead to a frequent practice of the hitherto prohibited behaviour pattern (Gopalaswami, 1953: 76).

(3) 'Value differentials' may not have been forceful enough to make a lasting alteration in the relevant societal arrangement by means of a legal sanction (such as, the failure to pass a law in British India against the practice of polygyny), but the corresponding behaviour pattern may have undergone extreme alteration (as in the case of polygyny, possibly because of the continually growing economic difficulty to maintain more than one wife).

Findings of this sort are *sui generis* to a 'developing society' since (a) the opinion attitude, idea, and the belief of the people are in a state of flux, and (b) causality in social change works in more ways than what can be comprehensively assumed or anticipated in the current state of our knowledge. With reference to many aspects in their life and living, the people learn in one way at home and in another way through formal education: and, then, realities may compel them to think in a third way when they grow up, and act in a fourth way. In the contemporary perspective, therefore, we are not in a position to draw an invariant relation between the emergence of 'value differentials' in a society and the *anticipated* change in the behaviour pattern of the people. Consequently, the 'value differentials' will denote their usefulness as contingent facts in the evaluation of social change, and they should be taken note of on that merit alone. The implication is untenable that they represent *ipso facto* a causal or a concomitant role in the ongoing process. Yet this is how social change is not infrequently anticipated for the 'developing societies', which places sociology in the realm of conjecture and speculation.

The speculative character of the study of social change in the 'developing societies' is brought out more forcefully with reference to two major fallacies associated with the last two of the four premises mentioned at the beginning of this discussion. They refer to the following contingencies (for details, see Mukherjee, 1968: 36–41, 46–50):

(1) Even though alteration in one behaviour pattern will begin a chain reaction, it is not justifiable to assume that alterations in certain other *specified* behaviour patterns will inevitably follow or, even if alterations take place to some or all the specified behaviour patterns, they may not register change to the expected manner.

(2) An altered behaviour pattern, or a set of altered behaviour patterns, is not necessarily a replacement of the previous behaviour pattern or patterns in the society. So that, *social accumulation*, instead of *successive replacement*, may be the essential character of the changes taking place in a society.

Both the fallacies are operative in India. The current course of industrial and rural development, and urbanization and spread of education, has certainly initiated a chain reaction in the society with reference to the newly emerged behaviour patterns. The chain, however, does not invariably follow the expected course or culminate in the anticipated target of social change. For example, it has not destroyed the joint family or the caste system, which industrialization and urbanization, in particular, were supposed to do. There is also no evidence to indicate that social change in these respects will take place in the near future. Even so, the disappearance of the joint family and the caste system has been repeatedly anticipated with certain drastic alterations in the societal arrangements, such as: (a) the introduction of railways and machineries by the British since the middle of the nineteenth century; (b) the enforcement of the Caste Disabilities Removal Act XXI of 1850, and additional rules and regulations to this effect afterwards; (c) the proclamation of Queen Victoria in 1858 that Indians 'of whatever race or creed, be freely and impartially admitted to offices in our services, the duties of which they may be qualified, by their education, ability, and integrity, duly to discharge'; (d) the rapid spread of English education and western liberal and scientific ideas since the middle of the nineteenth century; (e) the noticeable formation of a class of English-educated Indians, from about the end of the last century, with progressive and, in some cases, revolutionary ideas; (f) the disintegration of the subsistence economy in rural areas since about the beginning of the present century; (g) the growth of the Indian working class since the First World War; (h) the development of mass political movements since the 1920s; (i) the measures taken to develop India since 1947; and so on.

If we look into the social history of India we find that it is characterized by an assortment of different behaviour patterns, by their accumulation, adjustment and compromise, and not always be their successive replacement (Kapp, 1963: 30–40; Mukherjee, 1957: 59ff; 1968; 140ff; 1961: 157–167; 1965: 13–38; 185–213; 1969b). Changes are, no doubt, taking place in the society, but they do not necessarily destroy the existing social systems; at any rate, the governing ones. For example, what has happened, and is happening, with regard to the joint family and the caste system is that change takes place within the systems and this results in the emergence of various forms of joint family structures, many new *jatis* (caste-units); and within and between all these variants of family and caste structure, the newly emerged behaviour patterns are adjusted with those existing from earlier times.

This characteristic of 'unity in diversity' is possibly strongly underlined for India, since it bears a continued history over two thousand years. Similarities in this respect, however, are not unlikely in some other 'developing societies'; as for example, in Indonesia (Wertheim, 1956: 1ff). Also, possibly because of their course of conditional changes in a colonial or semi-colonial atmosphere in the recent past, the above four fallacies referring to sequential alteration and replacement of specified behaviour patterns are found applicable to virtually all 'developing societies'. A simple *sequential model of social change,* therefore, is inadequate for these societies when the phenomenon is studied in the contemporary perspective.

II

The model may be found ineffective for the contemporary analysis of social change in the 'developed' societies also, while, for all kinds of society, it may be appropriate for the study of social change in a historical perspective. In that case, change is a *matter of deduction* after it has taken place and new social formations have replaced new social formations have replaced the corresponding previous formations.[3] Within such a frame of reference, a set of indicators of social change may be formulated deductively; 'value differentials' in a society may be treated as causal or concomitant facts to explain change in the value system of the people and, subsequently, in their behaviour pattern; and a sequential relation may be drawn among the new and old behaviour patterns according to the schema of eventual replacement of the latter ones by the former.

If, however, social change is invariably regarded as a matter of deduction and any alteration in any behaviour pattern (as the consequence of any alteration in any societal arrangement) is considered as an evidence of 'social change', then the concept loses its analytical relevance for diagnostic investigations in the contemporary perspective. It will merely substantiate the obvious fact that any society, at a given point of time, is in a state of *dynamic equilibrium* and alterations are inevitably effected in a social organism. It is necessary, therefore, to distinguish between studies of social change from the *historical or the contemporary* perspective and as an *explanatory or a diagnostic* proposition. In the latter event, the fallacies we have discussed attain a crucial importance while, for the former, the four premises of social change may be considered in a straightforward sequence.

This distinction is particularly relevant to the investigation of social change in the 'developing societies' because the perspective is contemporary and the attempt is diagnostic. For our purpose, therefore, a deductive approach to the investigation of social change is inappropriate; and, correspondingly, the theories of social change, evolved out of this approach, would be inadequate. It would also be fallacious to employ any other theory deductively. Possibly because we do not pay serious attention to these two points, we are not consistently aware of the fallacies involved in a simple sequential analysis of social change.

The theories of social change have mostly been evolved out of the historical experience in the 'developed' societies, and in trying to explain how the West European societies have undergone change since the European renaissance and how the spillover of the social forces in the New World led to the development of the North American societies. A few of the painstaking theoreticians endeavoured to prove the general validity of their theories by applying their respective models of social change to other societies. The most rigorous of them have also pursued an inductive course of validation of their theories. However, with reference to the contemporary situation in the 'developing societies', we are still in the position exemplified by the Indian fable of seven blind men and the elephant. Under the circumstances, the deductive application of any theory of social change (which may be attempted covertly or overtly) will not be useful.

To be sure, the 'developing societies' are not respectively unique. Social science has progressed far enough to preclude a discussion like what Lenin and Plekhanov had to undertake with reference to Mikhailovsky's and Danielson's unique characterization of the Russian society (Lenin 1894; 1899; Plekhanov 1895). Each of the 'developing societies', however, will exhibit some specific characteristic of its own, while the categorization of these societies as different from the 'developed' societies may denote certain characteristics of particularity. Universality in the development of sociology, therefore, will not be attained by a-contextual and imitative application of any theory on these societies. Instead, empirical research on the mechanics of these societies (viz., *what, how,* and *why* of their statics and dynamics) will lead us to this goal.

In this venture, social research in the 'developing societies' can make a profitable use of the current theories of social change provided they are not upheld *ipso facto* but are employed to formulate hypotheses for testing in the fields of variation duly specified by their place, time, and object dimensions. For example, to maximize the contended difference among the theories prevailing today, hypotheses may be formulated in light of the Marxian and Weberian concepts of social dynamics, and these hypotheses may be tested in the same field of variation. Pursuantly, the procedure for testing the hypotheses will follow from an inductive-inferential course of research based on the logic of probability. This is a long drawn process, but there is no short-cut to success, however brilliant the short-cuts may appear for a short while.

In order to draw objective and unambiguous generalizations from this approach, we require a commonly agreed frame of reference which locates a set of hierarchically structured units of observation, analysis and inference. The constitution of the frame will improve along with the course of research, as we learn successively from the limitations of the earlier undertakings. To begin with, however, the smallest of the relevant units of observation and analysis may be given by Max Weber's concept of *social action*: 'Action is social insofar as, by virtue of the subjective meaning attached to it by the acting individual (or individuals), *it takes account of the behaviour of others and is thereby oriented in its course*' (Weber, 1947: 80; emphasis added).

To the anti-Weberians this ultimate point of reference may appear to be subjectivistic and equivocal. However, Marx also stated 'Social activity and social mind by no means exist *only* in the form of activity or mind which is *manifestly social*' (Bottomore and Rubel, 1963: 91). Moreover, we are not concerned with actions at random. As Homans very aptly said 'It is hard to believe that social scientists could have worked out many generalizations about the behaviour of men in groups, if there had been no persistences in this behaviour' (Homans, 1950: 311). For our purpose, therefore, individual actions must be affiliated to one or another set of mutually distinct but analogous social actions, and this set will characterize a specific *behaviour pattern*. On this premise also we may muster a general agreement; for, as Marx said: 'What is society, whatever its form may be? The product of men's reciprocal action' (Marx, 1846).

Proceeding on this basis, we may consider a set of mutually distinct but analogous behaviour patterns to denote a specific *social relationship*. Here again, we may muster agreement among different ideologies and orientations towards social research. For example, Weber wrote: 'The term "social relationship" will be used to denote the behaviour of a plurality of actors insofar as, in its meaningful content, the action of each takes account of that of the others and is oriented in these terms. The social relationship thus consists entirely and exclusively in the existence of a *probability* that there will be, in some meaningfully understandable sense, a course of social action' (Weber, 1947: 107). Marx had stated, correspondingly: 'The production of life, both of one's own in labour and of fresh life in procreation, now appears as a double relationship: on the one hand as a natural, on the other as a social relationship. By social we understand the co-operation of several individuals, no matter under what conditions, in what manner and to what end' (Marx, 1942: 18).

Following therefrom, a set of mutually distinct but analogous social relationships will denote an *institution*, which comprises specifically patterned actions and relationships in reference to what Malinowski characterized as an 'organized, powerful system of human effort and achievement' (Malinowski, 1944: 51). Defined in this manner, the concept or institution will conform to an agreed characterization of this phenomenon among social scientists and, thus, register a relevant landmark in the hierarchically structured configuration of units to constitute the required frame of reference; as employed, for instance, by Marx and Weber (see, for some relevant comments, Gerth and Mills, 1959: 65–66).

Next, the particular characteristics of a set of mutually distinct but analogous institutions will refer to a specific *social group*; and a set of these mutually distinct but analogous social groups will define a society bounded by its three dimensions of identification in place, time, and object.

The tiers of social actions, behaviour patterns, social relationships, institutions, and social groups will, thus, express the mechanics of any society. The content of these hierarchically structured units, and their interrelationships, may be differently emphasized by the persons concerned according to their ideological orientation, terms of reference to social research, and methodology. It has been argued, for instance, that Weber was 'polemical against… the Marxist use of objective meanings of social action irrespective of the awareness of the actor' (Gerth and Mills, 1958: 58). It is true that Marx was primarily interested in the social relations of production (Marx, 1859). The institutions may be examined in the sociological sense or, restrictedly, in the juridical sense by different persons or by the same person in different contexts of research (see, for Weber's comment on this point, Rheinstein, 1954: 157–58). The social groups, as identified in the present context, may be regarded as one of the many empirical possibilities to identify groupings in a society. These variations, however, are either subsequent or external to the proposed unit-characterization of the sociological phenomena of social action, behaviour pattern, social relationship, institution, and social group. Also the hierarchical structuring of these units of observation, analysis and inference is not affected by any differential emphasis put on their contents. These tiers, therefore, may represent the frame of reference required to specify a field of variation in an objective and accountable manner, and irrespective of any intrinsic evaluation of the current theories of social change.

The field may comprise one or more than one society, provided they are identified in terms of their place, time, and object dimensions. The constitution of the field will then remain flexible in theory and unconstrained in practice, while the appraisal of social change will be based upon the relations drawn unrestrictedly among the ascertained characteristics of social actions, behaviour patterns, social relationships, institutions, and social groups. Namely: which one of them deserve priority of attention? What are their respective and relative role in social dynamics? Which of them are, therefore, *relevant*, *necessary*, or *sufficient* to evaluate social change in the given society?

For this course of research the field will be conceived to comprise, theoretically, infinite but enumerable varieties of social actions, and the *null hypothesis* will be that no change takes place in their respect. The inductive-inferential approach can, then, be pursued the most effectively. For, in practice, all the social actions in the given field cannot be brought under examination. *Alternate hypotheses*, proposed in light of the current theories and our *a priori* knowledge on the society under reference, will, therefore, focus our attention on particular sets of social action. So that, over a time-series projected backwards from, say, t_n to t_k, we may examine the cause and the characteristics of variation in the social actions from their individual operation – and through their impact on behaviour patterns, social relationships institutions, and operation of social groups – to the configuration of the total field, the society or the societies under reference.

The test of hypotheses will require a research design which is based on the concept of statistical probability and which is conducive to multivariate analysis of the quantitative and/or qualitative data, as found appropriate and available (cf. Mukherjee and Bandyopadhyay, 1964: 259–82). The course of objective and unambiguous test of the hypotheses will then indicate the usefulness of taking particular sets of social action into account and suggest, further, the necessity of considering others from the total field of variation. The content of the field, therefore, will not suffer from subjective constraints and will yield ever more precise and comprehensive information on social change, as the course of research is successively improved and enlarged.

In this context, the distinction drawn between change by replacement and casual fluctuations around a central tendency becomes relevant to any research undertaking, for: (a) the casual fluctuations lead to what has been described as social accumulation, and (b) when a course of accumulation reaches a critical point, without sequential transformation, the result is frustration, chaos, imbalance, and disorganization, as exemplified in some ways or other in ritually all 'developing societies' today.

In order to be comprehensive in this respect, we should take into account three modes of social change, which with reference to two mutually distinct but analogous social actions, behaviour patterns, etc., may be posed as follows: (a) x is removed from the social scene by force, with or without x' being deliberately introduced in its place; (b) x disappears without replacement or is replaced by x' in a situation which is not deliberately induced and achieved; and (c) x survives with x' by accumulation in a situation which may or may not have been deliberately induced. The first and the second possibilities refer to a historically accomplished phenomenon; the only difference between them is that for the former we merely *state* the resultant change, and for the later we *deduce* it from empirical investigation. The third possibility, on the other hand, is the one which we are primarily concerned with; and, in this case, change becomes a *matter of inference* to be drawn on a probability basis. For which could be considered as 'change' over the time period ($t_i \ldots t_i$) could also be considered casual fluctuations around the basic behaviour pattern over the time period ($t_i \ldots t_i \ldots t_n$). Correspondingly, the inference on change over the time period ($t_{(n+1)} \ldots t_r$) may be superseded by the inference of casual fluctuations over the time period ($t_i \ldots t_i \ldots t_n$, $t_{(n+1)} \ldots t_r$), in which the nature and degree of fluctuations may have varied among themselves over the total time period.

A suitable example to this effect is the previously mentioned recurrent inference drawn on the disintegration and disappearance of the caste system in India under a broad categorization of the temporal point as, say: t_i = the onset of the Bhakti movement in about the twelfth century; t_i = the final phase of development of the movement in about the seventeenth century; t_n = the eighteenth and the first phase of the nineteenth century $t_{(n+1)}$ = the second half of the nineteenth century; and t_r = 1947 to the present (see, for details, Mukherjee, 1958: 182–91, 313–28, 423–29). Such a situation calls for empirical investigations on the basis of 'no change' as the null hypothesis and the alternate hypotheses formulated in light of our *a priori* knowledge on the phenomenon and the prevailing theories on the origin, development, and persistence of the caste system in the society.

The formulation of alternate hypotheses in reference to the prevailing theories on a social phenomenon may not be a simple task since there may be a general agreement among the contending viewpoints on the constituents of the phenomenon. In that case, difference may be noticed in the allocation of relative importance to the various factors producing and sustaining the phenomenon in the society or in the assumption of varying intensity of their regression upon one another. It is necessary to underline this point because, more often than not, social research on the 'developing societies' is pursued on the basis of sweeping generalization on one or another theory or a deductive selection of a particular course of argument in any one of them. What is required, instead, is a content analysis of the writings, which record the development of respective theories, as a prelude to the formulation of the alternate hypotheses. This is a painstaking and time-consuming task, but it should be an obligatory part of social research if the development of sociology is not to be distorted by dogmatic adherence to any particular theory, dissipated by the so-called 'open minded' and 'hit and run' method of empirical research, or rendered futile by imaginary or sterile polemics.

For example, both Marx and Weber were of the opinion that the caste system of India formed a syndrome of economic, social, and ideological factors (cf. Marx, 1853a; 1949: I, 350–52; Weber, 1958: 101–33). The difference between Marx and Weber in this context, therefore, may be obtained in their attribution of decisive importance to one or the other factor in the origin, development, and persistence of the societal phenomenon. Thus, to quote a few of their significant statements in this respect:

Marx: 'The primitive forms of property necessarily dissolve into the relation of property to the different objective elements conditioning production: they are the economic basis of different forms of community, and in turn presuppose specific forms of community. These forms are significantly modified once labour itself is placed among the *objective conditions of production* (as in slavery and serfdom). …[Where] the particular kind of labour – i.e., its craft mastery and consequently property in the instrument of labour – equals property in the conditions of production, this admittedly excludes slavery and serfdom. However, it may lead to an analogous negative development in the form of a caste system' (Marx, 1964: 101–02.).

Weber: 'All factors important for the development of the caste system operated singly elsewhere in the world. Only in India, however, did they operate conjointly under special Indian conditions: the conditions of a conquered territory within ineffable, sharp, "racial" antagonisms made socially visible by skin colour. ... [This] well-integrated, unique social system could not have originated or at least could not have conquered and lasted without the pervasive and all-powerful influence of the Brahmans. It must have existed as a finished idea long before it conquered even the greater part of North India. The combination of caste legitimacy with *karma* doctrine, thus with the specific Brahmanical theodicy – in its way a stroke of genius – plainly is the construction of rational ethical thought and not the production of any economic "condition" ' (Weber, 1958: 131).

Marx: 'When the crude form in which the division of labour appears with the Indians and Egyptians calls forth the caste system in their state and religion, the historian believes that the caste system is the power which has produced this crude social from. While the French and the English at least hold by the political illusion, which is moderately close to reality, the Germans move in the realm of the "pure spirit", and make religious illusion the driving force of history' (Marx, 1942: 30).

Weber: '...what was decisive for the Hindu caste system in particular was its connection with a belief in transmigration, and especially its connection with the tenet that any possible improvement in one's chances in subsequent incarnations depended on the faithful execution in the present lifetime of the vocation assigned him by virtue of his caste status.... Among the Hindus, the Biblical emphasis echoed in Luther's injunction, "Remain stead-fast in your vocation", was elevated into a cardinal religious obligation and was fortified by powerful religious sanctions' (Weber, 1965: 42–43).

Marx: 'We know that the municipal organization and the economical basis of the village communities has been broken up, but their worst feature, the dissolution of society into stereotyped and disconnected atoms, has survived their vitality.... Modern industry, resulting from the railway system will dissolve the hereditary divisions of labour, upon which rest the Indian castes, those decisive impediments to Indian progress and Indian power' (Marx, 1853b).

Weber: 'Modern industrial capitalism, in particular the factory, made its entry into India under the British administration and with direct and strong incentives. But, comparatively speaking, how small is the scale and how great the difficulties.... So long as the *karma* doctrine was unshaken, revolutionary ideas or progressivism were inconceivable... . It was impossible to shatter traditionalism, based on caste ritualism anchored in *karma* doctrine, by rationalizing the economy' (Weber, 1958: 113–14, 123).

It follows from the issues we have discussed so far that the content and the manner of examination of social change in the contemporary perspective and as a diagnostic proportion are reduced, ultimately, to interpretation and prediction. It need not, however, be conjectural. Hence, to be precise and objective in drawing appropriate inferences, we cannot depend on the four sequential premises enumerated at the beginning of this discussion. We cannot, on the other hand, consider any societal change as social change. In between these two extreme situations, therefore, the following set of questions should provide us with the guidelines to pursue our researches unambiguously and fruitfully:

(1) What is the rationale behind the selection of a set of social actions for observation and analysis: that is, what are the alternate hypotheses put forward against the null hypothesis of 'no change', and why?
(2) How have the relations among the selected social actions been drawn to represent particular behaviour patterns, social relationships, institutions, social groups, and, ultimately, the total field = the society or the societies under reference?
(3) How precise are the parameters to define the *place* and the *object* under reference; and what is the rationale behind the time-series taken into account (e.g., $t_n \ldots t_k$, $t_j \ldots t_a$) and why?
(4) What is the nature of alterations, over the time-series, in the societal arrangements which have altered one or a set of the specified social actions, behaviour patterns, etc.?
(5) What are the specific characteristics of the altered social actions, behaviour patterns, etc., over the time-series; and how and why have they altered?
(6) What is the chain of alteration effected by the altered social actions, behaviour patterns, etc., over the time-series?
(7) Has that chain been ascertained precisely, unambiguously, and comprehensively at the existing state of our knowledge; and is the design of research amenable to a better appraisal of the chain of alteration in the future along with our ever accumulating knowledge in this respect?
(8) How and why has the chain of alteration taken a particular configuration over the time-series, and not any other?

(9) What is the likely configuration of this chain of alteration in the immediate future, as can be predicted objectively?
(10) How can we make our predictions increasingly efficient in light of our continually increasing knowledge on the subject?

III

Let us now examine the concept of social development. While the concept of social change is in vogue for some years, the concept of social development has been introduced fairly recently to appraise the dynamics of the 'developing societies'. This is an improvement in research methodology, for the latter was submerged in the former and social change was implicitly meant for 'development'. Social change was, thus, a value-loaded concept which hampered its objective evaluation even more than what has already been discussed. Social development, however, remains a value-charged concept, having the implication of particular kinds of social change from a particular base and towards an ultimate goal.

Attempts are now being made – significantly by the economists and statisticians – to enumerate the content of social development under subject-categories like nutrition, shelter, health, education, leisure and recreation, security, and opulence level (Drewnowski, 1967: 131–34); or under the categories like output and incomes, conditions of production, levels of living, attitudes towards life and work, institutions, and policies (Myrdal, 1968: III, 1960). These attempts help us to ascertain social development on the basis of precise and objective information (e.g., McGranahan, 1969: 1–22) in place of its superficial and esoteric evaluation. They will not, however, make the concept of social development value-free.

The values are imposed by the respective social philosophies of development. This is obvious when the world is dichotomized into the 'free' sector and its counterpart, or when a three-fold distinction is drawn among the western world, the Socialist World, and the Third World. It is also implied when human society is dichotomized as capitalist and communist; trichotomized as monopoly-capitalistic, bourgeois-democratic, and socialistic; and so on. 'Value considerations' in social development may be further indicated by the distinction drawn within any one of these sectors; for example, by the Russian and the Chinese outlook within the gamut of socialist development. Also, another social philosophy may totally upset the accepted constellation of development indicators for an 'affluent' society. For example, the growth of GNP, rise in per capita incomes, increasing levels of investment, industrialization and urbanization, etc., will be of no relevance to the Gandhian outlook of social development.

The concept of a 'welfare society' or faith in the overall 'humanitarian values' also will not impose an equal 'value-load' on all possible courses of social development and, thus, make the concept of social development operationally value-free. Consensus on such a concept or understanding will be obtained only at the level of such generalized truths as 'all men are mortal'. In effect, on the other hand, differential emphasis on the developmental measures will depend on 'value considerations' of the politicians, planners, reformers, etc., in a local, regional or the global perspective, even when they subscribe to a specific kind, and a particular brand, of social philosophy. The 'developing societies' furnish, currently, many examples of this kind.

Conceptually as well as operationally, therefore, we cannot consider that social development is value-free. Bendix has attempted to override this problem by distinguishing between a 'nominal' and the 'real' definition of 'development'. To quote Bendix (1964: 5–6): 'There is nothing inherently wrong about using the history of western societies as the basis of what we propose to mean by *development* – as long as the purely nominal character of this definition is understood. The history of industrial societies must certainly be one basis for our definition in this field. Trouble arises only when it is assumed that these are "real" definitions, that development can mean only what it has come to mean in some western societies.'. Such an attempt, however, only further substantiates the fact that social development is a value-loaded concept. Therefore, in place of ignoring or bypassing the inherent characteristic of this phenomenon, we should consider the point: how efficiently we may employ the concept of social development to appraise the dynamics of the 'developing societies' under the proviso that it is value-loaded.

'Tradition to modernity' is the schema frequently employed now-a-days to evaluate social development. This is a useful schema so long as we adhere to its basic connotation that tradition denotes the base of particular kinds of social change and modernity denotes the goal of these changes. Usually, however, we do not specify the contents of 'tradition' and 'modernity', and consider them to be axiomatic. For example, Deutsch (1961: 493) defined 'social mobilization' as 'an overall process of change, which happens to substantial parts of the population in countries which are moving from traditional to modern ways of life'. We need not discuss the overall fallacy of this approach since it has already been pointed out (Mshvenieradze, 1964: III, 33–37). It would, however be useful to note additionally that the schema stimulates the image in the mind of many social scientists that the 'developing societies' of Asia, Africa, Oceania, and South America are 'traditional' and the 'developed' societies of West Europe and North America are 'modern'. This dichotomy is implicit, and occasionally explicit, in the writings of several reputable social scientists (e.g., Black, 1966: 1–55; Shils, 1962: 7–11). Even to countries like the USSR and Japan they may accord a 'developed' status in parenthesis, while China is hardly ever mentioned in this context. The upshot is that the schema loses its objectivity, ignores the inherent dynamism of any society at any time-period, and conforms to a particular course of ideology and action.

Insofar as the concept of modernity is concerned, doubts about the usefulness of equating it to the 'social, political, and economic characteristics of western democracies' has already been expressed (Nettl and Robertson, 1968: 42). Equally it is necessary to examine the utility of a blanket characterization of the 'developing societies' as traditional, and to specify how the schema of 'tradition to modernity' can be employed fruitfully. For, if we treat 'tradition' as a value-free concept and as merely referring to that body of social actions, behaviour patterns, social relationships, and institutions of a social group (or of the society *en bloc*), which has been transmitted from the past to the present, then the schema loses its analytical relevance. There is not a single society, at any point of time and space, which has not a tradition behind it. If, on the other hand, 'tradition' is regarded on *its own merit* as a value-charged concept, then the hitherto applied dichotomy of tradition and modernity cannot but resurrect the concept of 'primitive' and 'civilized' which is an anathema to the 'modern' man and is also unreal as representing discrete entities. For the schema, therefore, tradition acquires a meaning only as *subjunctive* to modernity, and at denoted by that body of transmitted facts which is antithetical to the purposively conceived characteristics of modernity.

Viewed in this manner, the tradition (or, more appropriately, the traditionalism) of a society cannot be specified by some innate characteristics like the lack of achievement orientation, joint family system, the caste system of India or any ascriptive system in other 'developing societies', and so on. Correspondingly, modernity cannot be denoted by certain generalized concepts or attributes like rationality, nuclear family organization, etc. The procedure may give a wrong characterization of what is transmitted or provide those indicators of modernization which are irrelevant or even harmful to the desired course of social development.

For example, according to the Brahmanical tradition, which has permeated into virtually all sectors of the Indian society, all social actions fall under one of the four categories of *dharma* (relating to religious practices), *artha* (relating to wealth and material well-being), *kama* (relating to the fulfillment of desire), and *moksa* (relating to ultimate salvation). The evaluation of any social action, however, refers to whether it is a *dharma* action (i.e., righteous) or an *adharma* (i.e., not-*dharma*) action. The category *moksa,* in this context, consumes all actions. Therefore, the 'traditional' social actions categorized as *artha* and *kama* but evaluated as *dharma* can be achievement-oriented at any time period, and this possibility is reinforced by the fact that the gamuts of *dharma* and *adharma* actions are not immutable. Otherwise we fail to explain instances like that a Brahmin working even at the production bench of a shoe factory does not consider himself to commit an *adharma* action, which he would reckon to have done if he was earning his livelihood as a cobbler.

Thus, the lack of achievement-orientation *per se* is not a characteristic of the so-called Indian tradition, as we are sometimes told in course of an imitative and a-contextual application of a model of modernization. What we should consider, instead, is whether the 'traditional' achievement-orientation in the society is conducive or not to the desired course of social development. Similar situations should be searched for other 'developing societies' in place of trying to establish an 'achieving society' on an utopian basis.

If we pursue the example of 'traditional' social actions in India, we find that the consequence of *dharma* and *adharma* actions is assessable in the future perspective according to the doctrine of *karma* and the theory of reincarnation of souls. Accordingly, the contemporary actions are cumulative and the net effect on the presumed next birth is derived by subtracting the total consequence of *adharma* actions from that of *dharma* actions. Causality or concomitance of all these actions is not specific to the place (*sthana*), time (*kala*), and object (*patra*). So that, within the 'traditional' set-up, certain *adharma* actions can be performed with impunity since they will be expatiated by the corresponding performance of suitable *dharma* actions. Rationality, in the contemporary situation, can thus be purposively applied to optimize the relation between ends and means, without moving out of the sphere of 'traditional' ideology and action. Possibly, it is only in this or a similar manner that many apparent incongruities in the 'developing societies' can be duly explained; for example, the 'anti-social' activities of many 'achieving' persons; the contradictory role of the entrepreneurs in their economic *versus* ideological life, of the elites in their social versus political life; and so on. Rationality *per se*, therefore, is not a suitable indicator of any course of modernization.

The assumed role of the caste system to obstruct modernization of India, and of similar ascriptive systems in other 'developing societies', should also be examined in terms of their actual effect on the programme to attain the particular goal of modernity. The facts like that the people identify themselves by caste, rank, or religion, or that the political parties make use of the caste, rank, or the religious affiliation of the people to gain votes in elections, are inconsequential until we learn how and why that action or behaviour pattern obstructs a particular course of social development. There are ample evidence to substantiate the fact that the 'traditional' modes of identification in many 'developing societies' serve as a cloak to represent specific class or economic interest in the contemporary situation (see Mukherjee, 1957 for the situation in West Bengal). We also notice, contextually, that political parties with religious or similar appellations are not common in many 'developed' societies.

On the other hand, suppositions like that the joint family system hinders social development may be irrelevant or have a harmful effect on that very sense of development in the given conditions. For example, the frequently found joint family in India is of a two or three generation lineal structure with the principal or the only provider for the family located at: (a) the top most generation level, or (b) at the intermediate level, if the top is represented by the widowed 'mother' or old-age 'parent(s)' (Mukherjee, 1969b: 75–97). In both cases, therefore, the maintenance of the joint structure may hinder a course of modernization if: (a) it is in a position to provide economic and the corresponding opportunities to all able bodied persons, (b) more than one such person is found in the respective families, and (c) these persons are found to relinquish or undermine the opportunities offered to them in favour of a partial or a fully parasitic existence upon their parent(s) earnings. These three conditions are rarely met with simultaneously in India or other 'developing societies', while the second form of joint family structure denotes that: (a) its maintenance may be an inevitable burden on the nuclear sub-unit since the old people cannot be provided for in any other way, or (b) it is a boon to the working couple since their children can be looked after by the 'grandparent(s)' when they are out to earn for the family. Thus, the formation of nuclear family organization is not necessarily an indicator for even the commonly implied goal of modernization. Goode (1963: 2) also noted: 'Just *how* industrialization or urbanization affects the family system, or how the family system facilitates or hinders these processes, is not clear.'

Many more examples can be cited to substantiate the obvious fact that, at the present state of our knowledge of the 'developing societies', traditionalism and modernization cannot be indicated by a set of attributes evolved out of an a-contextual theoretical construct. Just as modernity cannot be comprehended in one and the only way, and the traditionalism of a society is predicated by a specific characterization of social development, so that attributes of traditionalism and modernization will have to be formulated for each society from empirical investigations. And, if we accept this aspect of reality, we find that the enforced dichotomy of 'developing' and 'developed' societies loses its meaning for social research. No society is finally developed, whatever may be the chosen goal of social development. Also, the so-called 'developed' societies may choose a different goal of development. Either way, an objectively formulated schema of 'tradition to modernity' is applicable to any and all world societies.

A discussion on the relative merits of different goals of social development is beyond our present term of reference. We may note, however, that the appraisal of any course of social development in a society will primarily require answering the following questions:

(1) What is the goal of social development, and why that goal has been chosen?
(2) What is the immediate target of social development, what are the successive targets, and how are they sequentially related?
(3) What are the necessary social actions, behaviour patterns, social relationships, institutions, and social groups for the realization of the successive targets and, eventually, the ultimate goal of social development?
(4) What are the characteristics and intensity of the social actions, etc., which are found currently in the society and which are inimical to those formulated for (3) above?
(5) How and why have the social actions, etc., under (4) been transmitted from the past? What are their traditional roots and current viability? And, how can they be replaced by those under (3)?
(6) What is, therefore, the programme of the desired course of development? How can it be communicated to the people, and how can they be motivated to strive for it?

The answer to these questions will provide the basis to examine social change in the given society in an induced situation. The questions posed earlier to appreciate social change *per se* will, therefore, follow in order to evaluate the dynamics of the society precisely, unambiguously, and comprehensively.

IV

Pursued in this manner, the development of sociology in each society will have a specificity of its own. It will require an intrinsic knowledge of each society with reference to what it was, what it is, and what it should be: a point which, with reference to India, has been discussed elsewhere in some details (Mukherjee, 1969a). In terms of the prevailing dichotomy, the available experience from the 'developed' societies will help us in this pursuit of knowledge in the 'developing societies'; but that experience, crystallized in the currently available theories, cannot be imposed upon the latter to look for certain selected traits of change and development, of traditional and modernity. On the contrary, a true grasp of the reality in the latter group of societies will enrich the currently available theories and practice and, thus, lead to the development of world sociology.

Universality of science has not been attained in any discipline without an objective comprehension of its particular manifestations. History tells us that apparently irreconcilable theories and practice have reached synthesis at higher levels of effectiveness with our ever-accumulating knowledge on the analogous systems of variation. The process has been particularly manifest in the last few decades in the economic science and technology. A proper development of sociology in the 'developing societies', therefore, will not only be useful to the respective societies but also to the world society at large.

Notes

1. For example what should be the comparable points of reference to ascertain inter-generational occupational mobility? Why a correlation analysis between family types and fertility rates is often proved to be fallacious? How can we appraise a course of nuclearization of joint family structures since the increasing incidence, over time, of nuclear to joint family structures in a society may be due to the fission of joint structures or change in the demographic profile of the people with reference to their age of effective marriage, fertility pattern, expectation of life, etc.? (see, for details, Mukherjee, 1968: 45–46, 48–50, 1969b: 49–73).
2. There is also the point that the imputation of 'value differentials' from the given fact may be wrong because: (a) the informants may not have crystallized opinions or attitudes on the subject under reference but are obliged to furnish *some* information, or (b) they may be

able to guess and supply the 'desirable' answers without actually subscribing to their professed views on the way of life, family, marriage, caste, religion, etc. (see, for some details, Mukherjee, 1968: 34–35, 46). Either way, thus is a problem for social research *per se*, as noted for a corresponding situation with reference to premise 1. We need not, therefore, discuss it in exclusive reference to the 'developing societies'.

3. For example: (a) the former social structure of India, which was based on the four *varnas*, was replaced, at one stage of her history, by a matrix of an increasingly large number of *jatis*; (b) the emergence of the Bahima aristocracy and Bahera serfs replaced the previous social relations of the Bahimas and the Baheras when the kingdom of Ankole came into being in Africa in the pre-British days; (c) the majority of the peoples in Uganda had passed beyond the tribal stage and were in the feudal stage of historical development (with tendencies among the Banganda and some other people towards further change) when the British occupied their territory; and so on (see for details, Oldenberg, 1897: 267–290; Oberg, 1950: 121–162; Mukherjee, 1956: 46–101).

References

Alatas, Syed Hussein, 1969, 'The Captive Mind in Development Planning', paper submitted to the 11th World Conference of the Society for International Development, New Delhi, 14–17 November.

BBC (British Broadcasting Corporation), 1959, 'The Public and the Programmes', London, BBC.

Becker, Howard and Barnes, Harry Elmer, 1952, *Social Thought from Lore to Science*, Washington DC, Harren Press.

Bendix, Reinhard, 1964, *Nation-building and Citizenship*, New York, John Wiley and Sons Inc.

Black, C.E., 1966, *The Dynamics of Modernization*, New York, Harper and Row.

Bottomore, T.B. and Rubel, Maximilien, 1963, *Karl Marx: Selected Writings in Sociology and Social Philosophy*, London, Pelican.

Deutsch, K.W., 1961, 'Social Mobilization and Political Development', *American Political Science Review*, 55(3): 493–514.

Drewnowski, Jan, 1967, 'Some Suggestions for Measuring Social Variables', *Social Change and Economic Growth*, Paris, Development Centre of the Organization for Economic Co-operation and Development.

Gerth, H.H. and Mills, C. Wright (Eds), 1958, *From Marx Weber: Essays in Sociology*, New York, Oxford University Press.

Goode, William J., 1963, *World Revolution and Family Patterns*, London, Collier-Macmillan Limited.

Gopalaswami, R.A., 1953, Census of India, 1951, I (IA), New Delhi, Government of India Press.

Homans, George C., 1950, *The Human Group*, New York, Harcourt Brace and Co.

Kapp, K. William, 1963, *Hindu Culture, Economic Development and Economic Planning in India*, Bombay, Asia Publishing House.

Karve, I., and Ranadive, J.S., 1965, 'The Social Dynamics of a Growing Town and its Surrounding Area', Poona, Deccan College.

Lenin, V.I., 1894, *What the 'Friends of the People' Are and How They Fight the Social-Democrats* (English translation), Moscow, Foreign Languages Publishing House.

—, 1989, *The Development of Capitalism in Russia* (English translation), Moscow, Foreign Languages Publishing House.

Malinowski, B., 1944, *A Scientific Theory of Culture and Other Essays*, North Carolina, North Carolina University Press.

Marx, Karl, 1846 'Letter to P.V., Annenkov' in Karl Marx, *The Poverty of Philosophy* (English translation), Moscow, Foreign Languages Publishing House.

—, 1853a, 'British Rule in India', *New York Daily Tribune*, June 25, 1853.

—, 1853b, 'The Future Results of British Rule in India', *New York Daily Tribune*, August 8, 1853.

—, 1859, Preface, *A Contribution to the Critique of Political Economy* (English translation), Moscow, Foreign Languages Publishing House.

—, 1942, *The German Ideology*, London, Lawrence and Wishart.

—, 1849, *Capital: A Critical Analysis of Capitalist Production*, Vol. I, London, George Allen and Unwin.

—, 1964, *Pre-Capitalist Economic Formations*, London, Lawrence and Wishart.

McGranahan, Donald V. (Director), 1969, 'Research Notes', Geneva, United Nations Research Institute for Social Development.

Mshvenieradze, V.V., 1964, 'Objective Foundations of the Development of Society: Critical Study of Some Sociological Theories', 'Transactions of the Fifth World Congress of Sociology', Louvain (Belgium), International Sociological Association, Vol. III, 33–37.

Mukherjee, Ramkrishna, 1956, *The Problem of Uganda: A Study in Acculturation*, Berlin, Akademie-Verlag.

—, 1957, *The Dynamics of a Rural Society*, Berlin, Akademie-Verlag.

—, 1958, *The Rise and Fall of the East India Company*, Berlin, Verlag der Wissenschatten.

—, 1961, 'Caste and Economic Structure in West Bengal in Present Times', Saksena, R.N. (Ed), *Sociology, Social Research and Social Problems in India*, Bombay, Asia Publishing House, 157–167.

—, 1965, *The Sociologist and Social Change in India Today*, New Delhi, Prentice-Hall.

—, 1968, 'Some Observations on the Diachronic and Synchronic Aspects of Social Change', *Social Science Information*, Paris, 7 (1): 31–55.

—, 1969a, 'Empirical Social Research on Contemporary India', *Social Science Information*, Paris, 8 (6).

—, 1969b 'Family in India: A Perspective' (mimeo), Calcutta, Sociological Research Unit, Indian Statistical Institute.

Mukherjee, Ramkrishna and Bandyopadhay, Suraj, 1964 'Social Research and Mahalanobisis D.' in: Rao, C.R. (Ed), *Contributions to Statistics*, Calcutta, Statistical Publishing Society and Oxford, Pergamon Press.

Myrdal, Gunnar, 1968, *Asian Drama*, London, Allen Lane the Penguin Press.

Nettl, J.P. and Robertson, Roland, 1968, *International Systems and the Modernization of Societies*, London, Faber and Faber.

NHK (NHK Public Opinion Research Institute), 1969, 'Public Opinion Research of NHK', Tokyo, NHK.

NORC (National Opinion Research Centre), 1948, *Radio Listening in America*, New York, Prentice Hall.

Oberg, K., 1950, 'The Kingdom of Ankole in Uganda', in Fortes, M. Evans-Pritchard, E.E. (Eds), *African Political Systems*, London, Oxford University Press.

Odaka, K, 1964, 'Traditionalism and Democracy in Japanese Industry', Transactions of the Fifth World Congress of Sociology, Louvain (Belgium), International Sociological Association, Vol. III, 39–49.

Oldenberg, H, 1897, 'Zur Geschichte des indischen Kastenwestns', *Zeitschrift der Deutschen Morgenlandischen Gesellschaft*, 51: 267–290.

Plekhanov, G., (Beltov, N), 1895, *The Development of the Monist View of History*, (English translation), Moscow, Foreign Languages Publishing House.

Rheinstein, Max (Ed.), 1954, *Max Weber on Law in Economy and Society*, Cambridge (Massachusetts), Harvard University Press.

Russet, Bruce M., Alker Jr, Haavward R., Deutsch Karl W. Lasswell, Harold, D., 1964, *World Handbook of Political and Social Indicators*, New Haven and London, Yale University Press.

Shils, Edward, 1962, *Political Development in the New States*, Mouton and Co., Netherlands.

Weber, Max, 1947, *The Theory of Social and Economic Organization*, London, William Hodge and Co.

—, 1958, *The Religions of India*, Glencoe (Illinois), The Free Press.

—, 1965, *The Sociology of Religion*, London, Methuen and Co.

Wertheim., W.F., 1956, *Indonesian Society in Transition*, The Ifague, Bandung, W. van Hoeve.

14

History and Sociology

A.M. Shah

Whatever else sociologists, including social anthropologists, might do they do many things – the core of their discipline consists of observation and analysis of contemporary behaviour of groups, classes and categories of people through a variety of instruments such as census, survey, questionnaire, interview, and participant observation or intensive fieldwork.[1] All of these instruments help observe behaviour for short periods of time, ranging from just one day of a census of population to normally a year or two of fieldwork. Nevertheless, most sociologists stretch the span of time to make general statements about the society under observation, if not about many societies belonging to a particular type, and even about all human societies. They tend to make these statements in the present tense, presuming they are applicable for all time – past, present and future.

In their moment of awareness that a lot of time passes between their observation of behaviour and their analyzing and reporting on it – that they are reporting on what is already past – they try to satisfy themselves by saying that the present tense they use is the special 'anthropological, ethnographic, or sociological present'. This is a reflection of the explicit or implicit claim of sociology to being a 'science'.

The synchronic analyses of society are usually guided by the idea of structure, which entails the notion of continuity, if not permanence. Only the less ambitious sociologists talk about time-bound structures, and accept that statements of structure are as if in the present. Otherwise, the structuralists as such, particularly those who follow Claude Levi-Strauss, talk of structures as timeless, eternal models, and deny the value of history in understanding society and culture. On closer examination, these so-called timeless structures turn out to be time-bound, or to be only heuristic devices. To some they have only an aesthetic value. With the passing away of primitive society everywhere in the world, an ahistorical study of society has become unreal and irrelevant. This is not to say that there really was primitive society without history. In any case, the synchronic studies of society acquire wider significance and meaning when viewed in the context of the historical heritage of society.

Students of social change do not deny the value of history in studying social change, since the very notion of change is diachronic, involving the past and present. However, closer examination of many statements of social change would reveal that their authors have not bothered to base them on sound, if any, historical knowledge. They try to disentangle the present and the past from what they think to be disparities or contradictions in the on-going social scene. Such disentangling is inevitably involved in deriving propositions of change from synchronic data such as that of a census of survey. Frequently such disentangling is guided by the scholar's own explicit ideological preferences or implicit habitual perceptions. Sometimes the scholar relies on the people's own perceptions of the past. When he does take recourse to history, frequently it is nothing but worn out cliches, learnt by him from text-books of history during his school or college days, or the so-called truths inherited from the so-called authorities in the social sciences. Somewhat careful – should I say clever – scholars glorify them as hypotheses of change. Historical myths masquerading as social scientific hypotheses and theories abound in the social sciences.

The sociological study of contemporary India, whether from the angle of structure or of change, requires an adequate understanding of Indian history. This does not mean that a sociologist has to be conversant with the history of all the periods and of all aspects of society. However, a thorough understanding of the conditions at the beginning of British rule and of major changes during this rule, seems to be essential. For a fuller understanding of certain aspects such as religion, a knowledge of longer periods would be essential.

Many sociologists and other intellectuals concerned with the health and strength of modern India, resort to thinking that many of our modern institutions and organizations do not work as well as we would like them to because we have not inherited them from the past, and that they are not allowed to work by the structures and institutions we have inherited from the past. Usually, many facile assumptions about the past are involved in such thinking, and the diagnosis of ills therefore tends to be wrong. A simplistic comparative sociology also lurks in the background of such thinking.

Social sciences in India should be rooted firmly in history for another reason also. I doubt if there is any society, including the most primitive, which does not have a historical consciousness. We have only to identify the particular pattern of historical consciousness in a society. In India, there have been articulators of historical consciousness from the Vedic time. The Rgvedic society had two major articulators – the Brahman and the bard (Suta, Magadha).[2] The latter was included among the twelve close associates, the *ratnins*, jewels, of the Raja and became important in later periods on account of his association with genealogies and myths, both oral and written, legitimizing the status of many groups, particularly the Kshatriyas. Basically, the same institution has survived with different names in different parts of India.[3] The Brahmans, bards and a number of other cultural specialists have spread historical consciousness even among the illiterate villagers and tribals throughout the length and breadth of India.

While a great deal has been written about the Brahman's role, there is little analysis of the role of the non-Brahman legitimizers of status like the bard who have operated through a basically historical medium and idiom. One would like to know in particular whether there has been conflict between the Brahman and the non-Brahman legitimizers and how people have made use of the conflict.

The so-called modern and secular history – the professional historian's history – has become an additional element in the historical consciousness of the people of India, among not only the elite but the ordinary people as well. We should realize that history has been taught directly or indirectly in schools and collages since the early nineteenth century,[4] and the literate Indian also spreads his text-book ideas of the past to his illiterate fellow villagers, castemen and kinsmen. The traditional articulators of history such as the Brahman and the bard have also been absorbing the secular historian's history, constructing their own historical paradigms and transmitting them to the people.

Such absorption is not at all difficult, because after all the historian's history when transformed into school text-books and popular literature is essentially a set of myths, or cultural texts, to use modern anthropological jargon. In consequence, there is far more historical consciousness among the people of India than what both historians and sociologists might think. It is possible that this consciousness is fragmented and partisan. But when the people themselves have a high degree of historical consciousness, the sociologist studying them can ill afford to be ahistorical.

While sociologists are increasingly realizing the importance of historical knowledge in understanding contemporary India, they also feel that they do not always get the kind of history they would like to have from historians. I would not like to slip into a homily to historians; a lot of welcome changes have been taking place among them in recent years, and moreover, I do not claim to have read a lot of historical literature. I would therefore mention only what I have missed in many historical writings.

First of all, I have missed in many historical works a sensitivity to Indian ethnography. They have indulged in generalizations about Indian society without taking into account the diversity of the social composition of the population. It is possible that the historical sources are silent on certain sections of the population. However, if we know from the ethnography of modern India that certain tribes and castes form a large proportion of the population, they cannot be presumed to be non-existent in the past in large numbers, unless historical sources prove otherwise. Similarly, if a historian is writing about marriage and if we know that the custom of bride price is prevalent in many castes and tribes today, the historian should not say, on the basis of references to bridegroom price in some historical source, that the latter was the generally prevalent custom in the entire society. I am not saying that historians should write history backwards, but only that they should cultivate a greater sensitivity to Indian ethnography. The historians would serve not only an intellectual but also a social purpose if they tell their readers a little more about what their works do not portray.

In recent years, Indian history has quite rightly moved away from its dominant concern with unique events such as wars and elite persons such as kings, queens and generals, towards a concern with ordinary people and with basic social structures and institutions. However, many historical works seem to assume that in dealing with cultural and social phenomena one can derive one's insights from one's common sense, in effect, from one's experience as a member of Indian society rather than from the systematic knowledge built up by sociologists about a number of structures and institutions. Many historians do not seem to take seriously the so-called continuity of Indian culture and civilization about which they themselves talk so frequently. Even in the case of discontinuities, they seem to ignore the fact that comparative sociology has built up systematic knowledge about an enormous variety of social structures and institutions around the world. Some historians seem to think that the only systematic knowledge about society available to them is Marxist sociology.

Whatever the limitation of history, serious sociological treatment of history is essential for sound sociology. If sociologists do not get the kind of history they need from historians, the solution is not to reject history but to enter into a dialogue with historians. To carry on such dialogue effectively, the first necessity is for every sociologist to become aware of the dimension of time involved in all sociological analysis. Secondly, at least a few sociologists should carry out hard historical research so as to demonstrate in however small a way the kind of history sociologists need. Such a dialogue would enrich both history and sociology.

Notes

1. There is virtually no distinction between sociology and social cultural anthropology in India.
2. See Romila Thapar, *From Lineage to State*, Oxford University Press, Bombay, 1985, pp. 60, 113, 120, 130, 131, 136–37.
3. See, for example, A.M. Shah and R.G. Shroff, 'The Vahivancha Barots Gujarat: A Caste of Genealogists and Mythographers', *Journal of American Folklore*, 71 (1958), pp. 246–76. Reprinted in Milton Singer (ed.), *Traditional India: Structure and Change*, American Folklore Society, Philadelphia, 1959, pp. 40–70.
4. Sociology has not had this privilege. It began to be taught at the post-graduate level in just two or three universities around 1912, and spread to a large number of universities first at this level and then at the undergraduate one only after 1950. It began to be taught at the higher secondary school level (11th and 12th classes) in only a few schools around 1976.

15

Gandhian Social Thought in Relation to Non-Violence and Social Change

Narendra K. Singhi

I
SOCIAL CHANGE AND IDEOLOGY

Social change at some level and degree is as characteristic of man's life in organized systems, as is orderly persistence (Aron, 1968: 4). It could be viewed both in totality and fragments and can be analyzed at both the levels. Social change has to be seen as a significant alteration of social structure (pattern of social action and interaction) including consequences and manifestations of such structures embodied in norms (rules of conduct), values and cultural products symbols (Moore, 1968: 366).

Analysis of social change poses a variety of problems in relation to its complex manifestation. The dimensions on which the phenomenon could be analyzed are varied and multiple and involve a number of variables and beg diverse nature of questions.

There are certain changes which are directionless and express a pattern of fluctuation (Sorokin, 1947: 6–7). Certain other changes reveal a direction, which could be so analyzed as to depict a consistent pattern. In terms of consequences on the general social structure, certain social change does not make any meaningful difference to the prevailing social structure; while consequences of certain other social change have far-reaching implications for the social structure, whereby change in one part leads to changes in other parts consequently. Such cumulative, multiplicating and complex consequences help in the maintenance of social equilibrium, or alternatively leads to the disintegration of the system. Many social changes come about without any deliberate attempt but result due to interplay of several forces existing in the social milieu. Social changes alternatively are planned and based on a programme which is implemented or has the potentiality of being implemented by a unit, be that a group, institution or person.

The other dimension of social change relates to the mechanism which brings about social change. Since the eighteenth century, social theorists have tried on the whole to explain most forms of social change in terms of a single factor (Cohen, 1968: 178). The other approach has been that of multicausality. The emphasis on the former is on a single factor to which empirical consequences are attributed or to which potentiality of consequences is assigned. The mechanism could be conceived as abstract-theoretical entity posited in the realm of ideas and ideology or it could be conceived as concrete objective phenomenon which is empirically considered to be instrumental in bringing about change. In the later case, combination of many factors is considered necessary, both for causation of social change as well as for empirical examination and delineation of factors involved thereto in social change.

Tendency to change is inherent in all human societies for the following two reasons:

(1) Culture is dynamic and interactional merger of various cultural traits or variables of human living, lead to the emergence of a different phenomenon, which in its wake necessitates new process of adjustment. All social systems in course of time develop needs which are structurally not meetable from within the system.

(2) The reflective nature of man has made him aware of problems, which are created, solved, recreated and resolved in new form and shape. This process has been going on. This is largely because of the fact that humanity so far did not have had overall and lasting solution. The internal constraints of personality at psychic level are influenced by the prevailing strains of culture and social system. This is the result of seeing either the dysfunctions of societal phenomena or expression of dissatisfaction with prevailing situation, despite the capacity of existing elements to maintain the system. The system thus continues to exist but through reflective realization and delineation of ignored and non-visible inadequacies, a new perception is obtained.

In this sense, social change is related to the problematic disjunctions of various societal elements on the one hand and reflective perception of non-problematic given inadequacy of man and society on the other.

The awareness about it thus taken in the form of ideology, which in the hands of intellectuals or thinkers meet the rigour of logico-rational analysis and in its diffusionist stage, gets cognitive-emotive acceptance by a large number of people. The ideologist innovators are thus basically motivated to change the existing social order due to its perceived imperfections and disintegrative consequences. An ideology is constructed by meaningfully integrating the diverse array of thoughts into a coherent structure or by academic exposition of thoughts at intellectual plane by systematic analysis.

These ideologies have been either predominantly socio-economic and political, wherein social changes have been contemplated through state or have relied on liberalism and democracy, assuming the inherent rationality of man. Democracy and communism are major ideologies connected with the political system, which are designed to change the social structure. The goals include aspects of economic redistribution, social justice and shift of control in the economic management. These ideologies either provide individual freedom and liberty or subordinate human beings to a greater force of state by extracting his freedom of expression and liberty. Each ideology conceives of certain means, through which change is to be managed. Broadly the ideologies have either emphasized, ignored or rejected the element of violence or non-violence as a part of means-mechanism in achieving the goal.

Gandhi's ideology is predominantly and essentially based on non-violence, which has been considered as an instrument to bring about desired social change. Non-violence is thus conceived as a monocratic abstract – theoretical mechanism, which can have overt manifestation through concrete operational plans. At theoretical level, its analysis has been considered to be explicit and logical while its concretization at societal level is considered operationally dubious by people not wedded to this ideology.

Thus, so far we have discussed the nature of social change and the meaning and role of ideology and their mutual relationship. We are further concerned in this paper with the examination of Gandhi's ideology of non-violence, interpreted integrally and comprehensively by him, as a mechanism to bring about social transformation.

For this analysis, we have dealt with the following aspects: (a) examination of the concept of non-violence as interpreted by Gandhi at theoretical level, (b) delienation of major areas wherein Gandhi's mechanism of non-violence was to be operationalized, (c) Gandhi's strategy of social change with its instruments of overt action, (d) Gandhi's charismatic impact and operative failure of his ideology, (e) explanation for the operative failure of all ideologies, and (f) the relation of structural changes to the psychic-spiritual development of man.

II
THE CONCEPT OF NON-VIOLENCE

The concept of non-violence can be put to analysis on various dimensions. According to Unnithan and Singh (1965: III), the traditions of non-violence could be analyzed at: (a) the mystical and theological level, (b) the philosophical level, (c) the ethical level, and (d) the sociological and psychological level. We are concerned here primarily with the sociological interpretation of the concept of non-violence and evaluation of Gandhi's non-violence as a social ethics and a central mechanism of social change. Unnithan and Singh (1965: 20) maintain that non-violence is not only a functional requirement of the society but also the psychological need of individuals. A society cannot maintain its order unless the violence is reduced to the point necessary for structural integration and processual facilitation of a social system. On the other hand, no social system has empirically eliminated violence altogether so that the structural components of a social system do not experience any tension whatsoever. Historically, different epochs in history have had predominance of either of the two polar elements, operating at the various levels of human society.

The positive tradition on non-violence is activistic which lays down standard of norms to be cultivated by its followers and in its passive form it refers to avoidance of certain types of behaviour (Unnithan and Singh, 1965: 29). In its positive form, it emphasizes inculcation of certain values like kindness, generosity, love and universal brotherhood for regulation of human relationship. Non-violence in its passive from refers to non-killing at physical level and refraining form hurting the feelings and sentiments of others through speech and action and social level and not to entertain violent thoughts at psychological level. Non-killing in its broader sense includes not only the human beings but also the living non-human objects of the cosmos.

Sociologically, non-violence has no mysticism of yoga or other spiritual phenomenon but expresses itself on social-human plane dealing primarily with human relationship at an integral level.

Analysis of Gandhi's writings and speeches on non-violence reveals that the phenomenon of non-violence has an integral meaning for him. The following typified interpretations can be formulated:

1. Non-violence, as a part of his instrumentality of action, whereby it takes the form of basic social ethics for all changes. Gandhi believed that non-violence has to be made effective through action and activities. It has to be a means for realization of the goals of both the actor and the collectivity. Non-violence in terms of its application has not to be partialized through its application in certain sectors of life and its activities but it has to be creed and belief for all spheres of human activities – political, economic, social, cultural, personal.
2. Non-violence to him was supreme human value, when he characterized it as pure love. Non-violence thus becomes an expression of love, which in its broadest sense encompasses the total humanity and is not confined to the 'neighbourhood concept'. Such a love is considered to be the fullest expression of man's altruism.
3. Non-violence to Gandhi was a psychic force as he (1952: 4) said that the strength of non-violence as a force comes from indomitable will. It has to be part of one's conviction which comes through conscious internalization of this value which forms core of one's consciousness.
4. Non-violence to Gandhi has a transcendental reference as he equated it with truth and God. The conviction and ideology of non-violence was deified.

The ideology of non-violence has as its components not only activistic elements dealing with human relationship on a composite and integral manner but also transcendental reference on its being equated with truth and God. Gandhi conceived of life as consisting not only of mundane physical manifestation but encompassing the supernatural phenomenon and thus viewed life integrally.

In terms of specific areas, apart from the variety of meanings in which non-violence has been used by Gandhi, we could delineate three broad areas where Gandhi operationalized non-violence as a social ethics. He both preached and practised non-violence in these areas. These three areas are: (a) political field, (b) social field, and (c) economic field.

Political Field

Non-violence was the means which was adopted and put to use for the fight for independence. It was a potent force which was continuously used by Gandhi in his all political moves for the independence of the country. Gandhi further rejected the concept of power in the political system and advocated complete devolution and decentralization of power. His conception of stateless society was based on the moral base for all political changes. Gandhi's contribution in the political field was not confined to fight for independence but they conceived of a programme of political order both with reference to Indian situation and its peculiarities, and also a universalistic approach with reference to the general and basic problem of power and political systems.

Social Field

Gandhi conceived of a Sarvodaya social order in which the basis of order is harmony. The evils of industrialization and technology have far-reaching negative consequences, hence their use has got to be specific and limited. An industrial society which brings a series of human problems in its wake was rejected by Gandhi. High human values and harmonious relationship were of greater significance to Gandhi, than comforts and luxuries, which became problematic in their consequences. Gandhi, as a keen observer of Indian society, had delineated various social problems like eradication of untouchability, upliftment of women, removal of casteism, emphasis on social justice and imposition of prohibition. Gandhi not only had a conscientious concern about the problems but also had a programme for positive action for tackling them vigorously. He saw the pervasion of certain traditional social institutions in the Indian society and led a vigorous attach on their evil consequences. He judiciously glorified the past and duly recognized and emphasized equality, liberty, fraternity and democracy for building the new social order.

Economic Field

Gandhi advocated eradication of poverty by way of advocating a normative economics, which gets self-expression through limitations of wants. Multiplication of wants and erratic competitiveness make the economic goal the only goal of human existence and social order. Gandhi realized the importance of village social system and advocated the idea of village self-sufficiency.

His idea of trusteeship asserts that the rich shall use what is reasonably required for personal need and will act as a trustee for the use of society. Trusteeship provides a means of transforming the present capitalist order of society into an egalitarian one by giving the present owning class a chance to reform (Gandhi, 1952).

Gandhi's conception of social change thus was broad and so encompassing as to include all significant areas of human activities which are put to structural strains leading to individual anxieties, deprivations, deviations and resignation.

III
GANDHIAN STRATEGY OF SOCIAL CHANGE

The operationalization of Gandhi's ideas and ideology has been well conceived by him through certain channels. Gandhi did not give any ideology as a thinker or philosopher through systematic writings or theoretical preachings. He was concerned with action and not merely with the formulation of ideas. He continuously experimented with putting his ideas into action both in his personal life as well as whenever he led a mass movement. His ideas become more perceptible and meaningful when judged in their relevance to their concretization.

His approach has been directed all along towards mass movement. In his mass movement, people of all shades, religion, caste and communities found their way in. He appealed to all sections of the society and adjusted with ease with the people and groups of even opposite composition and character. He took care of the lowest rung of society and took in confidence the wealthiest persons. He himself possessed superb simplicity and an extra ordinary capacity to identify with the masses, which helped him in mobilizing them for social movement. His sensitivity to human problems and capacity to empathy with diverse people was remarkable which led to easy mutual identification. He spoke in a language and style which suited the masses. He gave religious interpretations to all human-societal phenomena. His personality and influence grew charismatic.

Mass movement which was the basis of Gandhi's strategy became a great success, for Gandhi gave a leadership through externalization of his internalized thoughts. The gap between what he preached and practised was non-existent. The masses never doubted his sincerity of purpose. Gandhi used the instrument of *satyagraha* and civil disobedience not only to fight an alien rule but to bring justice. *Satyagra*ha was for him a method of meeting aggression, settling conflicts and bringing about social and political changes. He made *satyagraha* the moral equivalent of war. The ultimate and the most potent in the armory of *satyagraha* was fasting (Dhawan, 1957: 146). Fasting was used as a penance for purification over not only one's own deeds but also those of others. According to Dhawan (1957: 147), it was thus a means of resisting injustice and coverting the evil doer.

Gandhi's non-violence was primarily a strategy to bring about social change immediately in context with the contemporous social system and his expression and interpretation of non-violence were continuously enumerated and explained in his writings and speeches. His ideas – written and spoken – were systematized and logically categorized by some of his followers and interpretators leading to the formulation of 'Gandhism' as an ideology, having non-violence as a central theme, which was both an end and means and a way of life – both at the level of society and personality system.

IV
THE CHARISMATIC INFLUENCE AND OPERATIVE FAILURE OF THE IDEOLOGY

The deified adoration and influence of a charismatic leader and diffused acceptance of his ideology in operation, leading to institutionalization at the societal level or internalization at personal level are two different things. The masses in human history have affectively adored and deified certain human beings, have made them 'heroes' and in some cases assigned them God-like qualities or made them Gods. This popular expression is neither based on logico-rational analysis nor objective calculation, for the common man in the form of collectivity, is hardly capable of attempting such an analysis. Such symbolism projected on an individual, helps people in reinforcing their belief in the uncommon geniousness and exceptional and uncanny ability. There is psychological comfort through reinforcement of belief in the 'goodness'.

Evaluation of Gandhi's success reveals that he succeeded in making a tremendous personal impact on the people and evoked their highest reverence. But his ideology, which was put to constant use by him, did not alter the social structure, in a way, which could be in consonance with his ideology. In effect thus Gandhi could not diffuse non-violence at the societal level to make it part of either social structure or action process of even significant minority.

It is true that Gandhi's rejection of affluence and emphasis on simplicity was a part of his wider vision of a total world social order. The problems created by materialism and affluence have concerned various social thinkers like Sorokin (1958), Eric From (1963) and Mumford (1958). Widespread technolization and urbanization have created problems of alienation, formalistic impersonality, mass society, and subtle hypocracy, generated by emphasis on success goals. In such societies an undercurrent of new norms which are technically expedient have extensively replaced the institutionalized norms, thus leading to conditions of anomie. The evils of materialism and extensive materialization through machine and technology, according to Gandhi, could be eliminated by emphasis on simplicity and negation of technology.

We have, however, reached a stage in the evolution of human society where acceptance of two imperatives – to produce as much as possible through mastering of the forces of nature and to treat the numbers of society as equals have been accepted by a large number of thinkers (Aron, 1968: 3).

Mastery of nature would necessitate technological advancement which in turn shall lead to material prosperity and opulence. Gandhi's rejection of material prosperity and partial negation of matter was misreading of history and misunderstanding of the positive power of science and technology. Any ideology, if it has to be operationally successful and effective, has to accept the logic of the fact of the inevitability and necessity of technological advancement and material progress.

The material progress has led to another set of ideology emphasizing economic equality and equality of opportunities for all. Such ideologies occupy dominant place in the contemporary thought (Aron, 1968: 3). However, it is a fact that egalitarian ideal has precluded any effective stabilization of modern societies. They are being continually unsettled by the progress of science and technology, with the result that three principal kinds of inequality result and exist, according to Aron (1968: 4): (a) socio-economic inequality which depends on the part played by the individual in the production process and in the distribution of the income, (b) socio-political inequality, dependent on the part played by the individuals separately or as members of a group in the management of public affairs, and (c) national inequality, as in the case of sovereign states or a larger collectivity within which groups co-exist differentiated by language, culture, skin color, birth, etc. The modern society is torn by the class struggle in capitalistic social structure. In state owned means of production, there is political exploitation and exploitation of personality, as freedom is denied to individuals. Passive masses and all powerful elites are becoming clearly demarcated in all societies (Aron, 1968: 6).

Rejection of material progress, a call to go back to nature, artificial limitation of wants and desires, emphasis of simplicity is undermining of the unfolding and growth of the creative genius of man. What is important is the rational and just appropriation of such advancement, taking into consideration the entire humanity.

The elimination of psychological and structural dysfunctions arising out of material progress need not be attempted by negation of material growth. This is not a solution as it would mean not only negation of material progress but also blocking the creative ability of man.

Gandhi's ideology and ideas of non-violence, apart from his personal preaching and practice, in its various form, could have been carried out through constitutional and legal means, in the policy divisions of free India. It is a fact that the structural framework which was sought to be created after independence, by those who were close associates of Mahatma, was not based on Gandhi's essential ideas of village upliftment, economic distribution, removal of social problems, education and political programming. Efforts by some of his followers, on non-governmental basis, specially for village upliftment and ushering of Sarvodaya Samaj, have also been unsuccessful and have failed to inspire people.

V
EXPLANATION FOR THE OPERATIVE FAILURE OF IDEOLOGIES

The failure of operationalization of the ideology of a person who received unprecedented reverence during his own life and a band of large number of followers, raises the basic question – why it is that Gandhi's ideology as a mechanism of social change has failed to operationalize itself or failed to usher in a transformed era in society. It would be more appropriate to widen this question and ask, why it is so that various ideologies fail and have failed in achieving their goals of social transformation. These ideologies in the sense that either in their operation they create problems which need further solutions or they fail as in practice they are found impractical. The reasons for such failures could be located into either of the two factors: (a) there is something inherent in the content of ideology which is responsible for its failure, and (b) there are structural universals which do not adopt to the ideology or the institutional sub-structure of the contemporary society in which the ideology is nourished and propagated lags much behind the requirements of the normative system contained in the teachings of these philosophers and saints.

Gandhi's experiment – as he liked to call it – was a great achievement at the level of self or ego. Gandhi himself internalized his own values and made a truthful expression of them in his all actions. There was never a gap between his preaching and practice. But at the level of collectivity it was hardly got internalized as a part of the value system and put into action by plurality of actors.

The crux of the problem is thus related to a wider question relating to any ideology conceived and practised by the originator of the ideology. Excepting ritualistic expression or deification, alternatively dogmatic acceptance, an ideology in its programmatic expression makes superfluous or transitory changes or creates new problems or falls highly short of achieving major and essential goals.

VI
RELATION OF STRUCTURAL CHANGES TO THE PSYCHIC-SPIRITUAL DEVELOPMENT OF MAN

There has been unprecedented social change of diverse type and with greater rapidity, as a result of rapid scientific and technological advancement, in the last century. Such an advancement is cumulative and in its manifestation tends to grow with each successive stage multiplicitly. In terms of difference and certain types of advancement, it is an epoch-making era. But the problematic areas have also enlarged and multiplied, and are equally significant. All of these factors – the cruciality of the period, the evolving of alternative solutions, the diversity of choices – expressed through various types of ideologies – many of which have been programmatically tried and their resultant illusions – logically lead us to examine the view that all structural changes are related to the psychic development of man.

Humanity has attained the present stage of evolution, having gone through the earlier stages from matter to life, to mind. Till now, advent of a developed thinking mind in the evolutionary process of matter, life and mind had been effected not by the self-aware aspiration, intention, will or seeking of the living being, but subconsciously on subliminally by the automatic operation of nature (Sri Aurobindo, 1963: 29). The present evolutionary stage has witnessed emergence of mind and it is believed that the next stage of evolution can come by man's own efforts. This presupposes transformation in man's consciousness. For any change to come, at the structural and societal levels, change in the very consciousness of man is a basic prerequisite. This change has to come not merely at an individual level but also at the general societal level, without this all changes having attempted through ideology (a) with either fall short of goals, (b) create more problems in the process of solving them, or (c) be almost ineffective at general societal level.

References

Aron, Raymond, 1968, *Progress and Disillusion*, London, Paul Mall Press.

Cohen, Percy, 1968, *Modern Social Theory*, London, Heinemann Educational Book Limited.

Dhawan, Gopinath, 1957, *The Political Philosophy of Mahatma Gandhi*, Ahmedabad, Navajivan Publishing House.

From, Eric, 1963, *The Same Society*, London, Routledge and Kegan Paul.

Gandhi, M.K., 1952, *My Non-violence*, Ahmedabad, Navajivan Prakashan.

Ghosh, Sri Aurobindo, 1963, *The Future Evolution of Man*, London, George Allen and Unwin.

Moore, Wilbert, 1968, (Editor David L. Sills), *International Encyclopedia of the Social Sciences*, Volume 10, The Macmillan Company and Free Press.

Mumford, Lewis, 1958, *The Culture of Cities*, London, Seeker and Warburg.

Sorokin, P., 1947, *Society, Culture and Personality*, New York, Harper.

Sorokin, P.A., 1958, *The Reconstruction of Humanity*, Bombay, Bhartiya Vidya Bhawan.

Unnithan, T.K.N. and Singh, Yogendra, 1965, *Report on Tradition of Non-violence in East and West*, UNESCO sponsored: unpublished.

16

Professions and Their Co-optation in State and Polity

The Case of Legal Profession

J.S. Gandhi

THE ARGUMENT: THESIS AND ITS VARIANT

Theory of the role that both 'profession' and 'law' play in the process of state-engineered social change inheres the well familiar phenomenon of the extension of state's domain into diverse sectors of civic life or, as it is also sometime euphemistically called, 'the increasing governmentalization of civic life'. This is indeed a global trend rather than one confined to the *developing* or the *underdeveloped* world. Even in the western world, as its history for the past six to seven decades reveals, state has come to wield responsibility in several spheres of life which earlier used to be 'matters of private concern'. It has thus come to play its role, as it were, as a benign big brother, providing health insurance or free medical care and a host of other services and amenities such as free or subsidized education, free legal aid, etc. This process, as has been rightly stylized by some, has resulted from the 'the explosion of popular aspirations'.[1] In this journey towards approximating a 'populistic paradise', professions have continued to be a useful ally of the state. As Halliday in his study of the Chicago Bar Association convincingly illustrates, state (which in his analysis means the state of Chicago) has co-opted the Bar into several of its role-positions in order to ward off its crises arising mainly from its incapacity to meet growing popular expectations and aspirations. He recognizes this process as one of professional empowerment. The argument may not sound all that impressive to the dialectists, but the facts are indisputably there for any one to see. But, whether this process in itself and in all circumstances leads to professional 'empowerment' as such is indeed a different question and remains to be examined a bit closely.

In the Indian context, in view of the evidence that we examine here, the 'co-optation' thesis gets corroborated – but only obliquely, since the role of professions apparently extends much beyond 'bailing the state' out of the crises of inadequacy. The argument developed here seeks to show that the professions in the Indian society have a generalized *cruciality/criticality* vis-à-vis the wider polity and not just the *state* alone. Also, that the professions, here, i.e., specifically in the Indian context, seem to be doing so by way of aiding, assisting and even mobilizing such forces as tend to restore the constitutionality and democratic functioning of the polity otherwise threatened by the self-willed behaviour of the state and some of its allied groups.

Another variation from the 'co-optation' thesis lies in that the professions (in our usage here, the 'legal' profession in specific) do not get co-opted into the state functioning so much as a result of its collectivistic professional urge or a deliberate initiative to capture a nitch in the power-polity. Instead, they find a place in the state or central legislatures as a result of their salability to the gate-keepers of these and related political institutions because of their astute mastery over the art of 'persuading', 'presentation', 'negotiation' and 'bargaining'. That is why one finds professionals (particularly the lawyers) everywhere in the Indian polity, i.e., in the state as well as national legislatures; in the opposition as well as in the party-in-power. In addition, professions in India are coming to have some visible presence in the public life and seem to be working in the protection of democracy and the allied institutions.

From the data that we produce here, the case of Indian lawyers promoting their life-chances through participation in the Indian polity seems to be pure and simple an illustration of *zweckrationality*, used and pursued purely in the service of 'individual' and 'personal' interests rather than in the support of capitalistic interests, as the patent Marxian thesis would have it, or in the larger professional interests as the functionalists would have it. In other words, the professionals are spurred by a pure and simple attitude of 'instrumentalizing' the existing opportunity-structure in furtherance of their self-interests through occupying available power-positions within the polity. And this, they seem to be doing, in their *individual* capacities rather than as self-conscious members of the professional collectivity. We intend to pursue this line of argument using whatever scanty or symbolic data are available from the contemporary Indian social and political scene.

THE EVIDENCE

First set of evidence will be provided on the professionals (particularly the lawyers) who preponderate the legislatures – primarily the national and also of some states. The evidence suggests that the professionals play an exceedingly significant role in the law-making which in fact is the crucial and substantive wherewithal of the functioning democracies. As we shall see, the 'heavy' representation of professionals is definitely out of keeping with the massive illiteracy and poverty of the people who have elected them. For the national legislatures, the data pertain to the national parliaments (called Lok Sabha in the Indian context) constituted till prior to November 1989. As for the states[2] are concerned, it is only in a very few cases that such details about the legislators are compiled regularly. As such, we have been able to present these data in a rather sampled manner. We present below the data starting with the data on the national legislature first.

Professionals in National Legislature

As we can see from the table below, as many as one-third to one-half of the total Lok Sabha members at all times were drawn from the 'professions'. This is only when we count such 'professions' as conform more closely to the professional ideal type under the theory of professions.[3] This also needs to be appreciated that Indian economy continues to be basically an agricultural economy with

Table 1

Professionals in Various Lok Sabhas

(percentage of professionals to total membership)

Professions	1st ls	2nd ls	3rd ls	4th ls	5th ls	6th ls	7th ls	8th ls
Lawyers	35.6	30.5	24.5	17.5	20.5	23.4	22.2	19.1
Teachers	9.9	11.3	5.8	6.5	7.1	8.4	6.7	7.7
Medicos	4.9	3.5	3.0	2.8	1.7	1.9	1.9	4.0
Engineers			0.9	1.4	1.2	0.9	1.1	0.8
Total (Professions)	50.4	45.3	34.2	28.2	30.5	34.6	31.9	31.6

* ls = Lok Sabha.

** Adopted from Socio-Economic Background of Lok Sabha Members, Monograph Series, 10. Subash C. Kashyap, New Delhi, 1987, pp. 9–10.

over three-fourth of the population living in villages. Consequently, the web of social relations in the Indian society are perceived to be multiplex or *gemeinschaft* type. Despite this, professions continue to dominate in the top national forum, i.e., national legislature which is vested with most significant decision-making. A closer scrutiny of the process of cabinet-making reveals that professions do not merely stuff the national legislature, but also occupy some of the most crucial portfolios such as home, foreign affairs, finance, industry, etc. This is borne out by the analysis of Mrs. Gandhi's last cabinet (i.e., the seventh Lok Sabha) as well as Rajiv's last cabinet (i.e., the eighth cabinet). For example:

> Mrs. Gandhi's cabinet in 1980 was comprised total of 41 ministers including herself; out of this lawyers accounted for 19 or 46.3 per cent of the total cabinet. Further, the top layer of her ministry, i.e., comprising *cabinet rank* ministers, was constituted of 19 ministers, out of which 12 or 63 per cent were lawyers and were vested with such important portfolios as external affairs, finance, agriculture, information and broadcasting, law, education, etc.... . In Rajiv's cabinet, constituted for the first time after the elections, 25 out of 50 ministers were lawyers. Out of a total of 15 ministers of the *cabinet rank* (i.e., the top layer), 10 or 66.6 per cent were lawyers. Further, important portfolios such as home affairs, education, industry, energy, banking and insurance and information and broadcasting, etc., were put under the charge of lawyer-members.[4]

Even though the main burden of evidence in the preceding section is on the legal profession, yet the argument holds that 'professions' occupy a central and pivotal position in the management of the state, which engages in deliberate and planned social change. It needs no argument or citation to prove that the Indian State faces the stupendous task of meeting a wide-range of popular expectations and aspirations which assume ever larger proportions day-by-day. Thus, Halliday's argument of 'profession-state' nexus in the cause of steering a crisis-ridden state holds in the Indian context as well. However, professions seem to serve an additional function here – that of reinforcing political legitimacy vis-à-vis the masses. This applies not merely to the party-in-power but also to other political parties who are contending for 'power' within the political system. Law-professionals come especially handy for this role.

This is so because of their professionally ingrained forensic capabilities; the parties find in them the best spokesmen for their policies – both inside and outside the legislature. Their role, in selling their policies to the illiterate and semi-literate masses of the Indian society can hardly be overemphasized.[5]

Professionals in State Legislatures

As stated above, the data on the legislators in the various states are not systematically collected and preserved. Such data are absolutely essential for the verification, refutation or qualification of the 'co-optation' thesis since all the 25 states which constitute the democratic polity are characterized by different socio-economic indices such as literacy, demographic profile, level of industrial growth, etc. As such, each situation would constitute a crucial testing ground for the validation of the thesis advanced above regarding the participation of professionals in the polity. But in view of the paucity of the systematic data at present, such decisive judgement on the thesis can only be held in suspension. We, therefore, present below a comparative profile for three contiguous states of Haryana, Punjab and Himachal Pradesh for the legislative assemblies of 1972 and 1977 for which data are available to us. Incidentally, all these three states are geographically close to country's capital and were all constituting the state of bigger 'Punjab' in the pre-partition (i.e., pre-1947) days of British India.

Table 2

Professions in Some Select State Legislatures

Legislature	Lawyers	Other profs.	Total profs.	Total legislators
Haryana[6]				
1972	21	1	22	81
	(25.9%)		(27.16%)	
1977	34	2	36	91
	(36.9%)		(39.1%)	
Himachal Pradesh[7]				
1972	17	3	20	68
1982	18	3	21	69
	(26.08%)		(30.4%)	
Jammu and Kashmir[8]	27	2	29	77
1984	(35.6%)		(37.6%)	
Assam[9]	24	2	26	126
1985	(19.04%)		(20.6%)	

PROFESSIONS IN THE TRANSFORMATION OF CONTEMPORARY SOCIETY

It has been well emphasized in many studies that professionals, particularly the lawyers, have played a crucial role in shaping the contemporary history of India and many other ex-colonies. Among others, they have lead the independence movement against the British, and organized a nation-wide popular upsurge against them. They were central participants in the political affairs of the country and still are today. A barrister was the first president of the Indian National Congress, which led the freedom struggle, and the practitioners at Bombay High Court were important party leaders at that time. Some lawyers gave up their careers to assist Mahatma Gandhi. In his Champaran projecting for investigating the exploitation of the Indian peasants by the British Indigo planters (Schmitthener, 1968–69).[10] I have described elsewhere (Gandhi, 1982)[11] the participation of lawyers in Punjab who protested against the repressive legislation in Punjab and were subject to very humiliating and specially vindictive measures after the Amritsar massacre. Although there was disagreement as to whether to co-operate with British institutions or not, some lawyers pursued equality in the courts, and others gained experience in provincial and municipal councils, thereby acquiring a sense of political and administrative realism.[12,13]

India freed itself from the British yoke and the lawyers opened their chapter of socio-political participation in free India, by playing a formative and sheet-anchor role in constitution-making. Those who played probably the most prominent role were nearly all lawyers, noteworthy among them being Pandit Jawaharlal Nehru (the first Prime Minister of free India), Sardar Patel (the Home Minister in Pandit Nehru's cabinet), B.R. Ambedkar (later, Pandit Nehru's Law Minister) and Rajendra Prasad (the first President of free India). A perusal of the proceedings of the Constituent Assembly[14] reveals clearly how some of the very basic percepts of the Indian Constitution such as secularism, equalitarian-egalitarian ideology were expounded, elaborated and incorporated by the lawyer-members of the assembly.[15,16]

A remarkable continuity is observable between the pre-independence and post-independence situation in so far as the centrality of lawyers in the Indian polity is concerned. As Lalit Bhasin,[17] in his analysis of lawyers who played a significant role in the freedom struggle of India (184 in all), reports, nearly half of such lawyers 'ultimately occupied important positions in free India'.[18]

However, the two situations also mark an important discontinuity, especially in terms of the post-independence *instrumental orientation* of the lawyers' rationale of their participation towards the Indian polity. This is clear from the fact that the post-independence profile of political participation of the legal professionals show a markedly conscious tendency among them towards 'career-building' through their participating in the polity.[19] This can be understood from a pure and simple manifestation of their professional *brief keeper's* tendency. Accordingly, one finds them lend their support events such policies as are patently against the values they are professionally supposed to uphold – such as values of legalism, constitutionality, human rights, etc.[20]

Evidence from the Neighbouring Kingdom of Nepal[21]

It is indeed curious that despite the fact that a nation-wide referendum had already voted the continuation of the monarchy-led partyless national panchayat system as late as 1980, a popular insurgence demanding a multi-party democratic system had been continuously shaping, as if subterraneously. It surfaced only recently during the last couple of months and shook the monarchy from its very roots. At the existing stage of information, the kind, even though having conceded the demand in principle (after initial trial of strength with the protesters and their leaders – in which over 200 people were shot dead) continues to prevaricate and 'improvise' bargaining strategies with the popular leaders so as to occupy the centre of the political stage and fill the newly proposed set-up with his stooges. In all this turmoil that has gone by in the recent days and weeks, the observers attribute a crucial role to various professions and their organizations. As one, Ashwani Bhatnagar, writing for the Times of India News Service (April 18, 1990), reports:

> Kathmandu, April 17. Professional groups have emerged as a crucial factor in Nepali politics right from the launching of Movement for Restoration of Democracy (MRD) to the events leading to the dissolution of Rashtriya Panchayat yesterday. *Professionals have played the role of a pressure group both on the political parties as well as on the royal palace.*
>
> Teachers, lawyers, chartered accountants, doctors, paramedicals along with a number of other professional groups combined together to complement and support the efforts of the Nepali Congress and the Left Front to beget democratic systems in this monarchical Himalayan kingdom. In fact, the professionals claim

that they acted as a catalyst in bringing out political reform and fought shoulder to shoulder with political workers during the entire span of about one and a half years during which the trickle of discontent transformed itself into a mountain torrent.

There may not be a significant parallel between the Himalayan Nepal and India apart from the common cultural bond of Hinduism, but a close nexus between the educated and professional elites of these two contiguous nations during the last hundred years or so and also the historicity of professions' engagement in India's independence movement, may have contributed to this seminal role that professions are currently playing in the Nepalese democratic movement. Even so, the Nepalese situation is marked by a markedly greater solidarity among various professions in their effort to pressurize the polity for a popular political change than even has been the case in India. Inferentially, therefore, as far as the current indications go, professions in Nepal seem to engage themselves much more self-consciously in the overall process of activating a systemic change than their counterparts in India have been at any stage of India's history. What really explains this important differential is not clear at the present stage of analysis, but surely this is an important pointer towards differential modes of integration between history, contemporaneity and polity in different structural settings.

PROFESSIONS IN CONFRONTATION WITH THE STATE

Some trends which have been visible lately evidence a confrontationists' posture on the part of the legal profession[22] vis-à-vis state with the putative purpose of guarding the constitutional guarantees and rights of the citizens against their possible erosion by the state or by some other powerful group or groups. This phenomenon which has been studied at length elsewhere[23] by the author has resulted from a combined effort of lawyers, judges, writers and social workers mostly during the last one decade. All these categories of individuals have rallied around the movement carrying a blanket name of 'public interest litigation'. Significantly enough, this emergent culture blossomed luxuriously during post-1978 phase when some of the most liberal judges like Justice P.N. Bhagwati, Justice Krishna Iyer, Justice D.A. Desai served their terms as judges of the Supreme Court of India (the first of these, i.e., Justice Bhagwati also served as Chief Justice of the Supreme Court of India). During their terms, many liberal-minded lawyers with a strong activist orientation filed petitions on behalf of such categories of persons as labourers, landless and bonded workers, women, pavement and slum-dwellers whose fundamental rights were under threat of violation by some acts of omission or commission by the state or some other powerful interests. This was done by them through a liberal and imaginative interpretation of fundamental rights as incorporated in the constitution. As it has been studied at length by the author elsewhere (mentioned in f.n. 23 in the preceding), the entertainment of these petitions by the court has often meant lot of embarrassment to the various organs of the state – the executive, police, bureaucracy and the lower judiciary. Quite often, the decisions already taken by the state on the issues involved in these 'human rights' petitions had to be reversed consequent upon the verdict given by the court on these petitions.

Some of the crucial changes which were crafted into the Indian legal system in its dynamic functioning as a result of these petitions are almost epoch-making. For example, the legally imperative principle of *locus standi* was waived by the judges in the case of public interest litigation. As a result of this, any individual or body which feels exercised on the denial of some fundamental rights to the poor, resourceless and the disadvantaged could file a petition on their behalf in a court of law, even though the petitioner may not have been formally engaged by the aggrieved. Further, during the period when Justice Bhagwati held the office of the Chief Justice, simple post-cards sent in mail by the aggrieved and the indigent individuals to any of the Supreme Court judges were treated by them as 'petitions' and given 'priority listing', ahead of the cases normally due for hearing. This phase in the history of Indian legal system as well as the Indian society can indeed be said to be remarkable – nay, even radical. This is despite the fact that only the thinnest portion of the total bar in the country engaged itself in such litigation and also despite the fact that the Supreme Court engaged itself only episodically in these large-hearted accommodations to the needy and the exploited poor. But, despite all this euphoria, the court never moved to lay down some enduring norms, accommodating such public interest petitions. As a result, in the post-Bhagwati phase, the euphoria created by the explosion of public interest litigation during the period under mention has substantially waned mainly because of a lack of enthusiasms and initiative on the part of subsequent judiciary in the Supreme Court – a situation which seems to send dissuasive signals even to the bar to engage in such litigation. All this, however, does not mean that the profession's confrontation with the state has completely died down. On the contrary, some new varieties of litigations with the potential of causing embarrassment to the state have surfaced. For example, some lawyers have started specializing in the area of ecology-protection litigation and file petitions on behalf of several newly sprung environment protection organizations. Such cases are mounted mostly against the state engaged as it is in the construction of massive dams, industrial and power-generation projects. The petitions are mostly made under articles of the constitution which tend to protect life, liberty and livelihood of the people, since most of such projects entail disturbing the existing ecological balance in these areas and also disrupting the modes of livelihood of the affected people.

CONCLUDING OBSERVATIONS

In this brief article, I have examined some scanty data to take a look at the nature and range of professional participation in the Indian polity and to consider them in the context of one of the existing theoretical perspectives (e.g., Halliday's thesis referred in the text) that the *state empowers the professions by co-opting them into its functioning in order to tide over crises created by explosion of popular expectations and aspirations*. The data considered here relate to professional representation in the national as well as state legislatures. The level and magnitude of professional (especially 'legal') representation brought out in the analysis is indeed quite impressive, especially for a country with as low a level of literacy as 36.23 per cent.[24] The explanation for this lies partly in history, in that the current legal as well as educational system in India is a continuation of the British colonial legacy, i.e., the host of legal-juridical institutions with which they ruled India for approximately two hundred years. In addition, the populistic democratic polity is more amenable to manipulation by better-trained, technically-equipped, forensic-expert professionals than to the rest of the populace. But, all this need not by itself open the portals of legislatures to them – a necessary condition, which is provided by their utility and serviceability to various political parties who need them, for their very survival in a popular democracy, as effective spokesmen for their policies both within and outside the legislatures.

Much against the narrow theoretical confines of 'co-optation thesis', as the data examined (primarily from India, but also from the neighbouring state of Nepal) suggests, professions' role is not confined merely to 'buttressing' the state in its crisis management but also extends much beyond that to the wider polity. They are found engaged at times in saving the state from itself, i.e., from its misdoings and unwarranted deflections from the constitutional format and agenda. They seem to accomplish this by mobilizing public opinion (e.g., Nepal) or by pressurizing judiciary to bring about restoration of legalism and constitutionality (as in India). But that does not mean that professions are exercised over these issues as a collectivity or that members of the professions do or do not pursue or promote breach of constitutionality while in government or in the opposition. Available facts and evidence suggest that the aforesaid pressures are put on the state and the government only by a minuscular portion of the professional fraternity; but, despite this, the said pressures are effective and sometimes have a telling effect in quelling the rot and blackmail that some powerful forces tend to perpetrate on the generality of the people, using state as an apparatus and a tool. At least, in view of the data examined here, the empowerment thesis does not stand in its original shape and colour but gets substantially moderated and modified. Even if some sort of pressure on the state brings professions into co-optation with the state, power stays away from them in as much as they do not work as a collectivity and with the requisite solidarity so as to perpetuate for themselves a position of power and 'reckoning' in the political system. But, despite all this, they do exercise a distinct political influence – though sporadically and episodically, so strong as to give a sudden twist and turn to the social history, as for example is happening in the contemporary Nepal. This becomes possible, obviously on account of, at least, a formal *commitment* on the part of the state to rule as per a specifiable minima of rules: legality or constitutionality. Because, when the state errs on these minima, the professions can and do expose it before the people either through exhortations and mobilization or by activating the rational-legal institutional framework to which the state is committed, at least formally.

Notes

1. Terrence C. Halliday, *Beyond Monopoly: Lawyers, State Crises and Professional Empowerment*, The University of Chicago Press, Chicago, 1987.
2. India has a total of 25 states which comprise the Union of India.
3. One may refer here to theoreticians such as Carr Saunders and P.A. Wilson (*The Professions*, Frank Case and Company, 1964); Talcott Parsons (e.g., 'Professions and Social Structure' in his *Essays in Sociological Theories*, Glencoe, III; The Free Press, 1954). Also, see some of the more recent ones such as C. Turner and M.N. Hodge, 'Occupations and Professions' in J.A. Jackson, *Professions and Professionalization*, Great Britain Cambridge University Press.
4. J.S. Gandhi, *Sociology of Legal Profession, Law and Legal System: The Indian Setting*, Gian Publishing House, Delhi, 1987.

5. 'Lawyers and Polity in India: Historical and Contemporary Context' in J.S. Gandhi, ibid., p. 9.
6. (i) Haryana Vidhan Sabha, *Who's Who 1972*, Haryana Vidhan Sabha Secretariat, Chandigarh, 1974.
   (ii) Haryana Vidhan Sabha, *Who's Who 1977*, Haryana Vidhan Sabha Secretariat, Chandigarh, 1979.
7. (i) *Who's Who 1972* Himachal Pradesh Government, Simla, 1974.
   (ii) *Who's Who 1982*, Himachal Pradesh Government, Simla, 1984.
8. Jammu and Kashmir Legislative Assembly (1983–89) *Who's Who-1984*, Jammu and Kashmir Legislative Assembly Secretariat, Srinagar, 1985.
9. Eighth Assam Lok Sabha (1985–90), *Who's Who*, Assam Legislative Assembly Secretariat, Guwahati, 1986.
10. Samuel Schmitthener, 'A Sketch of the Development of Legal Profession in India', *Law and Society Review*, 3, 1968–69, p. 337.
11. J.S. Gandhi, *Lawyers and Touts: A Study in the Sociology of Legal Profession*, Hindustan Publishing Corporation, 1982.
12. J.S. Gandhi, 'Past and Present: A Sociological Portrait of the Indian Legal Profession' in Richard Abel and Philip S.C. Lewis (eds.), *Lawyers in Society*, University of California Press, Berkeley, 1988, pp. 369–82.
13. 'How does one explain this deep involvement of the lawyers in the independence movement? A variety of factors seemed to have played their part in shaping this orientation of their's. First of all, their proficiency to deal with the British through the interpretation of their very laws gave them an honorific status among their own people, and a respectable status among the British. This fell in tune with the natural demeanour and disposition of the aristocratic-feudal class to which most of them had belonged for several generations. Secondly, as a close reading of the memoirs of some of the leading leaders of the free Indian reveals, most of them clearly foresaw the imminence of the British withdrawal from India and thus a clear possibility that they might occupy the front-ranking positions in the political system of free India.' See J.S. Gandhi, 'Lawyers and Polity in India: Historical and Contemporary Context' in his *Sociology of Legal Profession, Law and Legal System: The Indian Setting*, Gian Publishing House, Delhi, 1987.
14. B.Shiva Rao, *The Framing of India's Constitution*, Vol. 1–V, The AIPA, New Delhi, 1968.
15. J.S. Gandhi, op. cit., 1987, p. 6.
16. 'So fundamental was their contribution that even some of the well-known ambiguities in the Indian Constitution, such as the uncertainty regarding the primacy of the *fundamental rights* or the *directive principles of the state policy*, owe their origin to a formalistic rather than a substantive-historic understanding and expostulation of the Indian social reality on the part of the lawyers who incorporated these terms into the Indian Constitution'. See J.S. Gandhi, op. cit., pp. 6–7.

17. Lalit Bhasin, *Lawyers in the Freedom Struggle of India*, Delhi Art Press, Delhi, 1985.
18. J.S. Gandhi, op. cit., 1988, p. 377.
19. Ibid.
20. Support to this assertion comes from an analysis of public pronouncements made by lawyers-in-government between 1975 to 1981. Incidentally, this period saw the installation of first-ever non-Congress (i.e., Janata) government at the centre and also the re-installation of the Congress government led by Mrs. Gandhi in 1980, after the fall of the Janata government. As the analysis reveals, lawyers holding important ministerial positions in both the governments (which were, to an extent, 'ideologically' – diverse), lent equal support to such policies of their governments as entailed abridgement of the civil liberties guaranteed to the people under the constitution. (This analysis is available in author's 'Lawyers and Polity in India: Historical and Contemporary Context' in his *Sociology of Legal Profession, Law and Legal System*, op. cit., pp. 10–13.
21. Nepal is a Himalayan kingdom located in the north of India. A land-locked and a traditional Hindu country, it has an area of 1,47,121 kms., and a population of 1,64,65000 (in 1984). 'During medieval times the country was divided into various principalities, each under the rule of a hereditary Raja. The founder of modern Nepal, Prithvi Narayan Shah (1769), consolidated them under his rule. From 1846, even though Shah dynasty continued, country's *de facto* control passed on to the Rana Prime Minister. In 1951, the Rana regime was overthrown and King Tribhuvan promised introduction of democracy in Nepal. His son King Mahendra later proclaimed a new constitution in 1959 and late B.P. Koirala, leader of the Nepali Congress became the first elected Prime Minister of Nepal. However, the government was dissolved by a royal decree in December 1960 and the partyless panchayat system of government introduced. A nationwide referendum held on May 2, 1980 decided continuance of partyless panchayat system'. (Taken from Nepal Fact Sheet issued by the Nepal Embassy in New Delhi in 1988).
22. The term 'profession' is being used here rather loosely, not only to denote lawyers but also various other categories of trained lawyers such as judges, law-columnists and law-writers as well as law-teachers who may be making use of their legal expertise in a variety of occupations they pursue. This departure from the traditional definitional position is being proposed here for reasons of 'relevance' in as much as all these categories of 'trained lawyers' seem to be similarly oriented in adopting an anti-government and sometime even anti-state stance, in the protection of the rights of the citizens.
23. J.S. Gandhi, 'Phenomenology of Emergent Culture' in his *Sociology of Legal Profession, Law and Legal System*, op. cit., pp. 138–62.
24. *India – 1988–89*, A Reference Manual, Publication Division, Ministry of Information and Broadcasting, Government of India, New Delhi, 1989.

17

Dialectic of Tradition and Modernity in the Sociology of D.P. Mukerji

T.N. Madan

I

In this essay I make an attempt of briefly examine some central ideas in the work of the late Dhurjati Prasad Mukerji (1894–1961).[1] He was one of the founding fathers of sociology in India and taught during the second quarter of the century at the Lucknow University, where it was my privilege to have been his student. I do believe that if an intellectual is worth commemorating through the means of a memorial lecture, then his work is worthy of serious consideration. It is an obligation, an expression of the sincerity of the gesture of commemoration and, in fact, the best homage we many pay such a scholar and thinker. This should not, however, mean uncritical acceptance of the ideas under examination. DP (to refer to Professor Mukerji by the 'name' by which he was best known among his friends, colleagues and students alike) would have never approved of that.

I should like to mention here that I have another reason for wanting to turn to DP's own work. It so happens that considerable misrepresentation of this work has occurred in recent years; one would ignore what is said informally, but some grievous distortions have appeared in print.[2] In fact, two tendencies are noticeable. The more general of these has been to simply ignore DP's work. His books are out of print and not readily available in libraries, but where they are to be found they are not read. They rarely find a place in courses of studies. A reason for this may well be the contemporary concern with immediate goals and with a narrow empiricism. Be that as it may, this neglect is quite unjust and not only to him but, in fact more so, to ourselves, precisely because he ever was a critic of narrow dogmatism. Moreover, how can we hope to build sound scholarly traditions in India if we do not take the work of our predecessors seriously? Surely, their experience should be as relevant to our tasks of today, if not more so, as the concerns of intellectuals in other parts of the world.

Then there is the misrepresentation I mentioned, arising out of a casual acquaintance with DP's work. It would seem that not only his critics but also some of his admirers have arrived at evaluations of his work without studying it closely. This is harder to explain and, needless to stress, it is the more dangerous tendency.

DP's work demands to be seriously examined as was done, for instance, in his lifetime by one of the very ablest of his students and colleagues, Prof. A.K. Saran (see Saran, 1959 and 1965). I undertake here to make a small contribution to this important task in the hope more of perhaps persuading others to do the same, and do it better, than in the conviction that I personally can do it well.

II

The theme I have chosen for discussion is the relationship of tradition and modernity in DP's thought. It is true that this bipolarity is now becoming quite outmoded. Yet, I think, there would be a consensus among intellectuals and policy-makers in defining our endeavours today as a nation as the quest for modernization: or, as DP would have put it, the effort to give a push to history towards the next higher stage. We may have become weary of the concept of modernization, but the important question is, have we carefully formulated the reasons for this weariness? And did we earlier develop adequately the argument for modernization and examine its nature and scope?

I am not sure we have done these things; and it is my belief that DP is an excellent guide not only in the clarification of the concept of modernity but also in this self-questioning. He drew attention to some of the hazards that attent the task; and his own work illustrates others. Thus, he would have argued that our modernity is spurious, a sham, and indeed a major obstacle in the path of genuine modernization; but his criticism ultimately fails to point to a satisfactory solution. I should like to construct this argument in some detail.

Let me begin with DP's early work to examine the seeds of his ideas regarding tradition and modernity that came to flower later on. It is interesting to note here that he considered his first two books, *Personality and the Social Sciences* (1924) and *Basic Concepts of Sociology* (1932), 'personal documents' – products of his endeavour to formulate an adequate concept of social science. From the very beginning he organized his ideas around the notion of personality. He took up the position that the abstract individual should not be the focus of social science theories, and pleaded for a 'wholistic', psycho-sociological approach. It was this 'synthesis of the double process of individuality and the socialization of the uniqueness of individual life, this perfect unity' that he called personality (1924: ii).

Looking back at his work of a lifetime, he said in his presidential address to the First Sociological Conference in 1955 that he had come to sociology from economics and history because he was interested in developing his personality through knowledge (1958: 228). The office of a comprehensive social science, transcending the prevailing compartmentalization of social sciences, was conceived to be the development of an integrated though many-facted personality. This is an idea which, as A.K. Saran (1962: 167) has pointed out, is 'in some ways parallel to the ideal suggested by Moore in his *Principia Ethica*'.

Thus, at the very beginning of his intellectual career, DP committed himself to a view of knowledge and of the knower. Knowledge was not, as he put it, mere 'matter-of-factness' but ultimately, after taking the empirical datum and the scientific method for its study into account, philosophic (1932: iv-v). Economics had to be rooted in concrete social reality, that is, it had to be sociological; sociology had to take full cognizance of cultural specificity, that is, it had to be historical; history had to rise above a narrow concern with the triviality of the gone-by events through the incorporation in it of a vision of the future, that is, it had to be philosophical. Given such an enterprise, it is obvious that the knower had to be a daring adventurer with a large vision rather than a timid-seeker of the safety of specialization. He pointedly asked in the mid-forties:

> We talk of India's vivisection, but what about the vivisection of knowledge which has been going on these years in the name of learning, scholarship and specialization? A 'subject' has been cut off from knowledge, knowledge has been excised from life, and life has been amputated from living social conditions. It is really high time for sociology to come to its own. It may not offer *the* truth. Truth is the concern of mystics and philosophers. Meanwhile, we may as well be occupied with the discipline which is most truthful to the wholeness and the dynamics of the objective human reality. (1946: 11)[3]

The philosophical approach which DP wished cultivated was that of rationalism of 'practical and speculative reason'. Reason was to be understood as a tool, 'not of understanding merely, but of the development of personality' (1932: x). It seems a reasonable conjecture, though one could hardly assert it, that at this time DP may have been under the influence of the teachings of Hegel. In fact, such an influence seems to have persisted till the very end, prominently in his concern with reason and human dignity, his attitude towards the past, wanting to preserve whatever was judged as valuable in it, and his fascination with dialectics. But, then, these values could also have been imbibed from the Hindu Upanishadic tradition.

III

DP's concern in the 1920s and 1930s was with the mental make-up of modern Indian intellectuals and their world-view, which he rightly judged to be a borrowal of the western liberal outlook with its various preoccupations, most notably the notions of 'progress' and 'equality'. These and the related concepts of 'social forces' and 'social control' were subjected to critical analysis in *Basic Concepts of Sociology*. It is in his discussion of the relation of 'progress' to 'personality' that, it seems to me, we come across early intimations of his later view on the nature of modernization.

Rejecting the evolutionist notion of 'progress' as a natural phenomenon, DP stressed the element of 'purpose' in the life of human beings. Development is not growth, he admonished us, but the broader process of the unfolding of potentialities (in this he followed Hegel and Marx though he did not say so explicitly), and added that the 'emergence of values and their dynamic character' must receive adequate consideration (1932: 9). He further wrote:

> Progress can best be understood as a problem covering the whole field of human endeavour. It has a direction in time. It has various means and tactics of development. Fundamentally, it is a problem of balancing of values.
>
> The scope of the problem is as wide as human society, and as deep as human personality. In so far as human values arise only in contact with human consciousness at its different levels, the problem of progress has unique reference to the changing individual living in a particular region at a particular time in association with other individuals who share with him certain common customs, beliefs, traditions, and possibly a common temperament. (1932: 15)

It seems to me permissible to derive from the foregoing statement the conclusion that 'modernization' is the special form which 'progress' takes for people in the Third World countries today. If this is granted,[4] then the following words need to be pondered (1932: 29–30):

> Progress...is...a movement of freedom.... What is of vital significance is that our time-adjustments should be made in such a way that we should be free from the necessity of remaining in social contact for every moment of our life. This is an important condition of progress. In leisure alone can man conquer the tyranny of time, by investing it with a meaning, a direction, a memory and a purpose. Obstacles to leisure, including the demands of a hectic social life, often mistaken for progress, must be removed in order that the inner personality of man may get the opportunity for development. This is why the Hindu philosopher wisely insists on the daily hour of contemplation, and after a certain age, a well-marked period of retirement from the turmoil of life. The bustle of modern civilization is growing apace and the need for retirement is becoming greater.

The above passage has a contemporary ring; and it is very relevant. If we paraphrase it, using words and phrases that are in use today, we get a succinct reference to the unthinking craving for and the human costs of modernization, including alienation, to the values of individual freedom and human dignity, and to social commitment. For DP progress was, as I have already quoted him saying, a problem of balancing of values; and so is modernization. When we introduce values into our discourse, and the rationalist perspective that DP recommended will have it in no other way, we are faced with the problem of the hierarchy of values, that is with the quest for ultimate or fundamental values. For these DP turned to the Upanishads, to *shantam, shivam, advaitam,* that is, peace, welfare, unity.

> The first is the principle of harmony which sustains the universe amidst all its incessant changes, movements and conflicts. The second is the principle of co-ordination in the social environment. The third gives expression to the unity which transcends all the diverse forms of states, behaviours and conflicts, and permeates thought and action with ineffable joy... . On this view, progress ultimately depends on the development of personality by a conscious realization of the principles of harmony, welfare and unity. (1932: 35)

This appeal to Vedanta, while discussing the western notion of progress, is a disconcerting characteristic of DP's thought throughout. He sought to legitimize it by calling it 'synthesis', which itself he described as a characteristic of the historical process, the third stage of the dialectic triad. He thus evaded, it would seem, a closer examination of the nature and validity of synthesis. Its existence was assumed and self-validating. One's disappointment and criticism of DP's position is not on the ground of the source of this trinity of values – I am reminded of the research student at an Indian university who told me of her deep disappointment that DP was at heart a Hindu – but on the ground that harmony, welfare and unity are too vague and esoteric, as they make their elusive appearance in DP's discourse; and he does not show how they may be integrated with such values of the West as are embodied in its industrial civilization. On the positive side, however, it must be added that DP's preoccupation with ultimate values should be assessed in the light of his deep distrust of the installation of science as the redeemer of mankind and of scientific method (based on a narrow empiricism and exclusive reliance on inductive inference) as the redeemer of social sciences.

IV

I have heard it said that DP's intellectual life reveals a striking lack of continuity between his early work, when he was interested almost exclusively in broad conceptual issues rather than in understanding the nature and problems of Indian society, and his later work, when he became increasingly immersed in India. Also, it is asserted that this transition in his ideas was marked by a growing salience of a Marxist, or pseudo-Marxist (depending upon the critic's own ideological position), orientation in his work. That the emphases in his work changed with the passage of time may not be denied – and what is wrong with that – but to maintain that there is a sharp break in the two phases of his work would seem to be an overstatement.

DP, it would seem, was always and deeply influenced by the social environment around him. To the extent to which the society in which he lived was undergoing change, to that extent there was a discernible change in his intellectual concerns also, and he was conscious of this. He even wrote about it: 'In my view, the thing changing is more real and objective than change per se' (1958: 241). He was a very sensitive person, and many of those who knew him intimately will recall how a turn in events – whether of the university, the city, the country or the world – would cast a gloom on him or bring him genuine joy. He had an incredible capacity for intense subjective experience; it perhaps killed him in the end. (One of his favourite books was Goethe's *Werther*). In all his writings he addressed himself to his contemporaries: he had an unstated contempt for those who write for posterity with an eye on personal fame and some kind of immortality, and I think he was right in this attitude.[5]

It would seem that what DP was most conscious of in his earlier writings was the need to establish links between the traditional culture of which he was a proud though critical inheritor and the modern liberal education of which he was a critical though appreciative product. The two – Indian culture and modern education – could not stay apart without each becoming impoverished – as indeed had been happening – and therefore had to be synthesized in the life of the people in general and of the middle classes and the intellectuals in particular. In this respect, DP was a characteristic product of his times. He was attracted by the image of the future which the West held out to traditional societies and, at the same time, he was attached to his own tradition, the core of which was the Hindu tradition. The need to defend what he regarded as the essential values of this tradition thus became a compelling concern, particularly in his later writings.

Dualities never ceased to bother DP, and he ever sought to resolve the conflict implicit in persistent dualism through transcendence. This transcendence was to him what history was all about – or ought to be. But history was not for him a tablet already etched on, once for all, and for each and every people. Hence, his early criticism that, in the hands of Trotsky, Lenin and Bukharin, history had degenerated into 'pure dialectic' (1932: 184). This criticism was repeated by him again and again. In 1945, he complained that the Marxists had made the 'laws of dialectics' behave like the 'laws of *karma*'

> predetermining every fact, event and human behaviour in its course; or else, they are held forth as a moral justification for what is commonly described as opportunism. (1945: 18)

For DP historiography was meaningless unless it was recognized that the decision to 'write history' entailed the decision to 'act history' (1945: 46). And history was being enacted in India in the 1930s, if it ever was during DP's lifetime, by the middle classes and, under their leadership, by the masses. What they were doing increasingly bothered him, for history had not only to be enacted but to be enacted right. The question of values could not be evaded. The middle classes whose intellectual life was his concern in his earlier work were also his concern in his later work, but now it was their politics that absorbed him. In this respect, his concern avowedly with himself was in fact sociological, for he believed that no one is an island unto himself but embedded not merely in his class but in his total socio-cultural environment. The focus was on modern Indian culture and the canvas naturally was the whole of India.

V

Modern Indian Culture: A Sociological Study was first published in 1942, and a second revised edition was completed in 1947, the year of independence, but also of partition. It was written under the impending shadow of the vivisection of India; anguish and sorrow are the mood of the book. The problem, as he saw it, was first to explain why the calamity of communal division had befallen India, and then to use this knowledge to shape a better future. Sociology had to be the handmaiden of history and it was no mean role; indeed it was a privilege. His analysis led him to the conclusion that a distortion had entered into the long-established course of Indian history and crippled it. The happening responsible for this was British rule. But let me first quote DP's succinct statement of the character of modern Indian culture:

> As a social and historical process... Indian culture represents certain common traditions that have given rise to a number of general attitudes. The major influences in their shaping have been Buddhism, Islam, and western commerce and culture. It was through the assimilation and conflict of such varying forces that Indian culture became what it is today, neither Hindu nor Islamic, neither a replica of the western modes of living and thought nor a purely Asiatic product. (1948: 1)

In this historical process, synthesis had been the dominant organizing principle and the Hindu, the Buddhist and the Muslim had together shaped a worldview in which, according to DP, 'the fact of Being was of lasting significance'. His favourite quotation from the Upanishads was *charaiveti*, keep moving forward. This meant that there had developed an indifference to 'the transient and the sensate' and a preoccupation with the subordination of 'the little self' to and ultimately its dissolution in 'the Supreme Reality' (1948: 2). This worldview DP called 'the mystical outlook'. He maintained that Islam could have on its arrival in India shaken Hindu society in its very roots but Buddhism served as a cushion. Buddhism itself had failed to rend Hindu society as under and had succeeded only in rendering it more elastic. Muslim rule was an economically progressive force but, on the whole, it brought about only a variation in the already existent socio-economic structure (1948: 65–67) and provided no real alternatives to native economic and political systems. 'The Muslims just reigned, but seldom ruled' (1948: 24).

British rule, however, did prove to be a real turning point in as much as it succeeded in changing the relations of production, or to use DP's own words, 'the very basis of the Indian social economy' (1948: 24). New interests in land and commerce were generated; a new pattern of education was introduced; physical and occupational mobility received a strong impetus. Overshadowing all these developments, however, was the liquidation of an established middle class and 'the emergence of a spurious middle class'

> who do not play any truly historical part in the socio-economic evolution of the country, remain distant from the rest of the people in professional isolation or as rent receivers, and are divorced from the realities of social and economic life… . Their ignorance of the background of Indian culture is profound… . Their pride in culture is in inverse proportion to its lack of social content. (1948: 25)

It was this middle class which helped in the consolidation of British rule in India but later challenged it successfully; it was also this same middle class which brought about the partition of the country. Its rootlessness made it a 'counterfeit class' and therefore its handiwork (whether in the domain of education and culture, in the political arena, or in the field of economic enterprise) had inevitably something of the same spurious quality. 'The politics and the culture of a subject country', DP wrote, 'cannot be separated from each other' (1948: 207). To expect such an 'elite' to lead an independent India along the path of genuine modernization, DP asserted with remarkable prescience, would be unrealistic. He warned that before they could be expected to remake India, modernize it, the elite themselves must be remade. And he wrote a forthright, if not easy prescription for them: 'conscious adjustment to India traditions and symbols' (1948: 215), for 'culture cannot be "made" from scratch' (1948: 214).

It is important to understand why he made this particular recommendation, why he wanted the withdrawal of foreign rule to be accompanied by a withdrawal into the self which, let me hasten to add, was quite different from a withdrawal into the past or inaction. DP was not only *not* a revivalist, he was also keenly aware of the imminent possibility of revivalism and its fatal consequences. He noted that it would be the form that political hatred disguised as civil hatred would take after independence. But he was not hopeless, for he fondly believed that revivalism could be combated by giving salience to economic interests through a 'material programme' that would cut across communal exclusiveness. He envisaged India's emancipation from the negative violence of the constrictive primordial loyalties of religion and caste through the emergence of class consciousness (1948: 216). He was silent on class conflict, however, and his critics may justifiably accuse him of not seeing his analysis through to its logical conclusion. His optimism was the sanguine hope of an Indian liberal intellectual rather than the fiery conviction of a Marxist revolutionary.

In any case, we know today, three decades after DP's expression of faith on this score, that class does not displace caste in India. Nor do they co-exist in compartments: they combine but they do not fuse. DP's vision of a peaceful, progressive India born out of the 'union' of diverse elements, of distinctive regional cultures rather than out of the type of 'unity' that the British imposed from above, however, remains eminently valid even today. The *accommodation* of various kinds of conflicting loyalties within a national framework, rather than national *integration*, is the strategy which new African and Asian states faced with cultural pluralism are finding to be both feasible and advantageous. We all know how Pakistan broke up in 1971 (see Madan, 1974).

DP's plea for a reorientation to tradition was, then, of a positive nature – an essential condition for moving forward, for restoring historical dynamism, for reforging the broken chain of the socio-cultural process of synthesis. Employing Franklin Gidding's classification of traditions into primary, secondary and tertiary, he suggested that by the time of the British arrival, Hindus and Muslims had yet not achieved a full synthesis of traditions at all levels of social existence. There was a greater measure of agreement between them regarding the utilization and appropriation of natural resources and to a lesser extent in respect of aesthetic and religious traditions. In the tertiary traditions of conceptual thought, however, differences survived prominently.

It was into this situation that the British moved in, blundering their way into India, and gave Indian history a severe jolt. As already stated, they destroyed indigenous merchant capital and the rural economy, pushed through a land settlement based on alien concepts of profit and property, and established a socially useless educational system. Such opportunities as it did create could not be fully utilized, DP said, for they cut across India's traditions, and 'because the methods of their imposition spoilt the substance of her need for new life' (1948: 206).

VI

At this point it seems pertinent just to point out that, while DP followed Marx closely in his conception of history and in his characterization of British rule as uprooting, he differed significantly not only with Marx's assessment of the positive consequences of this rule but also with Marx's negative assessment of the pre-British traditions. It is important to note this because some Marxists have claimed DP on their side, despite his repeated denials that he was a Marxist; he claimed to be only a 'Marxologist' (Singh, 1973: 216). Some non-Marxists also have, it may be added, described DP as a Marxist.

It will be recalled that Marx had in his articles on British rule in India asserted that India had a long past but 'no history at all, at least no known history';[6] that its social condition had 'remained unaltered since its remotest antiquity'; that it was 'the British intruder who broke up the Indian handloom and destroyed the spinning-wheel'; that it was 'British steam and science' which 'uprooted, over the whole surface of Hindustan, the union between agriculture and manufacturing industry.' Marx had listed England's 'crimes' in India and proceeded to point out that she had become 'the unconscious tool of history' whose actions would ultimately result in a 'fundamental revolution'. He had said (Marx and Engels, 1959: 31):

> England had to fulfil a double mission in India: one destructive and other regenerating – the annihilation of old Asiatic society, and the laying of the material foundations of western society in India.

Thus, for Marx, as for so many others since his time, including Indian intellectuals of various shades of opinion, the modernization of India had to be its westernization.

As has already been stated above, DP was intellectually and emotionally opposed to such a view about India's past and future, where it came from Marx or from liberal bourgeois historians. He refused to be ashamed of or apologetic about India's past. The statement of his position was unambiguous (1945: 11):

> Our attitude is one of humility towards the given fund. But it is also an awareness of the need, the utter need, of recreating the given and making it flow. The given of India is very much in ourselves. And we want to make something worthwhile out of it....

Indian history could not be made by outsiders: it had to be enacted by Indians. In this endeavour they had to be not only firm of purpose but also clear-headed. He wrote:

> Our sole interest is to write and to act Indian history. Action means making; it has a starting point – this specificity called India; or if that be too vague, this specificity of the contact between India and England or the West. Making involves changing, which in turn requires (a) a scientific study of the tendencies which make up this specificity, and (b) a deep understanding of the crisis (which marks the beginning no less than the end of an epoch). In all these matters, the Marxian method... is likely to be more useful than other methods. If it is not, it can be discarded. After all, the object survives. (1945: 46)

'Specificity' and 'crisis' are the key words in this passage; the former points to the importance of the encounter of traditions and the latter to its consequences. When one speaks of tradition, or of 'Marxist specification', one means, in DP's words, 'the comparative obduracy of a culture-pattern'. He expected the Marxist approach to be grounded in the specificity of Indian history (1945: 45, 1946: 162 ff), as indeed Marx himself had done by focusing on capitalism, the dominant institution of western society in his time. Marx, it will be said, was interested in precipitating the crisis of contradictory class interests in capitalist society (1945: 37). DP, too, was interested in movement, in the release of the arrested historical process, in the relation between tradition and modernity. He asked for a sociology which would 'show the way out of the social system by analyzing the process of transformation' (1958: 240). This could be done by focusing first on tradition and only then on change.

> The first task for us, therefore, is to study the social traditions to which we have been born and in which we have had out being. This task includes the study of the changes in traditions by internal and external pressures. The latter are mostly economic... Unless the economic force is extraordinarily strong – and it is that only when the modes of production are altered – traditions survive by adjustments. The capacity for adjustment is the measure of the vitality of traditions. One can have a full measure of this vitality only by immediate experience. Thus, it is that I give top priority to the understanding (in Dilthey's sense) of traditions even for the study of their changes. In other words, the study of Indian traditions... should precede the socialist interpretation of

changes in Indian traditions in terms of economic forces. (1958: 232)

This brings us to the last phase of DP's work. Before I turn to it, however, I should mention that Louis Dumont also has drawn our attention to an unresolved problem in DP's sociology. He points out that one's 'recognition of the absence of the individual in traditional India' obliges one to 'admit with others that India has no history' for 'history and the individual are inseparable'; it follows that 'Indian civilization [is]...unhistorical by definition' (Dumont, 1967: 239). Viewed from this perspective, DP's impatience with the Marxist position is difficult to justify. In fact, it is rather surprising that, having emphasized the importance of the group as against the individual in the Indian tradition, and of religious values also, DP should have opted for a Marxist solution to the problems of Indian historiography (see Dumont, 1967: 231) and for a view of India's future based on synthesis. he hovered between Indian tradition and Marxism and his adherence to Marxist solutions to intellectual and practical problems gained in salience in his later work which was also characterized by a heightened concern with tradition.[7]

VII

For DP the history of India was not the history of her particular form of class struggle because she had experienced none worth the name. The place of philosophy and religion was dominant in this history, and it was fundamentally a long-drawn exercise in cultural synthesis. For him 'Indian history was Indian culture' (1958: 123). India's recent woes, namely, communal hatred and partition, had been the result of the arrested assimilation of Islamic values (1958: 163); he believed that 'history halts unless it is pushed' (1958: 39).

The national movement had generated much moral fervour but, DP complained, it had been anti-intellectual. Not only had there been much unthinking borrowal from the West, there had also emerged a hiatus between theory and practice as a result of which thought had become impoverished and action ineffectual. Given his concern for intellectual and artistic creativity, it is not surprising that he should have concluded: 'politics has ruined our culture' (1958: 190).

What was worse, there were no signs of this schism being healed in the years immediately after independence. When planning arrived as state policy in the early fifties, DP expressed his concern, for instance in an important 1953 paper on 'Man and Plan in India' (1958: 30–76), that a clear concept of the new man and a systematic design of the new society were nowhere in evidence. As the years passed by, he came to formulate a negative judgement about the endeavours to build a new India, and also diagnosed the cause of the rampant intellectual sloth. He said in 1955:

> I have seen how our progressive groups have failed in the field of intellect, and hence also in economic and political action, chiefly on account of their ignorance of and unrootedness in India's social reality. (1958: 240)

The issue at stake was India's modernization. DP's essential stand on this was that there could be no genuine modernization through imitation. A people could not abandon their own cultural heritage and yet succeed in internalizing the historical experience of other peoples; they could only be ready to be taken over. He feared cultural imperialism more than any other. The only valid approach, according to DP, was that which characterized the efforts of men like Rammohun Roy and Rabindranath Tagore, who tried to make the main currents of western thought and action... run through the Indian bed to remove its choking weeds in order that the ancient stream might flow (1958: 33).

DP formulated this view of the dialectic between tradition and modernity several years before independence, in his study of Tagore published in 1943, in which he wrote:

> The influence of the West upon Tagore was great... but it should not be exaggerated: it only collaborated with one vital strand of the traditional, the strand that Ram Mohan and Tagore's father... rewove for Tagore's generation. Now, all these traditional values Tagore was perpetually exploiting but never more than when he felt the need to expand, to rise, to go deeper, and be fresher. At each such stage in the evolution of his prose, poetry, drama, music and of his personality we find Tagore drawing upon some basic reservoir of the soil, of the people, of the spirit and emerging with a capacity for larger investment. (1972: 50)[8]

This crucial passage holds the key to DP's views on the nature and dynamics of modernization. It emerges as a historical process which is at once an expansion, an elevation, a deepening and a revitalization – in short, a larger investment – of traditional values and cultural patterns, and not a total departure from them, resulting from the interplay of the traditional and the modern. DP would have agreed with Michael Oakeshott, I think, that the principle of tradition 'is a principle of continuity' (1962: 128).[9] From this perspective, tradition is a condition of rather than an obstacle to modernization; it gives us the freedom to choose between alternatives and evolve a cultural pattern which cannot but be a synthesis of the old and the new. New values and institutions must have a soil in which to take root and from which to imbibe character. Modernity must therefore be defined in relation to, and not in denial of, tradition.[10] Conflict is only the intermediate stage in the dialectic triad: the movement is toward *coincidenia oppositorum*. Needless to emphasize, the foregoing argument is in accordance with the Marxist dialectic which sees relations as determined by one another and therefore bases a 'proper' understanding of them on such a relationship.

Synthesis of the opposites is not, however, a historical inevitability. It is not a gift to a people unasked or merely for the asking: they must strive for it self-consciously, for 'culture is an affair of total consciousness' (1958: 189), it is a 'dynamic social process, and not another name for traditionalism' (1958: 101–02). History for DP was a 'going concern' (1945: 19), and the value of the Marxist approach to the making of history lay in that it would help to generate 'historical conviction' (1958: 56), and thus act as a spur to fully awakened endeavour. The alternative to self-conscious choice-making is mindless imitation and loss of autonomy and, therefore, dehumanization, though DP did not put it quite in those words.

Self-consciousness, then, is the form of modernization. Its content, one gathers from DP's writings in the 1950s, comprises nationalism, democracy, the utilization of science and technology for harnessing nature, planning for social and economic development, and the cultivation of rationality. The typical modern man is the engineer, social and technical (1958: 39–40). DP believed that these forces were becoming ascendant:

> This is a bare historical fact. To transmute that fact into a value, the first requisite is to have active faith in the historicity of that fact... . The second requisite is social action... to push... consciously, deliberately, collectively, into the next historical phase. The value of Indian traditions lies in the ability of their conserving forces to put a brake on hasty passage. Adjustment is the end-product of the dialectical connection between the two. Meanwhile is tension. And tension is not merely interesting as a subject of research; if it leads up to a higher stage, it is also desirable. The higher stage is where personality is integrated through a planned, socially directed, collective endeavour for historically understood ends, which means... a socialist order.

> Tensions will not cease there. It is not the peace of the grave. Only alienation from nature, work and man will stop in the arduous course of such high and strenuous endeavours. (1958: 76)

In view of this clear expression of faith (it is that, not a demonstration), it is not surprising that DP should have told Indian sociologists (in 1955) that their 'first task' was the study of 'social traditions' (1958: 232), and should have reminded them that traditions grow through conflict.

It is in the context of this emphasis on tradition that his specific recommendation for the study of Mahatma Gandhi's views on machines and technology, before going ahead with 'large-scale technological development' (1958: 225), was made. It was no small matter that from the Gandhian perspective, which stressed the values of wantlessness, non-exploitation and non-possession, the very notions of economic development and underdevelopment could be questioned (1958: 206). But this was perhaps only a gesture (a response to a poser), for DP maintained that Gandhi had failed to indicate how to absorb 'the new social forces which the West had released' (1958: 35); moreover, 'the type of new society enveloped in the vulgarized notion of Rama-rajya was not only non-historical but anti-historical' (1958: 38). But he was also convinced that Gandhian insistence on traditional values might help to save India from the kind of evils (for example, scientism and consumerism) to which the West had fallen prey (1958: 227).

The failure to clearly define the terms and rigorously examine the process of synthesis, already noted above, reappears here again and indeed repeatedly in DP's work. The resultant 'self-cancellation', as Gupta (1977) puts it, 'provided a certain honesty and a certain pathos to DP's sociology'. In fact, he himself recognized this when he described his life to A.K. Saran as 'a series of reluctances' (Saran, 1962: 169). Saran concludes that DP 'did not wish to face the dilemma entailed by a steadfast recognition of this truth', that the three world views – Vedanta, western liberalism, Marxism – which all beckoned to DP 'do not mix'.[11] One wonders what his autobiography would have been like.

VIII

I hope to have shown in this necessarily brief presentation that, despite understandable differences in emphasis, there is on the whole a remarkable consistency in DP's views on the nature of modernization. Not that consistency is always a virtue but that in this case it happens to be true. Genuine modernization, according to him, has to be distinguished from the spurious product and the clue lies in its historicity. The presentation of the argument is clear but it is not always thorough and complete, and may be attacked from more than one vantage point.

Saran (1965), for instance, has rightly pointed out that DP does not subject the socialist order itself to analysis and takes its benign character on trust, that he fails to realize that a technology- oriented society cannot easily be non-exploitative and not anti-man, that the traditional and the modern worldviews are rooted in different conceptions of time, that traditional ideas cannot be activated by human effort alone, that given our choice of development goals we cannot escape westernization, and so forth. It seems to me that DP's principal problem was that he let the obvious heuristic value of the dialectical approach overwhelm him and failed to probe deeply enough into both the requirements of theory building and of the examination of empirical reality. He fused the method and the datum.

I do want to suggest, however, that DP's approach has certain advantages as compared to the others that are current in modernization studies. An examination of modernization theories in general is outside the scope of this essay; I will therefore make only a rather sweeping generalization about them. They seem to me to fall into two very broad categories. There are, firstly, what we may call the 'big bang' theories of modernization, according to which tradition and modernity are mutually exclusive, bipolar phenomena. This entails the further view that before one may change anything at all, one must change everything. The examples that come to mind are many, but Gunnar Myrdal's *Asian Drama* (1968) is notable. This view is, however, unfashionable now, and to that extent sociology has moved forward.

Secondly, there are what we may call the 'steady state' theories of modernization, according to which modernization is a gradual, piecemeal process, involving compartmentalization of life and living; it is not through displacement but juxtaposition that modernization proceeds. Examples are too numerous to be listed here (but see Singer, 1972 and Singh, 1973). As a description of the empirical reality, the latter approach is perhaps adequate, but it creates a serious problem of understanding, for it in effect dispenses with all values except modernity; and modernity is defined only vaguely by reference to what has happened or is happening elsewhere – industrialization, bureaucratization, democratization, etc.

By this latter view, one is committed to the completion of the agenda of modernization; and hence the boredom, the weariness and the frustration one sees signs of everywhere. The gap between the 'modernized' and the 'modernizing', it is obvious, will never be closed. No wonder, then, that social scientists already speak of the infinite transition – an endless pause – in which traditional societies find themselves trapped. Moreover, both sociology and history teach us, if they teach us anything at all, that there always is a residue, that there always will be traditional and modern elements in the cultural life of a people, anywhere, anytime.

The virtue or a dialectical approach such as DP advocated would seem to be that it reveals the spuriousness of some of the issues that the other approaches give rise to. At the same time, it may well be criticized as an evasion of other basic issues. I might add, though, that it does provide us with a suggestive notion, one which we may call *generative* tradition, and also a framework for the evaluation of ongoing processes. All this, of course, needs elaboration, but the present essay is not the place for such an undertaking. Suffice it to say, the notion of generative tradition involves a conception of 'structural' time more significantly than it does that of 'chronological' time. 'Structural' time implies, as many anthropologists have shown, a working out of the potentialities of an institution. Institutions have a duration in 'real' time, but this is the surface view; they also have a deeper duration which is not readily perceived because of the transformations they undergo.

IX

To conclude the task I set myself in this essay was to give an exploratory exposition of a selected aspect of D.P. Mukerji's sociological writings, using as far as convenient his own words. I chose to organize some of the available materials around the theme of 'tradition and modernity' because it occupied an important place in his work and also because it survives as a major concern of contemporary sociology. Taking DP's work as a whole, one soon discovers that his concern with tradition and modernity, which became particularly salient during the 1940s and remained so until the end, was in fact a particular expression of a larger, and it would seem perennial, concern of westernized Hindu intellectuals. This concern, manifested in a variety of ways, was with the so-called apologetic patterns of the Hindu renaissance (see Bharati, 1970). Hence, the urge for a synthesis of Vedanta, western liberalism and Marxism.

I have referred very briefly to DP's fascination with the Marxist method as also his insistence that he was not a Marxist. This needs a deeper examination than I am competent to undertake. What is clear, however, is that DP should not be claimed to be on this or that side of the fence without actually demonstrating such a stance. In this regard, his overwhelming emphasis on synthesis needs to be examined.

An equally important and difficult undertaking would be the elaboration and specification of DP's conception of the content of tradition. Whereas he establishes, convincingly I think, the relevance of tradition to modernity at the level of principle, he does not spell out its empirical content except in terms of general categories, such as those suggested by Giddings and already quoted above. One has the uncomfortable feeling that he himself operated more in terms of intuition and general knowledge than a deep study of the texts. A confrontation with tradition through fieldwork in the manner of the anthropologist, was, of course, ruled out by him, at least for himself. His tribute to G.S. Ghurye as the 'only Indian sociologist today', whilst others were 'sociologists in India' (1955: 238), is to be understood in this light. Also required is an examination of the general indifference of Indian sociologists to DP's plea for the study of tradition. Mukherjee (1965) has a suggestive first essay on this problem, but much more needs to be done. There is work to do for many of us.

Notes

1. As is well known, D.P. Mukerji wrote both in Bengali and in English, but I have read only his English works. In this essay I have drawn mainly on four of his five monographs and three of his four collections of essays. The excluded books are *Problems of Indian Youth* (1946), a collection of essays and addresses, and *Introduction to Indian Music* (1945). References to his works are by date alone; references to other sources are by author's name and date.
2. See, for example, Srinivas and Panini (1973). This fairly long essay contains only two paragraphs about D.P. Mukerji (pp. 189–90), and nearly every statement in them is either factually incorrect or otherwise misleading. It is indeed surprising that the authors should suggest that DP 'viewed the processes of change under British rule as similar to changes under earlier alien rulers' or that they should think that he changed his views about 'synthesis' in his later writings. His concern for the cultural 'specificity' of India is misrepresented as an emphasis on 'uniqueness', and this after they have themselves drawn attention to the influence of Marxism on DP.

3. Cp. Eliot (1940), *Two Choruses from the 'Rock'*: 'Where is the life we have lost in living?/Where is the wisdom we have lost in knowledge?/ Where is the knowledge we have lost in information?'

   I would like to record here that the most lasting impression that DP made on me, as indeed on many other students of his, was of his luminous conviction that genuine scholarship was socially useful no less than personally satisfying, that the life of ideas was not for the contended and the lazy but only for the sceptical and the restless, and that the life on an intellectual was an honourable life and intellectuals were the very salt of the earth. Given the contemporary cynicism about and among intellectuals, DP's faith needs reassertion. The rewards he sought were large, and so were the risks. I have often heard him criticized as a dilettante; I only wish these critics would go beyond DP and examine the costs of their own narrow concerns and the little underlying faiths. He himself would have asked for no more.
4. K.P. Gupta (1977) objects to such a formulation: 'I think it is undesirable to link the concepts of "social progress" and modernization… because it (the linkage) provides a convenient bridge to legitimize the shift from the universal concern with progress in all societies to the narrower and prejudicial concern solely with the Third World development.'
5. I am reminded of R.G. Collingwood who wrote in his famous autobiography that good writers always write for their contemporaries (Collingwood, 1970: 39).
6. As is well known, Marx owed this judgement about India to Hegel.
7. Ramakrishna Mukherjee writes in a personal communication (1977) that my analysis does justice neither to Marx's views on Indian history nor to DP's 'basic adherence to the principles of Marxism'.
8. DP drew an interesting and significant contrast between Bankim Chandra Chatterjee and Rabindranath Tagore. He wrote (1972: 75–76): '[Bankim] was a path-finder and a first class intellect that had absorbed the then current thought of England. His grounding in Indian thought was weak at first; when it was surer…. [it] ended in his plea for a neo-Hindu resurgence. Like Michael Madhusudan Dutt, Bankim the artist remained a divided being. Tagore was more lucky. *His saturation with Indian traditions was deeper; hence he could more easily assimilate a bigger dose of western thought*' (emphasis added).
9. Marx, it will be recalled, had written (in 1853) of the 'melancholy' and the 'misery' of the Hindu arising out of the 'loss of his old word' and his separation from 'ancient traditions' (Marx and Engels, 1959: 16). The task at hand was to make the vital currents flow. That this could be done by re-establishing meaningful links with the past would have been emphasized, however, only by an Indian such as DP. I suspect DP would have sympathized with Oakeshott's assertion that the changes a tradition 'undergoes are potential within it' (1962: 128), his fascination with Marxism notwithstanding.

10. Many contemporary thinkers have expressed similar views. See, e.g., the motto of this essay taken from Popper (1963: 122). Or Schneider (1974: 205): 'Social life is meaningful; new meanings are established with reference to old meanings and grow out of them and must be made, in some degree, congruent with them; and exchange, whenever and wherever it occurs, must be articulated with the existing system of meanings.'
    Shils (1975: 203–204) puts it somewhat differently: 'One of the major problems which confronts us in the analysis of tradition is the fusion of originality and traditionality. T.S. Eliot's essay "Tradition and Individual Talent", in *The Sacred Wood,* said very little more than that these two elements co-exist and that originality works within the framework of traditionality. It adds and modifies, while accepting much. In any case, even though it rejects or disregards much of what it confronts in the particular sphere of its own creation, it accepts very much of what is inherited in the context of the creation. It takes its point of departure from the "given" and goes forward from there, correcting, improving, transforming.'
    Cp. also Husserl's relatively more complex notion *sitftung,* that is foundation or establishment, which, as Merleau-Ponty has pointed out, helps us understand the rich and enduring character of cultural creations. Merleau-Ponty (1964: 59) writes: 'It is thus that the world as soon as he has seen it, his first attempts at painting, and the whole past of painting all deliver up a *tradition* to the painter – that is, Husserl remarks, *the power to forget origins* and to give to the past not a survival, which is the hypothetical form of forgetfulness, but a new life, which is the noble form of memory.'
11. It may be noted though that in his earlier writings DP had shown a greater wariness regarding the possibility of combining Marxism with Hindu tradition. Referring to the 'forceful sanity' of the 'forceful sanity' of the 'exchange of rights and obligations' on which Hindu society was organized, he had written (1932: 136): '... before Communism can be introduced, national memory will have to be smudged, and new habits acquired. *There is practically nothing in the traditions on which the new habits of living under an impersonal class-control can take root'* (emphasis added).

References

Bharati, Agehananda, 1970, 'The Hindu Renaissance and its Apologetic Patterns', *The Journal of Asian Studies* 29: 267–87.

Collingwood, R.G., 1970, *An Autobiography,* London, Oxford.

Dumont, Louis, 1967, 'The Individual as an Impediment to Sociological Comparison and Indian History', in B. Singh and V.B. Singh, (eds.),

Social and Economic Change: Essays in Honour of Professor D.P. Mukherji, Bombay, Allied.

Eliot, T.S., 1940, *The Waste Land and other Poems.*, London, Faber and Faber.

Gupta, K.P., 1977, Personal communication.

Madan, T.N., 1974, 'The Dialectic of Ethnic and National Boundaries in the Evolution of Bangladesh', in S. Navalakha, (ed.), *Studies in Asian Social Development*, New Delhi, Vikas.

—, 1977, 'First D.P. Mukerji Memorial Lecture: The Dialectic of Tradition and Modernity', *National Herald* (New Delhi and Lucknow), 10 and 17 April, 1977.

Marx, Karl and F. Engels, 1959, *The First Indian War of Independence*, Moscow: Foreign Publishers.

Merleau-Ponty, M., 1964, *Signs*, Translated by R.C. McCleary, Evanston, North-Western University Press.

Mukerji, D.P., 1924, *Personality and the Social Sciences*, Calcutta, The Book Company.

—, 1932, *Basic Concepts in Sociology*, London, Kegan Paul.

—, 1945, *On Indian History; A Study in Method*, Bombay Hind Kitabs.

—, 1945a, *Introduction to Indian Music*, Bombay, Hind Kitabs.

—, 1946, *Views and Counterviews*, Lucknow, Universal.

—, 1946a, *Problems of Indian Youth*, Bombay, Hind Kitabs.

—, 1948, *Modern Indian Culture*, Bombay, Hind Kitabs.

—, 1952, 'Sociology in Independent India', *Sociological Bulletin* 1(I): 13–27.

—, 1955, 'Social Research', in K.M. Kapadia, (ed.), *Professor Ghurye Felicitation Volume*, Bombay, Popular Prakashan.

—, 1958, *Diversities*, New Delhi, People's Publishing House.

—, 1972, *Tagore: A Study*, Calcutta, Manisha.

Mukherjee, Ramakrishna, 1965, 'Role of Tradition in Social Change', in *The Sociologist and Social Change in India*, New Delhi, Prentice-Hall.

—, 1977, Personal communication.

Myrdal, Gunnar, 1968, *Asian Drama, An Inquiry into the Poverty of Nations*, 3 vols., New York, Pantheon.

Oakeshott, Michael, 1962, *Rationalism in Politics and Other Essays*, London, Methuen.

Popper, Karl R., 1963, *Conjectures and Refutations*, London, Routledge and Kegan Paul.

Saran, A.K., 1959, 'India' in J.S. Roucek, *Contemporary Sociology*, London, Peter Owen.

—, 1962, 'D.P. Mukerji, An Obituary', *Eastern Anthropologist* 15(2): 167–69.

—, 1965, 'The faith of a modern intellectual', in T.K.N. Unnithan et al. (eds.), *Towards a Sociology of Culture in India*, New Delhi, Prentice-Hall.

Scheider, D.M., 1974, 'Notes toward a Theory of Culture', in K. Basso and H. Selby, (eds.), *Meaning in Anthropology*, Albuquerque, University of New Mexico Press.

Shils, Edward, 1975, 'Tradition' in *Centre and Periphery: Essays in Macrosociology*, Chicago, Chicago University Press.

Singer, Milton, 1972, *When a Great Tradition Modernizes*, New York, Praeger.

Singh, Yogendra, 1973, *Modernization of Indian Tradition*, Jaipur, Rawat Publications.

Srinivas, M.N. and M.N. Panini, 1973, 'The Development of Sociology and Social Anthropology in India', *Sociological Bulletin* 22(2): 179–215.

18

G.S. GHURYE ON CULTURE AND NATION-BUILDING

C.N. VENUGOPAL

The purpose of this paper is to discuss in some detail G.S. Ghurye's perspective on the theme of nation-building. He started his academic career as an ethnographer. He had been trained in ethnography at Cambridge University where he studied for his Ph.D. (1919–22). After he settled down as a teacher in the Department of Sociology, School of Economics, Bombay University (in the 1920s), he wrote a number of books and papers on such diverse themes as family and kinship, urban centres and Indian tribes. He also wrote a number of descriptive works on religion and culture and on political and social tensions in post-independent India. As a historical-indologist Ghurye wrote on Vedic India, Indian costumes, dance and architecture. His early training in Sanskrit made him predisposed to view the classical literary and religious works as an important source of values and ideals.

Although Ghurye was not a political scientist, he averred that culture and polity could not be separated. Today, often the two terms 'nation' and 'state' are used interchangeably. But these terms stand for different sets of meanings. The state is an entity with formal properties; it has explicit characteristics such as a constitution and territorial sovereignty, and judicial, administrative and coercive authority. In contrast, the nation is a constellation of mainly implicit meanings and subjectivist constructions. The abstruse theorist, Talcott Parsons, spoke of four core elements in the social system designated by the acronym AGIL (Adaptation, Goal Attainment, Integration and Latent Pattern Maintenance). The last named denotes an unmanifest state which is a repository of values, ideals and symbols (Mennell, 1974: 152). The term 'latent' implies that the nation has the capacity not only to sustain itself but also achieve self-renewal in the event of crises. Ghurye's use of cultural attainments as indicators of Indian nationalism was rooted in his perceptions which he shared with many other educated Hindus. For him, cultural output was the foundation on which the nation-state could be built in free India.

Ghurye's methodology may be broadly described as an exercise in the sociology of knowledge. In the West, the sociology of knowledge developed around the theories of Max Scheler, Karl Mannheim, George Lukacs and, in more recent times, Peter Berger, Michael Mulkay and H. Collins (Dant, 1991; Mannheim, 1952). In general, the sociology of knowledge rests on a critique of the positivistic epistemology which held sway over the English-speaking countries in the West. Deriving from Cartesian theory, the positivists validated knowledge in terms of dichotomies, viz., true and false, subjective and objective, etic and emic. The critics of positivism pointed out that human life-in contrast to the natural world – is infinitely variable. It is characterized by reflexivity (ego's introspection of or reflection on a cultural object), contingency (partial or complete variation due to historical and cultural factors), and collective subjectivist perceptions which modified the validation of knowledge leading to a relativist rather than an absolute certification of knowledge. In recent years, relativism has been applied to the field of science as well. For instance, science is influenced by political or economic expediency and scientists are susceptible to personal influences (ethnocentricism, hostility towards new ideas, reluctance to admit error, plain jealousy, etc.). The certainty in the realm of natural science has been questioned by a noted philosopher of science, P.K. Feyerabend, who takes a relativist position (1981).

Karl Mannheim wrote extensively on the neglect of culture which he described as atheoretical reality. The richness of human culture is glossed over as intangible or non-rational by positivistic epistemology. He proposed an alternative epistemology based on the recognition of atheoretical reality. He became a controversial figure in academic circles over his new epistemology (Walter, 1967: 342–48). Combining the insights of the sociology of knowledge and phenomenology, Peter Berger has referred to the process in which knowledge is produced through shared objectivity or inter-subjectivity (1967: 1–87). According to him, knowledge is able to transcend its particularistic properties through cultural objectification. He cited language as an objectified cultural product.

I would like to make a few observations on the growth of knowledge in the Indian context. Unlike China where practical knowledge was emphasized, India showed a bent towards theoretical or speculative knowledge. The philosophical systems in India were diversified on account of their different approaches to the problem of validity of knowledge. Vedanta and Mahayana Buddhism followed an idealistic epistemology which held empirical knowledge as false or misleading; according to it true knowledge was mystical or spiritual. Lokayata, Samkhya, Vaisesika and Mimamsa followed an empirical epistemology in varying terms which affirmed knowledge gained through nature. The Jainas followed a relativist epistemology which led to the doctrine of partial truths.

Chattopadhyaya (1964: 1–27) has remarked that many Indian philosophical systems have retained magico-religious ideas which were derived from primitive sources. He has also noted that 'ethnological ferment' or clash of ideas led to the emergence of new systems of thought such as Buddhism. Some of the philosophical works outlining these different approaches were incorporated into the *vidyas* (Indian systems of knowledge); these were Vedanta (which included a number of Upanishads), Mimamsa, Vaisesika and Samkhya. The members of the ruling class were given instruction in the philosophies mentioned above; in turn, royal patronage was extended to the philosophers. Some of the rulers also held debates in their court in which the relative merits of different philosophies were assessed. Competition and rivalry marked the relations among different philosophies. These developments testify to the vibrancy of Indian philosophy which existed in conjunction with the *vidyas*. It is perhaps relevant to mention that in India a number of rulers or members of wealthy households chose to become monks, thereby giving up their worldly comforts. Idealist philosophy imparted through the *vidyas* probably contributed to this kind of voluntary asceticism.

Ghurye wrote a number of essays on the sociology of knowledge, some of which are included in *Anthropo-Sociological Papers* (1963a). He had shown interest in the systems of knowledge developed by Aristotle, Bacon and Comte. He discussed the Indian systems of knowledge descriptively without going into epistemological or analytical quest. However, in my understanding, Ghurye's writings in general, i.e., his paper on the *vidyas*, his works on caste, ethnicity, religion, culture and the like, can be placed within the sociology of knowledge. There are two reasons for this: (a) he viewed the growth of knowledge in India in relation to contingent (historical and cultural) factors; and (b) he used the plural sources of knowledge (sacred texts, historical documents, folk beliefs and practices, etc.) as valid grounds for his sociological descriptions. In the rest of this paper, I have drawn heavily on some of his ideas expressed in his collection of essays (ibid.). It is my view that these essays reveal his nationalistic sentiments and that he perceived culture – which is the domain of feeling, emotions and spirit – through a subjectivistic angle. Two of his noted contemporaries, Benoy Kumar Sarkar and Nirmal Kumar Bose, seemed to share with him the nationalistic approach to the study of society in India.

CASTE AND ETHNICITY

Although Ghurye did not theorize on caste, he was interested in the description of caste in its various aspects. He meticulously presented data on the evolution of Indian castes and the processes of fission and fusion which characterized castes through the centuries. One of his main assumptions was that in the diachronic sense the caste system provided an integrative framework for the numerous ethnic groups which inhabited India. Derived from the caste system were two institutional units: *gotra* and *charana* which were more specific aggregates of people. Of these two, *gotra* was not confined to one caste, as people of many castes could claim descent from the same eponymous *rishi*.

While Ghurye was convinced of the usefulness of caste in previous times he was upset over the proliferation of caste-sponsored associations. In his book, *Caste and Race in India*, he referred to the anti-Brahmin ferment which made a far-reaching impact on the backward class movement in India (1969: 355–403). Further, Ghurye stated that India in the post-independent phase was heading towards a kind of pluralism[1] reminiscent of J.S. Furnivall's analysis of Burma and Indonesia (ibid.: 404–60). This pluralism had set in motion an aggressive competition among the castes for securing a larger share of the national pie.[2] Fragmentation of interests was giving a fillip to the process of cultural disintegration of India. The inter-caste rivalries and the rise of numerous caste blocks were undermining national unity.

Ghurye's ethnography of caste included both detailed and specific works. Writing on the *Scheduled Tribes* (1963) in general, Ghurye referred to the process of Hinduization which was occurring in south-central India. The tribes of this region, such as the Bhils, Gonds, Mundas, Oraons and Santals, were in close interaction with Hindu society. He wrote:

> While sections of these tribes are properly integrated in the Hindu society, very large sections, in fact the bulk of them, are

> rather loosely integrated... only very small sections, living in the recesses of hills and the depths of forests, have not been more than touched by Hinduism. Under the circumstances, the only proper description of these peoples is that they are the imperfectly integrated classes of Hindu society. (1963b: 19)

In this region, it was not possible to treat caste and tribe as belonging to separate categories. He regarded the tribals as backward Hindus who had somehow missed assimilation into the mainstream Hindu society. He advocated a policy of assimilation of tribes into mainstream not only in economic terms but also in moral and cultural terms (Venugopal, 1986: 305–14). Ghurye regretted the prevalence of certain vices such as drinking and loose sexual morals among the tribals. While he advocated a Hindu model for tribal integration, he omitted to mention the role of Christian missions in the ethical reform of tribals in this region.

So far as the tribes inhabiting the north-east are concerned, Ghurye proposed a programme for their political assimilation into the national mainstream. He was not against political autonomy but desired a strong federal government at the centre which could be effective in containing tribal dissidence. He was alarmed by the intransigence of rebel groups among the tribes of the north-east. He was apprehensive that if separatism in the north-east was not curbed the political future of India would be in peril. In regard to other frontier regions like Punjab, Ghurye thought along similar lines (1977a). It may be observed here that his perspective on nationalism was wanting in two respects. First, he did not adequately appreciate the contribution of Buddhism and Jainism to cultural nationalism in India. Second, he did not document the contributions of Muslims and Christians to India's nation-building.[3]

Ghurye collected vast data on social tensions in free India (1968a). In his references to communal tensions, he seemed to single out the role of Muslims. It is in order to note a few relevant facts on the Muslims. Pre-conquest Islam entered India in two distant places: the north-west (Sind and Punjab) and the south-west (Kerala). This Islam was mainly of the Arabic variety and its followers lived in amity and goodwill with the local populace. In the north-west, Sufism paved the way for Hindu-Muslim interaction in religious and cultural spheres. In the south-west, the Muslims built up effective trade networks linking India to the Middle East, West Asia and Africa. The frenzied or arbitrary acts of some north Indian Muslim rulers who were of Central Asian origin could be traced to their deviance from the basic tenets of Islam (Hussain, 1978: 74–77). The communal tensions in the southern parts of India were less morbid than in north India in the pre-colonial era. Even in the north, prior to British rule, communalism did not take on the form of a holocaust. In sum, Indian Muslims are a heterogeneous lot, divided on ethnic, sectarian and regional lines but united only by their monotheistic faith. Ghurye resorted to a reductive approach in his assessment of social tensions. This assumes poignance in view of the fact that he was erudite and few Indians could match his intellectual acumen.

INDIAN UNITY

Ghurye showed his deep concern for the unity of India (1963a: 141–255). The two outstanding features which unified India were Brahmi script and Sanskrit language. The scripts of most Indian languages were derived from the Brahmi. Sanskrit became not only the language of sacred texts but also a medium for inter-regional contact. In this respect, it provided an unbroken unity for India till the decline of Hindu polity. With the evolution of regional languages Sanskrit receded somewhat. Ghurye mentioned marriage as another unifying factor in India. Apart from its institutional role in relation to caste and kinship, it was a political instrument of much significance. He wrote:

> From a hoary past... royal families of the people of northern India, have married into similar families from all parts of India. In their marital behaviour the royal families have demonstrated their unity from Gandhara (the North-West Frontier Province) and Sauvira (Northern Sindh) to Kamarupa (Assam) on the one hand and Vidharba (Berar) and Dravidadesa (Madura) on the other. (1963a: 242)

He noted that these marital alliances were adversely affected following the decline of Hindu rule owing to Islamic conquest and British colonialism. Along with the marital relationship, there was the ritualistic unity provided by the *asvamedha* sacrifice in which a horse, as the symbol of monarchic power, wandered all over the country. These dynastic and ritualistic unities were influential in the emergence of cultural nationalism.

A few inferences can be drawn on the basis of the foregoing statements made by Ghurye. In India, there was no monolithic political hegemony in the proto-historical period. Marital alliances among the ruling families brought together not only bigger and smaller rulers but also cut across *varna* and *jati* lines through the practice of hypergamy.[4] These alliances were mostly adapted by the rulers to contain seething political and social tensions. Besides, the sacrifice confirmed mainly the *symbolic* authority of the overlord. The monarch neither enslaved nor subordinated the 'conquered' rulers.

According to Ghurye, the evolution of India's unity stemmed considerably from the acculturative process. The interactions between Aryans and non-Aryans, Aryans and Dravidians, and castes and tribes promoted religious and cultural efflorescence. The major deities of India – Shiva, Vishnu and Shakti – were symbols of ethnic groups which were incorporated into a single religious complex (1968b). The Aryanization of the south by Skanda (God) and Agastya (*rishi*) gave a fillip to Tamil language which became an important literary vehicle (1977b). The acculturative process lost its fervour after the decline of Hindu polity. Concluding his essay on Indian unity, Ghurye noted that free India was facing many uncertainties. The linguistic division of states had become inevitable, but he hoped that unity could still be preserved in cultural and political terms. He wrote:

> To guard against the legitimate and healthy realization of linguistic separateness, miltating against the overall homogeneity of political India, there must be comparable central organization for intellectual and cultural life… . On the political and administrative side, we can trust to our political leadership to devise appropriate techniques to see that the various groups above referred to feel at home as one political unit, leaving enough scope to manage their own affairs without interference and yet subject to such wise supervision and even guidance as may keep the centre strong and respected. (1963a: 249)

A brief comment may be made here on Ghurye's thinking on India's unity. His scholarship notwithstanding, his view of Indian society was slanted in favour of Hinduism. The nationalist Muslims who participated in India's struggle for freedom and the many Christians who devoted their time and energy for the expansion of medical welfare and education in India were also contributing to the process of nation-building. Existentially, just as Hindus are internally stratified, Muslims and Christians are also divided along sectarian, linguistic and regional lines. Nevertheless, all these three groups are mentally rooted in religio-cultural integrative systems of their own. Thus, Indian unity represents a unique case wherein integration has been carried on simultaneously by different groups. Ghurye fell short of his life-long ambition to arrive at a model of national integration because of his cognitive dissociation with non-Hindu cultural motifs. In free India, some pro-Hindu militant groups have upheld a model of nationalism which equates Hinduism with nationalism. This attempt made by them has ignored the truly outstanding characteristic of the Indian nation: its compositeness!

INDIAN VALUES

In his treatment of values, Ghurye (1963a: 256–78) mainly relied on the Hindu tradition which enjoined upon people to follow a given scheme. For instance, it was an obligation on the part of Hindus to pay debts to Gods, ancestors and teachers. Emphasis was placed upon the pursuit of four ends called *purusarthas – dharma, artha, kama and moksha;*[5] the Hindu's life was divided into four stages: student, householder, anchorite and renunciate. In the Indian domain of values there was an emphasis on the triads. Of the four ends the first three were regarded as more important, while among the four stages the last two, anchorite and renunciate, were practically merged into each other. He stated that the psychological, ethical and theological aspects of Indian values were expressed through triads.[6] He wrote:

> On the mental side, the sacred lore is declared to be *Trayi Vidya*, that is, three-fold knowledge comprised in the *Rigveda, Yajurveda* and *Samaveda*. Then we have the three categories of *mana, buddhi, ahamkara* and the three qualities of *sattva, rajas, tamas.* On the ethical side we have self-control (*dama*), charity (*dana*) and compassion (*daya*). The creation of these last three values is presented in the *Brihadaranyaka Upanishad* as being the work of Prajapati, the creator, himself in relation to his pupils: Gods, men and demons. Alternatively, as in the passage already quoted from the *Chhandogya Upanishad*, religious duty has three components or factors, namely, sacrifice (*yanja*), study (*adhyayana*) and charity (*dana*). On the theological side, in the Vedic age we have three steps of Vishnu and, in the post-Vedic, the three mighty Gods, Brahma, Vishnu and *Mahesa*. (1963a: 261)

Ghurye noted two interludes in the evolution of Indian values: the Upanishadic quest for inner perfection and the Ashokan policy of compassion and goodwill towards all sentient beings. Besides, there was a continuous interaction between folk and elite groups in India which gave rise to a syncretic culture. It is not only the elites who influenced the folk, but also vice versa. However, this interaction brought about a moral elevation among the folk. For instance, many of the Bhakti sects in India had a discernible folk origin but they invariably elevated folk beliefs and practices to a higher ethical plane. Hence, the Bhakti sects stood on an intermediate ground between Sanskritic culture on the one hand and folk culture on the other. To illustrate the moral aspect, he compared two Indo-European cultures: India and Greece. Just as Aryans interacted with the non-Aryans who were followers of the Phallic cult, the Greeks too came in contact with the people of Crete who followed the same cult. The Greeks retained this cult with much of its coarseness, while in India the *linga* became a symbol of sanctity and faith.

Ghurye concluded his discussion of Indian values by referring to *jatras*, gambling and drinking, which were popular among both folk and elite. Although there was a recreational element in these diversions, gambling and drinking claimed many victims among gentry and commoners alike. While the vices were denounced by the early law-givers such as Manu, Kautilya advised the rulers to regulate them in order to derive revenue from them. Thus, Ghurye viewed the elite-folk distinctions as fluid.

INDIAN SYSTEMS OF KNOWLEDGE

In the following preamble I have attempted to introduce the reader to the Indian systems of knowledge as I understand them. In common with the pre-modern West, Indian systems of knowledge called *vidyas* were designed to cater to the elite groups – most of whom belonged to the three upper *varnas*; the *vidyas* excluded from their purview artisans, peasants and the like. In India, knowledge was mostly imparted from *guru* to *shishya*. Even if the *guru* had several *shishyas*, the relationship between teacher and student was dyadic. The learning was acquired by students in hermitages which were scattered across the country in austere surroundings. In contrast to China, where imperial examinations were conducted on an impersonal basis, the Indian way of instruction was personalized. As previously noted, an individual's life was focused on the clearance of debts to Gods, ancestors and teachers. Hence, after learning, the student remained indebted to the teacher in a personal as well as in a scholastic sense.

The impetus to *vidyas* stemmed from the desire of members of the ruling class to acquire education. Besides, one significant reason was the absence of the divine right of the king in India. The ruler as a person was human and fallible; yet the rulership was divine. India and ancient Greece were among the few countries which encouraged the political aspirants to learn. Even when rulership was acquired, it did not confer on the Hindu ruler the authority to legislate. The consent of his councillors was taken by the ruler for decisions pertaining to the governance of his realm. By contrast, in the western divine right theory, the ruler was infallible and he could legislate at will. Another factor which limited the ruler's authority in India was the political autonomy of villages.

There is no doubt that the Hindu ruler acquired *de jure* status through learning. Hence, royal patronage was extended to *gurukulas* all over India. A Marxist theory of recent years states that the dominant group has used education as an instrument of control over the people: the educational system reproduces the dominant values among the subordinate groups. This theory seems to have limited applicability to India (past or present), although it has been useful in the analysis of some colonies (Bacchus, 1990: 93–114) ruled over by external powers. In a heterogeneous society like India there are different dominant groups and multiple hierarchies depending on contingent factors such a regional and cultural variations, etc. The *gurukulas* were not centralized under a common educational authority. Besides Hindu *gurukulas*, the Buddhist and Jaina centres of learning imparted education to pupils on their own terms. In pre-independent India, in spite of British rule, missionary and nationalist schools and colleges offered different patterns of education. During India's struggle for freedom, colleges and universities were founded by Indian nationalists often in defiance of the foreign rulers. Even in free India there are different orientations in education.

The Indian *vidyas* appear to have arisen from pluralistic sources: economic, religious and literary. Sarkar, who wrote extensively on Hindu positivism (1937: 6), felt that much harm had been done in the western assessment of India's culture. Only certain aspects such as otherworldliness of Indians were emphasized. This was due to the application of 'monistic' methodology which measured everything in terms of western standards. Sarkar's 'positivism' opted for a synthetic approach in which the material and the spiritual could be balanced. His pluralistic methodology differed from any monistic interpretation of culture be it economic, political or mystico-religious (ibid.: 40). In Vedic culture, the sacrifices and ceremonies were regarded as instrumental in helping a mortal acquire divine status. For instance, Indra was a divine functionary who acquired his position through ritualistic effort. Sarkar wrote: 'The texts as a rule tell us in so many words that a person becomes divine through certain actions, ceremonial or otherwise, and that divinity is but [a] consequence and not the cause or antecedent' (ibid.: 152).

In Indian polity the acquisition of *vidyas* enabled the ruler to achieve divinity. The dominant theme of Indian culture is that the ruler sustains the earth and protects it because of his divine qualities. The acquisition of *vidyas* was similar to the performance of sacrifice as it conferred divinity on the ruler. But the educational process was profoundly linked to the *guru*'s role. *Vidyas* acquired without the *guru* were not valid. Also, the *guru*'s displeasure of curse was feared by all seekers of learning. The subjectivistic nature of Indian education is revealed through such beliefs. In the formulations of *vidyas* the personality of the system-builder left a discernible imprint on the selection of subjects. Besides, as there was a dyadic relationship between teacher and student, some part of the instruction remained esoteric or secretive. It is a well-known fact that till recently the Vedas were taught mostly through verbal communication. It was regarded as *infra dig* for a member of the elite group to read Veda from a written text.

Ghurye was keenly interest interested in the development of knowledge. Writing on Aristotle and Bacon (1963a: 289–302) he noted that these Occidental philosophers of the pre-Comtean era strove for establishing a hierarchy of knowledge system in which theology occupied a superordinate status. The present-day distinction between sacred and secular pursuits was not marked in this era. These early writers used the terms 'arts' and 'science' more or less synonymously. The quest for knowledge was the common factor in these two spheres. Ghurye too used the two terms interchangeably. I will now refer briefly to his discussion of *vidyas* (ibid.: 303–51) which was an attempt to explore the speculative and the practical dimensions of knowledge. He wrote:

> The first enumeration of branches of knowledge or *vidyas* occurs at about the end of the Vedic period; the second much more incidental than the first, about the 2nd century B.C., the third, very purposeful, illustrating all viewpoints except perhaps the last, can be placed in the period, second to the fourth century A.D., the fourth, ascribed to the 9th century A.D. is almost unique in many ways; the fifth, of doubtful dating though a simple enumeration and an uninspiring one, is entirely unique. The sixth is from an acute philosopher and appears to have been entirely an analytical and intellectual activity. Its added interest, though a mere coincidence, is that the author, an ascetic living on the banks of the *Ganga* (Ganges) was a junior contemporary of Francis Bacon and lived only about a quarter of a century after him. (1963a: 304)

In the formulation of *vidyas* such names as Yajnavalkya, Patanjali, Kautilya, Sukra, Rajasekara and Madhusudana Saraswati were associated. The last named author was the 'acute philosopher' mentioned above. The revision of *vidyas* six times implies that there were contingent factors in Hindu society which made it necessary. This also reveals that the cultural heritage was subjected to a kind of 'self-criticism'.

The *vidyas*, which totaled thirty-two, were a compendium of different topics which included speculative, ritualistic, marital and practical sciences. To mention a few: Vedas and allied sacred literature, systems of philosophy such as Mimamsa, Samkhya and Vaisesika, eighteen Puranas, *ayurveda, arthasastra, dharmasastra, itihasa,* political knowledge, archery and related martial arts. The accretion of knowledge-components from 16 to 32 indicated that the *vidyas* were responsive to changing needs. A common element in the *vidyas* was the inclusion of introspective or spiritual knowledge. The sacred and the secular, mundane and supernatural subjects were prescribed in different combinations under each revised scheme of learning.

Ghurye credited Kautilya with devising a system of knowledge based on a dual purpose: (a) to instruct the ruler in arts and science; and (b) to inculcate in the ruler a balance or equipoise which would help him in ruling over his subjects. In his *vidyas* Kautilya placed emphasis on non-idealistic philosophy such as Samkhya, Mimamsa and Tarka. He gave relatively less importance to *dharmasastra* which emphasized libational and sacrificial aspects. He placed a premium on *varta* (commerce) and *dandaniti* (policy of coercion) for these were required to make the ruler practical in his outlook and effective in his rule. It was clear that Kautilya desired that the ruler would wield coercive power rather than piously uphold *dharma*. The threat of foreign influx into India seemed to make him reorient the values. The patronage of rulers to learning stimulated cultural output in India in a variety of subjects. For instance, mathematics, logic, works in grammar and poetics, *ayurveda* and *silpasastra* (architecture) attained a high level.

Ghurye felt that the decline of Hindu polity in the Gupta Age (6th century A.D.) led to the eclipse of *vidyas*. But he noted that for a long time thereafter, i.e., up to the 10th or 11th century, the quest for knowledge continued at non-macro levels, especially regional centres. It is in these centres that subjects such as mathematics, logic and *ayurveda* developed. Sarkar (1937: 91) took a different position in regard to the effectiveness of Hindu polity. According to him, even after Islamic rule was founded in north India, Hindu polity thrived for nearly six to seven centuries in Rajputana, south India and other regions. Even if the political system declined in a formal sense, there were some cultural alternatives. In a recent paper (Venugopal, 1990: 305–14), I have attempted to show that some of the reformist sects in India provided a political alternative in the regional settings. Ethnic turbulence and normative breakdown were brought under control by these sects. As such Ghurye's view may be regarded as nostalgia for the classical Hindu polity.

CONCLUSION

In today's march toward globalization and apocalyptic developments in science and technology, when the nation has declined in importance, Ghurye's perspective on nation-building may indeed seem out of place. But still the nation remains a powerful symbol of people all over the world. Toynbee remarked that nationalism is akin to a religious force. It can produce a collective impulse strong enough to mobilize people on a large scale. There is no doubt that Ghurye was disillusioned by the turn of events after the decline of Hindu polity. Of course, it is not possible to renew the Hindu nation as Ghurye desired it. Nevertheless, if a pluralistic nation is accepted as a programme for the future, it will be necessary to arrive at a new synthesis of Indian values: Hindu Buddhist, Jaina, Christian, Muslim, Parsi, etc. The fact that the Indian nation has survived numerous economic and political crises has shown that the composite culture of India has a great tenacity. Not merely political will but cultural revitalization is the need of the nation.

Notes

1. There are at least three ways in which pluralism can be defined. First, there is the popular usage of the term which denotes heterogeneity of groups in a given country. Second, the Americans define it as indicating the presence of groups which are 'equi-distant' from the centre of power and authority. Third, Furnivall uses the term of characterize the co-existence of ethnic groups in a market economy *without* cultural integration.
2. S.L. Sharma writes: 'Reduced to its essentials, casteism represents a curious compound of ethnic identity and modern interests, with ethnic collectivity using the ideology and technology of modernization to the furtherance of its economic and political interests' (1990: 42).

3. T.K. Oommen writes: 'Although pre-conquest Islam and pre-colonial Christianity existed in India, hardly anybody seems to acknowledge it, not even the intellectuals. This is not to deny that the bulk of Muslim and Christian conversions took place after conquest and colonization. But to spotlight attention only on this is to castigate and stigmatize these religious collectivities and to thwart the authentic nature of Indian religious pluralism. More importantly, an overwhelming majority are converts from local castes and tribes and hence natives of this country; only their religion is foreign' (1986–59).
4. S.C. Dube writes: 'According to legend, Rukmini whom Krishna married, belonged to Arunachal Pradesh; Hidimba, whom Bhima married, was a Naga; and Arjuna was married to Chitrangada from Manipur and to Ulupi from Nagaland' (1990: 15).
5. *Moksha* assumed importance mostly in the post-Vedic period; the Upanishads reacted against the prevailing ritualism and advocated the discovery of self. *Moksha* refers to the release of a person from the cycle of births and deaths.
6. Structuralist methodology attempts to analyze society in terms of binary oppositions. Perhaps Ghurye's insistence on triads indicates a different dimension of Indian reality.

References

Bacchus, M.K., 1990, 'A Critical Review and Analysis of Early Developments in Education in the British West Indian Colonies', *Sociological Bulletin*, 39 (1 and 2): 93–114.

Berger, Peter L., 1967, *Social Reality of Religion*, Harmondsworth, Penguin.

Chattopadhyaya, D., 1964, *Indian Philosophy*, New Delhi, People's Publishing House.

Dant, Tim, 1991, *Knowledge, Ideology and Discourse*, London, Routledge.

Dube, S.C., 1990, *Indian Society*, New Delhi, National Book Trust.

Feyerabend, P.K., 1981, *Problems of Empiricism*, Cambridge, Cambridge University Press.

Ghurye, G.S., 1963, *Scheduled Tribes*, Bombay, Popular.

—, 1968a, *Social Tensions in India*, Bombay, Popular.

—, 1968b, *Gods and Men*, Bombay, Popular.

—, 1969, *Caste and Race in India*, 5th Edition, Bombay, Popular.

—, 1977a, *Whither India*? Bombay, Popular.

—, 1977b, *Agastya and Skanda: A Study in Indian Acculturation*, Bombay, Popular.

Hussain, Abid, S., 1978, *The National Culture of India*, Delhi, National Book Trust.

Mannheim, Karl, 1952, *Essays in the Sociology of Knowledge*, New York, Oxford University Press.

Mennell, Stephen, 1974, *Sociological Theory: Uses and Unities*, New York, Praeger Publishers.

Oommen, T.K., 1986, 'Insiders and Outsiders in India: Primordial Collectivism and Cultural Pluralism in Nation-building', *International Sociology*, 1 (1): 53–74.

Sarkar, B.K., 1937, *The Positive Background of Hindu Sociology*, Allahabad, Sacred Book of the Hindu Series.

Sharma, S.L., 1990, 'The Salience of Ethnicity in Modernization', *Sociological Bulletin*, 39 (1 and 2): 33–44.

Venugopal, C.N., 1986, 'G.S. Ghurye's Ideology of Normative Hinduism: An Appraisal', *Contributions to Indian Sociology* (n.s.), 20 (2): 305–14.

—, 1990, 'Reformist Sects and the Sociology of Religion in India', *Sociological Analysis*, 51 (5): 77–78.

Walter, Benjamin, 1967, 'The Sociology of Knowledge and the Problem of Objectivity', in L. Gross (ed.), *Sociological Theory: Inquiries and Paradigms*, New York, Harper International, pp. 335–57.

19

Toward Reconstructing National Traditions in Sociology

Dan A. Chekki

It is a common assumption that sociology has a universally relevant theory, methodology, and an international professional identity. This assumption is challenged on the grounds that sociology can only be relevant if its theory and methodology are appropriate to a socio-cultural milieu of a nation. The purpose of this paper is to examine the endogenous and exogenous forces that have influenced the development of sociology in India. It is intended to demonstrate that the nationalization issue within the discipline of sociology in India has resulted in an identifiable Indian sociology movement. The multicausal contextual and dependency models will be employed to explain how the national disciplinary community has been greatly influenced by paradigms and approaches to sociology emphasized in other countries. Furthermore, the Indian sociology movement in search of the content of a distinctly Indian sociological perspective would be delineated.

Based on the sociology of knowledge perspective developed by Marx (1963) and Mannheim (1936 and 1952), contemporary sociologists such as Merton (1968 and 1972) and Coser (1971) suggest that the development of sociological knowledge be related to the social, economic, and political conditions of the society in which it emerges. Whereas Parsons (1959) and Bierstedt (1981) believe that ideas are relatively autonomous in the stream of history and are more dependent upon antecedent ideas than they are upon the social, economic, or political circumstances prevailing at the time of their appearance.

This study attempts to examine these viewpoints in the light of the process of institutionalization of sociology and socialization of sociologists in India. The purpose of this analysis is to show how sociology in India has not only developed in response to its social milieu but also has been influenced by American sociology. The trend toward universalization of sociology, in recent decades, seems to imply the acceptance of American sociology which itself is said to be ethnocentric, culture-bound, and parochial. In this context, a question is often raised: Is American sociology relevant to the national-cultural context of India?

Different models have been used to analyze the nature and development of sociology in various countries. For instance, the institutional model considers sociology within the context of educational institutions where university structures, traditions, and rivalries influence the shape of the sociological enterprise. This model is well illustrated in the works of Ben-David (1966) and Shils (1970).

The ideological congruence model demonstrates the influence of societal values and ideologies in the nature, conception and development of sociology. Mannheim (1936 and 1952), Myrdal (1958), Mills (1959), Friedrichs (1970) and Gouldner (1971) exemplify this model in their works. The contextual analysis model is intradisciplinary in its forms and it deals with the dominance, decline and fall of major paradigms, theoretical schools, shifts and conflicts, fads and fashions, leadership and control of intellectual means of production in sociology and other disciplines. Kuhn (1970), Wiley (1979), Mullins (1973), and Ritzer (1981) have explained this model.

A dependency model has emerged on the basis that the main centres of sociological dominance, power and prestige, and influence are located outside the boundaries of a national social science community. This model has been successfully used by Lamy (1976), Atal (1976), Sharma (1982), Loubser (1982), and Hiller (1980). This external orientation is attributed to the underdevelopment of the internal disciplinary community as well as to the hegemony and strength of the external disciplinary community. There is a growing concern expressed in terms of the vertical relationship between social scientists in Europe and North America and those in the Third World; the dependency of the latter upon the former; there is implicit recognition of intellectual imperialism and neo-colonial exploitation involved. This academic intellectual imperialism is not only characteristic of the kind of dependency relations characteristic of the Third World but also between the United States and Canada as well as between America and Australia and a few other industrialized countries.

In the context of dependency theory and world system theory, American sociology forms the 'core' whereas sociologies of India and Canada tend to be associated with the 'peripheral' and/or 'semi-peripheral' units in a system of global sociology.

Through the centuries, the Indian philosophy of life and ethos stated in the sacred scriptures, philosophical schools of thought, and religious traditions have been vital parts of the major social institutions, ideals, and values. Indian society has manifested cultural unity amidst diversity resulting from processes of internal differentiation and importation and adaptation of foreign cultures. Over the ages, continuity of traditions and changes are characteristic of Indian society and culture.

It is demonstrated that the rise and growth of sociology in India was deeply interwoven with the radical reorientation of the social-intellectual milieu during the Renaissance, the Revolution, and independence in India (Ishwaran, 1965; Nandy, 1971). In the early years of the twentieth century, the precursors of sociology such as Arobindo Ghosh, B.K. Sarkar, Tilak, Gokhale, Ranade, Mohandas Gandhi and many others tried to link sociology with religion, politics, economics and nationalism. Positivism, values and the non-empirical modes of inquiry with a reformist and at times revolutionary flavor did continue to influence social thought.

In the 1920s, with the institutionalization of sociology first at the University of Bombay and later at Lucknow, Calcutta and Mysore universities, Indian sociology adopted theoretical conceptions of society and culture and research methods from the western sociology and anthropology. Prior to independence, sociology in India was primarily influenced by historical, indological, anthropological, humanistic as well as positivistic approaches. During this period (1920–1947), Indian sociology emerged as a result of the traditional and the modern, and of the endogenous and exogenous forces.

Saran (1958) observed that the development of sociological thought in India has been cotemporaneous with her contact with the western culture resulting in three different responses: (a) a total rejection of the modern western civilization and a return to the traditional principles, (b) a synthesis of two cultures, and (c) a tendency to interpret and justify traditional concepts and institutions in terms of modern rationalistic-positivistic ideas.

It was only after 1947 when India attained independence from the British rule that sociology, under the changing socio-cultural milieu, began to experience significant growth. The national leaders and planners, in their zeal to modernize the country, perceived the role of sociology, along with the other social sciences, in the task of national reconstruction and development. The University Grants Commission and the Research Programmes Committee of the Planning Commission gave impetus to sociology. These federal government agencies provided grants to various universities and sponsored research on problems of development and change. This initiative by the government accelerated the pace of institutionalization and professionalization of sociology in terms of both teaching and research.

During the post-independence period there has been a rapid growth of colleges and universities (Rao, 1978). An overwhelming majority of universities – both old and new – have introduced sociology; and the proportion of students, teachers, graduates and doctorates in sociology has increased dramatically.[1] Moreover, sociology in most universities and colleges in India today, by and large, has become independent of other relatively well-established disciplines such as history, economics, political science, philosophy and psychology. The distinct sociological approach and method used by sociologists in the study of social phenomena and problems is illustrated by the growth of teaching and research in various branches of sociology. It should be recognized, however, that in the Indian context it is difficult to distinguish sociological and social anthropological modes of inquiry and analysis.[2] Despite the increasing acceptance of the scientific sociological approach (positivism), sociology in India has tended to combine different approaches and perspectives such as the philosophical, historical-indological, anthropological and humanistic.

Two noticeable trends in Indian sociology have originated because of strong influences from western countries. From the British, Indian sociology developed a trend which is social anthropological. The social anthropological approach stems from the fact that the British upon which the Indians were academically dependent before independence, had made much more progress in social anthropology than they had in sociology (Bottomore, 1962). Social anthropology was given impetus also because of the administrative purposes it could serve for government such as investigations of tribal people and because of the suitability of anthropological methods for studying many of India's social institutions and problems. This British influence, especially if Indian scholars have been trained in Britain, has led to an emphasis on rural studies while many urban social phenomena remain without adequate research, although this rural emphasis may be justifiable considering that a large majority of India's population lives in villages.

Since independence, American influences have been instrumental in charting the course of Indian sociology. American influences do not represent a coherent body of thought but are more felt in the areas of methodology and techniques. Following the stress on empiricism found in American sociology some Indian scholars have begun to use the idea of testing hypotheses and have adopted statistical tools. Along with American empiricism has come the notion that sociological investigations should be objective. The acceptance or rejection of objectivity as a desirable goal for research has generated much debate because a number of prominent Indian sociologists, especially those with the philosophical tendencies, are of the opinion that because man's behaviour and experience cut across many dimensions and metaphysical speculations as regards man and society... that furnishes the ultimate postulates of all social sciences and social action (Mukherjee, 1961). Saksena (1961) believes that the philosophical elements of Indian sociology are necessary in that they provide a continuum between the past and the present.

During the first twenty-five years after independence, sociology in India expanded quite dramatically. The number of universities teaching sociology has increased greatly as well as the number of students enrolled in sociology courses, the number of colleges and universities teaching sociology programmes, and the number of M.A. and Ph.D. degree awarded has increased. The publication of sociological researches has also greatly increased along with the increases in the number of Indian sociologists. It appears that despite influences of American empiricism there has been little use of computers and quantitative or statistical methods. Little theoretical development of methodological innovation has taken place, although a few ideas more recently are being developed which are uniquely suited to the Indian context. Possibly, because of the vastness of India, and probably because of lack of initiative and funding for macro level research projects, most studies have taken a microscopic rather than a macroscopic view, while most of the work which has been done at the micro level has not been organized or synthesized to yield generalizations for all of India. Thus, comparative studies have been conducted either between India and other countries or among regions in India (Chekki, 1975 and 1978).

The development of Indian sociology was classified under a time-sequence of 1920–40, and the 1950s, 1960s and 1970s with the 'pioneers', 'modernizers', 'insiders', and 'pace-makers' versus 'non-conformists' playing distinctive roles in the respective periods (Mukherjee, 1977). It is stated that the pioneers' approach was synoptic and their theoretical formulations, though not precise enough, had a good deal of inductive power to generalize from a multidimensional comprehension of social reality in the historical, contemporary and futuristic perspectives.

For the modernizers social change was an ideology not only a matter for theoretical comprehension. The research orientation of the modernizers was essentially pragmatic and explained social change in modern India in terms of the complementary processes of 'sanskritization' and 'westernization'.

The modernizers could not produce better, or even any significant sociological theory on the basis of a comprehensive appraisal of social reality in India. Moreover, Mukherjee (1977) notes that the deductive and simplistic methodology of the dominant section of the modernizers produced a fragmentary or distorted appraisal of social reality. The methodology of the other section of the modernizers which followed the theory and practice dominating American rural sociology in the 1950s, was sophisticated but not necessarily efficient in the Indian context because of its uncritical acceptance. In any event, the modernizers, though helped to considerably broaden the data base of Indian sociology, did not succeed in producing a better understanding of social reality.

During this period, sociologists exhibited various value preferences and research orientations. The structural-functional approach has been a dominant mode of analysis. A few sociologists, such as Mukherjee, Desai, Saran, followed Marxist approach for sociological analysis (Desai, 1981).

In the 1960s, sociologists influenced by the outlook of the behavioural science as then prevalent in the United States adopted a holistic approach and participated in interdisciplinary research with other social scientists. The 1960s appeared in a large measure to be a continuation of the 1950s in the mode and manner of social research but with more specialization of the discipline, diversification of its thematic content in the Indian context, and the adoption of appropriate methodology for micro-sociology.

Despite changes in the 1960s, the optimism of the 1950s regarding the ushering in of change in India through rapid economic growth was found to be an illusion. There was also a growing realization among some sociologists that the kind of sociology advocated and accepted since the 1950s was not adequate to understand the dynamics of Indian society. In place of an imitative development of Indian sociology, the indigenization of Indian sociology was demanded not merely in form but also in content. Marxist approach has not been well received by the policy makers and by a majority of social scientists. However, a group of young sociologists wish to make Indian sociology effective in changing reality.

In the 1960s and 1970s sociologists in India seem to have been influenced both by capitalist and socialist ideologies. During these two decades increasing numbers of sociological researches were sponsored and supported by the Planning Commission and the University Grants Commission to propose and/or evaluate various government initiated programmes of development and change.[3] Indian sociologists tended to follow either a value neutral, scientific objectivity stance or a value committed action orientation. A few sociologists, however, tried to combine both these approaches.

In the late 1970s, it appears that there has been a better co-ordination of theory and research than ever attained before. This is exemplified by (a) more critical concept formation, (b) search for new avenues to appraise social reality, and (c) reconsideration of the modes of studying the society which were advocated by the pioneers.

As a result of the unprecedented growth of sociology as an academic discipline in the post-independence era, a number of problems arose. Universities and colleges experienced the need for qualified teachers, and shortage of funds for hiring sociologists, and the need for indigenous course materials in Indian languages, and had to contend with the problems of medium of instruction.

Regarding the modernization of syllabi in sociology Indian sociologists have arrived at a consensus that the cognitive contents of the courses must primarily be grounded into the Indian concrete reality and its history. Another area of consensus is that at higher levels the courses may be more diversified with greater theoretical and substantive contents emphasizing regional, national and international comparative approaches. Indian sociologists have also recognized the undesirability of a completely standardized uniform structure of syllabi for all regions of the country, although a basic minimum is considered to be necessary.

A need for teaching materials that are relevant to the Indian social milieu and/or derived from social researches in India is being felt. This need is more pronounced as far as teaching materials in Indian languages are concerned. Likewise, Indian sociologists have tried to re-examine teaching methods and have been experimenting with a medium of regional language instruction in different parts of the country. The committees appointed by the University Grants Commission have recommended seminars and workshops and exchange programmes for faculty, production of teaching materials in regional languages and the restructuring of the examination and evaluation system for significant improvements in teaching-learning sociology in India. These efforts have tended to contribute to the indigenization of sociology movement.

The impact of American sociology on Indian sociology during the past three decades has been quite significant. Since the mid-1950s increasing exchange of scholars between the United States and India increased use of American sociology textbooks, together with aid for research from Ford, Rockefeller and other American foundations and the Fullbright programme have had their influence on the growth of sociology in India (Chekki, 1984).

Several Indian scholars either trained in the United States or exposed to American sociology have been responsible for the diffusion of American sociology in India. The dominant theoretical framework, i.e., structural-functionalism that was prevalent in the United States during the 1950s and early 1960s was readily accepted by many sociologists in India. Likewise, the characteristic features of American sociology, such as heavy emphasis on empirical research and quantitative research methods, were emulated by Indian sociologists. This apparent dependence of Indian sociology on American sociology seems to reflect a situation of intellectual imperialism (Uberoi, 1968). Desai (1981) points out that during the 1950s and early 1960s for academic position a foreign degree, or even a stay abroad without any degree was considered more acceptable by the universities and they filled up many positions in the university departments. He called these foreign-returned sociologists as a 'priestly' category not in a derogatory sense but in a functional sense.

Namboodiri also observes that in the post-1950 period, Indian sociology became increasingly 'westernized' by accepting structural-functionalism as the best guide for analysis of data. With the proliferation of American collaboration in empirical research, several Indian sociologists, however, have been quite critical of wholesale acceptance of American sociological theories and research methods without considering their relevance to Indian social and cultural milieu.[4]

From 1960 onwards, Indian sociologists turned their attention away from the micro-sociological models in order to free themselves from external influences and develop their own model of thinking about reality (Singh, 1979). Marxist and neo-Marxian theoretical orientations began to influence the Indian sociological tradition.

During the 1970s American sociology continued to influence Indian sociology but in a more selective way than it was initially presumed. This selective reception of sociological knowledge from the United States and other external sources is in accordance with India's tradition of adoption and modification of foreign culture elements without losing its own identity. As such, Indian sociology, despite American influence since independence, has retained its unique character.

Indian sociology has been growing as a mixture of various endogenous and exogenous intellectual traditions. The substantive content of sociology has ranged from tribal peasant to urban industrial communities, reflecting diverse social realities in India. It is evident that the multidimensional nature of Indian sociology is characteristic of its multifaceted socio-cultural environment.

While in the 1970s American sociology experienced considerable competition, controversy, debate and confrontation among different theoretical schools and research methodologies, Indian sociology has been, with a few exceptions, remained less conflict-ridden than American sociology. Instead of ideological-theoretical-methodological controversies and battles, what we find in contemporary Indian sociology is a tolerance for different perspectives and trend toward synthesis of various kinds of sociologies prevalent in India and abroad. Obviously, this process has not contributed to a sociology of India that can be recognized as a photocopy of American sociology.

Indeed, some India sociologists have advocated a distinct sociology for India with its own concepts, theories and methods of inquiry. While others have maintained that Indian sociology is distinct only in terms of its focus, and research emphasis. It is believed that with the development of universalistic and synthetic sociology, with a place in it for diverse patterns of sociology, Indian sociology can unfold itself at its creative best, and also contribute its share to the development of a world sociology (Nandy, 1971).

The recent trends characteristic of the 1970s do indicate that Indian sociology has been developing theoretical concerns and comparative perspectives by using native categories and testing several hypotheses derived from Weberian, Marxist and other theoretical paradigms (Singh, 1979). These theoretical orientations are being applied to the Indian social reality rather innovatively and in this process Indian sociologists are generating new theoretical insights by challenging classical sociological theories.

Another notable trend during the 1970s has been a series of studies on the problems of the disadvantaged groups such as scheduled tribes and scheduled castes (ex-untouchables) and their education, unemployment and poverty, women's studies, inequality, social indicators, etc., sponsored by the Indian Council of Social Science Research (ICSSR). These studies have provided useful data for planning. In theoretical terms, there has been considerable attention focused on alternate models of development in the Indian context. The ICSSR has also sponsored a series of training courses in research methodology and has provided fellowships, research and publication grants to scholars.

During the 1970s, the number of American scholars engaged in research in India has declined. The Government of India discovered that the CIA and other agencies of the US government have not only been supporting research but also using research data for political and military purposes. Consequently, the Government of India imposed restrictions on American sponsored research and researchers.

Sociologists from India and abroad have advocated different kinds of sociologies or at least seem to have different conceptions of what Indian sociology is or ought to be. Under the title 'For a Sociology of India', Dumont and Pocock (1957) initiated a discussion presenting a distinct view of sociology of India in the hope of eliciting comments from colleagues. In their opinion, the first condition for a sound development of a sociology of India is found in the establishment of the proper relation between it and classical indology. While claiming, in principle, that a sociology of India lies at the point of confluence of sociology and indology they referred to a small band of scholars who have combined both effectively. Dumont and Pocock postulate that India is one and it can be understood as a single system of ideas or values through an analysis of the values of Hinduism.

Bailey (1959) disagrees with Dumont and Pocock on their conception of Indian sociology as a form of culturology that is too narrow a perspective. Bailey is interested in the study of Indian social phenomena from the comparative point of view. The debate for a sociology of India revolves round several theoretical, methodological, and substantive issues pertaining to Indian sociology. For instance, Damle (1965) makes a plea for the use of the Parsonian frame of reference for the study of Indian sociology. Madan (1966) raises the question: Why is it that Indian sociologists have not been interested in examining the theoretic assumptions underlying their studies? He thinks that the Indian sociologist has been a victim of history (the colonial situation) and of positivist orientation of western sociology, leading to his peculiar intellectual sloth. For him there cannot be many sociologies, but sociological understanding must take account of social specificity. Moreover, it is asserted that the Indian sociologist has not made a significant contribution to the development and refinement of sociological concepts.

This deficiency makes Uberoi (1968) remark: 'Until we can concentrate on decolonization, learn to nationalize our problems and take our poverty seriously, we shall continue to be both colonial and unoriginal. A national school, avowed and conscious, can perhaps add relevance, meaning and potency to our science; continued assent to the international system cannot.'

A common thread that binds a group of sociologists in this debate is a belief that the patterns of Indian social structure are so unique that they require a special sociology of India asking different questions but using similar western methods to answer them (Unnithan, 1967). Kantowsky (1969), while expressing critical comments with reference to Indian sociology, notes that 'Indian sociologists, when they quote Talcott Parsons does not prove that the structural-functional analysis has stood the test within the Indian milieu. Rather it indicates an adaptive process of many Indian social scientists to the rules of the dominant caste within the Euro-American social science game'. He asserts that studies in developing countries should try to make their relevance clear not only in regard to practical questions but also to the theoretical problems of the social sciences in general. For Kantowsky it is impossible to make any general scientific statement without proper reference to intercultural data. Therefore, there is no need to distinguish the 'sociology of developing countries' from the 'sociology of industrial countries'. In the same vein it is maintained that Indian sociology is distinctive only in terms of its focus and research emphasis (Atal, 1976). The strategy of parochialization is not a proper response to the parochial sociology of the West.

While recognizing the existential roots of scientific propositions and paradigms intuitively formulated by scientists Singh (1979) thinks of the possibility of an Indian sociology based on concepts and propositions derived from the study of Indian society. However, 'the sociological propositions which would form the basis of Indian or any other national sociology would of course have less theoretic power than those of general sociology'.

Narain (1971) observes that in having a history of its own, surely Indian society is not unique and he seems to imply that there is no need for sociology of India with its own concepts, theories, and methods. He agrees with Bailey that Indian society, granting all its uniqueness, must still be seen in the context of the general principles of sociology. Because of the inadequacy of the methods of national science in dealing with meanings, values, and behaviour of humans he hopes to bring about a fruitful marriage between the scientific and humanistic approaches in sociology.

Ahmed (1972) demonstrates the pronounced tendency among sociologists to equate Hindu society with India and neglect of other religious groups and sects. He argues that greater attention must be paid to non-Hindu societies if the aim is to build a comprehensive sociology of India. 'Until then', he notes, 'we may have Hindu, Muslim or Christian sociologies, but hardly a sociology of India'.

In the mid-1960s the seminar on 'Sociology for India' raised the question: Should sociology for India be an altogether independent discipline both in theory and method and apply itself to the analysis of the typical social phenomena of the Indian society or should it be a general body of concepts and theory with the help of which both general as well as specific problems of any social phenomenon. Indian or non-Indian could be analyzed and interpreted? The papers presented and the discussion that followed challenged and rejected the possibility of a typical or particularistic Indian sociology.

However, Saksena (1962) maintained that Indian sociology cannot be divorced from metaphysical thinking and it cannot be entirely objective in its content (Saksena, 1962). It is also suggested that Indian sociology should focus its attention on problems of basic conceptualization within the frame of Indian social data (Srivastava, 1966). The lack of concepts applicable to Indian social phenomena is noted and 'middle range' studies instead of 'grand generalizations' are considered to be adequate to the empirical reality of Indian social phenomena (Mohan, 1975).

The cultural diversity of India is reflected in Indian sociology. There is a lack of consensus among Indian sociologists as to whether sociology in India should be historical-indological, empirical, functional, dialectic, microscopic or macroscopic and so on. The advocates of sociological particularism aim at developing concepts, theories, and methods arising out of and relevant to social reality in India. Whereas the advocates of sociological universalism tend to accept theories and methods from the western countries.

Borrowing from the West – primarily the US – it is believed, fosters intellectual dependency and 'Indian sociology degenerates into replicative, deductive, intellectual enterprise; an exercise merely of testing the cross-cultural validity of the western models and formulations rather than inductive initiatives leading to independent conceptual formulations springing from close observations of indigenous phenomena' (Rao and Rao, 1977). Furthermore, it is argued that this task of merely testing the cross-cultural validity of the western models reduces the Indian sociological community to the position of a mass consumer of western sociology by providing a market for its output.

Indian sociology, Unnithan argues, must follow an integrative 'middle path' between 'sociological universalism' and 'sociological regionalism', adopting sociological concepts to the peculiarities of Indian social phenomena. Namboodiri (1980) recognizes some of the unique characteristics of Indian society such as the heavy concentration of population in villages, with a caste structure and a joint family system and spiritual and moral ideas like *dharma, karma, moksha*, etc., which should be taken into account when studying social processes in India. But for him it does not follow that in order for sociology to be concerned with history and cultural contexts sociological methods and models have to be society-specific.

This debate and controversy surrounding the nature of the Indian sociology movement tends to encompass three different camps of sociologists: (a) those who advocate for distinct concepts, theories, and methods appropriate for the study of Indian society; (b) those who wish to consider sociology as a universal science with common concepts, theories and methods that can be used to study any society including Indian; and (c) integration and adaptation of sociological concepts, theories and methods to the peculiarities of Indian phenomena.

As a reaction to a western, especially American, sociological view of social phenomena that has prevailed in India, a movement of indigenization has set in motion aimed at the interpretation and understanding of social reality with due regard to the historical and cultural specificities. For Madan (1979), 'indigenization stands for the effort to cultivate self-awareness, to see ourselves not as others would see us, but as we may also see ourselves'. Here, the outsider's view of reality alone is considered inadequate and at times distorted because the problem lies in the western view of scientific or objective knowledge of human behaviour at the cost of its meaning and significance to the actors themselves.

The issue is not merely one of a dichotomy between 'outsider's vs. insider's view' of reality posed by Merton (Madan, 1972). 'The outsider's view', in the case of India as reported by Madan, 'was enthroned as the exclusively valid vision. It became the truth.' Concomitantly involved therein was a relationship of dependency extended from the political areas to the intellectual circles.

In this context indigenization is neither meant to be parochialization nor a means to an end but its goal is the self-conscious definition of research worthy questions and the enrichment of the social sciences as instruments of general understanding and of practical action in historically specific situations: theoretical universals must illumine concrete problems. This indigenization movement seems to incorporate a new vision of mankind – a non-exploitative relationship among humans and harmonious relationship between humans and the biosphere.

American sociology is considered to be largely regressive in imparting a conservative and superficially empiricist influence on social research in India (Verma, 1979). Therefore, social scientists in India are asked to take a clearly anti-imperialistic stance and devote their energies to the emancipation of the masses from the shackles of colonialism and neo-colonialism. Furthermore, it is argued that social inquiry should be relevant to problems of the masses and to the enrichment of life in India. These critical reflections and new directions seem to be the basis for Dube (1977) to comment that 'there has been a visible unease within Indian sociology about its direction and purpose'.

The preceding analysis of the process of institutionalization of sociology in India suggests that the discipline has developed beyond its traditional moorings. While exposed to internal socio-cultural processes as well as external forces, especially to the hegemonic influence of American sociology, the sociology of India has tried to retain its unique sociological tradition of a synthetic approach in theory, method, and substantive research. More importantly, sociology in India has reacted to external intellectual domination by way of an indigenization movement.

The Indian sociology movement does not encompass the sociological enterprise as a whole in India but to those specific endeavours of 'Indianizing' the discipline, minimizing its imported connotations, and developing conceptual framework and theoretical perspectives that emanate from the study of Indian society. This movement emphasizes not only the need to use distinct concepts, theories, and methods for the study of Indian society but also the necessity of rationalization of sociology curriculum and creating textbooks and course materials that are relevant to the cultural milieu.

Furthermore, in developing an Indian sociological perspective which reflects the facts and values of a unique national context, the movement tends to encourage an Indian contribution to global sociology. This movement also serves as a case study in the sociology of knowledge by demonstrating the importance of a national context in relativizing and shaping sociological practice and theorizing.

The increasing urbanization and industrialization, the rapid expansion of the post-secondary educational system, the increasing differentiation of sociology from history, economics, political science and psychology, and the dominant American influence on India's economy and the social sciences contributed to a set of forces in which a new wave of national consciousness emerged among a group of sociologists.

Perhaps the most significant single factor to account for the Indian sociology movement was a developmental one. The relatively recent and rapid growth of discipline of sociology in India was due to a new acceptance of sociology as an autonomous field of inquiry in Indian universities and colleges, and rapid increase of students enrolled in sociology courses.

With the size of the college and university sociological community increasing and with the greater stability and institutionalization of sociology departments, Indianization can be considered a form of consciousness raising by a sociological community that had now reached a level of organizational maturity and that needed to sensitize itself to mutual problems and its collective existence.

The major focus of the Indianization movement has been on the creation of distinct perspectives emerging from the Indian social context. This movement tends to emphasize an Indian sociological perspective based on an 'approach' that is holistic, macro sociological, interdisciplinary, and generated from the distinctive characteristics of Indian society.

The Indian sociology movement has been a challenge to place sociological research into the national context in which sociality takes place. This, in turn, it is believed, would make it possible to develop different or at least additional theoretical perspectives than currently available in sociology in India. Furthermore, this effort would or should change sociology from an imported to a more indigenous discipline. In as much as the Indian sociology movement emphasizes research done on critical aspects of Indian society and stresses Indian content in instruction, it contributes to national self-understanding. The macro sociological perspective seemed to have become important at a time when the fabric of society was being threatened by tensions and conflicts resulting from regional, religious, caste, and language differences within the country and increasing fears of American influence. The Indian sociology movement in its attempt to develop a distinct theoretical thrust strives to engage in creative and independent reflection emerging from the intensive study of a particular society.

Weber and Mannheim emphasized the relativity of the sociological perspective. With the growth of the discipline in India, theoretical models emerging from the American environment were being re-examined for their appropriateness in the Indian social context. In response to the comparative strength of sociology in the United States and the post-Second World War efforts to emulate American sociology, several national sociological communities have gone through an indigenization phase. Among the many national sociological communities, Canada serves as a good example of indigenization movement in sociology. Reaction in India, however, appears to have been unique because of the socio-economic and historical context that differs greatly from the United States.

To the extent that the Indian sociology movement represents a struggle for differentiation from American sociology, it is co-extensive with the national need for economic independence. But more than that, it is an attempt to create a sociological perspective that not only emerges from the study of Indian society but that reflects the social processes which are unique to Indian society.

Despite numerous distinctive features of Indian society, how original can such a sociological perspective be at the global level? What aspects of sociology can be prominently Indian and what aspects universal? What effects do strong regional, religious, caste, linguistic identities have on a national sociology? To what extent is sociology in India impoverished if it does not develop a national sociology? These and other questions need to be confronted in terms of their epistemological and disciplinary implications.

The development of sociology as a discipline and as a field of scholarly endeavour in India influenced by the European and American traditions of sociological analysis can be characterized as a dialectical one in which the European or more specifically the British model maintained the upper hand prior to 1945 and the American model since the end of the Second World War. These trends reflect a situation of dependency on the part of sociology in India and within the nation as a whole. Only in the 1960s has sociology in India sought to develop at more indigenous character as the result of an enlarged and strengthened professional community.

The context in which this movement took place was both international and international. At an international level within the discipline, numerous minority sociologies (e.g., black sociology, radical sociology, feminist sociology) arose to challenge the universality of science motif in sociology. Sociology in other nations (e.g., Canada, Australia) also sought paradigms and sociological foci that were more relevant to social life in their national and cultural contexts.

The end result of dependency has been the co-existence and frequent conflict of both European and American sociological traditions and sociological traditions in India. Reaction to the foreign paradigm has more often consisted of a new emphasis in research on specific aspects of Indian society than it has meant total rejection of the alien paradigmatic approach. In that sense, sociology in India seems to have developed a synthetic approach with a strong emphasis on India's historical and cultural characteristics. The contextual and dependency models of disciplinary development sketched at the outset have been used to demonstrate the shape that sociology has taken at the various phase of its development in modern India.

The sociology of knowledge thesis developed by Marx, Mannheim, Merton and Coser, among others, that the development of sociological knowledge is related to the socio-economic, and political conditions of the society in which it emerges is supported in the case of Indian sociology. More importantly, from the foregoing, it is quite obvious that the dependency/world system model finds adequate support from this study in that American sociology constituting the 'core' has had considerable power and influence in creating a state of dependency on the part of the 'peripheral' and 'semi-peripheral' sociology of India.

After more than two decades of the emergence of the Indian sociology movement it is best to speak on an Indian sociological perspective as still in the process of formation. However, certain features appear to be crystallizing. There are differences of opinion as to the nature of Indian sociology. It is suggested by some sociologists that it should use a Marxist approach, while others have argued for a blend of various indigenous and non-indigenous perspectives. Despite these differences, the challenge seems to lie in applying preferred perspectives critically to an analysis of Indian society. Indian sociology will be made distinctive by what it contributes to the analysis of society. And in contributing to an understanding of a particular society, an explicit contribution should be made to the fund of disciplinary knowledge about societies in general.

It is reasonable to argue that whereas nationalism in science is unscholarly, the comprehension of national societies is not. The facts that Indian society is both similar and unique in relation to other societies makes us realize that whatever emerges from the Indian sociological perspective should be part of a global sociology so that cross-national data and theory can be compared and tested. If the

Indian sociology movement is to be more than merely an exercise in consciousness raising, the Indian sociological perspective(s) must continue to crystallize so that it can be one of the critical frameworks into which data might be organized to make sociology in India both societally relevant and productive in the context of global sociology. In other words, it would be necessary to develop an Indian sociology that is historically informed, theoretically sophisticated, and comparatively oriented.

Notes

1. M.N. Srinivas attributes the recent popularity of sociology to the greatly increased exposure of Indian students to American universities and to a belated realization of insufficiency of a purely economic approach to development.
2. According to Srinivas, a distinction between sociology and social anthropology in India does violence to social reality.
3. The government bureaucrats and politicians in India, however, have paid very little attention to social science research because it is considered too academic.
4. For instance, Yogendra Singh, S.L. Sharma, T.N. Madan, T.K.N. Unnithan, among others, have questioned the relevance of the Western sociological theories to reality in India.

References

Ahmed, I., 1972, 'For a Sociology of India', *Contributions to Indian Sociology*, Vol. 6.

Atal, Y., 1976, 'Sociology in the Indian Campus' in G.R. Gupta (ed.), *Main Currents in Indian Sociology*, Vol. I, New Delhi, Vikas.

Bailey, F.G., 1959, 'For a Sociology of India'?, *Contributions to Indian Sociology*, Vol. 3.

Ben-David, J. and R. Collins, 1966, 'Social Factors in the Origin of a New Science', *American Sociological Review*, Vol. 31.

Bierstedt, R., 1981, *American Sociological Theory: A Critical History*, New York, Academic Press.

Bottomore, T.B., 1962, 'Sociology in India', *British Journal of Sociology*, Vol. 13.

Chekki, D.A., 1975, *The Social System and Culture of Modern India*, New York and London, Garland Publishing.

—, 1978, *The Sociology of Contemporary India*, Columbia, Missouri, South Asia Books.

Coser, L.A., 1971, *Masters of Sociological Thought*, New York, Harcourt.

Damle, Y.B., 1965, 'For a Theory of Indian Sociology', *Sociology in India*, Agra, Institute of Social Sciences, Agra University.

Desai, A.R., 1981, 'Relevance of the Marxist Approach to the Study of Indian Society', *Sociological Bulletin*, Vol. 30, No. 1.

Desai, I.P., 1981, 'Craft of Sociology in India: An Autobiographical Perspective', *Economic and Political Weekly*, February 7, and February 14.

Dube, S.C., 1977, 'Indian, Sociology at the Turning Point', *Sociological Bulletin*, Vol. 26, No. 1.

Dumont, L. and D. Pocock, 1957, 'For a Sociology of India', *Contribution to Indian Sociology*, Vol. I.

Friedrichs, R.W., 1970, *Sociology of sociology* New York, The Free Press.

Gouldner, A., 1971, *The Coming Crisis of Western Sociology*, New York, Avon.

Hiller, H.H., 1980, 'Paradigm Shifts, Indigenization, and the Development of Sociology in Canada', *Journal of the History of the Behavioural Sciences*, Vol. 16.

Ishwaran, K., 1965, 'The Sociology of Sociology', *International Journal of Comparative Sociology*, Vol. 6.

Kantowsky, D., 1969, 'A Critical Note on the Sociology of Developing Countries', *Contributions to Indian Sociology*, Vol. 3.

Kuhn, T.S., 1970, *The Structure of Scientific Revolutions*, Chicago, University of Chicago Press.

Lamy, P., 1976, 'The Globalization of American Sociology: Excellence or Imperialism', *American Sociologist*, Vol. II.

Loubser, J.J., 1982, 'The Need for the Indigenization of the Social Sciences', paper presented at the Tenth World Congress of Sociology, Mexico City.

Madan, T.N., 1966, 'For a Sociology of India', *Contributions to Indian Sociology*, Vol. 9.

—, 1979, 'Indigenization of Social Sciences', *ICSSR Newsletter*, April-September.

Mannheim, K., 1936, *Ideology and Utopia*, New York, Harcourt, Brace and World.

—, 1952, *Essays in Sociology of Knowledge*, London, Routledge and Kegan Paul.

Marx, K. and F. Engels, 1963, German Ideology, New York, International Publishers.

Merton, R.K., 1968, *Social Theory and Social Structure*, New York, The Free Press.

—, 1972, 'Insiders and Outsiders: A Chapter in the Sociology of Knowledge', *American Journal of Sociology*, Vol. 78, No. 1.

Mills, C. Wright, 1959, *The Sociological Imagination*, New York, Oxford University Press.

Mohan, R.P., 'Contemporary Sociology in India', in R.P. Mohan and D. Martindale (eds.), 1975, *Handbook of Contemporary Developments in World Sociology*, Westport, C.T. Greenwood.

Mukherjee, R., 1977, 'Trends in India Sociology', *Current Sociology*, Vol. 25, No. 3.

Mukerjee, R.K., 'Presidential Address', in Saksena, R.N. (ed.), 1961, *Sociology, Social Research and Social Problems*, New York, Asia.

Mullins, N.C., 1973, *Theories and Theory Groups in Contemporary American Sociology*, New York, Harper and Row.

Myrdal, G., 1958, *Values in Social Theory*, London, Routledge and Kegan Paul.

Namboodi, N.K., 1980, 'On Sociology in India: Yesterday, Today and Tomorrow', *Social Forces*, Vol. 59, No. 1.

Nandy, S.K., 1971, 'Aspects of Development of Sociology in India: A Study in the Sociology of Sociology', in E.A. Tiryakian (ed.), *The Phenomenon of Sociology*, New York, Appleton-Century Crofts.

Narain, D., 1971, 'For a Sociology of India: Some Observations', *Contributions to Indian Sociology*, Vol. 5.

Parsons, T., 1959, 'An Approach to the Sociology of Knowledge', *Transactions of the Fourth World Congress of Sociology*, IV, Louvian, International Sociological Association.

Rao, M.S.A. et.al., 1978, *Report of the Status of Teaching of Sociology and Social Anthropology*, New Delhi, University Grants Commission.

Rao, S.V.V.S. and C.R.P. Rao., 1977, 'Reflections on the Crisis of Indian Sociology', *Sociological Bulletin*, Vol. 26, No. 2.

Ritzer, G., 1981, *Toward An Integrated Sociological Paradigm*, Boston, Allyn and Bacon.

Saksena, R.N., 1962, 'Some Observations of Sociology in India', *American Sociological Review*, Vol. 27.

Saran, A.K., 1958, 'Sociology in India', J.S. Roucek (ed.), *Contemporary Sociology*, New York, Philosophical Library.

Sharma, S.l., 1982, 'Western Theory and Indian Reality: The Question of Relevance', paper presented at the Tenth World Congress of Sociology, Mexico City.

Shils, E., 1970, 'Tradition, Ecology and Institution in the History of Sociology', *Daedalus*, Vol. 99.

Singh, Y., 1979, 'On the History of Sociology in India', in Mullick, M., (ed.), *Social Inquiry: Goals and Approaches*, New Delhi, Manohar.

Srivastava, R.N., 1966, 'Sociology for India: Some Consideration', *Indian Journal of Social Research*, Vol. 7, No. 3.

Uberoi, J.P.S., 1968, 'Science and Swaraj', *Contributions to Indian Sociology*, New Series 2.

Unnithan, T.K.N., et. al., (eds.), 1967, *Sociology for India*, New Delhi, Prentice-Hall.

Verma, S.C., 1979, 'Social Inquiry for What'? in Mullick, M., op. cit.

Wiley, N., 1979, 'The Rise and Fall of Dominating Theories in American Sociology', in Snizek, W. et.al., (eds.), *Contemporary Issues in Theory and Research*, Westport, Greenwood.

20

Dialectics Between Theory and Social Reality

Y.B. Damle

Social science in general and sociology in particular has a very unenviable brief to handle. It is indeed well-known that the very discipline of sociology developed in response to the challenges faced by the western industrial civilization. It is often said that sociology is under crisis, without realizing that the very purpose of sociology has historically been to come to grips with the existing crisis. This is not to say that other social sciences do not face a similar challenge; for instance, economics, political science or psychology. In his preface to the symposium on *Crisis and Contentions in Sociology*, Bottomore (1975: 6) has very rightly stated that 'sociology is a part of the general culture and subject to all the influences that arise from the clash of interest and the diversity of cultural orientations'. If any discipline is so engulfed by any crisis, which emerges every now and then, it is likely to find itself wanting in providing clear-cut solutions to such crisis. Apart from suggesting solutions to the crisis, sociology is also called upon to be a critical reflection upon society. In trying to maintain its distinctive character of the interrelatedness of various components like the cultural, economic, political, moral, and psychological, it is not unlikely that sociology would undertake rather ambitious types of enquiry, instead of drawing upon both the material as well as insights provided by different social sciences mentioned above.

While other social sciences such as economics and political science in particular tend to deal with markedly logical action and behaviour, of course by making a variety of assumptions, sociology tries to provide a logic to understand a peculiar blend of logical and non-logical action. It is the logic of situations which is emphasized rather than logic in its abstract form of reasoning. Actor, the central figure in sociological analysis, apart from the social system, tries to be a 'person' and he does not want to be straight jacketed into the performance of roles. Actor, so-called, wants to control the situation and he values freedom of all kinds, such as freedom from want, domination and manipulation by others, who are so imperiled by their status position and by their machinations. Thus, apart from the dialectics between logical and non-logical, there is also the problematic relationship between actor, person, system, etc. Atkinson (1972: 2) has very trenchantly complained that 'in attaining respectability, sociology has come increasingly to ignore its critical task and its initial subject matter – the understanding of ordinary living people'. Emphasis on constraint and order and sociology of choice has tended to neglect conflict, which is inherent in the contradictions referred to above. Gouldner (1971: 40, 47) also emphatically stressed the importance of personal reality and social theory and also the importance of sentiments and ideologies very rightly.

Theory (sociological) is a set of logically interrelated concepts and propositions about social reality. Merton, though sceptical about universal generalizations in sociology, emphasizes the importance of general sociological orientations. He states that 'sociological concepts have to be tightly tested empirically and have to be put forward in a set of ordered propositions' (1957: 90). Of course, in his characteristic manner, he has very rightly cautioned students of sociology to continuously test every concept and even every semblance of sociological theory empirically. According to him, theoretic pertinence of any theory results, when it is conceptualized, in abstraction of a higher order, so that a possibility of universal propositions can be increased. However, he cautions that precision by itself is not a sufficient proof of any theoretical proposition (ibid.: 85–101). By and large, theory is expected to provide a comprehensive description of the existing social reality in all its complexities and interrelatedness. Thus, it has to be exploratory and inductive. Theory is also expected to provide analysis and explanation of the existing reality, where it is called upon to resort to deduction by the use of concepts and logically interrelated propositions. It is only then that theory can help prediction of possible events. As if this was not a tall enough assignment, more often than not, theory also tends to be prescriptive in its ambition, where the understanding and insight provided by theory is expected to provide guidelines for appropriate action. It may be argued that in its prescriptive role, theory usually ceases to function and is reduced to *ad hoc* solutions to trivial problems, but it cannot also be denied that sometimes the presence and persistence of a particularly popular, fashionable, analysis which, if loaded with ideological conviction, may be resorted to for resolving every kind of problem including the appropriate transformation of a system. Importance of both inductive and deductive approach is thus emphasized and it is also seen as to how the predictive aspect of theory is laden with difficulties, because of the lack of really universal propositions which transcend the bonds of space and time. Equally well or perhaps more strongly it should be stated that prescriptive domination of theory is considerably more difficult because of its ideological underpinnings, which in addition are couched under a unilinear perspective for viewing social reality. It is indeed well-known that the various laws propounded about social and economic development are rooted in a particular historical context and as such, have failed to click with vastly differing situations and needs, particularly in connection with the so-called Third World societies. Therefore, the various purposes of theory, as enlisted above, do not belong to the same level of rigour and development and as such cannot be relied upon to take the expected cognizance of social reality.

THEORY AND SOCIAL REALITY

Theory has to facilitate an understanding of social reality in all its complexities. The problem of complexity of social reality can be wished away by assuming a coherent unified and composite society, i.e., social system or structure. The conception of unified society, social system, social structure emphasizes the importance of sociality of every individual and the efficacy of various social arrangements and institutions, which though ostensibly performing the task, needs satisfaction of all the members of society, also are more prominently, agencies of social control and sanctions. Socialization of individuals to adopt them to the system is a first requisite, although it is indeed a commonplace of sociology that due to various cultural and structural reasons, the required degree of socialization would not be forthcoming. Even a cursory look at any social institution makes us aware that it would be wrong to imagine that no institution is homogeneous, and, therefore, not really coherent or consistent as far as the various groups – strata of people are concerned. Even secular education, in spite of all the efforts made to provide a common syllabus and examination system is far from homogeneous, which is very well-known, leave aside the institutions of marriage, family, religion, stratification, etc. Several assumptions were made about inevitable sequence as well as determinateness of processes like urbanization, industrialization and modernization, which also, on a further scrutiny, have proved to be without strong foundation. The First World expects itself to provide a model both for the Second and the Third World and for the last particularly so. A kind of unilinearity is implicit in this formulation. It is also expected that every society will try to change and develop itself economically, socio-culturally and politically without falling apart – again an assumption based on a particular historical experience of the West. It is customary to forget that the very process of change and development necessitates an increasing access, if not equal access, to the various facilities implicit in the process of change and development, which again is not the case and that is why the various attempts made for development create more imbalances and, therefore, also pose the problem of conflict rather than an orderly change and development. Change and development have to be both systemic and systematic – neither of which is borne out by empirical reality. Systemic change means change in the 'core institutions' of society, as Lockwood puts it. Systematic change means a rationally planned and programmed change which can be effected so as to bring forth the desired results. Even in this case, the empirical reality does not support such a claim. Without socialization, conformity to the existing mechanisms – norms, values, patterns of behaviour, interaction and relationship would again not be possible. It is here that one would question the kind of overemphasis on social facts which are regarded as both given and immutable like physical, geographical environment by Durkheim. On the other hand, as mentioned earlier, every individual wants to alter the existing system of relationship, hierarchy, stratification and power, so as to make life congenial for himself or herself. Whether or not everyone is able to control the situation in which he or she finds himself or herself to his or her complete satisfaction, there is no denying the persistence of efforts he or she makes in this direction. In his remarkably lucid and incisive analysis of anomie and social structure, Merton (1957: 131–94) has drawn our attention to this poignant fact. Apart from deviance which is generally disapproved, Merton also emphasizes both the possibility and probability of rebellion against the existing social system – arrangements, relations, ideas, interests and values play a very significant role in impelling members of a society to express their resentment against the existing arrangements, which may even take the shape of appropriate ideological justification for mobilizing to bring about systemic change.

Some of the important authors mentioned above like Gouldner, Atkinson, and Bottomore have also questioned this basic premise of social structure on which sociological theory has so far rested. Thus, Gouldner (1971: 40) draws our attention to the importance of taking into account personal reality rather than social reality in the construction of social theory. He, therefore, challenges the autonomy of social structure as domain assumptions of sociological theory (ibid.: 51). Of course, Gouldner is both candid and careful enough to point out as to how even Soviet sociology has, apparently paradoxically, accepted the mandate of societal integration which is a very important assumption and requirement of western sociological theory (ibid.: 465). Atkinson (1972: 6) has addressed himself to the task of examination of the individual person, situational logic and the elements of situational analysis. The sociological view of the individual, his action, the meaning he gives to that action and its significance for other people is reassessed in the light of this analysis. Inevitably, we are forced to explore choice, and the extent to which the individual shapes and controls his social situation. This forces us to reconstruct the sociological view of the relationship between the individual and social structure and indeed to question the very concept of 'structure itself'.

Atkinson has very rightly questioned complete common denominator being provided by class to any individual and asserts that every individual tries to meet other people on his own terms (Damle, 1984). In fact, social structures are kaleidoscopic in their nature, instead of being unified. Individual interaction is characterized a great deal by co-operation, consensus and conflict depending upon the needs of his situation. In a way therefore, it should be emphasized in all seriousness that what was taken for granted, namely, social structure as a functioning composite, unified and accepted reality, really should be taken as a point of departure and as such questioned from time to time.

NECESSITY AND VARIOUS MODALITIES OF CHANGING SOCIAL STRUCTURE

Social structure cannot be unified or composite, because inherently it is based on division of labour, which is linked with stratification. It is indeed well-known that different units of society are not only differentiated but also discriminated against on the basis of age, sex, ethnicity, ranking of occupations, possession of power, authority and domination or its absence. While it may be argued that the existing system of stratification is accorded legitimacy by all those who are the beneficiaries of the system of stratification, there is also a continuous rejection and challenge posed to the system of stratification, naturally by the 'have nots'. It should be further pointed out that such discontent and the necessary efforts made to challenge and change the system of stratification is not confined to the 'have nots' only, but individuals from the 'haves' also develop this feeling which is transformed into conviction by rational analysis as well as intellectual and moral conviction, which again is a function of evolving appropriate ideology. As mentioned earlier, social space and time adds another dimension to the heterogeneity of social structure which paves the way for changing it. Continuous emphasis placed on open society and the resulting competition which is inherently unequal, gives rise to the disequilibrium. It is customary to emphasize contradictions in a society mainly pertaining to the material plane. However, it is equally important to emphasize contradictions on ideational plane as well, which makes it difficult for persons belonging to different strata and groups to accept the dominant ideational matrix. Due to modern technology, particularly the influence of mass media and of course the efforts made to make a society more and more open, one comes across the phenomenon of reference group behaviour. While the reference group behaviour does not necessarily pose a threat to the existing order, lack of access to the means, due to which one can acquire control over one's situation, opens an avenue for not only discontent but also for challenging the existing arrangements. The ideology of open society and structural constraints to realize the same in practice, in which every kind of society, whether it is based on freedom of enterprise or is a centrally planned economy and polity, would necessitate mobilization by the deprived and disprivileged too, to develop modalities to alter the arrangements for their benefit. The ideology of open society further sharpens the phenomenon of relative deprivation which adds an edge to not only dissatisfaction and discontent, but also to the necessity of mobilization. That is how social movements encompassing dissent, protest and transformation start. Yet there is no denying the fact that the state, in the sense of ruling or dominating groups in a society, by anticipating such discontent, dissatisfaction and the likelihood of the emergence of social movements, may throw certain sops and try to nip in the bud any concerted movement. Both Gouldner and Atkinson have pointed out the concept of welfare state as a very significant example of efforts to assuage the feeling of discontent and dissatisfaction amongst people. All the same, even a cursory glance at the working of the welfare state in various kinds of systems does not warrant our pinning of complete faith in the efficacy of the welfare state in permanently avoiding any possibility of social movement. It can be said, without much fear of contradiction, that every state has an inherent tendency to not only discriminate between various interest groups but to perpetuate such discrimination and differentiation with the help of the authority it may enjoy or even more so with the help of the use of power, e.g., discrimination between urban and rural, elite and common people, industry and agriculture and so on. As such the functioning of a welfare state is not acceptable in the long run. There is thus a dialectics between structure and the efforts made to perpetuate it in all its differentiation, discrimination and inequities and the efforts made to challenge and change it. Viewed from this angle, Alain Touraine's (1981) emphasis that social structures should be looked at as social movements, acquires significance.

Thus, the importance of examining social structure or system from the point of view of its being unacceptable to certain sections of society and the relevant efforts made to change it, even though unsuccessfully, should really constitute the agenda of sociological theory; otherwise such theory may not have any relevance to the existing and ever changing reality. Due to the kalaedoscopic nature of social structure, social reality is not only heterogeneous but presents a picture of competing, not to say conflicting views from which it is perceived and lived. This is certainly not to underrate the efforts made by the state – ruling elite either to maintain the status-quo or to provide the palliatives, so that the urge to fight for radical transformation is not only watered down, but can also be neutralized, although temporarily.

INDIAN SOCIAL REALITY

Sociology as an academic discipline was introduced by the British, more specifically by Patrick Geddes in Bombay University in 1919. Patrick Geddes was greatly concerned with urban planning and as such even here the introduction of the discipline was in a way in response to the prospective crisis. While G.S. Ghurye, the first incumbent of the Chair in Sociology in Bombay University was certainly concerned with the crisis created by the British rule, and as such mainly addressed himself to the study of traditional and time honoured institutions like caste, family and kinship, religion, urban civilization, integration of the 'so-called' aboriginees in the wider stream (Hindu civilization) and the challenges forced by the British rule. Radhakamal Mukherjee was greatly concerned with the imbalance, not to say crisis, created in Indian society by the British rule, seen in the field of industrialization, emerging dehumanization and crisis of values. D.P. Mukerji also felt a threat to the erstwhile pattern of integration and adjustment in Indian society by the British rule and later on after independence focused his attention on the capitalist path of planning and development and advocated adoption of the Marxian methodology to overcome such crisis. Ramakrishna Mukherjee pinpointed attention on the breakdown of village economy and society. D.R. Gadgil very pointedly analyzed the breakdown of the handicraft industry in India as a result of British rule and the impoverishment of India. Of course, the impoverishment of India was very sharply focused by Dadabhai Naoroji, M.G. Ranade and others, but it was Tarlok Singh who wrote directly on 'Poverty and Social Change'. Of course, Vinay Kumar Sarkar had written very incisively on the capacity of the Indian society to integrate diverse cultural elements which was *rudely* stopped by the intrusion of the British rule.

Thus, in India too, sociology was concerned with dealing with crisis situations. Tacit acceptance of a historical approach by some scholars in the post-independence period and undue emphasis on integration had made the study of sociology rather unrealistic. On the other hand, atheoretical and *adhoc* studies undertaken with a view to provide solutions to trivial problems like the adoption of smokeless *chullahs* or pit latrines also posed a threat to the discipline of sociology. As is well known, the persistent economic and political crisis in India in the late sixties and seventies again called for a critical examination of sociological concepts, postulates and theories (Damle, 1984).

The foregoing discussion about the viability of the concept of social structure and the increasingly felt necessity of emphasizing the importance of contradictions inherent in a given social structure and therefore, emergent conflict and concerned effort to transform the structure are illustrated with reference to Indian society. I am fully aware that this exercise is confined purely to illustrations and comprehensive discussion is deferred.

SOME CHARACTERISTICS OF INDIAN SOCIETY

In a society, which has a very long protracted history and also a formidable (subcontinental) geography, it would be both necessary and realistic to take cognizance of substructures while indulging in structural analysis. Indian society cannot be understood except in terms of sub-structures and the various levels at which it exists and functions, right from the most sophisticated level to the most antiquated.

Several efforts have been made to document the working of various institutions like marriage, family, religion, property, inheritance, education, economy and polity and in their quest for arriving at a modicum of structural, universal propositions, several amendments have to be made both in terms of historicity and the geographical spread of the people, not to say the technology practised by them. There is also a bewildering variety of various social mechanisms and regulations underlying these institutions mentioned broadly. This only means again that neither the institutions nor the structure can be regarded as homogeneous. Several formulations are made about the dichotomy between simple and complex society, unilinear development, evolution or mutation, uniliner (determinate) development or skipping certain stages which is particularly noticed in the case of ideas, ideologies and even advanced learning in India. It needs to be stated that additionally and ideologically Indian society has accepted certain norms and ethical principles which took the West a couple of centuries both to evolve and accept. Similarly high technology and science have also been the watchwords for India, although confronted with mass illiteracy. The multifaceted and multilayered Indian social reality, therefore, needs to be tested more carefully using various theoretical propositions.

Dealing with Indian society, it becomes even more pertinent to be conscious of the dimensions of space and time, because one is apt to blur these dimensions and lose track of the diachronic aspect of the existing social reality. It would not be wrong to say that even in present times there are certain units and groups in Indian society which do not belong to social space exemplified by time and vice versa. On the other hand, some individuals and groups have already turned themselves to the twenty-first century in terms of their educational equipment, mental make-up and capacity for innovation, risk taking and proneness to attitudinal and mental change. In the Indian context, the group to which one belongs is specially important in terms of ethnicity, caste, religion and language. It would not be wrong to say that these groupings also reflect cultural, economic, technological, political and social institutionwise differentiation, hierarchy, discrimination and domination. As for institutions, the obvious example which comes to one's mind is marriage and kinship, various differentiations made on the basis of sex, age, education, occupation, income, status and power. In spite of these groupings and pigeon-holing of individuals into these groups and their respective status, there is absolutely no denying the fact that it would be erroneous to imagine that groupings determine completely and beyond repair the status and role relevant to them. Even in the purely religious and philosophical field, it is very well-known as to how the different categories (*varnas*) registered their demands not to say protest for throwing open the path of salvation to them. The emergence of the Bhakti movement in the four corners of India is too well known to need any further elaboration. Similarly, the fight for supremacy between the Brahmins and the Kshatriyas and the battles between Brahminism and Buddhism is also very well known. Access to education and knowledge of the resulting prestige and status had also been a bone of contention. In short, it can be said that, though not significant in terms of its magnitude, there has always been dissent, protest, if not a movement, to change the status of a role carrier and to demand the freedom attendant on the status of a 'person'.

STRUCTURE AS A COMPOSITE WHOLE

In Indian society, systematic efforts have been made to provide the composite system by facilitating integration through the division of labour based on caste. Notwithstanding the eulogizing of such division of labour and consequent integration of society, it should be mentioned that more often than not, such division of labour was anomic in its character and, therefore, failed to bring forth the required kind of integration. Further, the division of Indian society into rural and urban, agricultural and industrial has also meant schism in the social structure. This schism further divided the society, creating difficulties in the process of integration of Indian society. It would be unrealistic to imagine that the division of Indian society, along the lines mentioned above, was acceptable to all its participants. Both on account of ideational and material interests, such a division would not be acceptable, even though rejection of such division may not be always possible for those at the receiving end.

STRATIFICATION

Age, sex, caste, and class have been the time honoured bases of differentiation, hierarchy and discrimination. Additional complication is added by distinction between the achieved status and ascribed status, traditional and modern, sacred and secular, and particularly because of the interplay between these polarities, whereby what looks like achieved status is not really so. On further scrutiny, the same could be said about what is modern or what is secular. In one of my papers, I had written about the imposition of the achieved over the ascribed, modern over the traditional and so on. In fact, the dynamics between these polarities has to be taken note of, in order to understand the process of social mobility in Indian society or rather the impediments in the attainment of social mobility. However, it would be useful to remember that these bases have not been entirely acceptable to the various members of Indian society. Indian history is replete with instances of dissent, protest and social movements. It has been often said that social reforms have been specific to a given stratum, i.e., that social reforms particularly pertaining to age at marriage, education of women, independence of individuals and so on have been the major concerns and problems of higher castes, classes and urban based individuals, leaving high and dry the problem of structural change; which alone would eliminate the inequities inherent in the system based on caste, occupation, status, prestige and power. Even then, it must be remembered that launching of non-Brahmin mass movements in different parts of the country is quite symptomatic of the refusal to accept the system of stratification.

PATTERNS AND AVENUES OF MOBILITY

In spite of caste, being a major determinant of status, prestige and power, there have been several instances of certain careers and vocations being open to everyone such as the career of a ruler or that of a cultivator. Due to the exposure to new ideas and values, there has been a significant and appreciable rise in the level of aspirations with respect to modern education, secular jobs, urbanization and emancipation from the traditional constraints imposed by caste and stratification. One witnesses a proliferation of educational institutions amongst all castes and classes with a view to facilitate mobility. One cannot fail to witness the adroit use made of traditional loyalties, groupings and mechanisms like kinship, caste, solidarities based on ethnicity, religion and language, to further one's prospects on the secular plane, in monetization of village economy, making successful demands for getting a fair price for agricultural products and even more so by greater political participation in ruling and domination, modern higher education and secular jobs which alone can made possible freedom, dignity and a fair means of subsistence for the people. Reference group behaviour can be significantly noted (compare the state of Pulayas by Alexander in Kerala). However, it also cannot be denied that there are several limits to reference group behaviour which would really ensure the establishment of a civil society.

CIVIL SOCIETY

Civil society is characterized by the rule of law and by transition from the society based on status to that based on contract. Likewise, it is an open society and as such, it accepts the principle of competition rather than status quo. It should not, however, be forgotten that if competition is unequal it perpetuates contradictions which can be resolved only by conflict. Open society, as already mentioned, provides avenues for reference group behaviour, to which as we have already seen, there are limits. Phenomenon of relative deprivation acquires greater importance which enhances both competition and conflict.

In spite of the efforts to establish a civil society and, therefore, implementation of the rule of law, if there is the rule of dominant groups, where caste, ethnicity, economic and political power may play a significant role, then the rule of law would not be really effective in practice which is exemplified by lack of access to facility, lack of justice, etc. Since India has opted for a democratic framework, people's participation acquires a very vital importance and yet as various studies of development like economic, scientific, technological as well as political demonstrate, because of differential access to facilities, the process of development is neither coherent nor congruent. In fact, the very concept of development has been very rightly questioned and is increasingly regarded as questionable particularly when the concept is lifted from different historical experiences. Of course, we also note that access to facilities like education, status, prestige, and health is also limited, making the rule of law ineffective in the bargain.

STATE INTERVENTION

We have already noted as to how a welfare state can in a way subvert the logical culmination of contradiction in a social structure into radical movements. In the Indian case what we have is state intervention rather than a welfare state. Framing the constitution does not necessarily mean a tacit acceptance of new ideas and values enshrined about equality, freedom and human dignity, social justice, secularism and socialism. However, recourse was taken to legislation which as we known has not been properly implemented due to persistent pressure of vested interests – social, cultural, economic and political.

Calculations about vote catching have thwarted the process of the acceptance of a common civil code for all the constituents of

Indian society. The fiscal policies practised by the state, perpetuate the rural-urban, agricultural and industrial differences and discrimination so that the implementation of the constitution has become well-nigh impossible. The policy of co-optation in the political process has in a way taken the wind out of the sails of protest and mobilization by purchasing leaders from different strata of society, particularly the deprived and disprivileged. The failure to implement the rules enshrined in the constitution gives rise to the persistence of anomie which reflects structural contradictions, again emphasizing the point that the Indian social structure is *not* a composite, unified, integrated whole.

A great deal has been written about the importance of leadership; placing a good deal of faith in the capacity of the leaders to steer common masses to the desired goal, i.e., social justice, human dignity, freedom, secularism, rationality and so on. However, before pinning so much faith on the leadership, it is very important to inquire into the composition of the leadership. It would not be out of place to mention here that the various leaders of different social movements in India were *very* highly educated, urban-based and from the upper middle class. Even in respect of representative leadership through the ballot box, several studies point in the direction of the elitist composition of such representatives and leaders. Co-operation and collusion between various elites would certainly give rise to a situation where the common man will hardly have any say in the process of decision making, policy formulation and of course its implementation. Max Weber raised questions about legitimate authority and suggested ideal types – legal rational authority, traditional authority and charismatic authority. In India, we find various permutations and combinations of the three types of authority existing at different levels, rendering the situation more difficult to handle.

To overcome some of these contradictions, there has been a simultaneous working of various movements, such as labour movements both in the industrial and agricultural field, student movements, political movements and now a science movement – all with the avowed aim of proper social action to make minimum facilities available to everyone, so that the fruits of development can accrue to everyone, so that traditional dependency and exploitation can be sufficiently challenged, if not ended.

Thus, even with the help of a few illustrations from the Indian case, it can be said that 'social structure' has to be treated as a point of departure rather than as an existing and acceptable reality. Moreover, the utilization of segments of the structure for furthering one's prospects also means fragmentation of the 'structure'. Likewise, theories of unilinear and unidirectional development and the projected consequences for different social institutions such as family, kinship, caste and language has not been borne out in reality. As Merton has very thoughtfully and forcefully pointed out, empirical study is extremely necessary for revising, reformulating and even rejecting the existing theory. I would add that a critical and continuous examination of the theoretical presuppositions is called for.

References

Atkinson, Dick, 1972, *Orthodox Consensus and Radical Alternative*, New York, Basic Books Inc., Publishers.

Bottomore, Tom, (ed.), 1975, *Crisis and Contention in Sociology*, Sage Studies in International Sociology.

Damle, Y.B., 1982, *Caste, Religion and Politics in India*, New Delhi, Oxford and IBH.

—, 1984, *Problems and Perspectives in the Study of Sociology*, Presidential Address to the Indian Sociological Conference.

—, 1985, *Survey of Research in Sociology and Social Anthropology*, 1969–79, Indian Council of Social Science Research, Delhi, Satvahan.

—, 'Group Theory with Regard to Mobility Within Caste', in *Bulletin of Deccan College Research Institute*, Vol. 23.

Gouldner, Alvin, W., 1971, *The Coming Crisis of Western Sociology*, London/ New Delhi, Heinemann.

Merton, Robert K., 1957, *Social Theory and Social Structure*, Glencoe, Illinois, Free Press.

Touraine, Alain, 1981, *The Voice and the Eye – An Analysis of Social Movements*, Cambridge University Press, *Editions de la Maison des Sciences de I'Hommes*.

21

Indian Social Reality
For Paradigm-Bridging

H.C. Srivastava

PARADIGMATIC STATUS OF SOCIOLOGY IN INDIA

Is 'tradition fix' the logical universal of Indian sociology? From this question crop up a set of questions. What is the character of knowledge in Indian sociology? Is there any reigning paradigm or multiple-paradigm scheme?[1] Whether the paradigmatic scheme in Indian sociology is discrete, closed or open system paradigm. What is the presupposition of sociology in India? Whether the postulates of functionalism were really operationalized in Indian sociology or it is simple survey with discrete variables. What are the epistemological categories frequently employed in explanation? What basic categories of Indian sociology have been reinforced by categories in other social science discipline or vice versa? How is that, Indian sociologists are in search of the prime mover immanent in social structures? Social structure is *that* which determines end-means schema. What is *that*? *What* is value. In Indian sociology, *what* is tradition – 'great-little/east-west/ritual-secular/India-specific, universal'. Thus, sociological reasoning is either circular or tautological. This type of epistemological position, in spite of its explanatory value, delimits the scope and image of the subject-matter of sociology in India as it was in the post-French Revolution sociology in Europe. The scope and subject-matter of sociology should be enlarged to assimilate what is being done in other social science disciplines where a shift in paradigm has taken place. There are not a few but many in the profession who realize the need of paradigm shift. If there are 'emerging concerns' in Indian sociology then why not articulate them, lest sociology loses its credibility (an audience).

Indian 'specific tradition' was problematic to the so-called 'pioneers' of sociology in India but for the contemporary traditionalist in Indian sociology relativism[2] is not problematic. Indian tradition, for them, is adopting, modernizing, and evolving (like the Hegalian spirit). Tradition remains the core content of Indian sociology, other things are externalities. On the occasion of the Eleventh World Congress of Sociology,[3] a trend report entitled *Indian sociology* with sub-title *Social Conditioning and Emerging Concerns* was a published (Singh, 1986). Indian sociology, like the Pavolovian organism, is being conditioned by stimulus from outside it. The 'emerging concerns' are not its real concerns but irritants from stimulating interaction with political economy, social history, economics and world-system studies. The processes of 'conditioning' and 'emerging' are the externalities of Indian sociology. In other words, tradition as the inner core of Indian sociology should not be shifted, it is a metaphysical entity, a fetish.

Sociology in India began in combination rather than specialization in combination with economics, social philosophy, anthropology, indology and political philosophy. The active core of sociology became defensive exploring and establishing the positive aspects of Hinduism. It has, as yet, not been relieved of this burden. The trend thrives upon the sloganized search for something 'Indian' 'ours' against the western sociological concepts and methods. As if, Indian tradition is something else than an evolving process of acculturation. Some of the eminent men in the profession of sociology in India are in search of residual entity (subjective or transcendental) a priori as the indigenous 'something' against the western sociology. For them social science is not possible. The indigenous reality is *amnaya* (triangleness of triangle) like the substance of Spinoza.[4] This is non-issue in sociology. Sociology need not commit suicide in search of the ultimate symbol. The non-issue is tenaciously epistemic in nature. The so-called logico-philosophical approach (without logic) of Indian sociology culminated in archetypes (as structures of consciousness) of traditional thought. The archetypes of Great Tradition were discovered by Dumont. The reality of Indian tradition was not beautific. The logico-philosophical approach is regressive time and again like the Jungian racial unconscious mind for timeless elements in Indian tradition. Unlike the French structuralists interpreting psycho-analytical theories, Indian scholars of tradition are going beyond Dumont's *Homo Hierarchicus* to justify the indigenous search of tradition or tradition-like substance. The substance (residual, transcendental, archetypal) is not subject to logical scrutiny. 'Indianness' is the only logic. Sanskrit language is the only store-house of this knowledge.[5] Some of the scholars are so sure of the ultimate tradition in the East, as if, there was no tradition of transcendentalism in western philosophy and culture. For them Indianness is bliss. We fully respect such type of thinking and thinkers. Our contention is that sociology is 'wrong place' for them. The logico-philosophical approach, from its early start in Indian sociology, remained underdeveloped in hermeneutics. Only three names of exponents of this approach are mentioned (Singh, 1986: 12). Except one, the others made no substantive contribution. *Modernization of Indian Tradition* is the first and the last work in social historicism.[6]

Another serious confusion that emerged out of the logico-philosophical approach is 'social thought' identical with 'society' or 'culture'. No distinction is made between Hindu ethic, Manu's code (*varna-ashrama, dharma, karma, purusarthas*) and historical Indian society as such. Whereas ancient history and culture, as emerged in time-space, are hardly the concern of sociological teaching in India. This happened because the logico-philosophical approach has no sound epistemology to acquire and distinguish 'social thought' from 'social reality'. Ancient scriptures and *Puranas* are, no doubt, sources of history. Social reality in space-time dimension is constructed from these sources. Our sociologists do not believe in constructing social reality. They preserve a fictitious distinction between sociology and history. The art of sociology in India confused the image of value as image of fact.

Indian sociology, in general, adopted neo-positivism with a Weberian touch. It continues to search motivational spirit of social action, social type or social institutions. Attitude and values (as aspects of culture) are the major concern of contemporary sociological research to find out how motivation and social institutions have been 'caging' wholeness of life in terms of primordial loyalty. Even colonial history has no relevance to many sociologists. The community development programmes were evaluated exclusively in motivational terms by the Indian rural sociologists in accordance with the American sociological impact. One is surprised to note that many of the rural sociological studies were without reference to agrarian institutions (land use, tenancy rights and agricultural practices). They were mainly confined to caste and tradition. Even the human actors (the peasants) were absent from some of the reputed studies. Peasant movement studies are late entries in Indian sociology. Barring a few, structural-functional paradigms are not used by many. India remained a historyless society in Indian sociology along with the discrete variables.

The Marxist trend in Indian sociology was brushed aside. *The Rise and Fall of the East India Company*, or *Social Background of Indian Nationalism*[7] were valued more by the students of modern history and political science than the students of sociology. The pioneer Marxists were valued in Indian sociology for their non-Marxist works. For Indian sociology, India-in-history does not exist, only history of ideas exist as *India*. Dichotomous typical forms of sanskritic, de-sanskritic, great and little, mega, non-mega codes, crowd-commonality were conceived representing Indian culture and society. The real India, as formed from stone age to green revolution, found no place in Indian sociology. Social institutions, as variables, remained *hypothetical isolates*. The British government was quick to realize the inherent potentiality of sociology, therefore, it offered financial assistance in 1914 to Bombay University for starting the discipline of sociology. The same realization emerged upon the USA when in early fifties it made a distinction between plans of aggression and plans of defence. American foreign aid programmes of defence were conceived to meet the challenge of the communist appeal to the undeveloped people of subsistence economy and anti-capitalist animus. The American academic understanding about 'natural conservatism' of peasantry required social science guidance.[8] In order to cover 'all activities' of relatively industrialized countries in promoting the economic development of undeveloped countries 'social science guidance is needed by government agencies (of the United States and other countries) by international organization, by business concerns, and by private non-profit agencies, and it is needed in capital investment and business activities as well as in technical co-operation activities.'[9]

The sociologists were supposed to be 'the native intelligentsia' worthy of developing an ethos and system of values to combat communism. We do not subscribe to a conspiracy theory behind the American interest and thrust in sociology for India but the American ideology of modernization, so valued in the sixties, collapsed before the world-systems and dependencia paradigms. The paradigms of development or underdevelopment and neo-colonialism made irrelevant the impact from abroad syndrome. Sociology in India struggled in 'its overarching, symbolic, subjectivist and culturological tendency *than* the structures of political economy, power structure and social order' (Singh, 1986: 25). From *than* mentioned above, emerges the need for new paradigms for sociology in India today. In other words, the distinction between representation as social structure (Dumont and Pocock) and 'facts of behaviour' should be given up. Inter-culture and intra-culture comparability would not lead us beyond the diffusionist approach, enshrined in evolutionary or conflict models.

FOR PARADIGM-BRIDGING

'Convergence' and 'influence' on sociology are the terms used to denote what has been consistently done in other social science disciplines, such as economics and history (Singh, 1986: 26). The debate on the dominant mode of production in Indian agriculture, differentiation of peasantry, ancient and medieval social history and subaltern studies in social movement could be cited as instances. All these studies are explanatory in nature and based on paradigms quite different in Indian sociology. The structuralist-Marxist and structuralist-phenomenological subaltern studies (consciousness and culture of elite and non-elite) are presumed to have resemblance with Great and Little Traditions and their modernization in Indian sociological studies. Without being hypocritic, there is neither convergence nor influence but a lag to be bridged. One is tempted to quote a reviewer who locates 'lagging behind' syndrome of Indian sociology in functionalism and behavioural techniques and jargons.[10] What is worth paradigm-mix is not in sociology but outside sociology. A plea for convergence is an apologia, not intended reality.

The crucial issue is not successive paradigms in Indian sociology. A more viable proposition could be paradigm-bridging or integrated insights from different paradigms.[11] Theory-specific paradigms (Marxism, Freudian, Weberian, phenomenological, ethnomethodological, symbolic interactionist, exchange, etc.) are not common in Indian sociology. The reigning paradigm is discrete paradigm (ecological properties, size of groups, caste hierarchy, psychological characteristics, etc.) in Indian sociology. The closed system paradigms (interconnected elements) are seldom used. Tradition, either evolutionary, diffusionist or both, constitutes the only dimension of certain degree of unified paradigm. Diffusion of tradition into the base, or to say in Marxian terms, diffusion of super structure into the basic structure would have been a fruitful dimension of exploration, but Indian sociology had made no serious attempt on this dimension.

We refrain from saying what paradigms should be rejected. Our submission is to incorporate a few to achieve paradigm-bridging if viable in continuity of the existing paradigms.

Sociology in India is too much person-centric (attitude and values) and committed to social institutions as frozen data from history. Agrarian institutions (like tenancy, market, usuary, etc.) and contractual relationship are kept outside the social institutional matrix. Our contention is that *contractual relationship* should be given paradigmatic significance in Indian sociology (Srivastava and Chaturvedi, 1986).

The role of state in recombination of Indian society remains a neglected field in Indian sociology. Occasional reference to constitutionalism is not paradigmic. Caste remains the 'pope theory' of Indian sociology. Expanded presence of interventionist state in the process of social change could hardly be overlooked (Srivastava, 1987). The entrepreneurial role of state, so detrimental to social dynamics, deserves paradigmic significance to relieve Indian sociology from theoretic blindness.

World system is regarded as the instance of classic paradigm-shift in social science but sociology in India remained unmoved in its practice about world-system paradigms. The concept of westernization or modernization are no substitute to the phases of imperialism and phenomenon of neo-colonialism. There are so many slogans in world-system theorization. We do not insist upon accepting or rejecting one in favour of the other. Our submission is to study Indian society in world-system context.[12] World-system paradigms present a set of conditions of existence of national societies, particularly of the Third World. A nation-state, along with its national society, is deeply entrenched in the world-system. Sociology in India has to give adequate analytical significance to the 'response' of the nation-state and society to the world system factors.

A 'paradigmatic break' is interpreted often to mean introducing new paradigms. Sociology cannot start a-new. There are no sudden discoveries or inventions in social life to demolish existing matrix of knowledge in favour of the new. A sudden paradigmatic break is not viable in social science. Lag is possible in face of competitive paradigms. Paradigm-bridging may resolve the anomalies which the earlier paradigms failed to do.

Notes

1. Kuhn debunks the commonly held assumption that slow and steady increments of knowledge change science. Not cumulation but revolutions bring major changes in a science. A crisis stage occurs in the normal science leading to paradigm change. The paradigm is the broadest insight of consensus within a science and serves to differentiate one scientific community from another. Most sciences are dominated not by

single paradigm but multiple paradigms. Kuhn, Thomas, *The Structure of Scientific Revolution*, Chicago, University of Chicago Press, 1962.

2. The doctrine of uniqueness of historical meaning (tradition in Indian sociological context) creates an extreme epistemological relativism. 'It is maintained, therefore, that knowledge as a system of meanings cannot be properly appraised without rooting it to a given time, that moment or its formation in history.' Bershady Harold, *Ideology and Social Knowledge*, Bristol: Oxford Basil Blackwell, 1973, p. 29. Tradition in Indian sociology is distinct from Gadamer's hermeneutic concept of tradition or Wittgenstein's notion of forms of life.
3. Eleventh World Congress of Sociology was held at New Delhi on August 18–24, 1986.
4. The residual concepts of tradition (A.K. Saran) or *amnaya* (something a priori) beyond tradition may have meaning as the ultimate reality as metaphysical issue but this ultimate is non-issue in social sciences.
5. Hinduism and Brahmanical ideas and values have formed the core element of unity. Pramanick quotes G.S. Ghurye: 'I am a firm believer that whoever wants to do sociology in India in particular, must have a thorough grounding in Sanskrit literature. Latently, it is a plea for culture unity in India which is essentially the result of the Brahmans endeavour.' Pramanick, S.K., 'Historic Evolutionary Approach in Sociology of G.S. Ghurye', *Sociological Bulletin*, Vol. 31, No. 1, March 1982.
6. Singh, Yogendra, *Modernization of Indian Tradition*, Delhi, Thomson, 1973.
7. Mukherjee, Ramkrishna, *The Rise and Fall of the East India Company*, Berlin: Verlag der Wislen Schaften, 1958; and Desai, A.R., *Social Background of Indian Nationalism*, Bombay: Popular Prakashan, 1966.
8. 'During the 1950s, British and European influence on the Indian sociology declined. There was an ascendance of American influence both in academic and political domains.' Singh, Yogendra, *Indian sociology: Social Conditioning and Emerging Concerns*, Delhi: Vistaar Publications, 1986, pp. 98–99.
9. Haidyes, Sammuel, R., 'Personality and Culture in Point IV'; Watnick, Morris, 'The Appeal to Communism to the Underdeveloped People', in Haselitx, Berth, F. (ed.), *The Progress of Underdeveloped Area*, Chicago: University of Chicago Press, 1952, p. 204.
10. A survey report of International Sociological Associations Research Committee on Economy and Society observed: 'Practically all or 90 per cent of our respondents indicated that Marxist or neo-Marxist approaches are not often used in the study of the economy and society.' The reviewer comments: 'While in the West the post-behavioural revolution was proclaimed to have taken place about two decades ago, in India many social scientists continue to spend much of their time in learning behavioural techniques and jargon. The reason for such

backwardness seems to be that functionalism and behaviouralism constitute the best available ideology for our dependent monopoly capitalism.' Deva, Satya, 'Social Science of Dependency', *Economic and Political Weekly*, Vol. XXII, No. 46, November 14, 1987.

11. Eisenstadt and Curelaru, *The Form of Sociology: Paradigm and Crisis*, New York, 1976; Ritzer, George, *Toward an Integrated Paradigm*, 1981, *Passim*, Hill, Bckberg, Lee, 'The Paradigm Concept and Sociology: A Critical Review', *American Sociological Review*, Vol. 44, 1979.

    Srivastava, H.C., and M.K. Chaturvedi, *Rural Middlemen: Network of Patronage*, New Delhi: Ashish Publications, 1986.

    Srivastava, H.C., 'State and Path of Development in India', *Mainstream*, Vol. XXV, No. 35, May 16, 1987.

12. The world-system paradigms assumed that most significant social, economic and political phenomena in the modern world can be understood in terms of capital accumulation, hierarchical coreperiphery division of labour. World-system paradigms are directed toward a wide range of theoretical questions: 'These include social change and modernization, the transformation and evolution of the world-system, the development of capitalism, industrialization, and the national-state, the accumulation and distribution of wealth and rise of imperialism and dependency, and conflict and the leading political entities.' Thompson, W.R., (ed.), *Contending Approaches to World System*, London: Sage Publication, 1983, p. 184; Chaturvedi, M.K. and Srivastava, H.C., 'Underdevelopment and World Capitalist System', paper presented in Eleventh World Congress of Sociology, New Delhi, 1986.

References

Singh, Yogendra, 1986, *Indian sociology: Social Conditioning and Emerging Congress*, New Delhi: Vistaar Publications.

Srivastava, H.C. and Chaturvedi, M.K., 1986, *Rural Middlemen: Network of Patronage*, New Delhi, Ashish Publications.

Srivastava, H.C., 1987, 'State and Path of Development in India', *Mainstream*, Vol. 25, No. 35, May 16.

22

Sociology in India
A Sociology of Knowledge Perspective

Surendra Sharma

We intend to discuss sociology in India from the point of its theory, methodology and data in this paper. We shall limit our discussion mainly to the debate that has appeared in *Contributions to Indian Sociology* including the one in New Series, articles that have appeared in *Sociological Bulletin* and *Economic and Political Weekly* and a couple of other articles and books that have come out on this theme. The emphasis in the debate is on: whether sociology in India should concern itself with the study of values or it should study *relations*. The corollary of this question is: whether the approach would be indological (or culturological) or comparative. The main points of interest in a study are the *method* of study and the *material* to be studied. Now the question is: Is indology a history? Is indological study diachronic in nature? How far a study of relations would do justice to diachrony? The question whether Indian society should be studied 'from within' or 'from without' or from both 'within and without' has also been taken up in view of the 'complexity', 'diversity', and 'unity' of Indian society. This refers to what is known as 'home-made model' and 'external point of view'. In other words, it poses the problem of culturology versus positivism for studying Indian society. It is said that D.P. Mukerji had 'positive-cum-subjective' approach by combining the view from within (study of tradition) and the view from without (Marxology). This point is related to the nature of Indian sociology in regards to its universal versus specific nature.

What is the nature of sociology in India? There cannot be a straight answer to this question. It is Hindu sociology – is one view; it is Indian sociology – is another. It is indological or culturological or it is universal, (general) positivistic social science – is a different view. It has the hangover of British colonialism and the academic hegemony of the West on the one hand, and the input of the 'Hindu chauvinism' and Indian nationalism on the other.

How to arrange the material on the nature of Indian sociology from 1957 to 1982 (over a quarter century) in this paper is really a problem before us. There is no order in the debate over these years. The same questions and points have been raised back and forth. We shall take up the debate the way it has grown, but our main points of discussion would revolve round theory, method and data. Our impression is that the debate has concentrated more on theory and method than data. There has been an effort to classify the literature on Indian sociology from a theoretical perspective right from 1965.[1] Recently, Ramakrishna Mukherjee[2] and R.S. Khare[3] have also provided classifications of sociologists engaged in researches on India. We shall analyze these classifications and other analytic schemes.

A SOCIOLOGY OF VALUES OR A VALUE-LOADED SOCIOLOGY

Dumont and Pocock, in the first article of the first number of *Contributions to Indian Sociology*, suggest their viewpoint 'for a sociology of India'.[4] They write: 'In our opinion, the first condition for a sound development of a sociology of India is found in the establishment of the proper relation between it and classical sociology. We wish to show how on one side the construction of an *Indian sociology* (emphasis added) rests in part upon the existence of Indology and how, on the other hand, far from its results being confined to its own domain, it can hope in its turn to widen and deepen the understanding of India, present and past, to which indology is devoted.'[5]

They further observe: 'In principle, a sociology of India lies at the point of confluence of sociology and indology.'[6] R.N. Saxena agrees with this indological or scriptural basis of studying Indian society.[7] The basic premise of Dumont and Pocock is that 'India is one'[8], that 'the unity of India is a sort of common place'.[9] Castes are found throughout the country, and this speaks for India's *oneness*. They write in an assertive tone: 'Unity is found here above all *in ideas and values*'[10] (emphasis added). Unity is *social* in nature as *Indian society as a whole* could be seen by these ideas and values. Unity is found in terms of *relations* also (caste system is an evidence of this).

Dumont and Pocock accept the *relevance of* what they call *descriptive sociology* for India. Such a sociology is based on monographic field work by a trained anthropologist. However, this does not mean that an empirical group becomes a legitimate object of study. An empirical group or a segment of a caste or a village cannot be isolated from its milieu. Their view is that the primary principle of sociology forbids us to abstract a phenomenon from its social context.[11] In India, the relation between an empirical group and its environment is social in the strictest sense.[12] Thus, Dumont and Pocock do not approve the idea of conducting 'monographic' or 'regional' studies, or studies confining to a state or a linguistic group etc. Their view is that instead of highlighting regional or national diversities or differences, we should emphasize the common civilization or pan-Indian patterns.

In regard to 'descriptive sociology' they observe: 'to say description is to say understanding'.[13] This is true in three ways:

(1) because there are no sociological facts unless and until we speak of them, i.e., we express the data in sociological language;
(2) we do not claim to 'explain isolated traits', but tend to count for each of them by the system of which it is a part; and
(3) our primary object is a system of ideas.[14]

They formulate their view on Indian sociology in terms of interpretations of indological data as part of the entire system and its values. They further assert: 'It is a matter then, broadly speaking, of a sociology of values: first we must describe the common values and take care not to mix up facts of "representation" with facts of "behaviors".'[15] 'We must learn from the people themselves which modes of thinking we have the right to apply and which we should reject.'[16]

Thus, the *value-load* in Dumont and Pocock's thesis is to take for granted that (a) India is one; (b) indology is representative of people's behaviour or that it guides people's behaviour in a significant way; (c) unity in ideas and values is *social* in nature; (d) unity and differences cannot co-exist; and (e) people's mode of thinking and not their modes of actual relations should be taken as data. These points speak of Dumont and Pocock's value-load in sociology. Surprisingly, differences between North and South India, between literate and illiterate, between the rich and the poor, and between the powerful and the weak do not matter to Dumont and Pocock as all of them are guided by the same principle known as caste system. Caste is not simply a system of ideas and values. It is more than a ritualistic system. Historians have convincingly proved that it has been a dynamic system; its corporateness has been challenged from time to time; mobility and migration took place due to caste conflicts. All these and other vital facts have been ignored by these architects of 'a sociology of values'.

Some other points related to Dumont and Pocock's 'for a sociology of India' are: (a) the notion of purity and impurity; (b) caste as a system of values; (c) India's basic unity in terms of its social organization; and (d) hierarchy – the encompassing and the encompassed or institutionalized inequality. Sociology in India for Dumont and Pocock cannot go beyond an analysis of socio-religious values of Hindus. It is difficult to find out the 'real' purpose of their emphasis on indology as methodological tool and on 'values' as a frame of reference. These a priori constraints lead to serious distortions of Indian society, and their analysis amounts to 'reductionism'. What is 'ideal' is treated as 'real' and what is 'real' is neglected from the analysis. Let us now look at F.G. Bailey's review of Dumont and Pocock's view on 'for a sociology of India'.[17]

BAILEY'S CRITIQUE OF THE DUMONT-POCOCK APPROACH

F.G. Bailey in a critique of Dumont and Pocock's 'for a sociology of India' observes that their style is 'infectious', perspective is too narrow, and they define 'sociology' out of existence. They have designed a 'strait-jacket' for 'Indian sociology'. Bailey picks up a few points from Dumont and Pocock's essay related to their object of study, namely, *Indian society as a Whole*. Understanding is achieved by the abstraction of a system, the elements in this system are ideas – 'our primary object is a system of ideas'. Ideas are 'the principles that the people themselves give', and behind these principles are 'necessary but implicit links'.[18] Bailey thinks that one should not confine his analysis to the raw material (people's principles), and one should not concern only with abstracting out consistent elements. Bailey puts his view lucidly as follows: 'A valid sociological understanding can be achieved, given certain problems, by making abstractions immediately from behaviour or from other non-verbal information, and by using only our own concepts and evading the ideas of the people (supposing they have any idea, which is not always the case). In other words, sociology does not consist only of a sociology of values, and a part of our understanding can be derived from behaviour. This is not to deny that there is a sociology of values, but only to say that "what it is that people believe and think" is not the whole field of sociology, as the editors seem to me arguing.'[19] The editors feel that they have been misunderstood by Bailey. In a textual note, they write: 'in our view it can be argued that we make too much of ideas or that we put them unduly at the beginning, but not that we are exclusively after a "sociology of values".'[20]

Bailey's emphasis is on the understanding of 'structural facts' which is quite evident in his book *Caste and the Economic Frontier*.[21] Analysis of Indian society, as a system of values or ideas, becomes a strait-jacket, in which only a limited range of social phenomena can be fitted into. The ideas of 'unity', 'complexity' and 'people's principles' automatically do not make 'a sociology of values'. To treat Aryans and Dravidians, tribes and castes, caste and village, at par, would amount to utter ignorance of the 'complexity' of Indian society and denial of its historical ramifications. These are considered as 'distortions' by Bailey.[22] Tribe and village exist as sociological realities independent of the caste system. Bailey observes: 'One wonders also whether the editors would agree that those villages which are "isolated" have "sociological reality".'[23]

Dumont and Pocock do not explain why they have preferred indology or culturology 'for a sociology of India'. Is it not an attempt towards academic indoctrination of scholars interested in the study of Indian society? Is it that they think for the welfare of Indian sociology by bringing ideas which would reinforce and relegitimize India's caste system? While commenting on Iravati Karve's book *Kinship Organization in India,*[24] they suggest that Karve should choose between sociology and culturology. Bailey observes that 'this taunt could well be directed at themselves'.[25] Iravati Karve's work on kinship provides a wholesome analysis of the subject by combining indology and field work, unity and diversity, ideas and practices. It is a good example of anthropological phenomenology.

Bailey says that Dumont and Pocock talk of 'Indian sociology', but they do not talk of 'Indian chemistry'. They do not make a rigorous distinction between cultural and social facts. Their definition of cultural facts (values, ideas or caste) rules out *comparison* of India with other societies and within India with different components and segments. Thus, Bailey is not for a particularistic sociology. Bailey writes: 'The uniqueness is *scientifically* incomprehensible. The unique can be comprehended only intuitively or through a mystical experience. I forebear to suggest that the editors have had this experience although their style suggests it.'[26]

Bailey quotes Nadel that 'society' is a higher level of abstraction than is culture.[27] This is also accepted by Yogendra Singh in his analysis of 'modernization of Indian tradition'.[28] Bailey is quite forthright in his criticism of Dumont and Pocock's view and in advancing his own view about understanding of Indian society. He writes: 'In my view a knowledge of cultural values is only the beginning or the raw material of sociological analysis.'[29] Bailey's view is that one should make a sociological analysis of culture as one does of language, religion, etc. He feels that 'what the editors are advocating is not sociology at all, but a form of culturology'.[30] Only culturology can be made distinctively Indian. The editors use the phrase 'science of sociology', but it seems that they have used it for 'knowledge'.[31] The other point is that how 'science of sociology' could become 'Indian' sociology as a science deals in *systems*.[32] Bailey states: 'There can be no "Indian" sociology except in a "vague geographic sense", any more than there are distinctively Indian principles in chemistry or biology.'[33]

Finally, Bailey calls the editor's view a 'very odd kind of inverted ethnocentrism'.[34] The editors have not clearly expressed their view; their view is more of an assertion than evidence; and they have used an emotive language.[35] The editors express that Indian sociology is a branch of culturology. 'In fact, sociology in India is a part of sociology elsewhere.'[36] The editors' view that 'real structural changes' are a rare phenomenon is also not acceptable to Bailey.[37]

OTHER CRITIQUES OF DUMONT'S APPROACH AND DUMONT'S REPLY

Dumont and Pocock reply Bailey's criticisms of their 'for a sociology of India'.[38] Dumont also responds to A.K. Saran's review of Dumont and Pocock's position regarding Indian sociology,[39] and Dumont also gives his view on T.N. Madan's defence[40] of Dumont and Pocock in 'A Fundamental Problem in the Sociology of Caste'.[41] Let us take up some other important points of this debate which runs from 1957 to 1966. We have already discussed the main points of Dumont and Pocock's culturology and Bailey's structural analysis in this connection.

In their rejoinder to Bailey[42] the editors make it clear that sociology is a special kind of science and the sociologist looks at his data from without and from within.[43] Madan does not agree with Dumont and Pocock regarding the external point of view which they say the sociologist shares with the natural scientist.[44] Saran also expressed similar view before Madan. Saran writes: 'Social reality qua reality has no "outside" ...the only outside is its interpretation in terms of an alien culture...'[45] Madan accepts that there is a view from within the society studied, and here he agrees with Saran, but he is doubtful of the 'external point of view', which the editors share with the natural scientist.[46] Dumont admits a 'combine' of the two viewpoints. However, he does not agree either with Saran's or with Madan's criticism of their (Dumont and Pocock's) position.[47]

Madan makes two points: (a) that by taking an internal view one surrenders a 'truly external position', and (b) so far Dumont-Pocock maintain the external view, their position is not opposed to that of Bailey.[48] Thus, according to Madan, both Dumont-Pocock and Bailey's views may be subsumed under positivism. But Dumont raises questions about Madan's view. Dumont's view is that positivism exclusively refers to the 'external view', and this is not applicable to Dumont and Pocock as they take a serious cognizance of indology. However, Dumont feels that the external view can be combined with the internal view, and their position may be treated as *positivie-cum-subjective*. This is another modification we note in Dumont-Pocock position of 1957 by Dumont in 1966. Earlier we have referred to the modification that the editors are not exclusively after a 'sociology of values'. Dumont admits that they should have used the expression 'sociology of India' instated of 'Indian sociology'. They also admit that they were not aware of the fact that there was a periodical *The Indian Sociologist* in the early part of the twentieth century. It is regretted that they knew of B.K. Sarkar's *Hindu Sociology* only.[49]

Saran considers the combining of the internal and external views as *positivistic hybris*. Saran thinks that the interpretation of one culture in terms of another is simply meaningless, or ontologically nil. Different cultures cannot be compared. Man is an ontologically non-being abstraction. The one who looks from outside imposes perspective of his culture in understanding the other society. Saran writes: '...taking, in the name of science, modernity or objectivity, a firmly provincial standpoint for the study of traditional or tradition-haunted societies.'[50] Imtiaz Ahmad observes that studies on Hindus and their traditions are more than other communities. Indian nationalism is expressed in Hindu idiom. Indian sociology could be called a Hindu sociology.[51] However, this view is not quite true factually, and its logical conclusions are quite nasty in nature.

Dumont refers to Saran's view as 'cultural solipsism'. Dumont observes that 'duality' is necessarily a part of anthropological or sociological research. 'External view', comparison and objectivity are necessary parts of a 'proper' understanding of Indian society. Dumont's view is that if the western sociology had scientific temper and applied to Indian society as well construction of Indian sociology independent of that would have been a wrong attempt.[52] 'A Hindu sociology is a contradiction in terms...' Dumont disregards the role of socio-centrism in sociology. 'Sociology is one in its principle.'[53] Particularly reacting to Saran's observations, Dumont writes: 'What is actually found under its label may be good or bad, scientific or not, understanding or not; there may be found within it different tendencies; but there never will be two sociologies, let alone a sociology of solipsism.'[54] India can contribute to universal sociology both directly and indirectly. Global features of Indian society should be translated into sociological language. The Indian type of hierarchy, Dumont finds, is a universal tool for a better understanding of the modern western society itself.[55] Sociology reflects the social experience of mankind. Reacting to Saran, Dumont writes: 'Progressive Indians should be particularly alert against the danger of fake or "Hindu" sociology developing as a weapon obscurantism and reaction.'[56] Madan broadly agrees with Saran and responds to his criticism by Dumont.[57]

Apparently Dumont, Saran and Saxena might appear different from each other in regard to their perspectives about Indian sociology, but the result of their analyses has been the same. Dumont may talk of 'the external view' or 'positivist-cum-subjective' view, he ultimately praises *caste system* and its sanctions related to institutionalized inequality through the concept of *hierarchy*. He seeks approval of his view from Mauss and Hocart.[58] The first refers to the force of 'social' which is 'caste' in India, the latter writes about the ritualistic theory of caste. Hutton talks of functions of caste,[59] thereby meaning it as a beneficial institution. Not only Hutton, other British administrators-cum-ethnographers have also given an optimistic picture of caste and other institutions.[60] Perhaps this was the demand of the British Raj in India. The western scholars have defined caste and class as antithetical institutions and at the same time they have praised western society and class, and have defined caste as an archaic and oriental institution working against democratic ethos. But, at the same time, they have praised caste as a useful institution for Indian society.

Why such contradictory and biased views and definitions have been given by these western scholars is a question which should be taken up seriously and sincerely. Dumont can blame Saran for wrong 'hypothetical-deductive reasoning', for 'irrelevant quotations', and for his 'neo-Hindu creed',[61] but why Dumont gives such an enormous premium to culturology and caste system and its allied institutions remains a sort of mysticism. Why Indian caste system becomes a datum for Dumont to develop a global sociology? Dumont's absolutist view has its history in the study of Indian society. One concrete result is that differences, conflicts, interests, exploitations, uneven access to resources and opportunities have not become as relevant phenomena for sociological understanding. Study of these aspects would have given understanding for giving a challenge to the colonizers. Today it could give a challenge to the western sociology if caste was not studied on the line suggested by Hutton, Hocart, Dumont, etc. Dumont's polemics would not strengthen his view on Indian society. The question is: What approach is relevant for studying Indian society? Should the approach be Radcliffe-Brownian or Dumontian or Levi-Straussian or Marxian? It cannot be an approach based on scriptures or ancient texts. The question is not that 'ideas' are more important or 'relations' are more important from a methodological point of view. It is a question of having a real understanding of Indian society, its social formation, particularly of its contemporaneity to understand the present with clarity and reliability. Such an exercise has not so far been a part of the sociologist's infrastructure and understanding.

SOME MORE POINTS IN THE DEBATE 'FOR A SOCIOLOGY OF INDIA'

The debate on 'for a sociology of India' takes a different form after Dumont and Pocock stopped editing the *Contributions to Indian Sociology*. In fact, Dumont withdrew from it as he writes in 'A Farewell'[62] to *Contributions to Indian Sociology*. Let us once again state that the Marxist and neo-Marxist sociologists still did not join the debate in *Contributions*, and debate also did not remain as 'alive' as it was up to 1966. A couple of short articles have appeared and we shall give a brief resume of the post-1966 debate.

J.P.S. Oberoi looks at the aim and method of science as uniform and universal, but the problem of science is seen in relation to a given society. As such Oberoi writes: 'The sociology of knowledge is a study of urgent practical importance today, for some consideration of it should form the prolegomenon and background to the determination of particular priorities and objectives.'[63] Advancement of science cannot be separated from the advancement of independence in India. According to Oberoi, false cosmopolitanism and false humanitarianism must go. Srinivas prefers the concept of westernization in place of modernization because the former entails the values of humanitarianism and egalitarianism.[64] It is really an irony of our scholars that they have found human values in colonization of the Indian masses. Oberoi rightly observes that 'as a social institution science, national or international, cannot and does not live outside its era'.[65] '... Scientistic internationalism is a bridge of illusion, a cloak of comfort across the chasm.'[66]

Yogendra Singh takes a position[67] comparable with R.K. Merton's view[68] about nature of sociological theory. According to Singh, sociological theory in India does not have a 'formal' status of theory. Theory is rare, but approaches are far too many. There are typologies and classifications. Singh questions: 'Do we find a paradigm reflecting theoretic simplicity and power in Dumont's formulation of Indian sociology?' The other question is: 'Is the definitional range of his primitive concepts such that his sociology is able to (a) translate sociological data inter-culturally, and (b) deal with all the significant range of societal and cultural facts which are relevant to Indian sociology?'[69] Yogendra Singh's answer is 'no' to these questions. He does not accept Dumont's idea of 'functionally equivalent concepts'. 'Sociology of development'[70] and 'change' do not matter for Dumont. Singh states that 'Dumont is more concerned with system integration and maintenance than with change or conflict'.[71] For Singh sociology means a system of operational concepts and societal self-consciousness. 'Sociology is a science and its theoretic structure should not differ basically from natural sciences.'[72] According to Singh, the search for a sociology of India may not logically contradict the general and scientific nature of sociology.[73]

Dhirendra Narain is of the view that questions raised by Dumont-Pocock are not urgent and of a general nature as they refer to the relationship between history and sociology or between culture and society.[74] A number of important questions raised by Narain are as follows:

(1) Is the diachronic-synchronic polarity an analytical distinction or does this distinction really inhere in social reality?
(2) Is a wholly synchronic study possible?
(3) Does it not imply freezing time which is clearly out of question?
(4) If the wholly synchronic approach is not possible, what is the controversy about?
(5) Is a study historical if it spans centuries and not if it spans only decade(s)?

There are some more questions raised by Narain:

(1) Must one always go to the *very* beginning of a thing in order to fully understand its contemporary form and function(s)?
(2) Are there no strategic moments in time which can be used as convenient starting points?
(3) Is the whole past, undifferentiated into periods, equally valid for the understanding of everything in contemporary society?
(4) Must we always go to the ancient sources to understand everything in Indian society of today?[75]

Narain deals with both disciplinary and methodological questions. He is certainly not for diachrony at the cost of synchrony. He does not surrender sociology to history for generalization. He writes: 'By removing the absolute distinction between the diachronic and synchronic approaches, one also removes the need to surrender sociology to history. Good history is as much dependent on sociology as good sociology is dependent upon history.'[76] Narain is not for 'unique'. 'Concentration on the unique, inevitably tending to exclude, or at least reduce comparison and generalization, will surely limit knowledge and understanding.'[77]

Distinction between insider and outsider is not quite relevant for Narain as he observes that 'the fact of the matter is that a rank outsider has no way of feeling interested in a phenomenon to which he is a *total* outsider'.[78] An alliance between scientific and humanistic approaches can be brought out without saying that one is more powerful than the other. In nutshell, Narain is for a scientific approach which basically emphasizes study of the present, and if necessary, the relevant past is taken into account. Madan summarizes the debate in a recent number of *Contributions*,[79] and again agrees with Dumont's position about Indian sociology. However, Madan is unfair to a few important sociologists who have provided schema of studies on Indian society by sociologists and social anthropologists. Yogendra Singh's *Modernization of Indian Tradition*,[80] and his articles on Indian sociology have been ignored. Ramakrishna Mukherjee's earlier books and articles[81] and recent book on Indian sociology have also been left out. One gets the impression as if 'positivism' and 'culturology' alone have influenced and shaped sociology in India. Variants of Marxism and structural-functionalism and structuralist perspectives have been debated and tested by several scholars.

TOWARDS THEORY AND METHODOLOGY OF INDIAN SOCIOLOGY

We shall discuss the main points of theorization in Indian sociology within the specific context and milieu of Indian society. The immediate context is that India had colonial cognitive traditions in the past, and it has become an independent nation since 1947 and this provides it a new context and milieu. A sociology of knowledge perspective would demand examination of the continuity/discontinuity of the colonial/traditional approaches, concepts and methods of study. The units and themes of study are not independent of their context and milieu.

Yogendra Singh observes that even the debate whether sociology has universal concepts and techniques or it refers to culturally-oriented cognitive styles and structures could be seen in the context of the hangover of colonialism in independent India.[82] Today the tensions in Indian sociology are between (a) the 'master theory' or 'general theory' and 'conceptual schemes', and (b) 'universalism' of concepts and propositions and their 'particularism' or 'contextuality'. The third source of tension is the role of ideology in theory construction.[83]

Let us take up some more points of this important essay on ideology, theory and methods in Indian sociology by Singh which covers a period of a quarter century of sociology in India from 1952 to 1977. However, we have made use of literature on Indian sociology up to 1982. Singh divides this period into four parts:

(1) 1952 to 1960 – a period of adaptive changes and innovations.
(2) 1960 to 1965 – a period of significant shifts in theoretic priorities and the beginning of some critical tensions in theory and ideology of Indian sociology.
(3) 1965 to 1970 – a period of marked sociological self-awareness and growth of new directions in theoretical and substantive contributions.
(4) 1970 to 1977 – a period of new maturity and exploring both theoretically and substantively new horizons of knowledge.

These four periods correspond with four theoretic developments in Indian sociology. These theoretic orientations are: (a) philosophical, (b) culturological, (c) structural, and (d) dialectical-historical. Singh states that Indian sociologists have been less concerned with constructing metatheories or general theories, and they have been more prone to using conceptual schema for analysis of social problems.[84] Somewhat differently, this point has also been made by Madan while reacting on Dumont-Pocock's view on sociology of India.[85] Any way, Singh observes that the only exception is Radhakamal Mukherjee who proposes a *general integrated social sciences model for explanation and understanding of social realities* in the *Philosophy of Social Sciences*.[86] Singh states that some Marxist scholars, particularly A.R. Desai,[87] have used a general theory but have analyzed substantive realities from an ideological position rather than on the relative power of theoretical systems.[88]

The work of Radhakamal Mukerjee, D.P. Mukerji and A.K. Saran[89] are included in the philosophical orientation. Singh provides a detailed comparative analysis of these three different orientations on a continuum. Dumont, Srinivas, Singer and Marriott[90] are the chief representatives of the culturological approach. The structural theoretic orientation in Indian sociology refers to the writings of Bailey, Beteille, Agarwal, Arora, Bhatt, Brass, D'Souza, Joshi, R. Singh, P.N. Mukherji, I.P. Desai, M.S.A. Rao and a host of several other sociologists,[91] who have been working on social stratification, agrarian structures, social movements, kinship and family and disputes etc. Studies by D.P. Mukherji, Ramakrishna Mukherjee, A.R. Desai, Charles Bettleheim and by some economists and historians[92] could be included under dialectical-historical orientation.

Ideology, culture or tradition, structure and dialectics are the key concerns of these four theoretic orientations, respectively. There are a few points which one could take up for investigation: (a) The periods do not synchronize with the dominance or prominence of these approaches. The tendency of going back and forth is found in regard to these orientations. (b) It is assumed that the sociologists[93] took up mainly those problems for investigation which were of crucial significance and urgency for the people. The question whether the 'scientism' and fashions of the discipline guided the selection of research problems or the research was demanded by society for gaining understanding of its problems, has been left undecided by Singh. Singh inclines to have more concern for 'systematics of sociology' with a 'positivistic' bias rather than for ontologically determined concepts and categories. His love for systematization and classificatory skill could be seen in his writings from 1965 onwards.[94] However, he gives premium to the interaction between the general theories and culture-specific data. This is evidenced in Singh's book *Modernization of Indian Tradition*[95] and his 'trend reports' for ICSSR on social stratification[96] and social change[97] in India.

A somewhat different perspective is advanced by Singh in an earlier essay.[98] An assumed international 'reference model' of social science and the slow pace of Indian social transformation itself have conditioned the character and evaluation of Indian social sciences in general; and sociology and social anthropology in particular. Singh examines sociology in India from the perspective of the sociology of knowledge. He writes: 'The relationship between the conceptual and methodological baggage of the western social science and its relevance to an understanding of the historic-specific problems of various societies lies in the domain of the sociology of knowledge.'[99] How the western theoretic constructs, methodologies and techniques of research have been accepted by Indian sociology and to what extent they have gone well with historical specificities of Indian society is the most relevant question to be examined from the point of sociology of knowledge. A few questions are referred by Singh in the essay under discussion:

(1) What is the logical or substantive relevance of social science paradigms developed in a different historical context for another country which is historically and existentially different[100]
(2) How far have social sciences responded to the various phases of social structural transformation in India and the corresponding needs of a worldview and socio-cultural identity of their own society[101]
(3) How far have the existential conditions in India influenced their growth?[102]

A few statements may be picked up in the form of answers to the above questions from Singh's essay. Historically, the building blocks, both of social anthropology and sociology in India, are derived from the western colonialist interpretations of the Indian society. In its early phase, sociology had a deep imprint of the earlier colonial and ethnographic and social interpretative writings. 'Caste' was treated independent of 'tribe' and vice versa; village was looked at as isolated whole.[103] This was perhaps done for *promoting colonial power in India* (emphasis added). Thus, basic issues related to feudalism, agrarian structure, reforms and movements remained untouched to a large extent.

Like Madan,[104] Singh also observes: 'Imitative social science tradition in India was a logical result of this fragmentation of sociological apperception.'[105] G.S. Ghurye, Radhakamal Mukerjee and D.P. Mukerji realized the imposition of western social science and reacted to this by providing their own explanations for studying Indian society. Singh asks: 'Did this major historical change (India's independence) influence the social science paradigms in India?' 'Did social science mobilize itself to tackle the crucial issues of national consolidation and identity?'[106] Singh's answer to these is in the negative.

Our view is that we have undoubtedly two co-existent traditions in Indian sociology: (a) the colonialist, and (b) the imperialist. The 'nativist' tradition has not emerged as a challenge to the forceful 'combine' of the two traditions. However, the debate has started questioning the role and relevance of the continuity of colonial elements and the hegemony of the western social sciences paradigms in understanding Indian society.

Finally, Singh raises the question: 'What should be the role of social science and social scientists in contemporary India?'[107] He writes: 'My argument is not that we should give up the scientific spirit in social science researches and substitute ideology for it... I affirm that the task of science is to offer explanations of social phenomena in terms of prediction of causal relationships among various events. This should also hold good for the social sciences. The universalism of social science, however, in my opinion, ends at this point of formal structure and methodology. Beyond this, the nature of social science is governed by the historicity of societal conditions... . My argument is that whatever may be the sophistications achieved by a particular research endeavour, its problem selection and formulation of hypotheses is basically conditioned by the value-preferences of the researcher.'[108] Researcher becomes a 'variable' in terms of particular existential conditions – refers to sociology of knowledge perspective.

Singh cautions us against the international or western social science 'reference model' and its inherent concepts, tools and techniques, in other words, against 'methodological individualism' and social system ideology, and suggests greater use of history in sociological understanding.[109] Singh's this essay no doubt emphasizes the need for 'indigenization' of sociological understanding, but Singh is not prepared to bid a 'farewell' to the 'formal structure' and methodology of social science. The assumption that there is 'universalism of social science' is quite untenable. This 'universalism' could be called as 'particularism' of the British or American social science. Thus, Singh gives us cautious hints about the use of western social science paradigms and concepts, but his exposition is only a slightly different view from his earlier position.[110]

A couple of articles provide narrative accounts of the history of sociology or teaching of sociology in Indian universities and colleges.[111] We shall discuss the two modes of thinking, which have emerged in Indian sociology in the seventies. The one has a swing towards the Marxian approach and the other is non-Marxian way of sociological understanding. A few selected representatives of the two categories could be taken up to illustrate this point.

THE MARXIST AND THE NON-MARXIST DISPOSITIONS IN INDIAN SOCIOLOGY

Ramakrishna Mukherjee shows a strong Marxist disposition in his book *The Rise and Fall of the East India Company*,[112] but in his other book, *The Dynamics of a Rural Society*,[113] a modification of this disposition is evident as he uses 'interactional' relations between various classes as the device, by which the details of each class could be known to understand their differentiation. However, Mukherjee takes more of a methodological position than a Marxist or a modified

Marxist view for studying Indian society in an article 'Study of Social Change and Social Development in the Developing Societies'.[114] We shall refer this view of Mukherjee as his analysis combines both 'theory' and 'method' of study. Mukherjee claims his perspective to be both 'contemporary' and 'diagnostic'. He rejects the idea of a simple sequential model of social change. For Mukherjee 'developing societies' are not unique. He writes: 'Universality in the development of sociology, therefore, will not be attained by a contextual and imitative application of any theory on these societies. Instead, empirical research on the mechanics of these societies (viz., *what, how,* and *why* of their statics and dynamics) will lead us to this goal.'[115]

Mukherjee brings home this point by saying that the current theories can be used for formulating hypotheses for studying 'developing societies' in terms of their *place, time* and *object* dimensions. He refers to the use of the Marxian and the Weberian concepts of social dynamics. Mukherjee writes: 'In order to draw objective and unambiguous generalizations from this approach, we require a commonly agreed frame of reference which locates a set of hierarchically structured units of observation, analysis and inference.'[116] 'Indicators' of the problem under investigation may be formulated *deductively* in term of the *null hypotheses* (referring to no change) and the *alternate hypotheses* (referring to a time series). A *research design* is required based on the concept of statistical probability and multivariate analysis.[117] This leads to the research to collection of both quantitative and qualitative data-inductive investigation.

Mukherjee has a deep-seated desire to have a 'universality of science', by seeing its objective comprehensive particular manifestations. We would say that Mukherjee's approach suffers from a couple of limitations: (a) His deductive-inductive inferential approach becomes a strait-jacket, and it emphasizes too much of methodologism, and theoretical a priorism becomes inevitable; (b) existential determinism goes in the background and methodological nomology predominates; (c) a synthesis of value (frame of reference) and fact (actual research), diachrony and synchrony, structure and process, and quantitative and qualitative data is aimed at (as claimed by Mukherjee) but is not realized; and finally (d) the approach has not been put so far in practice, perhaps mainly due to its cumbersomeness.

In two subsequent articles,[118] Ramakrishna Mukherjee reinforces the view he develops about the study of social change and development in 'developing societies'. Four fundamental questions have to be answered in regard to the phenomena which a scientific discipline deals with: *what it is, how is it, why is it,* and *what will it be.* 'What' and 'how' refer to the understanding of social phenomena as entities or units, hence *descriptive stage* in social research. 'Why' refers to *explanatory stage*, and 'what will it be' refers to the *diagnostic stage*. The last stage follows from the first three questions and on the basis of probability denotes the structure, function and process of the contemporary phenomena in a dynamic perspective.[119] On this basis, Mukherjee distinguishes three stages in the historical development of Indian sociology as follows:

(1) Proto-professional stage of sociology prior to the twentieth century.
(2) Professional stage of descriptive and explanatory sociology in the first half of the present century.
(3) Currently needed stage of diagnostic sociology.[120]

The Indian sociology has reached at that critical point which demands diagnostic research and this would also enhance both *descriptions* and *explanation*. Mukherjee writes: 'In any scientific discipline an explanation may be: (a) relevant or irrelevant, if it is fallacious; (b) necessary or unnecessary, if it is *suri generis* to the given facts; (c) efficient or inefficient, if it is equivocal; and (d) sufficient or insufficient, if it is not comprehensive'. The possibilities from these four sets of characteristics are as follows:

(1) An explanation may not be relevant and therefore, not necessary, efficient and sufficient.
(2) An explanation may be relevant but not necessary and therefore, not efficient and sufficient.
(3) An explanation may be relevant and necessary but not efficient, and therefore, not sufficient.
(4) An explanation may be relevant, necessary and efficient, but not sufficient.
(5) An explanation may be relevant, necessary and efficient, but the demand of the discipline may be beyond explanation.[121]

Though Ramakrishna Mukherjee suggests a blue-print of *diagnostic sociology* with a view to make sociology as a 'relevant' discipline for understanding India's multifarious problems, yet he is not able to spell out a clear line of thinking. Often he seeks support from speeches and writings of D.P. Mukerji, but D.P. Mukerji's combination of 'tradition' and 'Marxology' is not the source of Ramakrishna Mukherjee's strength. He draws more from positivistically oriented 'logical and statistical' social sciences for understanding of Indian society.

Role of 'ideology' and deductive-positivistic orientation is again examined by Ramakrishna Mukherjee in another essay, 'The Sociologist and the Social Reality'[122] in having a dialectical appreciation of a problem with an *inductive-inferential orientation*. Mukherjee writes: 'The problem before us is not that sociology contains value-loads, but how we may objectively treat the differential value-loads for an ever more precise, comprehensive, and unequivocal appraisal of the social reality.' 'An inductive-inferential approach is "value-free" and it examines the "value-loaded" images about reality and of the researcher.'[123] Mukherjee does not plead for an 'Indian science of sociology', nor D.P. Mukerji did by studying Indian traditions.[124] Myrdal's study of the countries of Asia[125] with a common framework gives impression of developing an Asian sociology, but Mukherjee does not approve of this too. He says that he has been labelled a 'bourgeois-Marxist' or a 'Marxist-bourgeois', or merely a dilettante or purist, but he claims that he examines the role of ideology in understanding of social phenomena for achieving the status of a *diagnostic* discipline for sociology.[126] Finally, Mukherjee feels that the themes of research when diagnostically formulated would represent the issues of 'universal' appeal precisely and systematically, and this would also enhance causality and knowledge about social reality.

P.C. Joshi in his rambling 'reflections' on social science research in India[127] highlights the need for 'institutionalization of scientific activity' in independent India. Like Ramakrishna Mukherjee, a need for relating the 'general' features of science with 'specific' situation is emphasized by Joshi. However, Joshi does not offer a 'deductive-inductive-inferential' approach for social research as suggested by Mukherjee. Joshi stresses on rejection of western social science models and concepts, and insists on emergence of an 'involved' social scientist in India. But the perspective is not quite clear. He speaks of Myrdal's work as 'an immoral contribution to social science'.[128] A.R. Desai's work[129] has not been praised and only a passing reference is made that it has been unduly criticized by Dumont.[130] He talks of a 'scientific ethos', and seeks support for this idea from S. Andreski's book *Social Sciences as Sorcery*[131] which is full of polemics and negativism. Finally, Joshi claims to go along with D.P. Mukerji's approach, but he does not work on a sort of 'synthesis' of Indian tradition and Marxology. Eclecticism is pronounced in Joshi's treatment of the subject. For example, he makes a reference of Radhakamal Mukherjee, D.P. Mukherji and N.K. Bose's contributions to Indian sociology, but affords to forget G.S. Ghurye's contributions to Indian sociology and his catholicity in guiding his students in regard to their researches.

Prescriptions in sociology are abundantly available particularly suggesting renovation of concepts, formulation and reformulation of hypotheses and application of new techniques of research. One of the suggestions is that western social science would be used wherever it is found useful; another is that Marxist approach should be applied in a suitably modified fashion; and the third suggestion is that a structural-historical perspective should be adopted in place of culturological analysis of Indian society. Self-critical appraisal[132] is another advice extended to the Indian sociologist. Gouldner and Andreski are ready references to be suggested for conducting sociological researches in India.

A.R. Desai applies the Marxist approach to the study of 'nationalism' in India during the British rule.[133] He spells out historical-dialectical materialism and applies it to the study of various types of movements, rural and urban, caste and class structure, social mobility, education and other aspects. Though Desai's book was published in 1948, but it became more popular in the late sixties and the seventies perhaps due to increased consciousness of Indian social scientists toward societal self-consciousness. In the fifties and early sixties American structural-functionalism and British functionalism dominated social sciences in general and sociological researches in particular. However, Desai undeterred by these imperialistic influences continued to write on Indian society and state from the perspective of an involved scholarship.[134]

In his presidential address to the XV All-India Sociological Conference, A.R. Desai narrates about twenty-seven points referring to the assessment of Indian sociology.[135] Desai finds that the dominant sociological approaches in India are basically non-Marxist, and the Marxist approach has been rejected on the pretext of its being dogmatic, value-loaded and deterministic in nature. The non-Marxist approaches are phenomenological, ethnomethodological, culturological, etc.[136] The relevant approach, according to Desai, is the Marxist approach as it could help study of governmental policies, the classes entrenched into state apparatus and India's political economy. Desai writes: 'I wish the social science practitioners in India breakthrough the atmosphere of allergy towards this profound and influential approach and create climate to study the growing body of literature articulating various aspects of Marxist paradigm.' Marxist approach emphasizes the study of *property relations* to understand Indian society, the class character of the state and the path of development.[137]

Dumont commenting on Desai's *Social Background of Indian Nationalism*[138] writes: 'More than university thesis, it is an overgrown political pamphlet clad in a university gown.'[139] Dumont makes a scathing and unsparing attack on Desai's approach. In fact, Dumont hates not only a Marxist approach but also any other non-Marxist approach except his own. Dumont's approach to Indian society represents rank conservative ideology and it also smells of the self-proclaimed superiority of the western scholarship and western society.

Now let us look at some other observations on Indian sociology. Yogendra Singh's book *Modernization of Indian Tradition*[140] brought out a fundamental shift in the theorization about Indian society by an Indian sociologist. It is a very well documented and systematic study of social change in independent India. It has been taken seriously by scholars of both Marxist and non-Marxist hues. H.C. Srivastava[141] rates it as a significant landmark in Indian sociology. Sumit Chopra considers it a sort of 'establishment' or 'official' sociology.[142] Ramakrishna Mukherjee looks at the analysis of social change in India by Singh with a suspicion.[143] Analysis of interaction between religion and society in India's socio-historical context by K.P. Gupta is undertaken from a sociology of knowledge perspective.[144] Gupta recapitulates sociology of Hinduism. Saran is aware of 'what is "India" or "modern" in India's modernity'.[145] Gupta siding with Saran writes: 'India's modernity is Indian but not modern because it is still rooted in the Hindu tradition.'[146] Further, 'India's modernity is modern but not Indian because it is consciously seeking to imitate the modernized west'.[147] This has led to a 'synthesis ideology' in India. In this synthesis, 'rational' Hindus are supposed to be living in a westernized Indian society. 'In Indian sociology this ideology has prospered by accepting the weberian framework. Weber provided to Indian sociologists a typical Hindu framework for viewing and explaining social change in terms of inner thought process, rather than institutional reform.'[148]

Gupta considers Sarkar's *Hindu Sociology*, Srinivas' *Sanskritization* and Singh's *Modernization of Indian Tradition* as variations on the above theme. These sociologists draw a line between the Hindu religion and Hindu society, and the former remains intact, and the latter changes. Thus, 'modernity' is dissociated from religion. Gupta is unfair in clubbing Singh's thesis with Sarkar's Hinduistic and Srinivas' culturalistic understanding of Indian society. One finds a semblance of orthogenetic and heterogenetic sources of change, levels of change, namely, primary and secondary, and structures in which change takes place, namely, macro and micro. Thus, Singh's treatment of social change combines theory and empiricism and structure and culture.

A fuctionalist's perspective of sociology as a profession and sociologists as a professional community is given by D.A. Chekki.[149] Chekki analyzes their academic background, fields of interest, membership of professional organizations, nature of publications, etc. Momin examines the issue of 'identity' for Indian sociology. He writes: 'Indian sociology should have an active, humanistic and critical stance towards its subject-matter, but it should not get bogged down by revivalism and obscurantism.'[150] Indra Deva suggests use of folk and oral literature as data for sociological understanding. 'Social-anthropological approach' is considered as most suitable for studying Indian society.[151]

In a long essay, R.S. Khare discusses the problem of 'external' versus 'internal' view about sociology of India.[152] He raises certain questions about the debate 'for a sociology of India', and notes that sociology is seeking 'nationalist identity', 'outside' debate is seen as a major theoretical and methodological issue in Indian sociology.[153] The main dimensions of the debate are: (a) the insider's view from 'inside', (b) the outsider's view from 'inside', (c) the outsider's view from 'outside' and (d) the insider's view from 'outside'. These positions are represented by Saran, Dumont, Bailey and Srinivas, respectively.[154] This debate (on Indian sociology) has become a 'manageric' of diverse issues – as between indigenous and analytic models, positive sciences and historiography, 'inside' view and 'outside' view, duality of form and content, particularization and generalization, the conscious and the unconscious, and predominant ideology and the 'fact'.[155] A few more dimensions have been added such as 'science and swaraj', patterns of dominance and dependence, nationalism versus internationalism, synchronic and diachronic approaches, and the Hindu and the non-Hindu dimensions of the 'Indian' social sciences in general, and of sociology in particular.[156] Inside-outside dichotomy is clearly evident in Indian sociology. 'Inside' view is 'mechanical', and 'outside' is epistemological and structural. The 'mechanical' is more popular today, but Khare prefers for having the epistemological and structural view due to scientific and humanistic considerations.[157]

In a recent comprehensive review of 'Trends in Indian Sociology', Ramakrishna Mukherjee reiterates his point of view, namely, diagnostic perspective about Indian sociology.[158] The main questions are:

(1) What is it (enumeration of the phenomenon).
(2) How is it (classification).
(3) Why is it (causality).
(4) What will it be (probability).
(5) What should it be (desirability).

These five questions should interact in a sequential manner with a dialectical appreciation having both positive and negative points in regard to reality of phenomena. These questions refer to *descriptive, explanatory, diagnostic* and *prescriptive* explanations. All questions do not have equal weight and emphasis.[159]

Mukherjee gives a bibliography containing 712 references and all these are cited in the text. He traces history of sociology as a profession from 1920 till 1970s[160] He also refers a typology of the pre-professional stage of the intellectuals.[161] The sociologists are classified as: (a) pioneers (1920s-1940s), (b) modernizers (1950s), (c) insiders (1960s), (d) pace-makers (1970s), and (e) non-conformists (1970s). He analyzes a selected few from each category on the basis of the variables of value-preference, theoretical orientation, research orientation and contribution to sociology. Mukherjee claims that his diagnostic approach would bridge the gap between theory and research and integrate value and fact, and also a deductive-positivistic nature of sociology would be replaced by the inductive-inferential orientation.[162]

In the end, a few words about methodological orientations in Indian sociology. We have already debated 'inside' view and/or 'outside' view, positivistic versus indological orientation, diachronic versus synchronic approaches and other points including a *nationalist* view of methodological orientation in Indian sociology. Methodology comprises logic of enquiry and philosophy of science, techniques of operationalization of concepts and tools of research, problems of measurement and observation and finally questions of universality and particularity in tools of research that use symbolic linguistic categories for measurement and observation.[163] The concepts of methodology raise similar ideological issues and ethical questions of communication of values to the respondents and their use for desired goals of research. We often mention that 'participant observation' has come from Malinowski and Radcliffe-Brown's functionalism, 'village studies' from American anthropology, 'indology' from Weber and Dumont and 'history' from Marx as method of study.

The basic question is: Whether methods and techniques used in Indian sociology reflect the researcher's consciousness about research goals and refer to the character of the research objects or that it is a borrowed research instrument without referring either to research as such or to the objects of research. It is necessary to ask this question when we set out eyes on the use of participant observation, questionnaire and schedule cybernetic model, set theory, mathematical models, survey designs, and historical structural and comparative frameworks. T.N. Madan, in a trend report on research methodology,[164] covers the period from 1950 to 1970. Madan looks at methodology from the point of analytic power, objectivity and explanation, methods, techniques and tools, and analysis of data in social research. He also discusses the views of Radhakamal Mukerjee, D.P. Mukerji and A.K. Saran, along with Dumont, Bailey and Srinivas. The 'inside' view versus 'outside' view finds a prominent place in Madan's review. However, he bears his analysis on the studies of tribes, castes, village communities, family, urban centres, population studies based on a number of books and articles published in five well-known Indian journals of sociology.

Not much has been written on craft of sociology and social anthropology. Madan and Beteille have recently edited a volume on field experiences and encounters of social anthropologist.[165] I.P. Desai's article in *Economic and Political Weekly*, namely, 'Craft of Sociology in India: An Autobiographical Perspective'[166] is really refreshing and enrich our understanding of Indian sociology. Desai mentions three points about the early phase of Indian sociology:

(1) Methodology as a separate course was not learnt by any one of the sociologists of the second generation from Bombay University.
(2) Sociology was not understood as a science as it is understood today.
(3) Sociology was supposed to have a bearing on practical life and was future-oriented, that is, change-oriented.[167]

Desai's observations on the construction and use of questionnaire, sampling and tabulation, or in fact, survey research are really illuminating. Desai and Srinivas represented two different traditions in Indian sociology in the fifties at the University of Baroda. Srinivas was against the techniques of questionnaire and schedule, and use of statistics. Srinivas' strong point was his emphasis on field work method. Desai is against any kind of borrowed theories, concepts and research tools. His writings amply show this orientation. The new research technology in India has come due to constraints of Indian sociology itself and not due to any particular individuals. An assumed international reference model of social science and the slow pace of Indian social transformation have conditioned the character and evaluation of Indian social science in general and sociology and social anthropology in particular.

Notes

1. Yogendra Singh, 'Scope and Method of Sociology in India', in T.K.N. Unnithan, et.al. (eds.), *Sociology for India*, New Delhi: Prentice-Hall of India Private ltd., 1967, pp. 13–37; and 'Sociology for India: The Emerging Perspective' in ibid., pp. 165–83. See also Yogendra Singh, 'Disciplinary Growth of Sociology and Its Teaching in India', in *Sociology in India*, Agra, Institute of Social Sciences, Agra University, 1965, pp. 53–67.
2. Ramakrishna Mukherjee, 'Trends in Indian Sociology' *Current Society*, Vol. 25, No. 3, 1977.
3. R.S. Khare, '"Inside" Apropos of "Outside" some implications of sociological debate' in Giri Raj Gupta (ed.), *Main Current in Indian Sociology*, Vol. I, Delhi, Vikas Publishing House, 1976, pp. 20–58.
4. L. Dumont and D.F. Pocock, 'For a Sociology of India', *Contributions to Indian Sociology*, Vol. I, 1957, pp. 9–22.
5. Ibid., p. 9.
6. Ibid.
7. R.N. Saxena, 'A Sociology in India' in *Sociology in India*, op. cit., 1965, pp. 1–13.
8. Dumont and Pocock, op. cit., p. 11.
9. Ibid.
10. Ibid., 12.
11. Ibid.
12. Ibid.
13. Ibid., p. 13.
14. Ibid.
15. Ibid.
16. Ibid.
17. F.G., Bailey, 'For a Sociology of India'?, *Contributions to Indian Sociology*, No. III, 1959, pp. 88–101.
18. L. Dumont and D.F. Pocock, op. cit., pp. 10–11.
19. F.G. Bailey, op. cit., 1959, p. 90.
20. Ibid., p. 89.
21. F.G. Bailey, *Caste and the Economic Frontier*, Manchester, Manchester University Press, 1957.

22. F.G. Bailey, op. cit., 1959, p. 92.
23. Ibid., p. 96.
24. L. Dumont and D.F. Pocock, 'Kinship' (a review of Iravati Karve's Kinship Organization in India), *Contributions to Indian Sociology* Vol. I, 1957, p. 64.
25. F.G., Bailey, op. cit., 1959, p. 97.
26. Ibid., p. 98.
27. Cf. from Bailey, op. cit., 1959, p. 98.
28. Y. Singh, *Modernization of Indian Tradition*, Delhi, Thompson Press (India) Ltd., 1973, p. 17.
29. F.G. Bailey, op. cit., 1959, p. 98.
30. Ibid., pp. 98–99.
31. L. Dumont and D.F. Pocock, 'Village Studies', *Contributions to Indian Sociology*, No. 1, 1957, p. 41.
32. F.G. Bailey, op. cit., 1959, p. 99.
33. Ibid., p. 99.
34. Ibid., p. 100.
35. Ibid.
36. Ibid.
37. Ibid.
38. L. Dumont and D.F. Pocock, 'For a Sociology of India: A Rejoinder to Dr. Bailey', *Contributions to Indian Sociology*, No. 4, 1960.
39. See A.K. Saran's 'A Review of Contributions to Indian Sociology, No. IV', *Eastern Anthropologist*, Vol. XV, No. 1, 1962.
40. T.N. Madan, 'For a Sociology of India', *Contribution to Indian Sociology*, No. IX, 1966, pp. 9–16.
41. L. Dumont responds to A.K. Saran's criticisms and T.N. Madan's 'weak' defence of their (Dumont and Pocock's) position in 'A Fundamental Problem in the Sociology of Caste', *Contribution to Indian Sociology*, No. IX, 1966, pp. 17–32.
42. L. Dumont and D.F. Pocock, op. cit., 1960.
43. Ibid., p. 84.
44. T.N. Madan, op. cit., 1966, p. 12.
45. A.K. Saran, op. cit., 1962, p. 68.
46. T.N., Madan, op. cit., 1966, p. 12.
47. L. Dumont, op. cit., 1966, p. 22.
48. T.N. Madan, op. cit., 1966, pp. 11–12.
49. L. Dumont, op. cit, 1966, fn. 9, p. 23.
50. A.K. Saran, op. cit. 1962, p. 68.
51. Imtiaz Ahmad, 'For a Sociology of India', *Contributions to Indian Sociology* (NS), No. 4 (1972), p. 23.
52. Dumont, op. cit., 1966, p. 23.

53. Ibid., p. 23.
54. Ibid.
55. Ibid., p. 24.
56. Ibid., p. 25.
57. T.N. Madan, 'For a Sociology of India: Some Clarifications' *Contributions to Indian Sociology* (NS), 1967, pp. 90–93.
58. See Emile Durkheim and Marcel Mauss, *Primitive Classification* (translated from French into English by Rodney Needham), London, 1963 and A.M. Hocart, *Caste: A Comparative Study*, London, Mathew and Company, 1950.
59. J.H. Hutton, *Caste in India*, Bombay, Oxford University Press, 1963.
60. See K.L., Sharma, *Essays on Social Stratification*, Jaipur, Rawat Publications, 1980, pp. 1–25.
61. L. Dumont, op. cit., 1966, pp. 25–26.
62. L. Dumont and D.F. Pocock, 'A Farewell', *Contribution to Indian Sociology*, No. IX, 1966, pp. 7–8.
63. J.P. Singh Oberoi, 'Science and Swaraj', *Contribution to Indian Sociology* (NS), No. II, 1968, p. 119.
64. M.N. Srinivas, *Social Change in Modern India*, Berkeley, California University Press, 1966.
65. J.P. Singh Oberoi, op. cit., 1968, p. 120.
66. Ibid., p. 120.
67. Y. Singh, 'For a Sociology of India', *Contribution to Indian Sociology*, (NS), No. 4, 1970, pp. 140–44.
68. Y. Singh, op. cit., 1970, p. 142.
70. D. Kantowsky, 'For a sociology of India: A Critical Note on the Sociology of Developing Countries', *Contributions to Indian Sociology* (NS), No. 3, 1969, pp. 128–31.
71. Y. Singh, op. cit., 1970, p. 142.
72. Ibid.
73. Ibid., p. 143.
74. Dhirendra Narain, 'For a Sociology of India: Some Observations', *Contributions to Indian Sociology*, (NS), No. V, 1971, p. 131.
75. Ibid., pp. 131–32.
76. Ibid., p. 142.
77. Ibid., p. 133.
78. Ibid.
79. T.N. Madan, 'For a Sociology of India', *Contributions to Indian Sociology*, (NS), Vol. 15, Nos. 1 and 2, 1981, pp. 403–18.
80. Y. Singh, op. cit., 1973. See also his, 'The Role of Social Sciences in India: A Sociology of Knowledge', *Sociological Bulletin*, Vol. 22, No. 1, 1973, pp. 14–28.

81. Ramakrishna Mukherjee, 'Indian Sociology: Historical Development and Present Problems', *Sociological Bulletin*, Vol. 22, No. 1, 1973, pp. 29–58, See also his, op. cit., 1977.
82. Y. Singh, 'Ideology, Theory and Methods in Indian Sociology', Stein Rokkan (ed.), *A Quarter Century of International Social Science*, New Delhi, Concept Publishing House, 1979, pp. 291–314.
83. Ibid., p. 292.
84. Ibid., p. 293.
85. T.N. Madan, op. cit., 1966.
86. Radhakamal Mukerjee, *The Philosophy of Social Science*, Delhi, Macmillan Co., 1960.
87. A.R. Desai's *Social Background of Indian Nationalism* (1948) is referred in this context.
88. Y. Singh, op. cit., 1979.
89. See ibid., op. cit., 1979.
90. See ibid., pp. 298–301.
91. Ibid., pp. 301–04.
92. Ibid., pp. 304–06.
93. Ibid., pp. 306–09.
94. See Y. Singh, op. cit., (1965–67), 'Caste and Class: Some Aspects of Continuity and Change', *Sociological Bulletin*, Vol. XVIII, No. 2, 1968, pp. 165–86; and op. cit., 1973, 1974 and 1979.
95. Y. Singh, *Modernization of Indian Tradition*, op. cit., 1973.
96. See Y. Singh's 'Sociology of Social Stratification' in *A Survey of Research in and Social Anthropology*, Vol. I (ICSSR), Bombay, Popular Prakashan, 1974.
97. Y. Singh, 'Concepts and Theories of Social Change' in *A Survey of Research in Sociology and Social Anthropology*, Vol. I (ICSSR), ibid.
98. Y. Singh, *Sociological Bulletin*, op. cit., 1973.
99. Ibid., p. 15.
100. Ibid., p. 18.
101. Ibid., p. 20.
102. Ibid.
103. Ibid., p. 22.
104. T.N. Madan, op. cit., 1966.
105. Y. Singh, *Sociological Bulletin*, op. cit., 1973, p. 23.
106. Ibid., p. 23.
107. Ibid., p. 26.
108. Ibid.
109. Ibid., pp. 27–28.
110. Y. Singh, op. cit., 1967, pp. 13–37.

111. See, for example, M.N. Srinivas and M.N. Panini, 'The Development of Sociology and Social Anthropology in India', *Sociological Bulletin*, Vol. 22, No. 2 1973, pp. 199–215; M.N. Srinivas, 'Sociology and Sociologists in India Today', *Sociological Bulletin*, Vol. XIX, No. 1, 1970, pp. 1–10. See also C. Lakshmanna, 'Teaching and Research in Sociology in Indian', *Sociological Bulletin*, Vol. 23, No. 1, 1974, 1013; Ramakrishna Mukherjee, 'The Sociologist and the Social Reality', *Sociological Bulletin*, Vol. 23, No. 2, 1974, pp. 169–192; S.C. Dube, 'Indian Sociology at the Turning Point', *Sociological Bulletin*, Vol. 26, No. 1, 1977, pp. 1–13, R.N. Saxena (ed.) *Sociology, Social Research and Social Problems in India*, Bombay: Asia Publishing House, 1961; and M.S.A. Rao, 'Sociology in the 1980s', *Economic and Political Weekly*, Vol. XIV, No. 44, 1974, pp. 1810–15.
112. Ramakrishna Mukherjee, *The Rise and Fall of the East India Company*, Berlin, Akademie-Varlag, 1958.
113. Ramakrishna Mukherjee, *Dynamics of a Rural Society*, Berlin: Akademie-Verlag, 1957.
114. Ramakrishna Mukherjee, 'Study of Social Change and Social Development in the Developing Societies', *Economic and Political Weekly*, Vol. V, Nos. 29–31, 1970, pp. 1159–70.
115. Ibid., p. 1161.
116. Ibid.
117. Ibid., p. 1163.
118. See Ramakrishna Mukherjee, *Sociological Bulletin*, op. cit., 1973–74.
119. Ramakrishna Mukherjee, *Sociological Bulletin*, op. cit., 1973, p. 29.
120. Ibid., p. 31.
121. Ibid., pp. 39–47.
122. Ramakrishna Mukherjee, op. cit., 1974, pp. 169–92.
123. Ibid., pp. 182–83.
124. D.P. Mukerji, *Diversities*, Delhi, People's Publishing House, 1958.
125. Gunnar Mydral, *Asian Drama: An Inquiry into the Poverty of Nations*, Vol. I, Penguin Books, 1968.
126. Ramakrishna Mukherjee, op. cit., 1974, pp. 185–86.
127. P.C. Joshi, 'Reflections on Social Science Research in India', *Sociological Bulletin*, Vol. 24, No. 2, 1975, pp. 139–62.
128. Gunnar Myrdal, op. cit., 1968.
129. A.R. Desai, *Social Background of Indian Nationalism*, Bombay, Popular Prakashan, 1948.
130. P.C. Joshi, op. cit., 1975, p. 147.
131. Stanislav Andreski, *Social Sciences as Sorcery*, New York, St. Martinus Press, 1972.
132. Jayant K. Lele, 'Indian Sociology and Sociology in India: Some Reflections on Their Being', *Sociological Bulletin*, Vol. 30, No. 1, 1981, pp. 39–53.

133. A.R. Desai, op. cit., 1948.
134. See A.R. Desai, *State and Society in India: Essays in Dissent*, Bombay, Popular Prakashan, 1975.
135. A.R., Desai, 'Relevance of the Marxist approach to the study of Indian Society', *Sociological Bulletin*, Vol. 30, No. I, 1981, pp. 1–20.
136. Ibid., pp. 4–7.
137. Ibid., p. 11.
138. A.R. Desai, op. cit., 1948.
139. Louis Dumont, 'Nationalism and Communalism', *Contributions to Indian Sociology*, Vol. VII, 1964, p. 32.
140. Y. Singh, *Modernization of Indian Tradition*, op. cit., 1973.
141. H.C. Srivastava, 'Concept of Tradition in Indian Sociological Thought', *Social Scientist*, Vol. 3, No. 3, 1974, pp. 17–25.
142. Sumit Chopra, 'Old Wine in New Skins: Modernization of Indian Tradition', *Social Scientist*, Vol. 3, No. 4, 1974, pp. 78–84.
143. Ramakrishna Mukherjee, 'History and Tradition in Indian Society: Null and Alternate Hypotheses?', *Sociological Bulletin*, Vol. 24, No. 1, 1975, pp. 95–107.
144. Krishna Prakash Gupta, 'Sociology of Indian Tradition and Tradition of Indian Sociology', *Sociological Bulletin*, Vol. 23, No. 1, 1974, pp. 14–43.
145. Ibid., p. 37.
146. Ibid.
147. Ibid.
148. Ibid.
149. D.A., Chekki, 'The Sociology of Sociologists: An Empirical Study in the Sociology of Knowledge', *Sociological Bulletin*, Vol. 27, No. 2, 1978, pp. 131–53. See also T.B. Bottomore, 'Sociology in India', *British Journal of Sociology*, Vol. 13, June 1962, pp. 98–106; M.B. Clinard and J.W. Elder, 'Sociology in India: A Study in the Sociology of Knowledge', *American Sociological Review*, Vol. 30, August 1965, pp. 581–87; and R.N. Mukherjee and H. Mujumdar, 'Sociology in India', in H. Becker and H.E. Barnes (eds) *Social Thought from Lore to Science*, Vol. 2. Washington D.C.: Harren Press, pp. 1135–48.
150. A.R. Momin, 'Indian Sociology: Search for Authentic Identity', *Sociological Bulletin*, Vol. 27, No. 2, 1978, p. 169.
151. Indra Deva, 'Methodological Perspectives for the Study of Society' in Giri Raj Gupta (ed.) op. cit., (1976) pp. 75–98.
152. R.S. Khare, op. cit., 1976, pp. 19–58.
153. Ibid., p. 23.
154. Ibid., p. 24.
155. Ibid., p. 38.
156. Ibid., p. 39.

157. Ibid., pp. 52–57.
158. R.K. Mukherjee, op. cit., 1977.
159. Ibid., pp. 2–5.
160. Ibid., p. 18.
161. Ibid., p. 12.
162. Ibid., pp. 37–43.
163. Y. Singh, op. cit., 1979.
164. T.N. Madan, 'Research methodology' in *A Survey of Research in Sociology and Social Anthropology*, Vol. 3 (ICSSR), Bombay, Popular Prakashan, pp. 282–315.
165. T.N. Madan and Andre Beteille (eds.), *Encounter and Experience*, Delhi, Vikas, 1975.
166. I.P. Desai, 'Craft of Sociology in India: An Autobiographical Perspective', *Economic and Political Weekly*, Vol. XVI, No. 6, pp. 197–204 and Vol. XVI, No. 7, pp. 246–51.
167. Ibid., p. 197.

Contributors to this Volume

Chekki, Dan A., an eminent Canada-based sociologist.

Damle, Y.B., Former Professor of Sociology, Department of Sociology, Poona University, Pune.

Desai, I.P., Former Founder Director, Centre for Social Studies, Surat.

Dube, S.C., eminent Social Scientist, D-504, Purvasha, Mayur Vihar Group Housing Colony, New Delhi.

Gandhi, J.S., Professor of Sociology, Centre for the Study of Social Systems, Jawaharlal Nehru University, New Delhi.

Gupta, Dipankar, Professor of Sociology, Centre for the Study of Social Systems, Jawaharlal Nehru University, New Delhi.

Joshi, P.C., Professor, Institute of Economic Growth, New Delhi.

Lal, Sheo Kumar, Former Professor of Sociology, Jodhpur University, Jodhpur.

Madan, T.N., Professor, Institute of Economic Growth, New Delhi.

Mukherjee, Ramkrishna, National Fellow of ICSSR, Calcutta.

Oommen, T.K., Professor of Sociology, Centre for the Study of Social Systems, Jawaharlal Nehru University, New Delhi.

Pathy, Jaganath, Professor of Sociology, South Gujarat University, Surat.

Shah, A.M., Former Professor of Sociology, Delhi University, Delhi.

Sharma, S.L., Professor of Sociology, Punjab University, Chandigarh.

Sharma, Surendra, Centre for the Study of Social Systems, Jawaharlal Nehru University, New Delhi.

Shukla, Suresh Chandra, Former Professor, Indian Institute of Public Administration, New Delhi.

Singh, Nirmal, Former Professor of Sociology, Centre for the Study of Social Systems, Jawaharlal Nehru University, New Delhi.

Singhi, Narendra K., Professor and Head, Department of Sociology, University of Rajasthan, Jaipur.

Srivastava, H.C., Former Professor of Sociology, Banaras University, Varanasi.

Shrivastava, R.S., Associate Professor of Sociology, Jodhpur University, Jodhpur.

Uberoi, Patricia, Centre for the Study of Social Systems, Jawaharlal Nehru University, New Delhi.

Venugopal, C.N., Professor of Sociology, Centre for the Study of Social Systems, Jawaharlal Nehru University, New Delhi.

has not made a significant contribution to the development and refinement of sociological concepts.

This deficiency makes Uberoi (1968) remark: 'Until we can concentrate on decolonization, learn to nationalize our problems and take our poverty seriously, we shall continue to be both colonial and unoriginal. A national school, avowed and conscious, can perhaps add relevance, meaning, and potency to our science; continued assent to the international system cannot.'

A common thread that binds a group of sociologists in this debate is the belief that the patterns of Indian social structure are so unique that they require a special sociology of India asking different questions but using similar western methods to answer them (Unnithan, 1967). Kantowsky (1969), while expressing critical comments with reference to Indian sociology, notes that 'Indian sociologists, when they quote Talcott Parsons, do not prove that the structural-functional analysis has made its start within the Indian milieu. Rather it indicates an adaptation [illegible] by many Indian social scientists to the rules of the dominant game, that is, the Euro-american social science game'. He asserts that scholars in developing countries should try to make their [illegible] contributions not only in regard to practical questions but also to the theoretical problems of the social sciences in general. For Kantowsky it is impossible to make any general scientific statement without proper reference to cross-cultural data. Therefore, there is no need to distinguish the 'sociology of developing countries' from the 'sociology of industrial countries'. In the same vein it is maintained that Indian sociology is distinctive only in terms of its focus and research emphasis (Atal, 1976). The strategy of parochialization is not a proper response to the parochial sociology of the West.

While recognizing the existential roots of scientific propositions and paradigms [illegible] formulated by scientists Singh (1979) [illegible] Indian sociology based on concepts and theories [illegible] derived from the study of Indian society. However, 'the sociological propositions which would form the basis of Indian or any other national sociology would of course have less theoretical power than those of general sociology'.

[illegible] observes that [illegible] having a history of its own, surely Indian society is not unique and he seems to imply that there is no need for sociology of India with its own concepts, theories, and methods. He agrees with Bailey that Indian society, granting all its uniqueness, must still be seen in the context of the general principles of sociology. Because of the inadequacy of the methods of national science in dealing with meanings, values, and behaviour of humans [illegible] Change and Social Development in the Developing [illegible]. We shall refer this view of M[illegible] as his analysis combines both [illegible]

[illegible]

[illegible] social change and devel- [illegible] fundamental questions have to be answered [illegible] which a scientific

self-conscious definition of research-worthy questions and the enrichment of the social sciences as instruments of general understanding and of practical action in historically specific situations. Theoretical universals must illumine concrete problems. This indigenization movement seems to incorporate a new vision of mankind — a non-exploitative relationship among humans and harmonious relationship between humans and the biosphere.

American sociology is considered to be largely regressive in imparting a conservative and superficially empiricist influence on social research in India (Verma, 1979). Therefore, social scientists in India are asked to take a clearly anti-imperialist stance and devote their energies to the emancipation of the masses from the shackles of colonialism and neo-colonialism. Furthermore, it is argued that sociology should be relevant to problems of the masses and to the enrichment of life in India. These critical reflections and new directions seem to be the basis for Dube (1977) to comment that there has been a visible unease within Indian sociology and its theoretical perspectives.

The preceding analysis of the process of [illegible] of sociology in India suggests that the discipline has developed [illegible] its [illegible] shortcomings. While exposed [illegible] as well as external forces, especially to the [illegible] of American sociology, [illegible] sociological tradition of a [illegible] methods and substantive research [illegible] sociology in India has reacted to several [illegible] by way of the indigenization movement.

The Indian sociology movement [illegible] [illegible] the discipline [illegible] [illegible] study of Indian society [illegible] not only the need to [illegible]

Furthermore, the emerging all-Indian sociological perspective [illegible] This movement also serves as a case study [illegible] of knowledge by demonstrating the importance of [illegible] in influencing and shaping sociological practice and [illegible].